Children's Writer's
WORD
BOOK

Children's Writer's
WORD
BOOK

2ND EDITION

Alijandra Mogilner & Tayopa Mogilner

WRITER'S DIGEST BOOKS

Writer's Digest Books
An imprint of Penguin Random House LLC
penguinrandomhouse.com

Copyright © 2006 by Alijandra Mogilner and Tayopa Mogilner.

Printed in the United States of America

ISBN 978-1-58297-413-2

Edited by Amy Schell
Designed by Claudean Wheeler

ABOUT THE AUTHORS

Alijandra Mogilner started writing on a bet and sold her first piece of children's writing to the Children's Television Workshop publication "3-2-1 Contact" in 1982. Her work appeared regularly in that publication throughout the 1980s and early 1990s. Her work has been translated into at least 37 languages, and she has appeared in children's magazines, such as *Misha* (Russia), around the world. Besides writing for children, she has published several trade and text books and literally hundreds of magazine articles. She taught writing at the University of California at San Diego Extension and is currently an adjunct professor at Alliant International University. She serves on the Board of Directors of several companies including Faucon International Publications. She is married with three children and lives in California.

Tayopa Mogilner published her first story in a national publication at the age of 10 and had a regular column in a magazine by the age of 12. A graduate of Brandeis University, she works as an educator and author. She currently studies learning in the cognitive science department at the University of California at San Diego.

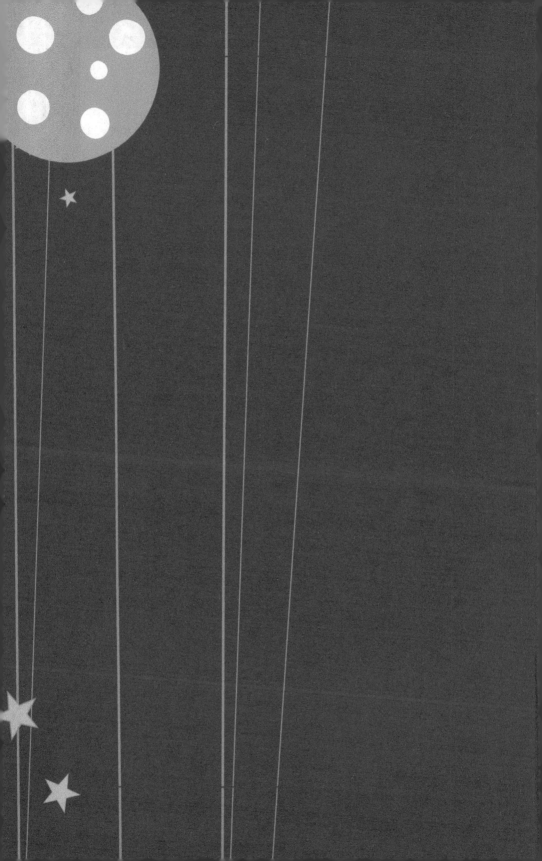

DEDICATION

Especially for Colin and Miles

ACKNOWLEDGMENTS

The road to this revised edition to the *Children's Writer's Word Book* has been a long one and has taken many turns. Wherever I have traveled my family has patiently helped me along the way, and I thank them all for their support and love. The world is a very different place than it was almost 15 years ago, but the people at F+W Publications are still kind and helpful, especially Jane Friedman, Amy Schell, Claudean Wheeler, and Robin Richie, who helped make this edition possible.

CONTENTS

INTRODUCTION

O ne of the wonderful things about dreaming of becoming a children's writer is that it is such a possible dream. Successful writers not only gain financially, but they also gain a loyal and generous readership. I can think of no more gracious and enthusiastic an audience than young readers. Children identify strongly with characters in their books and often want the same book read to them over and over again. That could be your book—the one that's dog-eared and tattered from being someone's cherished companion.

The original *Children's Writer's Word Book* set out to help authors achieve their goals of reaching young audiences. And with this new edition, the commitment to aiding authors is redoubled.

A great deal has happened in our world since *Children's Writer's Word Book* was first published in 1993. The World Wide Web has made dramatic changes in almost everyone's lives. We've discovered that there was once water on the surface of Mars and are planning to terraform that planet to make it livable for humans. Nanotechnology is already changing the landscape of medicine, and scientists have actually been able to teleport small amounts of matter from one place to another. Closer to home, concerns with ecology, disaster preparedness, mainstreaming in schools, and the expanded role most schools play in integrating children into problem solving in appropriate ways have been added to the classroom curriculum in many, if not most, schools.

With those changes, of course, came changes in children's literature and in the materials used in the classroom. Those changes include new words to express the new world in which we live, and they also include a change in emphasis on subject matter in juvenile publishing.

While horizons of knowledge keep expanding, and with it the language we use to talk about our world, successful children's writing requires more than just using the right vocabulary. To achieve your dream and become an author for this special audience, you first must understand the unique style necessary in children's writing. The clarity, simplicity, and rhythm that should be present in a children's book or story can be difficult to master. However, it's these very ingredients that will make your book one that is read over and over again.

Children's Writer's Word Book will help you choose words children will both understand and be challenged by, words that will help them perceive the world as it is and imagine worlds that could be. You, as a writer of children's literature, have a special commitment; along with the joy of creating for your readers comes the responsibility of writing honestly and clearly. This book will help you meet that responsibility. Anyone working in children's literature, young adult literature, or educational writing will find it an invaluable tool.

Educators will find the book useful in creating classroom materials, such as vocabulary lists, and for creative writing projects with students. Teachers and day-care professionals can use the lists as a reference when developing classroom material. Since the first edition of this book, there has been a rapid expansion in home schooling. Once reserved for children who were ill or for families who moved frequently, home schooling has expanded dramatically. Today, more than one million Web sites are devoted to the subject; and many states, such as California, now have online "Virtual Academy" resources for home schooling.

The aforementioned professionals and aspirants will refer again and again to specific word lists to spur ideas. The lists can stimulate creativity and verify your perception of what's appropriate. This book is for anyone who works with—or would like to reach—children and beginning readers, whether writing a story for fifth-grade boys or an adult reading text to improve literacy skills.

The original *Children's Writer's Word Book* has found a place both in the traditional classroom and in the home school environment. As a result, a variety

of resources have been added that will help both those who write for the commercial market and educators with a much smaller audience in mind.

While the specific areas of study identified in the grade sections are still accurate, several new areas have been added. These include national standards for reading and comprehension that will help both the author and the educator.

In part because of mainstreaming, disability issues are being introduced at the earliest levels. These books are aimed both at the nondisabled child and the affected child, to whom the disability or illness is explained. Along with this, issues of sensitivity to race, religion, and culture are being introduced variously, depending on the subject, from kindergarten through fifth grade.

Issues such as divorce and the concept of death (usually through the death of pets) are now being introduced in the first three years instead of being put off until fifth or sixth grade.

Ethnic, cultural pride, and bilingual books have increased in number, although they do not yet constitute a large percentage of the publishing world for juvenile readers. I expect this to grow dramatically in the next few years.

Fantasy and science fiction stories are being introduced at a younger age, and the science and technology curriculum has expanded for younger students. Thus, terms like *terraforming, browser,* and *URL* need to be added to the vocabulary. Dozens of new words were not contemplated in the original book. For example, the World Wide Web was just beginning to become popular at the time.

The increased saturation of the Internet in everyday life and the use of educational television and other technological resources have had a great impact on a child's vocabulary. Names of superheroes are recognized in reading, and concepts such as atomic energy and living in outer space are not unfamiliar to five-year-olds. The Internet is being introduced in kindergarten throughout the United States wherever the technology is available. Internet safety, ecology, and proposed changes in transportation, living areas, and even where people will live have become integrated into the school curriculum. The world, and society, will continue to change rapidly and will affect children at least as much as adults. Even the words used for the youngest reader have changed. *SUV* may now supplement *car,* and words such as *Web* (as in World Wide Web) and *space* have been added to the pre-k and kindergarten word list. The world of technology will continue to evolve ever more rapidly. Words and subjects that deal with new technologies should be considered appropriate for even the youngest readers if the author uses them carefully. If you want to use a new word, consider if it is popular enough in the culture where children would use it in their own daily vocabulary. If they would, it is probably safe to use.

As adults, we often forget that children can comprehend more than they can articulate, and we end up communicating to them below their level, leaving them bored. Or the opposite can happen: Children are growing up faster than we did and act very sophisticated although their vocabulary skills are undeveloped. Striking the balance between writing below or above their level is tricky. This book helps make the levels clear.

As a writer and teacher, I often needed to know what level a particular word or idea was and didn't know where to look. That's when I got the idea for a book I could turn to any time I had a question of this nature. As the idea evolved, it became focused on three areas: lists of specific words commonly introduced at each graded reading level, a thesaurus of these words listing synonyms with the level at which each is usually introduced, and a discussion of standard practices related to word usage in children's writing.

The result is what you now hold in your hands. *Children's Writer's Word Book* is a desk reference intended to be kept close by for frequent and immediate access. When you need to know if a word you want to use is appropriate for your young audience, or how long your sentences should be, consult this book.

The grade level at which the words presented here are introduced is usually derived from more than one graded source. When there was a discrepancy between standard sources, the words are listed under the grade in which they were most frequently introduced. If there was no clear consensus, the words in this book have a bias in favor of the earliest usage. If that sounds a little inexact, it is—the ultimate judge is the child, and every child is different, as are school districts and parents. All these factors contribute to a child's comprehension and vocabulary.

In your word choices and in your decisions about theme and concept, you'll frequently be using your own judgment. This book will simply help make that judgment more certain.

The words in the lists were compiled from a variety of graded readers, several basic word lists, and other sources, and then subjected to my own testing. Certified reading specialists who work with children in the California school system checked the lists. Then, several panels of grade-school children reviewed words I was uncertain about. Beyond this word-by-word analysis, I received more general help from professors of education at San Diego State University and others from the University of California at San Diego, where I taught writing at the extension.

As with the earlier edition of the book, new words have been added at the level they were found in standard literature rather than the level being chosen using a mathematical formula. I have depended upon publications by organizations like NASA to integrate the latest ideas into the standard list. Some new words such as *vertiport, microgravity, terraforming*, and *astrobiology* do not have equivalent words because they are new to the language. As a result, these words have been included with only their definitions.

Not surprisingly, most of the vocabulary changes have to do with science. Since *Word Book* was first published, we have seen the creation of the World Wide Web, the first explorations of Mars, DVDs, the widespread use of cell phones, and a plethora of other technologies that directly affect our lives and the lives of the children we write for and work with. You may find words for readers as young as second grade that are even new to you. One example is *rotorcraft*, a flying machine that gets its lift and thrust from rotor blades. Though one does not hear the word daily, NASA uses it in its illustrated books for second to fourth grade and in its online cartoons. Although it is unusual, at least at the moment, it is used nationally and deserves a place in any graded vocabulary listing.

While this book gathers words from a wide variety of sources, the lists include those words that educators and publishers generally agree should become a permanent part of children's word knowledge. Sources used to create the word lists are listed in the appendix.

HOW TO USE THIS BOOK

Children's Writer's Word Book is an easily read reference book—presenting word lists and a thesaurus set up to help, no matter how you write. In publishing, the classifications of children's literature are broader than the grade-by-grade method employed here. However, before generalizing, you must first understand some of the fine distinctions in ages, grade levels, and word usage. Because a picture book is for children ages two to eight, it's apparent the two-year-old will be listening to, not reading, the story. Somewhere in that span of six years, the child begins recognizing words; later she can recall the spelling of some of the words when the book is not in front of her. Obviously, this process of selection is different in each child.

So, when you're writing a picture book, look for words at or below the third-grade level. Limit the amount of third-grade-level words you use because they are understood by the fewest picture-book readers. Publishers' categories are further explained in the following chapter.

When writing for school-age children, you should be aware of the recent trend in publishing to classify books by level rather than grade. These level books span grades (level 1 being grades 1 and 2, for example) rather than being tied to a specific grade. If you deal with educational materials, you will find that sixth grade, traditionally part of elementary school and included here in that way, is now grouped with six through eight for middle school. Whether considered part of elementary school or middle school, the words, subjects, and concepts pretty well match those given in this expanded and revised edition.

There is also some movement toward taking the chapter book concept, in very short chapters, to grades one and two rather than waiting until level three or third grade.

Except at the kindergarten and first-grade levels, all permutations and tenses of a word are assumed to be introduced at the same time, with exceptions noted on the list. Even at the first-grade level, regular conjugations of a verb are introduced together. For example, only the word *choice* is given in the listings, but its presence indicates that *choose, chose,* and *chosen* may all be used. Word families, such as *chemical, chemist,* and *chemistry* or *absorb, absorbed, absorbent, absorbing,* and *absorption* are also introduced together. When a first-grade word changes radically, it may become a second-grade word; for example, *reason* is a first-grade word, but *unreasonable* would be considered a second-grade word because both a prefix and a suffix are appended to the root word. This is where that ever-sharpening judgment will come into play.

Subjects are also grouped. For example, the early history of the United States is usually taught during the fifth grade, and any words relating to that period are appropriate for the ten- to twelve-year-old child.

Word lists are least exact at the pre-reader/kindergarten and first-grade levels for several reasons. Children are first learning to read, and they learn selectively, based on what they're most interested in. Further, many children in this age group are not yet in a formalized educational setting. And, finally, regional, religious, and family influences are stronger than classroom influences at this stage.

Many unusual nouns and even made-up words are introduced in children's books, and all of them cannot (and should not) be presented here. Richard Scarry's books are often accompanied by elaborate illustrations that clearly identify these objects with pickle cars joining jeeps in a delightful hodgepodge that has nothing to do with reality. Dr. Seuss's words are often only nonsense (Zizzer-Zazzer Zuzz or Fiffer-feffer-feff) and are meant to teach alphabet and phonic skills. These joyful exercises in experimental language are presented carefully and underscore the idea that you can do almost anything you like if you do it in a context the reader can understand. Take a look at these books. You will see that they are carefully crafted and other conventions, such as sentence length, are carefully adhered to.

USING THE GRADED LISTS

Information on national standards and benchmarks at various grades has been included in this new version of the book. Benchmarks are standards that are critical to successful performance in subsequent grade or level courses. Recognized nationally, they are included here to give you an idea of what students at a particular level can be expected to know and, additionally, what kinds of materials might be used in the classroom as well as reading for enjoyment. Benchmarks and standards are set for many areas by either government agencies, such as NASA, or professional organizations; and those are the ones included here. You will find reading standards now included in this book, as well as pointers to resources for science, mathematics, technology, and other subjects.

Writers and teachers should note that many subject matter lessons, and the publishers that produce readings for these lessons, call out "content area" articles or stories. In content area reading, students are not learning to read but are reading to learn information. In this style, the last and first paragraphs summarize and rephrase the main concepts of the article. The reading level is lower than the grade or level to facilitate the acquisition of new concepts.

The section titled "Some Things You'll Need to Know" discusses the special requirements of children's writing and the standard practices in that field. It covers such subjects as optimal sentence lengths for particular age groups, when contractions and possessives are introduced, and other topics. In another section, words are grouped by grade—kindergarten through sixth. A short introduction to each grade gives you general guidelines for writing for that grade. Writing samples integrating this information with the appropriate vocabulary follow each list. These lists are best used as a springboard to create stories. Look through a specific word list. Certain words will pop out at you. Take the first word that you stop at and create a sentence. A story may follow, or, if not, try another word. The possibilities are limited only by your imagination.

Let's go to the kindergarten word list and use it as an example of developing a short passage. The following mini-story, "A Trip to the Store," was developed from that list.

> Mother said: Tell the family to get in the car. We're going to the store to pay the bill. I have some extra money. You can buy the hat you want. Your brother can have a book.
>
> Ben asked: Can I buy a cat?
>
> Mother said: No, you can't.
>
> Tom asked: Can we get some food?
>
> Mom asked: What do you want?
>
> Ben and Tom yelled: Pizza!
>
> Mom said: OK, pizza it is.

USING THE THESAURUS

The *Children's Writer's Word Book*'s thesaurus is similar to other thesauruses, except it features only words understood by children from kindergarten through middle school. If you have already written a story, or are in the middle of writing one, and are not certain if a particular word is appropriate for your intended audience, look up the word alphabetically to see if it "fits." If the word is listed but is too far off the mark, you will find other choices listed. For example, I wanted to make sure the following story was appropriate for second-grade readers:

> Lockheed is a company that makes rockets and jet planes. So, of course, when they need to deliver messages, they use airmail. However, they don't use an airplane to do it. They use pigeons! That's because Robert Nelson came up with an old-fashioned idea to solve a modern problem.

The only inappropriate words in this paragraph are *old-fashioned*, a third-grade word, and *deliver*, a fifth-grade word. I used the thesaurus to find an appropriate substitute for *deliver*, and in the revision, it became *send*, a first-grade word.

I simply dropped the word *fashioned* from *old-fashioned*. It changed the meaning slightly, but the story wasn't hurt in the process.

In the thesaurus, clauses and phrases are usually given the grade of the highest-level word in the phrase. Sometimes a phrase may have all first-grade or kindergarten level words, but, as a concept, may not be understood at that level. For example, in the phrase *as best he could*, all words are level K. But as a phrase, it may not be understood by a kindergarten reader, so bump it up to the first-grade level.

Some words are presented at one level but may have another meaning at a higher level. Young readers who are at the lower level will certainly be able to read the word, but it may well make no sense to them in context. It becomes a function of personal judgment. Consider that more sophisticated definition in the context of the subject matter to judge appropriate use.

GUIDELINES FOR USING WORDS NOT IN THIS BOOK

The words presented in the word lists and thesaurus should be considered a part of a child's basic and permanent reading vocabulary. That is, at the appropriate level children should know the word well enough to know how to pronounce the word and recognize the important meaning, or meanings, of the word when they see it. There will probably be many other words you wish to use that do not fall into this category and, thus, are not on these lists.

To check if such words are appropriate for your intended readers, look up similar words, or words in the same subject area, to get an idea if the reader will understand the one you want to use. Take, for example, this excerpt from a science story written for ten- to-twelve-year-olds about foods we will eat in the future:

> Many changes are already being made in the kind of food we eat. Many of you use imitation "bacon bits" or drink imitation milk. The new products are often made out of soybeans, sunflower seeds, or alfalfa. That is because they are high-protein crops.

Most of the words used in this example, including the plants, are listed in the thesaurus; however, *soybean* is not. The introduction to the graded word lists notes that almost all foods and plants have been introduced by fourth grade. So, we know it's safe to use *soybean* in this article.

You may not find the word you are looking for if its conjugation, tense, or form is different from the one listed. Look for the most basic form of the word. I have tried to use the present tense of the words here, but there are some exceptions.

English has many compound words, and most of them are not presented here. As a general rule, compound words are first introduced in second grade. After that, almost any compound word is acceptable as long as the two parts are already known to the reader. For example, the word *wildlife* is not listed in the thesaurus; however, *wild* is a second-grade word and *life* is introduced in first grade. Therefore, *wildlife* is all right to use in the second grade and beyond. If you have any question about a word, look up the two parts to see if they will be familiar to your audience. A few compound words, such as *myself* and *cannot,* can be used before second grade. The general rule here is that the compound word should be made up of easily recognizable words. The child must be familiar enough with the word so that he or she will recognize it even though it is combined with another word.

Sometimes a whole story will hinge on an unusual word or idea. In fact, you will often tell a story, or write an article, precisely because it is about something foreign, rare, or unusual. When you use an unusual word, it should be given with enough information so that the reader can understand its meaning.

For example:

> In Mexico, a small town is called a pueblo. Maria Lopez is a little girl who lives in a pueblo called Toco. Her parents are farmers. Every day Maria helps her parents.

The material in this book reflects my own years of experience as a children's writer. Much of it is information given to me over the years by kind and patient editors. I hope *Children's Writer's Word Book* becomes a key to opening the door to your own success and helps you realize your dream. Writing for children has been a real joy for me, and I hope it brings you the same kind of satisfaction.

SOME THINGS
YOU'LL NEED TO KNOW

MORE ON WORDS AND LANGUAGE

Unusual Words. To introduce words not in the child's standard vocabulary—foreign words, for example—if it is possible, give the definition first, then the word. It is also common practice to underline the word the first time it is used. Readers of any age tend to skip over unfamiliar words without trying to read them, getting the meaning from the context of the sentence. Giving the definition first makes it much easier to actually learn the new word.

Names. Nicknames for your characters can be highly desirable. They can help describe someone's personality or appearance with little or no exposition: "Hey, Red, come here!" "Go get Pokey so we can get started." They can also set the mood as hostile or friendly or describe the cultural set of an era or a nation. They are also excellent "tags" that help your reader remember or identify a character.

Unless it is important to the story, avoid connecting words like *tiny, little, bitty,* and *small* to the names of your protagonists. The tiny of Tiny Tim is central to the character and his problem. Believe me, Little Leroy and Bitsy Betty have problems, too, whether you intended them or not. Psychologically, the diminutive name takes away personal power and emasculates. Even names like Jimmy or Billy fall into this cabinet.

Nonsexist and Nonracist Terminology. It is good to use generic terminology instead of words that express gender bias. For example, use *mail*

pronoun *he*. Even though it is proper to use the masculine pronoun, try to vary it. You can also use the plural *they* or the neutral third person *you*. Both are widely used today to avoid more awkward constructions such as *he/she*. Another area to avoid in nonsexist writing is stereotypical roles, such as exclusively male doctors and exclusively female nurses in a hospital setting. Women and men should be treated the same in all types of stories, as should boys and girls. Again, stay away from stereotyping.

Diversity. Race, religion, and physical abilities are other areas where you should be sensitive to word usage. Use *African American* or *of African heritage* instead of *black*, and *Native American* instead of *Indian*. *Asian American* is preferable to *Oriental*; not all Muslims are Arabs; not all Arabs are Muslim; Hispanics are from the Americas, while Latinos are from any place that speaks Spanish. You get the idea; be sensitive, especially to offensive terminology, and seek out an authority when in doubt. Children enjoy reading about people like themselves, so it's good to have characters with diverse backgrounds.

As noted in the introduction, ethnic, cultural pride, and bilingual books, as well as books with disabled characters, have increased in number though they do not yet constitute a large percentage of the publishing world for juvenile readers. With the tremendous strides the world has taken toward globalization, diversity has become an important part of juvenile literature, and I expect this to grow dramatically in the next few years.

Tags. An editor may suggest you use a tag to help identify a character. Tags are actions or gestures a character typically uses that easily identify the person to the reader. A boy may toss his head when he gossips, a young girl may push up her glasses just before she throws a fast pitch. The tag may be used to build a character, be part of the problem, or identify a "mystery" person. For example, a boy may try to hide in the bushes or shadow a suspect while humming the song he always hums or sniffing a chronically runny nose. As noted before, nicknames are another good tag you can use to help describe a character.

THEME AND CONTENT

Character's Ages. The protagonist(s) of your story should be the same age as or a little older than the reader. Establish the age of the protagonist as soon as possible, and make sure your characters act appropriately for their ages.

Taboos. While the market is much more flexible than in the past, stay away from any positive portrayal of drugs, tobacco, alcohol, explicit sex, crime, and violence. Drunkenness particularly should never be portrayed in a humorous light.

You will find certain themes, while not actually taboo, difficult to sell. Animals that talk to people are almost impossible to sell—even as fantasy. *'Lil Toot* and *The Little Engine That Could* aside, anthropomorphizing inanimate objects also makes for a difficult sale. Stories that turn out to be only a dream are not often welcome, especially if waking up is used to solve a plot problem. Things that are too cute, too old-fashioned, or too common usually get the cold shoulder, too.

One of those not-taboo-but subjects is weight. There is currently a medical, political, and social focus on overweight children and youth that promises to have a very real impact on our culture. At the same time, eating disorders are a very real issue, especially with preteens and early teens. As a result, the subject of weight should be handled carefully—especially if it is not the focus of the story or book you are writing.

Fantasy and Fairy Stories. Fantasy is a healthy field for juvenile publishing. However, retelling such classics as *Thumbelina* or *The Goose Girl* in modern dress is sure to garner rejection slips instead of praise. If you are tempted to begin your story "Once upon a time," you should probably think about how it will fit in your target publisher's list.

Mystery. There is a great difference between adult and children's mysteries. Violence is generally out for any age group. For preteen readers, murder is out, and so are most dead bodies. The only corpses are generally ancient mummies that lend a creepy mood to a story. Missing treasure, old legends and secrets, theft, and even kidnapping have formed the core of wonderful juvenile mysteries. Many mystery books are elaborate puzzles the reader is meant to solve.

Science Fiction. Science fiction becomes popular around fourth or fifth grade when it is a venue for fast-paced adventure. With science making headlines daily and subjects such as space and ecology entering the standard curriculum by second or third grade, science fiction stories may well find a home in even younger markets. By the sixth grade, character

development becomes important. Science fiction is often a pleasant and charming way of explaining science or giving facts, but make sure its primary goal is to entertain.

Romance. Romance stories are popular with sixth graders on up. Contemporary stories often include urban themes such as gangs, alcohol, and sex. Today's teens are dealing with some serious situations, and books and stories that accurately reflect their world are popular.

Nonfiction. Nonfiction is popular with readers in the elementary level, and stories in trade books and magazines are often used in the classroom. Stories about scientific phenomena, the environment, history, and technology interest every age group but the very youngest. Current events and how-to books are welcome at the elementary and high school level.

Problem-Oriented Stories. Issues such as divorce and death (usually the death of a pet) are now being introduced in the first three years instead of, as when this book was first published, the fifth or sixth grade. These issues must be handled carefully, but they open up new markets for stories that deal with the modern child's reality.

AGE GROUPS AND READING LEVELS

This section covers the age groupings and categories of books that publishers recognize. First, let's discuss the age groups.

Level Books. Many books are now indicated by levels rather than by specific grades. For example, Level 1 is generally used for kindergarten through second grade. This three-grade spread recognizes that there is a wide range of normal abilities among students. The vocabulary used for the level is the middle one, in this case, first grade. Many children are ahead or behind the usual target vocabularies for grade and age, and level books allow the students to use materials that are appropriate for them without some of the social issues involved with reading material identified as being for a grade different from the one the student is in.

Preschool to Kindergarten. Preschool books that are self-readers constitute a much larger market than in the past. Early childhood education is a major focus of both state and national educational programs, and reading is a primary focus. Picture books and picture stories are the primary forms for school and home. As a result, the story that is meant to be read by a caregiver to the child, and is not appropriate as a self-reader as well, has become less common. While the most common sentence length for self-readers at this level is still about six words, some publishers now use longer sentences (up to fifteen words) for even these youngest readers. To do this, they break the sentences into smaller phrases that generally express a whole idea like the writing sample in the kindergarten section:

He ran after the kitten

when it came into the room.

The Primary Age Group. This group, which includes children from six- to eight-years-old, or first through third grades, reads the picture book, picture story, and easy-to-read book. More magazines are aimed at this age group than at younger children. The easy reader is meant for the child to read alone, and the target sentence length is five to six words, ten words maximum. All the words given in the kindergarten through third-grade word lists are appropriate to use when writing for this group. There is some movement toward taking the chapter book concept, in very short chapters, to grades one and two rather than waiting until level three or third grade, as is most common.

The Elementary Level. Traditionally this has included the eight- to twelve-year-olds, or the fourth through sixth graders. More and more often this now is used to identify third through fifth grade, or seven- through ten- or eleven-year olds. The target sentence length here is ten words. The longest length acceptable to conservative institutions is about twenty words. Sentence length is more flexible in books than in magazines. Fiction should have a lot of action, and both fiction and nonfiction should deal with the special interests and problems relevant to this age group. Most books written for this age group range between 20,000 and 40,000 words. Most magazines use stories ranging from 700 to 2,000 words and often have a page or two of short-shorts under 100 words.

Middle School Through High School. Middle school, a new addition to this book, includes the sixth through eighth grades. The two groups, middle school and high school, include twelve- to eighteen-year-olds. Sixth graders, or twelve-year-olds, always constituted a major portion of the readership. This is the time when reading problems often become serious problems. Hi-lo books (for high interest, low reading level) and other materials meant to help the student catch up to grade level are introduced here. Regular texts that are not in the hi-lo grouping use an adult vocabulary and sentence structure. Most books range from 25,000 to 55,000 words, and longer lengths are permissible. Popular fiction subjects include romance, mystery, suspense (mild horror), the supernatural, and humor. More magazines are aimed at this age group than at any other. Magazine stories range from 1,000 to 3,500 words. Eighty percent of this market is nonfiction and include age-related problems, interviews, and special interests.

WHAT KIND OF BOOK IS IT?

The terms that follow are commonly used by publishers to describe the different types of children's books.

Picture Books. There are basically three types of picture books. The first type of picture book is for babies to three-year-olds, has little text, and is often prepared by publishers in-house.

The next type is for toddlers to five-year-olds. The picture books must be kept short enough to be read aloud by an adult to a child at one sitting. They should have a happy ending and must use language that can be read aloud comfortably. Sentence length should also be determined by reading ease. If the book is meant to be an early self-reader, the target sentence length should be five to six words, and each page should lend itself to illustration that will help carry the story. Try to use mainly kindergarten and first-grade vocabulary. These books should take no more than twenty minutes to read.

The oldest group of picture book readers is for the five- to eight-year-olds. These books must have a story to tell. They should have a beginning, a middle, and an end. There should be a plot, but it should be simple. Children in this age group still like to be read to, and rhythm keeps them attentive.

Picture books may run from as few as 50 words to 1,500. Most picture books average 500 to 1,000 words. Books for the youngest listeners (through five years old) should take no more than twenty minutes to read; ten to fifteen minutes is preferred. Keep in mind the short attention span of the listener.

Picture Story. Picture stories are the picture books in which text carries the story. These are for the five- to eight-year-old. Picture stories tell a real story and have lots of action. If it is written for an adult to read to a child, sentence length is restricted only to that which is comfortable to read aloud, and the vocabulary should be such that the child can understand it, rather than read it.

The picture story is still heavily illustrated but has a more complicated plot than a picture book.

Easy-to-Read Books (also known as young readers). These books are intended for ages six to nine (grades one to three). Manuscripts are 500 to 2,000 words, with 1,000 to 1,500 words preferred. These books generally have about forty pages of text. Sentences should be five to six words in length, with a few up to eight words. When putting your story together, try not to break up phrases between lines. To make sure that you haven't done this and that your story is easy to read, read it out loud a few times. These books are for the child to read alone; if your book is meant to be read by an adult to a child, notify the publisher when you submit it.

Hi-Lo Books. The term *hi-lo* means high interest, low reading level. These books are purchased mainly by schools and are written for people learning to read or those who are reading behind grade level. They use a controlled vocabulary and a sentence length appropriate to the vocabulary level. They use a lot of action and dialogue. Romance, mystery, and heritage-based, culturally centered stories, as well as stories dealing with urban problems, are often welcome. Most of these books run from 400 to 1,200 words.

Many publishers want hi-lo books or other graded books but do not supply the word lists. It is here that the graded word lists in this book become invaluable. Sentence length is about ten to twelve words. Stories should be fast paced and have a tightly knit plot. You can write a hi-lo book on the second-grade level, but the story must be mature in theme.

Young Adult Novels. These books are written for readers aged twelve to eighteen. They are similar to mainstream novels except the protagonist is a teen or young adult, and the story is relevant to that age group.

TECHNICAL ITEMS THAT HELP YOU SELL

Word Count. One of the most common reasons magazines reject good manuscripts is the failure to include a word count at the top of the first page. The use of computers with their varying type faces, sizes, and spacing has made even standard formulas for computing word count unreliable. It may not matter with a one- or two-page piece, but editors are not going to sit and count the number of words in your work to see if it will fit their format.

Standard Format. There are individuals at writers' conferences and some articles and books that encourage you to have your manuscript stand out by using colored paper or type. Even more suggest that your manuscript should include the rights you are selling at the top of the first page or that it should include a copyright notice. Virtually all these items mark the author as an amateur. Manuscripts other than picture books should be double spaced on white paper with black ink using 12-point type in a standard font. If there is no notice of the rights being sold, the author is offering first publication rights in English in North America. Only if the author is offering something different should the subject of rights be broached, and then it should be explained in the cover letter. Copyright is automatic in the United States and many other countries as well.

Picture Books. The author needs to indicate each page of a picture book. In other words, the author should make it obvious what text goes with which picture and that each page is separate. The most practical way to do this is to give the line of text with three dots, or other obvious page maker, below it:

> The San Diego Zoo has pandas
>
> • • •

That way, a number of pages can be shown on a single manuscript page.

Bibliographies. Occasionally children's periodicals ask writers to submit lists of reference material to support their facts. Do keep track of your source material; do not submit it with your story until asked for it unless you know the periodical requires it. Books are another matter; reference material should be cited with any work of nonfiction or fiction.

OTHER TYPES OF WRITING

So far this book has primarily dealt with books. A great many other markets are available to authors who write for children, including magazines, radio and television, and the legitimate stage.

Features. A feature is a newspaper or magazine story that allows emotional involvement or entertains as well as informs. Such stories almost always make your audience feel something or want to do something. Feature stories really come into their own at the elementary level. Fourth-, fifth-, and sixth-grade magazines often use the feature story style to lend life to science, mathematics, and news stories. Educational inserts in daily newspapers and special educational newspapers also use these kinds of stories.

Fillers. A filler is a short article or story—usually under 500 words and often under 100. Fillers, such as games, riddles, and items of special scientific or human interest, are especially welcome in young children's periodicals. In broadcasting, fillers are short, nonessential stories kept on hand in case a program runs short. If you are helping to produce a children's television or radio news program, keep a number of these on hand and at the bottom of the reader's pile. Trivia about such things as the world's largest pizza or the biggest pair of shoes is interesting and can be carried week after week until needed.

Writing for Television. The existence of public-access cable television channels and the availability of reasonably priced videotaping equipment have created a variety of exciting opportunities for people throughout the country. Even the smallest schools often videotape students presenting a weekly news report or original drama to be shown on these television channels or for use in the classroom.

Television news and other productions that narrate silent videos the viewers are watching generally use a forty- to forty-five-space line for the script, typed in a double- or triple-spaced column down the right-hand side of the paper. Common margin settings are thirty for the left margin and seventy for the right margin. The placement allows the left side of the paper to be used to note what video accompanies the text. Each forty-space line takes about two seconds of on-air time to read. Triple spacing makes it easier for the reader to keep his place and the writer to edit the work.

Writing for Radio. Many schools now have their own FM radio broadcasting facilities or access to local college or commercial stations. It's easy to produce material for this medium according to professional industry standards; and like so many other things, it's just as easy for the children to learn the correct format as any other. Standard radio broadcast format uses a sixty-five-space line for typing. This line length makes timing your stories easy. Each group of sixteen lines takes about one minute to read aloud. It is assumed it takes 3.75 seconds to read each line.

Writing in Verse. Verse seems to be everywhere in children's publishing, yet it is sometimes very hard to sell. One of the problems is that verse must sound good when read out loud, and it needs to be easy to read for an extended period. Read your work into a tape recorder, have a friend read it to you, or take it to a writers' workshop. If you stumble or have trouble reading it smoothly and easily, go back to work. It is a lot easier to sell verse to a magazine because it is generally interspersed with other types of material. A good track record publishing verse in magazines will make it easier to sell a book written the same way.

Writing Plays. Children's plays can be written one of three ways: (1) with children as actors, (2) with adults as actors and children as the audience, and (3) with adults or teens as actors and young adults and teens as the audience. For younger children, action is important, just as it is in other forms of children's writing. As always, themes and protagonists must correlate with the intended audience.

A SPECIAL NOTE ON MAINSTREAMING

In part because of mainstreaming, disability issues are being introduced at the earliest levels. These books are aimed at both the nondisabled child and the affected child. Along with this, issues of sensitivity to race, religion, and culture are being introduced variously, depending on the subject, in preschool through fifth grade. Elementary and secondary school classrooms have become diverse settings all across the United States. Bilingual education programs have become multilingual, fewer children in what are considered ethnic minorities are dropping out of school, and more special needs children are being mainstreamed than ever before. Between 1998 and 2002, mainstreaming increased 10 percent. Presently 50 percent of disabled students are educated in regular classrooms.[1] Demographic changes have created a need for a language arts curriculum and other programs that meet the needs of the new student body.

In particular, this diversity has created the need for inclusive literature. In the first half decade of the new century, over 2,500 juvenile books depicting the disabled became available. These range from picture books to young adult novels. Some of these books deliberately do not fill any inclusion role, but are educational and meant to increase the understanding of a particular disability, and the behaviors associated with it, for students, teachers, and parents. Some are meant to help disabled children understand their own situations better.

Between 1966 and 1975, twice as many books dealing with disabilities were published as in the previous twenty-six years.[2] An even larger number of books were published after 1975, due, in large part, to Public Law 94-142 passed in November of that year.[3] This law was later updated to become the 1990 Individuals with Disabilities Education Act (IDEA). Owing in great part to these laws, millions of children are now participating in regular classrooms who would not have been fifty years ago.

Children's literature has played a special role in mainstreaming these children. Like ethnic integration, the desired result is for the disabled to be accepted as a normal part of the environment whether it is in school, at work, in public places, or at home. Children learn to expect what they see around them and learn their values and attitudes at a very young age. Literature, especially children's literature, helps form those attitudes that may last a lifetime. If children grow up expecting to see the disabled in their classroom and in their literature, the situation will psychologically become the normative state.

At the turn of the new century, approximately 5.8 million disabled children were mainstreamed into the U.S. educational system. The expectation is that mainstreaming of the disabled into the public school system will increase due, in part, to recent amendments in federal law that encourage that program to be extended to children as young as three years old.

Besides filling legal imperatives, literature that is inclusive can help make the lives of the disabled more inclusive. Scientific experiments show that exposure to the disabled, especially when cooperative or emotional interaction is involved, results in less prejudice and hostility. If the presence of the disabled in children's literature plays no other role than to inform and to help alleviate discrimination, it is well worth the effort to create and use these books.

Books like *Hearts of Gold: A Celebration of Special Olympics and Its Heroes*, *Extraordinary People with Disabilities*, *How It Feels to Live with a Physical Disability*, *Views from Our Shoes*, and *I Have a Sister, My Sister Is Deaf* are typical examples of the type of book meant either to communicate the idea that the disabled can succeed in life and what it is like to be, or live with, a person who is disabled. Publishers, especially academic publishers, have been encouraged to include people with disabilities in children's literature. To that end, publishers have sought books and other materials that will help teachers and students understand and accept differently-abled children in the classroom. Much of what has been published has been heavy handed, but some has taken its place among the best children's literature. It is a fairly new market that you may not have considered.

Many books including disability in the subject matter, like those mentioned, are nonfiction and meant to educate, but fiction is just as important in creating a sense of belonging and normalcy. Ideally, a character should just happen to be disabled rather than that being the main focus of the story or the only reason for the character's being present. While one does not usually think of Stephen King as an author of children's literature, *Cycle of the Werewolf* is an appropriate book for fifth graders and above, and an excellent example of an authentic portrayal of a protagonist who happens to be disabled. The great advantage of this kind of fiction is that it has a much wider market than the nonfiction whose market is almost exclusively in the educational community. The ability to cross markets can provide a much larger sales base for the author than a single market at any level.

NATIONAL STANDARDS AND BENCHMARKS

National standards and benchmarks have been created in a variety of fields. The reading standards included here apply directly to your work and can help you not only sell your work to a broad audience but also help you identify some of the criteria on which your work may be judged. These standards are also an excellent reference for both educators and people who home school.

There are also standards already in place for science, mathematics, technology, writing, and a wide variety of other subjects. While those may well help you with your work, they are not appropriate to include here in full. You will find a brief description of some resources to these areas following the reading and comprehension standards.

NATIONAL READING AND COMPREHENSION STANDARDS

National reading and comprehension standards are grouped with several grades: K–2, 3–5, and 6–8. Grades 4–6 used to be grouped, but because of the popularity of middle schools, the sixth grade is now normally included with the older grades. For a variety of reasons, ranging from multiple languages being spoken in a classroom to the impact of natural disasters (which cause stress and, often, interrupt education), reading comprehension testing shows that much of this middle school population struggles to understand materials traditionally targeted to the older elementary group.[1] Thus, the learning period for traditional reading skills has been expanded to include middle schools, and many, if not most, reading comprehension materials and tests group middle school with at least sixth grade. You will also find pre-k has been added due to the national effort for early childhood education. These pre-k standards are more for comprehension and reading readiness than for reading itself. Additionally, though kindergarten through second grades are grouped, you will find a separate kindergarten group specifically geared toward the youngest learners in the standard public school system.

It should be noted that the UK has developed very similar standards and benchmarks, and the American and British versions are virtually interchangeable.

PRE-KINDERGARTEN

National standards assume that, before entering kindergarten, a child will know the following skills:

1. The child should understand that written symbols, whether handwritten or in print, can convey meaning and represent spoken language.

2. The child should be able to associate sounds with written words.

3. The child should know the differences between letters, numbers, and words, and the significance of spaces between words.

4. The child should know that illustrations and pictures can convey meaning and add to the understanding of the written context.

5. The child should know that books should be held upright, that they have pages, and that they are read from front to back.

6. The child should know that, in English, print is read from left to right, top to bottom.

7. The child should know at least some letters of the alphabet.

8. The child should recognize some familiar words in print, such as her own first name.

9. The child should know how to spell his own first name.

10. The child should know that printed information is used in a variety of places such as books, letters, and food labels, and that each of those conveys information that serves a particular purpose.

11. The child should know familiar words and numbers in her environment such as stop signs, the names of stores, and street signs.

12. The child should be able to make simple predictions about upcoming events or outcomes in stories using illustrations and prior knowledge as a guide.

13. The child, gathering information from pictures, should be able to tell the general story presented in a book or pretend to read the story to himself or others.

14. The child should know that books have titles, authors, and sometimes illustrators.

15. The child should know what role the author plays (the writer of the story).

16. The child should know that the illustrator draws the pictures in the book.

17. The child should know the title is the name of the book.

18. The child should know the sequence of events in a story: what happens first, in the middle, and at the end.

19. The child should know the elements of a story such as the names of the characters, what happens in the story (the plot), where the story is set, and so on.

20. The child should understand the literal meaning of plays, poems, and stories.

21. The child should know the difference between fact and fiction, that is, real and make-believe.

22. The child should be able to tell stories from her own life and share her personal experiences.

23. The child should be able to use drawings to express thoughts, feelings, and ideas.

KINDERGARTEN

National standards assume that students will already have accomplished the skills listed as pre-K. During kindergarten, the following skills should be added:

1. Unlike the middle of the last century, children are now encouraged to use their imagination in many areas, including reading. Reading programs now encourage children to use mental images based on both the pictures and printed words to help them understand the text.

2. The student should be able to identify visual similarities and differences in words. For example, he should be able to see that the words boy and boys, or farm and farmer are similar and also be able to discriminate between them.

3. The student is expected to use the subject that she is reading about, as well as picture captions, the story title, and other clues, to aid comprehension and make predictions about what will happen in the story or what a specific character will do.

4. The student is encouraged to sound words out using basic elements of phonetic analysis such as common letter combinations, letter sounds, and word patterns to figure out unknown words.

5. The student should be able to distinguish between written letters, words, and sentences.

6. The student should know the alphabet well enough to be able to identify uppercase and lowercase letters out of alphabetical sequence.

7. The student should be able to associate specific sounds with specific letters.

8. The student should be able to verbalize consonant sounds when shown consonant letters.

9. The student should be able to recognize rhyming words, primarily consonant-vowel-consonant (CVC) words such as cat, hat, bat, rat.

10. The student should read selected sight words, such as doll and candy, very early in the year. By the end of the year, the student

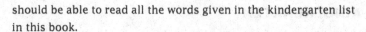

should be able to read all the words given in the kindergarten list in this book.

11. The student should be able to recall orally a series of three items that she is shown.

12. The student should be able to use words that signal sequence relationships such as first, next, and last; up, down, around; and over, under.

13. The student should be able to recognize simple word opposites such as boy and girl, left and right.

14. The student should be able to classify objects by characteristics such as color, size, shape, structure, and function.

15. The student should be able to put pictures in a sequence to tell a logical story.

16. The student should be able to interpret pictures to identify main idea, sequence of events, cause-effect, and to predict logical outcomes.

17. The student should be able to explain his own drawings and writings in a logical manner or to tell a story. This indicates that the student understands that illustrations and writing can have meaning.

18. The student's vocabulary should reflect an increasing range of knowledge and interests.

KINDERGARTEN THROUGH SECOND GRADE (LEVEL 1)

1. By first grade, the young reader has been introduced to syllables, basic prefixes, suffixes, and root words; and by second grade, to compound words, contractions, and spelling patterns. These are basic elements of structural analysis. At the appropriate levels, the child is expected to use these skills to decode unknown words.

2. Depending on the school and the teacher, in first or second grade, the student should be introduced to the idea of a dictionary. In first grade, a picture dictionary is most often used to determine the meaning of words the student does not understand.

28

3. The student is expected to understand, as well as read, level-appropriate words and vocabulary such as those given in this book's thesaurus. That may sound a little odd, but new readers are often able to sound out words without understanding what they mean.

4. When the young reader does not understand the text, she is expected to search for clues, identify where she has misread or misunderstood words or ideas, reread, and ask for help. Known as self-correction strategies, the student is expected to take an active part in the development of her reading skills.

5. Reading aloud is usually introduced in first grade. The student is expected to read familiar stories and poems fluently and with appropriate expression such as rhythm and meter, smooth flow, intonation, and pitch and tone by the time he is well into the second grade.

6. The student is also introduced to the basic characteristics of familiar types of books, including fairy tales, folktales, fiction, nonfiction, legends, fables, myths, poems, nursery rhymes, picture books, and predictable books.

7. The student should then be able to use these reading skills to understand these types of age-appropriate literature.

8. The beginning of literary analysis is introduced, and the student is expected to know about setting, main characters, main events, sequence, and problems in stories. The student is also expected to know the main ideas, or theme, of a story.

9. The student is expected to be able to relate his own personal experiences, including who was involved, what happened, the conflicts, and a general theme.

10. The student is expected to use the same skills and strategies to understand and interpret a variety of nonfiction and fiction texts, including written directions, signs, captions, and warning labels.

11. The student should understand the main idea and supporting details of simple expository writing.

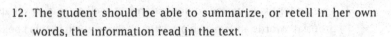

12. The student should be able to summarize, or retell in her own words, the information read in the text.

13. The student should be able to relate the new information to his own prior knowledge and experience.

14. The student is asked to use her imagination, based on the pictures and words in the text, to aid in understanding the material she is reading.

15. Meaning clues are introduced. That is, picture captions, the title of the writing, headings, and other hints are used to have the student make predictions about what is going to happen in a story or what a nonfiction piece will be about.

16. The student is expected to be able to use phonetic strategies to sound out and decode unknown words.

17. The student is expected to use structural analysis to better understand unknown words. Structural analysis includes breaking the words into syllables, identifying common prefixes and suffixes, finding root words, identifying compound words, and understanding contractions.

18. The student should be able to read and understand level-appropriate sight words and vocabulary such as those listed for her grade in this book.

19. The student should use self-correction strategies such as rereading and asking for help.

20. The student should practice reading aloud familiar stories, poems, and passages with fluency and expression.

21. The student is expected to be familiar with, and know the difference between, a variety of literary types, including fables, fairy tales, folktales, legends, myths, poems, nursery rhymes, nonfiction, and more general fiction.

22. The student should be able to identify setting, main characters, main events, sequence, and problems in stories.

THIRD THROUGH FIFTH GRADE (LEVEL 2)

1. In third grade, the idea of previewing materials to help understand the content is expanded by having the student skim the materials in addition to the clues formerly introduced.

2. Also introduced are the many reasons for reading such as for information, for pleasure, or to understand a specific viewpoint.

3. Along with making simple predictions about what the reading materials will be about, or what will happen, the student learns to revise her predictions when they are not correct.

4. The idea of foreshadowing is introduced in a simple way.

5. Phonic and structural analyses become more sophisticated, and syntactic structure and semantic context to decode unknown words such as vowel patterns, complex word families, and affixes are further introduced.

6. The idea of reading ahead and taking words in context are used to decode unknown words.

7. By at least the fourth grade, regular dictionaries are introduced, and the student is taught how to use a variety of other word reference materials such as a glossary and thesaurus to determine the meaning, pronunciation, and derivations of unknown words.

8. The student is introduced to synonyms, antonyms, homophones, and words with multiple meanings.

9. The student should monitor his own reading strategies and make modifications as needed like recognizing when he is confused by a section of text or questions whether the text makes sense.

10. The student should understand that she can adjust her reading speed to suit her purpose and the difficulty of the material.

11. The student should understand the author's purpose or point of view. For example, he should be able to identify whether the writer is trying to persuade or inform the reader.

12. The student should be able to select reading material of direct interest or use to her based on her knowledge of genres, authors, and why they are choosing the material.

13. The student should understand the basic concept of plot, including the main problem, conflicts, and resolutions.

14. Literature from other cultures is often introduced in the third and fourth grade. The student should understand the similarities and differences between those works and those from her own culture, including setting, what characters are expected to do, and the roles of people and nature.

15. The elements of character development in literary works are introduced. These include the differences between main and minor characters; stereotypical characters as opposed to fully developed characters; changes that characters undergo; the importance of a character's actions, motives, and appearance to plot and theme.

16. The student should know that themes and basic plots recur across literary works.

17. By fifth grade, the student should understand personification, alliteration, onomatopoeia, simile, metaphor, imagery, hyperbole, beat, and rhythm.

18. The student should be able to make connections between characters or basic events that she is reading about and people or events in her own life.

19. New kinds of literary works are introduced such as formal textbooks, biographies, letters, diaries, directions, and magazines.

20. The student should be able to explain the differences between different kinds of nonfiction materials, including biographies, diaries, directions, letters, magazines, and textbooks.

21. The student should be able to use the way information is organized in a text to find main ideas and specific information quickly. This means using topic sentences, graphics, summaries, and headings.

22. Along with using organizational hints within the text, the student is expected to learn to use the physical layout of the book, including the table of contents, index, glossary, and appendix, to find information in an efficient manner.

23. The student should be able to summarize and paraphrase information from a text, including the main idea and major supporting details.

24. The student should be able to draw from his previous knowledge and experience to respond to what he has read and to help understand new information.

25. The student should be able to explain different ways a work is organized or how information in the work is organized; for example, chronologically or sequentially. This also includes writing that is centered on organization such as compare and contrast, proposition and support, and cause and effect.

26. The student should be able to understand the function of chapter breaks in both fiction and nonfiction books.

27. The student should be able to identify different genres of fiction such as fantasy, folk tales, mainstream, and science fiction.

SIXTH THROUGH EIGHTH GRADE (LEVEL 3)

1. At this level, the student should be able to explain the reason she is reading a specific text. These reasons may include enjoyment, problem solving, skimming for facts, reviewing previous material, or understanding an issue or viewpoint.

2. The student should be introduced to the etymology of words fairly early in sixth grade if not before. This includes Latin and Greek roots, meanings of foreign words frequently used in English, and historical influences, as well as the individual origin of a particular word.

3. The now more sophisticated student should understand analogies, idioms, metaphors, and similes and be able to use them to infer the meaning of phrases.

4. The student should also use comparison and contrast, definitions, and examples to make sure he understands the meaning of individual words and to identify shades of meaning between synonyms.

5. The student should know denotative and connotative meanings of the reading material.

6. The student should understand the vocabulary of current events even if it is nonstandard for the age.

7. The student should be able to use references such as rhyming dictionaries, etymological dictionaries, and classification books.

8. Techniques for understanding confusing texts should have grown to include consulting other sources, representing abstract information as mental pictures, and drawing on background knowledge.

9. The student should be able to identify the ways in which an author uses language to persuade readers to his viewpoint or to accomplish another purpose. The student should be able to identify the use of emotion, appeal to authority, how word choice affects attitude, language structure, and other techniques.

10. The student should be able to form and express an opinion about what she has read and be able to respond to the text.

11. The student should be able to identify and understand complex elements of plot development such as the use of subplots, parallel episodes, and climax, as well as the development of conflict and resolution.

12. Similarly, the student should be able to identify and explain the elements of character development such as character traits, motivations, relationships between characters, stereotypes, and plot development. The student should also understand the development of characters through their actions, thoughts, words, and interaction with other characters.

13. The student should understand foreshadowing, flashback, the development of suspense or tension, and similar literary devices.

14. The student should understand that the way language is used in literature helps convey mood and meaning as well as create mental images. Some of the literary techniques include dialect, dialogue, irony, rhyme, symbolism, and tone. This should also include the actual sound of the word and how it interacts with other words, for example, alliteration; assonance; consonance; euphonious and cacophonous words; onomatopoeia; and figurative language such as similes, metaphors, personification, hyperbole, and allusion.

15. The student should also be aware that the structure of the writing can convey emotion and affect the tempo of the story. For example, very short sentences are often used to create tension or convey urgency while long sentences with adjectives are often used to slow the pace of a story.

16. The student should be able to explain the effect of an author's style, such as word choice and imagery, on the reader.

17. The student should be able to identify the point of view used in a literary text such as first or third person, limited and omniscient, and how that affects what the reader knows.

18. The student should be able to explain implied and recurring themes in literary works such as good versus evil; bravery; friendship; loyalty; and historical, cultural, and social themes.

19. The student should be able to see the similarities between the motivation of characters in a text, or the causes of complex events, and her own life and the world around her.

20. By sixth grade, the student should be able to follow map routes, order from a catalogue, use bus schedules and understand routes, and use telephone and other directories

21. The student should be able to make judgments on the quality of source materials, such as between standard newspapers and tabloids. The student should also be able to make critical judgments about, and know how to use, primary source materials such as letters and historical documents.

22. Besides being able to summarize read materials, the student should be able to properly quote materials and convey the author's viewpoint.

23. The student should be able to draw conclusions based on implicit, as well as explicit, information in a text.

24. The student should be able to differentiate between fact and opinion within the same text.

WHERE TO FIND INFORMATION ON OTHER STANDARDS AND BENCHMARKS

Science and Technology

Many, if not most, magazines for children now have science stories as a regular part of their content. Project 2061 of the American Association for the Advancement of Science is a long-term initiative dealing with K–12 science nationwide. The project is creating a coordinated set of reform tools and services—books, CD-ROMS, online resources, and workshops—to help educators work toward science literacy for all students, and is a wonderful resource for writers who want to enter that market. Find them at http://www.project2061.org.

The American Association for the Advancement of Science (AAAS) and MCI WorldCom offer lessons and Web resources organized around Project 2061 "Benchmarks for Science Literacy." They also provide the research that went into creating those benchmarks. They are found at http://www.sciencenetlinks.com/index.html.

National Science Education Standards have been developed by the National Research Council. The National Academy Press has the full text of these standards online at http://stills.nap.edu/html/nses.

The National Council for Geographic Education (NCGE) has created a program called "Geography for Life." It is the final report of the Geography Education Standards Project, which was funded through the NCGE by the U.S. Department of Education, the National Endowment for the Humanities, and the National Geographic Society. "Geography for Life" provides a set of guidelines for what students should know, and be able to do, by the end of grades 4 and 8. The URL is http://www.ncge.org/publications/tutorial/.

Content for the Study of Technology was created by the International Technology Education Association. They try to provide the basics of what every student needs to know about technology and what they should be able to do with it. They provide an organizational framework for an articulated program in technology from grades K–12 and a structure for teaching technology that can withstand the accelerating changes in our technological environment. Their "Standards for Technological Literacy: Content for the Study of Technology" can be found at http://www.iteawww.org/TAA/TAA.html.

The same group has developed National Educational Technology Standards (NETS). The primary goal of NETS is to enable those who write for or work with pre-K–12 education to have national standards for the educational uses of technology. The NETS project is working to integrate curriculum technology into the wider world of education. Though a work in progress at this time, the site will be of increasing use over the next several years. It is located at http://cnets.iste.org/.

Mathematics

The National Council of Teachers of Mathematics "Principles and Standards for School Mathematics" was released in 2000. The electronic version of the latest standards is available online. The document is designed to establish a broad framework to guide reform in school mathematics in the next decade for pre-K through grade 12. Find them at http://standards-e.nctm.org. For vignettes and lessons that help explicate the new standards, see the Illuminations Web site, published by NCTM and MCI WorldCom, at http://illuminations.nctm.org/.

Other Resources

The Council of Chief State School Officers (CCSSO) has made the full text of Key State Policies on K–12 Education available through searching http://www.ccsso.org/publications/index.cfm?init=1. Other publications that may be of interest through this site include "Alignment of Science and Mathematics Standards and Assessments in Four States."

A Compendium of Standards and Benchmarks for K–12 Education is available at http://198.17.205.11/standards-benchmarks/.

Each U.S. state has a department of education. Contact information and Web sites for each state and most territories are listed in the back of this book, in the Resources section. Many of the states and territories have standards and benchmarks online. Virtually all the online materials can be found by searching within the Web sites for standards, benchmarks, framework, or course of study. You can also find hotlinks to each state's education Web site online at http://www.census.gov/mso/www/educate/agencies.htm.

Footnote

[1] One survey in Southern California showed as many as fifty separate languages were spoken as primary, or first, languages by students in a single school district.

KINDERGARTEN

Social Changes. At one time, kindergarten was considered primarily a socialization process. Those days are gone. The federal government is promoting preschool education for all students. In a growing number of places in the country, children actually have to pass a reading competency test to "graduate" into first grade. Teachers now must teach reading skills, and there is a growing demand for stories for classroom use. This makes read-it-yourself literature even more relevant than before. There are also new subjects introduced at the earliest ages. While actual lessons on space exploration and ecology currently wait until second or third grade, the concepts are introduced here, and one should expect these subjects to be introduced formally in the future at even younger ages.

In the Classroom. Because of the ever-growing number of kindergartners who have attended preschool, some are able to read materials previously considered appropriate for first to third graders.

Health education begins, or continues, in kindergarten. Children are often given toothbrushes and encouraged to brush their teeth at school. Nutrition is discussed in terms of eating a good breakfast and drinking milk and personal hygiene is also promoted. If you can make these health issues fun or interesting, educational publishers and trade magazines such as *Highlights for Children* could turn into great marketplaces.

Words for holidays such as Halloween, Christmas, and Easter may seem too advanced for this level, but are, in fact, commonly used. Like many complicated picture books, they are understood in context and become recognized as "sight" reading words rather than "phonic" ones. Mother's Day, Valentine's Day, February as Black History Month, and President's Day have all come into major focus in schools. Even though they may not be vacation holidays, a great deal of time is devoted to talking, writing, and arts and crafts projects in celebration of these days. Poetry and short stories with themes geared to these minor holiday are a part of classroom learning.

Dinosaurs are popular with young children, but they are treated in a simplified manner here and formally introduced in second grade. However, dinosaurs are often a focus in the kindergarten classroom and are the basis of art projects, music, and developing reading and writing skills. They make good subjects for shape books or picture and coloring books. If you use the scientific names for the different species, or discuss subjects such as family, diet, or other behavior, be sure they're compatible with current opinions. For example, the brontosaurus is now generally accepted as not having really lived. Brontosaurus is actually just an Apatosaurus, whose head was replaced with the wrong skull.

Cooking is often used in the same way and provides hands-on experience that can lend extra dimensions to classroom learning.

Specific Vocabulary Development. The kindergarten student's vocabulary centers around one-syllable words, under six letters. The numbers one to ten and the primary colors are introduced in kindergarten. Seasons are also introduced (autumn is known as fall). Kindergartners know words like *the* and *a* as well as *tree* and, of course, *boy* and *girl*. Most publishers do not use contractions yet, and possessives are not commonly used either. The months and days of the week are not usually introduced until first grade.

The animals most commonly introduced at the kindergarten level are included in the following word list. Groups of animals and plants are particularly flexible. Please see the first- through third-grade lists for other animals that are introduced at the earliest levels.

Publishing. Schools primarily use picture books and magazines, which traditionally address the two- to eight-year-old child. Picture stories are also good for this group, although traditionally meant for the first- to third-grade child. Whether meant to be read aloud by an adult or alone by the child, the story line is carried more by text than by pictures in the picture story. These stories should have lots of action.

Books meant to be read by adults to the youngest listeners should take no more than twenty minutes to read; ten to fifteen minutes is preferred. The sentence length can vary but should be such that the child that is being read to can follow it easily. If the sentences are long, they should have breaks and pictures to keep the child in the story. The self-reader should have a sentence, or idea, length of five to six words. That means that a long sentence can be broken up into shorter phrases, but those phrases should convey a whole idea. For example, in a self reader the sentence, *It is best to have two when you go to the zoo*, might be broken up into *it is best to have two* as one idea phrase and *when you go to the zoo* and a second idea phrase.

Dialogue at this level is often set off by a full colon, rather than by quotation marks:

> Mother said: See the sun. Today will be fun.

Stories about other holidays that take into account our nation's cultural diversity are often eagerly sought. You may find Chinese New Year, Chanukah, and Kwanzaa have little or no competition in the marketplace, yet they provide a healthy market for the children's writer and excellent formats for creative writing exercises in class. Magazines, book publishers, and even newspapers often look for holiday material for children, and it's easier to sell stories about holidays that get less media coverage than Christmas and Easter.

Writing Samples. The following is a picture story meant for the adult to read to the kindergarten child. The dots indicate a picture or a page break and each of the ideas would be illustrated.

- There is one girl. One. And she wants to have fun.
- She can roll a ball,
- color,
- draw,
- ride a bus,
- play with the cat.
- She can walk the dog
- or play with her doll.
- But one, just one,
- cannot play bat the ball,

- or go fish
- or run, red, run.
- One, just one, cannot play house
- or school
- or store.
- It is best to have two when you go to the zoo
- or go for a walk
- or just want to talk.
- It is a good thing she has a brother.

To make this story into a self reader, the sentence, or idea phrase, length should be changed.

- There is one girl. One.
- And she wants to have fun.
- She can roll a ball.
- She can color.
- She can ride a bus.
- She can play with the cat.
- She can walk the dog.
- Or play with her doll.
- But one cannot play ball.
- Or play go fish.
- Or play run, red, run.
- One cannot play house.
- Or play school.
- Or play store.
- You need two for the zoo.
- Or to go for a walk.
- Or just to talk.
- She is glad she has a brother.

The sentences are not actually complete, but a period is often used to show a complete thought. Short sentences or idea phases are less daunting to a young reader. It gives them a feeling of accomplishment to finish a sentence unit and understand it.

KINDERGARTEN WORD LIST

a

a
about
above
act
acts
add
address
again
air
all
almost
alone
also
always
am
an
and
animal
answer
ant
any
are
arm
art
as
ask
at
ate
away
ax

b

baby
back
bad
ball
ban
barn
bat
bay
be
beach
bead
bear
beat
because
bed
bee
been
before
begin
bell
bent
best
better
big
black
blue
book
boss
both
box
boy
bring
brown
bug
bull
bunny
bus
but
buy
by

c

cab
cake
call
can
candy
cap
care
carry
chair
chicken
child
children
Christmas
church
circle
city
clean
close
cold
color
colt
come
coming
cookie
cop
cost
could
count
cow
crab
crayon
cry
cub
cup
cut

d

dad
daddy
dam
dark
day
dead
deer
do
doll
door
dot
down
dove
down
draw
dream
dress
drive
drop
duck

e

each
Easter
easy
eat

eel
egg
eight
elephant
elk
end
ever
every

f

face
fad
fall
family
fan
farm
farmer
father
fed
fan
feel
feeling
few
fight
fill
find
fire
fireman
fish
fit
five
food
floor
flower
fly
foot
for
found
four
fox

free
freely
frog
from
full
fun
fur

g

game
gap
garden
gave
gee
get
ghost
gift
giraffe
girl
give
glad
go
goat
gold
golden
goldfish
good
goose
got
grass
great
green
grow
gum
gun

h

had
hair
ham
Halloween

hand
happy
hard
has
hat
have
hay
he
head
health
hear
heard
heart
hello
help
hen
her
here
hers
hey
hi
him
hippo
his
hit
hog
hole
holiday
home
hop
hope
hot
house
how
hurt

i

I
ice
in

it
its

j

jam
jar
jet
Jew
job
juice
jump

k

keep
key
kid
kind
king
kiss
kite
kitten
koala

l

lad
lamb
land
lap
large
last
late
led
leg
lend
let
light
like
line
lion
lit
little

log	nap	picture	road
look	neat	pie	rob
lose	never	pig	robin
loss	new	pin	robot
lost	next	pizza	rock
lot	nine	plant	rocket
love	no	plate	room
low	not	play	round

m

	now	please	row
mad	number	pole	rule
made	nurse	pony	run
make	nut	poor	
making		pop	**s**

o

mall	of	present	sad
man	off	price	safe
manly	oh	pull	said
many	oil	pumpkin	same
mat	old	pup	saw
may	on	puppy	say
me	one	purple	school
meet	only	put	seal
meow	open		see

q

miss	or	quack	sell
mom	orange	queen	send
mommy	our	quiet	sent
money	out		set
monkey	owl	**r**	seven
moo	own	rabbit	she
moose	ox	ram	sheep
more		ran	shoe

p

mother		rat	shy
mouse	pad	read	sick
move	pal	red	side
Mr.	pan	reindeer	six
Mrs.	paper	rent	skunk
Ms.	party	rich	sky
my	pass	ride	sleep

n

	pat	right	small
name	pay	rip	snow
	people	river	snowball

snowman	tan	turkey	what
so	tap	turtle	when
soft	tax	TV	white
some	tell	two	White House
son	ten		who
song	tend	**u**	why
soon	thank	under	will
spider	Thanksgiving	up	win
spring	that	us	winter
stand	the	use	wish
star	their	used	witch
stick	them		with
sticker	then	**v**	woman
sticky	these	valentine	word
stood	they	van	work
stop	thing	very	worm
store	things		wow
story	this	**w**	write
strong	three	wait	
summer	tiger	walk	**y**
sun	to	wall	yard
sure	toe	want	yea
sweet	told	was	yellow
swim	top	water	yes
	town	wax	you
t	toy	way	your
tab	tractor	we	
table	train	wed	**z**
tag	tree	week	zebra
take	true	well	zip
talk	try	went	zipper
tall	tummy	were	zoo
		wet	

FIRST GRADE

Unlike the middle of the last century, children are now encouraged to use their imagination in many areas, including reading. One of the first things reading programs now encourage children to do is to use mental images based on both the pictures and printed word to help young readers understand the text. In a related strategy, they are expected to use the subject that they are reading about, picture captions, the story title, and other clues to aid comprehension and make predictions about what will happen in the story or what a specific character will do.

When *Word Book* was first published, phonics was only one of several popular strategies for teaching reading to the youngest children. As the new century takes off, phonics has returned to center stage, and children nationally are encouraged to sound words out using basic elements of phonetic analysis such as common letter combinations, letter sounds, and word patterns to figure out unknown words.

Social Changes. Although many first graders have been in all-day kindergarten, some are new to being away from home all day long, and all first graders are new to the sustained periods of concentration that are necessary in the first-grade classroom.

In the Classroom. While children learn the seasons and the numbers one to ten in kindergarten, the months, days of the week, and numbers over ten generally are introduced in first grade.

Almost all sports are introduced by name at this level. However, the technical details and rules are not generally introduced until third grade.

By the end of kindergarten, most children can sound out any three- or four-letter word. However, many of these words (such as *eve* or *dim*) are introduced later since they are somewhat abstract. (If a word seems overly sophisticated for your young audience, check the word list or the thesaurus sections in this book; the words listed there are taken from publishers' graded material.)

Specific Vocabulary Development. The prefix *un* is introduced for the simplest of words such as *unhappy, unfit,* or *undo.* The suffix *ing* is also introduced, and words such as *fishing, walking,* and *reading* are common. The past tense is also introduced. This includes irregular forms such as *know* to *knew* and *was* to *were,* as well as the addition of a simple *ed* such as *ask* to *asked* and *walk* to *walked.*

Possessives are introduced at the very beginning of the year. *Dad's hat* and *mother's dress* appear along with the other changes mentioned, which give the writer a great deal more flexibility than when writing for the youngest self-readers.

Contractions such *as I'd, I'll, I'm, I've, we're, can't,* and *won't* are introduced at this level.

The most commonly used compound words, such as *classroom* and *grandmother,* are introduced in first grade, but many schools wait until second grade even if the individual words are understood by the child. The key seems to be how familiar the reader is with the concept and how often the word is used in their everyday lives.

Publishing. The optimal sentence length is still around five to six words. However, as with all writing, length should vary throughout your story. Some publishers are now using longer sentences but use the strategy of breaking them up into five- or six-word lines. The longest sentence length used in a strictly graded text for this age is ten words. Parenthetical statements should be avoided. Sentence length is important because the early reader can become lost in the individual words and have trouble understanding the overall idea. The constraints on sentence length are eased by the ability to start sentences with such words as *and, because,* and *but.* Sentences at this level need to be whole ideas but do not necessarily need to conform to strictly correct adult standards.

If the story is written for an adult to read to a child, sentence length is only restricted to that which is comfortably read aloud in one breath. The vocabulary should be such that the child can easily understand it, but it is not constrained to a graded vocabulary.

There is a much larger periodical market for the primary group than there is for the very beginning reader. Very short articles or stories, known as fillers, are popular in magazines. These fillers are usually under 500 words and often under 100. One editor told me that "if you can make brushing your teeth fun, you can make a living the rest of your life." Games, riddles, and stories about good health habits, safety, science, and human interest pieces are especially welcome even in the most prestigious periodicals.

As mentioned earlier, most sports are understood by name at this level and are especially popular in literacy books for older readers. There is a great appetite for stories and nonfiction articles about everything from baseball to karate; however, the technical details and rules are not generally introduced until the reader achieves third-grade reading skills.

Like sports, simple mysteries and "friendly" ghost stories are popular among first graders or level 1 books. Many, if not most, of the fiction stories published for six- to eight-year-olds are fantasies, but retelling such classics as *The Goose Girl* in modern dress is sure to garner rejection slips instead of praise. Two areas that are popular are stories that show a child being able to help her family or community in a realistic manner and children dealing with minor problems in appropriate ways. Problems like the death of a gold fish or a divorce is acceptable if it is done with a light touch.

Books for teens and adults learning to read often start at the first-grade level rather than kindergarten. Most of these books are presented much like those for the young reader but with fewer pictures than those for children, and many are presented in a standard paperback format. They primarily feature romance, sports, suspense, nonviolent mysteries, and other high-interest subjects. They may also address such practical areas as working, social skills, and legal problems and how to solve them. The vocabulary, length, and style guidelines are uniform for the level no matter who the end user.

Writing Sample. The following story employs a popular subject—ghosts—and a popular genre—mystery. It also takes on a common "problem" for kids—moving. The sentences are within the ten-word limit, and the words are monosyllabic. Another theme present is adaptation. First graders adapt to full days of school work, and Tommy adapts to new surroundings:

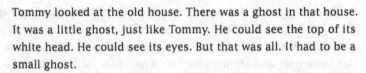

Tommy looked at the old house. There was a ghost in that house. It was a little ghost, just like Tommy. He could see the top of its white head. He could see its eyes. But that was all. It had to be a small ghost.

"This is OK. A ghost is fun," he said. "Moving here may be OK."

Tommy did not like to move. He did not want to move from the city. But his father was a park ranger. He worked at a beach park now so they all had to move.

His father liked the beach. So did his brother Bob. His mother loved their house. Most houses for rangers are not new. This one was new and it was big. Tommy was the only one who did not want to live there.

"But a ghost is really OK," he said. "The old house is OK. The new house may be OK, too."

FIRST GRADE WORD LIST

a

across
action
adult
afraid
afternoon
against
age
aged
ago
ahead
Air Force
aircraft
airfield
airplane
airport
airship
album
alike
alligator
almond
along
already
among
amount
anger
angry
another
anybody
anyone
anything
anyway
apartment

April
aquarium
aren't
armadillo
arms
Army
around
August
aunt

b

baboon
backing
bag
bake
balloon
band
bank
base
baseball
basket
basketball
bass
bath
bathe
bathroom
bathtub
batter
beached
beat
beautiful
beaver
become
beetle

beg
behind
being
belief
believe
belong
below
bend
beneath
berry
beside
besides
bet
between
beyond
bib
bid
bike
bill
bin
bit
bite
blackbird
blacktop
blaze
block
blood
blouse
blue jay
bluebird
board
boat
bobcat
body

bone
boom
boot
border
born
bottom
bow
bowl
boxer
brake
brave
break
breakfast
breath
breathe
bridge
bright
brother
buck
bud
build
building
bulldog
bulldozer
bullfrog
bull's-eye
bully
burglar
busy
button
buyer

c

cabin

cable
cage
calendar
camera
camp
campfire
canary
cannot
can't
card
careful
cart
catbird
catch
caterpillar
cave
cell
cent
certain
certainly
chart
chase
chat
chatter
check
chew
chief
chin
circle
choke
circus
clam
class
classroom
claw
clay
climb
clinic
clock

clothes
cloud
clown
club
coat
cob
cobra
cocoa
coke
computer
cone
Congress
cook
cool
cot
couldn't
country
cover
coyote
crawl
cream
creep
creeping
cricket
cripes
crocodile
cross
crown
cuff
cute
cutting

d

dab
dairy
dance
dandy
danger
dart

date
daughter
daylight
dead
dear
December
decide
deck
deed
deep
den
dent
desert
dew
didn't
different
dig
dill
dim
dime
dine
dinner
dip
direct
direction
dirt
discover
dish
dive
dock
doctor
does
doesn't
doing
done
don't
dope
dose
doubt

doubtful
dragon
drink
dropped
drove
drown
drug
drum
dry
dull
dumb
dummy
during
duty

e

eagle
ear
early
earth
east
eating
edge
eighteen
eighty
elf
else
English
enough
enter
escape
even
evening
everything
excellent
except
exercise
extra

f

fact
factory
fade
fair
fake
families
far
farming
fast
fat
favor
fear
fearful
feast
feat
feed
feet
fell
fellow
fence
fib
fifteen
fifth
fifty
fig
file
fin
finance
finding
fine
finger
finish
first
fishing
fix
flake
flew
float

flop
floppy disk
flow
fog
fold
follow
following
football
force
forest
forget
fork
form
forty
fourteen
fourth
France
freckles
French
Friday
friend
front
fry
funny

g

gab
gag
gang
gas
gate
gather
gay
gear
ginger
gingerbread
glass
glasses
gleam
glow

glue
gnaw
gobble
god
goddess
goes
gone
good-bye
gopher
gorilla
government
grandfather
grandmother
grasshopper
gray
grin
ground
group
grown-up
gruff
guard
guess
guide
gulp
gut
guts
guy
gym

h

hadn't
half
hall
hamster
happen
hard drive
hasn't
he'd
heat

heaven
heavy
helmet
helper
hem
here's
hero
hidden
hide
hint
hip
hold
homework
honey
honk
honor
hoof
hoot
hopped
horrible
hour
however
hug
huge
hum
hundred
hurried
hurry
husband

i

icon
I'd
idea
ill
I'll
illegal
I'm
important

inch
indeed
Indian
inside
instead
interest
into
isn't
it's
I've

j

jab
jack
January
jay
jeans
jeep
jell
jelly
joke
jot
joy
judge
jug
jumped
just

k

kangaroo
keeper
keg
keyboard
kick
kill
kin
kit
kitchen
kneel
knew

knife
know
known

l

labor
lack
lady
lag
lake
lamp
lass
later
law
lay
lead
leaf
learn
least
leather
leave
left
lens
leopard
letter
lick
lid
lie
life
lift
likely
likes
lily
lip
listen
live
lived
lives
living

lizard
llama
lock
long
longing
looked
looking
loud
loved
lovely
luck
lug
lumber
lunch

m

machine
machinery
magic
mail
mailbox
mailman
maker
mama
mane
map
March
march
Marines
mark
market
marry
marsupial
master
mastodon
matter
May
maybe
mayor

mean
meat
member
men
mend
mess
message
met
might
mike
mile
milk
mill
mind
mine
minus
minute
mist
mistake
mitten
mix
mixed
moment
Monday
monster
month
moon
mop
morning
moss
most
moth
mouth
movie
moving
much
mud
mug
muss

must
myself
mystery

n

nab
nag
napping
NASA
nation
native
nature
Navy
near
nearing
nearly
necessary
neck
need
neither
nervous
nest
newspaper
nice
nickel
night
nineteen
ninety
nip
nobody
nod
noise
none
north
nose
note
nothing
notice
November

nun
nuzzle

o

oak
oar
oat
object
ocean
October
octopus
office
officer
often
okay
older
once
onto
order
ostrich
other
otter
ought
outside
oval
oven
oversee

p

pack
paddle
pair
palace
panic
pants
papa
park
parrot
part
partridge

past
paste
path
patrol
paw
paying
payment
pea
peach
peacock
peck
peer
peg
pelican
pen
pencil
penguin
penny
perhaps
person
pest
pet
pick
pickle
piece
pigeon
pile
pill
pine
pink
pipe
pipeline
pit
place
plan
plane
player
playground
plenty

plop
pluck
plus
pocket
pod
point
poke
police
policeman
policewoman
pond
pool
popcorn
possible
post
postcard
pouch
power
practice
prepare
president
press
pretty
prince
princess
print
problem
promise
pub
public
Puritan
purpose
push
push-up

q

quail
Quaker
quarter

question	rid	scared	shore
quick	riddle	scene	short
quicksand	rig	schoolwork	shortly
quit	rim	score	shot
quite	ring	scout	should
	ripe	scream	shouldn't
r	ripen	screech	shout
raccoon	rise	search	shovel
race	roadbed	seat	show
rack	roar	second	shut
radish	rod	secret	sidewalk
rag	roll	seed	sight
rain	roof	seek	sign
raise	rooster	seem	silly
rake	rope	seesaw	silver
ranger	rose	Senate	simple
rap	rot	senate	sin
rate	rotorcraft	sense	since
rather	rub	sentence	sing
rattlesnake	rubber	September	sip
raw	rug	serve	sir
ray	rum	service	sister
reach	running	seventeen	sitting
ready	rut	seventy	sit-up
real		several	sixteen
reason	**s**	shake	sixth
receive	sack	shall	sixty
rectangle	sadness	shape	size
recycle	sag	shark	skate
reins	sail	sharp	skin
remain	sale	shave	skinny
remember	salt	sheet	slate
reply	sand	shell	slow
report	sap	shine	smart
require	Saturday	ship	smart house
rest	save	shirt	smile
return	sawmill	shiver	smoke
rib	scare	shock	snail
rice	scarecrow	shop	snake

sob	stream	team	tomorrow
soccer	street	tee	ton
social	strength	teeth	tonight
sock	string	telling	too
socks	stripe	tent	took
somebody	stroke	terrible	tool
someday	struggle	that's	toot
someone	study	themselves	tooth
something	stuff	there	touch
sometimes	stutter	therefore	touching
somewhere	subject	they'll	tow
sort	subtract	they're	toward
sound	such	thin	track
soup	suck	think	trade
south	sudden	third	trained
space	sugar	thirteen	trap
speak	suit	thirty	travel
spell	suitcase	those	tray
spill	sum	though	triangle
spin	Sunday	thought	trick
splash	sunny	thousand	trip
spoke	sunset	threw	troll
spoon	super	throat	trouble
sport	supply	through	troublemaker
spot	surprise	throw	truck
squirrel	swallow	Thursday	trust
stag	sweets	thus	truth
stake	swing	tick	tub
starfish		ticket	tuck
start	**t**	tickets	Tuesday
state		tide	tug
station	tack	tie	tune
stay	tail	tight	turn
step	taken	tile	twelve
still	tape	till	twenty
stock	taste	time	twist
stoplight	taxi	tin	type
stove	tea	tip	
strange	teach	together	
	teacher		

u

umpire
uncertain
uncle
understand
unfit
unhappy
uniform
unreal
until
unzip
uphill
upon
uptown

v

vertical
vet
view
visit
voice

w

wag
wake
walked
walking
walnut
walrus
wanted
war
warm
wash
wasn't
waste
watch
wee
wear
weather
wedding
Wednesday
weed
weigh
weight
weird
welcome
we'll
we're

west
whale
whatever
wheat
wheel
where
whether
which
while
whisper
whoever
whole
wick
wide
wife
wig
wind
window
wine
wing
wipe
wise
wit
within

without
wonder
wonderful
won't
wood
worked
worker
workman
world
worry
worse
would
wouldn't
writer
wrong

y

yam
yeah
year
yet
yip
you'll
young
yucca

SECOND GRADE

I n the second and third grades, the smallest number of new words are added to a new reader's vocabulary. The two grades together add the average number in each of the other grades. One change from the earlier edition of the book is the addition of the proper names of the most common dinosaurs. Previously, even though dinosaurs were very popular with even the youngest child, proper names were not used in graded literature until fifth grade. That is still true of the most unusual types, but the most common, such as Stegosaurus or Triceratops, are now introduced here. Additionally, children are introduced to science, particularly biology and ecology. Still, overall, this is a time to confirm skills and allow those who were not as ready to catch up.

Social Changes. One of the major changes common at this age is that most children have become less self-oriented than they were in kindergarten and even first grade. As a result, they have stopped generalizing characters, and individual personalities have become important in stories.

In the Classroom. A beginning study of the solar system is often part of the second-grade curriculum. The continents and the cardinal directions, north, south, east, and west, are generally taught in school, and there is usually some work with the world map.

Schools introduce their home state, other major states, and a few foreign countries by this level. These countries include major powers and nations that are near neighbors of the United States both physically and culturally. The best known states, such as New York, California, Florida, and Texas, are familiar to the second grader as he learns about the con-

tinental United States. More explanation or description may be needed in introducing difficult names or lesser known states. Canada and Mexico, which border the United States, and England, France, and Germany are introduced at this level. Nations currently in the news are often familiar to the second grader also.

Foreign or unusual words begin to be introduced in second grade. When including words that are not in the child's vocabulary, it is best to give the definition first and then the word. Readers tend to skip over unfamiliar words, getting the meaning from the context of the sentence. Giving the definition first makes it much easier to learn the new word; for example, a large open plain in Africa is called a savanna.

Specific Vocabulary Development. While some of the most common compound words were introduced in first grade, far more are introduced in second grade. At this point, any compound words that are made up of words the children already know may be used. Going beyond the standard list, you might name a Native American Redhorse or Whitesnake and still be well within the parameters of the age group. Some compound words in the word lists are listed at a higher grade level than where they usually would be placed. These words are listed at the levels at which they were actually used in graded texts. However, if the meaning is clear and the word is easily read, it can be used at a lower level.

Publishing. From this point on, the protagonist of your story should be at least the same age as, and preferably a little older than, the reader.

Since there are few illustrations in easy readers, you need to help your reader identify the characters and give her easy ways to remember each character. One way to do this is with tags, actions, gestures, or physical attributes that easily identify the person for the reader. One character might constantly be pushing up his glasses when he talks, or another's red hair and freckles may make her memorable.

Mysteries, adventures, and hero stories are very popular at this age. Vocabulary choice and sentence length are important because most books are aimed at self-readers. The ideal sentence length is still five or six words. However, some publishers have already increased the target sentence length to around ten words. Long passages of description are still unacceptable. There are many reasons to maintain a short sentence length, even if the publisher does not require it. The child reads one word at a time, then puts the words together to make a whole idea. The shorter the sentence is, the easier that process becomes. Thus, it is easier to understand. The inexperienced reader also gets a sense of accomplishment in successfully finishing and understanding a sentence.

Most books run between 1,000 and 1,500 words. The low end is 500 words, and the high end is 2,000. Most magazines aimed at this age group use stories ranging from 300 to 500 words but welcome short pieces also. One thousand words is almost certain to be too long for a magazine. Check your writer's guide lines or *Children's Writer's and Illustrator's Market* for individual length requirements; remember, publishers generally list the maximum number of words they want.

Second graders seem to be caught in the middle as far as books and magazines are concerned. They are neither at the beginning nor at the end of a period. Their interests, reading skills, and egos sometimes make reading picture books unacceptable, and heavily illustrated picture stories are often overlooked because they seem too "babyish." Even though the vocabulary goes beyond second grade, at this point the young reader or easy-to-read book comes into its own. The more adult presentation appeals to the seven- and eight-year-olds, and their reading skills are generally good enough that they no longer need the support provided by profuse illustrations.

Writing Samples. The following story asks the young reader to use her imagination. It also demonstrates how to introduce a new word, barnacle:

> Let's pretend you have an aquarium. What would you put in it? Would you put a cat in it? No. Cats don't live in water. Would you put a dog in it? No. Dogs don't live in water. Would you put a barnacle in it? You could. Barnacles live in water. But they aren't very pretty. They are small grayish sea animals. Would you put a fish in it? Yes. Fish live in water. Most fish are pretty. Some fish are beautiful. I think I like fish best. I would put them in my aquarium.

SECOND GRADE WORD LIST

a
aboard
accomplish
ace
actor
advance
afire
afloat
agree
aid
ale
allow
alphabet
although
antennae
Apatosaurus
appear
appearance
apply
ark
armload
arrive
arrow
arrowhead
article
artist
ashore
asteroid
atom
attempt
attention

b
bacteria
badger
banana
barber
basic
basis
batch
battle
beautify
beginner
belt
bicycle
bind
blackberry
blade
blame
blast
blow
bluebell
blueberry
bold
boob
bore
borrow
bother
bought
bound
braid
branch
brand
brass
bread
breadfruit
brook
broom
brownie
brush
bubble
bulb
bump
bun
bunt
bush
business
butter

c
candle
capital
captain
cardboard
carnival
carrot
cartoon
case
cash
cast
cause
cedar
cell phone
center
centigrade
centimeter
chance
change
character
charge
checkers
cheek
cherry
chest
chipmunk
chirp
chop
chrome
chubby
cider
cinnamon
claim
clear
clerk
click
cliff
clip
closet
clue
coal
coast
cockpit
cocoon
coffee
collie
colorful
comb
comma
command
commission
common
community
company

consider
continue
control
corn
corner
corny
cotton
craft
crash
crew
crib
crime
crop
crosswise
crow
crowd
cue
curl

d

dare
daydream
deal
department
desk
destroy
die
disagree
disk
dolphin
doorway
doughnut
downstairs
downtown
dresser
drift
drill
drip
due

dump
dust

e

earn
effort
either
elevate
elevator
elm
enemy
England
enjoy
equal
erase
everywhere
exact
example
expect
explain

f

fail
famous
feather
field
figure
fireworks
firm
fist
fitting
flash
flat
flaw
flight
flip
flock
flood
floss
foal

fool
foolish
forceful
forgive
forth
France
fresh
friendship
fright
frighten
frown
fruit
further

g

gain
gale
general
Germany
giant
good-night
govern
grade
grand
grant
grape

h

hale
hammer
handcuffs
handle
hang
harbor
harden
haste
hasty
hate
haunt
heavenly

herd
herself
himself
history
hive
hoe
hogan
hound
hunger
hungry
hunt

i

imagine
ink
Internet
invent
iron
island
itself
ivy

j

Japan
jellyfish
jingle
jog
journal

k

kilogram
knight
know-how
knowledge

l

ladder
language
larvae
lawn

lemon
length
lice
lighthouse
list
litter
load
lone
lonely
lord
lumbering
lumberman
lye

m

maize
malt
manner
maple
mask
measure
meek
melt
meter
method
middle
millimeter
misunder-
  standing
mix-up
moccasin
modern
mole
monument
mound
mount
mountain
movement
mule

multiply
mummy

n

nail
narrow
natural
nectar
neighbor
neighborhood

o

oarlock
objective
offer
onion
ounce
outstanding
ovenbird
overseas
overthrow

p

page
pail
pain
paint
parade
peel
period
phone
pinecone
pint
pitch
plain
pleasure
plentiful
pollen
poppy
porcupine

position
positive
pound
powerful
predator
preen
pretend
pride
produce
proud
prove
prowl
Pteranodon
puff
pupa

q

quart

r

rail
railroad
raindrops
rainfall
raspberry
rattle
realize
recess
record
refrigerator
refuse
remove
respect
result
roost
rote
roundhouse
rude
ruin

rush
rust

s

sandstone
season
sequoia
settle
sew
shade
share
shoemaker
sidekick
skateboard
skill
skip
slap
slide
smooth
snack
snap
snowstorm
soil
sonic
sorry
sour
spank
special
speech
spend
spinach
spirit
spool
sportsman
sportswoman
spray
spread
square
squash

squawk	sundown	tonic	vase
squeak	sunlit	toothpaste	vegetable
squirm	sunrise	toss	village
stair	suntan	total	violet
stamp	supper	toxic	virus
steak	suppose	trail	vote
steam	sweetness	trash	

W

wagon

steel	swish	treat	wasp
steep	system	trend	watchful
Stegosaurus		Triceratops	whom

t

stem		tryout	wild
stew	talent	tulip	wildcat
sting	taught	tunnel	wink
stink	tear	typewriter	withdraw
stomach	teaspoon	Tyrannosaurus	woodchuck
stone	teen	Rex	woodpecker
stool	telephone		

u

y

stork	termites	umbrella	
storm	thick	unless	yank
straw	thirsty	unpaid	yarn
strawberry	thorn	useful	yearly
strike	thoughtful	useless	yeast
success	thread		yew

v

suffer	throughout		yourself
suffering	tiny	vacation	youth
suggest	tire	valley	Yule
suggestion	tired	value	
	toilet		

65

THIRD GRADE

Ecology, which was introduced in a minor way in second grade, is now expanded. The groups establishing national standards and benchmarks recommend including information on solid waste and recycling. Quite a few schools have recycling programs, and some clever teachers have the children not only save items like aluminum cans but take a field trip to a recycling plant. The children see what happens to the materials they collect and can get money for what they have done. The money can go to a special fund for the school or to buying something for the classroom. One of the challenges is to make the children understand why handling trash is important, and interesting stories about this process may well find a variety of markets.

On a similar note, make sure you check current accepted science before dealing with greenhouse gases, global warming, or other controversial issues. Just as the fashions in teaching reading were in flux when the last edition of this book was written, opinions on some ecological issues are currently subject to change.

Disaster preparedness is now introduced in third grade along with an increase in health and safety issues. Natural disasters are more commonly dealt with in the classroom than terrorism. One can see the difference that education and preparedness make when studying how communities deal with the same or similar incidents. Knowing what to do in the case of fire, earthquake, flood, or high winds can save lives, and that educational process often starts in the classroom.

Diet is a particular focus now. Childhood obesity will probably be a political and social issue for ten, or more, years to come. The students are already familiar with the food pyramid, but knowing what calories are, or carbohydrates, and other issues generally wait for third grade. With today's emphasis on weight and health, the "Fat Albert" style of hero will probably be a hard sell, but be careful not to make fun of an overweight child. Personal attack, no matter what the fashion, is unacceptable.

Space, new types of transportation, and a world of future science are also introduced in second and third grades. Science fiction stories as a genre once waited for fourth or fifth grade, but are now welcome. The stories should be based on what we can expect in a real future and should explain what things like rotocars are or how they work.

Social Changes. Third graders begin identifying themselves with the world around them through attachments to objects such as toys. They begin to clearly prefer one thing to another. It is just this discovery of taste preferences that creates devoted fans. Whether it's Star Wars or the Little Mermaid, eight- and nine-year-old third graders are prime markets for toy manufacturers.

In the Classroom. Health, drug, and sex education are started early throughout the United States, and antidrug messages are often a part of the third-grade curriculum. In our culture, the word drug has generally taken on the connotation of being a narcotic or other controlled substance. In most schools, however, the idea has expanded to include caffeine, tobacco, and alcohol. It is wise to stay away from any positive portrayal of these substances, whether your work is aimed at an academic or popular market. The word *medicine* is generally used to specify the proper use of controlled substances.

Third graders do a lot of in-class reading and group reading. One of the popular classroom subjects is sports. The details, rules, and technical aspects of sports begin to be introduced at this level, and sports will remain a high-interest subject throughout all children's and young adult markets. Another ongoing interest is in mystery stories. While they are one of the most popular genres for young readers, there are a few rules you need to know. Too much violence is generally unacceptable for any juvenile writing. For preteens, murder is out, and so are most dead bodies. The only corpses generally are mummies that lend a safely creepy

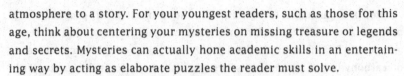

atmosphere to a story. For your youngest readers, such as those for this age, think about centering your mysteries on missing treasure or legends and secrets. Mysteries can actually hone academic skills in an entertaining way by acting as elaborate puzzles the reader must solve.

Specific Vocabulary Development. The prefixes *dis, ex,* and *re* are added at this level. For example, *disable, disadvantage, disallow, redo, reset,* or any other word already introduced may be used with these prefixes.

Hyphenated words such as *part-time, sit-ups, dry-eyed,* and *age-old* are introduced in third grade.

The suffix *ment* is also introduced at this level: *excitement, encouragement.*

You may use the name of almost any body part at this level. Ankles, knees, shoulders, and even abdomen join the simpler head, arms, and legs previously introduced. Individual bones and muscles are not understood yet.

Publishing. By third grade, children have reached the end of the primary reading level. They have some experience both reading and choosing books and are beginning to have a good idea of what type of story they like to read.

Your book title helps sell your story both by catching the reader's attention and giving him some idea of what the book is about. Mysteries or adventures often announce themselves with their title at this level: *The Mystery of the Golden Door, The Adventure of Aben-Go-Down.* The title can also announce whether the main character is a boy or a girl: *Paula Makes a Mess, Norman Joins the Circus.* It is true that most book titles are finally chosen by the publisher, but a carefully selected title may be part of what sells your book (and tells your publisher you understand the market) in the first place.

Juvenile publishing is one of the few areas where the commercial rights covered in every book contract may actually be exercised. Commercial rights cover the use of your story or characters for toys, posters, magnets, and a rather long list of other odd things. It doesn't happen often, but there are enough Sponge Bob, Elmo, and Batman t-shirts out there to make one hopeful. If you have not reserved commercial rights, all contracts for such items will go through your publisher, no matter how little they seem to resemble your book.

Writing Samples. The following writing sample demonstrates how to introduce words not in the vocabulary:

> Every day Maria helps her family. She feeds the chickens and rolls up the bed mats from the dirt floor of their one-room house. She also makes a flat bread called tortillas. The tortillas are cooked on top of the stove.
>
> One day Maria woke up early. She was sure something special was going to happen. Then she remembered what it was. Today the men from the town were going to buy bricks in the city. They would bring back the bricks to build an oven for the pueblo. Her father would go with them to help.
>
> With an oven, they could make bread called bolillos. They are very much like French rolls. Maria knew that they could make sweet rolls called pan dulces. And they could even make cookies and cakes!

THIRD GRADE WORD LIST

a

able
absolute
accept
accompany
account
active
actual
addition
additionally
adopt
advantage
adventure
advice
advise
afford
aim
alarm
alder (tree)
alfalfa
alive
amiss
amphibian
anemone
anew
angle
announce
announcement
apart
apparent
appeal
applesauce
appoint
approach

apron
arctic
area
argue
arithmetic
arrange
arrest
ash
aside
asleep
assure
astray
atop
attack
attend
author
authority
authorize
automobile
avenue
average
avocado
avoid
awake
awaken
aware
awful

b

bagpipe
bait
balance
bamboo
bandit
bang

banner
bar
bar code
bare
bark
barnacle
basement
beak
beam
beast
bedroom
behold
beneficial
benefit
bewilder
billboard
bitter
blackboard
blanket
bless
blind
bloodhound
bluebottle
boil
bond
bonfire
bookcase
bookkeeper
bottle
brag
brain
brat
breast
brief
broad

bucket
bulletin
bunch
burn
burning
burst
bury
busybody

c

calm
calories
campaign
cane
capitalize
capture
cardinal
carefree
carol
castle
catnip
cattle
central
century
chain
chapter
charm
cheap
cheat
cheer
cheese
chill
choice
choose
churn

citizen
civil
clever
clump
cobweb
code
coin
collect
colonel
colony
combine
comfort
comfortable
companion
comparable
compare
compel
complete
con
concern
concerning
conclude
condition
condor
conduct
connect
consent
consist
construct
content
contract
copy
coral
correct
couple
course
court
courtroom
crackle

crater
crawfish
create
creature
crystal
curb
curious
current
curse
curve

d

decision
decorate
decoration
delight
depend
diary
disabled
display
double
drag

e

ease
edit
educate
education
effect
egret
elect
electric
electricity
element
empty
engine
entire
entrance
entrap
Eskimo

establish
event
everybody
evil
exclaim
excuse
exist
exit
expense
experiment
explode

f

faint
faith
falcon
false
falter
fame
familiar
fancy
faraway
fare
farther
fashion
fate
fault
faultless
favorite
feature
fiber
final
fitness
flag
flame
flesh
flour
folk
footstep

forever
fortune
forward
fountain
frame
freedom
fume
funnel
furniture

g

gentle
gentleman
glacier
glance
gloom
glory
godfather
godmother
grace
gradual
grave
gray
greenery
greenhouse
greenhouse
    effect
greet
greyhound
groan
gross
guest

h

habit
handsome
hare
harm
hateful
headquarters

heal
hectic
heel
herald
hike
hippopotamus
hire
hiss
hobby
hockey
hollow
honest
horn
hospital
hotel
housekeeper
housework
hover
hovercraft
human
hump
hush

i

iceberg
ideal
immediate
impossible
improve
include
increase
independent
individual
inquire
instant
instrument
interrupt
invite
ivory

j

jacket
join
joined
journey
junk
justice
kingbird
kingdom
knock

l

label
league
lean
leaning
leap
lessen
lesson
level
liberty
library
limit
limpet
linen
linger
liquid
livestock
lobster
local
locate
location
loose

m

madness
magazine
magnet
magnetize

magnify
maid
main
major
majority
manufacture
mass
match
matching
meadow
meal
meaning
melon
memory
merchant
mere
merry
metal
midnight
military
million
mink
mistreat
misuse
model
moisture
mood
moral
moreover
motion
murder
mussel

n

needle
nestle
net
niece
noble

nor
noticeable
notify

o

obey
observe
occasion
occupy
occur
odor
official
oneself
onward
operate
operation
opinion
opossum
opportunity
oppose
opposite
ordinary
original
oriole
otherwise
outer space
owe

p

pace
parent
part-time
pattern
pause
peanut
perfect
perfume
permit
personal
picket

pity
plastic
plead
pleasant
pliers
poem
poison
polar
pollute
popular
population
porch
port
possess
pour
powder
pray
prayer
prefer
prevent
prevention
principal
prison
private
prize
proper
property
provide
prune
purchase
pure

q

quest

r

range
rear
recall
recent

recognize
reduce
regular
remind
reserve
rhinoceros
rinse
root
royal
rumble
rustle

s

sailor
saint
sake
salamander
salary
salmon
satin
satisfy
sauce
scale
scatter
scent
science
scientist
scrap
scrapbook
screw
screwdriver
secure
seize
self
separate
servant
sex
shadow
shame

shiny
shoot
shoplift
sigh
silent
silk
silkworm
sing
sink
skirt
skyrocket
slave
sleek
slip
slope
smash
smear
smell
society
soldier
solid
soul
spare
spark
speed
spice
spit
spite
sponge
sprinkle
spruce
sputter
squid
stage
standard
stare
steady
steal
stiff

stir
straight
stray
strip
student
stump
sturdy
style
sufficient
surface
surround
surrounding
survive
sway
sweat
sweater
swell

t

tale
tangle
task
tease
teenager
temple
tender
term
terrified
territory
terror
test
theater
thee
thigh
thud
thunder
thy
title
tone

tongue
tortoise
tour
tower
trace
tremble
tribe
trio
troop
tube
tuft
turnip
twice
twine
twirl

u

undertaking
union
unlimited
unto
unusual
upper
upset
upstairs
urchin
usual

V

vanish
vapor
veil

vest
volume
vulture

W

wage
wand
wander
warn
warning
watermelon
weak
wealth
weasel
westward
whenever
wire

witness
woodbine
wool
worn
worst
worth
worthless
wound
wrap
wrinkle
written

Y

yesterday

Z

zigzag

FOURTH GRADE

Social Changes. Fourth grade is a turning point in a child's development. Fourth graders are more independent and self-reliant. Homework is now considered their responsibility rather than one shared with parents. Most kids are able to read independently, and many begin to read on their own. Montessori programs often express the enthusiasm of the young reader as "exploding into reading." This describes many fourth graders well. The jump from the primary readers meant for the first four school years to the more sophisticated books aimed at fourth grade is almost an explosive one. Series books became popular in third grade because they give the reader confidence. In fourth grade, children often read simply for the pleasure of reading, whether they are adventure stories, mysteries, legends, or science fiction. Children often follow specific authors, such as Judy Blume, and buy book after book in a series such as Harry Potter or the Babysitters Club.

In the Classroom. Fourth grade now covers much, if not most, of the new technology that has developed over the past ten years: digital equipment, new communication systems, smart houses, and the cyber-world. Thus, you will find some words that were previously listed as fifth or sixth grade words used at this level. You can also feel free to use virtually any word from this new vocabulary whether you are talking about podcasting or using a workstation. Astronomy, geology, paleontology, and other types of science and space are usually taught in fourth or fifth grade. Science fiction becomes a popular leisure reading subject because it combines the newly acquired academic knowledge with fast-paced adventure.

Many words pertaining to American history are learned in fourth grade, as are the different U.S. states and the countries of the world. Many types of plants become familiar at this age also. The plants given in the word lists are the ones most commonly used in literature.

Local history is often introduced at this level. This means you can write about geographic areas such as the Rockies, the Great Plains, or New England because a large number of children will be exposed to these topics.

Native American history is also studied in many fourth-grade classrooms. It is good policy to use the correct names for indigenous groups rather than using the anglicized or Spanish names. For example, it's just as easy for children to learn the name Kummeai for the peaceful Native American tribe that lived in San Diego as it is to learn the Spanish name Degunios. It's also just as easy to use Native Americans, Native American Indians, or indigenous peoples, as it is to use Indians. Your awareness of ethnic language concerns will enrich the experience of your readers.

The new international economy and new breakthroughs in understanding disease have had an impact on health and fitness programs. Those experts helping shape the new curriculum recommend expanding fourth-grade education to include diet and the beginning of sex education. Specifically, standard programs now include information on AIDS and HIV, as well as smoking tobacco and drinking alcohol. Concepts of immunity, genetic links in disease, and disease control are also recommended for the age group.

Words pertaining to foods, cooking, and measurements are introduced by this level and are frequently taught as part of "fun" projects in cooking. Children often make cookies or holiday foods in earlier grades, but now cooking is integrated with mathematics and sociology. Multicultural festivals at schools often attempt to pull together a great variety of skills in a creative, exciting way.

Publishing. Whether it's space, videogames, or babysitting, both fiction and nonfiction for this age should deal with the special interests and problems of the eight- to twelve-year-old age group. Most books now range between 20,000 and 40,000 words. Typical magazine stories run between 700 and 2,000 words, but most publications also use a page or two of special-interest short-shorts under 100 words.

Even the most conservative publishers now use the ten-word sentence as a target, with a maximum length of about twenty words. Even if it's not required, you should not go too far beyond twenty words at a stretch because ideas become more difficult to follow. Almost all children are still reading one word at a time at this level, and they can actually forget the subject being talked about in a long sentence.

Be careful of using localized terminology, such as specific wildlife or customs unique to an area. For example, I once wrote a story on lighter-than-air vehicles—blimps to us old guys. I described an exciting new airship as looking "like a beach ball being carried on the back of a manta ray." My editor thought the description was too localized and kids in the Midwest wouldn't know what a manta ray was. We finally decided to say it looked "like a baseball with a handle attached."

Make sure you check your facts if you are writing about something you remember from a few years ago, but you do not keep up on the subject. Paleontology is an excellent example. Good old Brontosaurus had become an Apatosaurus in the 1990s, and the idea that many species may have been warm-blooded and herded in family became widely accepted by the turn of the millennia. Current opinions may disagree with what was once considered fact.

The elementary level, which covers fourth, fifth, and sixth grades, is the largest of all the markets for children's writers. Beyond sheer volume, your readers are loyal and appreciative. They write fan letters and buy or read all the books a favorite writer produces. That loyalty is the reason so many publishers want series books for this age. A few publishers won't even look at books that can't be made into a series, and presenting the possibility of a series in a book proposal may be a big plus with any publisher.

Fiction stories should have lots of action, and a carefully crafted modern plot is absolutely necessary at this point. Many manuscripts are rejected simply because the plots are weak or outdated. Take the time to find out what hobbies and sports are currently popular, what issues children have to deal with, and what their dreams are; it will go a long way in helping sell your book.

Science fiction is often a great way of explaining science concepts or imparting facts. As with any science fiction writing, your "hard science" facts must be correct.

Nonfiction comes into its own in fourth, fifth, and sixth grades. Magazines and books specialize in science, mathematics, world events, and much more. When you write for these markets, keep track of your source material in case you need to supply a bibliography or support a fact. Do not submit a bibliography with a manuscript written for a periodical unless you are asked to do so or you know the publisher requires it. *The Children's Writer's and Illustrator's Market* listings sometimes note if one is necessary. When writing a nonfiction book, reference material should be cited.

Writing Samples. The following excerpt demonstrates the fourth grader's new interest in nonfiction and world events:

> Towns are like families. The people who work give money to run the town. That year, more than half the people in South Renovo were out of work. That means they had over 50 percent unemployment. So the town didn't have much money to spend. It was so bad even the local YMCA had to shut down.
>
> It also meant Debra Burrows, the park director, had no money for summer projects. What she did have was over one hundred kids with nothing to do. She must have felt like Old Mother Hubbard. There were only two things left in the playground cupboard. They had two gallons of white glue and some paper. So the kids decided to see how long a paper chain they could make.

Later in the same story is this paragraph, capitalizing on the interest of readers learning about measurements:

> Some kids had odometers on their bikes. They used them to measure one-tenth of a mile along the playground fence. The kids then measured their work in picnic tables (six feet). When they finished a picnic table length, they laid it along the fence. Eighty-eight picnic tables made one fence length. The kids made about one fence length, or one-tenth of a mile, each day.

FOURTH GRADE WORD LIST

a

abandon
accident
accord
according to
accuse
accustom
acid
acorn
acquaint
acquire
ad
adapt
adept
admit
adobe
adore
advertise
advertisement
aerial
aerosol
affect
affection
afterward
agate
agriculture
AIDS
airfoil
alas
alcohol
aloe
aloud
alphanumeric

altar
alter
amber
ambition
amen
amend
amid
amethyst
amuse
analog
anchor
anchovy
angel
ankle
annual
antibiotic
antibodies
antler
anxiety
anxious
appetite
approve
arc
arch
arise
armor
arouse
artichoke
artificial
artificial
   intelligence
ascend
ashamed

aspen (tree)
assault
assemble
assist
assistance
assistant
astonish
astound
astrology
astronomy
atmosphere
au pair

b

backbone
background
backpack
backward
backwoods
bacon
ballast
ballet
baneberry
banquet
banyan
bareback
bargain
barley
baron
barrel
barren
bashful
basin
beard

beech
beet
behave
behavior
bellow
beloved
bench
birch
biscuit
bison
blackmail
blacksmith
blank
bleach
bleat
blizzard
bloodthirsty
bloom
blossom
blot
blur
blush
boast
bobbin
bodyguard
bolt
bonbon
boulevard
boundary
boundless
boyfriend
boyhood
breakers

breakwater
breed
breeze
brick
bride
bridesmaid
brilliant
broadsword
broccoli
broil
bronze
brooch
brood
broth
brow
buckeye
buddy
budge
bulge
bulk
bullet
bumble
bumblebee
bunk
bureau
butcher
buttonhole
buzzard

C

cabbage
cabinet
café
cameo
canal
candidate
cannibal
cannon
canoe

canyon
capable
cape
caper
carbon
career
caretaker
carload
carnation
carpenter
carpet
carton
carve
cask
casserole
Catholic
cauliflower
ceiling
celebrate
celery
cement
challenge
champion
channel
chap
chapel
charity
chemical
chess
chestnut
childhood
chili
Christ
Christian
cigar
cigarette
circuit
circular
civilization

clang
clank
clasp
climate
climate-
   controlled
cling
cloak
clone
cluster
clutch
clutter
coach
coarse
cock
collar
college
colonial
column
commit
communicate
commute
compass
compete
complain
composition
compound
compress
comrade
conceal
conceive
concrete
condemn
condo
condominium
conference
confess
conflict
confuse

congress
conquer
conscience
consequence
constant
constantly
constitute
consult
consume
contact
contest
continent
contrary
contrast
contribute
convenient
convert
convey
convince
copper
cord
corporal
corporation
costume
cottage
couch
courage
courtesy
cowardly
cowboy
crack
cracker
cradle
crayfish
crazy
creak
creek
crest
criminal

crunch
crush
crust
cube
cure
cyber

d

DNA
daily
data
datamining
deform
deserve
detect
detective
device
diamond
diet
differ
digits
digital
discontinue
distance
distant
district
divide
divorce
dumpling
dwarf
dwell
dwelling

e

earl
earnest
echo
economy
effective
elbow

electron
electronic
elevation
e-mail
elsewhere
embrace
embryo
emotion
emperor
empire
empress
enable
enclose
encounter
encourage
endeavor
endure
energy
engineer
enormous
entertain
enthusiasm
envy
epidemic
equator
ere
erect
errand
error
erupt
especially
estate
evergreen
exceed
exchange
excite
exhaust
exhibit
expedition

experience
explore
expose
extend
eyeglasses

f

Fahrenheit
fairy
fasten
fatal
fax
federal
fee
feeble
female
fetch
fever
fiber-optics
fiddle
fierce
film
fingernail
fission
flap
flatter
flavor
flipper
flourish
flush
flute
foam
foe
folly
fond
forbid
forecast
forehead
formal

formation
fortunate
fossil
foul
fowl
fraction
framework
frank
freeze
freezing
freight
frequent
freshwater
frock
frost
fuel
fugitive
fulfill
fulfillment
function
fund
fundamental
funeral
furious
furnace
furnish
fury
fuse
fusion

g

gallant
gallop
garb
garment
gasp
gene
generation
generous

genius
gesture
gill
girlfriend
glare
glide
glimpse
glitter
globe
glove
glum
gnash
goal
goggle
goggles
golf
gown
grab
graduate
grasp
grateful
gravel
gravity
greed
grim
grind
grip
grizzly
grove
growl
guilt
guilty
guitar
gulf

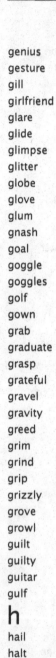

h

hail
halt
hamburger

handkerchief
harmonize
harmony
harness
harp
harvest
harvesting
hatch
haul
heap
hedge
heed
height
heir
hesitate
highway
hillside
hind
HIV
hood
hook
horizon
horrid
horrify
horror
host
hostile
howl
hull
humble
humor
hut
hyena

i

identify
idle
ignorant
illustration

image
immense
immortal
immunity
impose
imprint
income
indicate
ingredient
inlet
inn
insect
inspire
instruct
intelligence
intelligent
interactive
interface
interfere
intestine
issue

j

jail
jaw
jellybean
jest
joint
jolly
jungle
junior
jury

k

keen
kettle
knapsack
knead
kneel
knit

knot
knuckle

l

laboratory
lace
ladle
lame
lance
lane
lash
lasso
latch
latchkey
latitude
layer
lazy
leech
Lent
lest
liberal
lieutenant
lightweight
limb
limber
lime
limestone
loaf
loan
locality
lodge
logger
logo
longitude
luggage
lump
lung
luster

luxury
lynx

m

madam
magnificent
maiden
maim
maintain
majesty
male
mallard
manage
manager
mankind
mantel
mantle
marble
mare
marvel
marvelous
mash
mast
mate
mayonnaise
medal
medicine
melody
membrane
mercy
merit
mermaid
micro
microchip
microwave
migrant
mild
mingle
minister

minnow
mirror
mischief
miserable
misery
mistress
mixture
mob
mock
moderate
modest
moist
monk
Monsieur
moonbeam
moonlight
Mormon
mortal
motor
mourn
muffin
mulberry
mumble
mums
murmur
muscle
muse
museum
mushroom
musician
mustang
mustard
mutate
mutt
mutter
mystic
myth

n

naked
nanites
nano
nanometer
nanoparticle
nanowires
narcissus
nasturtium
nay
Nazareth
nebula
neglect
nephew
nettle
nevertheless
nibble
nightingale
nuclear
nucleus
numerous
nutmeg

o

o'clock
odd
offend
offensive
olive
opera
orbit
orchid
ore
organ
organic
organism
organize
ornament
outcome

outcry
outline
overlook
oyster

p

package
paprika
papyrus
parasite
paradise
parcel
pardon
parlor
parsley
parsnip
particular
pastel
pastor
patch
patent
patient
patriot
peak
pear
pearl
peasant
pebble
peculiar
peep
pepper
peppermint
percent
perch
perform
periodic
perish
persimmon
petrify

pheasant
photon
piano
pier
pierce
pike
pillow
pimento
pinch
pineapple
pioneer
planet
plaster
platform
plot
plow
plum
plunge
plural
pneumatic
polish
polite
political
politics
pomegranate
poodle
poplar
portion
potato
practical
prairie
preach
precious
preserve
pressure
prey
priest
principle
pro

probably
proceed
process
procession
proclaim
product
production
professor
profit
program
progress
project
prompt
pronounce
proof
prophet
proportion
propose
prospect
protect
protection
protest
provision
publication
publicity
publicize
publish
puma
pump
punch
punish
purse
puzzle

q
quake
qualify
quality
quantity

quarrel
queer
quiver

r
RNA
rabbi
rage
rapid
rare
realm
reap
rebuke
recover
redwood
reed
reflect
regard
region
register
reign
rejoice
relate
relation
relative
relax
relief
relieve
religion
remark
remedy
rend
renew
repair
repeat
represent
reproduce
reptile
request

rescue
resemble
resist
respecting
responsible
restless
retire
retreat
reveal
reverence
reverend
review
reward
rhubarb
ribbon
rifle
ripple
risk
rival
roam
roast
robe
rotate
rough
rouse
route

s
sacred
sacrifice
saddle
saffron
sage
sagebrush
salute
sardine
sassafras
sausage
sauté

scamper	slender	steed	tailor
scarce	slight	steer	tame
scoop	slither	stern	taro
scorn	slumber	stocking	telecommun-
scramble	sly	stomp	ications
scrape	snatch	stout	telegram
scratch	sneak	stovepipe	telescope
sculptor	snooze	strain	television
sculpture	soap	stretch	temper
scuttle	sober	structure	temperature
secretary	solar	stuck	tempt
section	solar system	stumble	terraform
seep	sole	stun	thatch
seldom	solve	stupid	theme
serious	sorcerer	submit	thence
severe	sore	sulfur	thermo-
shabby	sorrow	sumac	dynamics
shaft	source	summon	thicket
shallow	sovereign	superior	thistle
shelter	spear	support	thorough
shepherd	speck	surf	thrash
sheriff	spike	suspend	thrill
shield	spine	suspicion	throne
shift	splendid	swamp	thrust
showroom	splendor	swarm	thyme
shriek	split	swear	tingle
shrug	spoil	sweep	tiptoe
shudder	spur	swift	tobacco
shutter	spy	switch	toenail
sift	squire	swoop	toil
signal	squirt	sword	tomato
similar	stable	sycamore	towhead
simmer	staff	sympathy	traitor
sincere	stagger	syrup	tramp
sire	stain		transmit
situation	stalk	**t**	transmission
skeleton	stallion		tread
Skylab	startle	tablecloth	treason
slay	statue	tablespoon	treasure
		tackle	

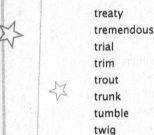

treaty
tremendous
trial
trim
trout
trunk
tumble
twig
twinkle

U

ugh
ugly
unceremonious
underground
universal
universe
university
upright
upward
urge
utter

V

vaccine
vaccination
vain
vale
valuable
various
vary
vast
veal
vein
vent
venture
verse
vessel
veterinarian
vice
victim
victory
video
video-
conference
violin
virtual
environment
virtual reality
virtually

virtue
visible
vision
volcano
vow
voyage

W

wade
warp
warrior
watercress
weapon
weary
weave
wedge
weep
whence
whereas
wherefore
whereupon
whip
whippoorwill
whirl
whisk

wicked
widow
width
Wi-Fi
wilderness
wilt
wobble
woe
workstation
worship
wrath
wreath
wreck

Y

ye
yield
yon
yonder

Z

zone

86

FIFTH GRADE

Social Changes. New studies have shown that many children who have been struggling with reading until now break through in fifth grade. For example, about 60 percent of children in the study who had dyslexia and were typically reading at a second-grade level at the beginning of the year jumped to tenth- or twelfth-grade level by the end of the year. That jump typifies other, fairly dramatic, changes in a fifth-grader's life. Fifth graders begin to embark on the stage of growth that changes their focus from home to peers. This is fully realized by sixth and seventh grades, but it begins in fifth grade. Friends' opinions can have as much influence now as a parent's. Those euphemistically called "early bloomers" begin to see secondary sexual characteristics change. Many students become interested in the opposite sex, whereas others don't see what all the fuss is about. In any event, fifth graders become more focused on the outside world than before.

One way to tap into this new maturity and outside interest is to have students put together "real" television broadcasts or other media shows. Even the smallest schools can now produce packages (a complete program on tape or digital video meant to function as a self-contained, finished unit) of news programs, original plays, or other material to run free of charge on a variety of venues. In the past, owing to the low cost and ease of accessibility, most of the time that meant television; however, the possibilities have been greatly expanded. Streaming online video, Web-based television and radio broadcasting, podcasting, and other new technologies provide great potential for sharing the student's talent with the entire world. Free Web sites and production programs make these kinds of projects more economically feasible than ever before.

In the Classroom. Current events generally become part of classroom learning and discussion in fifth grade. In most areas, fifth- or sixth-grade students have to memorize the states and their capitals. The children have a general idea of what each state is like, including their major agricultural and economic products.

Most animals can be recognized at this level; echidnas and platypuses join more familiar animals as good subjects for stories and articles. Many cities, countries, and sites are introduced by fifth grade. If you choose to write about an unusual country, you should be sure to place it geographically; tell your reader that Belize is in Central America and Ghana is on the west coast of Africa.

Prehistory is usually studied in fifth grade. Early man, cave paintings, fire and the development of civilization are often covered. Science teachers would like to make sure the children know that people did not keep dinosaurs as pets and that they actually know the eras these different species walked the earth. Even the most unusual dinosaurs, such as Cynognathus, are introduced with their proper name. New standards recommend that schools introduce earth sciences such as geology in a more sophisticated manner than in the past, including basic rock types and the scientific names of different geologic ages.

Ecology and environmentalism are major issues in children's magazines, text books, and general literature. These topics will remain important areas in children's publishing for many years to come.

Nonfiction subjects that are often introduced in fourth grade in a rather casual way, such as hard science and current events, now become very important both in the classroom and out.

Publishing. Become familiar with the magazines for this level. A large number of magazines cover everything from unusual animals and robots to ongoing peace and war negotiations to killer bees. Visit your local elementary school to see what magazines they carry.

For the teacher or writer, producing material for a television program (or the program itself) can engage students and readers in tremendously exciting projects in acting, reading, writing, and researching that have relevance to the children's lives. It also provides an excellent and growing market for those who want to write plays for children or work in other dramatic forms. It is just as easy to write for this medium correctly (and teach children to write for it correctly) as it is to produce something in a haphazard manner. Actually, most of the rules for broadcast writing are meant to make the material easier to use during production.

Another alternative market is working with children in the electronic media. That could include computer programs or radio broadcasting.

One of the ways to make news stories and other academic subjects relevant and interesting is called localization, that is, finding a local angle for the story. To do that, you might interview a family from a different country or cover a local ethnic festival. Localization is highly desirable in the classroom, in broadcast writing, and writing for local periodicals; but you must be careful not to assume that a broader audience will recognize, or be interested in, strictly local references. National magazines and books aimed at a national market are leery of any type of localization.

This is also a good place to become aware of your options that go beyond the "normal" forms of publishing. Many of these alternative markets are grouped under "electronic rights" in your book publishing contract. Unimportant until recently, they include the possibility of your work being included in computer databases or sent by fax. Some publishers are beginning to sell material only via electronic marketing. To find these publishers, look under the syndicates listing in *Writer's Market.*

Writing Samples. The following excerpt illustrates the technique of sneaking in a history lesson while actually telling a nonfiction story:

> The tales of lost missions in Mexico are told wherever treasure hunters get together. The stories usually start off telling about gold and jewels hidden in the missions. They often end up being about the curses that are supposed to protect the treasure.
>
> Most of these legends are, at best, flights of fancy. They grew out of daydreams and years of searching. Yet, the missions themselves are probably real. More than that, there is some proof the curses are real, too.

Later in the same piece, a geography lesson is incorporated:

> Mountains run down Mexico's west coast, and few people live there. Even in the south, where there is lots of water, there are only a few place names on the map. Most of the "towns" shown are really only ranches where you can get some rest.

FIFTH GRADE WORD LIST

a

abacus
abide
abode
abolish
abolition
abroad
abrupt
absence
absent
absorb
abundant
ache
achieve
acknowledge
acrobat
A.D.
adder
addict
adjust
adjustment
admiral
admire
adolescent
agent
agitate
agony
aide
airtight
albatross
alert
algae

alien
alight
Allah
allergic
allergy
allowance
alternate
altitude
amateur
amaze
Amazon
ambergris
ample
ancestor
annoy
ape
appreciate
apt
Arab
archaeology
Archaeozic Era
archer
arena
array
aspect
assign
associate
association
assort
assume
asthenosphere
athlete
attach

attitude
attract
aurora
austere
avenge
await

b

B.C.
B.C.E.
babe
badge
ballad
bane
banister
barbecue
barge
basalt
baton
battery
bawl
bayonet
bayou
bazaar
bedraggled
beef
beer
belly
berate
beseech
bestow
betray
billion

bishop
blemish
blend
blimp
blister
blond
boar
bobolink
bodily
bog
bomb
boomerang
boon
booth
borax
boulder
brace
bracelet
Brahman
breeches
bribe
brim
broadcast
broadcloth
brocade
bruise
budget
bundle
burden
burnoose
burrow
buzz

c

C.E.
cafeteria
calculate
Cambrian
camouflage
canine
canter
caramel
Carboniferous
carcass
careless
cargo
carnivore
carp
carriage
casual
cat scan
catalog
catalogue
cathedral
caution
cautious
cavity
celebration
celebrity
celestial
cellophane
ceremony
chagrin
chalk
chamber
chandelier
chant
Cenozoic
cherish
chickadee
chip

choir
chord
chorus
chow
chowder
chute
clambake
clamp
clan
clash
classic
clatter
cleat
clog
clot
coil
coliseum
collapse
cologne
combat
comedian
comedy
comet
comic
comment
commentator
commercial
commissar
committee
commodity
commonwealth
commotion
communism
compact
compassion
compassionate
competition
compliment

comprehend
compromise
conceited
concentrate
confront
conserve
console
conspicuous
constellation
contraceptive
consul
consumerism
contain
contemporary
contempt
contend
contrite
conversation
convict
cooperate
copal
correspond
corridor
cough
council
counsel
counter
countless
cram
crate
crease
Cretaceous
credit
cremate
crimson
critical
criticize
Cro-Magnon

crouch
cruel
cuddle
curtain
customer
cybernetics
cyberpunk
cyberspace
Cynognathus

d

damage
damp
dangle
dazzle
debris
decay
deceive
descendant
declare
decode
defeat
defend
degree
deity
dejected
delay
delegate
delegation
delicate
delicatessen
deliver
demand
demure
deny
depart
deposit
depress
depth

descend
descendant
design
desire
desperate
despise
destiny
destruction
destructive
detail
determine
develop
Devonian
devote
devotee
devour
dial
dialect
difficult
diplomat
disappoint
disbelief
discourage
discuss
disease
disguise
disgust
dishearten
disintegrate
dispense
dispose
disposition
distinctive
distress
domicile
dominant
dominate
dormitory

dough
downhearted
drain
drake
drama
dramatize
drape
droop
dune
dungeon
dusk

e

eager
earthenware
earthquake
eclipse
ecotourism
ecology
ecosystem
elaborate
elder
elderly
elegant
eliminate
embarrass
embarrassed
emblem
embroider
emerge
emergency
emission
emphasize
employ
encircle
encode
encyclopedia
enforce
engage

engrave
enlarge
enterprise
entitle
envelope
Eocene
Epoch
equip
equipment
equinox
erode
escort
essay
esteem
estimate
E.U.
European
    Community
eve
eventually
evidence
evident
examine
excavate
excess
execute
executive
exile
expand
expert
export
express
extinct
extraordinary
extraterrestrial
extreme
extremist

f

fable
fabric
facility
factor
fang
fascinate
fatigue
ferret
fertile
fertilizer
festive
festivity
fetish
fez
fiction
fiery
fife
filch
filter
fingerprint
firecracker
fizz
flamingo
flank
flea
flee
flicker
flint
flounder
focal
focus
folklore
ford
forego
foreign
foreigner
forge

fort
forthright
fortress
foundation
foxglove
fragrance
fragrant
frantic
fresco
fret
friar
fried
fringe
frizz
fro
frontier
fumble
fungus

g

Gaia
Gaia theory
gallery
gamble
gape
garrison
gaze
gazelle
gelatin
genial
genome
genuine
geographic
geography
geology
gigantic
gland
gloss
glee

gleeful
gloss
Glossopteris
gnarled
gnat
goldenrod
goldfinch
good-natured
gooseberry
gorge
gorgeous
gossip
gourd
grapefruit
graze
grease
grief
gripe
groom
groove
grub
grudge
grudgingly
grumble
gust
gymnasium
gymnast

h

half-mast
hardship
hardy
harsh
haunch
hearth
hearty
heave
hemp
herb

herbivore
hermit
heroic
herring
hindquarter
Hindu
hinge
hoarse
hoax
Holocene
holy
homespun
honeysuckle
hoop
hornet
hothouse
hotspot
hurl
hymn

i

identity
igneous
ignore
imitate
immature
imp
impatient
imperial
imply
import
impress
impression
impulse
incense
incident
incline
inclined
indifferent

indignant
induce
indulge
industry
infant
inferior
infinite
influence
inform
informal
information
inherit
initiate
injure
injury
inland
inner
innocent
innumerable
inscribe
insist
inspect
instance
instinct
institute
insult
insure
intent
interior
international
interpret
interview
intimate
introduce
invade
invest
investigate
ion

iris
irrigate
Islam
itch
item

j

jackal
jackdaw
jagged
jasper
jealous
jeer
jersey
jewel
jewelry
jovial
Jurassic
justification
juvenile

k

Kaiser
kindle
kingfisher
knave
Koran

l

lagoon
lair
landslide
lantern
launch
lawyer
lecture
ledge
lee
leek

legal
legend
legislation
leisure
license
lichen
lilac
limp
link
liquor
literature
lithosphere
locomotive
locust
loft
lofty
loom
loop
lope
lots
lotus
loyal
lull
lurch
lure
lurk
Lystrosaurus

m

mackerel
magician
magnetron
magnitude
magnolia
magpie
mainland
mammal
mammoth
mandarin

mango
manifest
mansion
manure
margin
marine
marigold
marine
marrow
marsh
marshal
mason
massive
mastiff
material
mathematical
mathematics
mature
mean (average)
meatloaf
mechanic
mechanical
mediate
medium
menace
mental
mention
Mesosaurus
Mesozoic
meteor
midge
milestone
mimosa
mineral
minor
minstrel
mint
miracle

Miocene
mirth
miser
misfortune
mislead
mission
Mississippian
moan
mode
modify
mold
molecule
molten
monarch
monastery
mongoose
monstrous
moor
mope
morsel
Moslem
mosque
motive
mush
musical
musk
musket
muskrat
mutton
mutual

n

napkin
naught
naughty
navigate
Neanderthal
Newtonian
noisy

nominate
nonetheless
nonfiction
nonsense
normal
nostril
notable
notch
notion
novel
novice
numeral
neutrino

o

oath
oatmeal
obstacle
obstinate
obtain
obvious
Oligocene
omnivore
onyx
opal
operator
opponent
optical
orchard
Ordovician
orient
ornithischians
orphan
osprey
outer
overflow
overtake
overwhelm
ozone

ozone hole

p

pagoda
paleontologist
Paleocene
Paleozoic
pallet
pane
Pangea
pantry
parakeet
parallel
paranormal
particle
partner
pasty
patron
pave
pavilion
peddler
penalty
penetrate
peril
permanent
Permian
persist
personality
persuade
petal
pewter
philosophy
phonograph
photograph
photosynthesis
phrase
physical
picnic
pilgrim

pillar
pilot
pimple
pirate
pistol
pivot
plague
plait
plank
plantation
plea
pleat
pledge
Pliocene
plod
plug
plunder
policy
poll
Pope
porridge
porter
portrait
pounce
poverty
prank
Precambrian
precaution
precise
prehistoric
prehistory
preoccupy
pretext
prevail
previous
prick
prim
primary

prime
primitive
prior
privilege
procure
profess
profession
profile
prolong
promenade
prominent
promote
promotion
pronghorn
prop
prosper
protein
protostar
prow
psychedelic
pulse
pulsars
pursuit
pyramid

q

quaint
quasars
Quaternary
quay
quote

r

radar
ragged
rally
ranch
raptor
rascal

rave
ravine
react
reality
receipt
reception
recite
reckless
reckon
recommend
recreation
reef
reel
refer
reform
refuge
refute
regiment
registration
regret
regulate
reject
release
relic
rely
remote
renaissance
renown
replace
reputation
research
resent
reside
residence
resident
resign
resin
resolution

resolve
resort
resource
respond
restaurant
restore
restrain
resume
retain
retort
revenge
reverse
revolt
revolution
revolve
revolver
rhythm
ridge
rigid
robust
roe
rogue
romance
roust
rubbish
rugged
ruinous
rumor
rural

S

Sabbath
saber
saber-toothed
sable
sally
sample
sapling
Saurischians

savage
scan
scar
scheme
scholar
scissors
scold
scorpion
screen
scroll
seam
sedimentary
Seismosaurus
selfish
semitropical
sensation
sensitive
sensitivity
sentiment
sentinel
sergeant
sermon
serpent
shaggy
shale
shaman
shatter
shear
sheer
shellfish
sherbet
shimmer
shipment
shipwreck
shove
shred
shrill
shrine

shrink
shuttle
siege
sieve
Silurian
site
sketch
skull
skyline
slab
slam
slaughter
sled
sleeve
slice
slim
slipper
slit
slob
sloth
slug
slugger
slump
smite
smog
snarl
sneeze
snorkel
snort
snout
snuggle
soak
solemn
solitary
solution
soothe
spar
sparkle

sparrow	sulky	theory	translate
spearhead	sullen	theropod	transparent
species	sultan	threat	transport
specific	summit	three-fourths	traverse
specimen	superintendent	threshold	treatment
spectacle	supernatural	throb	trench
spectacles	superstition	throng	Triassic
spectator	suppress	thrush	tribute
spiritual	supreme	thyself	trickery
splotch	surge	tilt	trifle
spout	surgeon	timber	triumph
sprint	surrender	timid	tropical
spurt	survey	tinge	trot
squat	suspect	tinker	trousers
squeeze	sustain	tinkle	trudge
stab	swagger	tint	tsunami
stalagmite	sweetmeat	tissue	turban
stall	swine	toast	turbulent
stampede	symbol	token	turf
stanza		tolerate	turquoise
starve	**t**	tomb	turret
stereoscope	tank	tomfoolery	tusk
stoop	Taoist	toolbox	tyranny
strait	taper	topic	tyrant
strand	target	torch	
strap	tariff	torment	**u**
streak	tarry	torrent	udder
stride	tart	torture	undoubtedly
strife	taunt	tote	unidentified
strive	tavern	tough	unit
stroll	tectonic	tourist	unite
strut	temporary	tournament	unity
stubborn	temptation	tradition	uproar
studio	tenant	traffic	
submarine	tendency	tragedy	**v**
substance	tense	trample	vacuum
substantial	terrace	transfer	vague
substitute	terrier	transform	vanity
	terrific		vault

venison
vertebrate
vex
vexation
vibrant
vibrate
viewpoint
vigor
vigorous
Viking
villain
violent
vital

volunteer

W

waft
wail
waltz
ward
ware
warehouse
warrant
wary
waver
weevil

welfare
wharf
wheeze
whiff
whimper
whine
wholesome
wholly
widespread
wigwam
willing
wince
wither

wont
worrisome
wouldst
wren
wriggle
wring
wrought

Y

yawn

Z

zinc

SIXTH GRADE
AND MIDDLE SCHOOL

Social Changes. Sixth grade is now commonly combined with seventh and eighth grades, or even ninth grade, to create a middle school. Most middle school students are preteens or young teenagers whose egos depend on being seen as that and not as children. Their social life is usually centered on groups of friends rather than on the family. They have favorite rock bands, and some have their own sources of income. Even though your reader may seem to have taken a giant step toward growing up, you should stay away from any positive portrayal of drugs, tobacco, alcohol, street language, explicit sex, graphic crime, or violence. Drunkenness should not be portrayed as humorous.

Because of their own changes, the readers are usually very aware of their appearance and, subsequently, how characters in stories look. Description is not only acceptable, it's desired.

In the Classroom. If they haven't already done so, most sixth-grade students are now required to memorize the states, their capitals, and their major economic contributions.

Overall, difficult subjects such as death and divorce are often dealt with at this level in a realistic way. Sixth grade also includes sex and health education. As a result, both in-school and leisure reading materials are often problem oriented.

Publishing. Easy-reading books (also called hi-lo for high interest, low reading) begin to appear at this level. Most children now have a fairly sophisticated reading vocabulary, and the low achiever has begun to slip between the cracks. The easy-reading book is one way schools and other

programs are trying to prevent that from happening. These books are written to cover readers from twelve-years-old through young adults, but they use a controlled vocabulary and sentence length appropriate to the lower vocabulary levels. These books are short and run from 400 to 1,200 words in length. They use a lot of action and dialogue, and often use sports, romance, mystery, and ethnic-urban problems as subjects for their stories.

Besides being a part of the elementary eight- to twelve-year-old market, the sixth grader is more and more often a real part of the high school market, and others in the middle school group are firmly in its grasp. The high school group officially targets the thirteen- to seventeen-year-olds, but many readers are somewhat younger. This group uses an adult vocabulary (as long as it is not too sophisticated) and sentence structure. Most books range from 25,000 to 55,000 words, and longer lengths are permissible. Popular fiction subjects include romance, suspense, mild horror, the supernatural, and humor.

More magazines are aimed at the elementary or middle school group than any other. Eighty percent of the magazine stories are nonfiction and include age-related problems, dress, dating, interviews, fads, and special interests. Periodical stories usually range from 1,000 to 3,500 words.

By sixth grade, it becomes important to the reader to know exactly how a character, especially a leading character, looks. The just-preteen reader identifies with the leading characters in the books she reads, and her concerns about her own appearance are directly transferred to those characters. Others in the middle school group want to know how a character dresses, what kind of makeup they wear, how they get around without mom driving, and other issues that help answer very personal questions. Do be careful when you describe your characters not to make them too much a part of a popular fad either in dress or in speech. Fads pass quickly, and your book may follow if the reader sees it as "too last year."

Writing Samples. The following example shows the increased description present in stories for this age group. Not only do readers now have longer attention spans, they want descriptive details and like to know how characters look:

> Elizabeth thought that it was impossible not to admire him. Yet, if you looked at his features one at a time, there was little special about him. He was slim for his 5 feet 10 inches. Besides his eyes,

his gold hair and beard were his best features. Elizabeth smiled to herself. She remembered how Bob had grown that beard.

The following excerpt from a nonfiction piece uses the longer sentence length and, again, more description than is found in books for younger readers:

One of the reasons we are not sure if these creatures are real is that their habitats are desolate mountain ranges. In Asia, the Abominable Snow Man is supposed to live in the areas that are permanently covered with snow. Its shaggy white coat is the perfect camouflage for its surroundings. In North America, Bigfoot's dark shaggy hair serves the same purpose, and, if it is real, it stays well hidden in the shadows and foliage.

SIXTH GRADE WORD LIST

a

abbey
abbot
abbreviate
abdomen
abduct
abhor
ablaze
abominable
abstain
abstract
absurd
abuse
accent
access
accessory
accommodate
accumulate
accurate
acquit
acute
adhere
adhesive
adjective
adjourn
administer
adorn
adrift
aggress
aggressive
agile
alias
alibi
alkaline

allege
alley
allied
alloy
ally
alto
alum
aluminum
a.m.
ambulance
ambush
ammonia
ammunition
amplify
anguish
animate
animated
anoint
anticipate
antique
anvil
apologize
apology
apparatus
ardent
arid
aristocrat
arrogant
assert
assertive
asthma
attain
attire
autobiography
autograph

automatic
aviation
awe
awkward

b

babble
bachelor
balcony
bald
ballot
barrier
befriend
behalf
belle
beverage
beware
bias
billiards
biography
biosphere
blink
blotch
bluff
blunt
bondage
bonnet
bonus
bounce
bouquet
bout
boycott
brandish
bravado
bravo

brew
brier
brig
brigantine
brink
brisk
bristle
bronco
brutal
brute
buckle
buckskin
buffet
buggy
bugle
bung
burlap
bust
bustle

c

calamity
calcium
calico
campus
cancel
cancer
canopy
canvas
capacity
caption
caravan
cartridge
cauldron
cavalry

Cayuse
cayuse
cemetery
census
cereal
certificate
certify
chancellor
characteristic
charcoal
chariot
chauffeur
chime
chronicle
chum
cinch
circumstance
cite
clamor
clause
clergy
client
clumsy
coax
cocaine
coffin
cog
collision
coma
combustion
commence
commend
compartment
compensation
competent
complex
complicate
comply
comprise

concede
concession
concord
condense
confederate
confide
confident
confidential
conform
confound
congratulate
congregation
conscious
conscript
conscription
constable
consternation
contaminated
contagious
contaminate
contemplate
contrive
controversy
convent
convention
conventional
cordial
core
cork
corps
corrupt
cosmetics
courtier
covert
covet
cowpuncher
craftsmanship
crag
cramp

crave
credible
credulous
creed
crepe
crescent
crevice
crotch
cultivate
cultivation
culture
cunning
curfew
custom
cutlass
cylinder

d

daft
damsel
dangerous
decapitate
decline
dedicate
deduce
defy
dehydrate
deliberate
demigod
demonstrate
depose
depression
derelict
desolate
detest
dethrone
devastate
diarrhea
diminutive

din
dire
disaster
discard
discipline
dispute
distaste
distinguish
distribute
disturb
draught
dread
dubious
duplicate
durable

e

ecstasy
eddy
ejaculate
elastic
emigrant
eminent
emphatic
enamel
enchant
encrust
endanger
endow
enlist
enliven
enrage
enraged
enrich
environment
episode
equivalent
err
essential

et cetera
etc.
evolution
exaggerate
excel
exclude
exclusive
exert
exhilarate
expel
expire
exploit
exquisite
exterminate
extravagant

f

faculty
famine
fathom
fauna
feces
fend
ferry
fervor
feud
fidelity
fixture
flail
flair
flare
fleece
fleet
flexible
fling
flirt
flora
floatation
flotsam

fluid
fluorescent
fluster
foliage
fore
forefather
foreman
foresight
foretell
forfeit
forlorn
former
formidable
formula
forsake
fortnight
fragile
fragment
frail
fraud
friction
frigid
frolic
furrow

g

gait
gallows
garage
garbage
gargle
garland
garnish
gaunt
germ
ghastly
gild
gin
gingerly

girdle
glaze
glen
glimmer
glisten
gnome
gospel
graham
grammar
grapeshot
grapple
grope
gruel
guarantee
guidepost
gully
gutter
guttural
gypsy

h

habitable
habitat
hackle
hark
haughty
hazard
headache
heathen
helm
hemisphere
hemlock
hereafter
hew
hideous
hinder
hither
hoarfrost
hoard

hoary
hoist
homage
horde
horizontal
hose
hue
hunch
hunker
hydrogen
hysteria
hysterical

i

identical
idiot
idol
idolize
ignite
illuminate
illusion
illustrious
immaculate
immigrant
immobile
impart
impetus
implement
impoverished
imprison
incapable
inconvenient
incredible
incredulous
index
indispensable
indoor
infect
inflect

ingenious
inhabit
initial
initiative
insane
inscription
insert
install
intend
intense
intensive
intention
internal
interval
intricate
intrude
invisible
involve
inward
irk
irregular

j

jaunty
jibe
jostle
joust

k

khaki
kilo

l

laden
lament
lapse
lard
lavish
leak
lease

legion
legitimate
levee
liable
limpid
listless
liter
literal
logic
loincloth
lounge
lowland
lunatic
lunge
lush
lust
lyre

m

ma'am
magistrate
malice
malignant
malinger
manuscript
mar
marquis
martyr
massacre
mattress
maturity
maxim
maximum
mechanism
meddle
meditate
melancholy
mellow
menu

merchandise
mesa
metropolitan
mimic
mince
miniature
minimalist
minimum
minority
miraculous
mobile
mobilize
momentum
monopoly
mortgage
motivate
motto
municipal
muster
mute
mutiny
muzzle
myriad

n

narrate
naturalist
negative
nerve
neuron
neutral
nitrogen
nook
nourish
nuisance
nymph

o

obligation
oblige

obscure
occupation
omen
ominous
omit
oppress
oracle
orchestra
ordain
outlandish
outrage
outright
outward
outwit

p

pageant
pamphlet
panel
pang
papier-mâché
paragraph
paleontologist
paralysis
paralyze
parish
parson
partial
partition
passion
passport
pastime
pathetic
patter
peal
pellet
peninsula
pension
perceive

perpetual
perplex
persecute
perspire
pestilence
petroleum
petticoat
petty
Pharaoh
phase
phenomenon
physics
piecemeal
pious
piteous
plateau
platter
plight
plume
plump
ply
p.m.
poach
poise
pomp
ponder
pork
postpone
poultry
precede
precipice
predict
preface
prejudice
preliminary
premise
prescribe
preside
presume

privateer
prod
profound
prohibit
propel
proprietor
province
prowess
prudent
pry
psalm
psychic
psychology
pulp

q

quarry
quench
query
quill
quilt
quirt

r

radiant
radiate
radical
radioactive
radius
raft
rafter
raid
ramble
ramp
rampart
random
ransom
rash
ratify
ratio

ravage
ravenous
ravish
razor
reassure
reclaim
recline
recollect
recompense
reconcile
recount
recourse
recruit
recur
redeem
redouble
refine
reflex
refrain
refresh
regain
regal
rehearse
reheat
relay
relish
reluctant
remnant
remonstrate
remorse
renounce
repel
repent
replenish
repose
reproach
repulse
requisition
respiration

respite
restrict
retrieve
revenue
revive
rhyme
ridicule
ridiculous
riot
rite
ritual
role
routine
rove
ruby
ruffle

s

saga
salesperson
saloon
salvation
sanction
sane
sapphire
satellite
satyr
saunter
savior
savor
savory
scabbard
scandal
scant
scarf
schedule
scoff
scope
scorch

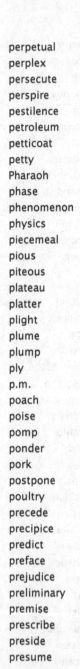

scour	soar	subtle	totter
scourge	socket	succession	towel
scow	sod	suckling	trait
scrub	sodden	suffice	tranquil
scull	sombrero	suffocate	transit
scurvy	sonnet	sundry	transom
seizures	spade	superb	treacherous
senior	span	supervise	treble
sensible	spasm	supple	tremor
serene	spectrum	surmise	trespass
serf	speculate	surmount	tribunal
serge	sphere	surpass	trigger
session	spire	surplus	trinket
shawl	splinter	swarthy	tripod
sheaf	sprawl	syllable	trophy
shelf	squadron	symphony	tropic
shirk	stack	symptom	troth
shrewd	stalwart		trough
shroud	stamen	**t**	truant
shun	staple		tumor
sickle	starch	tact	tumult
signature	stature	tactics	tunic
significant	stimulate	taint	tussle
signify	stitch	tankard	tutor
simulate	stockade	tapestry	twain
sinew	stow	tarpaulin	twang
skim	strangle	tawny	typical
slant	strategy	tedious	
slash	strenuous	tenement	**u**
sledge	stress	terminate	ultimate
slouch	stricken	tether	unanimous
smack	strict	text	unbidden
smother	stubble	texture	uncanny
smuggle	stud	thermometer	unique
snare	stunt	thresh	unison
sneer	subdue	thrift	unruly
snore	sublime	thrive	uphold
snuff	subsequent	toll	upholster
snug	subside	topple	upholstery
		tornado	

uranium
urgent
usher
utensil
utilize

V

vacant
valiant
valve
vamoose
vanquish
veer

vehicle
vengeance
venue
verdict
verge
version
veteran
vicinity
vicious
virgin
vivid
vocabulary

void
vomit

W

wallet
wallow
wan
warble
wardrobe
wasteland
weld
whim
whir

whiskey
whoop
wield
wile
withal
wizard
woo
wrench
wrest
wrestle
wretched
writ

writhe

Y

yearn
yelp
yoke
yore

Z

zeal
zealous
zephyr
zest

THESAURUS

This thesaurus is used like any other thesaurus—as a tool for substituting words. I've tried to include words from a range of grades; however, some times this is not possible. You'll find that at times you'll have to substitute phrases and clauses because no one word is accurate.

In the previous edition of this book, some words were listed only in a separate word list because they had no synonyms or there are no synonyms understood at sixth grade and below. In the current version, these words are included here, and the simple word list has been omitted for two reasons. First, many people did not use the word list and assumed that words not in the thesaurus section were left out. Second, many new words stand alone. These new words are often science and technology related. These words, such as *Wi-Fi*, are defined if it might be helpful to the writer, teacher, or parent who is using this book.

a (K): one (K)

abacus (5th): calculator (5th), computer (1st)

abandon (4th): desert (1st), discard (6th), forsake (6th), give up (K), leave (1st), quit (1st), reject (5th), surrender (5th), yield (4th) **B.** freedom (3rd), liberty (3rd), license (5th), recklessness (5th)

abbey (6th): convent (6th), monastery (5th)

abbot (6th): monk (4th), priest (4th)

abbreviate (6th): abstract (6th), condense (6th), contract (3rd), cut (K), cut down (K), lessen (3rd), reduce (3rd), shorten (2nd), shrink (5th)

abdomen (6th): belly (5th), gut (1st), stomach (2nd), tummy (K)

abduct (6th): kidnap (2nd), seize (3rd), steal (3rd)

abhor (6th): condemn (4th), despise (5th), detest (6th), hate (2nd), scorn (4th)

abide (5th): A. dwell (4th), live (K), reside (5th) **B.** endure (4th), survive (3rd), tolerate (5th) **C.** accept (3rd), cling (4th), continue (2nd), remain (2nd), stay (1st)

ablaze (6th): A. aglow (2nd), alight (5th), gleaming (1st) **B.** afire (2nd), aflame (2nd), burning (3rd), on fire (K)

able (3rd): A. capable (4th), competent (6th), qualified (4th) **B.** clever (3rd), expert (5th), intelligent (4th), smart (1st)

aboard (2nd): A. beside (1st) **B.** inside (K), on (K)

abode (5th): dwelling (4th), home (K), house (K), place (1st), residence (5th)

abolish (5th): blot out (4th), cancel (6th), destroy (2nd), exterminate (6th)

abolition (5th): cancellation (6th), destruction (6th)

abominable (6th): A. bad (K), inferior (5th), poor (K), sorry (2nd) **B.** cursed (3rd), detestable (6th), hateful (3rd), horrible (4th), horrid (4th), offensive (4th)

about (K): A. around (1st), near (1st) **B.** concerning (3rd), regard (4th), respecting (4th)

above (K): better (K), higher (1st), over (K)

abroad (5th): about (K), away (K), out (K), out of the country (K), overseas (2nd)

abrupt (5th): fast (1st), hasty (2nd), hurried (1st), quick (1st), sharp (1st), sheer (5th), speedy (3rd), steep (2nd), sudden (1st), unexpected (2nd)

absence (5th): lack (1st), need (1st), want (K)

absent (5th): gone (1st), lacking (1st), missing (K), not here (K), wanting (K)

absolute (3rd): A. clear (2nd), certain (1st), complete (3rd), entire (3rd), genuine (5th), outright (6th), perfect (3rd), real (1st), solid (3rd), sure (K) **B.** ideal (3rd), pure (3rd), simple (2nd), true (K), whole (1st)

absorb (5th): consume (4th), draw in (K), gather (1st), learn (1st), soak up (5th), swallow up (1st), take in (K)

abstain (6th): decline (6th), deny (5th), forego (5th), give up (K), quit (1st), refrain (6th), reject (5th)

abstract (6th): A. brief (3rd), part (1st), sketch (5th) **B.** divide (4th), remove (2nd), separate (3rd), take away (K) **C.** difficult (5th), general (2nd), ideal (3rd), universal (4th), vague (5th)

absurd (6th): comic (5th), dumb (1st), fantastic (6th), foolish (2nd), funny (1st), idiotic (6th), illogical (6th), ridiculous (6th), silly (1st), unreasonable (2nd)

abundant (5th): ample (5th), full (K), generous (4th), lush (2nd), more than enough (1st), plentiful (2nd)

abuse (6th): A. exploitation (6th), mistreatment (3rd) **B.** damage (5th), harm (3rd), hurt (K), injure (5th), mistreat (3rd), misuse (3rd), mock (4th), put down (2nd), ridicule (6th), spoil (4th), wrong (1st)

accent (6th): A. emphasize (5th), mark (1st), stress (6th) **B.** emphasis (5th), pitch (2nd), rhythm (5th), tone of voice (3rd), voice (1st)

accept (3rd): adopt (3rd), assume (5th), believe (1st), commence (6th), embrace (4th), get (K), receive (2nd), take (K)

access (6th): admit (4th), approach (3rd), door (K), entrance (3rd), entry (3rd), gate (1st), nearing (1st), route (4th), way (K)

accessory (6th): A. aide (5th), helper (1st) **B.** decoration (3rd), jewelry (5th), ornament (4th), trim (4th)

accident (4th): casualty (5th), chance (2nd), disaster (6th), injury (5th), misadventure (3rd), misfortune (3rd), mistake (1st), twist of fate (3rd)

accommodate (6th): A. adjust (5th), fit (K), suit (1st) **B.** aid (2nd), assist (4th), help (K)

accompany (3rd): attend (3rd), combine (3rd), conduct (3rd), connect (3rd),

escort (5th), go with (K), join (3rd), link (5th)

accomplish (2nd): achieve (5th), close (K), complete (3rd)

accord (4th): A. award (5th), bestow (5th), grant (2nd) **B.** admit (4th), agree (2nd), allow (2nd), consent (3rd), permit (3rd) **C.** agreement (2nd)

according to (4th): as stated by (1st), in conformity with (6th)

account (3rd): A. article (2nd), report (1st), story (K), tale (3rd) **B.** cause (2nd), motive (5th), reason (1st), sake (3rd) **C.** regard (4th), value (2nd), worth (3rd)

accumulate (6th): assemble (4th), collect (3rd), gather (1st), keep (K), multiply (2nd)

accurate (6th): A. careful (1st), particular (4th) **B.** correct (3rd), exact (2nd), faultless (3rd), precise (5th), right (K), true (K), without error (4th)

accuse (4th): blame (2nd), charge (2nd), fault (3rd)

accustom (4th): A. adapt (4th), adjust to (5th) **B.** acquaint (4th), harden (2nd), season (2nd)

ace (2nd): A. achieve (5th), best (K), get it (K), win (K) **B.** card (1st), eleven (1st), expert (5th), one (K), shark (1st), top (K)

ache (5th): A. sadness (1st), sorrow (4th), suffer (2nd) **B.** hurt (K), pain (2nd), pang (6th)

achieve (5th): accomplish (2nd), ace (2nd), complete (3rd), conquer (4th), do (K), effect (3rd), finish (1st), fulfill (4th), get (K), manage (4th), perform (4th), win (K)

acid (4th): bitter (3rd), harsh (5th), sour (2nd), tart (5th)

acknowledge (5th): accept (3rd), admit (4th), allow (2nd), answer (1st), concede (6th), declare (5th), grant (2nd), profess (4th), reveal (4th)

acorn (4th)

acquaint (4th): accustom (4th), advise (3rd), educate (3rd), inform (5th), instruct (4th), introduce (5th), mention (5th), teach (1st)

acquire (4th): assume (5th), attain (6th), buy (K), gain (2nd), get (K), obtain (5th), purchase (3rd), secure (3rd), take (1st), win (K)

acquit (6th): clear (2nd), excuse (3rd), find not guilty (4th), forgive (2nd), free (K), pardon (4th), release (5th)

acrobat (5th): gymnast (5th), tumbler (4th)

across (1st): astride (6th), crosswise (2nd), opposite to (3rd), over (1st), span (6th)

act (K): A. behave (4th), do (K), operate (3rd), perform (4th) **B.** imitate (5th), pretend (2nd) **C.** action (1st), deed (1st), dramatize (5th), function (4th), play (K), task (3rd), work (K) **D.** law (1st)

acts (K)

action (1st): A. act (K), behavior (4th), conduct (3rd), deed (1st) **B.** cause (2nd), fulfillment (4th), motion (3rd), movement (2nd), operation (3rd), process (4th), work (K)

active (3rd): alert (5th), alive (3rd), busy (1st), energetic (4th), moving (1st), productive (3rd), wide-awake (3rd)

actor (2nd): A. agent (5th), doer (K) **B.** player (K), thespian (6th)

actual (3rd): certain (1st), nonfiction (5th), present (K), real (1st), true (K)

acute (6th): aware (3rd), critical (5th), cutting (1st), intense (6th), keen (4th), pointed (1st), serious (4th), severe (4th), sharp (1st)

A.D. (5th)

ad (4th): advertisement (4th), announcement (3rd), promotion (5th), publication (4th), publicity (4th)

adapt (4th): accustom (4th), adjust (5th), alter (4th), change (2nd), conform (6th), fit (K), harmonize (4th), modify (5th), qualify (4th), regulate (5th), suit (1st)

add (K): addition (3rd), attach (5th), calculate (5th), combine (3rd), connect (3rd), enlarge (5th), fasten (4th), figure (4th), plus (1st), sum (1st), total (2nd)

adder (5th): snake (1st)

addict (5th): A. devotee (5th), one who surrenders to (5th) **B.** accustom (4th), have a habit (3rd), surrender to (5th)

addition (3rd): add (K), calculation (5th), extra (1st), mathematics (5th), plus (1st), sum (1st), total (2nd)

additionally (3rd): also (K), besides (1st), furthermore (3rd)

address (K): A. home (K), house (K), location (3rd) **B.** aim (3rd), direct (1st), point (1st) **C.** appeal (3rd), greet (3rd), speak to (1st), speech (2nd), talk to (K)

adept (4th): able (3rd), capable (4th), expert (5th), good (K), skilled (2nd)

adhere (6th): attach (5th), cling (4th), combine (3rd), fasten (4th), glue (1st), hold to (1st), join (3rd), link (5th), paste (1st), stick (K), tape (1st), unite (5th)

adhesive (6th): glue (1st), paste (1st), sticky (K), tape (1st)

adjective (6th)

adjoin (6th): attach (5th), connect (3rd), contact (4th), join (3rd), link (5th), meet (K), next to (K)

adjourn (6th): close (K), end (K), interrupt (3rd), leave (1st), postpone (6th), quit (1st), stop (K)

adjust (5th): accommodate (6th), accustom (4th), adapt (4th), alter (4th), change (2nd), correct (3rd), fit (K), fix (1st), modify (5th), move (K), regulate (5th), suit (2nd), vary (4th)

adjustment (5th): allowance (5th), change (2nd), concession (6th)

administer (6th): A. dispense (5th), give (K) **B.** conduct (3rd), control (2nd), direct (1st), furnish (4th), manage (4th), operate (3rd), oversee (1st), run (K), supervise (6th)

admiral (5th): A. flag officer (1st) **B.** butterfly (1st)

admire (5th): adore (4th), appreciate (5th), desire (5th), esteem (5th), prize (3rd), regard (4th), respect (2nd), value (2nd)

admit (4th): A. allow (2nd), let in (K), permit (3rd) **B.** acknowledge (5th), agree (2nd), concede (6th), confess (4th), reveal (4th)

adobe (4th)

adolescent (5th): A. immature (5th), inexperienced (4th) **B.** juvenile (5th), teen (2nd), teenager (3rd), youth (2nd)

adopt (3rd): acquire (4th), assume (5th), choose (3rd), embrace (4th), receive (1st), take in (K)

adore (4th): admire (5th), cherish (5th), honor (1st), idolize (6th), love (K), prize (3rd), respect (2nd), worship (4th)

adorn (6th): beautify (1st), decorate (3rd), dress up (K), ornament (4th), trim (4th)

adrift (6th): A. aimless (3rd), uncertain (1st), unstable (4th) **B.** at sea (1st), drifting (2nd), floating (2nd)

adult (1st): A. grown-up (1st) **B.** aged (1st), developed (5th), mature (5th), ripe (1st)

advance (2nd): aid (2nd), assist (4th), develop (5th), further (2nd), help (K), lift (1st), progress (4th), promote (5th), propel (6th), speed (3rd)

advantage (3rd): A. edge (1st) **B.** beneficial (3rd), benefit (3rd), improvement (3rd), power (1st), useful (2nd)

adventure (3rd): exploit (6th), feat (1st), risk (4th), thrill (4th), trip (1st), undertaking (3rd), venture (4th)

advertise (4th): announce (3rd), promote (5th), publicize (4th)

advertisement (4th): ad (4th), announcement (3rd), promotion (5th)

advice (3rd): caution (5th), counsel (5th), intelligence (4th), opinion (3rd), suggestion (2nd), teaching (1st), warning (3rd)

advise (3rd): acquaint (4th), caution (5th), counsel (5th), guide (1st), persuade (5th), recommend (5th), suggest (2nd), urge (4th)

aerial (4th): A. antenna (2nd) **B.** in the air (K)

aerosol (4th)

affair (2nd): A. circumstance (6th), event (3rd), incident (5th), occasion

(3rd), party (K) **B.** business (2nd), concern (3rd), matter (2nd)

affect (4th): A. act (K), fake (1st), pretend (2nd), simulate (6th) **B.** alter (4th), change (2nd), drive (1st), impress (5th), influence (5th), move (K), stir (3rd), sway (3rd), touch (1st), transform (5th)

affection (4th): devotion (5th), emotion (4th), feeling (K), fondness (4th), leaning (3rd), love (K), passion (6th), warmth (2nd)

afford (3rd): A. allow (2nd), bear (K), manage (4th) **B.** accord (4th), bestow (5th), confer (4th), furnish (3rd), give (K), grant (2nd), offer (2nd)

afire (2nd): aflame (2nd), on fire (K)

aflame (2nd): afire (2nd), burning (3rd), on fire (K)

afloat (2nd): A. in the air (K), on air (K) **B.** adrift (6th), at sea (1st), drifting (2nd), floating (2nd), on board (1st)

afraid (1st): anxious (4th), fearful (1st), frightened (2nd), scared (1st), shy (1st), timid (5th)

after (K): back (1st), behind (1st), below (1st), following (1st), later (1st), next (K), rear (3rd), then (K)

afternoon (1st): evening (1st), p.m. (6th)

afterward (4th): later (1st), subsequently (6th), when it was over (K)

again (K): another time (1st), in addition (3rd), once more (1st), repeatedly (4th)

against (1st): A. beside (1st), touching (1st) **B.** contrary (4th), disagree (2nd), opposed to (3rd)

agate (4th)

age (1st): A. era (6th), period (2nd) **B.** develop (5th), grow old (K), mature (6th), ripen (1st), season (2nd), years (1st)

aged (1st): adult (1st), mature (5th), old (K), seasoned (2nd)

agent (5th): actor (2nd), executive (5th), instrument (3rd), medium (5th), operator (5th), vehicle (6th), worker (1st)

aggress (6th): assault (4th), attack (3rd), invade (5th), provoke (6th)

aggressive (6th): assertive (6th), attacking (3rd), forceful (2nd), invading (5th), offensive (4th), pushy (1st)

agile (6th): flexible (6th), limber (4th), supple (6th), swift (4th)

agitate (5th): disturb (6th), excite (4th), move (K), rock (K), shake (1st), shock (1st), stir (3rd), sway (3rd), upset (3rd)

ago (1st): before (1st), earlier (1st), gone (1st), past (1st), previous (5th)

agony (5th): A. struggle (1st) **B.** ache (5th), anguish (6th), distress (5th), grief (5th), hurt (K), misery (4th), pain (2nd), suffering (2nd), torment (5th), trial (4th)

agree (2nd): accord (4th), acknowledge (5th), conform (6th), consent (3rd), correspond (5th), harmonize (4th)

agriculture (4th): cultivation (6th), farming (1st), gardening (K), harvesting (4th)

ahead (1st): A. forward (3rd) **B.** before (K), first (1st), in front (1st)

aid (2nd): A. gift (K), relief (4th) **B.** assist (4th), back (1st) **C.** assistance (4th), backing (1st), help (K), support (4th)

aide (5th): assistant (4th), helper (1st)

AIDS (4th)

aim (3rd): A. address (K), direct (1st), focus (5th), point (1st) **B.** design (5th), end (K), goal (4th), intent (5th), level (3rd), object (1st), objective (2nd)

air (K): A. express (5th), proclaim (4th), reveal (4th), say (K), tell (K), utter (4th), vent (4th), voice (1st) **B.** feeling (K) **C.** atmosphere (4th), oxygen (4th), ozone (5th)

Air Force (1st)

aircraft (1st)

airfield (1st) : airport (1st), landing strip (3rd)

airfoil (4th)

airplane (1st): aircraft (1st), airship (1st), jet (K), plane (1st)

airport (1st): airfield (1st), field (2nd), landing strip (3rd)

airship (1st): aircraft (1st), airplane (1st), jet (K)

airtight (5th): closed (K), sealed (1st), self-contained (5th)

alarm (3rd): A. bell (K), horn (3rd), whistle (4th) **B.** alert (5th), amaze (5th), astound (4th), frighten (2nd), horrify (4th), scare (1st), shock (1st), startle (4th), surprise (1st), terrify (3rd), upset (3rd), warn (3rd)

alas (4th): oh my (K), pity (3rd), too bad (1st), woe (4th)

albatross (5th)

album (1st): book (K), chronicle (6th), record (2nd), register (4th), scrapbook (3rd)

alcohol (4th): ale (2nd), beer (1st), liquor (5th), spirits (2nd), wine (1st)

alder (tree) (3rd)

ale (2nd): beer (1st), malt (2nd)

alert (5th): A. active (3rd), awake (3rd), aware (3rd), lively (2nd), wide-awake (3rd) **B.** alarm (3rd), awaken (3rd), call attention to (2nd), notify (3rd), warn (3rd)

alfalfa (3rd)

algae (5th)

alias (6th): also known as (1st), false name (3rd), name (K), pen name (1st)

alibi (6th): defense (5th), excuse (3rd), explanation (2nd), justification (5th), pretext (5th), reason (2nd)

alien (5th): A. foreigner (5th), immigrant (6th), outsider (1st), stranger (1st) **B.** different (1st), foreign (5th), hostile (4th), outside (1st), strange (1st), unknown (2nd) **C.** spaceman (1st)

alight (5th): A. descend (6th), dismount (3rd), get off (K) **B.** bright (1st), lit (K), shining (3rd) **C.** land (K), perch (5th), roost (2nd)

alike (1st): comparable (3rd), equivalent (6th), identical (6th), matching (3rd), same (K), similar (4th)

alive (3rd): A. breathing (1st), existing (3rd), live (1st), living (1st) **B.** active (3rd), alert (5th), animated (6th), dynamic (5th), vital (5th)

alkaline (6th)

all (K): every (K), total (2nd)

Allah (5th): the Arabic name of God

allege (6th): assert (6th), claim (2nd), declare (5th), imply (5th), insist (5th), proclaim (4th), profess (5th), say (K), state (1st)

allergic (5th): averse (6th), sensitive (5th)

allergy (5th): reaction (5th), sensitivity (5th), weakness (3rd)

alley (6th): back street (1st), lane (4th), path (1st), road (K), walkway (3rd)

allied (6th): associated (5th), cooperative (5th), joined (3rd), parallel (5th), related (4th), similar (4th), together (1st)

alligator (1st)

allow (2nd): A. acknowledge (5th), admit (4th), concede (6th) **B.** endure (4th), go along (1st), let (K), permit (3rd), stand (K), tolerate (5th), yield (4th) **C.** accord (4th), give (4th), grant (2nd)

allowance (5th): A. amount (2nd), money (K), portion (4th), share (2nd), wages (3rd) **B.** adjustment (5th), agreement (2nd), change (2nd), concession (6th), consent (3rd)

alloy (6th): combination (3rd), compound (4th), mixture (4th)

ally (6th): A. join (3rd), side with (1st) **B.** associate (5th), friend (1st), partner (5th)

almond (1st)

almost (K): approaching (3rd), barely (3rd), just about (1st), nearing (1st), nearly (1st)

aloe (4th)

alone (K): apart (3rd), individual (3rd), lone (2nd), lonely (2nd), only (K), remote (5th), separate (3rd), single (3rd), sole (4th), solitary (5th), unique (6th)

along (1st): beside (1st), in accordance (5th), in the direction (1st), next to (K), throughout (2nd), with (K)

aloud (4th): audible (6th), clearly (2nd), out loud (1st), plainly (2nd), spoken (2nd)

alphabet (2nd): code (3rd), letters (1st), signs (1st), symbols (5th)

alphanumeric (4th): using both letters and numbers

already (1st): before (K), by now (1st), previously (5th), so soon (K), yet (1st)

also (K): additionally (3rd), and (K), as well (K), besides (1st), furthermore (3rd), moreover (3rd), together with (1st), too (1st)

altar (4th): platform (4th), table (K), temple (3rd)

alter (4th): adapt (4th), adjust (5th), amend (4th), change (2nd), correct (3rd), mix (1st), modify (5th), transform (5th), vary (4th)

alternate (5th): change (2nd), change off (2nd), other (1st), periodic (4th), rotate (4th), substitute (5th), switch (4th)

although (2nd): but (K), however (3rd), though (2nd)

altitude (5th): A. elevation (4th), height (4th), upward (4th) **B.** peak (4th), point (1st), top (K)

alto (6th)

alum (6th)

aluminum (6th)

always (K): constantly (4th), ever (K), every time (1st), forever (3rd), regularly (3rd)

a.m. (6th): morning (1st)

am (K): are (K), be (K), exist (3rd)

amateur (5th): beginner (2nd), learner (1st), novice (5th), unpaid (2nd)

amaze (5th): astonish (4th), astound (4th), bewilder (3rd), confound (6th), perplex (6th), shock (1st), stun (4th), wow (1st)

Amazon (river) (5th)

Amazon (5th): warrior (4th)

ambassador (5th): delegate (5th), diplomat (4th), minister (4th)

amber (4th): A. resin (5th), sap (1st) **B.** gold (K), yellow (K)

ambergris (5th)

ambition (4th): A. aim (K), dream (K), goal (4th) **B.** desire (5th), drive (1st), hope (K), need (1st), wish (K)

ambulance (6th): emergency vehicle (6th)

ambush (6th): assault (4th), attack (3rd), entrap (3rd), snare (6th), surprise (1st)

amen (4th): so be it (K), truly (1st), yes (K)

amend (4th): adapt (4th), adjust (5th), alter (4th), change (2nd), correct (3rd), modify (5th), reform (5th)

amid (4th): among (1st), center (2nd), during (1st), in (K), mixed (1st)

amethyst (4th)

amiss (3rd): astray (3rd), bad (K), faulty (3rd), off (K), wrong (1st)

ammonia (6th)

ammunition (6th): arms (1st), bullets (4th), guns (K), rifles (4th), shells (1st), weapons (4th)

among (1st): amid (4th), between (1st), in (K), mixed (1st), surrounded (3rd), within (1st)

amount (2nd): A. measure (2nd), part (1st), portion (4th) **B.** count (K), number (K), sum (1st), total (2nd), whole (1st)

amphibian (3rd)

ample (5th): big (K), enough (1st), generous (4th), huge (1st), liberal (4th), many (K), much (1st), plenty (1st), sufficient (3rd), unlimited (3rd)

amplify (6th): broaden (3rd), develop (5th), enlarge (5th), exaggerate (6th), expand (5th), extend (4th), increase (3rd), overdo (1st)

amuse (4th): charm (3rd), entertain (4th), interest (1st), please (K)

an (K): one (K)

analog (4th): a device where data is represented by continuously variable, measurable quantities, such as a second hand on a clock

anarchy (5th): disorder (3rd), mess (1st), riot (6th), without discipline (6th), without laws (1st)

ancestor (5th): forefathers (6th), parent (3rd), relative (4th)

anchor (4th): A. prop (5th), weight (1st) **B.** attach (5th), fix (1st), grasp (4th), hold (1st), moor (5th), secure (3rd) **C.** base (1st)

anchovy (4th)

ancient (3rd): antique (6th), elderly (5th), old (K)

and (K): also (K), too (1st)

anemone (3rd)

anew (3rd): again (1st), newly (1st), once more (K), renew (4th)

angel (4th): fairy (4th), good (K), heavenly (2nd), spirit (2nd)

anger (1st): **A.** annoy (5th), bother (2nd), vex (5th) **B.** annoyance (5th), rage (4th), vexation (5th)

angle (3rd): **A.** catch (1st), fish (K) **B.** corner (2nd), curve (3rd) **C.** aspect (5th), attitude (5th), side (K), slant (6th), viewpoint (5th)

angry (1st): annoyed (5th), cross (1st), enraged (6th), frantic (5th), mad (K), vexed (5th), violent (5th)

anguish (6th): ache (5th), agony (5th), distress (5th), grief (5th), heartache (6th), hurt (K), misery (4th), pain (2nd), regret (5th), sorrow (4th), suffering (2nd), torment (5th), torture (5th)

animal (K): **A.** bodily (5th), brutal (6th), physical (5th) **B.** beast (3rd), creature (3rd), mammal (5th)

animate (6th): alive (3rd), create (3rd), enliven (6th), moving (1st)

animated (6th): active (3rd), alert (5th), alive (3rd), busy (1st), dynamic (5th), energetic (4th), live (1st), lively (1st), moving (1st)

ankle (4th)

announce (3rd): advertise (4th), broadcast (5th), communicate (4th), declare (5th), inform (5th), post (1st), proclaim (4th), promote (5th), publish (4th), state (1st), tell (K)

announcement (3rd): ad (4th), bulletin (3rd), promotion (5th), publicize (4th), statement (2nd)

annoy (5th): anger (1st), badger (2nd), bother (2nd), fret (5th), pester (2nd), trouble (1st), vex (5th), worry (1st)

annual (4th): once a year (1st), every year (1st), yearly (2nd)

anoint (6th): bless (3rd), choose (3rd), oil (K)

another (1st): **A.** different (1st), other (1st) **B.** an extra (1st), one more (K)

answer (K): **A.** acknowledgment (5th), retort (5th) **B.** acknowledge (5th), defend (5th), refute (5th), respond (5th)

ant (K)

antennae (2nd)

antibiotic (4th): a drug that fights bacterial infections

antibodies (4th)

anticipate (6th): await (5th), expect (2nd), forecast (4th), foretell (6th), hope (K), predict (6th), prevent (3rd), stop (K)

antique (6th): ancient (3rd), elderly (5th), old (K), one hundred years old (1st)

antler (4th): horn (3rd), rack (1st)

anvil (6th)

anxiety (4th): anguish (6th), care (K), concern (3rd), doubt (5th), dread (6th), fear (1st), trouble (1st), worry (1st)

anxious (4th): nervous (1st), restless (4th), suffering (2nd), worried (1st)

any (K): all (K), every (K), one (K), some (K), whatever (1st), whichever (2nd)

anybody (1st): anyone (1st), everybody (3rd), everyone (1st), whoever (1st), whomever (2nd)

anyone (1st): anybody (1st), everybody (3rd), everyone (1st), whoever (1st), whomever (2nd)

anything (1st): any item (5th), any one thing (K), everything (1st), whatever (1st)

anyway (1st): however (3rd), nevertheless (4th), so (K)

apart (3rd): aside (3rd), away (1st), disjointed (4th), distant (4th), far (1st), private (3rd), secret (1st), separate (3rd), singly (3rd)

apartment (1st): abode (5th), chamber (5th), condo (1st), condominium (2nd), flat (2nd), dwelling (4th), rental (1st), room (K)

Apatosaurus (2nd)

ape (5th): copy (3rd), imitate (5th), mock (4th)

apologize (6th): beg pardon (4th), confess (4th), regret (5th)

apology (6th): alibi (6th), amend (4th), excuse (3rd), explanation (2nd), make amends (4th), reason (2nd)

apparatus (6th): a fixture (6th), construction (3rd), device (4th), equipment (5th), instrument (3rd), machinery (1st), mechanism (6th), tool (1st)

apparent (3rd): clear (2nd), evident (2nd), noticeable (3rd), obvious (5th), plain (2nd), visible (4th)

appeal (3rd): A. entreaty (6th), petition (5th), plea (5th), prayer (3rd), request (4th), suit (1st) **B.** address (K), ask (K), beg (1st), plead (5th), pray (3rd), sue (1st) **C.** attract (5th), charm (3rd), draw (K), fascinate (5th), lure (5th), magnetism (3rd), pull (K)

appear (2nd): A. look (K), look as if (K), look like (K), seem (1st) **B.** arrive (2nd), emerge (5th), rise (1st)

appearance (2nd): A. arrival (2nd), coming (K), emergence (5th) **B.** attitude (5th), look (K)

appetite (4th): craving (6th), desire (5th), hunger (2nd), longing (1st), lust (6th), passion (6th), taste (1st)

apple (K)

applesauce (3rd)

apply (2nd): A. employ (5th), use (K) **B.** add (K), lay on (1st), stick (K) **C.** ask (K), beg (1st), request (4th), seek (1st)

appoint (3rd): choose (3rd), commission (2nd), determine (5th), elect (3rd), name (K), set (K)

appreciate (5th): A. comprehend (5th), detect (4th), realize (2nd), recognize (3rd), understand (1st) **B.** admire (5th), cherish (5th), like (K), prize (3rd), respect (2nd), treasure (4th), value (2nd)

approach (3rd): A. address (3rd), greet (3rd) **B.** begin (K), start (1st) **C.** advance (2nd), near (1st)

approve (4th): A. allow (2nd), authorize (3rd), certify (6th), commend (6th) **B.** admire (5th), like (K), value (2nd)

April (1st)

apron (3rd): cover (1st), skirt (3rd)

apt (5th): A. adept (4th), clever (3rd) **B.** fitting (2nd), inclined (5th), likely (1st), proper (3rd)

aquarium (1st): pond (1st), pool (1st), tank (5th)

Arab (5th)

arc (4th): arch (4th), bend (K), bow (1st), curve (3rd)

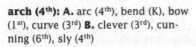

arch (4th): A. arc (4th), bend (K), bow (1st), curve (3rd) **B.** clever (3rd), cunning (6th), sly (4th)

archaeology (5th)

Archaeozic Era (5th): the time from 3,800 million years to 2,500 million years ago

archer (5th)

arctic (3rd): cold (K), freezing (4th), frigid (6th), frozen (4th), polar (3rd)

ardent (6th): eager (5th), enthusiastic (4th), intense (6th), passionate (6th), severe (4th), zealous (6th)

are (K): A. am (K), exist (3rd), to be (K) **B.** currently doing (3rd)

area (3rd): belt (2nd), district (4th), locality (4th), part (1st), range (3rd), region (4th), section (4th), space (1st), territory (3rd), vicinity (6th), zone (4th)

arena (5th): area (3rd), coliseum (5th), field (2nd), stage (3rd), sports stadium (4th), venue (6th) aren't (1st)

argue (3rd): discuss (5th), dispute (6th), explain (2nd), object (1st)

arid (6th): bald (6th), bare (3rd), barren (5th), dry (1st), scorched (6th)

arise (4th): A. ascend (4th), come up (K), elevate (2nd), go up (K), lift (1st), rise (1st), soar (6th), **B.** appear (2nd), beginning, emerge (5th), genesis, start (1st)

aristocrat (6th): gentleman (3rd), lady (1st), lord (2nd), noble (3rd), nobleman (3rd)

arithmetic (3rd): computation (6th), figures (2nd), math (5th), mathematics (5th), numbers (K)

ark (2nd): boat (1st), ship (1st)

arm (K): A. branch (2nd), extension (4th), limb (4th), part (1st) **B.** equip (5th), weapon (4th)

armadillo (1st)

armload (2nd): bunch (3rd), enough (K), full (K), lots (K), plenty (1st)

armor (4th): cover (1st), defend (5th), protection (4th), shield (4th)

arms (1st): A. ammunition (6th), guns (K), weapons (4th) **B.** equips (5th) **C.** extensions (4th), limbs (4th), parts (1st)

army (1st): A. legion (6th), military (3rd), soldiers (3rd) **B.** bunch (3rd), horde (6th), host (4th), mob (4th), swarm (4th)

around (1st): about (K), all over (K), encircle (5th), near (1st), outside (1st), surrounding (3rd)

arouse (4th): alarm (3rd), alert (5th), awaken (3rd), compel (3rd), get up (K), motivate (6th), provoke (6th), roust (5th)

arrange (3rd): A. accommodate (6th), decide (1st), plan (1st), settle (2nd) **B.** align (5th), array (5th), class (1st), group (1st), line up (K), organize (4th), order (1st), sort (2nd)

array (5th): A. attire (6th), dress (K) **B.** align (5th), arrange (3rd), battery (5th), line up (K), order (1st), place (K), spread out (2nd)

arrest (3rd): capture (3rd), catch (1st), detain (5th), halt (4th), imprison (6th), jail (4th), seize (3rd), stop (K), take (K)

arrive (2nd): appear (2nd), come (K), happen (1st), land (K), occur (3rd)

arrogant (6th): haughty (6th), proud (2nd), self-important (2nd), vain (4th)

arrow (2nd): arm (K), focus (5th), point (1st), pointer (1st), signal (4th), weapon (4th)

arrowhead (2nd)

art (K): ability (3rd), craft (2nd), cunning (6th), skill (2nd)

artichoke (4th)

article (2nd): account (3rd), clause (6th), detail (5th), item (5th), object (1st), piece (1st), story (K), thing (K), unit (5th)

artificial (4th): fake (1st), false (3rd), faux (6th), imitation (5th), man-made (1st), manufactured (3rd), mock (4th), unreal (1st)

artificial intelligence (4th): the ability of a computer to perform tasks that are thought to require intelligence such as decision making

artist (2nd)

as (K): because (K), similarly (4th), since (1st), so (K)

ascend (4th): arise (4th), climb (1st), elevate (2nd), float (1st), go up (K), incline (5th), lift (1st), mount (2nd), raise (1st), rise (1st), soar (6th)

ash (3rd): coal (2nd)

ashamed (4th): embarrassed (5th), humbled (4th), shy (1st), uneasy (1st)

ashore (2nd): beached (1st), grounded (1st), on land (K), on shore (1st)

aside (3rd): A. apart (3rd), away (K), beside (1st), other than (1st) **B.** beside (1st), by (K), next to (K), parallel (5th)

ask (K): demand (5th), examine (5th), expect (2nd), inquire (3rd), question (1st), request (4th)

asleep (3rd): idle (4th), nap (K), napping (1st), resting (1st), sleeping (1st), snoozing (4th)

aspect (5th): angle (3rd), appearance (2nd), look (K), point of view (2nd), quality (4th), slant (6th)

aspen (tree) (4th)

asphalt (5th): blacktop (1st), street (1st)

assault (4th): attack (3rd), batter (1st), beat (1st), pound (2nd), raid (6th)

assemble (4th): collect (3rd), compose (4th), gather (1st), put together (1st), summon (4th)

assert (6th): allege (6th), claim (2nd), declare (5th), profess (5th), push (1st), state (1st)

assertive (6th): aggressive (6th), pushy (1st), strong (1st)

assign (5th): appoint (3rd), award (5th), give (K), grant (2nd), name (K), set (K)

assist (4th): accommodate (6th), aid (2nd), help (K), support (4th)

assistance (4th): aid (2nd), backing (1st), help (K), relief (4th), support (4th)

assistant (4th): aide (5th), clerk (2nd), helper (K), maid (3rd), secretary (4th)

associate (5th): A. companion (3rd), friend (1st), partner (5th) **B.** connect (3rd), join (3rd), link (5th), mix (1st), relate (4th)

association (5th): A. companionship (3rd), friendship (2nd), union (3rd) **B.** club (1st), group (1st), society (3rd)

assort (5th): class (1st), grade (2nd), list (2nd), organize (4th), separate (3rd), sort (1st)

assume (5th): A. acquire (4th), adopt (3rd), take on (K) **B.** gather (1st), guess (1st), presume (6th), suppose (2nd), theory (5th), think (1st)

assure (3rd): assert (6th), insure (5th), secure (3rd), support (4th)

asteroid (2nd)

asthenosphere (5th): a zone of the earth's mantle that lies beneath the lithosphere and consists of several hundred kilometers of deformable rock

asthma (6th)

astonish (4th): amaze (5th), astound (4th), surprise (1st). See astound.

astound (4th): amaze (5th), astonish (4th), bewilder (3rd), confound (6th), perplex (6th), stun (4th)

astray (3rd): amiss (3rd), false (3rd), mistaken (1st), off (K), wrong (1st)

astride (6th): across (1st)

astrology (4th)

astronaut (4th): pilot (5th), star man (K)

astronomy (4th)

at (K): in (K), near (1st), on (K), upon (1st), within (1st)

ate (K)

athlete (5th): acrobat (5th), sportsman (2nd), sportswoman (2nd)

atmosphere (4th): A. condition (3rd), feel (K), feeling (K), setting (2nd) **B.** air (1st), ozone (5th)

atom (2nd): bit (1st), molecule (5th), particle (5th)

atop (3rd): high (K), on top (K), summit (5th)

attach (5th): add (K), adhere (6th), adjoin (6th), fasten (4th), fix (1st), join (3rd), link (5th), pin (K), stick (K), stop (K)

attack (3rd): aggress (6th), ambush (6th), assault (6th), battle (2nd), charge (2nd), fight (K), raid (6th)

attain (6th): accomplish (2nd), achieve (5th), acquire (4th), fulfill (4th), gain (2nd), get (K), realize (2nd), secure (3rd), win (K)

attempt (2nd): begin (K), initiate (5th), start (1st), strive (5th), tackle (4th), try (K)

attend (3rd): A. go to (K), visit (1st) **B.** mind (1st), nurse (K), watch (1st)

attention (2nd): alertness (5th), awareness (3rd), focus (5th), note (1st), notice (3rd), observe (3rd), regard (4th)

attire (6th): A. adorn (6th), array (5th), dress up (K) **B.** clothes (1st), dress (K), garb (5th)

attitude (5th): angle (3rd), appearance (2nd), bearing (2nd), feeling (K), position (2nd), slant (6th), thought (1st), view (2nd)

attract (5th): charm (3rd), draw (K), engage (5th), fascinate (5th), invite (3rd), lure (5th), pull (K)

au Pair (4th)

audible (6th): aloud (6th), heard (K), out loud (1st)

August (1st)

aunt (1st)

aurora (5th): dawn (1st), daybreak (2nd), morning (1st), sunrise (2nd), sunup (2nd)

austere (5th): bare (3rd), formal (4th), grim (4th), harsh (5th), plain (2nd), severe (4th), stern (4th), stiff (3rd), strict (6th)

author (3rd): composer (4th), creator (3rd), maker (1st), writer (1st)

authority (3rd): A. adept (4th), expert (5th), knowledgeable (3rd), master (1st) **B.** control (2nd), force (1st), power (1st), rule (K)

authorize (3rd): A. establish (3rd), institute (5th) **B.** allow (2nd), let (K), permit (3rd)

autobiography (6th): confessions (6th), diary (3rd), history (2nd), journal (2nd), memory (3rd)

autograph (6th): name (K), signature (6th)

automatic (6th): habit (3rd), mechanical (5th), reflex (6th), self-acting (3rd), set (K), trained (1st)

automobile (3rd): car (K)

autumn (3rd): fall (K), harvest (4th)

avenge (5th): punish (4th), repay (K), revenge (5th)

avenue (3rd): approach (3rd), boulevard (4th), lane (4th), road (K), street (1st), way (K)

average (3rd): center (2nd), common (2nd), mean (5th), middle (2nd), normal (5th), ordinary (3rd), typical (6th), usual (3rd)

aviation (6th): flight (2nd), flying (K)

avocado (3rd)

avoid (3rd): escape (2nd), shun (6th), skirt (3rd)

await (5th): abide (5th), expect (2nd), stay (2nd), wait for (K)

awake (3rd): alert (5th), alive (3rd), aware (3rd), conscious (6th), up (K), watchful (2nd)

awaken (3rd): arouse (4th), roust (5th), waken (1st), wake up (1st)

award (5th): A. bonus (6th), medal (4th), prize (3rd), trophy (6th) **B.** allow (2nd), bestow (5th), give (K), grant (2nd), present (K)

aware (3rd): A. familiar (3rd), informed (5th), know (1st) **B.** alive (3rd), awake (3rd), conscious (6th)

away (K): abroad (5th), absent (5th), far (1st), gone (1st), not here (K), there (1st)

awe (6th): astonishment (4th), bewilderment (3rd), fear (1st), respect (2nd), reverence (6th), surprise (1st), wonder (1st)

awful (3rd): bad (K), dreaded (6th), fearful (2nd), horrible (4th), terrible (3rd)

awhile (5th)

awkward (6th): coarse (4th), clumsy (6th), rough (4th), rude (2nd), uneasy (1st)

ax (K): A. pick (1st) **B.** chop (2nd), cut (K), hack (6th), split (4th)

axis (4th): center line (2nd)

B.C. (5th): Before Christ

B.C.E. (5th): Before Common Era

babble (6th): chatter (1st), gab (1st), gossip (5th), talk (K)

babe (5th): baby (K), girl (K), infant (5th), tot (2nd)

baboon (1st)

baby (K): A. humor (4th), indulge (5th), pet (1st), spoil (4th) **B.** babe (5th), child (K), infant (5th), newborn (1st)

bachelor (6th): man (K), single (3rd)

back (K): A. behind (1st), other side (1st), reverse (5th) **B.** spine (4th) **C.** aid (2nd), assist (4th), help (K), support (4th)

backbone (4th): A. back (1st), spine (4th) **B.** character (2nd), courage (4th), guts (1st), resolve (5th), spirit (2nd)

background (4th): A. conditions (3rd), experience (4th) **B.** distance (4th), environment (6th), horizon (4th), setting (2nd), surroundings (3rd)

backing (1st): aid (2nd), assistance (4th), encouragement (4th), help (K), relief (4th), support (4th)

backpack (4th): bag (1st), knapsack (4th)

backward (4th): awkward (6th), inside out (1st), reverse (5th), wrong (1st)

backwoods (4th): country (1st), forest (2nd), frontier (5th), outback (1st), wild (2nd), wilderness (4th), woods (1st)

bacon (4th): A. ham (K), pork (6th) **B.** earnings (2nd), money (K), wages (3rd)

bacteria (2nd)

bad (K): A. broken (1st), false (3rd), faulty (3rd), soiled (2nd), wrong (1st) **B.** not good (K), poor (K) **C.** dreadful (6th), evil (3rd), harmful (3rd), ill (1st), rotten (1st)

badge (5th): button (1st), crest (4th), identification (4th), mark (1st), patch (4th), sign (1st)

badger (2nd): annoy (5th), bait (5th), bother (2nd), disturb (6th), pester (2nd), provoke (6th), trouble (1st), vex (5th)

bag (1st): A. backpack (4th), purse (4th), sack (1st), suitcase (1st) **B.** capture (3rd), catch (1st), pack (1st), snare (6th), trap (1st)

bagpipe (3rd)

bait (3rd): badger (2nd), charm (3rd), heckle (3rd), interest (1st), lure (5th), tease (3rd), trap (1st)

bake (1st): boil (3rd), burn (3rd), cook (1st), dry (1st), hot (K), roast (4th), scorch (6th)

balance (3rd): A. arrange (3rd), order (1st), organize (4th), total (2nd) **B.** difference (1st), extra (1st), rest (1st) **C.** calm (3rd), poise (6th), stability (4th), steadiness (3rd)

balcony (6th): porch (3rd), railing (2nd)

bald (6th): bare (3rd), hairless (K), naked (4th), nude (6th), obvious (5th), open (K), plain (2nd)

ball (K): A. dance (1st), party (K) **B.** blast (2nd), fun (K) **C.** globe (4th), orb (4th), sphere (6th)

ballad (5th): poem (3rd), song (K)

ballast (4th): balance (3rd), level (3rd), steady (3rd), weight (1st)

ballet (4th): dance (1st)

balloon (1st): A. fatten (1st), fill out (1st), grow (K), rise (1st), swell (3rd) **B.** ball (K), bubble (2nd)

ballot (6th): ticket (1st), vote (2nd)

bamboo (3rd)

ban (K): bar (3rd), condemn (4th), disallow (2nd), forbid (4th), prevent (3rd), prohibit (6th), reject (5th), stop (K)

banana (2nd)

band (1st): A. bond (3rd), collect (3rd), gather (1st), group (1st), tie (1st), troop (3rd), unite (5th) **B.** belt (2nd), cord (4th), ribbon (4th)

bandit (3rd): criminal (4th), gangster (1st), pirate (5th), robber (K), thief (3rd)

bane (5th): curse (3rd), pain (2nd), poison (3rd), problem (1st), trouble (1st), wrong (1st)

baneberry (4th)

bang (3rd): A. hit (K), pound (2nd), slam (5th), smash (3rd) **B.** boom (1st), crash (2nd), explode (3rd), thud (3rd)

banister (5th): pole (K), post (1st), rail (2nd)

bank (1st): A. bar (3rd), incline (5th), reef (5th), shore (1st), slope (3rd) **B.** collect (3rd), gather (1st), heap (4th), mass (3rd), pile (1st) **C.** depend (3rd), rely (5th), save (1st), trust (1st)

banner (3rd): flag (3rd), ribbon (4th), streamer (1st)

banquet (4th): dinner (1st), feast (1st), meal (3rd), meeting (1st), party (K)

banyan (4th)

bar (3rd): A. pole (K), rod (1st), shaft (4th), stick (K) **B.** saloon (6th), tavern (5th) **C.** ban (K), block (1st), dam (K), forbid (4th), prohibit (6th)

bar code (3rd): computer readable codes that give information about products

barbecue (5th): A. banquet (4th), feast (1st), party (K) **B.** bake (1st), cook (1st), roast (4th), toast (5th)

barber (2nd): A. haircutter (1st) **B.** cut (K), shave (1st), trim (4th)

bare (3rd): A. reveal (4th), show (1st), strip (3rd), uncover (1st) **B.** arid (6th), bald (6th), naked (4th), plain (2nd), simple (1st), unadorned (6th)

bareback (4th)

bargain (4th): A. arrange (3rd), deal (2nd), settle (2nd) **B.** agreement (2nd), contract (3rd), deal (2nd), understanding (1st)

barge (5th): A. force (1st), interrupt (3rd), intrude (6th), push (1st) **B.** boat (1st), float (1st)

bark (3rd): A. covering (1st), shell (1st), skin (2nd) **B.** howl (4th), yap (1st)

barley (4th)

barn (K): stable (4th), stall (5th)

barnacle (3rd)

baron (4th): aristocrat (6th), gentleman (3rd), nobility (3rd), royalty (3rd)

barrel (4th): cask (4th), keg (1st), tank (5th)

barren (4th): arid (6th), bald (6th), bare (3rd), dead (1st), dry (1st), empty (3rd), naked (4th), scarce (1st)

barrier (6th): bar (3rd), block (1st), wall (K)

basalt (5th): a hard, dense, dark volcanic rock

base (1st): bottom (1st), foot (K), home (K), low (K), stand (K), support (4th)

baseball (1st)

basement (3ʳᵈ): cellar (1ˢᵗ)

bashful (4ᵗʰ): backward (4ᵗʰ), modest (4ᵗʰ), shy (K), timid (5ᵗʰ)

basic (2ⁿᵈ): base (1ˢᵗ), fundamental (4ᵗʰ), main (3ʳᵈ), primary (5ᵗʰ)

basin (4ᵗʰ): bowl (1ˢᵗ), depression (6ᵗʰ), pan (K), sink (3ʳᵈ)

basis (2ⁿᵈ): base (1ˢᵗ), cause (2ⁿᵈ), foundation (5ᵗʰ), ground (1ˢᵗ), law (1ˢᵗ), support (4ᵗʰ)

basket (1ˢᵗ): box (K), case (2ⁿᵈ), pouch (1ˢᵗ)

basketball (1ˢᵗ)

bass (1ˢᵗ)

bass (1ˢᵗ): A. singer (1ˢᵗ) **B.** low pitch (2ⁿᵈ) **C.** guitar (1ˢᵗ) **D.** palm fiber (4ᵗʰ)

bat (K): A. blow (1ˢᵗ), hit (K), smack (6ᵗʰ) **B.** baton (5ᵗʰ), club (1ˢᵗ), stick (K)

batch (2ⁿᵈ): array (5ᵗʰ), bunch (3ʳᵈ), bundle (5ᵗʰ), group (1ˢᵗ), mess (1ˢᵗ), set (K)

bath (1ˢᵗ): dip (1ˢᵗ), shower (4ᵗʰ), wash (1ˢᵗ)

bathe (1ˢᵗ): clean (K), rinse (3ʳᵈ), shower (4ᵗʰ), wash (1ˢᵗ)

bathroom (1ˢᵗ): restroom (K), toilet (2ⁿᵈ), washroom (1ˢᵗ)

bathtub (1ˢᵗ): basin (5ᵗʰ), tub (1ˢᵗ)

baton (5ᵗʰ): bat (K), rod (1ˢᵗ), stick (K), wand (3ʳᵈ)

batter (1ˢᵗ): A. dough (5ᵗʰ), paste (1ˢᵗ) **B.** beat (1ˢᵗ), fighter (K), hitter (1ˢᵗ), pound (2ⁿᵈ), smack (6ᵗʰ)

battery (5ᵗʰ): array (5ᵗʰ), group (1ˢᵗ), set (K), stand (1ˢᵗ)

battle (2ⁿᵈ): action (1ˢᵗ), argument (3ʳᵈ), combat (5ᵗʰ), discussion (5ᵗʰ), fight (K), war (1ˢᵗ)

bawl (5ᵗʰ): bellow (4ᵗʰ), cry (K), exclaim (3ʳᵈ), howl (4ᵗʰ), roar (1ˢᵗ), shout (1ˢᵗ)

bay (K): A. bark (3ʳᵈ), cry (K), howl (4ᵗʰ), scream (1ˢᵗ), yell (K) **B.** inlet (4ᵗʰ), harbor (2ⁿᵈ)

bayonet (5ᵗʰ): blade (2ⁿᵈ), knife (1ˢᵗ)

bayou (5ᵗʰ): creek (4ᵗʰ), marsh (5ᵗʰ), swamp (4ᵗʰ)

bazaar (5ᵗʰ): fair (1ˢᵗ), market (2ⁿᵈ)

be (K): A. last (K), remain (1ˢᵗ), stay (1ˢᵗ) **B.** am (K), exist (3ʳᵈ), happen (1ˢᵗ), live (1ˢᵗ), occur (3ʳᵈ)

beach (K): bank (1ˢᵗ), coast (2ⁿᵈ), land (K), shore (1ˢᵗ), strand (1ˢᵗ)

beached (1ˢᵗ): ashore (2ⁿᵈ), stranded (5ᵗʰ)

bead (K): bubble (2ⁿᵈ), dot (K), drop (K), jewel (5ᵗʰ), pearl (4ᵗʰ)

beak (3ʳᵈ): bill (1ˢᵗ), nose (1ˢᵗ)

beam (3ʳᵈ): A. board (1ˢᵗ), plank (5ᵗʰ), stick (K) **B.** flash (2ⁿᵈ), gleam (1ˢᵗ), ray (1ˢᵗ), streak (5ᵗʰ)

bear (K): A. birth (1ˢᵗ), bring (K), carry (K), drop (K), give (K), lay (1ˢᵗ), produce (2ⁿᵈ), transfer (5ᵗʰ) **B.** force (1ˢᵗ), press (1ˢᵗ), push (1ˢᵗ) **C.** endure (4ᵗʰ), hold (1ˢᵗ), stand (K), support (4ᵗʰ), yield (4ᵗʰ)

beard (4ᵗʰ): A. hair (K), face hair (K) **B.** brave (1ˢᵗ), challenge (4ᵗʰ), dare (2ⁿᵈ), defy (6ᵗʰ)

beast (3ʳᵈ): animal (K), creature (3ʳᵈ), hog (K), mammal (5ᵗʰ), pig (K)

126

beat (1st): A. accent (6th), pulse (5th), rhythm (5th), tone (3rd) **B.** assault (4th), hit (K), pound (2nd), punch (4th), strike (2nd), swat (3rd), whip (4th) **C.** conquer (4th), defeat (5th), win (K)

beautiful (1st): attractive (5th), fair (1st), great (K), handsome (3rd), lovely (1st), pretty (1st)

beautify (2nd): adorn (6th), decorate (3rd), polish (4th)

beaver (1st)

because (K): as (K), due (2nd), for (K), since (2nd), so (K)

become (1st): change (2nd), grow into (1st), happen (1st), occur (3rd), transform (5th)

bed (K): A. retire (4th), sleep (K) **B.** bunk (4th), cot (1st), couch (4th), cradle (4th), crib (2nd)

bedraggled (5th): dirty (1st), messy (1st), soil (2nd), worn (3rd)

bedroom (3rd)

bee (K)

beech (4th)

beef (5th): cattle (3rd), meat (1st)

been (K): was (K), were (1st)

beep (K): honk (1st), squeak (5th)

beer (5th): alcohol (4th), ale (2nd), malt (2nd)

beet (4th): red (K)

beetle (1st)

before (K): ahead (1st), earlier (1st), forward (3rd), in advance (2nd), previous (5th), sooner (K)

befriend (6th): accept (3rd), familiarize (3rd), like (K), make friends (1st), protect (4th), take in (K)

beg (1st): ask (K), beseech (5th), persuade (5th), seek (1st)

begin (K): initiate (5th), start (1st)

beginner (2nd): amateur (5th), novice (5th), student (3rd)

behalf (6th): for (K), represent (4th)

behave (4th): act (K), conduct (3rd), conform (6th), function (4th), perform (4th)

behavior (4th): action (1st), bearing (K), conduct (3rd), habits (3rd)

behind (1st): A. back (4th), support (4th) **B.** after (1st), afterwards (4th), following (1st), later (1st)

behold (3rd): eye (K), look at (K), notice (1st), observe (3rd), see (K), stare (3rd), view (2nd), watch (1st)

being (1st): A. animal (K), beast (3rd), body (1st), creature (3rd), thing (K) **B.** animation (6th), existence (3rd), individual (3rd), personality (5th)

belief (1st): conviction (5th), credence (6th), credit (5th), faith (3rd), tenet (6th), think (1st), trust (1st)

believe (1st): A. accept (3rd), credit (5th), have faith (3rd), know (1st), think (1st) **B.** assert (6th), certainty (2nd), claim (2nd), maintain (2nd)

bell (K): alarm (3rd), chime (6th), curve (3rd), mark (1st), ring (1st), signal (4th)

belle (6th): beautiful (1st), girl (K)

bellow (4th): howl (4th), roar (1st), shout (1st), yell (K)

belly (5th): abdomen (6th), gut (1st), stomach (2nd), tummy (K)

belong (1st): A. hold (1st), own (K), possess (3rd) **B.** apply (2nd), member of (1st), relate (4th)

beloved (4th): admired (5th), adored (4th), cherished (5th), dear (1st), favorite (3rd), loved (1st)

below (1st): beneath (1st), lower (1st), under (K), underground (4th)

belt (2nd): A. hit (K), punch (4th), strike (2nd) **B.** area (3rd), region (4th), zone (4th) **C.** band (1st), cinch (6th), encircle (5th), fasten (4th), sash (6th), tie (1st)

bench (4th): seat (1st), stall (5th)

bend (1st): A. mold (5th), shape (1st), twist (1st) **B.** arch (4th), bow (1st), circle (K), curve (3rd), hook (4th)

beneath (1st): below (1st), down (K), under (K), underneath (4th)

beneficial (3rd): helpful (1st), valuable (4th)

benefit (3rd): advantage (3rd), aid (2nd), help (K), improve (3rd), profit (4th), service (1st)

bent (K): A. aptitude (3rd), gift (1st), talent (2nd) **B.** curved (3rd), twisted (1st)

berate (5th): chew out (1st), criticize (5th), curse (3rd), put down (2nd), scold (5th)

berry (1st)

beseech (5th): ask (K), beg (1st)

beside (1st): against (1st), bordering (1st), close (K), nearby (1st), next to (K), other than (1st), parallel (5th)

besides (1st): additionally (3rd), also (K), furthermore (3rd), too (1st)

best (K): ace (2nd), choice (3rd), excellent (1st), finest (1st), prime (5th), superb (6th), superior (4th), top (K)

bestow (5th): afford (3rd), confer (4th), favor (1st), give (K), grant (2nd), hand (K), pass (K)

bet (1st): gamble (5th), risk (4th), stake (1st)

betray (5th): deceive (5th), double cross (3rd), give away (K), mislead (5th), reveal (4th), sell out (1st)

better (K): A. advance (2nd), improve (3rd), raise (1st) **B.** good (K), preferable (4th), superior (4th)

between (1st): amid (4th), among (1st), in the middle (2nd), joining (3rd), linking (5th)

beverage (6th): drink (1st), liquid (3rd), refreshment (6th)

beware (6th): be careful (1st), caution (5th), mind (1st), watch out (1st)

bewilder (3rd): confound (6th), confuse (4th), mystify (4th), puzzle (4th)

beyond (1st): farther (3rd), outside (1st), over (K), past (1st)

bias (6th): point of view (2nd), prejudice (6th), slant (6th), view (2nd)

bib (1st): apron (3rd), drape (5th), napkin (5th)

Bible (K)

bicycle (2nd): bike (1st)

bid (1st): offer (2nd), propose (4th), suggest (2nd)

big (K): giant (2nd), grand (2nd), great (K), heavy (1st), huge (1st), large (K), vast (4th)

bike (1st): bicycle (2nd), spin (1st), travel (1st)

bill (1st): A. act (K), law (1st), notice (1st) **B.** account (3rd), check (1st), record (2nd) **C.** beak (4th)

billboard (3rd): ad (4th), advertisement (4th), sign (1st)

billiards (6th): pool (1st)

billion (5th)

bin (1st): basket (1st), box (K), case (2nd), can (K), container (5th), drawer (1st)

bind (2nd): attach (5th), connect (3rd), fasten (4th), hold (1st), link (5th), strap (5th), tie (1st)

binoculars (6th): scope (6th), sights (1st), telescope (4th)

biography (6th): history (2nd), life story (1st)

biology (4th)

biosphere (6th)

birch (4th)

bird (K)

birthday (K)

biscuit (4th): bun (2nd), cookie (K), cracker (4th), sweet (K)

bishop (5th): churchman (1st), clergyman (6th), holy man (5th)

bison (4th)

bit (1st): atom (5th), detail (5th), dot (K), fraction (4th), piece (1st), speck (4th), trace (3rd)

bite (1st): attack (3rd), gnaw (1st), nip (1st)

bitter (3rd): A. mocking (4th), scornful (4th), unhappy (K) **B.** acid (4th), sour (2nd), tart (5th), unsweet (K)

black (K): A. African (5th) **B.** dark (K), evil (3rd), inky, night (1st), sinful (1st)

blackberry (2nd)

blackbird (1st)

blackboard (3rd)

blackmail (4th): A. force (1st), make (K) **B.** bribe (5th), ransom (6th), steal (3rd)

blacksmith (4th)

blacktop (1st): asphalt (5th)

blade (2nd): edge (1st), knife (1st), sword (4th)

blame (2nd): A. responsibility (4th) **B.** accuse (4th), criticize (5th), fault (3rd)

blank (4th): bare (3rd), clean (K), empty (3rd), nothing (1st), plain (2nd), vacant (6th), void (6th)

blanket (3rd): A. conceal (4th), enclose (1st) **B.** comforter (3rd), cover (1st), quilt (4th)

blast (2nd): A. bellow (4th), honk (1st), horn (3rd) **B.** force (1st), injure (5th), ruin (5th)

blaze (1st): A. bright (1st), flash (2nd), gleam (1st), glow (1st) **B.** burn (3rd), fire (K), flame (3rd)

bleach (4th): fade (1st), pale (3rd), whiten (1st)

bleat (4th): cry (K), yelp (6th)

blemish (5th): A. damage (5th), injure (5th) **B.** defect (5th), flaw (2nd), mark (1st), pimple (5th), spot (1st), stain (4th)

blend (5th): combine (3rd), compound (4th), mix (1st)

bless (3rd): anoint (6th), make sacred (4th), pray (3rd), thank (K), wish well (K)

blimp (5th): airship (1st), balloon (1st)

blind (3rd): A. ignorant (4th), unaware (3rd) **B.** sightless (1st)

blink (6th): flicker (5th), wink (2nd)

blister (5th): boil (3rd), bulge (4th), burn (3rd), pimple (5th), swelling (3rd)

blizzard (4th): snow storm (2nd), wind (1st)

block (1st): A. brick (4th), cube (4th), piece (1st) **B.** bar (3rd), dam (K), restrain (5th), stop (K)

blond (5th): fair (1st), pale (3rd), yellow (K)

blood (1st): family (K), life (1st), red (K)

bloodhound (3rd)

bloodshed (4th): battle (2nd), death (3rd), massacre (6th), murder (3rd), war (1st)

bloodthirsty (4th): brutal (6th), fierce (4th), savage (5th)

bloom (4th): blossom (4th), flower (K), grow (1st), thrive (6th)

blossom (4th): A. grow (K) **B.** bloom (4th), flower (K)

blot (4th): A. dry (1st), soak up (5th) **B.** blemish (5th), brand (2nd), mar (6th), mark (1st), smear (3rd), stain (4th)

blotch (6th): blemish (5th), mark (1st), spot (1st), stain (4th)

blouse (1st): shirt (1st), top (K)

blow (1st): A. blast (2nd), sound (1st) **B.** hit (K), punch (4th), slap (2nd) **C.** breeze (4th), sail (1st) **D.** enlarge (5th), expand (5th)

blue (K): A. sky (K) **B.** rare (4th), sad (K), unhappy (1st)

blue jay (1st)

bluebell (2nd)

blueberry (2nd)

bluebird (1st)

bluebottle (3rd)

bluff (6th): A. fool (2nd), tease (3rd), trick (1st) **B.** blunt (6th), cliff (2nd), hill (K), open (K), plain (2nd)

blunt (6th): A. dull (1st), rounded (K) **B.** open (K), plain (2nd), rude (2nd), short (1st)

blur (4th): A. soil (2nd), stain (4th) **B.** out of focus (5th), unclear (2nd)

blush (4th): color (K), glow (1st), redden (K)

boar (5th)

board (1st): A. beam (3rd), panel (6th), plank (5th), wood (1st) **B.** close (K), nail down (2nd) **C.** accommodate (6th), feed (1st), house (K), lodge (4th)

boast (4th): brag (3rd), crow (2nd), pride (2nd)

boat (1st): ark (2nd), canoe (4th), ship (1st)

bobbin (4th): spool (2nd)

bobcat (1st)

bobolink (5th)

bodily (5th)

body (1st): A. being (1st), creature (3rd), person (1st) **B.** bunch (3rd), group (1st), mass (3rd) **C.** build (1st), figure (1st), frame (1st), skeleton (4th)

bodyguard (4th): guard (1st), protector (4th)

bog (5th): marsh (5th), swamp (4th)

boil (3rd): A. bubble (2nd), pimple (5th), sore (4th) **B.** anger (1st), simmer (4th), steam (2nd), stew (2nd)

bold (2nd): adventurous (3rd), brave (1st), confident (6th), courageous (4th), daring (2nd), fearless (1st)

bolt (4th): A. block (1st), latch (4th), lock (1st), tie (1st) **B.** jump (K), run (K), start (1st)

bomb (5th): A. explosive (3rd), mine (1st) **B.** assault (4th), attack (3rd), explode (3rd)

bonbon (4th): candy (K), surprise (1st), sweet (K), treat (2nd)

bond (3rd): A. agreement (2nd), guarantee (6th), security (3rd) **B.** connection (3rd), link (5th), restraint (5th), tie (1st)

bondage (6th): restraint (5th), slavery (3rd)

bone (1st)

bonfire (3rd): fire (K)

bonnet (6th): hat (K)

bonus (6th): award (5th), extra (1st), gift (K), present (K), prize (3rd), reward (4th)

boo (K)

boob (2nd): clumsy (6th), idiot (6th), stupid (4th)

book (K): literature (5th), magazine (3rd), publication (4th)

bookcase (3rd)

bookkeeper (3rd): accountant (3rd), clerk (2nd), recorder (2nd)

boom (1st): bang (3rd), blast (2nd), clap (2nd), explosion (3rd), roar (1st), rumble (3rd)

boomerang (5th): A. stick (K) **B.** return (2nd), reverse (5th)

boon (5th): advantage (3rd), benefit (3rd), extra (1st), favor (2nd), gift (K), present (K), tip (1st)

boot (1st): A. fire (K), terminate (6th) **B.** kick (1st) **C.** foot cover (1st), shoe (K)

booth (5th): closet (2nd), counter (5th), room (K), stall (5th), stand (K)

borax (5th)

border (1st): boundary (4th), brim (5th), edge (1st), line (K), margin (5th), rim (1st)

bore (2nd): A. drill (2nd), penetrate (5th), punch (4th) **B.** annoy (5th), burden (5th), tire (2nd), wear out (1st)

born (1st)

borrow (2nd): ask (K), beg (1st), take (K), use (K)

boss (K): A. control (2nd), direct (1st), lead (1st) **B.** chief (1st), employer (5th), head (K), manager (4th), supervisor (6th)

both (K): each (K), including (3rd), two (K)

bother (2nd): annoy (5th), bait (5th), irk (6th), pester (2nd), trouble (1st), vex (5th)

bottle (3rd): container (5th), glass (1st), package (4th)

bottom (1st): base (1st), foot (K), ground (1st), rest (1st), support (4th)

bought (2nd): acquired (4th), purchased (3rd)

boulder (5th): rock (K), stone (2nd)

boulevard (4th): avenue (3rd), road (K), street (1st), strip (3rd), way (K)

bounce (6th): drop (K), fire (K), hop (K), jump (K), leap (3rd), spring (K)

bound (2nd): A. connected (3rd), fastened (4th), held (1st), restrained (5th), tied (1st) **B.** hop (K), jump (K), leap (3rd) **C.** meant (1st), ought (1st)

boundary (4th): border (1st), edge (1st), frame (3rd), frontier (5th), limit (3rd), line (K), outline (4th)

boundless (4th): eternal (4th), infinite (5th), unending (2nd), unlimited (3rd), vast (4th)

bouquet (6th): A. fragrance (5th), incense (5th), odor (3rd), perfume (3rd), scent (3rd), smell (3rd) **B.** arrangement (3rd), bunch (3rd), cluster (4th), flowers (1st)

bout (6th): A. shift (4th), spell (2nd), turn (1st) **B.** fight (K), match (3rd), meet (K)

bow (1st): A. defer (6th), submit (4th), yield (4th) **B.** kneel (4th) **C.** bend (K), curve (3rd), flex (6th)

bowl (1st): A. strike (2nd), throw (1st) **B.** crater (3rd), depression (6th) **C.** basin (4th), dish (1st), sink (3rd), tub (1st)

box (K): A. carton (4th), case (2nd), package (4th) **B.** cuff (1st), hit (K), punch (4th) **C.** enclose (4th), pack (1st), seal (K)

boxer (1st): fighter (1st)

boy (K): child (K), lad (K), male (4th), youth (2nd)

boycott (6th): avoid (3rd), block (1st), ignore (5th), prevent (3rd), shun (6th)

boyfriend (4th): chum (6th), friend (1st), lover (1st), mate (4th), pal (K)

boyhood (4th): childhood (4th), youth (4th)

brace (5th): A. couple (3rd), pair (1st) **B.** band (1st), prop (5th), support (4th)

bracelet (5th): band (1st), circle (K), encircle (1st)

brag (3rd): boast (4th), crow (2nd)

Brahman (5th)

braid (2nd): curl (2nd), knit (4th), weave (4th), wind (1st)

brain (3rd): intelligence (4th), mind (1st), reason (1st)

brake (1st): limit (3rd), slow (1st), stop (K)

branch (2nd): limb (4th), twig (4th)

brand (2nd): A. label (3rd), mark (1st), stamp (3rd), tag (K) **B.** class (1st), kind (K), make (K)

brandish (6th): display (4th), flourish (4th), shake (1st), show (1st), swing (1st), wave (K)

brass (2nd): A. metal (3rd) **B.** bravery (1st), nerve (1st), strength (2nd)

brat (3rd): child (K), imp (5th), kid (K)

bravado (6th): boasting (4th), bragging (3rd)

brave (1st): A. challenge (4th), dare (2nd), defy (6th), encounter (4th), meet (K), oppose (3rd) **B.** courageous (4th), unafraid (1st)

bravo (6th): cheer (3rd), cry (K), hazah (6th)

bread (2nd): A. money (K) **B.** dough (5th), living (1st), loaf (4th)

breadfruit (2nd)

break (1st): A. gap (K), opening (1st), space (1st), split (4th) **B.** bust (6th), crack (4th), destroy (2nd), shatter (5th)

breakers (4th): waves (1st)

breakfast (1st)

breakwater (4th): barrier (6th), reef (5th), wall (K)

breast (3rd): chest (2nd), front (1st)

breath (1st): air (K), breeze (4th), wind (1st)

breathe (1st): A. share (2nd), tell (K), whisper (1st) **B.** gasp (4th), puff (2nd)

breeches (5th): pants (1st), trousers (5th)

breed (4th): cultivate (6th), generate (4th), grow (K), mate (4th), produce (2nd), raise (1st), reproduce (4th)

breeze (4th): air current (3rd), wind (1st)

brew (6th): A. ale (2nd), beer (5th) **B.** plan (1st), think (1st), spin (1st) **C.** cook up (1st), mix (1st), soak (1st), stew (2nd)

bribe (5th): pay (K), ransom (6th), tip (1st)

brick (4th): block (1st)

bride (4th): mate (4th), partner (5th), wife (1st)

bridesmaid (4th)

bridge (1st): connect (3rd), cross (1st), join (3rd), link (5th), span (6th)

brief (3rd): A. communicate (4th), inform (5th), tell (K) **B.** compact (5th), fast (1st), quick (1st), short (1st), sudden (1st), swift (4th)

brier (6th): bush (2nd), root (3rd), wood (1st)

brig (6th): jail (4th), prison (3rd)

brigantine (6th)

bright (1st): A. intelligent (4th), smart (1st) **B.** brilliant (4th), clear (2nd), light (K), quick (1st), shining (1st)

brilliant (4th): bright (1st), gleaming (1st), glittering (4th)

brim (5th): border (1st), brink (6th), edge (1st), margin (5th), rim (1st)

bring (K): bear (K), carry (K), deliver (5th), get (K), fetch (4th), take (K), transport (5th)

brink (6th): border (1st), boundary (4th), edge (1st), margin (5th), rim (1st)

brisk (6th): abrupt (5th), active (3rd), agile (6th), fast (1st), quick (1st), sharp (1st)

bristle (6th): A. hair (K) **B.** parade (2nd), strut (5th), swagger (5th)

broad (3rd): deep (1st), entire (3rd), extended (4th), full (K), large (K), vast (4th), whole (1st), wide (1st)

broadcast (5th): advertise (4th), announce (3rd), circulate (4th), distribute (6th), proclaim (4th), publish (4th)

broadcloth (5th)

broadsword (4th)

brocade (5th)

broccoli (4th)

broil (4th): barbecue (5th), cook (1st), fight (K), flame (3rd), heat (1st), toast (5th)

bronco (6th): horse (K)

bronze (4th): cover (1st), gild (6th), plate (1st)

brooch (4th): pin (K)

brood (4th): A. fret (5th), fuss (1st), mourn (4th), sorrow (4th), stew (2nd), sulk (5th), worry (1st) **B.** band (1st), children (K), group (1st), litter (2nd), nest (1st), pups (K), young (1st)

brook (2nd): A. creek (4th), stream (3rd) **B.** allow (2nd), bear (K), endure (4th), stand (K), suffer (2nd), tolerate (5th)

broom (2nd)

broth (4th): liquid (3rd), soup (1st)

brother (1st): associate (5th), relative (4th)

brow (4th): brink (6th), edge (1st), overhang (4th), peak (4th), rim (1st), top (K)

brown (K): A. cook (1st), fry (1st) **B.** beige (3rd), chestnut (4th), chocolate (4th), tan (K)

brownie (2nd): A. elf (1st), fairy (4th) **B.** cake (1st) **C.** Scout (1st)

bruise (5th): A. blemish (5th), mark (1st) **B.** beat (1st), hurt (K), pound (2nd), sore (4th), wound (3rd)

brush (2nd): A. broom (2nd) **B.** graze (5th), rub (1st), skim (6th), touch (1st)

brutal (6th): cold (K), rough (4th), rude (2nd)

brute (6th): animal (K), beast (3rd), creature (3rd), monster (1st)

bubble (2nd): ball (K), balloon (1st), bead (K), burp (3rd), drop (K)

buck (1st): A. challenge (4th), go against (1st), oppose (3rd) **B.** bound (2nd), hop (K), jump (K), leap (3rd) **C.** deer (K), stag (1st) **D.** youth (2nd)

bucket (3rd): barrel (4th), can (K), cask (4th), drum (1st), keg (1st), pail (2nd), pan (K), tub (1st)

buckeye (4th)

buckle (6th): A. bend (K), bow (1st), bulge (4th), flex (6th), fold (1st) **B.** clasp (4th), clip (2nd), fasten (4th), hook (4th)

buckskin (6th): hide (1st), leather (1st)

bud (1st): bloom (4th), flower (K), shoot (3rd)

buddy (4th): chum (6th), friend (1st), mate (4th), pal (K)

budge (4th): go (K), move (K), push (1st), shift (4th), stir (3rd)

budget (5th): cost (4th), expense (3rd), plan (1st), program (4th)

buffet (6th): A. cafeteria (5th), dinner (1st), restaurant (5th) **B.** beat (1st), blow (1st), hit (K), pound (2nd), rap (1st), slap (2nd), strike (2nd)

bug (K): A. insect (4th) **B.** annoy (5th), badger (2nd), bother (2nd), problem (1st)

buggy (6th): coach (4th), wagon (2nd)

bugle (6th): brass (2nd), horn (3rd)

build (1ˢᵗ): A. body (1ˢᵗ), figure (4ᵗʰ), form (1ˢᵗ), frame (3ʳᵈ), shape (1ˢᵗ) **B.** construct (3ʳᵈ), create (3ʳᵈ), develop (5ᵗʰ), erect (4ᵗʰ), establish (3ʳᵈ), found (K), increase (3ʳᵈ), make (K), start (1ˢᵗ)

building (1ˢᵗ): house (K), lodge (4ᵗʰ), structure (4ᵗʰ)

bulb (2ⁿᵈ): A. light (K) **B.** root (3ʳᵈ) **C.** swelling (3ʳᵈ)

bulge (4ᵗʰ): A. extend (4ᵗʰ), project (4ᵗʰ), rise (1ˢᵗ), stick out (K), swell (3ʳᵈ) **B.** bump (2ⁿᵈ), lump (4ᵗʰ), swelling (3ʳᵈ)

bulk (4ᵗʰ): A. greater part (K), most (1ˢᵗ) **B.** mass (3ʳᵈ), volume (3ʳᵈ), weight (1ˢᵗ)

bull (K): A. bunk (4ᵗʰ), nonsense (5ᵗʰ) **B.** steer (5ᵗʰ)

bulldog (1ˢᵗ)

bulldozer (1ˢᵗ)

bullet(s) (4ᵗʰ): lead (1ˢᵗ), rocket (K), shell (1ˢᵗ), shot (1ˢᵗ)

bulletin (3ʳᵈ): announcement (3ʳᵈ), journal (2ⁿᵈ), newsletter (1ˢᵗ), newspaper (3ʳᵈ), notice (1ˢᵗ), publication (4ᵗʰ), review (4ᵗʰ)

bullfrog (1ˢᵗ)

bull's-eye (1ˢᵗ): center (2ⁿᵈ), exactly (2ⁿᵈ), target (5ᵗʰ)

bully (1ˢᵗ): A. attack (3ʳᵈ), bulldoze (1ˢᵗ), menace (5ᵗʰ), pick on (1ˢᵗ), rule (K) **B.** brat (3ʳᵈ), tough guy (5ᵗʰ)

bumble (4ᵗʰ): fumble (5ᵗʰ), hesitate (4ᵗʰ), stumble (4ᵗʰ)

bumblebee (4ᵗʰ)

bump (2ⁿᵈ): A. lump (4ᵗʰ), bulge (4ᵗʰ), hump (3ʳᵈ), rise (1ˢᵗ) **B.** bang (3ʳᵈ), hit (K), jar (K), knock (3ʳᵈ), meet (K)

bun (2ⁿᵈ): biscuit (4ᵗʰ), roll (1ˢᵗ)

bunch (3ʳᵈ): A. collect (3ʳᵈ), gather (1ˢᵗ), tie up (1ˢᵗ) **B.** batch (2ⁿᵈ), bouquet (6ᵗʰ), bundle (5ᵗʰ), clump (3ʳᵈ), cluster (4ᵗʰ), collection (3ʳᵈ), group (1ˢᵗ), pack (1ˢᵗ), set (K)

bundle (5ᵗʰ): A. collect (3ʳᵈ), gather (1ˢᵗ) **B.** batch (2ⁿᵈ), box (K), bunch (3ʳᵈ), cluster (4ᵗʰ), pack (1ˢᵗ)

bung (6ᵗʰ): cork (6ᵗʰ)

bunk (4ᵗʰ): A. junk (3ʳᵈ), nonsense (5ᵗʰ), rot (1ˢᵗ), rubbish (5ᵗʰ) **B.** bed (K), cot (1ˢᵗ), couch (4ᵗʰ), sleep (K)

bunny (K): hare (5ᵗʰ), rabbit (K)

bunt (2ⁿᵈ): hit (K), push (1ˢᵗ), tap (K)

burden (5ᵗʰ): charge (2ⁿᵈ), cross (1ˢᵗ), duty (1ˢᵗ), load (2ⁿᵈ), responsibility (4ᵗʰ), tax (K), weight (1ˢᵗ)

bureau (4ᵗʰ): A. department (2ⁿᵈ), division (4ᵗʰ), section (4ᵗʰ) **B.** cabinet (4ᵗʰ), chest (2ⁿᵈ), dresser (2ⁿᵈ)

burglar (1ˢᵗ): criminal (4ᵗʰ), robber (K), thief (3ʳᵈ)

burlap (6ᵗʰ): homespun (5ᵗʰ), sacking (1ˢᵗ)

burn (3ʳᵈ): A. fire (K), flame (3ʳᵈ) **B.** long (1ˢᵗ), thirst (2ⁿᵈ) **C.** hurt (K), sore (4ᵗʰ)

burning (3ʳᵈ): afire (2ⁿᵈ), aflame (2ⁿᵈ), baking (1ˢᵗ), broiling (4ᵗʰ), on fire (K), roasting (4ᵗʰ)

burnoose (5ᵗʰ): hair net (3ʳᵈ), hat (K), scarf (6ᵗʰ)

burrow (5ᵗʰ): A. dig (1ˢᵗ), mine (1ˢᵗ), scoop (4ᵗʰ), shovel (1ˢᵗ) **B.** cave (1ˢᵗ), den (1ˢᵗ), hole (K), lair (5ᵗʰ), recess (2ⁿᵈ)

burst (3rd): blow (1st), break (1st), explode (3rd), shatter (5th), smash (3rd)

bury (3rd): conceal (4th), cover (1st), hide (1st)

bus (K): A. vehicle (6th), wagon (2nd) **B.** move (K), transport (5th)

bush (2nd): brier (6th), plant (K), shrub (4th)

business (2nd): company (2nd), employment (5th), job (K), occupation (6th), profession (5th), trade (2nd), work (K)

bust (6th): A. head (1st), sculpture (4th) **B.** break (1st), destroy (2nd), explode (3rd), shatter (5th)

bustle (6th): hurry (1st), motion (3rd), movement (2nd), rush (2nd)

busy (1st): active (3rd), intent (5th), involved (6th), occupied (3rd)

busybody (3rd): gossip (5th), informer (5th), nosy (1st), talker (K)

but (K): although (2nd), however (3rd), yet (1st)

butcher (4th): A. grocer (4th) **B.** cut up (K), destroy (2nd), kill (1st), massacre (6th), slaughter (5th), slay (4th)

butter (2nd): spread (2nd)

button (1st): clasp (4th), close (K), fasten (4th), hook (4th)

buttonhole (4th)

buy (K): acquire (4th), get (K), obtain (5th), pay for (K), purchase (3rd)

buyer (1st)

buzz (5th)

buzzard (4th)

by (K): along (1st), near (1st), over (K), through (1st), with (K)

C.E. (5th): Common Era

cab (K): carriage (5th), taxi (1st)

cabbage (4th)

cabin (1st): cottage (4th), house (K)

cabinet (4th): box (K), chest (2nd), closet (2nd)

cable (1st): cord (4th), line (K), rope (1st)

cafe (4th): restaurant (5th)

cafeteria (5th): buffet (6th), restaurant (5th)

cage (1st): A. enclose (4th), restrain (5th) **B.** box (K), jail (4th), pen (1st)

cake (K): A. bun (2nd), cookie (K), treat (2nd) **B.** compact (5th), harden (1st), thicken (2nd)

calamity (6th): accident (4th), agony (5th), disaster (6th), torture (5th), trouble (1st)

calcium (6th)

calculate (5th): add (K), compute (1st), count (5th), determine (5th), figure (1st), sum (1st)

calendar (1st): day book (K), log (K), record (2nd)

calf (K)

calico (6th): cloth (1st), cotton (2nd), print (1st)

call (K): A. ask (K), invite (3rd), shout (1st), summon (4th), telephone (2nd), yell (K) **B.** name (K), order (1st), pronounce (4th) **C.** stay (1st), visit (1st)

calm (3rd): peaceful (4th), quiet (K), serene (6th), still (1st), tranquil (6th)

calories (3rd)

Cambrian (5th): of or belonging to the geologic time, system of rocks, or sedimentary deposits of the first period of the Paleozoic Era

came (K)

camel (K)

camera (1st)

cameo (4th): A. carving (4th), pin (K) **B.** appearance (2nd), walk-on (K)

camouflage (5th): conceal (4th), cover (1st), disguise (5th), hide (1st), mask (2nd)

camp (1st): A. site (5th), tent (5th) **B.** settle (2nd), sleep (K), stop (K)

campaign (3rd): A. operation (3rd), plan (1st) **B.** canvas (6th), run (K)

campfire (1st)

campus (6th): grounds (1st), school (K), site (5th)

can (K): A. able (3rd), capable (4th) **B.** container (5th), jar (K), tin (1st)

canal (4th): channel (4th), path (1st), pipe (1st), tube (3rd), waterway (1st)

canary (1st)

cancel (6th): ban (K), call off (K), deny (5th), end (K), halt (4th), stop (K)

cancer (6th): growth (K), malignant (6th), tumor (6th)

candidate (4th): nominee (5th), politician (4th), runner (K), seeker (1st)

candle (2nd): flame (3rd), light (K)

candy (K): chocolate (4th), sweets (K)

cane (3rd): pole (1st), stick (K), support (4th)

canine (5th): dog (K), tooth (1st)

cannibal (4th): man-eater (K), monster (1st)

cannon (4th): gun (K), law (1st), order (1st), rule (2nd)

cannot (1st): can't (1st), not able (3rd), unable (2nd)

canoe (4th): boat (1st)

canopy (6th): cover (1st), drape (5th), shade (2nd), top (1st)

can't (1st): not able (3rd), unable (3rd)

canter (5th): jog (2nd), ride (K), trot (5th)

canvas (6th): base (1st), burlap (6th), sail (1st), tarpaulin (6th)

canyon (4th): divide (4th), gorge (5th), ravine (5th), split (4th), valley (2nd)

cap (K): A. bonnet (6th), hat (K) **B.** cover (1st), lid (1st), top (K)

capable (4th): able (3rd), adept (4th), can (K), clever (3rd), competent (6th), skilled (2nd)

capacity (6th): A. extent (4th), size (1st), volume (3rd) **B.** ability (3rd), gift (K), skill (2nd), talent (2nd)

cape (4th): A. cloak (4th), cover (1st), wrap (3rd) **B.** peninsula (6th), point (1st), tip (1st)

caper (4th): dance (1st), hop (K), joke (1st), play (K), plot (4th), prank (5th), skip (2nd), theft (3rd), trick (1st)

capital (2nd): A. investment (5th), money (K) **B.** center (2nd), chief (1st), funds (4th), leading (1st), main (3rd), primary (5th), support (4th), top (K)

capitalize (3rd): exploit (6th), realize (2nd), take advantage of (3rd), use (K)

captain (2ⁿᵈ): chief (1ˢᵗ), direct (1ˢᵗ), headmaster (1ˢᵗ), lead (1ˢᵗ), officer (1ˢᵗ)

caption (6ᵗʰ): explanation (2ⁿᵈ), heading (1ˢᵗ), legend (5ᵗʰ), tag (K), title (3ʳᵈ)

capture (3ʳᵈ): carry off (K), catch (1ˢᵗ), snare (6ᵗʰ), snatch (4ᵗʰ), take (K), trap (1ˢᵗ)

car (K): automobile (3ʳᵈ), cab (K), vehicle (6ᵗʰ)

caramel (5ᵗʰ): candy (K), sweet (K)

caravan (6ᵗʰ): group (1ˢᵗ), line (K), train (K)

carbon (4ᵗʰ)

Carboniferous (5ᵗʰ): of, belonging to, or denoting a geologic division of the Paleozoic Era following the Devonian and preceding the Permian

carcass (5ᵗʰ): body (K), frame (3ʳᵈ), shell (1ˢᵗ)

card (1ˢᵗ): identification (4ᵗʰ), postcard (1ˢᵗ)

cardboard (2ⁿᵈ)

cardinal (3ʳᵈ): A. red (K) **B.** churchman (K) **C.** chief (1ˢᵗ), highest (K), main (3ʳᵈ), prime (5ᵗʰ) **D.** ball player (1ˢᵗ)

care (K): attention (2ⁿᵈ), charge (2ⁿᵈ), concern (3ʳᵈ), love (K), protection (4ᵗʰ), worry (1ˢᵗ)

career (4ᵗʰ): employment (5ᵗʰ), job (K), living (1ˢᵗ), occupation (6ᵗʰ), trade (1ˢᵗ), work (K)

carefree (3ʳᵈ): cheerful (3ʳᵈ), gay (1ˢᵗ), happy (K), worry free (1ˢᵗ)

careful (1ˢᵗ): accurate (6ᵗʰ), alert (5ᵗʰ), detailed (5ᵗʰ), exacting (2ⁿᵈ), strict (6ᵗʰ), thorough (4ᵗʰ)

careless (5ᵗʰ): casual (5ᵗʰ), messy (1ˢᵗ), rude (2ⁿᵈ), thoughtless (1ˢᵗ)

caretaker (4ᵗʰ): housekeeper (3ʳᵈ), keeper (1ˢᵗ), manager (4ᵗʰ)

cargo (5ᵗʰ): carload (4ᵗʰ), contents (3ʳᵈ), freight (4ᵗʰ), load (2ⁿᵈ)

carload (4ᵗʰ): cargo (5ᵗʰ), contents (3ʳᵈ), load (2ⁿᵈ)

carnation (4ᵗʰ)

carnival (2ⁿᵈ): ball (K), celebration (5ᵗʰ), circus (1ˢᵗ), fair (1ˢᵗ), festival (5ᵗʰ), party (K)

carnivore (5ᵗʰ)

carol (3ʳᵈ): A. poem (3ʳᵈ), song (K), tune (1ˢᵗ) **B.** sing (1ˢᵗ)

carp (5ᵗʰ): A. blame (2ⁿᵈ), complain (4ᵗʰ), criticize (5ᵗʰ), gripe (5ᵗʰ) **B.** goldfish (K)

carpenter (4ᵗʰ): builder (1ˢᵗ), contractor (3ʳᵈ)

carpet (4ᵗʰ): cover (1ˢᵗ), flooring (2ⁿᵈ), rug (1ˢᵗ)

carriage (5ᵗʰ): body (1ˢᵗ), buggy (6ᵗʰ), car (K), coach (4ᵗʰ), frame (3ʳᵈ), wagon (2ⁿᵈ)

carrot (2ⁿᵈ)

carry (K): bear (K), cart (K), deliver (5ᵗʰ), give (K), lift (1ˢᵗ), move (K), push (1ˢᵗ), support (4ᵗʰ), tote (5ᵗʰ), transport (5ᵗʰ)

cart (1ˢᵗ): A. truck (1ˢᵗ), wagon (2ⁿᵈ) **B.** carry (1ˢᵗ), lift (1ˢᵗ), move (K), tote (5ᵗʰ)

carton (4ᵗʰ): box (K), case (2ⁿᵈ), container (5ᵗʰ), package (4ᵗʰ)

cartoon (2nd): A. animation (6th), movie (1st) **B.** drawing (1st), picture (K), sketch (5th)

cartridge (6th): bullet (4th), case (2nd), holder (1st), insert (6th), shell (1st)

carve (4th): chip (5th), cut (K), engrave (5th), fashion (3rd), sculpture (4th), shape (1st)

case (2nd): A. action (1st), event (3rd), example (2nd), illustration (4th), lawsuit (5th), statement (1st), suit 1 **B.** box (K), carrier (2nd), carton (4th), cover (1st), protector (4th)

cash (2nd): change (2nd), coins (3rd), money (K)

cask (4th): barrel (4th), case (2nd), keg (1st)

casserole (4th): A. dish (1st) **B.** food (K), mixture (4th)

cast (2nd): A. pitch (2nd), throw (1st), toss (2nd) **B.** arrange (3rd), mold (5th), shape (1st) **C.** discard (6th), junk (3rd), scrap (3rd) **D.** assembly (4th), company (2nd), group (1st)

castle (3rd): mansion (5th), palace (1st)

casual (5th): A. accidental (4th), chance (2nd) **B.** cool (1st), relaxed (4th)

cat (K)

cat scan (5th): computed axial tomography: the use of computer processing to transform a series of x-rays into a three-dimensional image

catalog (5th): A. book (K), bulletin (3rd) **B.** count (K), list (2nd), number (K), sort (1st)

catalogue (5th): same as catalog

catbird (1st)

catch (1st): A. come down with (1st), get (K), obtain (5th) **B.** grasp (4th), understand (1st) **C.** capture (3rd), gain (2nd), grab (4th), snare (6th), trap (1st) caterpillar (1st)

cathedral (5th): church (K), temple (3rd)

catholic (4th): universal (4th), worldwide (1st)

catnip (3rd)

cattle (3rd): animals (K), beef (2nd), cows (K), herd (2nd)

cauldron (6th): kettle (4th), pot (K)

cauliflower (4th)

cause (2nd): A. beginning (1st), reason (2nd), start (1st) **B.** author (3rd), compel (3rd), create (3rd), make (K), produce (2nd)

caution (5th): A. alertness (5th), care (1st), concern (3rd), thought (1st) **B.** advise (3rd), alert (5th), tell (K), warn (3rd)

cautious (5th): alert (5th), careful (1st), wary (5th)

cavalry (6th): army (1st), horse troop (3rd), riders (K), soldiers (3rd)

cave (1st): A. give in (K) **B.** cavity (5th), chamber (5th), hole (K), hollow (3rd)

cavity (5th): cave (1st), hole (K), hollow (3rd)

Cayuse (6th): a Native American Nation

cayuse (6th): horse (K)

cease (3rd): close (K), end (K), finish (1st), quit (1st), stop (K)

cedar (2ⁿᵈ)

ceiling (4ᵗʰ): cover (1ˢᵗ), lid (1ˢᵗ), roof (1ˢᵗ)

celebrate (4ᵗʰ): A. honor (1ˢᵗ), keep (K), observe (3ʳᵈ) **B.** party (K), play (K)

celebration (5ᵗʰ): holiday (K), party (K), ritual (6ᵗʰ)

celebrity (5ᵗʰ): fame (3ʳᵈ), glory (3ʳᵈ), honor (2ⁿᵈ)

celery (4ᵗʰ)

celestial (5ᵗʰ): A. sky (1ˢᵗ), stars (5ᵗʰ) **B.** heavenly (1ˢᵗ), holy (5ᵗʰ)

cell (1ˢᵗ): booth (5ᵗʰ), chamber (5ᵗʰ), closet (2ⁿᵈ), cocoon (2ⁿᵈ), compartment (6ᵗʰ), room (K), stall (5ᵗʰ)

cell phone (2ⁿᵈ)

cellar (1ˢᵗ): basement, (3ʳᵈ), below stairs (2ⁿᵈ)

cellophane (5ᵗʰ)

cement (4ᵗʰ): A. concrete (4ᵗʰ), plaster (4ᵗʰ) **B.** adhere (6ᵗʰ), bond (3ʳᵈ), glue (1ˢᵗ), join (3ʳᵈ), paste (1ˢᵗ)

cemetery (6ᵗʰ): field (2ⁿᵈ), plot (4ᵗʰ)

Cenozoic (5ᵗʰ)

census (6ᵗʰ): count (1ˢᵗ), figures (1ˢᵗ), study (2ⁿᵈ)

cent (1ˢᵗ): coin (3ʳᵈ), penny (1ˢᵗ)

center (2ⁿᵈ): core (6ᵗʰ), focus (5ᵗʰ), middle (2ⁿᵈ)

centigrade (2ⁿᵈ)

centimeter (2ⁿᵈ)

central (3ʳᵈ): A. main (3ʳᵈ), principal (3ʳᵈ) **B.** core (6ᵗʰ), focus (5ᵗʰ), middle (2ⁿᵈ)

century (2ⁿᵈ): A. one hundred years (1ˢᵗ) **B.** age (1ˢᵗ), period (2ⁿᵈ)

cereal (6ᵗʰ): breakfast (1ˢᵗ), grain (3ʳᵈ), meal (3ʳᵈ)

ceremony (5ᵗʰ): observance (3ʳᵈ), rite (6ᵗʰ), ritual (6ᵗʰ), service (1ˢᵗ)

certain (1ˢᵗ): A. particular (4ᵗʰ), single (3ʳᵈ), special (2ⁿᵈ) **B.** confident (6ᵗʰ), positive (2ⁿᵈ), sure (K)

certainly (1ˢᵗ): surely (1ˢᵗ), positively (2ⁿᵈ)

certificate (6ᵗʰ): award (5ᵗʰ), bill (1ˢᵗ), note (1ˢᵗ), paper (6ᵗʰ)

certify (6ᵗʰ): authorize (3ʳᵈ), support (4ᵗʰ), uphold (6ᵗʰ)

chagrin (5ᵗʰ): A. embarrassment (5ᵗʰ), irritation (6ᵗʰ) **B.** annoy (5ᵗʰ), embarrass (5ᵗʰ), shame (3ʳᵈ), vex (5ᵗʰ)

chain (3ʳᵈ): A. bond (3ʳᵈ), control (2ⁿᵈ), fasten (4ᵗʰ), links (5ᵗʰ), restraint (5ᵗʰ), tie (1ˢᵗ) **B.** course (3ʳᵈ), series (4ᵗʰ), train (K)

chair (K): A. bench (4ᵗʰ), seat (1ˢᵗ), stool (2ⁿᵈ) **B.** govern (1ˢᵗ), lead (1ˢᵗ)

chalk (5ᵗʰ): crayon (K), marker (1ˢᵗ), pencil (1ˢᵗ)

challenge (4ᵗʰ): A. problem (1ˢᵗ), puzzle (4ᵗʰ) **B.** disagree (2ⁿᵈ), dispute (6ᵗʰ), question (1ˢᵗ) **C.** call (K), dare (2ⁿᵈ)

chamber (5ᵗʰ): apartment (1ˢᵗ), cell (1ˢᵗ), room (1ˢᵗ)

champion (4ᵗʰ): back (K), conqueror (4ᵗʰ), defend (5ᵗʰ), hero (1ˢᵗ), leader (1ˢᵗ), victor (4ᵗʰ), winner (1ˢᵗ)

chance (2ⁿᵈ): A. accident (4ᵗʰ), fortune (3ʳᵈ), luck (1ˢᵗ) **B.** dare (2ⁿᵈ), risk

(4th), try (K) **C.** opportunity (3rd), turn (1st)

chancellor (6th): head (K), leader (1st)

chandelier (5th): lamp (1st), light (K)

change (2nd): A. adjustment (5th), growth (1st) **B.** coins (3rd), money (K) **C.** adapt (4th), adjust (5th), alter (4th), amend (4th), differ (4th), fix (1st), modify (5th)

channel (4th): bed (K), canal (4th), course (3rd), passage (3rd), path (1st), road (K), tube (3rd), way (K)

chant (5th): A. carol (3rd), intone (3rd), say (K), sing (1st) **B.** hymn (5th), song (K), tune (1st)

chap (4th): lad (K), mate (4th), man (K)

chapel (4th): church (K), house of worship (4th), temple (3rd)

chapter (3rd): division (4th), part (1st), portion (4th), section (4th)

character (2nd): A. essence (6th), personality (5th), quality (4th) **B.** code (3rd), figure (1st), label (3rd), mark (1st), symbol (5th) **C.** being (1st), individual (3rd), person (1st), role (1st), someone (1st)

characteristic (6th): aspect (5th), bent (K), feature (3rd), leaning (3rd), quality (4th), style (3rd), symptom (6th), tone (3rd), trait (6th)

charcoal (6th): A. burned wood (3rd) **B.** gray (1st)

charge (2nd): A. care (K), control (2nd), protection (4th), rule (K), supervision (6th) **B.** attack (3rd), direct (1st), run (K), rush (2nd), storm (2nd) **C.** accuse (4th), blame (2nd) **D.** ask (K), ask

a price (K), command (2nd), cost (K), credit (5th), expect (2nd), impose (4th), price (K)

chariot (6th): carriage (5th), coach (4th)

charity (4th): benefit (3rd), courtesy (4th), favor (1st), gift (1st), kindness (K), love (K), service (1st)

charm (3rd): A. appeal (3rd), attractiveness (5th), beauty (1st), grace (3rd) **B.** bewitch (1st), delight (3rd), enchant (6th)

chart (1st): guide (1st), map (1st), outline (4th), plot (4th)

chase (1st): follow (1st), hunt (2nd), pursue (5th), run after (K), track (1st), trail (2nd)

chat (1st): babble (6th), converse (5th), gossip (5th), talk (K)

chatter (1st): babble (6th), chat (1st), gab (1st), gossip (5th), talk (K)

chauffeur (6th): driver (1st)

cheap (3rd): A. bargain (4th), inexpensive (3rd), low (K) **B.** junky (3rd), poor (K), shabby (4th), tacky (1st)

cheat (3rd): deceive (5th), exploit (6th), fake (1st), fraud (6th), hoax (5th), steal (3rd), trick (1st)

check (1st): A. look into (1st), notice (1st), study (1st), test (3rd) **B.** arrest (3rd), control (2nd), curb (3rd), interrupt (3rd), stay (1st), stop (K)

checkers (2nd)

cheek (2nd): A. face (K) **B.** gall (4th), nerve (1st)

cheer (3rd): A. enthusiasm (4th), fun (K), gaiety (1st), good spirits (2nd) **B.**

chant (5th), clap (2nd), cry (K), encourage (4th), shout (1st), yell (K)

cheese (3rd)

chef (4th): cook (1st)

chemical (4th)

cherish (5th): adore (4th), love (K), prize (3rd), treasure (4th), worship (4th)

cherry (2nd)

chess (4th)

chest (2nd): A. breast (3rd), front (1st) **B.** bureau (4th), cabinet (4th), carton (4th), crate (5th)

chestnut (4th)

chew (1st): A. bite (1st), eat (K), gnaw (1st), nibble (4th) **B.** study (2nd), think (1st)

chick (K)

chickadee (5th)

chicken (K): chick (2nd), fowl (4th), hen (K)

chief (1st): A. first (1st), head (K), important (1st), main (3rd), necessary (1st), primary (5th), principal (3rd), supreme (5th), vital (5th) **B.** boss (K), key (K), leader (1st)

child (K): adolescent (5th), kid (K), minor (5th), youth (2nd)

childhood (4th): adolescence (5th), growing up (K), youth (2nd)

children (K)

chili (4th): stew (2nd)

chill (3rd): arctic (3rd), brisk (6th), cold (K), cool (1st), freezing (4th), frigid (6th), icy (1st)

chime (6th): alarm (3rd), bell (K), clang (4th), ring (1st)

chin (1st)

chip (5th):A. bit (1st), piece (1st) **B.** break (1st), carve (4th), chop (2nd)

chipmunk (2nd)

chirp (2nd): chime (6th), peep (4th), tweet (4th)

chivalry (6th): bravery (1st), courage (4th), daring (2nd), fairness (1st), gallantry (4th), goodness (K), manners (2nd)

chocolate (4th)

choice (3rd): A. decision (2nd), desire (5th), opinion (3rd), preference (3rd), selection (4th), will (K) **B.** elegant (5th), favorite (3rd), fine (1st), good (K), rare (4th) **C.** solution (5th), vote (2nd), way out (K)

choir (5th): chorus (5th), singers (1st)

choke (1st): clog (5th), close (K), cover (1st), gag (1st), smother (6th), strangle (6th)

choose (3rd): appoint (3rd), elect (3rd), favor (2nd), nominate (5th), pick (1st), prefer (3rd), select (4th), sort (1st), take (K)

chop (2nd): ax (K), chip (5th), cut (K), divide (4th), hew (6th), mince (6th), slice (5th)

chord (5th)

chorus (5th): choir (5th), singers (1st)

chow (5th): eat (K), food (K)

chowder (5th): broth (4th), soup (1st)

Christ (4th)

Christian (4th)

Christmas (K)

chrome (2ⁿᵈ): metal (3ʳᵈ), plate (K), silver (1ˢᵗ)

chronicle (6ᵗʰ): account (3ʳᵈ), article (2ⁿᵈ), diary (3ʳᵈ), history (2ⁿᵈ), journal (2ⁿᵈ), log (K), record (2ⁿᵈ), report (1ˢᵗ), story (K)

chubby (2ⁿᵈ): fat (1ˢᵗ), plump (6ᵗʰ), portly (5ᵗʰ)

chum (6ᵗʰ): buddy (4ᵗʰ), companion (3ʳᵈ), friend (1ˢᵗ), mate (4ᵗʰ), pal (K), partner (5ᵗʰ)

church (K): chapel (4ᵗʰ), place of worship (4ᵗʰ), temple (3ʳᵈ)

churn (3ʳᵈ): beat (1ˢᵗ), blend (5ᵗʰ), mix up (1ˢᵗ), stir (3ʳᵈ), turn (1ˢᵗ), whip (4ᵗʰ)

chute (5ᵗʰ): channel (4ᵗʰ), course (3ʳᵈ), passage (4ᵗʰ), path (1ˢᵗ), slide (2ⁿᵈ)

cider (2ⁿᵈ): apple juice (K)

cigar (4ᵗʰ)

cigarette (4ᵗʰ)

cinch (6ᵗʰ): A. belt (2ⁿᵈ), grasp (4ᵗʰ), hold (1ˢᵗ), tighten (2ⁿᵈ) **B.** certain (1ˢᵗ), easy (1ˢᵗ), sure (K)

cinnamon (2ⁿᵈ)

circle (K): A. ball (K), disk (2ⁿᵈ), sphere (6ᵗʰ), wheel (1ˢᵗ) **B.** associates (5ᵗʰ), friends (1ˢᵗ) **C.** encompass (4ᵗʰ), group (1ˢᵗ), spin (1ˢᵗ), surround (3ʳᵈ), turn (1ˢᵗ)

circuit (4ᵗʰ): connection (3ʳᵈ), journey (3ʳᵈ), path (1ˢᵗ), round (K), route (4ᵗʰ), surround (3ʳᵈ), tour (3ʳᵈ), way (K)

circular (4ᵗʰ): A. circle (K), curved (3ʳᵈ), global (4ᵗʰ), indirect (2ⁿᵈ), round (K), spherical (6ᵗʰ) **B.** advertisement (4ᵗʰ), booklet (2ⁿᵈ), bulletin (3ʳᵈ), pamphlet (6ᵗʰ), sheet (1ˢᵗ)

circumstance (6ᵗʰ): A. event (3ʳᵈ), happening (1ˢᵗ), incident (5ᵗʰ), occurrence (3ʳᵈ) **B.** detail (5ᵗʰ), fact (1ˢᵗ), factor (5ᵗʰ), feature (3ʳᵈ), item (5ᵗʰ), point (1ˢᵗ), surroundings (3ʳᵈ)

circus (1ˢᵗ): carnival (2ⁿᵈ), fair (1ˢᵗ), show (1ˢᵗ)

cite (6ᵗʰ): call (K), invite (3ʳᵈ), name (K), number (K), quote (5ᵗʰ), recount (6ᵗʰ), repeat (4ᵗʰ), summon (4ᵗʰ), tell (K)

citizen (3ʳᵈ): national (2ⁿᵈ), native (1ˢᵗ), resident (5ᵗʰ), subject (3ʳᵈ)

city (K): area (3ʳᵈ), metropolis (6ᵗʰ), town (K)

civil (3ʳᵈ): gentle (3ʳᵈ), mannerly (2ⁿᵈ), polite (4ᵗʰ), thoughtful (2ⁿᵈ)

civilization (4ᵗʰ): community (2ⁿᵈ), culture (6ᵗʰ), society (3ʳᵈ)

claim (2ⁿᵈ): A. allegation (6ᵗʰ), assertion (6ᵗʰ) **B.** deed (1ˢᵗ), title (3ʳᵈ) **C.** allege (6ᵗʰ), assert (6ᵗʰ), declare (5ᵗʰ), demand (5ᵗʰ), maintain (4ᵗʰ), state (1ˢᵗ)

clam (1ˢᵗ)

clambake (5ᵗʰ): A. steam (2ⁿᵈ) **B.** gathering (1ˢᵗ), meeting (K), party (K)

clamor (6ᵗʰ): bellow (4ᵗʰ), noise (1ˢᵗ), racket (2ⁿᵈ), roar (1ˢᵗ), uproar (5ᵗʰ)

clamp (5ᵗʰ): clasp (4ᵗʰ), grasp (4ᵗʰ), hold (1ˢᵗ), lock (1ˢᵗ), vise (4ᵗʰ)

clan (5ᵗʰ): family (K), group (1ˢᵗ), house (K), tribe (3ʳᵈ)

clang (4ᵗʰ): bang (3ʳᵈ), chime (6ᵗʰ), clank (4ᵗʰ), ring (1ˢᵗ)

clank (4ᵗʰ): See clang.

clap (2ⁿᵈ): A. cheer (3ʳᵈ) **B.** blow (1ˢᵗ), hit (K), knock (3ʳᵈ), slap (2ⁿᵈ)

clash (5ᵗʰ): A. bang (3ʳᵈ), clang (4ᵗʰ), noise (1ˢᵗ) **B.** battle (2ⁿᵈ), collision (6ᵗʰ), conflict (4ᵗʰ), fight (K), war (1ˢᵗ)

clasp (4ᵗʰ): catch (1ˢᵗ), fasten (4ᵗʰ), grab (4ᵗʰ), hold (1ˢᵗ), hook (4ᵗʰ)

class (1ˢᵗ): A. course (3ʳᵈ), study (1ˢᵗ), lesson (3ʳᵈ) **B.** division (4ᵗʰ), grade (2ⁿᵈ), group (1ˢᵗ), level (3ʳᵈ), rank (3ʳᵈ), realm (4ᵗʰ), society (3ʳᵈ), type (1ˢᵗ)

classic (5ᵗʰ): remarkable (4ᵗʰ), superior (4ᵗʰ), top (K)

classroom (1ˢᵗ)

clatter (5ᵗʰ): bang (3ʳᵈ), clamor (6ᵗʰ), crash (2ⁿᵈ), din (6ᵗʰ), noise (1ˢᵗ), racket (2ⁿᵈ), rattle (2ⁿᵈ)

clause (6ᵗʰ): A. condition (3ʳᵈ), provision (4ᵗʰ), requirement (2ⁿᵈ), terms (3ʳᵈ) **B.** article (2ⁿᵈ), paragraph (6ᵗʰ), sentence (1ˢᵗ), verse (4ᵗʰ)

claw (1ˢᵗ): A. hoof (1ˢᵗ), paw (1ˢᵗ), talon (6ᵗʰ) **B.** divide (4ᵗʰ), hook (1ˢᵗ), scratch (4ᵗʰ), spur (4ᵗʰ), tear (2ⁿᵈ)

clay (1ˢᵗ): earth (1ˢᵗ), ground (1ˢᵗ), mud (1ˢᵗ), soil (2ⁿᵈ)

clean (K):A. neat (K), nice (1ˢᵗ), pure (3ʳᵈ), spotless (1ˢᵗ) **B.** cleanse (2ⁿᵈ), dress (K), launder (6ᵗʰ), polish (4ᵗʰ), wash (1ˢᵗ)

clear (2ⁿᵈ): A. apparent (3ʳᵈ), distinct (5ᵗʰ), plain (2ⁿᵈ), readable (3ʳᵈ) **B.** cut (K), make vacant (6ᵗʰ), remove (2ⁿᵈ), rid (1ˢᵗ) **C.** clean (K), fair (1ˢᵗ), light (K), shiny (3ʳᵈ), sunny (1ˢᵗ) **D.** bare (3ʳᵈ), barren (4ᵗʰ), open (K), transparent (5ᵗʰ), void (6ᵗʰ)

cleat (5ᵗʰ)

clergy (6ᵗʰ): pastor (4ᵗʰ), priest (4ᵗʰ), reverend (4ᵗʰ)

clerk (2ⁿᵈ): accountant (3ʳᵈ), assistant (4ᵗʰ), cashier (3ʳᵈ), official (3ʳᵈ), secretary (4ᵗʰ)

clever (3ʳᵈ): brilliant (4ᵗʰ), gifted (1ˢᵗ), handy (1ˢᵗ), intelligent (4ᵗʰ), knowing (1ˢᵗ), resourceful (5ᵗʰ), skilled (2ⁿᵈ), sly (4ᵗʰ), smart (1ˢᵗ), talented (2ⁿᵈ), witty (1ˢᵗ)

click (2ⁿᵈ): beat (1ˢᵗ), clack (2ⁿᵈ), snap (2ⁿᵈ), tap (K), tick (1ˢᵗ)

client (6ᵗʰ): buyer (1ˢᵗ), customer (5ᵗʰ), follower (1ˢᵗ), patron (5ᵗʰ), shopper (1ˢᵗ), user (1ˢᵗ)

cliff (2ⁿᵈ): bank (1ˢᵗ), bluff (6ᵗʰ), edge (1ˢᵗ), ridge (5ᵗʰ), slope (3ʳᵈ)

climate (4ᵗʰ): A. atmosphere (4ᵗʰ), feel (K), mood (3ʳᵈ), spirit (2ⁿᵈ) **B.** condition (3ʳᵈ), environment (6ᵗʰ), temperature (4ᵗʰ), weather (1ˢᵗ)

climate-controlled (4ᵗʰ): having temperature and humidity regulated by a heating and cooling system

climb (1ˢᵗ): advance (2ⁿᵈ), ascend (4ᵗʰ), go up (K), mount (2ⁿᵈ), rise (1ˢᵗ), scale (3ʳᵈ), soar (6ᵗʰ)

cling (4ᵗʰ): adhere (6ᵗʰ), bond (3ʳᵈ), hold (1ˢᵗ), hug (1ˢᵗ), stick (K)

clinic (1ˢᵗ): hospital (3ʳᵈ), ward (5ᵗʰ)

clip (2ⁿᵈ): A. cut (K), shave (1ˢᵗ), shorten (1ˢᵗ), snip (4ᵗʰ), trim (4ᵗʰ) **B.** clasp (4ᵗʰ), fastener (4ᵗʰ), hook (4ᵗʰ), latch (4ᵗʰ) **C.** part (1ˢᵗ), piece (1ˢᵗ), sample (5ᵗʰ), scrap (3ʳᵈ) **D.** attach (5ᵗʰ), catch (1ˢᵗ), connect (1ˢᵗ), fasten (4ᵗʰ), pin (K)

cloak (4th): **A.** cape (4th), coat (1st), wrap (3rd) **B.** cover (1st), hide (1st), mask (2nd), secret (1st)

clock (1st): measure (2nd), timer (1st), watch (1st)

clog (5th): block (1st), clot (5th), congest (4th), dam (K), hinder (6th), jam (K), obstruct (5th), stop up (K)

clone (4th): any organism whose genetic information is identical to that of a "mother organism" from which it was created, or an exact replica of all or part of another thing

close (K): **A.** bolt (4th), fasten (4th), seal (K), secure (3rd), shut (1st) **B.** bind (2nd), connect (3rd), join (3rd), tie (1st) **C.** like (K), similar (4th) **D.** bordering (1st), friendly (1st), intimate (5th), near (1st), neighboring (2nd), small (1st), stuffy (1st), tight (1st)

closet (2nd): box (K), cabinet (4th), cell (1st), cupboard (2nd), hide (1st), locker (3rd), room (K)

clot (5th): clog (5th), gel (5th), lump (4th), mass (3rd), thicken (2nd)

clothes (1st): array (5th), attire (6th), dress (K), garments (4th)

cloud (1st): **A.** fog (1st), mist (1st), vapor (3rd) **B.** bewilder (3rd), confuse (4th), cover (1st), darken (1st), depress (5th), dim (1st)

clown (1st): **A.** fool (2nd), joker (1st) **B.** entertain (4th), perform (4th), play (K), show off (1st)

club (1st): **A.** bat (K), baton (5th), stick (K) **B.** association (5th), group (1st), organization (4th), society (3rd)

clue (2nd): **A.** feeling (K), idea (1st) **B.** hint (1st), sign (1st), suggestion (2nd)

clump (3rd): batch (2nd), bunch (3rd), bundle (5th), cluster (4th), join (3rd), knot (4th), pack (1st), unite (5th)

clumsy (6th): awkward (6th), halting (4th), rough (4th), slow (1st)

cluster (4th): **A.** batch (2nd), bunch (3rd), bundle (5th), clump (3rd), collection (3rd), knot (4th), pack (1st) **B.** collect (3rd), gather (1st), group (1st), unite (5th)

clutch (4th): **A.** clasp (4th), grab (4th), hold (1st), possess (3rd), seize (3rd), snatch (4th) **B.** brood (4th), nest (1st)

clutter (4th): disorder (2nd), mess (1st), trash (2nd)

coach (4th): **A.** direct (1st), educate (3rd), guide (1st), instruct (4th), support (4th), teach (1st), train (K) **B.** buggy (6th), car (K), carriage (5th), vehicle (6th)

coal (2nd): a natural dark brown to black material used as a fuel

coarse (4th): bumpy (2nd), crude (5th), gross (3rd), rough (4th), rugged (5th), sandy (1st)

coast (2nd): **A.** beach (K), shore (1st), shoreline (1st) **B.** drift (2nd), float (1st), glide (4th), sail (1st), slide (2nd)

coat (1st): **A.** cloak (4th), cover (1st), jacket (3rd), wrap (3rd) **B.** fur (K), hide (1st), wool (3rd) **C.** cover (1st), paint (2nd)

coax (6th): beg (1st), charm (3rd), encourage (4th), urge (4th)

cob (1st)

cobra (1st)

cobweb (3rd)

cocaine (6th)

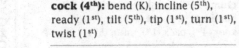

cock (4th): bend (K), incline (5th), ready (1st), tilt (5th), tip (1st), turn (1st), twist (1st)

cockpit (2nd)

cocoa (1st): chocolate (4th), beverage (6th)

cocoon (2nd): cell (1st), chamber (5th)

code (3rd): A. creed (6th), ethics (5th), law (1st), philosophy (5th) **B.** hide (1st), mark (1st), symbolize (5th)

coffee (2nd)

coffin (6th): box (K)

cog (6th): wheel (1st)

coil (5th): circle (K), curl (2nd), roll (1st), rotate (4th), spring (K), wind (1st), wrap (3rd)

coin (3rd): A. cash (2nd), money (K) **B.** create (3rd), invent (2nd), make (K), mint (5th)

coke (1st)

cold (K): A. arctic (3rd), chilly (3rd), cool (1st), freezing (4th), frigid (6th), frosty (4th), icy (1st) **B.** abrupt (5th), hostile (4th), unfriendly (1st)

coliseum (5th): field (2nd), sports stadium (4th),

collapse (5th): break (1st), cave in (1st), downfall (2nd), explode (3rd), fail (2nd), faint (3rd), fall (K), fold (1st), ruin (5th)

collar (4th): A. neckpiece (1st) **B.** arrest (3rd), corner (2nd), grab (4th), grasp (4th), seize (3rd)

collect (3rd): accumulate (6th), assemble (4th), bunch (3rd), gather (1st), harvest (4th), pack (1st), save (1st), take in (K)

college (4th): institute (5th), school (K), university (4th)

collie (2nd)

collision (6th): bump (2nd), clash (5th), crash (2nd), hit (K), impact (6th), meeting (K), wreck (4th)

cologne (5th): perfume (3rd), scent (3rd)

colonel (3rd)

colonial (4th)

colony (3rd): community (2nd), settlement (2nd), society (3rd)

color (K): A. hue (6th), shade (2nd), tint (5th), tone (3rd) **B.** badge (5th), banner (3rd), flag (3rd)

colorful (2nd): entertaining (4th), intense (6th), interesting (3rd), lively (1st), vivid (6th)

colt (K)

column (4th): A. pillar (5th), pole (1st), post (1st), support (4th) **B.** editorial (3rd), news story (1st) **C.** line (K), list (2nd), row (K)

coma (6th)

comb (2nd): A. arrange (3rd), brush (2nd), fix (1st), straighten (3rd) **B.** inspect (5th), rake (1st), search (1st), separate (3rd)

combat (5th): assault (4th), attack (3rd), battle (2nd), beat (1st), contest (4th), encounter (4th), fight (K), meet (K), oppose (3rd), war (1st)

combine (3rd): A. blend (5th), fuse (4th), mix (1st) **B.** accompany (3rd), band (1st), compound (4th), group (1st), join (3rd), pool (1st), unite (5th)

combustion (6th): burning (3rd), explosion (3rd), flame (3rd), ignite (6th)

146

come (K): A. appear (2nd), approach (3rd), arrive (2nd), near (1st) **B.** happen (1st), evolve (6th), occur (3rd)

comedian (5th): clown (1st), comic (5th), joker (1st)

comedy (5th): funny (1st), humor (4th), jest (4th), joke (1st), wit (1st)

comet (5th)

comfort (3rd): A. calm (3rd), ease (3rd), peace (1st) **B.** cheer (3rd), console (5th), snuggle (5th), strengthen (2nd)

comfortable (3rd): easy (K), happy (K), peaceful (1st), secure (3rd), snug (6th), warm (1st)

comic (5th): absurd (6th), amusing (4th), funny (1st), humorous (4th), laughable (2nd), silly (1st)

coming (K)

comma (2nd)

command (2nd): A. commission (2nd), demand (5th), direct (1st), force (1st), order (1st) **B.** control (2nd), govern (1st), manage (4th), regulate (5th), rule (2nd) **C.** ability (3rd), skill (2nd)

commence (6th): begin (K), commit (4th), lead (1st), organize (4th), origin (4th), start (1st)

commend (6th): approve (4th), celebrate (4th), compliment (5th), praise (4th), recognize (3rd), recommend (5th)

comment (5th): explain (2nd), observe (3rd), note (1st), remark (1st), statement (1st)

commentator (5th)

commercial (5th): A. ad (4th), advertisement (4th), bulletin (3rd) **B.** merchant (3rd), of business (2nd), of trade (4th), public (1st)

commissar (5th)

commission (2nd): A. appoint (3rd), authorize (3rd), charge (2nd), command (2nd), license (5th), name (K), order (1st) **B.** allowance (5th), cut (K), part (1st), percentage (4th), piece (1st), share (2nd) **C.** board (1st)

commit (4th): A. do (K), perform (4th), practice (1st) **B.** assure (3rd), dedicate (6th), entrust (3rd), pledge (5th), promise (1st), swear (4th)

committee (5th): association (5th), board (1st), commission (2nd), council (5th)

commodity (5th): article (2nd), item (5th), merchandise (6th), thing (K)

common (2nd): A. average (3rd), everyday (2nd), general (2nd), normal (5th) **B.** both (K), joint (4th), shared (2nd)

commonwealth (5th)

commotion (5th): confusion (4th), disorder (3rd), disturbance (6th), turmoil (5th), uproar (5th), upset (3rd)

communicate (4th): contact (4th), converse (5th), inform (5th), make known (1st), mention (5th), say (K), speak (1st), talk (K), tell (K), utter (4th)

communism (5th)

community (2nd): colony (3rd), group (1st), neighborhood (2nd), public (1st), settlement (2nd), society (3rd), town (K), village (2nd)

commute (4th): A. drive (K), travel (1st), trip (1st) **B.** alter (4th), change (2nd), exchange (4th), modify (5th), transform (5th)

compact (5th): close (K), condensed (6th), crowded (2nd), firm (2nd), hard (1st), small (1st), tight (1st)

companion (3rd): associate (5th), buddy (4th), chum (6th), escort (5th), friend (1st), mate (4th), pal (K), partner (5th)

company (2nd): A. association (5th), companionship (3rd) **B.** business (2nd), corporation (4th), group (1st) **C.** guest (3rd), party (K), visitor (1st)

comparable (3rd): alike (1st), near (1st), resembling (4th), similar (4th)

compare (3rd): associate (5th), contrast (4th), equate (3rd), explain (2nd), liken (1st), match (3rd), parallel (5th), relate (4th), sort (2nd)

compartment (6th): box (K), cabinet (4th), cell (1st), department (2nd), locker (3rd), nook (6th), place (1st), space (1st), stall (5th)

compass (4th): A. achieve (5th), acquire (4th), gain (2nd), obtain (5th) **B.** circle (K), hem (1st), ring (1st), surround (3rd)

compassion (5th): care (K), pity (4th), sympathy (4th), tenderness (3rd), understanding (1st)

compassionate (5th): caring (1st), gentle (3rd), loving (1st), sympathetic (4th), tender (3rd), understanding (1st), warm (1st)

compel (3rd): cause (2nd), command (2nd), control (2nd), drive (1st), force (1st), influence (5th), make (K), order (1st), require (1st)

compensation (6th): A. earnings (2nd), income (4th), pay (K), payment (1st), salary (3rd), wages (3rd) **B.** amends (4th), fee (4th), fine (1st), penalty (5th), return (2nd)

compete (4th): battle (2nd), challenge (4th), contest (4th), counter (5th), dispute (6th), fight (K), meet (K), oppose (3rd), strive (5th), struggle (1st)

competent (6th): able (3rd), capable (4th), effective (4th), fit (K), qualified (4th), skillful (2nd)

competition (5th): battle (2nd), challenge (4th), contest (4th), game (K), match (3rd), meet (K), rivalry (4th), tournament (5th)

complain (4th): criticize (5th), disapprove (4th), fault (3rd), gripe (5th), grumble (5th), object (1st), protest (4th)

complete (3rd): A. all (K), entire (3rd), every (K), perfect (3rd), whole (1st) **B.** achieve (5th), close (K), end (K), finish (1st), terminate (6th)

complex (6th): A. complicated (6th), compound (4th), difficult (5th), intricate (6th), involved (6th) **B.** structure (4th), system (2nd)

complicate (6th): confuse (4th), involve (6th), mix (1st), puzzle (4th), snare (5th)

compliment (5th): A. commend (6th), flatter (4th), honor (1st) **B.** courtesy (4th), flattery (4th), praise (4th), tribute (5th)

comply (6th): agree (2nd), consent (3rd), go along (1st), mind (1st), obey (3rd), submit (4th), yield (4th)

composition (4th): A. article (2nd), essay (5th), paper (K), theme (4th) **B.** blend (5th), compound (4th), creation (3rd), union (3rd)

compound (4th): A. add (K), blend (5th), combine (3rd), mix (1st) **B.** combination (3rd), mixture (4th) **C.** complex (6th), intricate (6th), many (K), multiple (2nd)

comprehend (5th): conceive (4th), decode (5th), get (K), grasp (4th), know (1st), perceive (6th), see (K), understand (1st)

compress (4th): bind (2nd), compact (5th), condense (6th), contract (3rd), cram (5th), crowd (2nd), deflate (6th), force (1st), pinch (4th), press (1st), shrink (5th), squeeze (5th), tighten (1st)

comprise (6th): compound (4th), contain (5th), cover (1st), include (3rd), involve (6th), make up (1st), span (6th)

compromise (5th): adjust (5th), agree (2nd), arrange (3rd), concession (6th), give in (K), settle (2nd), trade (2nd), yield (4th)

computer (1st)

comrade (4th): associate (5th), buddy (4th), chum (6th), companion (3rd), friend (1st), mate (4th), partner (5th)

con (3rd): A. against (1st) **B.** negative (6th), no (K) **C.** cheat (3rd), deceive (5th), mislead (5th), plot (4th), sting (2nd), trick (1st)

conceal (4th): bury (3rd), camouflage (5th), cover (1st), disguise (5th), harbor (2nd), hide (1st), mask (2nd), obscure (6th), screen (1st), shelter (4th), shield (4th), veil (3rd)

concede (6th): acknowledge (5th), admit (4th), allow (2nd), comply (6th), confess (4th), give up (K), grant (2nd), let (K), recognize (3rd), release (5th), yield (4th)

conceited (5th): arrogant (6th), not humble (4th), proud (2nd), self-important (3rd), stuck-up (4th),

vain (4th)

conceive (4th): create (3rd), fancy (3rd), form (1st), imagine (2nd), invent (2nd), plan (1st), plot (4th), realize (2nd), think up (1st)

concentrate (5th): A. absorb (5th), give attention (2nd), ponder (6th), think (1st) **B.** center (2nd), compact (5th), condense (6th), focus (5th)

concern (3rd): A. apply (2nd), have to do with (K), relate to (4th) **B.** care (K), doubt (5th), regard (4th), thought (1st), trouble (1st), worry (1st) **C.** affair (2nd), business (2nd)

concerning (3rd): about (K), in regard (4th), relating to (4th)

concession (6th): A. allowance (5th), apology (6th), surrender (5th) **B.** favor (2nd), gift (K), grant (2nd) **C.** business (2nd), lease (6th)

conclude (3rd): A. cease (3rd), close (K), complete (3rd), end (K), finish (1st), halt (4th), stop (K), terminate (6th) **B.** decide (1st), determine (5th), gather (1st), guess (1st), think (1st)

concord (6th): accord (4th), agreement (2nd), friendship (1st), harmony (4th), peace (2nd)

concrete (4th): certain (1st), particular (4th), real (1st), single (3rd), solid (3rd), specific (5th), substantial (5th)

condemn (4th): blame (2nd), charge (2nd), convict (5th), criticize (5th), curse (3rd), find guilty (4th), judge (1st), sentence (1st)

condo (4th): apartment (1st), attached house, condominium (2nd), dwelling (4th), flat (2nd), home (K), rental (1st)

condominium (4th): apartment (1st), attached house (5th), condo (1st), dwelling (4th), flat (2nd), home (K), rental (1st)

condense (6th): compact (5th), concentrate (5th), contract (3rd), shorten (1st), shrink (5th). See also compress.

condition (3rd): A. qualify (4th), requirement (2nd), term (3rd) **B.** disease (5th), illness (1st) **C.** fix (1st), shape (1st), situation (4th), state (1st), status (6th)

condor (3rd)

conduct (3rd): A. actions (1st), behavior (4th), ethics (5th) **B.** direct (1st), operate (3rd), run (K) **C.** accompany (3rd), escort (5th), guide (1st), lead (1st), take (K)

cone (1st)

confederate (6th): associate (5th), helper (1st), partner (5th)

conference (4th): assembly (4th), convention (6th), council (5th), interview (5th), meeting (1st), session (6th)

confess (4th): acknowledge (5th), admit (4th), concede (6th), grant (2nd), own (K), reveal (4th), tell (K)

confide (6th): A. reveal (4th), tell (K) **B.** believe (1st), depend on (3rd), trust (1st)

confident (6th): assured (3rd), certain (1st), cheerful (3rd), convinced (4th), poised (6th), positive (2nd), secure (3rd), sure (K)

confidential (6th): close (K), intimate (5th), personal (3rd), private (3rd), secret (1st)

conflict (4th): battle (2nd), clash (5th), competition (5th), contest (4th), disagreement (2nd), fight (K), match (3rd), rivalry (4th), struggle (1st), war (1st)

conform (6th): accept (3rd), adapt (4th), adjust (5th), correspond (5th), fit (K), match (3rd), square (2nd)

confound (6th): amaze (5th), astonish (4th), bewilder (3rd), confuse (4th), mystify (4th), perplex (6th), puzzle (4th), surprise (1st)

confront (5th): challenge (4th), defy (6th), encounter (4th), face (K), meet (K), tackle (4th)

confuse (4th): bewilder (3rd), cloud (1st), complicate (6th), disorder (3rd), mix (1st), mystify (4th), puzzle (4th), scramble (4th)

congratulate (6th): celebrate (4th), cheer (3rd), great (K), praise (4th), support (4th)

congregation (6th): assembly (4th), community (2nd), conference (4th), followers (1st), gathering (1st), members (2nd)

Congress (1st)

congress (4th): meeting (K), interaction (6th)

connect (3rd): add (K), adjoin (6th), associate (5th), attach (5th), bind (2nd), bridge (1st), fasten (4th), join (3rd), link (5th), relate (4th), tie (1st), unite (5th)

conquer (4th): achieve (5th), beat (1st), best (1st), crush (4th), defeat (5th), dominate (5th), master (K), overcome (2nd), triumph (5th), vanquish (6th), win (K)

conscience (4th): ethics (5th), honesty (3rd), justice (3rd), morality (3rd), virtue (4th)

conscious (6th): A. deliberate (6th), intentional (5th), known (1st), planned (1st), realized (2nd) **B.** alert (5th), awake (3rd), aware (3rd), know (1st), thinking (1st)

conscript (6th): call (K), elect (3rd), impress (5th), name (K), obtain (5th), recruit (6th), register (4th), select (4th)

conscription (6th)

consent (3rd): accept (3rd), agree (2nd), allow (2nd), approve (4th), authorize (3rd), comply (6th), grant (2nd), let (K), license (5th), permit (3rd)

consequence (4th): A. fame (3rd), importance (1st), significance (6th), value (2nd) **B.** effect (3rd), outcome (4th), reaction (5th), result (2nd)

conserve (5th): economize (4th), guard (1st), maintain (4th), preserve (4th), protect (4th), save (1st), shield (4th)

consider (2nd): A. ponder (6th), review (4th), study (2nd), think about (1st), wonder (1st) **B.** heed (4th), judge (1st), mind (1st), note (1st)

consist (3rd): A. ingredients (4th), involve (5th), make up (K) **B.** agree (2nd), conform (6th), fit (K)

console (5th): A. calm (3rd), cheer (3rd), comfort (3rd), relieve (4th), support (4th) **B.** cabinet (4th), furniture (3rd)

conspicuous (5th): noticeable (2nd), obvious (5th), outstanding (2nd), prominent (5th)

constable (6th): officer (1st), marshal (5th), policeman (1st), sheriff (4th)

constant (4th): A. devoted (5th), faithful (3rd), loyal (5th), true (K) **B.** continuous (2nd), even (1st), lasting (1st), regular (3rd), same (K), set (K), steady (3rd), uniform (1st)

constantly (4th): always (1st), forever (3rd)

constellation (5th): group (1st)

consternation (6th): alarm (3rd), astonishment (4th), bewilderment (3rd), confusion (4th), dread (6th), fear (1st), horror (4th), panic (1st), terror (3rd)

constitute (4th): A. are (K), compose (4th), form (1st), is (K), make up (1st), to be (K) **B.** compound (4th), create (3rd), establish (3rd), institute (5th)

contraceptive (5th): something that prevents conception

construct (3rd): build (1st), compose (4th), erect (4th), frame (3rd), make (K), process (4th), shape (1st)

consul (5th): ambassador (5th), delegate (5th), diplomat (5th), representative (4th)

consult (4th): advise (3rd), ask (K), communicate (4th), confer (4th), consider (2nd)

consume (4th): A. fascinate (4th), hold (1st) **B.** absorb (5th), destroy (2nd), eat (K), use (K), waste (1st)

consumerism (5th): A. the theory that an increasing consumption of goods is economically beneficial **B.** a movement advocating greater protection of the interests of consumers

contact (4th): call (K), collide (6th), communicate (4th), connection (3rd), meet (K), reach (1st), touch (1st)

contaminated (6th): unclean (2nd), impure (3rd), polluted (3rd)

contagious (6th): catching (1st), infectious (6th), spreading (2nd)

contain(ed) (5th): control (2nd), curb (3rd), enclose (4th), have (K), hold

(1st), include (3rd), incorporate (4th), restrain (5th)

contaminate (6th): poison (3rd), pollute (3rd), soil (2nd), spoil (4th), taint (6th)

contemplate (6th): A. aim (3rd), design (5th), intend (6th), plan (1st), purpose (4th) **B.** consider (2nd), meditate (4th), ponder (6th), reflect (4th), study (2nd), think (1st), watch (1st)

contemporary (5th): at the same time (1st), current (3rd), living (1st), modern (2nd), present day (K)

contempt (5th): disgust (5th), dislike (1st), distaste (6th), hate (2nd), mock (4th), scorn (4th)

contend (5th): A. assert (6th), believe (1st), hold (1st), maintain (4th), say (K) **B.** battle (2nd), compete (4th), fight (K), oppose (3rd), quarrel (4th)

content (3rd): A. cheerful (3rd), happy (K), pleased (1st), satisfied (3rd) **B.** filling (1st), insides (1st), volume (3rd) **C.** cheer (3rd), comfort (3rd), meaning (1st), satisfy (3rd), substance (5th)

contest (4th): A. disagree (2nd), dispute (6th), oppose (3rd) **B.** battle (2nd), conflict (4th), competition (5th), event (3rd), fight (K), game (K), match (3rd), meet (K), struggle (1st), tournament (5th), war (1st)

continent (4th): A. controlled (2nd), pure (3rd), restrained (6th) **B.** one of the principal land masses of the earth

continue (2nd): carry on (K), endure (4th), keep on (K), last (K), persist (5th), proceed (4th), remain (2nd), stay (1st)

contract (3rd): A. agreement (2nd), bargain (4th), pledge (5th), treaty (4th),

understanding (1st) **B.** condense (6th), decline (6th), shrink (5th), wither (5th)

contrary (4th): contradict (4th), different (1st), headstrong (2nd), hostile (4th), opposite (3rd), unruly (6th)

contrast (4th): compare (3rd), conflict (4th), differ (4th), oppose (3rd), parallel (5th), stand apart (3rd), vary (4th)

contribute (4th): bestow (5th), fund (4th), give (K), grant (2nd), pledge (5th)

contrite (5th): grief-ridden (5th), regretful (5th), remorseful (6th), repentant (6th), sorry (4th)

contrive (6th): construct (3rd), design (5th), frame (3rd), imagine (2nd), invent (2nd), plan (1st), scheme (5th)

control (2nd): administer (6th), conduct (3rd), direct (1st), dominate (5th), govern (1st), guide (1st), lead (1st), manage (4th), power (1st), rule (K), supervise (6th)

controversy (6th): argument (3rd), contention (5th), disagreement (2nd), dispute (6th), quarrel (4th)

convenient (4th): close (K), easy (1st), handy (2nd), helpful (2nd), near (1st), practical (4th), ready (1st), simple (2nd), usable (3rd)

convent (6th): abbey (6th)

convention (6th): A. custom (6th), tradition (5th) **B.** gathering (1st), meeting (1st) **C.** contract (3rd), deal (2nd)

conventional (6th): common (2nd), correct (3rd), customary (6th), formal (4th), normal (5th), ordinary (3rd), proper (3rd), traditional (5th)

conversation (5th): chat (1st), dialogue (5th), discussion (5th), talk (K)

convert (4th): A. adjust (5th), change (2nd), exchange (4th), persuade (5th), switch (4th), trade (2nd) **B.** believer (1st), follower (1st)

convey (4th): carry (K), deed (1st), move (K), send (K), shift (4th), take (K), transmit (4th), transport (5th)

convict (5th): A. condemn (4th), prove guilty (4th), sentence (1st) **B.** criminal (4th), offender (4th), prisoner (3rd), villain (5th)

convince (4th): assure (3rd), compel (3rd), demonstrate (6th), persuade (5th), prove (1st), reason (1st), sway (3rd)

cook (1st): bake (1st), boil (3rd), broil (4th), heat (1st), roast (4th), sauté (4th), warm (1st)

cookie (K)

cool (1st): A. calm (3rd), collected (3rd), serene (6th), tranquil (6th) **B.** chilly (3rd), cold (K), frigid (6th), icy (1st)

cooperate (5th): agree (2nd), agreeable (2nd), cooperative (5th), help (K), helpful (K), unite (5th), work with (K)

cop (K): officer (1st), police (1st)

copal (5th)

cope (6th): accept (3rd), contend (2nd), deal with (2nd), live through (1st), manage (4th)

copper (4th): penny (1st)

copy (3rd): ape (K), carbon (4th), duplicate (6th), imitate (5th), mock (4th)

coral (3rd)

cord (4th): line (K), rope (1st), string (1st), twine (3rd)

cordial (6th): friendly (1st), gracious (3rd), pleasant (3rd), sincere (4th), sympathetic (4th), warm (1st)

core (6th): center (2nd), heart (K), middle (2nd), nucleus (4th)

cork (6th): cap (K), lid (1st), stopper (1st), top (K)

corn (2nd)

corner (2nd): A. angle (3rd), bend (1st), edge (1st) **B.** area (3rd), part (1st), region (4th) **C.** control (2nd), difficulty (5th), jam (K), mess (1st), monopoly (6th), plight (6th), trap (1st), trouble (1st)

corny (2nd): feeble (4th), foolish (2nd), humor (4th), silly (1st)

corporal (4th): actual (3rd), animal (K), flesh (3rd), material (5th), physical (5th), real (1st), true (K)

corporation (4th): association (5th), business (5th), company (2nd), firm (2nd), institution (5th)

corps (6th): association (5th), band (1st), crew (2nd), group (1st)

correct (3rd): A. adjust (5th), alter (4th), amend (4th), better (K), improve (3rd), modify (5th), remedy (4th) **B.** accurate (6th), exact (2nd), precise (5th), right (K)

correspond (5th): A. agree (2nd), comply (6th), conform (6th), jibe (6th) **B.** communicate (4th), write (K)

corridor (5th): alley (6th), hall (1st), lane (4th), passage (4th), path (1st)

corrupt (6th): A. dishonest (3rd), evil (3rd), false (3rd) **B.** pollute (3rd), ruin (5th), soil (2nd), warp (4th), wreck (4th)

cosmetics (6th): makeup (1st)

cost (K): A. harm (3rd), hurt (K), injure (5th) **B.** charge (2nd), price (K), value (2nd), worth (3rd)

costume (4th): clothing (1st), disguise (5th), dress (K), mask (3rd), uniform (1st)

cot (1st): bed (K)

cottage (4th): cabin (1st), house (K)

cotton (2nd): fabric (5th), soft (K)

couch (4th): A. seat (1st) **B.** put (K), site (5th)

cough (5th): choke (1st), gag (1st), gasp (4th)

could (K): able (3rd). Also see can.

couldn't (1st): unable (3rd)

council (5th): administration (6th), assembly (4th), board (1st), commission (2nd), committee (5th), congress (4th)

counsel (5th): advise (3rd), direct (1st), guide (1st)

count (K): add (K), compute (1st), number (K)

counter (5th): against (1st), contrary (4th), opposed (3rd), opposite (3rd)

countless (5th): abundant (5th), infinite (5th), legion (6th), many (K), numerous (4th)

country (1st): A. farm land (K), suburban (6th) **B.** nation (2nd)

couple (3rd): A. pair (1st), two (K) **B.** put together (1st), yoke (6th)

courage (4th): boldness (2nd), bravery (1st), daring (2nd), heart (K), heroism (5th), pluck (1st), spirit (2nd), strength (2nd)

course (3rd): A. passage (4th), path (1st), route (4th), way (K) **B.** class (1st), plan (1st), program (4th), subject (3rd) **C.** bearing (1st), direction (1st), heading (1st), trend (2nd)

court (3rd): attract (5th), bid (1st), charm (3rd), invite (3rd)

courtesy (4th): civil (3rd), gallant (4th), kindness (K), manners (2nd)

courtier (6th): gallant (4th), gentleman (3rd), noble (3rd)

courtroom (3rd): arena (5th), chambers (5th)

cover (1st): A. camouflage (5th), hide (1st), protect (4th), shield (4th) **B.** contain (5th), include (3rd), take (K) **C.** blanket (3rd), cap (K), case (2nd), coat (1st), lid (1st), shroud (6th), surface (3rd), top (K), veil (3rd), wrap (3rd)

covert (6th): camouflage (5th), concealed (4th), covered (1st), disguised (5th), hidden (1st), secret (1st), unseen (1st)

covet (6th): crave (6th), desire (5th), envy (4th), lust (6th), resent (5th), want (K), yearn for (6th)

cow (K): A. an animal **B.** bully (1st), embarrass (5th), frighten (2nd)

cowardly (4th): afraid (1st), fearful (1st), frightened (2nd), scared (1st), timid (5th)

cowboy (4th)

cowpuncher (6th)

coyote (1st)

crab (K): complain (4th), snap (2nd), sulk (5th)

crack (4th): break (1st), burst (3rd), crevice (6th), hit (K), rend (4th), shatter (5th), snap (2nd), split (4th)

cracker (4th): biscuit (4th), chip (5th)

crackle (3rd): snap (2nd)

cradle (4th): bed (K), crib (2nd), hold (1st), rock (K), snuggle (5th)

craft (2nd): art (K), boat (1st), cunning (6th), skill (2nd), talent (2nd), trade (2nd), vessel (4th)

craftsmanship (6th): ability (3rd), skill (2nd), workmanship (3rd)

crag (6th): cliff (2nd)

cram (5th): fill (K), force (1st), pack (1st), push (1st), ram (K), stuff (1st)

cramp (6th): A. clamp (5th), grab (4th) **B.** pain (2nd), pang (6th), spasm (6th)

crash (2nd): accident (4th), bang (3rd), collision (6th), destroy (2nd), failure (2nd), finish (1st), hit (K), ruin (5th), shatter (5th), smash (3rd), wreck (4th)

crate (5th): box (K), carton (4th), case (2nd), container (5th)

crater (3rd): depression (5th), hole (K), opening (K)

crave (6th): covet (6th), demand (5th), desire (5th), hunger (2nd), long for (1st), lust (6th), need (1st), require (1st), want (K), yearn (6th)

crawfish (3rd)

crawl (1st): A. creep (1st), slow (1st), trail (2nd) **B.** swim (K)

crayfish (4th)

crayon (K)

crazy (4th): absurd (6th), insane (6th), mad (K), silly (1st)

creak (4th): squeak (2nd)

cream (1st): A. grease (5th), oil (K) **B.** beat (1st), defeat (5th), mash (4th) **C.** best (K), nobility (3rd), royalty (3rd)

crease (5th): edge (1st), fold (1st), pleat (5th), ridge (5th)

create (3rd): cause (2nd), construct (3rd), design (5th), develop (5th), device (4th), engineer (4th), establish (3rd), institute (5th), invent (2nd), make (K), produce (2nd)

creature (3rd): animal (K), being (1st), individual (3rd), monster (1st)

Cretaceous (5th): of or belonging to the geologic time, system of rocks, and sedimentary deposits of the third and last period of the Mesozoic Era

credible (6th): assured (3rd), believable (1st), certain (1st), conceivable (4th), convincing (4th), dependable (3rd), reliable (5th), true (K), trusty (1st)

credit (5th): A. believe (1st), have faith in (3rd), trust (1st) **B.** assign (5th), belief (1st), charge (2nd), reputation (5th)

credulous (6th): believing (2nd), foolish (2nd), trusting (1st)

creed (6th): belief (1st), faith (3rd), religion (4th)

creek (4th): river (K), stream (3rd)

creep (1st): crawl (1st), prowl (2nd), slither (4th), sneak (4th)

creeping (1st): crawling (1st), sneaking (4th)

cremate (5th): burn (3rd)

crepe (6th): A. pancake (1st) **B.** fabric (5th), fiber (3rd)

crescent (6th): circle (K), curve (3rd), moon (1st)

crest (4th): edge (1st), peak (4th), rise (1st), top (K)

crevice (6th): break (1st), crack (4th), gap (K), split (4th)

crew (2nd): bunch (3rd), gang (1st), herd (2nd), party (K), race (1st), row (4th), staff (4th), team (1st)

crib (2nd): bed (K), cradle (4th)

cricket (1st)

crime (2nd): harm (3rd), hurt (K), offense (4th), sin (1st), vice (4th), wrong (1st)

criminal (4th): convict (5th), illegal (1st), offender (4th), prohibited (6th)

crimson (5th): red (K), ruby (6th), scarlet (4th)

cripes (1st): gee (K), gosh (1st), wow (K)

critical (5th): A. difficult (5th), negative (6th), severe (4th) **B.** acute (6th), essential (6th), important (1st)

criticize (5th): accuse (4th), blame (2nd), charge (2nd), complain (4th), condemn (4th), crab (K), fault (3rd), reproach (6th), scold (5th)

crocodile (1st)

Cro-Magnon (5th)

crop (2nd): A. bounty (5th), harvest (4th), produce (2nd), yield (4th) **B.** clip (2nd), cut (K), shorten (1st), snip (4th), trim (4th)

cross (1st): A. angry (1st), furious (1st), mad (K), upset (3rd) **B.** betray (5th), cheat (3rd), deceive (5th), deny (5th) **C.** bridge (1st), meet (K), span

(6th), transport (5th), travel (1st), traverse (5th)

crosswise (2nd): across (1st), side to side (K)

crotch (6th): angle (3rd), bend (K), fork (1st)

crouch (5th): bend (K), crawl (1st), hunch (6th), stoop (5th)

crow (2nd): boast (4th), brag (3rd), show off (1st)

crowd (2nd): A. bunch (3rd), gathering (1st), group (1st), mass (3rd), mob (4th), pack (1st), throng (5th) **B.** crush (4th), jam (K), press (1st), push (1st), shove (5th), squeeze (5th), swarm (4th)

crown (1st): cap (K), point (1st), summit (5th), top (K)

cruel (5th): brutal (6th), fierce (4th), hard (K), harsh (5th), mean (1st), savage (5th), severe (4th), stern (4th), strict (6th), tough (5th), unkind (2nd)

crunch (4th): chew (1st), crush (4th), gnaw (1st), grind (4th), mash (4th), smash (3rd)

crush (4th): bruise (5th), defeat (5th), grind (4th), mash (4th), pound (2nd), powder (3rd), press (1st), push (1st), put down (2nd), smash (3rd), squash (2nd), stomp (4th), squeeze (5th)

crust (4th): A. case (2nd), coating (1st), covering (1st), outside (1st), rind (4th), shell (1st), skin (1st), surface (3rd) **B.** the outermost solid layer of a planet or moon

cry (K): address (K), announce (3rd), howl (4th), moan (5th), sob (1st), weep (4th), whimper (5th), whine (5th), yell (K)

crystal (3rd): clear (2nd), glass (1st), rock (K), transparent (5th)

cub (K): A. bear (K), pup (K), puppy (K) **B.** baby (K), boy (K), child (K), lad (K) **C.** Scout (1st)

cube (4th): block (1st), box (K), square (2nd)

cuddle (5th): cradle (4th), hold (1st), hug (1st), love (K), pet (1st), snuggle (5th), squeeze (5th), touch (1st)

cue (2nd): clue (2nd), guide (1st), hint (1st), indicator (4th), key (K), lead (1st), mark (1st), prompt (4th), remind (3rd), sign (1st), signal (4th), tip (1st)

cuff (1st): A. band (1st), edge (1st) **B.** box (K), hit (K), punch (4th), slap (2nd), strike (2nd)

cultivate (6th): breed (4th), develop (5th), further (2nd), grow (1st), improve (3rd), nurse (K), promote (5th), rear (3rd), teach (1st), train (K)

cultivation (6th): A. agriculture (4th), farming (1st), gardening (K) **B.** development (5th), improvement (3rd), teaching (1st)

culture (6th): A. customs (6th), habits (3rd), society (3rd), tradition (5th), ways (K) **B.** background (4th), breeding (4th), civilization (4th), cultivation (6th), education (3rd), polish (4th), taste (1st)

cunning (6th): A. clever (3rd), crafty (4th), foxy (1st), sly (4th), smart (1st), tricky (1st) **B.** craft (2nd), skill (2nd)

cup (K): A. bowl (1st), can (K), glass (1st), mug (1st) **B.** bend (K), depression (6th)

curb (3rd): A. block (1st), check (1st), control (2nd), limit (3rd), restrain (5th), restrict (6th), stop (K) **B.** border (1st),

boundary (4th), edge (1st), margin (5th), ridge (5th), rim (1st)

cure (4th): correct (3rd), fix (1st), repair (4th)

curfew (6th): bedtime (K), deadline (2nd)

curious (3rd): interested (1st), questioning (1st), wondering (1st)

curl (2nd): bend (K), coil (5th), curve (3rd), hook (4th), turn (1st), twist (1st), wind (1st)

current (3rd): A. drift (2nd), flow (1st), pull (K), river (K), stream (3rd), tide (1st) **B.** actual (3rd), contemporary (5th), immediate (3rd), popular (3rd), present (K), universal (4th)

curse (3rd): A. evil (3rd), plague (5th), scourge (6th) **B.** abuse (6th), condemn (4th), punish (4th), ruin (2nd), swear (4th)

curtain (5th): A. cover (1st), hide (1st), shield (4th) **B.** blind (3rd), drape (5th), screen (1st), shade (2nd), shutter (4th), wall (K)

curve (3rd): arc (4th), arch (4th), bend (K), bow (1st), coil (5th), curl (2nd), orbit (4th), turn (1st), twist (1st)

custom (6th): form (1st), habit (3rd), law (1st), manners (2nd), practice (1st), rite (6th), ritual (6th), tradition (5th), use (K), way (K)

customer (5th): buyer (1st), client (6th), patron (5th), shopper (2nd)

cut (K): A. hurt (K), injure (5th), wound (3rd) **B.** carve (4th), rip (K), scratch (4th), slash (6th), slice (5th), slit (5th), tear (2nd) **C.** piece (1st), portion (4th), section (4th) **D.** canal (4th), channel (4th), division (4th), furrow (6th), groove (5th), hew (6th), trim (4th)

cute (1st): funny (1st), precious (4th), pretty (1st), sweet (K)

cutlass (6th): blade (2nd), saber (5th), sword (4th)

cutting (1st)

cyber (4th): a prefix used in a growing number of terms to describe new things that are being made possible by the spread of computers

cybernetics (4th): the study of communication and control **A.** acute (6th), keen (4th), sharp (1st) **B.** bit (1st), part (1st), particle (5th), piece (1st)

Cyberpunk (4th): a genre of science fiction that draws heavily on computer science ideas

Cyberspace (4th): the nonphysical terrain created by computer systems

cylinder (6th)

Cynognathus (5th)

DNA (4th)

dab (1st): bead (K), bit (1st), dot (K), drop (1st), fragment (6th), pat (K), pinch (4th), poke (1st), speck (4th), spot (1st)

dad (K): daddy (K), father (K), papa (1st), pop (K)

daft (6th): confused (4th), crazy (4th), dazed (5th), foolish (2nd), insane (6th), mad (K), silly (1st), simple (1st)

daily (4th): common (2nd), customary (6th), everyday (1st), normal (5th), ordinary (3rd), regular (3rd), routine (6th), usual (3rd)

dairy (1st)

dam (K): bar (3rd), block (1st), clog (5th), halt (4th), hinder (6th), hold (1st), jam (K), obstruct (5th), prevent (3rd), stop (K)

damage (5th): A. destruction (5th), disaster (6th), loss (K) **B.** abuse (6th), destroy (5th), harm (3rd), hurt (K), impair (6th), injure (5th), loss (K), ruin (2nd)

damp (5th): foggy (1st), juicy (1st), misty (1st), moist (4th), watery (1st), wet (K)

damsel (6th): girl (K), lady (1st), lass (1st), maiden (4th), miss (K)

dance (1st): A. ball (K), ballet (4th), prom (5th) **B.** bounce (6th), hop (K), rock (K), spin (1st), swing (1st), whirl (4th)

dandy (1st): fine (1st), great (K), swell (3rd)

danger (1st): chance (2nd), hazard (6th), menace (5th), peril (5th), risk (4th), threat (5th)

dangerous (6th): hazardous (6th), perilous (5th), risky (4th), threatening (5th), uncertain (1st), unsafe (1st)

dangle (5th): drop (K), hang (2nd), suspend (4th), swing (1st), trail (2nd)

dare (2nd): A. challenge (4th), defy (6th), face (K) **B.** bear (K), brave (1st), endure (4th), meet (K), provoke (6th), risk (4th)

dark (K): black (K), dim (1st), dull (1st), gloomy (3rd), obscure (6th), shady (2nd), shadowy (3rd)

dart (1st): A. arrow (2nd), spear (4th) **B.** fly (K), rush (2nd), sail (1st), shoot (3rd), speed (3rd)

data (4th): information (5th)

database (4th): a body of information that can be searched to answer questions usually using a computer program

datamining (4ᵗʰ): data processing using searches and statistical algorithms to discover patterns and correlations in databases

date (1ˢᵗ): A. appointment (3ʳᵈ), engagement (5ᵗʰ), meeting (1ˢᵗ), reservation (3ʳᵈ) **B.** day (K), period (2ⁿᵈ), season (2ⁿᵈ), time (1ˢᵗ)

daughter (1ˢᵗ): child (K), female (4ᵗʰ), girl (K)

day (K): A. light (K) **B.** date (1ˢᵗ), time (1ˢᵗ)

daydream (2ⁿᵈ): dream (K), idea (1ˢᵗ), imagine (2ⁿᵈ), thought (1ˢᵗ), wish (K)

daylight (1ˢᵗ): light (K), morning (1ˢᵗ), sun (K), sunshine (1ˢᵗ)

dazzle (5ᵗʰ): A. shine (1ˢᵗ), sparkle (5ᵗʰ) **B.** amaze (5ᵗʰ), astonish (4ᵗʰ), blind (3ʳᵈ), confound (6ᵗʰ), confuse (4ᵗʰ), stun (4ᵗʰ)

dead (1ˢᵗ): gone (1ˢᵗ), not alive (3ʳᵈ), still (1ˢᵗ)

deal (2ⁿᵈ): A. assign (5ᵗʰ), deliver (5ᵗʰ), give (K), share (2ⁿᵈ) **B.** agreement (2ⁿᵈ), bargain (4ᵗʰ), contract (3ʳᵈ)

dear (1ˢᵗ): A. costly (1ˢᵗ), expensive (3ʳᵈ), priceless (1ˢᵗ), valuable (4ᵗʰ) **B.** admired (5ᵗʰ), beloved (4ᵗʰ), favorite (3ʳᵈ), loved (1ˢᵗ), precious (4ᵗʰ)

debris (5ᵗʰ): junk (3ʳᵈ), mess (1ˢᵗ), rubbish (5ᵗʰ), ruins (2ⁿᵈ), trash (2ⁿᵈ), waste (1ˢᵗ)

decapitate (6ᵗʰ): behead (2ⁿᵈ), chop off (2ⁿᵈ)

decay (5ᵗʰ): decline (6ᵗʰ), fail (2ⁿᵈ), rot (1ˢᵗ), spoil (4ᵗʰ), waste (1ˢᵗ)

deceive (5ᵗʰ): cheat (3ʳᵈ), con (3ʳᵈ), fool (2ⁿᵈ), lie to (2ⁿᵈ), mislead (5ᵗʰ), trick (1ˢᵗ)

December (1ˢᵗ)

descendant (5ᵗʰ): child (K)

decide (1ˢᵗ): consider (2ⁿᵈ), determine (5ᵗʰ), judge (1ˢᵗ), make up your mind (1ˢᵗ), resolve (5ᵗʰ), settle (2ⁿᵈ), weigh (1ˢᵗ)

decision (3ʳᵈ)

deck (1ˢᵗ): A. floor (K), porch (3ʳᵈ) **B.** adorn (6ᵗʰ), decorate (3ʳᵈ), grace (3ʳᵈ), ornament (4ᵗʰ)

declare (5ᵗʰ): announce (3ʳᵈ), assert (6ᵗʰ), claim (2ⁿᵈ), express (5ᵗʰ), inform (5ᵗʰ), proclaim (4ᵗʰ), profess (5ᵗʰ), publish (4ᵗʰ), say (K), state (1ˢᵗ)

decline (6ᵗʰ): A. deny (5ᵗʰ), reject (5ᵗʰ), resist (4ᵗʰ), turn down (1ˢᵗ) **B.** descend (6ᵗʰ), go down (K), slant (6ᵗʰ), slope (3ʳᵈ)

decode (5ᵗʰ): read (K), understand (1ˢᵗ)

decorate (3ʳᵈ): adorn (6ᵗʰ), beautify (2ⁿᵈ), ornament (4ᵗʰ)

decoration (3ʳᵈ): ornament (4ᵗʰ), trim (4ᵗʰ)

dedicate (6ᵗʰ): bless (3ʳᵈ), devote (5ᵗʰ), focus (5ᵗʰ), give (K), offer (2ⁿᵈ), surrender (5ᵗʰ)

deduce (6ᵗʰ): conclude (3ʳᵈ), gather (1ˢᵗ), infer (5ᵗʰ), think (1ˢᵗ), understand (1ˢᵗ)

deed (1ˢᵗ): A. achievement (5ᵗʰ), act (K), action (1ˢᵗ), assign (5ᵗʰ), exploit (6ᵗʰ), feat (1ˢᵗ), job (K), task (3ʳᵈ), transfer (5ᵗʰ), work (K) **B.** title (3ʳᵈ)

deep (1ˢᵗ): A. absorbed (5ᵗʰ), fascinated (5ᵗʰ), involved (6ᵗʰ), lost in (K) **B.** difficult (5ᵗʰ), hidden (1ˢᵗ), instinctive (5ᵗʰ), mysterious (1ˢᵗ), unclear (2ⁿᵈ) **C.** intent (5ᵗʰ), obscure (6ᵗʰ), profound (6ᵗʰ), serious (4ᵗʰ), sincere (4ᵗʰ)

deer (K)

defeat (5ᵗʰ): beat (1ˢᵗ), best (K), conquer (4ᵗʰ), crush (4ᵗʰ), destroy (2ⁿᵈ), dominate (5ᵗʰ), master (1ˢᵗ), overthrow (6ᵗʰ), ruin (2ⁿᵈ), (5ᵗʰ), stop (K), vanquish (6ᵗʰ)

defend (5ᵗʰ): A. argue (3ʳᵈ), justify (3ʳᵈ), maintain (4ᵗʰ) **B.** guard (1ˢᵗ), police (1ˢᵗ), protect (4ᵗʰ), shelter (4ᵗʰ), shield (4ᵗʰ), support (5ᵗʰ)

deform (4ᵗʰ): distort (6ᵗʰ), flaw (6ᵗʰ), warp (4ᵗʰ)

defy (6ᵗʰ): brave (1ˢᵗ), challenge (4ᵗʰ), dare (2ⁿᵈ), disobey (3ʳᵈ), face (K), ignore (5ᵗʰ)

degree (5ᵗʰ): A. class (1ˢᵗ), grade (2ⁿᵈ), level (3ʳᵈ), rank (3ʳᵈ), status (6ᵗʰ) **B.** amount (2ⁿᵈ), measure (2ⁿᵈ), size (1ˢᵗ), strength (1ˢᵗ)

dehydrate (6ᵗʰ): arid (6ᵗʰ), desiccate (6ᵗʰ), dry (1ˢᵗ), dry out (1ˢᵗ), parch (6ᵗʰ),

deity (5ᵗʰ): god (1ˢᵗ)

dejected (5ᵗʰ): blue (K), depressed (5ᵗʰ), gloomy (3ʳᵈ), melancholy (6ᵗʰ), sad (K), unhappy (K), weary (4ᵗʰ)

delay (5ᵗʰ): hold (1ˢᵗ), linger (4ᵗʰ), slow (1ˢᵗ), suspend (4ᵗʰ), wait (K)

delegate (5ᵗʰ): A. assign (5ᵗʰ), charge (2ⁿᵈ), enable (4ᵗʰ) **B.** representative (4ᵗʰ)

delegation (5ᵗʰ): A. assignment (5ᵗʰ), mission (5ᵗʰ) **B.** board (1ˢᵗ), body (1ˢᵗ), commission (2ⁿᵈ), group (1ˢᵗ)

deliberate (6ᵗʰ): A. consider (2ⁿᵈ), intend (5ᵗʰ), plan (1ˢᵗ) **B.** designed (5ᵗʰ), intentional (5ᵗʰ), planned (1ˢᵗ), willful (5ᵗʰ)

delicate (5ᵗʰ): dainty (5ᵗʰ), elegant (5ᵗʰ), frail (6ᵗʰ), gentle (3ʳᵈ), rare (4ᵗʰ), slight (K), small (K), smooth (2ⁿᵈ), soft (K), thin (1ˢᵗ), weak (3ʳᵈ)

delicatessen (5ᵗʰ): cafe (4ᵗʰ), restaurant (5ᵗʰ)

delight (3ʳᵈ): enjoyment (2ⁿᵈ), pleasure (2ⁿᵈ)

deliver (5ᵗʰ): A. bring (K), give (K), send (1ˢᵗ) **B.** address (K), announce (3ʳᵈ), say (K), speak (1ˢᵗ) **C.** free (K), hand (K), release (5ᵗʰ), save (1ˢᵗ)

demand (5ᵗʰ): ask (5ᵗʰ), claim (2ⁿᵈ), insist (5ᵗʰ), need (1ˢᵗ), order (1ˢᵗ), request (4ᵗʰ), require (2ⁿᵈ)

demigod (6ᵗʰ)

demonstrate (6ᵗʰ): exhibit (4ᵗʰ), explain (2ⁿᵈ), prove (1ˢᵗ), show (1ˢᵗ)

demure (5ᵗʰ): bashful (4ᵗʰ), meek (2ⁿᵈ), quiet (K), shy (1ˢᵗ)

den (1ˢᵗ): A. library (3ʳᵈ), study (2ⁿᵈ) **B.** bar (3ʳᵈ), tavern (5ᵗʰ) **C.** burrow (5ᵗʰ), cave (1ˢᵗ), lair (5ᵗʰ)

dent (1ˢᵗ): crease (5ᵗʰ), depression (6ᵗʰ), dip (1ˢᵗ)

deny (5ᵗʰ): contradict (4ᵗʰ), decline (6ᵗʰ), disprove (3ʳᵈ), object (1ˢᵗ), refuse (2ⁿᵈ), reject (5ᵗʰ), resist (4ᵗʰ)

depart (5ᵗʰ): exit (3ʳᵈ), flee (5ᵗʰ), go (K), leave (1ˢᵗ), move (1ˢᵗ)

department (2ⁿᵈ): branch (2ⁿᵈ), division (4ᵗʰ), office (1ˢᵗ), section (4ᵗʰ), unit (5ᵗʰ)

depend (3rd): lean (3rd), rely (5th), trust (1st)

depose (6th): dethrone (4th), kick out (1st), unseat (2nd)

deposit (5th): leave (1st), place (1st), sediment (4th), set (K)

depress (5th): A. dent (1st), lower (K) **B.** deject (5th), discourage (5th), downcast (5th), drain (5th), oppress (6th), tire (2nd), weary (4th)

depression (6th): A. blue (1st), despair (6th), discouraged (5th), gloom (3rd), low (K), sadness (2nd) **B.** cavity (5th), hollow (3rd)

depth (5th): deepness (1st), middle (2nd), range (3rd), scope (6th), span (6th), substance (5th), width (4th)

derelict (6th): A. beggar (2nd), tramp (4th) **B.** abandoned (4th), careless (5th), deserted (1st), desolate (6th), discarded (6th), left (1st), negligent (4th), reckless (5th), rejected (5th)

descend (5th): alight (5th), decline (6th), dismount (3rd), fall (K), go down (K), land (K), lower (1st)

descendant (5th): child (K), next generation (4th), heir (4th)

desert (1st): A. abandon (4th), betray (5th), due (2nd), forsake (6th), ignore (5th), leave (1st), quit (1st), reject (5th) **B.** badlands (3rd), wasteland (6th)

deserve (4th): merit (4th), reward (4th), worthy (3rd)

design (5th): aim (3rd), arrange (3rd), develop (5th), draw (K), form (1st), goal (4th), intend (6th), mean (1st), plan (1st), plot (4th), sketch (5th)

desire (5th): ambition (4th), covet (6th), crave (6th), hope (K), long (1st), want (K), wish (K)

desk (2nd): table (K)

desolate (6th): alone (K), bare (3rd), deserted (3rd), forlorn (6th), lone (2nd), lonely (2nd), ruined (2nd), solitary (5th)

desperate (5th): A. bold (2nd), daring (2nd), rash (6th), reckless (5th) **B.** critical (5th), urgent (6th) **C.** dire (6th), hopeless (2nd)

despise (5th): detest (6th), hate (2nd), look down on (1st), mock (4th), scorn (4th)

destiny (5th): chance (2nd), end (K), fate (3rd), fortune (3rd), future (5th), lot (K), luck (1st)

destroy (2nd): abolish (5th), crush (4th), damage (5th), destruct (2nd), erase (2nd), exterminate (6th), kill (1st), ruin (2nd), slaughter (5th), smash (3rd), spoil (4th), wreck (4th)

destruction (5th): damage (5th), ruin (2nd), wreckage (4th)

destructive (5th): evil (3rd), harmful (3rd), killing (1st), negative (6th), ruinous (5th)

detail (5th): A. fact (1st), item (5th), part (1st), particular (4th), point (1st) **B.** detect (4th), exact (2nd), find (K), list (2nd), locate (3rd), note (1st), notice (2nd)

detect (4th): catch (1st), find (K), glimpse (4th), spot (1st), spy (4th)

detective (4th): investigator (5th)

determine (5th): conclude (3rd), decide (1st), establish (3rd), find (K), fix (1st), learn (1st), resolve (5th), rule (K), settle (2nd), solve (4th)

detest (6th): despise (5th), dislike (K), hate (2nd), scorn (4th)

dethrone (6th): overthrow (6th), unseat (1st)

devastate (6th): destroy (2nd), overwhelm (5th), ravage (6th), ruin (2nd), spoil (4th), waste (1st), wreck (4th)

develop (5th): advance (2nd), age (1st), bloom (4th), grow (K), increase (3rd), mature (5th), progress (4th), ripen (1st)

device (4th): equipment (5th), instrument (3rd), machine (1st), tool (1st)

Devonian (5th): of or belonging to the geologic time, system of rocks, or sedimentary deposits of the fourth period of the Paleozoic Era

devote (5th): bless (3rd), commit (4th), concentrate (5th), dedicate (6th), give (K), offer (2nd), pledge (5th), promise (1st)

devotee (5th): addict (5th), believer (1st), follower (1st)

devour (5th): consume (4th), destroy (2nd), eat (K), finish (1st), ravage (6th), swallow (1st)

dew (1st): moisture (3rd)

dial (5th): A. adjust (5th), call (K), select (4th), spin (1st), tune (1st) **B.** circle (K), disk (2nd), indicator (4th)

dialect (5th): accent (6th), language (2nd), speech (2nd), tongue (3rd)

diamond (4th)

diarrhea (6th)

diary (3rd): account (3rd), history (2nd), journal (2nd), log (1st), notes (1st), record (2nd)

did (K)

didn't (1st)

die (2nd): cease (3rd), end (K), expire (6th), fade (K), pass away (K), perish (4th), stop (K), weaken (3rd)

diet (4th): A. fast (1st), reduce (3rd), slim (5th), trim (4th) **B.** food (K), meals (3rd)

differ (4th): A. disagree (3rd), oppose (3rd) **B.** change (2nd), contrast (4th), unlike (2nd), vary (4th)

different (1st): A. contrary (4th), distinct (5th), separate (3rd) **B.** extraordinary (5th), strange (1st), unusual (3rd)

difficult (5th): annoying (5th), awkward (6th), challenging (4th), complex (6th), demanding (5th), hard (1st), not easy (K), puzzling (4th), tough (5th), trying (1st), unpleasant (3rd)

dig (1st): A. enjoy (2nd), like (K), understand (1st) **B.** burrow (5th), mine (1st), scoop (4th), shovel (1st) **C.** archeology site (5th)

digits (4th): A. numbers (K) **B.** fingers or toes (1st)

digital (4th): A. a device that displays information, such as a picture, using individual dots **B.** relating to a device that can read, write, store, or show information that is represented in numerical form **C.** operated or done with the fingers

dill (1st)

dim (1st): cloudy (1st), dark (K), faint (3rd), foggy (1st), pale (3rd), shadowy (3rd), unclear (2nd), weak (3rd)

dime (1st)

diminutive (6th): little (K), short (1st), small (K), tiny (2nd)

din (6ᵗʰ): blast (2ⁿᵈ), clamor (6ᵗʰ), noise (1ˢᵗ), racket (1ˢᵗ), uproar (5ᵗʰ)

dine (1ˢᵗ): banquet (4ᵗʰ), dinner (1ˢᵗ), eat (K), feast (1ˢᵗ)

dinosaur (K)

dinner (1ˢᵗ): feast (1ˢᵗ), meal (3ʳᵈ), supper (2ⁿᵈ)

dip (1ˢᵗ): A. ladle (6ᵗʰ), lower (1ˢᵗ), plunge (4ᵗʰ), scoop (4ᵗʰ) **B.** bathe (1ˢᵗ), soak (5ᵗʰ), submerge (5ᵗʰ)

diplomat (5ᵗʰ): ambassador (5ᵗʰ), counselor (5ᵗʰ), go-between (1ˢᵗ)

dire (6ᵗʰ): acute (6ᵗʰ), awful (3ʳᵈ), critical (5ᵗʰ), disastrous (6ᵗʰ), dreadful (6ᵗʰ), evil (3ʳᵈ), fearful (1ˢᵗ), frightful (2ⁿᵈ), grave (3ʳᵈ), horrible (4ᵗʰ), ominous (6ᵗʰ), terrible (1ˢᵗ), tragic (5ᵗʰ), urgent (6ᵗʰ)

direct (1ˢᵗ): address (K), aim (3ʳᵈ), boss (K), control (2ⁿᵈ), manage (4ᵗʰ), supervise (6ᵗʰ)

direction (1ˢᵗ): A. charge (2ⁿᵈ), control (2ⁿᵈ), instruction (4ᵗʰ) **B.** bearing (2ⁿᵈ), control (2ⁿᵈ), course (3ʳᵈ), lead (1ˢᵗ), location (3ʳᵈ), movement (2ⁿᵈ), position (2ⁿᵈ), way (K)

dirt (1ˢᵗ): mud (K), sand (1ˢᵗ), stain (4ᵗʰ)

disabled (3ʳᵈ): broken (1ˢᵗ), hurt (K), injured (5ᵗʰ), ruined (2ⁿᵈ), weakened (3ʳᵈ)

disagree (2ⁿᵈ): argue (3ʳᵈ), contrast (4ᵗʰ), disagree (2ⁿᵈ), oppose (3ʳᵈ), vary (4ᵗʰ)

disappoint (5ᵗʰ): depress (5ᵗʰ), fail (2ⁿᵈ), let down (K), sadden (2ⁿᵈ)

disaster (6ᵗʰ): calamity (6ᵗʰ), misadventure (4ᵗʰ), tragedy (5ᵗʰ). See accident.

disbelief (5ᵗʰ): challenge (4ᵗʰ), distrust (3ʳᵈ), doubt (5ᵗʰ), rejection (5ᵗʰ)

discard (6ᵗʰ): cast (2ⁿᵈ), dispose of (5ᵗʰ), junk (3ʳᵈ), reject (5ᵗʰ), rid (1ˢᵗ), scrap (3ʳᵈ), throw (1ˢᵗ), toss (2ⁿᵈ), trash (2ⁿᵈ)

discipline (6ᵗʰ): coach (4ᵗʰ), control (2ⁿᵈ), correct (3ʳᵈ), direct (1ˢᵗ), drill (2ⁿᵈ), educate (3ʳᵈ), guide (1ˢᵗ), harden (K), instruct (4ᵗʰ), punish (4ᵗʰ), rule (K), school (K), teach (1ˢᵗ), train (K)

discontinue (4ᵗʰ): abandon (4ᵗʰ), cease (3ʳᵈ), end (K), quit (1ˢᵗ), stop (K)

discourage (5ᵗʰ): A. caution (5ᵗʰ), hinder (6ᵗʰ), warn (3ʳᵈ) **B.** dishearten (5ᵗʰ), sadden (2ⁿᵈ)

discover (1ˢᵗ): determine (5ᵗʰ), find (K), locate (3ʳᵈ), notice (1ˢᵗ), recognize (3ʳᵈ), uncover (1ˢᵗ)

discuss (5ᵗʰ): chat (1ˢᵗ), confer (4ᵗʰ), converse (5ᵗʰ), go over (K), speak (1ˢᵗ), talk (K)

disease (5ᵗʰ): complaint (4ᵗʰ), condition (3ʳᵈ), illness (2ⁿᵈ), sickness (2ⁿᵈ)

disguise (5ᵗʰ): A. camouflage (5ᵗʰ), deceive (5ᵗʰ), hide (1ˢᵗ) **B.** cloak (4ᵗʰ), costume (4ᵗʰ), mask (2ⁿᵈ)

disgust (5ᵗʰ): aversion (4ᵗʰ), offend (4ᵗʰ), revolt (5ᵗʰ), shock (1ˢᵗ), sicken (2ⁿᵈ)

dish (1ˢᵗ): container (5ᵗʰ), dip (1ˢᵗ), ladle (6ᵗʰ), plate (K), platter (6ᵗʰ), serve (1ˢᵗ)

dishearten (5ᵗʰ): discourage (5ᵗʰ), deject (5ᵗʰ), depress (5ᵗʰ), dull (1ˢᵗ)

disintegrate (5ᵗʰ): decay (5ᵗʰ), fall apart (3ʳᵈ), rot (1ˢᵗ), spoil (4ᵗʰ)

disk (2ⁿᵈ)

dispense (5ᵗʰ): administer (6ᵗʰ), distribute (6ᵗʰ), divide (4ᵗʰ), give out (K), share (2ⁿᵈ)

display (3ʳᵈ): arrange (3ʳᵈ), exhibit (4ᵗʰ), present (3ʳᵈ), show (1ˢᵗ), stage (3ʳᵈ)

dispose (5ᵗʰ): A. cast (2ⁿᵈ), junk (3ʳᵈ), rid (1ˢᵗ), scrap (3ʳᵈ), throw away (1ˢᵗ), toss (2ⁿᵈ), trash (2ⁿᵈ) **B.** arrange (3ʳᵈ), assort (5ᵗʰ), order (1ˢᵗ), range (3ʳᵈ) **C.** affect (4ᵗʰ), bend (K), bias (6ᵗʰ)

disposition (5ᵗʰ): humor (4ᵗʰ), mood (3ʳᵈ), nature (1ˢᵗ), spirit (2ⁿᵈ), temper (4ᵗʰ)

dispute (6ᵗʰ): argue (3ʳᵈ), disagree (3ʳᵈ), discuss (5ᵗʰ), fight (K), oppose (3ʳᵈ), quarrel (4ᵗʰ)

distance (4ᵗʰ): A. length (2ⁿᵈ), measure (2ⁿᵈ), range (3ʳᵈ), reach (1ˢᵗ), remove (2ⁿᵈ), scope (6ᵗʰ), space (1ˢᵗ), stretch (4ᵗʰ) **B.** reserve (3ʳᵈ), restraint (5ᵗʰ) **C.** future (5ᵗʰ), horizon (4ᵗʰ)

distant (4ᵗʰ): A. apart (3ʳᵈ), far (1ˢᵗ), remote (5ᵗʰ), removed (2ⁿᵈ), separate (3ʳᵈ) **B.** cold (K), composed (4ᵗʰ), faint (3ʳᵈ), unemotional (4ᵗʰ), unfriendly (2ⁿᵈ)

distaste (6ᵗʰ): contempt (5ᵗʰ), disgust (5ᵗʰ), dislike (2ⁿᵈ), horror (4ᵗʰ), repulsion (6ᵗʰ)

distinctive (5ᵗʰ): individual (3ʳᵈ), one of a kind (K), separate (3ʳᵈ), special (2ⁿᵈ), unique (6ᵗʰ), unusual (3ʳᵈ)

distinguish (6ᵗʰ): brand (2ⁿᵈ), group (1ˢᵗ), individualize (4ᵗʰ), mark (1ˢᵗ), rate (1ˢᵗ), separate (3ʳᵈ), set apart (3ʳᵈ), sort out (2ⁿᵈ)

distress (5ᵗʰ): agony (5ᵗʰ), grief (5ᵗʰ), hardship (5ᵗʰ), misery (4ᵗʰ), sadness (1ˢᵗ), sorrow (4ᵗʰ), suffering (2ⁿᵈ), worry (1ˢᵗ)

distribute (6ᵗʰ): bestow (5ᵗʰ), deal (2ⁿᵈ), deliver (5ᵗʰ), give (K), hand out (K)

district (4ᵗʰ): area (3ʳᵈ), community (2ⁿᵈ), division (4ᵗʰ), neighborhood (2ⁿᵈ), region (4ᵗʰ)

disturb (6ᵗʰ): bother (2ⁿᵈ), disorder (2ⁿᵈ), disorganize (4ᵗʰ), interrupt (3ʳᵈ), move (K), shift (4ᵗʰ), trouble (1ˢᵗ), unsettle (2ⁿᵈ), upset (3ʳᵈ)

dive (1ˢᵗ): descend (6ᵗʰ), drop (K), fall (K), jump (K), leap (3ʳᵈ), plunge (4ᵗʰ)

divide (4ᵗʰ): cut (K), distribute (6ᵗʰ), part (1ˢᵗ), separate (3ʳᵈ), sort (1ˢᵗ), split (4ᵗʰ)

divorce (4ᵗʰ): divide (4ᵗʰ), part (1ˢᵗ), separate (3ʳᵈ), split (4ᵗʰ)

do (K): accomplish (2ⁿᵈ), achieve (5ᵗʰ), act (K), execute (5ᵗʰ), fix (1ˢᵗ), happen (1ˢᵗ), make (K), manage (4ᵗʰ), perform (4ᵗʰ), satisfy (3ʳᵈ), work (K)

dock (1ˢᵗ): A. moor (5ᵗʰ), park (1ˢᵗ) **B.** pier (4ᵗʰ), wharf (5ᵗʰ)

doctor (1ˢᵗ): A. healer (3ʳᵈ), physician (5ᵗʰ), surgeon (5ᵗʰ) **B.** fix (1ˢᵗ), heal (3ʳᵈ), repair (4ᵗʰ), treat (2ⁿᵈ)

does (1ˢᵗ): A. acts (K), commits (4ᵗʰ), executes (5ᵗʰ), performs (4ᵗʰ), practice (1ˢᵗ) **B.** mimic (6ᵗʰ) **C.** suffice (6ᵗʰ), suit (1ˢᵗ)

doesn't (1ˢᵗ)

dog (K)

doing (1ˢᵗ): achieving (5ᵗʰ), action (1ˢᵗ), deed (1ˢᵗ), feat (1ˢᵗ), working (K)

doll (K): figure (1ˢᵗ), girl (K)

dolphin (1ˢᵗ)

domicile (5th): abode (5th), dwelling (4th), home (K), house (K), location (3rd), place (1st), shelter (4th)

dominant (5th): A. main (3rd), major (3rd), paramount (5th), primary (5th), uppermost (4th) **B.** aggressive (6th), boss (K), commanding (2nd), controlling (2nd), ruling (2nd)

dominate (5th): boss (K), command (2nd), control (2nd), rule (K)

done (1st): complete (3rd), finished (1st), over (K), through (1st)

donkey (K)

don't (1st)

door (K): entrance (3rd), entry (3rd), gate (1st), opening (K)

doorway (2nd): entrance (3rd), entry (3rd), gate (1st), opening (K)

dope (1st): A. dumb (1st), dummy (1st), foolish (2nd), stupid (4th) **B.** drugs (1st)

dormitory (5th): apartment (1st), bedroom (3rd)

dose (1st): measure (2nd), portion (4th), quantity (4th)

dot (K): dab (1st), drop (K), point (1st), speck (4th), spot (1st)

double (3rd): A. by two (K), pair (1st), twice (3rd) **B.** duplicate (6th)

doubt (1st): A. question (1st), suspect (5th) **B.** concern (3rd), fear (1st), suspicion (4th)

doubtful (1st): questionable (3rd), suspect (5th), suspicious (4th), uncertain (2nd), undecided (1st)

dough (5th): A. money (K) **B.** batter (1st), paste (1st)

down (K): A. bleak (4th), blue (K), gloomy (3rd), idle (4th), ill (1st), sad (K), sick (K), unhappy (1st) **B.** below (1st), beneath (1st), low (K), under (K)

doughnut (2nd)

dove (K)

down (K)

downhearted (5th): blue (K), depressed (6th), gloomy (3rd), sad (K), unhappy (1st)

downstairs (2nd)

downtown (2nd)

Dr. (K)

drag (3rd): A. carry (K), draw (K), haul (4th), pull (K), tow (1st) **B.** lag (1st), limp along (5th), trail (2nd)

dragon (1st)

drain (5th): clear (2nd), draw off (1st), empty (3rd), exhaust (4th), reduce (3rd), sap (1st), take (K)

drake (5th)

drama (5th): play (K), skit (3rd), theater (3rd), tragedy (5th)

dramatize (5th): act (K), stage (3rd)

drape (5th): cloak (4th), cover (1st), curtain (5th), hang (2nd), hide (1st)

draught (6th): drink (1st), measure (2nd)

draw (K): A. deadlock (3rd), tie (1st) **B.** cartoon (2nd), outline (4th), sketch (5th), trace (3rd) **C.** attract (5th), lure (5th), pull (K)

dread (6th): alarm (3rd), fear (1st), horror (4th), panic (1st), worry (1st)

dream (K): daydream (2nd), fantasy (6th), idealize (3rd), plan (1st), think (1st), vision (4th)

dress (K): A. clothe (1st), deck (1st), put on (K) **B.** attire (6th), clothing (1st), costume (4th), garment (4th), outfit (2nd)

dresser (2nd): cabinet (4th), chest (2nd), closet (2nd)

drift (2nd): A. current (3rd), flow (1st), progress (4th), run (K), tend (K) **B.** adrift (6th), aim (3rd), drifting (2nd), goal (4th), intent (5th), meaning (1st)

drill (2nd): A. exercise (1st), practice (1st), test (3rd) **B.** coach (4th), teach (1st), train (K) **C.** bore (2nd), grind (4th), pierce (4th), punch (4th)

drink (1st): consume (4th), draw (K), gulp (1st), sip (1st), swallow (1st)

drip (2nd): drop (K), leak (6th), mist (1st), seep (4th)

drive (K): A. ride (K), take (K), taxi (1st) **B.** energy (4th), power (1st), spirit (2nd) **C.** aim (3rd), control (2nd), move (K), push (1st), urge (4th)

droop (5th): curve (3rd), drop (K), fade (1st), fall (K), hang (2nd), sag (1st), sink (3rd), wilt (4th), wither (5th)

drop (K): A. descend (6th), dive (1st), fall (K), lower (1st), plunge (4th), sink (3rd), tumble (4th) **B.** abandon (4th), desert (1st), leave (1st), unload (2nd) **C.** bead (K), bubble (2nd)

dropped (1st)

drove (1st): cattle (3rd), group (1st), herd (2nd), pack (1st). See drive.

drown (1st): descend (6th), flood (2nd), sink (3rd), submerge (5th), swamp (4th)

drug (1st): A. chemical (4th), dope (1st), medicine (4th), narcotic (4th) **B.** blunt (6th), dull (1st), poison (3rd)

drum (1st): A. barrel (4th), keg (1st), tom-tom (1st) **B.** beat (1st), pound (2nd), tap (K)

dry (1st): arid (6th), baked (1st), bare (3rd), hard (K), powdery (3rd)

dubious (6th): doubtful (5th), questionable (2nd), uncertain (2nd), unsure (K), vague (5th)

duck (K): A. avoid (3rd), dodge (3rd), hide (1st) **B.** dip (1st), dive (1st), dunk (3rd), submerge (5th)

due (2nd): earned (2nd), fit (K), in for (K), merited (4th), needed (1st), owed (3rd), payable (K), required (2nd), rightful (2nd)

dull (1st): A. blunt (6th) **B.** boring (2nd), lazy (4th), monotonous (5th), slow (1st), stupid (4th), tiring (2nd)

dumb (1st): quiet (K), silent (3rd), speechless (2nd)

dummy (1st): doll (K), figure (1st), model (3rd)

dump (2nd): discard (6th), reject (5th), throw out (1st), toss (2nd), trash (2nd), unload (2nd)

dumpling (4th)

dune (5th): hill (K), pile (1st), sand (1st)

dungeon (5th): cell (1st), cellar (1st), chamber (5th), prison (3rd)

duplicate (6th): A. copy (3rd), double (3rd), reproduce (4th) **B.** doubled (3rd), reproduction (5th), similar (4th)

durable (6th): enduring (4th), lasting (1st), permanent (5th), stable (4th), steady (3rd), strong (K)

during (1st): at the same time (1st), meanwhile (3rd), through (1st), throughout (2nd), while (1st)

dusk (5th): afternoon (1st), dark (K), dim (1st), end of day (K), evening (1st), obscure (6th), sunset (1st)

dust (2nd): dirt (1st), earth (1st), loam (4th), sand (1st)

duty (1st): A. assignment (5th), job (K), profession (5th), task (3rd), work (K) **B.** care (K), charge (2nd), obligation (6th), responsibility (4th)

dwarf (4th): A. midget (4th) **B.** overpower (3rd), reduce (3rd), stunt (6th)

dwell (4th): live (1st), lodge (4th), remain (1st), reside (5th), settle (2nd), stay (1st)

dwelling (4th): abode (5th), domicile (5th), home (K), house (K), residence (5th)

dye (2nd): A. change color (2nd), decorate (3rd) **B.** color (K), shade (2nd), tint (5th), tone (3rd)

dynamic (5th): active (3rd), alive (3rd), brisk (6th), forceful (2nd), powerful (2nd), vital (5th)

dynamite (6th): A. terrific (5th), wonderful (1st) **B.** explosive (3rd), great (K), powerful (2nd), strong (K)

each (K): all (K), any (K), every (K), individual (3rd), separate (3rd)

eager (5th): alert (5th), animated (6th), anxious (4th), bright (1st), enthusiastic (4th), excited (4th), hopeful (K), in a hurry (1st), inspired (4th), lively (5th), wishful (K)

eagle (1st)

ear (1st)

earl (4th): gentleman (3rd), noble (3rd)

early (1st): A. ancient (3rd), antique (6th), original (3rd), previous (5th) **B.** ahead (1st), before (K), immediate (3rd), soon (K), too soon (K)

earn (2nd): deserve (4th), gain (2nd), get (K), make (K), merit (4th), obtain (5th), rate (1st), win (K)

earnest (4th): concentrated (5th), dedicated (6th), determined (5th), devoted (5th), grave (3rd), intense (6th), passionate (6th), serious (4th), sincere (3rd), sober (4th), solemn (5th)

earth (1st): A. globe (4th), planet (4th), sphere (6th), world (1st) **B.** one world (1st), people (K), the whole world (1st), world (1st) **C.** clay (1st), dirt (1st), ground (1st), land (K), loam (4th), mud (1st)

earthenware (5th): clay (1st), pottery (4th)

earthquake (5th): earth tremor (6th), shock (1st)

ease (3rd): A. capability (4th), skill (2nd) **B.** aid (2nd), calm (3rd), clear (2nd), help (K), lessen (3rd), lighten (K), reduce (3rd), relax (4th), relieve (4th), rest (1st), smooth (3rd) **C.** calm (3rd), comfort (3rd), content (3rd), effortless (2nd), grace (3rd), leisure (5th), peace (1st), rest (1st), smooth (2nd)

east (1st)

Easter (K)

easy (K): breeze (4th), cinch (6th), clear (2nd), comfortable (3rd), free (K), gentle (3rd), loose (3rd), no problem (1st), no sweat (3rd), obvious (5th), restful (2nd), simple (2nd), uncompli-cated (6th)

eat (K): bite (1st), chew (1st), consume (4th), crunch (4th), devour (5th), dine (1st), feast (1st), gobble up (1st), gulp down (1st), nibble (4th), snack (2nd), swallow (1st), wolf (K)

eating (1st)

eaves (6th): edges (1st), gutter (6th), rims (1st), roof (1st)

echo (4th): A. copy (1st), mimic (6th), mock (4th), repeat (4th), restate (2nd), return (1st) **B.** fake (1st), imitation (5th), mirror (4th)

eclipse (5th): cloud (1st), conceal (4th), cover (1st), darken (1st), dim (1st), hide (1st), mask (2nd), screen (1st), shadow (3rd)

ecotourism (5th): tourism involving travel to areas of ecological interest for the purpose of learning about the environment

ecology (5th): A. the science of the relationships between organisms and their environments; also called bio-nomics. **B.** the relationship between organisms and their environment

ecosystem (5th): an area comprised of organisms and the environment functioning as a unit

economy (4th): business (2nd), fi-nance (4th)

ecstasy (6th): delight (3rd), excite-ment (4th), happiness (K), joy (1st), paradise (4th), pleasure (2nd), rapture (6th), thrill (4th)

eddy (6th): circle (K), current (3rd), rotate (4th), spin (1st), whirl (4th), whirlpool (4th)

edge (1st): advantage (3rd), border (1st), boundary (4th), brink (6th), end (K), frame (3rd), head start (1st), limit (3rd), rim (1st)

edit (3rd): adapt (4th), change (2nd), revise (6th), rewrite (2nd)

educate (3rd): acquaint (4th), coach (4th), inform (5th), instruct (4th), pre-pare (1st), train (K)

education (3rd): development (5th), direction (1st), information (5th), in-struction (4th), schooling (1st), teach-ing (1st), training (1st)

eel (K)

effect (3rd): A. accomplish (2nd), achieve (5th), follow (1st) **B.** conse-quence (4th), feeling (K), impression (5th), product (4th), result (2nd)

effective (4th): in order (1st), useful (2nd), working (1st)

effort (2nd): achievement (5th), act (K), action (1st), activity (3rd), energy (4th), exertion (6th), muscle (4th), try (K), work (K)

egg (K): A. seed (1st) **B.** provoke (6th), push (1st), urge (4th)

egret (3rd)

eight (K)

eighteen (1st)

eighty (1st)

either (2nd): one or the other (1st)

ejaculate (6th): call out (K), expel (6th), fire (K)

elaborate (5th): A. complete (3rd), complicated (6th), decorated (3rd), detailed (5th), elegant (5th) **B.** amplify (6th), develop (5th), enlarge (5th), expand (5th), explain (2nd), improve (3rd), increase (3rd), polish (4th), refine (6th)

elastic (6th): flexible (6th), springy (1st), stretchy (4th)

elbow (4th): A. bend (K), crazy bone (4th), corner (2nd), fold (1st), funny bone (1st) **B.** bulldoze (1st), bump (2nd), hit (K), push (1st), shove (5th)

elder (5th): older (1st)

elderly (5th): ancient (3rd), mature (5th), old (K)

elect (3rd): A. exclusive (6th), special (2nd) **B.** choose (3rd), pick (1st), select (4th), vote (2nd)

electric (3rd): exciting (4th), moving (K), rousing (4th), stirring (3rd), thrilling (4th)

electricity (3rd)

electron (4th)

electronic (4th): battery powered (5th), electric powered (3rd), mechanical (5th)

elegant (5th): choice (3rd), elaborate (5th), excellent (1st), exquisite (6th), fine (1st), lovely (1st), noble (3rd), rare (4th), simple (2nd)

element (3rd): detail (5th), feature (3rd), fragment (6th), ingredient (4th), item (5th), member (1st), part (1st), piece (1st), portion (4th), section (4th), unit (5th)

elephant (K)

elevate (2nd): arise (4th), ascent (4th), enrich (6th), improve (3rd), lift (1st), rise (1st)

elevation (4th): altitude (5th), height (4th), hill (K), mountain (2nd), peak (4th)

elevator (2nd): lift (1st)

elf (1st): brownie (2nd), fairy (4th), goblin (4th), gnome (6th)

eliminate (5th): abolish (5th), do away with (K), drop (K), erase (2nd), exclude (6th), get rid of (1st), put an end to (K)

e-mail (4th): messages sent over a computer network such as the Internet

elk (K)

elm (2nd)

else (1st): or (K), other (1st)

elsewhere (4th): another place (1st), not here (K), there (1st)

embrace (4th): accept (3rd), adopt (3rd), cuddle (5th), hug (1st), nuzzle (1st), snuggle (5th), squeeze (5th), welcome (1st)

embarrass (5th): distress (5th), fluster (6th), make uncomfortable (3rd), shame (3rd)

embarrassed (5th): A. ashamed (4th), ill at ease (3rd), timid (5th) **B.** bother (2nd), upset (3rd)

emblem (5th): badge (5th), banner (3rd), crest (4th), flag (3rd), mark (1st), representation (4th), seal (K), sign (1st), symbol (5th)

embryo (4th): developing (5th), seed (1st), unborn (1st)

embroider (5th): add to (K), decorate (3rd), elaborate (5th), needlework (3rd), sew (2nd)

emerge (5th): appear (2nd), arise (4th), begin (K), come out (K), develop (5th), exit (3rd), happen (1st), loom (5th), show (1st), start (1st)

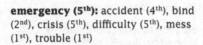

emergency (5th): accident (4th), bind (2nd), crisis (5th), difficulty (5th), mess (1st), trouble (1st)

emigrant (6th): alien (5th), foreigner (5th)

eminent (6th): celebrated (4th), elevated (2nd), famous (2nd), honorable (1st), honored (1st), noble (3rd), noted (1st), outstanding (2nd), renowned (6th), respected (2nd)

emission (5th)

emotion (4th): affection (4th), feeling (K), love (K), passion (6th)

emperor (4th): king (1st), ruler (2nd)

emphasize (5th): accent (6th), stress (6th)

emphatic (6th): bold (2nd), clear (2nd), critical (5th), earnest (4th), important (1st), intense (6th), plain (2nd), strong (K), urgent (6th)

empire (4th): kingdom (3rd), nation (2nd)

employ (5th): apply (2nd), hire (3rd), out to work (K), sign (1st), use (K)

empress (4th): queen (K)

empty (3rd): abandoned (4th), blank (4th), hollow (3rd), lacking (1st), unreal (1st), vacant (6th), void (6th)

enable (4th): aid (2nd), allow (2nd), assist (4th), energize (4th), equip (5th), establish (3rd), help (K), let (K), qualify (4th), strengthen (1st)

enamel (6th): A. coat (1st), decorate (3rd), finish (1st), paint (2nd), plate (1st) **B.** coating (1st), glaze (6th), polish (4th)

enchant (6th): bewitch (3rd), captivate (3rd), catch (1st), charm (3rd), fascinate (5th), win (K)

encircle (5th): circle (K), embrace (4th), encompass (4th), enclose (4th), ring (1st), surround (3rd)

enclose (4th): cage (1st), close (K), contain (5th), encircle (5th), fence (1st), imprison (6th), include (3rd), insert (6th), pen (1st), wall (K)

encode (5th): hide (1st), puzzle (4th), symbolize (5th)

encounter (4th): A. greeting (3rd), joining (3rd), meeting (K), struggle (1st) **B.** brush (2nd), bump (2nd), confront (5th), face (K), join (3rd), meet (K)

encourage (4th): animate (6th), assure (3rd), cheer (3rd), excite (4th), fire up (K), influence (5th), inspire (4th), motivate (6th), reassure (6th), root (3rd), support (4th), urge (4th)

encrust (6th): bread (2nd), cover (1st)

encyclopedia (5th)

end (K): A. aim (3rd), close (K), completion (3rd), conclusion (3rd), effect (3rd), ending (K), extreme (5th), finish (1st), goal (4th), limit (3rd), outcome (4th), purpose (1st), reason (1st), result (2nd) **B.** abandon (4th), complete (3rd), conclude (3rd), destroy (2nd), die (2nd), finish (1st), limit (3rd), quit (1st), settle (2nd), stop (K), term (3rd), terminate (6th)

endanger (6th): chance (2nd), dare (2nd), risk (4th)

endeavor (4th): A. attempt (2nd), labor (2nd), striving (5th), struggle (1st), work (K) **B.** attempt (2nd), effort (2nd), strive (5th), struggle (1st), try (K), work (K)

endow (6th): award (5th), bestow (5th), confer (4th), contribute (4th), enrich (6th), equip (5th), give (K), grant (2nd), invest (5th), present (K), provide (3rd), supply (1st)

endure (4th): allow (2nd), bear (K), continue (2nd), encounter (4th), hold (1st), last (K), meet (K), permit (3rd), persist (5th), remain (2nd), stand (K), stay (1st), suffer (2nd), survive (3rd), wait (K)

enemy (2nd): attacker (3rd), foe (4th), hostile (4th), opponent (5th), rival (4th)

energy (4th): action (3rd), bounce (6th), calorie (3rd), enthusiasm (4th), fire (K), force (1st), glow (1st), heat (1st), muscle (4th), passion (6th), power (1st), push (1st), spirit (2nd), strength (2nd)

enforce (5th): boss (K), bully (1st), cause (2nd), compel (3rd), control (2nd), demand (5th), direct (1st), force (1st), fulfill (4th), implement (6th), maintain (4th), make (K), perform (4th), pressure (4th), realize (2nd), require (1st), sanction (6th)

engage (5th): agree (2nd), attract (5th), battle (2nd), catch (1st), charm (3rd), commit (4th), contest (4th), contract (3rd), draw (K), encounter (4th), entertain (4th), fascinate (5th), hold (1st), interest (1st), meet (K), occupy (3rd), pledge (5th), promise (1st), pull (K), win (K)

engine (3rd): machine (1st), motor (4th)

engineer (4th): accomplish (2nd), achieve (5th), arrange (3rd), conduct (3rd), design (5th), direct (1st), do (K), guide (1st), handle (2nd), lead (1st), make (K), manage (4th), perform (4th), plan (1st), produce (2nd), run (K), steer (5th)

English (1st)

engrave (5th): brand (2nd), carve (4th), cut (K), fix (1st), imprint (4th), line (K), lodge (4th), mark (1st), print (1st), stamp (2nd)

enjoy (2nd): appreciate (5th), like (K), love (K), relish (6th)

enlarge (5th): add (K), develop (5th), double (3rd), expand (5th), extend (4th), grow (K), heighten (4th), increase (3rd), lengthen (2nd), magnify (3rd), mature (5th), multiply (2nd), spread (2nd), stretch (4th), swell (3rd), thicken (2nd), widen (1st)

enlist (6th): compel (3rd), employ (5th), engage (5th), hire (3rd), join (3rd), obtain (5th), pull in (K), recruit (6th), secure (3rd), volunteer (5th)

enliven (6th): animate (6th), brighten (1st), cheer (3rd), energize (4th), excite (4th), fire up (K), inspire (4th), refresh (6th), renew (4th), restore (5th), revive (6th), rouse (4th), stir (3rd), thrill (4th), vitalize (5th), waken (1st)

enormous (4th): gigantic (3rd), huge (1st), immense (4th), mammoth (5th), massive (5th), monstrous (5th), vast (4th)

enough (1st): abundant (5th), ample (5th), plenty (1st), sufficient (3rd)

enrage (6th): anger (1st), fire up (K), incense (5th), madden (2nd), provoke (6th)

enraged (6th): angry (1st), cross (1st), fuming (3rd), mad (K), violent (5th)

enrich (6th): better (K), brighten (1st), contribute (4th), decorate (3rd), develop (5th), endow (6th), improve (3rd), make rich (K), polish (4th), refine (6th), sharpen (1st)

enter (1st): admit (4th), begin (K), board (1st), go in (K), insert (6th), introduce (5th), intrude (6th), invade (5th), penetrate (5th), pierce (4th), start (1st)

enterprise (5th): adventure (3rd), attempt (2nd), business (2nd), cause (2nd), company (2nd), corporation (4th), courage (4th), effort (2nd), energy (4th), feat (1st), force (1st), plan (1st), power (1st), project (4th), push (1st), store (K), struggle (1st), task (3rd), work (K)

entertain (4th): absorb (5th), amuse (4th), charm (3rd), clown (1st), engage (5th), enliven (6th), feed (1st), house (K), interest (1st), joke (1st), occupy (3rd), please (K), shelter (4th), welcome (1st)

enthusiasm (4th): abandon (4th), animation (6th), confidence (6th), delight (3rd), determination (5th), ecstasy (6th), emotion (4th), energy (4th), excitement (4th), fire (K), hope (K), life (1st), passion (6th), spirit (2nd), vigor (5th), zeal (6th)

entire (3rd): absolute (3rd), all (K), clear (2nd), complete (3rd), extended (4th), full (K), pure (3rd), sheer (5th), total (2nd), whole (1st)

entitle (5th): address (K), call (K), enable (4th), label (3rd), let (K), license (5th), owe (2nd), qualify (4th), term (3rd)

entrance (3rd): A. attract (5th), charm (3rd), dazzle (5th), delight (3rd), enchant (6th), interest (1st), please (K) **B.** access (6th), admission (4th), approach (3rd), beginning (2nd), door (K), drive (K), entry (2nd), gate (1st), hall (1st), invasion (5th), lane (4th), opening (K), path (1st), penetration (5th), porch (3rd), ramp (6th), road (K), route (4th), start (1st), way (K)

entrap (3rd): bait (3rd), catch (1st), fool (2nd), net (3rd), reveal (4th), trap (1st), trick (1st)

envelope (5th): case (2nd), cloak (4th), container (5th), cover (1st), mask (2nd), wrap (3rd)

environment (6th): atmosphere (4th), background (4th), conditions (3rd), habitat (6th), mood (3rd), setting (2nd), surroundings (3rd)

envy (4th): A. jealousy (5th), resentment (5th), rivalry (4th) **B.** covet (6th), crave (6th), desire (5th), resent (5th), want (K), wish for (K)

Eocene (5th): of or belonging to the geologic time, rock series, or sedimentary deposits of the second epoch of the Tertiary Period

epidemic (4th)

episode (6th): action (1st), adventure (3rd), chapter (3rd), division (4th), event (3rd), experience (4th), happening (1st), scene (1st), story (K)

Epoch (5th): a unit of geologic time that is a division of a period

equal (2nd): A. match (3rd), partner (5th), peer (1st), rival (4th), similar (4th), steady (3rd) **B.** alike (1st), equivalent (6th), identical (6th), like (K), same (K)

equator (4th): center (2nd)

equip (5th): arm (K), prepare (1st), provide (3rd), stock (1st), store (K), supply (1st)

equipment (5th): furniture (3rd), gear (1st), machinery (2nd), material (5th), supplies (1st), tools (1st), utensils (6th), weapons (4th)

equinox (5th)

equivalent (6th): alike (1st), equal (2nd), identical (6th), like (K), match (3rd), same (K)

era (6th): age (1st), day (K), period (2nd), reign (4th), rule (K), time (1st)

erase (2nd): abolish (5th), cancel (6th), eliminate (5th), remove (2nd), rub out (1st)

ere (4th): before (K)

erect (4th): A. elevated (2nd), standing (1st), straight (3rd), tall (K) **B.** assemble (4th), build (1st), construct (3rd), create (3rd), elevate (2nd), form (1st), make (K), raise (1st)

erode (5th): corrode (6th), eat away (K), wear (1st)

err (6th): mistake (1st)

errand (4th): assignment (5th), duty (1st), job (K), task (3rd), trip (1st), work (K)

error (4th): err (6th), flaw (2nd), mistake (1st)

erupt (4th): blow up (1st), ejaculate (6th), explode (3rd)

escape (1st): A. daydream (2nd), exit (3rd), flight (2nd), freedom (3rd), opening (K), release (5th), vacation (2nd) **B.** flee (5th), fly (K), run (K)

escort (5th): A. assistant (4th), guide (1st), leader (1st), protector (4th) **B.** accompany (3rd), conduct (3rd), direct (1st), guide (2nd), lead (1st)

Eskimo (3rd)

especially (4th): exceptional (3rd), mainly (3rd), mostly (1st), particularly (4th), special (2nd), unusually (3rd)

essay (5th): article (2nd), attempt (2nd), effort (2nd), paper (K), struggle (1st), theme (4th), try (K),

work (K)

essential (6th): absolute (3rd), basic (5th), fundamental (4th), important (1st), main (3rd), necessary (1st)

establish (3rd): build (1st), create (3rd), fix (1st), form (1st), found (K), install (6th), make (K), organize (4th), set (K), settle (2nd), start (1st)

estate (4th): home (K), land (K), mansion (5th), property (3rd), residence (5th), will (K)

esteem (5th): A. approval (4th), favor (1st), love (K), regard (4th), respect (2nd) **B.** admire (5th), appreciate (5th), honor (K), regard (4th), respect (2nd), treasure (4th), value (2nd)

estimate (5th): figure (2nd), guess (1st), judge (1st), value (2nd)

et cetera (6th): and (K), so forth (2nd), so on (K)

etc. (6th): See et cetera.

eternal (4th): constant (4th), endless (1st), fixed (1st), immortal (4th), infinite (5th), perpetual (6th), permanent (5th)

E.U. (5th): European Community

European Community: (5th) European nations that have made agreements to work closely together politically and economically

evacuate (5th): leaving a place in an orderly fashion; especially for protection

eve (5th): beginning (1st), evening (1st), night before (1st)

even (1st): balanced (3rd), constant (4th), equal (2nd), flat (2nd), horizontal (6th), level (3rd), like (4th), same (K), similar (4th), smooth (2nd), stable (4th), steady (3rd), straight (3rd), uniform (1st)

evening (1st): eve (5th), night (1st), p.m. (6th), sundown (K), sunset (1st)

event (3rd): act (K), action (1st), deed (1st), episode (6th), experience (4th), happening (1st), incident (5th), outcome (4th), result (2nd)

eventually (5th): finally (3rd), last (K), ultimately (6th)

ever (K): always (K), constantly (4th), eternally (4th), forever (3rd)

evergreen (4th)

every (K): all (K), any (1st), each (K)

everybody (3rd): all (K), everyone (1st)

everyone (1st): all (K), everybody (1st)

everything (1st): all (K)

everywhere (2nd)

evidence (5th): demonstrate (6th), facts (1st), ground (1st), information (5th), proof (1st), show (1st), support (4th)

evident (5th): apparent (3rd), clear (2nd), exposed (4th), obvious (5th), plain (2nd)

evil (3rd): A. mischief (4th), misery (5th), sin (1st), wickedness (4th) **B.** bad (K), dark (K), foul (4th), horrible (1st), mean (1st), villainous (5th), wicked (4th)

evolution (6th): creation (3rd), change (2nd), development (5th), growth (K)

exact (2nd): A. command (2nd), demand (5th), require (2nd) **B.** accurate (6th), careful (K), correct (3rd), flawless (2nd), precise (5th), right (K)

exaggerate (6th): boast (4th), brag (3rd), elaborate (5th), enrich (6th), stretch (4th)

examine (5th): inspect (5th), investigate (5th), observe (3rd), question (1st), research (5th)

example (2nd): case (2nd), ideal (3rd), illustration (4th), model (3rd), pattern (3rd), sample (5th), specimen (5th), standard (3rd)

excavate (5th): dig (1st)

exceed (4th): dominate (5th), eclipse (5th), excel (6th), pass (K), surpass (6th)

excel (6th): eclipse (5th), exceed (4th), pass (K), surpass (6th)

excellent (1st): great (K), ideal (3rd), perfect (3rd), outstanding (2nd), superior (4th), terrific (5th), wonderful (1st)

except (1st): but (K), excluding (6th), however (3rd), minus (1st), not (K)

excess (5th): beyond (1st), overflow (5th), surplus (6th), too much (1st)

exchange (4th): trade (2nd)

excite (4th): agitate (5th), animate (6th), arouse (4th), awaken (3rd), egg on (K), encourage (4th), energize (4th), inspire (4th), provoke (6th), rally (5th), revive (6th), rouse (4th), spark (3rd), stir (3rd)

exclaim (3rd): cry (K), shout (1st)

exclude (6th): bar (3rd), eliminate (5th), forbid (4th), forget (1st), eliminate (5th), prevent (3rd), reject (5th), remove (2nd), rule out (K), shut out (1st)

exclusive (6th): choosy (3rd), elect (3rd), elegant (5th), fancy (3rd), individual (3rd), particular (4th), select (4th), single (3rd), special (2nd)

excuse (3rd): acquit (6th), alibi (6th), apology (6th), claim (2nd), explanation (2nd), forgive (2nd), pardon (4th), reason (2nd)

execute (5th): achieve (5th), cause (2nd), complete (3rd), engineer (4th), finish (1st), manage (4th), perform (4th), produce (2nd)

executive (5th): boss (K), director (1st), head (K), leader (1st), manager (4th), president (1st), principal (3rd)

exercise (1st): A. movement (2nd), sports (1st), work (K) **B.** drill (2nd), employ (5th), practice (1st), use (K), utilize (6th), work out (K)

exert (6th): attempt (2nd), employ (5th), labor (2nd), struggle (1st), sweat (3rd), trouble (1st), use (K), work (K)

exhaust (4th): drain (5th), fatigue (5th), tire (2nd), weary (4th)

exhibit (4th): A. display (3rd), show (1st) **B.** demonstrate (6th), display (3rd), expose (4th), parade (2nd), reveal (4th), show (1st)

exhilarate (6th): animate (6th), brighten (1st), cheer (3rd), encourage (4th), delight (3rd), energize (4th), enliven (6th), inspire (4th), revive (6th), thrill (4th)

exile (5th): ban (K), expel (6th), separate (3rd)

exist (3rd): be (K), breathe (1st), endure (4th), live (1st), remain (1st), survive (3rd)

exit (3rd): A. escape (1st), flee (5th), fly (K) **B.** departure (5th), door (K), gate (1st), leave (1st), opening (K), quit (1st), way out (K)

expand (5th): amplify (6th), enlarge (5th), fatten (1st), increase (3rd), multiply (2nd), spread (2nd), stretch (4th), swell (3rd)

expect (2nd): await (5th), hope (K), look (K)

expedition (4th): adventure (3rd), safari (4th), trip (1st)

expel (6th): exile (5th), throw out (1st)

expense (3rd): amount (2nd), charge (2nd), cost (1st), fee (4th), price (K), rate (1st)

experience (4th): A. adventure (3rd), happening (1st), life (1st) **B.** endure (4th), episode (6th), live (1st), try (K), undergo (2nd), understand (1st)

experiment (3rd): explore (4th), question (1st), sample (5th), try (1st)

expert (5th): artist (2nd), authority (3rd), genius (4th), knowledgeable (3rd), master (1st)

expire (6th): complete (3rd), conclude (3rd), die (2nd), end (K), fail (2nd), finish (1st), pass (K), run out (K), stop (K), terminate (6th)

explain (2nd): excuse (3rd), discuss (5th), interpret (5th), justify (3rd), teach (1st)

explode (3rd): blow up (1st), dynamite (6th)

exploit (6th): A. use (K) **B.** achievement (5th), act (K), deed (1st), feat (1st)

explore (4th): examine (5th), experiment (3rd), inspect (5th), search (1st)

export (5th): send (K), ship (1st)

expose (4th): display (3rd), exhibit (4th), find (K), parade (2nd), reveal (4th), show (1st), uncover (1st)

express (5th): air (K), announce (3rd), say (K), speak (1st), specific (5th), tell (K), utter (4th), voice (1st)

exquisite (6th): delicate (5th), elegant (5th), intense (6th), perfect (3rd), rare (4th)

extend (4th): draw out (K), enlarge (5th), expand (5th), lengthen (2nd), spread (2nd), stretch (4th)

exterminate (6th): abolish (5th), erase (2nd), kill (1st), remove (2nd)

extinct (5th): dead (1st), exterminated (6th), gone (1st), lost (K), nonexistent (4th), past (1st), vanished (3rd)

extra (1st): more (K), plus (1st), surplus (6th)

extraordinary (5th): choice (3rd), rare (4th), special (2nd), strange (1st), surprising (1st)

extraterrestrial (5th): a term to describe anything that does not come from earth

extravagant (6th): absurd (6th), excessive (5th), extreme (5th), lavish (6th), silly (1st)

extreme (5th): excessive (5th), greatest (K), least (1st), most (1st), smallest (K), total (2nd)

extremist (5th): a person who holds extreme views

eye (K): see (K), study (2nd), watch (1st)

eyeglasses (4th): glasses (1st), spectacles (5th)

fable (5th): fiction (5th), myth (4th), story (K), tale (3rd)

fabric (5th): material (5th)

face (K): A. expression (5th), features (3rd), front (1st) **B.** confront (5th), encounter (4th), meet (K)

facility (5th): ease (3rd), factory (1st), plant (K)

fact (1st): certainty (1st), information (5th), reality (5th), truth (1st)

factor (5th): agent (5th), component (4th), element (3rd), ingredient (4th), instrument (3rd), part (1st)

factory (1st): facility (5th), plant (K), shop (1st)

faculty (6th): A. ability (3rd), gift (K), power (1st), talent (2nd) **B.** instructor (4th), teacher (1st)

fad (K): craze (4th), fashion (3rd), rage (4th), style (3rd), trend (2nd)

fade (1st): lessen (3rd), thin (2nd), vanish (3rd), wither (5th)

Fahrenheit (4th)

fail (2nd): fault (3rd), lose (K)

faint (3rd): A. fall (K), pass out (K) **B.** light (K), weak (3rd)

fair (1st): A. carnival (2nd), exhibit (4th), market (1st), show (1st) **B.** average (3rd), beautiful (1st), blond (5th), common (2nd), just (1st), light (K), medium (5th), ordinary (3rd), pale (3rd), pretty (1st)

fairy (4th): angel (4th), brownie (2nd), elf (1st), gnome (6th)

faith (3rd): belief (1st), church (K), conviction (4th), creed (6th), loyalty (5th), religion (4th), trust (1st)

fake (1st): A. cheat (3rd), fraud (6th) **B.** lie (1st), make up (1st), pretend (2nd), trick (1st)

falcon (3rd)

fall (K): A. autumn (3rd) **B.** drop (1st), sink (3rd)

false (3rd): deceit (5th), mistaken (1st), not true (K), untrue (1st), wrong (1st)

falter (3rd): hesitate (4th), pause (3rd), shake (1st), stumble (4th), waver (5th)

fame (3rd): celebrity (5th), glory (3rd), honor (1st), renown (6th)

familiar (3rd): close (K), common (2nd), intimate (5th), well-known (1st)

families (1st)

family (K): clan (5th), relatives (4th)

famine (6th): hunger (2nd), starvation (5th)

famous (2nd): celebrated (5th), renowned (6th), well-known (1st)

fan (K): follower (1st)

fancy (3rd): A. decorated (3rd), elaborate (5th), elegant (5th) **B.** dream (K), enjoy (2nd), like (K), love (K) **C.** fantasy (6th), whim (6th)

fang (5th): tooth (1st)

fantastic (6th): absurd (6th), extravagant (6th), extreme (5th), fanciful (4th), odd (4th), strange (1st)

far (1st): away (K), distant (4th), faraway (3rd), remote (5th)

faraway (3rd)

fare (3rd): A. cost (K), fee (4th), price (K) **B.** banquet (4th), food (K), menu (6th)

farm (K): cultivate (6th), grow (K), till (1st)

farmer (K): peasant (4th)

farming (1st): agriculture (4th), cultivation (6th), tilling (1st)

farther (3rd): beyond (1st), further (2nd), past (1st)

fascinate (5th): attract (5th), captivate (3rd), charm (3rd), enchant (6th), engage (5th)

fashion (3rd): A. fad (K), manner (2nd), method (2nd), rage (4th), trend (2nd) **B.** create (3rd), form (K), make (K), manufacture (3rd)

fast (1st): rapid (4th), speedy (3rd), swift (4th)

fasten (4th): add (K), attach (5th), bind (2nd), connect (3rd), fix (1st), join (3rd), link (5th), secure (3rd), tie (1st)

fat (1st): chubby (2nd), plump (6th), stout (4th)

fatal (4th): deadly (2nd)

fate (3rd): certainty (1st), destiny (5th), fortune (3rd)

father (K): dad (K), daddy (K), papa (1st)

fathom (6th): grasp (4th), plumb (5th), sound (1st), understand (1st)

fatigue (5th): drained (5th), exhaustion (4th), tiredness (2nd), weariness (4th)

fault (3rd): A. error (4th), flaw (2nd), mistake (1st), vice (4th) **B.** a point where the earth's surface can move (earthquake) usually at or near the boundaries of two continental plates

faultless (3rd): ideal (3rd), perfect (3rd), pure (3rd)

fauna (6th): animal (K), nature (2nd)

favor (1st): A. gift (K), good deed (1st), kindness (K), present (2nd) **B.** aid (2nd), assist (4th), encourage (4th), help (K), like (K), support (4th)

favorite (3rd): popular (3rd), preferred (3rd), selected (4th)

fax (4th): (short for facsimile) the communication between remote locations via the telephone system

fear (1st): alarm (3rd), dread (6th), fright (2nd), horror (4th), panic (1st)

fearful (1st): afraid (1st), frightened (2nd), scared (5th), shy (1st), timid (5th)

feast (1st): A. dine (1st), eat (K) **B.** banquet (4th), carnival (2nd), celebration (4th), meal (3rd)

feat (1st): achievement (5th), act (K), adventure (3rd), deed (1st), exploit (6th)

feather (2nd): pad (K), secure (3rd), soften (2nd)

feature (3rd): characteristic (6th), detail (5th), mark (1st), property (3rd), quality (4th), trait (6th)

feces (6th): bowels (4th), bowel movement (4th), dung (4th), excrement (6th)

February (1st)

fed (K): A. nourished (6th), provisioned (4th) **B.** filled (1st), furnished (4th), gave (K), provided (3rd), put in (K)

federal (4th): government (1st), national (2nd)

fee (4th): bill (1st), charge (2nd), cost (K), fare (3rd), pay (K), price (K), salary (3rd), wage (3rd)

feeble (4th): delicate (5th), fragile (6th), frail (6th), weak (3rd)

feed (1st): A. dine (1st), gratify (4th), graze (5th), nourish (6th), provision (4th) **B.** fill (K), furnish (4th), give (K), provide (3rd), put in (K)

feel (K): handle (2nd), pet (1st), touch (1st)

feeling (K): affection (4th), emotion (4th), hint (1st), impression (5th), passion (6th), pity (3rd), reaction (5th), sensation (5th), sympathy (4th), touch (1st)

feet (1st)

fell (1st)

fellow (1st): brother (1st), equal (2nd), friend (1st), male (4th), man (K), member (2nd), peer (1st), sister (1st)

female (4th): girl (K), lady (1st), woman (K)

fence (1st): A. cage (1st), pen (1st) **B.** cage (1st), enclose (4th), surround (3rd), wall (1st)

fend (6th): bar (3rd), defend (5th), fight (K), prevent (3rd)

ferret (5th): hunt (2nd), search (1st), seek (1st)

ferry (6th): A. boat (1st), ship (1st) **B.** carry (1st), transfer (5th)

fertile (5th): fruitful (2nd), productive (4th), rich (K), seeded (1st)

fertilizer (5th)

fervor (6th): delight (3rd), enthusiasm (4th), excitement (4th), passion (6th), zeal (6th)

festive (5th): decorated (3rd), happy (K), joyous (1st), merry (3rd)

festivity (5th): celebration (4th), party (K)

fetch (4th): capture (3rd), catch (1st), get (K), grab (4th), retrieve (6th)

fetish (5th): charm (3rd)

feud (6th): argument (3rd), disagreement (2nd), fight (K), quarrel (4th)

fever (4th): A. fire (K), heat (1st), temperature (4th) **B.** excitement (4th)

few (K): little (K), not many (K), scarce (4th), small (K), three (K)

fez (5th): cap (K), hat (K)

fib (1st): A. misrepresent (4th), withhold (1st) **B.** falsehood (4th), lie (2nd), story (K), untruth (2nd), tale (3rd)

fiber (3rd): component (4th), fabric (5th), material (5th), substance (5th), thread (2nd), weave (4th)

fiber-optics (4th): a system where light or image is transmitted by bunches of flexible glass or plastic fibers

fiction (5th): fable (5th), false (3rd), myth (4th), not real (1st), story (K), tale (3rd)

fiddle (4th): A. play (K), toy with (K) **B.** bow (1st), violin (4th)

fidelity (6th): allegiance (6th), devotion (5th), faith (3rd), loyalty (5th), steadiness (3rd)

field (2nd): area (3rd), domain (5th), park (1st), range (3rd), space (1st), territory (3rd)

fierce (4th): cruel (5th), grim (4th), harsh (5th), intense (6th), savage (5th), violent (5th), wild (2nd)

fiery (5th): A. blazing (1st), flaming (3rd), glowing (1st), heated (1st) **B.** eager (5th), fierce (4th), peppery (4th), spirited (2nd)

fife (5th): flute (5th), pipe (1st)

fifteen (1st):

fifth (1st):

fifty (1st):

fig (1st):

fight (K): attack (3rd), battle (2nd), combat (5th), conflict (4th), confront (5th), contest (4th), dispute (6th), match (3rd), war (1st)

figure (2nd): A. design (5th), form (1st), image (4th), outline (4th), picture (K), sculpture (4th), shape (1st) **B.** add (K), amount (2nd), body (1st), calculate (5th), cost (2nd), sum (1st), total (2nd)

filch (5th): lift (1st), rob (1st), steal (3rd), take (K), thieve (3rd)

file (1st): alphabetize (2nd), line up (K), organize (4th), rank (3rd), row (K), sort (2nd)

fill (K): crowd (2nd), feed (1st), furnish (4th), occupy (3rd), provide (3rd), supply (1st)

film (4th): base (1st), coat (1st), cover (1st), layer (4th), thin (2nd)

filter (5th): clean, drain (5th), screen (1st), strain (4th)

fin (1st):

final (3rd): closing (1st), end (K), last (K)

finance (1st): A. aid (2nd), fund (4th), pay for (K) **B.** banking (1st), cash (2nd), economics (4th), loan (4th), money (K)

find (K): discover (1st), get (K), locate (3rd), notice (1st)

finding (1st): award (5th), conclusion (3rd), decision (1st)

fine (1st): charge (2nd), delicate (5th), good (K), penalize (5th), pure (3rd), quality (4th), small (K), tiny (2nd)

finger (1st): identify (4th), point out (1st)

fingernail (4th)

fingerprint (5th)

finish (1st): accomplish (2nd), achieve (5th), attain (6th), close (K), complete (3rd), do (K), end (K)

fire (K): A. energy (4th), power (1st) **B.** blaze (1st), burn (3rd), flame (3rd), light (K), spark (3rd)

firecracker (5th)

fireman (K): fire fighter (1st)

fireworks (2nd): explosion (3rd), fire (K), storm (2nd)

firm (2nd): A. hard (K), solid (3rd), steady (3rd), stiff (3rd) **B.** business (2nd), company (2nd)

first (1st): beginning (2nd), best (K), earliest (1st), main (3rd), primary (5th), start (K), top (K)

fish (K): angle (3rd), cast (2nd), hunt for (2nd), look for (K), search for (1st)

fishing (1st)

fission (4th)

fist (2nd): grab (4th), grasp (4th), grip (4th), hand (K), hit (K), ram (K), seize (3rd)

fit (K): A. correct (3rd), proper (3rd) **B.** adapt (4th), adjust (5th), apt (5th), attack (3rd), change (2nd), healthy (1st), prepare (1st), ready (1st), spasm (6th), strong (K), suit (2nd)

fitness (3rd): good shape (1st), health (K), hearty (5th), vigor (5th)

fitting (2nd): appropriate (4th), correct (3rd), proper (3rd), right (K)

five (K)

fix (1st): adjust (5th), alter (4th), attach (5th), cement (4th), establish (3rd), fasten (4th), mend (1st), plight (6th), secure (3rd), set (K)

fixture (6th): device (4th), instrument (3rd)

fizz (5th): buzz (5th), hiss (3rd), swish (2nd)

flag (3rd): banner (3rd), colors (K), signal (4th), streamer (3rd)

flail (6th): beat (1st), fight (K), flounder (5th), thrash (4th), whip (4th)

flair (6th): ability (3rd), brilliance (4th), class (1st), gift (K), learning (3rd), skill (2nd), style (3rd), talent (2nd)

flake (1st): bit (1st), chip (5th), peel (2nd), skin (1st)

flame (3rd): blaze (1st), brilliance (4th), fire (K), glare (4th), gleam (1st), glow (1st), spark (3rd)

flamingo (5th)

flank (5th): border (1st), bound (2nd), curb (3rd), edge 1, side (K), wall (K)

flap (4th): edge (1st), fold (1st)

flare (6th): A. direct (1st), guide (1st), signal (4th) **B.** blaze (1st), burst (3rd), dart (1st), flame (3rd), flash (2nd), explode (3rd), glow (1st)

flash (2nd): blaze (1st), flame (3rd), flare (6th), glare (4th), gleam (1st), glitter (4th), spark (3rd)

flat (2nd): A. even (1st), level (3rd), smooth (2nd) **B.** apartment (1st), condo (1st), condominium (2nd), flat (2nd), rental (1st), room (K)

flatter (4th): compliment (5th), fawn (5th), glorify (3rd), praise (4th)

flavor (4th): taste (1st)

flaw (2nd): blemish (5th), fault (3rd), mark (1st), scar (5th), spot (1st), stain (4th)

flea (5th)

flee (5th): escape (2nd), fly (K), leave (1st), run (K), take off (1st)

fleece (6th): covering (1st), hide (1st), skin (1st), wool (3rd)

fleet (6th): fast (1st), quick (1st), rapid (4th), speedy (3rd), swift (4th)

flesh (3rd): animal (K), body (1st), physical (5th), skin (1st)

flew (1st)

flexible (6th): agile (6th), bendable (1st), elastic (6th), limber (4th), plastic (3rd), pliable (6th), springy (2nd)

flicker (5th): flame (3rd), flare (6th), flash (2nd), gleam (1st), glimmer (6th), glitter (4th), sparkle (5th), twinkle (4th), waver (5th)

flight (2nd): A. departure (5th), trip (1st) **B.** gliding (4th), sailing (1st), soaring (6th)

fling (6th): cast (2nd), hurl (5th), shoot (3rd), throw (1st), toss (2nd)

flint (5th): rock (K), stone (2nd)

flip (2nd): A. easy (K), light (K), pert (1st), tactless (6th) **B.** fling (6th), revolve (5th), toss (2nd), turn (1st), twist (1st)

flipper (4th): fin (1st), paddle (1st), turner (1st)

flirt (6th): pet (1st), play (K), tease (3rd), toy (K)

float (1st): drift (2nd), glide (4th), hover (3rd), rest on (1st), sail (1st), swim (K)

flock (2nd): assembly (4th), bunch (3rd), congregation (6th), crowd (2nd), group (1st), herd (2nd), swarm (4th)

flood (2nd): cover (1st), drown (1st), excess (5th), flow (1st), overflow (5th), stream (1st), tide (1st), waves (K)

floor (K): base (1st), bottom (1st), deck (1st), platform (4th)

flop (1st): drop (K), fall down (K), flounder (5th), limp (5th)

floppy disk (1st)

flora (6th): foliage (6th), greenery (3rd), plants (K)

floss (2nd): fiber (3rd), string (1st), thread (2nd),

floatation (6th)

flotsam (6th): debris (5th), pieces (1st)

flounder (5th): flail (6th), flop (1st), plunge (4th), struggle (1st), stumble (4th), trash (2nd), trip (1st),

tumble (4th)

flour (3rd)

flourish (4ᵗʰ): A. display (3ʳᵈ), shake (1ˢᵗ), show (1ˢᵗ), wave (1ˢᵗ) **B.** brandish (6ᵗʰ), grow (K), succeed (2ⁿᵈ), thrive (6ᵗʰ)

flow (1ˢᵗ): arise (4ᵗʰ), current (3ʳᵈ), issue (4ᵗʰ), run (K), start (1ˢᵗ), stream (3ʳᵈ), tide (1ˢᵗ)

flower (K): A. flourish (4ᵗʰ), grow (K), prosper (5ᵗʰ) **B.** bloom (4ᵗʰ), blossom (4ᵗʰ), bud (1ˢᵗ), flora (6ᵗʰ)

fluid (6ᵗʰ): juice (K), liquid (3ʳᵈ), water (K)

fluorescent (6ᵗʰ): glowing (1ˢᵗ), shining (1ˢᵗ)

flush (4ᵗʰ): A. wash (1ˢᵗ) **B.** bloom (4ᵗʰ), blush (4ᵗʰ), color (K), red (K), rosy (1ˢᵗ)

fluster (6ᵗʰ): agitate (5ᵗʰ), bother (2ⁿᵈ), confound (6ᵗʰ), confuse (4ᵗʰ), disturb (6ᵗʰ), excite (4ᵗʰ), upset (3ʳᵈ)

flute (5ᵗʰ): fife (5ᵗʰ), pipe (1ˢᵗ)

fly (K): bolt (4ᵗʰ), dart (1ˢᵗ), drift (2ⁿᵈ), float (1ˢᵗ), hang (2ⁿᵈ), hover (3ʳᵈ), sail (1ˢᵗ), soar (6ᵗʰ)

foam (4ᵗʰ): bubbles (2ⁿᵈ), fizz (5ᵗʰ)

foal (2ⁿᵈ): colt (K)

foam (4ᵗʰ): froth (4ᵗʰ), lather (4ᵗʰ)

focal (5ᵗʰ)

focus (5ᵗʰ): A. aim (3ʳᵈ), direct (1ˢᵗ), point (1ˢᵗ) **B.** center (2ⁿᵈ), core (6ᵗʰ), heart (K)

foe (4ᵗʰ): enemy (2ⁿᵈ), opponent (5ᵗʰ), rival (4ᵗʰ)

fog (1ˢᵗ): A. cloud (1ˢᵗ), mist (1ˢᵗ), overcast (2ⁿᵈ), smog (5ᵗʰ), vapor (3ʳᵈ) **B.** darken (2ⁿᵈ), dim (1ˢᵗ), obscure (6ᵗʰ)

fold (1ˢᵗ): bend (K), crease (5ᵗʰ), double (K), flap (4ᵗʰ), tuck (1ˢᵗ), turn (1ˢᵗ)

foliage (6ᵗʰ): flora (6ᵗʰ), greenery (3ʳᵈ), leaves (1ˢᵗ), plants (K)

folk (3ʳᵈ): family (K), parents (3ʳᵈ), people (K), relatives (4ᵗʰ)

folklore (5ᵗʰ): fairy tales (4ᵗʰ), history (2ⁿᵈ), stories (1ˢᵗ)

follow (1ˢᵗ): A. accept (3ʳᵈ), adopt (3ʳᵈ), mind (1ˢᵗ), obey (3ʳᵈ) **B.** chase (1ˢᵗ), go after (1ˢᵗ), pursue (5ᵗʰ), replace (5ᵗʰ), succeed (2ⁿᵈ), trail (2ⁿᵈ)

following (1ˢᵗ): admirers (5ᵗʰ), after (1ˢᵗ), behind (1ˢᵗ), devotees (5ᵗʰ), fans (K), later (1ˢᵗ), next (K), succeeding (2ⁿᵈ)

folly (4ᵗʰ): foolish (2ⁿᵈ), humor (4ᵗʰ), idiocy (6ᵗʰ), joke (1ˢᵗ), madness (3ʳᵈ), mistake (1ˢᵗ), nonsense (5ᵗʰ), stupidity (4ᵗʰ)

fond (4ᵗʰ): affectionate (4ᵗʰ), loving (1ˢᵗ), sweet on (K)

food (K): bread (2ⁿᵈ), diet (4ᵗʰ), meals (3ʳᵈ)

fool (2ⁿᵈ): A. deceive (5ᵗʰ), trick (1ˢᵗ) **B.** clown (1ˢᵗ), dummy (1ˢᵗ), idiot (6ᵗʰ), silly (1ˢᵗ)

foolish (2ⁿᵈ): careless (5ᵗʰ), crazy (4ᵗʰ), dumb (1ˢᵗ), ill-advised (3ʳᵈ), silly (1ˢᵗ), simple (1ˢᵗ), unwise (1ˢᵗ)

foot (K): base (1ˢᵗ), bottom (1ˢᵗ), foundation (5ᵗʰ), prop (5ᵗʰ), support (4ᵗʰ)

football (1ˢᵗ)

footstep (3ʳᵈ): footprint (1ˢᵗ), mark (1ˢᵗ), step (1ˢᵗ), stride (5ᵗʰ)

for (K): as (K), because (K), belonging to (1st), concerning (3rd), during (1st), fit to (K), to (K)

forbid (4th): ban (K), deny (5th), eliminate (5th), not allow (2nd), outlaw (1st), prevent (3rd), prohibit (6th), reject (5th), stop (K)

force (1st): A. command (2nd), compel (3rd), insist (5th), order (1st), pressure (4th), push (1st), require (2nd), shock (1st), strain (4th) **B.** energy (4th), might (1st), power (1st), strength (1st), violence (5th)

forceful (2nd): aggressive (6th), intense (6th), powerful (2nd), pushy (1st), strong (K)

ford (5th): cross (1st)

fore (6th): ahead (1st), before (K), first (1st), front (1st)

forecast (4th): A. prediction (6th) **B.** anticipate (6th), foretell (6th), guess (1st), predict (6th)

forefather (6th): ancestor (5th), creator (3rd), parent (3rd)

forego (5th): avoid (3rd), give up (K), quit (1st), refrain (6th)

forehead (4th): brow (4th), front (1st)

foreign (5th): alien (5th), odd (4th), outside (1st), peculiar (4th), strange (1st), unfamiliar (3rd)

foreigner (5th): alien (5th), immigrant (6th), outsider (1st), stranger (1st)

foreman (6th): boss (K), director (1st), manager (4th), overseer (1st), supervisor (6th)

foresight (6th): A. understanding (5th), vision (4th) **B.** care (K), caution (5th), prudence (6th), readiness (1st)

forest (1st): brush (2nd), grove (4th), woods (1st)

foretell (6th): forecast (4th), indicate (4th), predict (6th), prophesy (5th), see (K)

forever (3rd): always (K), constantly (4th), endlessly (3rd), ever (K), without end (1st)

forfeit (6th): give up (K), lose (3rd)

forge (5th): A. copy (3rd), counterfeit (6th), duplicate (6th), imitate (5th), reproduce (4th) **B.** beat (1st), fabricate (6th), fashion (3rd), form (1st), make (K), manufacture (3rd), pound (2nd)

forget (1st): ignore (5th), never mind (1st), not remember (1st), overlook (4th), skip (2nd)

forgive (2nd): acquit (6th), clear (2nd), erase (2nd), excuse (3rd), overlook (4th), pardon (4th)

fork (1st): A. tool (1st), utensil (6th) **B.** give (K), lift (1st) **C.** branch (2nd), divide (4th), separate (3rd), split (4th)

forlorn (6th): alone (K), depressed (5th), gloomy (3rd), grim (4th), hopeless (2nd), lonely (2nd), lonesome (3rd), miserable (4th), sad (K), solitary (5th), unhappy (K)

form (1st): A. ceremony (5th), method (2nd), process (4th), rite (6th), ritual (6th), system (2nd) **B.** forge (5th), make (K) **C.** figure (4th), frame (3rd), outline (4th), shape (1st)

formal (4th): A. ceremonial (5th), dress up (K), fancy (3rd) **B.** conventional (6th), exact (2nd), fixed (1st), standard (3rd), stiff (3rd)

formation (4th): A. design (5th), figure (2nd), outline (4th), pattern (3rd), shape (1st) **B.** beginning (2nd), creation (3rd), start (1st), system (2nd)

former (6th): before (K), earlier (2nd), first (1st), gone (1st), late (K), old (K), past (1st), previous (5th), prior (5th)

formidable (6th): alarming (3rd), awe-inspiring (4th), difficult (5th), frightening (2nd), horrifying (4th), huge (1st), imposing (4th), scary (1st), strong (K), wild (2nd)

formula (6th): method (2nd), pattern (3rd), recipe (4th), rules (K), system (2nd)

forsake (6th): abandon (4th), deny (5th), desert (1st), leave (1st), quit (1st), reject (5th)

fort (5th): camp (1st), castle (3rd), fortress (5th), stronghold (3rd)

forth (2nd): away (K), forward (3rd), onward (3rd), out (K)

forthright (5th): blunt (6th), direct (1st), frank (4th), honest (3rd), honorable (3rd), just (1st), open (K), outspoken (K), straight (3rd)

fortnight (6th): two weeks (K)

fortress (5th): castle (3rd), fort (5th), shelter (4th)

fortunate (4th): advantageous (4th), beneficial (3rd), favorable (4th), good (K), happy (K), lucky (K)

fortune (3rd): A. income (4th), money (K), wealth (3rd) **B.** accident (4th), chance (2nd), destiny (5th), fate (3rd), luck (1st)

forty (1st)

forward (3rd) : A. flip (2nd), pushy (1st), rude (2nd) **B.** advanced (2nd), ahead (1st), early (1st) **C.** ahead (1st),

before (K), in front (1st), onward (3rd), toward (1st)

fossil (4th): bones (1st), remains (1st), skeleton (4th)

foul (4th): A. mistake (1st), out of bounds (2nd) **B.** contaminate (6th), mess up (1st), pollute (3rd), soil (2nd), stain (4th) **C.** dirty (1st), offensive (4th), soiled (2nd), stained (4th), unclean (K)

found (K): build (1st), create (3rd), set up (K), start (1st)

foundation (5th): A. basis (2nd), cause (2nd), reason (1st) **B.** base (1st), bottom (1st), ground (1st) **C.** association (5th)

fountain (3rd): jet (K), source (4th), spray (2nd), spring (K)

four (K)

fourteen (1st)

fourth (1st)

fowl (4th): bird (K), chicken (K), hen (K), poultry (6th)

fox (K)

foxglove (5th)

fraction (4th): bit (1st), fragment (6th), part (1st), piece (1st), section (4th), slice (5th)

fragile (6th): delicate (5th), fine (1st), frail (6th), slight (4th), weak (3rd)

fragment (6th): bit (1st), chip (5th), fraction (4th), part (1st), piece (1st), remnant (6th), section (4th), slice (5th), splinter (6th)

fragrance (5th): bouquet (6th), incense (5th), odor (3rd), perfume (3rd), scent (3rd), smell (3rd)

fragrant (5ᵗʰ): perfumed (3ʳᵈ), scented (3ʳᵈ), spicy (3ʳᵈ), sweet-smelling (3ʳᵈ)

frail (6ᵗʰ): delicate (5ᵗʰ), fine (1ˢᵗ), fragile (6ᵗʰ), infirm (2ⁿᵈ), sickly (K), slender (4ᵗʰ), slight (4ᵗʰ), thin (1ˢᵗ), unwell (K), weak (3ʳᵈ)

frame (3ʳᵈ): A. body (1ˢᵗ), structure (4ᵗʰ), support (4ᵗʰ) **B.** assemble (4ᵗʰ), build (1ˢᵗ), construct (3ʳᵈ), contrive (6ᵗʰ), create (3ʳᵈ), devise (4ᵗʰ), edge (1ˢᵗ), erect (4ᵗʰ), fabricate (6ᵗʰ), invent (2ⁿᵈ), make (K), raise (1ˢᵗ), set up (K), surround (3ʳᵈ)

framework (4ᵗʰ): frame (3ʳᵈ), skeleton (4ᵗʰ), structure (4ᵗʰ)

France (1ˢᵗ)

frank (4ᵗʰ): blunt (6ᵗʰ), candid (4ᵗʰ), clear (2ⁿᵈ), forthright (5ᵗʰ), free (K), genuine (5ᵗʰ), honest (3ʳᵈ), open (K), plain (2ⁿᵈ), sincere (4ᵗʰ)

frantic (5ᵗʰ): crazy (4ᵗʰ), furious (4ᵗʰ), hysterical (6ᵗʰ), insane (6ᵗʰ), mad (K), raving (5ᵗʰ), upset (3ʳᵈ), wild (2ⁿᵈ)

fraud (6ᵗʰ): cheat (3ʳᵈ), deception (5ᵗʰ), fake (1ˢᵗ), hoax (5ᵗʰ), trickery (5ᵗʰ)

freckles (1ˢᵗ): dots (K), spots (1ˢᵗ)

free (K): acquit (6ᵗʰ), clear (2ⁿᵈ), frank (4ᵗʰ), idle (4ᵗʰ), independent (3ʳᵈ), liberate (4ᵗʰ), loose (3ʳᵈ), open (K), release (5ᵗʰ), unbound (4ᵗʰ), untied (1ˢᵗ)

freedom (3ʳᵈ): independence (3ʳᵈ), leisure (5ᵗʰ), liberation (4ᵗʰ), liberty (3ʳᵈ), license (5ᵗʰ), range (3ʳᵈ), release (5ᵗʰ), scope (6ᵗʰ)

freely (K): candidly (4ᵗʰ), frankly (4ᵗʰ), generously (4ᵗʰ), openly (1ˢᵗ)

freeze (4ᵗʰ): chill (3ʳᵈ), cool (1ˢᵗ), frost (4ᵗʰ), glacial (3ʳᵈ), ice (1ˢᵗ), refrigerate (2ⁿᵈ)

freezing (4ᵗʰ): arctic (5ᵗʰ), cold (1ˢᵗ), frigid (6ᵗʰ), icy (K)

freight (4ᵗʰ): burden (5ᵗʰ), cargo (5ᵗʰ), haul (4ᵗʰ), load (2ⁿᵈ), luggage (4ᵗʰ), weight (1ˢᵗ)

French (1ˢᵗ)

frequent (4ᵗʰ): common (2ⁿᵈ), constant (4ᵗʰ), normal (5ᵗʰ), often (1ˢᵗ), regular (3ʳᵈ), repeated (4ᵗʰ), usual (3ʳᵈ)

fresco (5ᵗʰ): painting (2ⁿᵈ)

fresh (2ⁿᵈ): alert (5ᵗʰ), different (1ˢᵗ), energetic (4ᵗʰ), hearty (5ᵗʰ), modern (2ⁿᵈ), new (K), novel (5ᵗʰ), original (3ʳᵈ), recent (3ʳᵈ), unusual (3ʳᵈ), vital (5ᵗʰ)

freshwater (4ᵗʰ): lake (1ˢᵗ), river (K), stream (3ʳᵈ)

fret (5ᵗʰ): agitate (5ᵗʰ), agitation (3ʳᵈ), agonize (5ᵗʰ), annoyance (5ᵗʰ), complain (4ᵗʰ), friction (6ᵗʰ), irritation (6ᵗʰ), worry (1ˢᵗ), writhe (6ᵗʰ)

friar (5ᵗʰ): brother (1ˢᵗ), father (K), monk (4ᵗʰ)

friction (6ᵗʰ): argument (3ʳᵈ), clash (5ᵗʰ), dispute (6ᵗʰ), fight (K), rub (1ˢᵗ)

Friday (1ˢᵗ)

fried (5ᵗʰ): cooked (1ˢᵗ), sautéed (4ᵗʰ)

friend (1ˢᵗ): ally (6ᵗʰ), associate (5ᵗʰ), buddy (4ᵗʰ), companion (3ʳᵈ), comrade (4ᵗʰ), mate (4ᵗʰ), pal (K), partner (5ᵗʰ), peer (1ˢᵗ)

friendship (2ⁿᵈ): accordance (4ᵗʰ), affection (4ᵗʰ), agreement (2ⁿᵈ), fondness (4ᵗʰ), harmony (4ᵗʰ)

fright (2ⁿᵈ): A. horrify (4ᵗʰ), shock (1ˢᵗ), startle (4ᵗʰ) **B.** alarm (3ʳᵈ), anxiety (4ᵗʰ), dread (6ᵗʰ), fear (1ˢᵗ), horror (2ⁿᵈ), panic (1ˢᵗ), terror (3ʳᵈ)

frighten (ed) (2ⁿᵈ): afraid (1ˢᵗ), alarmed (3ʳᵈ), fearful (1ˢᵗ), horrified (4ᵗʰ), scared (1ˢᵗ), shocked (1ˢᵗ), terrified (3ʳᵈ)

frigid (6ᵗʰ): arctic (3ʳᵈ), cold (K), cool (1ˢᵗ), formal (4ᵗʰ), frosty (4ᵗʰ), glacial (3ʳᵈ), icy (2ⁿᵈ), prim (5ᵗʰ), remote (5ᵗʰ)

fringe (5ᵗʰ): border (1ˢᵗ), decoration (3ʳᵈ), edge (1ˢᵗ), end (K), rim (1ˢᵗ), verge (6ᵗʰ)

frizz (5ᵗʰ): curl (2ⁿᵈ)

fro (5ᵗʰ): away (K), back (K), from (K)

frock (4ᵗʰ): clothes (1ˢᵗ), dress (K)

frog (K)

frolic (6ᵗʰ): fun (K), gaiety (1ˢᵗ), merriment (3ʳᵈ), mirth (5ᵗʰ), play (K), prank (5ᵗʰ), sport (1ˢᵗ)

from (K)

front (1ˢᵗ): entrance (2ⁿᵈ), exterior (5ᵗʰ), face (K), fore part (6ᵗʰ)

frontier (5ᵗʰ): borderland (1ˢᵗ), boundary (4ᵗʰ), fringe (5ᵗʰ), limit (3ʳᵈ)

frost (4ᵗʰ): chill (3ʳᵈ), coldness (K), cool (1ˢᵗ), freeze (4ᵗʰ), frigidity (6ᵗʰ), ice (1ˢᵗ)

frown (2ⁿᵈ): glare (4ᵗʰ), grimace (4ᵗʰ), scowl (6ᵗʰ)

fruit (2ⁿᵈ): crop (2ⁿᵈ), harvest (4ᵗʰ), outcome (4ᵗʰ), result (2ⁿᵈ), reward (4ᵗʰ), yield (4ᵗʰ)

fry (1ˢᵗ): brown (K), burn (3ʳᵈ), sauté (4ᵗʰ), toast (5ᵗʰ)

fuel (4ᵗʰ): A. coal (2ⁿᵈ), gas (1ˢᵗ), gasoline (1ˢᵗ), oil (K) **B.** energy (4ᵗʰ), feed (1ˢᵗ), nourish (6ᵗʰ)

fugitive (4ᵗʰ): brief (5ᵗʰ), deserter (1ˢᵗ), escapee (1ˢᵗ), passing (2ⁿᵈ), runaway (1ˢᵗ), short-lived (1ˢᵗ), transient (6ᵗʰ)

fulfill (4ᵗʰ): accomplish (2ⁿᵈ), achieve (5ᵗʰ), complete (3ʳᵈ), execute (5ᵗʰ), finish (1ˢᵗ), implement (6ᵗʰ), obey (3ʳᵈ), observe (3ʳᵈ), perfect (3ʳᵈ), realize (2ⁿᵈ)

fulfillment (4ᵗʰ): achievement (5ᵗʰ), action (1ˢᵗ), performance (4ᵗʰ), realization (2ⁿᵈ)

full (K): abundant (5ᵗʰ), armload (2ⁿᵈ), complete (3ʳᵈ), enough (1ˢᵗ), limit (3ʳᵈ), maximum (6ᵗʰ), plenty (1ˢᵗ), solid (3ʳᵈ), total (2ⁿᵈ), whole (1ˢᵗ)

fumble (5ᵗʰ): flounder (5ᵗʰ), miss (K), slip (3ʳᵈ), stumble (4ᵗʰ)

fume (3ʳᵈ): A. fret (5ᵗʰ), rage (4ᵗʰ), stew (2ⁿᵈ) **B.** smell (3ʳᵈ), smoke (1ˢᵗ), stink (2ⁿᵈ), vapor (3ʳᵈ)

fun (K): cheer (3ʳᵈ), delight (3ʳᵈ), jest (4ᵗʰ), mirth (5ᵗʰ), play (K), pleasure (2ⁿᵈ), recreation (5ᵗʰ), sport (1ˢᵗ)

function (4ᵗʰ): duty (1ˢᵗ), job (K), operate (3ʳᵈ), perform (4ᵗʰ), purpose (1ˢᵗ), role (6ᵗʰ), use (K)

fund (4ᵗʰ): A. finance (1ˢᵗ), pay (K), support (4ᵗʰ) **B.** account (3ʳᵈ), accumulation (6ᵗʰ), grant (2ⁿᵈ), investment (5ᵗʰ), savings (1ˢᵗ), supply (1ˢᵗ)

fundamental (4ᵗʰ): base (1ˢᵗ), basic (2ⁿᵈ), bottom (1ˢᵗ), essential (6ᵗʰ), initial (6ᵗʰ), necessary (1ˢᵗ), original (3ʳᵈ), primary (5ᵗʰ)

funeral (4ᵗʰ): burial (3ʳᵈ), ceremony (5ᵗʰ), farewell (3ʳᵈ), rite (6ᵗʰ)

fungus (5th): mold (5th), mushroom (4th)

funnel (3rd): channel (4th), direct (1st), pour (3rd)

funny (1st): amusing (4th), clever (3rd), comic (5th), humorous (4th), jolly (4th), laughable (3rd), odd (4th), queer (4th), strange (1st), weird (1st)

fur (K): coat (1st), covering (1st), hair (K)

furious (4th): angry (1st), crazed (4th), heated (1st), mad (K), raging (4th), storming (2nd), violent (5th), wild (2nd)

furnace (4th): fireplace (2nd), heater (2nd), oven (1st)

furnish (4th): equip (5th), give (K), provide (3rd), supply (1st)

furniture (3rd): equipment (5th)

furrow (6th): channel (4th), groove (5th), row (K), rut (1st), trench (5th), truck (1st)

further (2nd): A. abroad (5th), away (K), farther (3rd) **B.** besides (1st), likewise (1st), moreover (3rd), then (K) **C.** advance (2nd), aid (2nd), assist (4th), forward (3rd) , help (K), nourish (6th), promote (5th), push (1st)

fury (4th): anger (1st), fit (K), furor (4th), passion (6th), rage (4th), violence (5th)

fuse (4th): blend (5th), combine (3rd), dissolve (4th), melt (2nd), unite (5th), wed (K), weld (6th)

fusion (4th)

fuss (1st): ado (2nd), agitation (5th), annoy (5th), argument (3rd), bother (2nd), complain (4th), fight (K), fret (5th), to-do (2nd)

future (5th): coming (K), down (K), expected (2nd), next (K), outlook (4th), probable (4th), prospect (4th), the road (1st), tomorrow (1st)

gab (1st): chatter (1st), gossip (5th), talk (K)

gag (1st): A. jest (4th), joke (1st) **B.** hold back (1st), restrain (5th), suppress (5th), tie (1st), trick (1st)

Gaia (5th): earth (1st)

Gaia theory (5th): a theory stating that earth acts like a living system that self-regulates

gain (2nd): A. benefit (3rd), interest (1st), profit (4th), reward (4th), use (K) **B.** achieve (5th), acquire (4th), advance (2nd), carry (K), gather (1st), get (K), improve (3rd), make (K), obtain (5th), reap (4th), win (K)

gait (6th): pace (3rd), step (1st), stride (5th), walk (K)

gale (2nd): air current (3rd), disturbance (6th), wind (1st)

gallant (4th): bold (2nd), brave (1st), chivalrous (6th), civil (3rd), courteous (4th), courtly (3rd), gentle (3rd), polite (4th), unafraid (1st)

gallery (5th): corridor (5th), hall (1st), museum (4th), passage (4th)

gallop (4th): canter (5th), hurry (1st), run (K), rush (2nd), trot (5th)

gallows (6th)

gamble (5th): A. chance (2nd), hazard (6th), try (K) **B.** bet (1st), risk (6th), wager (3rd)

game (K): challenge (4th), contest (4th), match (3rd), recreation (5th), sport (1st)

187

gang (1st): association (5th), crowd (2nd), gathering (1st), group (1st), team (1st)

gap (K): A. blank (2nd), emptiness (3rd), void (6th) **B.** break (1st), canyon (4th), cavity (5th), crack (K), hole (K), separation (3rd), space (1st), split (4th)

gape (5th): gaze (5th), show astonishment (4th), stare (3rd)

garage (6th): shelter (4th), storage (2nd)

garb (5th): attire (6th), clothes (1st), costume (4th), dress (K)

garbage (6th): leavings (1st), rejects (5th), remains (1st), waste (2nd)

garden (K): A. cultivate (6th), farm (K), plant (K) **B.** plants (K), plot (4th), yard (K)

gargle (6th): rinse (3rd)

garland (6th): crown (1st), flowers (K), loop (5th), wreath (4th)

garment (4th): attire (6th), clothes (1st), cover (1st), dress (K), garb (5th), shirt (1st)

garnish (6th): adorn (6th), beautify (2nd), deck (1st), decorate (3rd), dress up (K), ornament (4th), top (K)

garrison (5th): A. fort (5th), post (1st) **B.** guard (1st), preserve (4th), protect (5th) **C.** division (4th), unit (5th)

gas (1st): fuel (4th), steam (2nd), vapor (3rd)

gasp (4th): breath (1st), gulp (1st), short breath (1st)

gate (1st): access (6th), door (K), entry (2nd), opening (K), portal (5th)

gather (1st): accumulate (6th), assemble (4th), collect (3rd), take in (K)

gave (K)

gaunt (6th): lean (3rd), skinny (1st), thin (1st)

gay (1st): animated (6th), bright (1st), cheerful (3rd), cheery (3rd), gleeful (5th), happy (K), joyful (1st), joyous (1st), lively (2nd), merry (3rd), up (K)

gaze (5th): look at (1st), notice (1st), stare (3rd)

gazelle (5th)

gear (1st): A. apparatus (6th), equipment (5th), material (5th), outfit (1st), paraphernalia (6th), rig (1st), tackle (4th), tools (1st) **B.** toothed wheel (1st) **C.** rigging (1st) **D.** clothing (1st)

gee (K): gosh (1st), wow (K)

gelatin (5th)

gene (4th)

general (2nd): common (2nd), most (1st), overall (3rd), universal (4th)

generation (4th): age (1st)

generous (4th): ample (5th), lavish (6th), liberal (4th), open (K)

genial (5th): cordial (6th), friendly (1st), good natured (1st), pleasant (3rd), sociable (2nd)

genius (4th): brilliance (4th), brains (3rd), gift (K), intelligence (4th), sharpness (1st), talent (2nd), wisdom (1st)

genome (5th): A. the total genetic information contained in a set of chromosomes **B.** an organism's genetic material

gentle (3rd): considerate (2nd), delicate (5th), kind (K), mild (4th), peaceful (1st), soft (K), tender (3rd), thoughtful (2nd)

gentleman (3rd): aristocrat (6th), man (K), noble (3rd)

genuine (5th): pure (3rd), real (1st), simple (1st), sincere (4th), true (K)

geographic (5th)

geography (5th)

geology (5th)

germ (6th): bug (K), dirt (1st), disease (5th)

German (2nd)

Germany (2nd)

gesture (4th): motion (3rd), move (K), signal (4th), wave (K)

get (K): ace (2nd), acquire (4th), attain (6th), carry (K), collect (2nd), come by (K), earn (2nd), gain (2nd), gather (1st), obtain (5th), receive (1st)

ghastly (6th): awful (3rd), dreadful (6th), frightening (2nd), frightful (2nd), horrible (4th), horrid (4th), scary (1st), sickening (K), terrible (1st), ugly (4th)

ghost (K): image (4th), specter (6th), spirit (2nd)

giant (2nd): big (K), enormous (4th), fat (1st), grand (2nd), great (K), huge (1st), large (K), vast (4th)

gift (K): A. ability (3rd), flair (6th), genius (4th), intelligence (4th), talent (2nd) **B.** favor (1st), offering (2nd), present (K), prize (3rd), tip (1st)

gigantic (5th): See giant.

gild (6th): adorn (6th), coat (1st), cover (1st), decorate (3rd), paint (2nd), plate (K)

gill (4th)

gin (6th): bait (3rd), lure (5th), net (3rd), trap (1st)

ginger (1st)

gingerbread (1st)

gingerly (6th): attentively (2nd), carefully (5th), guardedly (1st), shyly (K), timidly (5th)

giraffe (K)

girdle (6th): belt (2nd), circle (K), enclose (4th), ring (1st), surround (3rd), wrap (3rd)

girl (K): child (K), female (4th), lass (1st), maid (3rd), miss (K), woman (K), young lady (1st)

girlfriend (4th): buddy (4th), chum (6th), friend (1st)

give (K): bestow (5th), confer (4th), contribute (4th), impart (6th), leave (1st), offer (2nd), present (K), transfer (5th)

glacier (3rd)

glad (K): cheerful (3rd), delighted (3rd), gay (1st), happy (K), jolly (4th), joyful (2nd), merry (3rd), pleased (K)

glance (3rd): A. bounce off (6th), skim (6th), touch (1st) **B.** brush (2nd), glimpse (4th), look (K), observe (3rd), peak (4th), notice (1st), see (K), view (2nd)

gland (5th)

glare (4th): A. dark look (1st), frown (K), gaze (5th), stare (3rd) **B.** blaze (1st), flame (3rd), flare (6th), gleam (1st), light (K), shine (1st)

glass (1st): A. cup (K), tumbler (3rd) **B.** mirror (4th), pane (5th), window (1st)

glasses (1st): eyeglasses (4th), lenses (1st), spectacles (5th)

glaze (6th): color (K), gloss (5th), luster (4th), paint (2nd), polish (4th), sheen (6th)

gleam (1st): flash (2nd), glint (6th), glitter (4th), glimmer (6th), shine (1st), spark (3rd), sparkle (5th), twinkle (4th)

glee (5th): cheer (3rd), delight (3rd), happiness (K), joy (1st), mirth (5th), pleasure (2nd)

gleeful (5th): joyous (1st), overjoyed (1st), sunny (6th). See glee.

glen (6th): gap (K), valley (2nd)

glide (4th): coast (2nd), drift (2nd), float (1st), graze (5th), move (K), roll (1st), slide (2nd), slip (3rd)

glimmer (6th): beam (3rd), glare (4th), gleam (1st), glitter (4th), shine (1st), spark (3rd)

glimpse (4th): glance (3rd), look (K), peek (2nd), see (K)

glisten (6th): flare (6th), flash (2nd), glance (3rd), gleam (1st), glimmer (6th), glint (6th), glitter (4th), shine (1st), sparkle (5th), twinkle (4th)

glitter (4th): See glisten.

globe (4th): ball (K), earth (1st), sphere (6th), world (1st)

gloom (3rd): darkness (K), depression (6th), low spirits (2nd), melancholy (6th), misery (4th), sadness (2nd), shadow (3rd)

glory (3rd): credit (5th), fame (3rd), honor (1st), success (2nd), victory (4th)

gloss (5th): shine (1st)

Glossopteris (5th): the Glossopteridales are an extinct group of seed plants that arose during the Permian on the great southern continent of Gondwana

glove (4th): clothe (2nd), cover (1st), fit (K)

glow (1st): brightness (1st), brilliance (4th), flare (6th), glare (4th), light (K), radiance (6th), shine (1st)

glue (1st): A. adhesive (6th) **B.** adhere (6th), cement (4th), paste (1st), seal (K), stick (K)

glum (4th): depressed (5th), down (K), gloomy (3rd), silent (3rd), sulky (5th), sullen (5th)

gnarled (5th): bent (K), bumpy (2nd), knotted (4th), twisted (1st)

gnash (4th): bite (1st), gnaw (1st), grind (4th), scrape (3rd)

gnat (5th)

gnaw (1st): bite (1st), chew (1st), grind (4th)

gnome (6th): brownie (2nd), dwarf (4th), elf (1st), fairy (4th)

go (K): act (K), advance (2nd), depart (5th), follow (1st), leave (1st), move (K), operate (3rd), pass (K), perform (4th), reach (1st), run (K), shift (4th), vanish (3rd), work (K)

goal (4th): aim (3rd), end (K), ideal (3rd), object (1st), purpose (1st), target (5th)

goat (K)

gobble (1st): cram (5th), devour (5th), eat (K), stuff (1st)

goblin (4th): brownie (2nd), elf (1st), fairy (4th), gnome (6th)

god (1st)

goddess (1ˢᵗ)

godfather (3ʳᵈ)

godmother (3ʳᵈ)

goes (1ˢᵗ)

goggle (4ᵗʰ): glare (4ᵗʰ), look (K), look hard (1ˢᵗ), see (K), stare (3ʳᵈ), view (2ⁿᵈ)

goggles (4ᵗʰ): glasses (1ˢᵗ), spectacles (5ᵗʰ)

gold (K): A. metal (3ʳᵈ), yellow (K) **B.** fortune (3ʳᵈ), money (K), riches (K), wealth (3ʳᵈ)

golden (K)

goldenrod (5ᵗʰ)

goldfinch (5ᵗʰ)

goldfish (K): carp (5ᵗʰ)

golf (4ᵗʰ)

gone (1ˢᵗ)

good (K): capable (4ᵗʰ), competent (6ᵗʰ), correct (3ʳᵈ), genuine (5ᵗʰ), honest (3ʳᵈ), just (1ˢᵗ), moral (3ʳᵈ), noble (3ʳᵈ), positive (2ⁿᵈ), real (1ˢᵗ), right (K), virtue (4ᵗʰ)

good-bye (1ˢᵗ): farewell (3ʳᵈ), see you (1ˢᵗ)

good-natured (5ᵗʰ): agreeable (2ⁿᵈ), cheerful (3ʳᵈ), easygoing (1ˢᵗ), gentle (3ʳᵈ), good (K), kind (K), obliging (6ᵗʰ), polite (4ᵗʰ)

good-night (2ⁿᵈ): good-bye (1ˢᵗ), farewell (3ʳᵈ)

goose (K)

gooseberry (5ᵗʰ)

gopher (1ˢᵗ)

gorge (5ᵗʰ): A. canyon (6ᵗʰ), gulf (4ᵗʰ) **B.** cram (5ᵗʰ), fill (K), gobble up (1ˢᵗ), stuff (1ˢᵗ)

gorgeous (5ᵗʰ): attractive (5ᵗʰ), beautiful (1ˢᵗ), dazzling (5ᵗʰ), grand (2ⁿᵈ), great (K), perfect (3ʳᵈ), pleasant (3ʳᵈ), splendid (4ᵗʰ), super (1ˢᵗ)

gorilla (1ˢᵗ)

gospel (6ᵗʰ): A. certainty (1ˢᵗ), fact (1ˢᵗ), truth (1ˢᵗ) **B.** belief (1ˢᵗ), word (K)

gossip (5ᵗʰ): chatter (1ˢᵗ), earful (1ˢᵗ), report (1ˢᵗ), rumor (5ᵗʰ), small talk (1ˢᵗ), talk (K)

got (K)

gourd (5ᵗʰ)

govern (2ⁿᵈ): boss (K), command (2ⁿᵈ), control (2ⁿᵈ), order (1ˢᵗ), rule (K)

government (1ˢᵗ): authority (3ʳᵈ), in charge (2ⁿᵈ), leadership (1ˢᵗ), management (4ᵗʰ), rulers (K)

gown (4ᵗʰ): attire (6ᵗʰ), cape (4ᵗʰ), dress (K), frock (4ᵗʰ), garb (5ᵗʰ), garment (4ᵗʰ), mantle (4ᵗʰ), robe (4ᵗʰ)

grab (4ᵗʰ): capture (3ʳᵈ), catch (1ˢᵗ), clutch (4ᵗʰ), grasp (4ᵗʰ), seize (3ʳᵈ), take (4ᵗʰ)

grace (3ʳᵈ): beauty (1ˢᵗ), charm (3ʳᵈ), elegance (5ᵗʰ), manners (1ˢᵗ), polish (4ᵗʰ)

grade (2ⁿᵈ): A. angle (3ʳᵈ), bank (1ˢᵗ), hill (K), slant (6ᵗʰ) **B.** class (1ˢᵗ), degree (5ᵗʰ), mark (1ˢᵗ), measure (2ⁿᵈ), merit (4ᵗʰ), rank (3ʳᵈ), rating (1ˢᵗ), scale (3ʳᵈ), score (1ˢᵗ), value (2ⁿᵈ), worth (3ʳᵈ)

gradual (3ʳᵈ): by degree (5ᵗʰ), even (1ˢᵗ), orderly (1ˢᵗ), regular (2ⁿᵈ), slowly (1ˢᵗ), steady (3ʳᵈ)

graduate (4th): A. achieve (5th), pass (K), succeed (2nd) **B.** make the grade (2nd), one who passed (1st), one who succeeded (2nd) **C.** grade (2nd), mark off (1st), order (1st), range (3rd)

graham (6th)

grain (3rd): bit (1st), cereal (6th), particle (5th), piece (1st), scrap (3rd), seed (1st), speck (4th), wheat (1st)

grammar (6th): basics (5th), laws (1st), principles (4th), rules (1st), speech (2nd), system (2nd), talk (K)

grand (2nd): big (K), great (K), imposing (4th), impressive (5th), large (K), lofty (5th), magnificent (4th), noted (1st), splendid (4th), stately (2nd), superb (6th)

grandfather (1st): forefather (6th), granddad (1st), grandpa (1st), relative (4th)

grandmother (1st): grandma (1st), granny (1st), relative (4th)

grant (2nd): A. contribution (4th), favor (1st), gift (K), offering (2nd) **B.** admit (4th), agree (2nd), concede (6th), consent (3rd) **C.** allow (2nd), award (5th), bestow (5th), furnish (4th), give (1st), offer (2nd), present (K), provide (3rd), supply (1st)

grape (2nd)

grapefruit (5th)

grapeshot (6th)

grapple (6th): battle (2nd), fight (K), grasp (4th), press (1st), scuffle (5th), secure (3rd), seize (3rd), squeeze (5th), struggle (1st), take hold (1st), wrestle (6th)

grasp (4th): A. comprehend (5th), get (K), realize (2nd), understand (1st)

B. catch (1st), clutch (4th), grab (4th), hold (1st), secure (3rd), seize (3rd), take (K)

grass (K): green (K), lawn (2nd), sod (6th)

grasshopper (1st)

grateful (4th): appreciate (5th), obliged (6th), thankful (2nd)

grave (3rd): A. grim (4th), sober (4th), solemn (5th), thoughtful (1st), unsmiling (1st) **B.** burial ground (3rd), tomb (5th) **C.** important (1st), serious (4th), vital (5th)

gravel (4th): sand (1st), stones (2nd)

gravity (4th): A. force (1st), pull (K), weight (1st) **B.** grimness (4th), importance (1st), seriousness (4th)

gray (1st): cloudy (1st), colorless (1st), dark (K), gloomy (3rd), overcast (2nd), pale (3rd), smoky (1st)

graze (5th): brush (2nd), feed (1st), pasture (5th), scrape (4th), touch (1st)

grease (5th): butter (2nd), fat (1st), oil (K)

great (K): big (K), gigantic (5th), huge (1st), important (1st), large (K), magnificent (4th), wonderful (1st). See also grand.

greed (4th): hunger (2nd), itch (5th), longing (1st)

green (K): immature (5th), new (K), unskilled (2nd), young (1st)

greenery (3rd): foliage (6th), flora (6th), leaves (2nd), plants (1st)

greenhouse (3rd)

greenhouse effect (3rd): warming that results when solar radiation is trapped by the atmosphere; caused by atmospheric gases that allow sunshine to pass through but absorb heat that is radiated back from the warmed surface of the earth

greet (3ʳᵈ): address (K), hail (4ᵗʰ), hello (K), wave to (K), welcome (1ˢᵗ)

grey (3ʳᵈ): See gray.

greyhound (3ʳᵈ)

grief (5ᵗʰ): ache (5ᵗʰ), agony (5ᵗʰ), anguish (6ᵗʰ), distress (5ᵗʰ), heartache (6ᵗʰ), hurt (K), misery (4ᵗʰ), pain (2ⁿᵈ), sorrow (4ᵗʰ), suffering (2ⁿᵈ), woe (4ᵗʰ)

grim (4ᵗʰ): bad (K), dark (K), depressing (5ᵗʰ), evil (3ʳᵈ), firm (2ⁿᵈ), forbidding (4ᵗʰ), hard (K), harsh (5ᵗʰ), merciless (4ᵗʰ), severe (4ᵗʰ), stern (4ᵗʰ)

grin (1ˢᵗ): laugh (1ˢᵗ), smile (1ˢᵗ)

grind (4ᵗʰ): A. toil (4ᵗʰ), work (K) **B.** crush (4ᵗʰ), grate (4ᵗʰ), scrape (4ᵗʰ), smash (3ʳᵈ)

grip (4ᵗʰ): clutch (4ᵗʰ), grasp (4ᵗʰ), hold (1ˢᵗ), possess (3ʳᵈ), seize (3ʳᵈ)

gripe (5ᵗʰ): A. distress (5ᵗʰ), trouble (1ˢᵗ), worry (1ˢᵗ) **B.** complain (4ᵗʰ), find fault (3ʳᵈ), object (1ˢᵗ)

grizzly (4ᵗʰ): awful (3ʳᵈ), chilling (3ʳᵈ), ghastly (6ᵗʰ), grim (4ᵗʰ), horrible (1ˢᵗ), horrid (4ᵗʰ), ugly (4ᵗʰ)

groan (3ʳᵈ): complain (4ᵗʰ), moan (5ᵗʰ), mourn (4ᵗʰ), sigh (3ʳᵈ), sob (1ˢᵗ)

groom (5ᵗʰ): A. brush (2ⁿᵈ), clean (K), maintain (4ᵗʰ) **B.** husband (1ˢᵗ)

groove (5ᵗʰ): crack (4ᵗʰ), line (K), rim (1ˢᵗ)

grope (6ᵗʰ): clasp (4ᵗʰ), clutch (4ᵗʰ), feel (K), grab (4ᵗʰ), grasp (4ᵗʰ), seize (3ʳᵈ)

gross (3ʳᵈ): A. all (K), complete (3ʳᵈ), entire (3ʳᵈ), whole (1ˢᵗ) **B.** disgusting (5ᵗʰ), plain (2ⁿᵈ), raw (1ˢᵗ), rude (2ⁿᵈ) **C.** extreme (5ᵗʰ), glaring (4ᵗʰ), large (K), obvious (5ᵗʰ), outright (1ˢᵗ), total (2ⁿᵈ)

ground (1ˢᵗ): base (1ˢᵗ), clay (1ˢᵗ), earth (1ˢᵗ), fix (1ˢᵗ), foundation (5ᵗʰ), install (6ᵗʰ), root (3ʳᵈ), set (K), settle (2ⁿᵈ), soil (2ⁿᵈ)

group (1ˢᵗ): array (5ᵗʰ), band (1ˢᵗ), batch (2ⁿᵈ), class (1ˢᵗ), classify (1ˢᵗ), club (1ˢᵗ), company (2ⁿᵈ), crew (2ⁿᵈ), file (1ˢᵗ), organization (4ᵗʰ), pack (1ˢᵗ), rank (3ʳᵈ), set (K), tribe (3ʳᵈ)

grove (4ᵗʰ): forest (2ⁿᵈ), orchard (5ᵗʰ), woods (1ˢᵗ)

grow (K): breed (4ᵗʰ), enlarge (5ᵗʰ), expand (5ᵗʰ), get bigger (1ˢᵗ), increase (3ʳᵈ), mature (5ᵗʰ), raise (1ˢᵗ)

growl (4ᵗʰ): bark (3ʳᵈ), complain (4ᵗʰ), howl (4ᵗʰ), moan (5ᵗʰ), roar (1ˢᵗ), snarl (5ᵗʰ), threaten (3ʳᵈ)

grown-up (1ˢᵗ): adult (1ˢᵗ), big (K), grown (1ˢᵗ), mature (5ᵗʰ)

grub (5ᵗʰ): dig (K), explore (4ᵗʰ), mine (1ˢᵗ), spade (6ᵗʰ), worm (5ᵗʰ)

grudge (5ᵗʰ): covet (6ᵗʰ), envy (4ᵗʰ), jealousy (5ᵗʰ), malice (6ᵗʰ), offense (4ᵗʰ), resent (5ᵗʰ), resentment (5ᵗʰ), spite (3ʳᵈ)

grudgingly (5ᵗʰ)

gruel (6ᵗʰ): oatmeal (5ᵗʰ), porridge (5ᵗʰ)

gruff (1ˢᵗ): bluff (6ᵗʰ), blunt (6ᵗʰ), grumpy (5ᵗʰ), harsh (5ᵗʰ), hoarse (5ᵗʰ), rude (2ⁿᵈ), sour (6ᵗʰ), sullen (5ᵗʰ)

grumble (5ᵗʰ): complain (4ᵗʰ), fuss (1ˢᵗ), growl (4ᵗʰ), roar (1ˢᵗ), snarl (5ᵗʰ)

guarantee (6th): bond (3rd), certify (6th), contract (3rd), oath (5th), promise (1st), secure (3rd), warrant (5th)

guard (1st): cover (1st), defend (5th), defender (5th), guide (1st), keep watch (1st), make safe (K), patrol (1st), protect (4th), save (1st), secure (3rd), shield (4th), supervise (6th)

guess (1st): believe (1st), figure (2nd), reckon (3rd), surmise (6th), theory (5th), think (1st)

guest (3rd): caller (1st), company (2nd), visitor (1st)

guide (1st): advise (3rd), counsel (5th), escort (5th), guard (1st), instruct (4th), lead (1st), model (3rd), navigate (5th), pattern (3rd), pilot (5th), rule (K), steer (5th), teach (1st)

guidepost (6th)

guilt (4th): blame (2nd), contrition (5th), fault (3rd), regret (5th), remorse (6th), sorrow (4th)

guilty (4th): contrite (5th), criminal (4th), sinful (1st), unholy (5th), wrong (1st)

guitar (4th)

gulf (4th): break (1st), canyon (6th), hole (K), inlet (4th), opening (K), sea (1st), space (1st)

gully (6th): canyon (4th), valley (2nd)

gulp (1st): devour (5th), guzzle (1st), swallow (1st)

gum (K): adhesive (6th), glue (1st)

gun (K): cannon (4th), pistol (5th), revolver (5th), rifle (4th), shotgun (1st)

gust (5th): blast (2nd), blow (1st), breath (1st), breeze (4th), burst (3rd), puff (2nd)

gut (1st): abdomen (6th), belly (5th), stomach (2nd)

guts (1st): bravery (3rd), courage (4th), nerve (1st), spirit (2nd)

gutter (6th): ditch (2nd), drain (5th), eaves (6th), rut (1st), sewer (2nd), spout (5th)

guttural (6th): gruff (1st), hoarse (5th), thick (2nd), throaty (2nd)

guy (1st): boy (K), buddy (4th), chap (4th), fellow (1st), male (4th), man (K), mate (4th)

gym (1st): arena (5th), court (3rd), gymnasium (5th)

gymnasium (5th): arena (5th), court (3rd), gym (1st)

gymnast (5th): acrobat (5th), tumbler (4th)

gypsy (6th): drifter (2nd), migrant (4th), tramp (4th), wanderer (3rd)

habit (3rd): A. addiction (5th), weakness (3rd) **B.** bent (1st), disposition (5th), pattern (3rd), practice (1st), routine (6th), rut (1st), way (K) **C.** attire (6th), costume (4th), custom (6th), dress (K), uniform (1st)

habitable (6th): livable (3rd), warm (1st)

habitat (6th): area (3rd), environment (6th), ground (1st), locality (4th), range (3rd), region (4th), surroundings (3rd), territory (3rd), vicinity (6th)

hackle (6th): A. feathers (2nd), hairs (K) **B.** chop (2nd)

had (K)

hadn't (1st)

hail (4th): address (K), call (K), cry out (1st), greet (3rd), hello (K), meet

(K), receive (1st), salute (4th), shout (1st), signal (4th), welcome (1st), yell (K)

hair (K): bristle (6th), coat (1st), fiber (3rd), fur (K), mane (1st), thread (2nd)

hale (2nd): A. drag (3rd), pull (K), tow (1st) **B.** fit (K), healthy (1st), hearty (5th), mighty (1st), robust (5th), strong (K), sturdy (3rd), vigorous (5th), well (K)

half (1st): hemisphere (6th), part (1st)

half-mast (5th)

hall (1st): corridor (5th), entry (3rd), passage (4th), way (K)

Halloween (K)

halt (4th): arrest (3rd), cease (3rd), close (K), end (K), falter (3rd), hinder (6th), quit (1st), restrain (5th), stall (5th), stop (K)

ham (K)

hamburger (4th)

hammer (2nd): beat (1st), club (1st), hit (K), pound (2nd), slap (2nd), strike (2nd)

hamster (1st)

hand (K): aid (2nd), assist (4th), deliver (5th), employee (5th), furnish (4th), give (K), help (K), helper (1st), pass (K), present (K), produce (2nd), workman (1st)

handcuffs (2nd): manacles (5th), restraints (5th), shackles (5th)

handkerchief (4th): napkin (5th), tissue (5th)

handle (2nd): carry (K), feel (K), finger (1st), grip (4th), heave (5th), hold (1st), lift (1st), pat (K), shaft (4th), stroke (1st), touch (1st)

handsome (3rd): A. free (K), generous (4th), liberal (4th), unselfish (5th) **B.** attractive (5th), beautiful (1st), fair (1st), good-looking (2nd), lovely (1st), pretty (1st)

hang (2nd): dangle (5th), suspend (4th), swing (1st)

happen (1st): become (1st), chance (2nd), come about (1st), occur (3rd), result (2nd), turn up (1st)

happy (K): cheerful (3rd), delighted (3rd), fortunate (4th), glad (1st), jolly (4th), joyful (2nd), jovial (5th), lighthearted (2nd), lucky (K), merry (3rd), pleased (1st)

harbor (2nd): A. house (K), lodge (4th), port (1st), refuge (5th), shelter (4th) **B.** cloak (4th), conceal (4th), cover (1st), guard (1st), hide (1st), protect (4th)

hard (K): A. difficult (5th), tough (5th) **B.** compact (5th), firm (4th), solid (3rd), strong (K)

hard drive (1st): (computer)

harden (2nd): cement (4th), set (K), solidify (4th), toughen (5th)

hardship (5th): burden (5th), difficulty (5th), harm (3rd), hurt (K), need (1st), neglect (4th), plight (6th), ruin (2nd), stress (6th)

hardy (5th): fit (K), healthy (1st), hearty (5th), mighty (1st), robust (5th), strong (K), sturdy (3rd), vigorous (5th), well (1st)

hare (3rd)

hark (6th): hear (K), listen (1st), notice (1st), pay attention (2nd)

harm (3rd): abuse (6th), damage (5th), hurt (K), ill (1st), injure (5th), injury

(5th), pain (2nd), spoil (4th), torment (5th), woe (4th), wound (3rd)

harmonize (4th): adapt (4th), agree (2nd), compose (4th)

harmony (4th): agreement (3rd), balance (3rd), order (1st), unity (5th)

harness (4th): A. reins (1st), yoke (6th) **B.** control (2nd), hold (1st), tie (1st)

harp (4th): complain (4th), persist in (5th), repeat (4th)

harsh (5th): coarse (4th), rough (4th)

harvest (4th): collect (3rd), cultivate (6th), gather (1st), reap (4th)

harvesting (4th): cultivating (6th), farming (1st)

has (K)

hasn't (1st)

haste (2nd): eagerness (5th), enthusiasm (4th), hurry (1st), impatience (5th), quickness (2nd), rapidity (4th), rush (2nd), speed (3rd)

hasty (2nd): brisk (6th), careless (5th), fast (1st), quick (1st), rapid (4th), rash (6th), speedy (3rd), sudden (1st), swift (4th), urgent (6th)

hat (K): bonnet (6th), cap (K), crown (1st)

hatch (4th): A. door (K), escape (1st), opening (1st) **B.** breed (4th), conceive (4th), devise (4th), plan (1st), scheme (5th)

hate (2nd): despise (5th), detest (6th), dislike (2nd)

hateful (3rd): cursed (4th), evil (3rd), hideous (6th), horrible (1st), mean (1st), repulsive (6th), wicked (4th)

haughty (6th): arrogant (6th), lordly (2nd), proud (2nd), self-important (2nd), vain (4th)

haul (4th): convey (4th), drag (5th), draw (K), heave (5th), lift (1st), lug (1st), move (K), pull (K), tow (1st), transport (5th)

haunch (5th): hip (1st), side (K), thigh (3rd)

haunt (2nd): burden (5th), linger (4th), possess (3rd), trouble (1st), visit (1st), worry (1st)

have (K): own (K), possess (3rd)

hay (K): feed (1st), straw (2nd)

hazard (6th): accident (4th), danger (1st), dare (2nd), endanger (6th), gamble (5th), offer (2nd), risk (4th), threat (5th), venture (4th)

he (K)

he'd (1st)

head (K): A. crown (1st), face (K), front (1st) **B.** boss (K), chief (1st), leader (1st), manager (4th), master (1st), president (1st), principal (3rd), supervisor (6th)

headache (6th): pain (2nd), problem (1st)

headquarters (3rd): base (1st), office (1st), station (1st)

heal (3rd): cure (4th), doctor (1st), improve (3rd), make well (2nd), mend (1st), recover (4th), remedy (4th), renew (4th), repair (4th), restore (5th)

health (K): fitness (3rd), power (1st), strength (1st), vitality (5th), well-being (2nd)

heap (4th): A. bulk (4th), mass (3rd), pile (1st) **B.** accumulate (6th), gather

(1st), mound (2nd), reserve (3rd), stack (6th), stock (6th), supply (1st)

hear (K): attend (3rd), hark (6th), heed (4th), learn of (2nd), listen to (2nd), notice (1st), regard (4th)

heard (K)

heart (K): A. center (2nd), core (6th), focus (5th), middle (2nd) **B.** emotion (4th), feeling (K), kindness (1st), love (K), passion (6th), spirit (2nd), soul (3rd)

heartache (6th): agony (5th), anguish (6th), grief (5th), hurt (K), misery (4th), pain (2nd), problem (1st), sadness (1st), sorrow (4th), suffering (2nd), torment (5th), woe (4th)

hearth (5th): fireplace (2nd), home (K)

hearty (5th): ardent (6th), cordial (6th), earnest (4th), friendly (2nd), healthy (1st), sincere (4th), sound (1st), vigorous (5th), warm (1st)

heat (1st): bake (1st), cook (1st), fever (4th), furor (5th), passion (6th), roast (4th), warm (1st), warmth (2nd)

heathen (6th): primitive (5th), not Christian (3rd), savage (5th), unsophisticated (5th)

heave (5th): cast (2nd), fling (6th), haul (4th), hurl (5th), launch (5th), lift (1st), raise (1st), throw (1st), toss (2nd), tug (1st)

heaven (1st): delight (3rd), ecstasy (6th), paradise (4th), rapture (6th)

heavenly (2nd): blessed (4th), delightful (3rd), glorious (4th), good (K), holy (5th), ideal (3rd), sainted (3rd)

heavy (1st): ample (5th), big (K), bulky (4th), huge (1st), immense (4th), large (K), massive (5th), weighty (2nd)

hectic (3rd): burning (3rd), busy (1st), excited (4th), feverish (4th), furious (4th), stormy (3rd), wild (2nd)

hedge (4th): border (1st), cheat (3rd), cover (1st), edge (1st), fence (1st), halt (4th), hesitate (4th), hold back (1st), limit (3rd), restrain (5th)

heed (4th): care (K), caution (5th), consider (2nd), consideration (3rd), guard (1st), note (1st), obey (3rd), observe (3rd), pay attention to (2nd), remember (1st), respect (2nd), think (1st)

heel (3rd): A. back (K), bottom (1st), end (K), foot (K), hoof (5th), last (K), remnant (6th), trail (2nd) **B.** cad (6th) **C.** dog (K), follow (1st), hound (2nd), pursue (5th), tag (K), trail (2nd) **D.** cant (6th), incline (5th), lean (3rd), list (2nd), tilt (5th), slant (6th), rake (1st), slope (3rd), tip (1st)

height (4th): altitude (5th), ceiling (4th), elevation (4th), extreme (5th), high point (2nd), length (2nd), limit (3rd), loftiness (5th), tallness (1st)

heir (4th): assign (5th), child (K), ward (5th)

hello (K): greetings (3rd), hi (K), salutations (4th)

helm (6th): control (2nd), head (K), reins (1st), throne (4th), wheel (1st)

helmet (1st)

help (K): advance (2nd), aid (1st), assist (4th), benefit (3rd), contribute (4th), employee (5th), hand (K), maintain (4th), relief (4th), save (1st), servant (3rd), service (1st), support (4th), use (K)

helper (1st): aid (1st), ally (6th), assistant (5th), attendant (4th), patron (5th), supporter (5th)

197

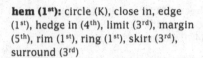

hem (1ˢᵗ): circle (K), close in, edge (1ˢᵗ), hedge in (4ᵗʰ), limit (3ʳᵈ), margin (5ᵗʰ), rim (1ˢᵗ), ring (1ˢᵗ), skirt (3ʳᵈ), surround (3ʳᵈ)

hemisphere (6ᵗʰ): half (1ˢᵗ), part (1ˢᵗ)

hemlock (6ᵗʰ)

hemp (5ᵗʰ)

hen (K): chicken (K), fowl (4ᵗʰ)

hence (3ʳᵈ): from now on (2ⁿᵈ), so (K), then (K), thence (4ᵗʰ), therefore (2ⁿᵈ), thus (1ˢᵗ)

her (K)

herald (3ʳᵈ): air (K), announce (3ʳᵈ), omen (6ᵗʰ), pioneer (4ᵗʰ), proclaim (4ᵗʰ), scout (1ˢᵗ), signal (4ᵗʰ), symptom (6ᵗʰ)

herb (5ᵗʰ): spice (3ʳᵈ)

herbivore (5ᵗʰ)

herd (2ⁿᵈ): A. bunch (3ʳᵈ), flock (2ⁿᵈ), group (1ˢᵗ), pack (1ˢᵗ) **B.** collect (3ʳᵈ), crowd (2ⁿᵈ), gather (1ˢᵗ)

here (K): present (K), now (K)

hereafter (6ᵗʰ): after this (K), finally (3ʳᵈ), forever (3ʳᵈ), from now on (K), heaven (1ˢᵗ), hence (3ʳᵈ), in the future (5ᵗʰ), later (1ˢᵗ), paradise (4ᵗʰ),

here's (1ˢᵗ)

hermit (5ᵗʰ): holy man (5ᵗʰ), monk (4ᵗʰ)

hero (1ˢᵗ): champion (4ᵗʰ), ideal (3ʳᵈ), idol (6ᵗʰ), model (3ʳᵈ), star (K), victor (4ᵗʰ)

heroic (5ᵗʰ): adventurous (3ʳᵈ), bold (2ⁿᵈ), brave (1ˢᵗ), courageous (4ᵗʰ), daring (3ʳᵈ), gallant (4ᵗʰ), grand (2ⁿᵈ), great (K), noble (3ʳᵈ), valiant (6ᵗʰ)

herring (5ᵗʰ)

hers (K)

herself (2ⁿᵈ)

hesitate (4ᵗʰ): delay (5ᵗʰ), falter (1ˢᵗ), hang back (3ʳᵈ), hedge (4ᵗʰ), pause (3ʳᵈ), put off (2ⁿᵈ), stall (5ᵗʰ), waver (5ᵗʰ)

hew (6ᵗʰ): axe (K), carve (4ᵗʰ), chop (2ⁿᵈ), clip (5ᵗʰ), cut (K), hit (K), sculpt (4ᵗʰ), slash (6ᵗʰ), trim (4ᵗʰ)

hey (K)

hi (K): greetings (3ʳᵈ), hello (K), hey (K), salutations (4ᵗʰ)

hidden (1ˢᵗ): concealed (4ᵗʰ), covered (1ˢᵗ), covert (6ᵗʰ), masked (3ʳᵈ), obscure (6ᵗʰ), secret (1ˢᵗ), unclear (3ʳᵈ)

hide (1ˢᵗ): A. coat (1ˢᵗ), fur (K), skin (1ˢᵗ) **B.** conceal (4ᵗʰ), disguise (5ᵗʰ), harbor (2ⁿᵈ), retire (4ᵗʰ), screen (1ˢᵗ), veil (3ʳᵈ), withdraw (2ⁿᵈ)

hideous (6ᵗʰ): awful (3ʳᵈ), disgusting (5ᵗʰ), foul (4ᵗʰ), hateful (3ʳᵈ), horrid (4ᵗʰ), monstrous (5ᵗʰ), offensive (4ᵗʰ), repellant (6ᵗʰ), repulsive (6ᵗʰ), terrible (1ˢᵗ), ugly (4ᵗʰ), vile (6ᵗʰ)

high (K): costly (1ˢᵗ), elevated (2ⁿᵈ), expensive (3ʳᵈ), lofty (5ᵗʰ), noble (3ʳᵈ), prominent (5ᵗʰ), raised (1ˢᵗ), remote (5ᵗʰ), steep (2ⁿᵈ), tall (K), towering (4ᵗʰ)

highway (4ᵗʰ): avenue (3ʳᵈ), boulevard (4ᵗʰ), drive (K), freeway (2ⁿᵈ), road (K), street (1ˢᵗ), strip (3ʳᵈ)

hike (3ʳᵈ): climb (1ˢᵗ), march (1ˢᵗ), plod (5ᵗʰ), stroll (5ᵗʰ), tramp (4ᵗʰ), trudge (5ᵗʰ), walk (K)

hill (K): bluff (6ᵗʰ), climb (1ˢᵗ), elevation (4ᵗʰ), heap (4ᵗʰ), incline (5ᵗʰ), mound (2nd), pile (1st), ramp (6th), slope (3rd)

hillside (4th)

him (K)

himself (2nd)

hind (4th): A. back (K), end (K), final (3rd), rear (3rd) **B.** after (K) **C.** red deer (K) **D.** fish (K) **E.** laborer (1st), unsophisticated (6th), worker (1st)

hinder (6th): bar (3rd), block (1st), dam (K), delay (5th), halt (4th), interfere (4th), limit (3rd), obstruct (5th), prevent (3rd), stop (K)

hindquarter (5th): back (1st)

Hindu (5th)

hinge (5th): center (2nd), depend (3rd), hang (2nd), joint (4th), pivot (5th), rest (1st), rotate (4th), turn (1st)

hint (1st): clue (2nd), cue (2nd), idea (1st), omen (6th), signal (4th), suggestion (2nd), warning (3rd)

hip (1st): aware (3rd), bottom (1st), bright (1st), clever (3rd), cool (1st), current (3rd), flank (5th), side (K), smart (1st)

hippo (K)

hippopotamus (3rd)

hire (3rd): A. earnings (3rd), fee (4th), salary (3rd), wage (3rd) **B.** employ (5th), engage (5th), lease (6th), rent (K), pay (K), use (K)

his (K)

hiss (3rd): buzz (5th), mock (4th), scorn (4th), taunt (5th), whisper (1st)

history (2nd): background (4th), biography (6th), chronicle (6th), legend (5th), past (1st), record (2nd), story (K), tale (3rd)

hit (K): beat (1st), box (1st), bump (2nd), club (1st), collide with (6th), pound (2nd), punch (4th), slap (2nd), slug (5th), smack (6th), spank (2nd), strike (2nd), tap (K)

hither (6th): far (1st), there (1st)

HIV (4th)

hive (2nd): house (K)

hoarfrost (6th)

hoard (6th): accumulate (6th), amass (3rd), heap (4th), hide (1st), pile (1st), reserve (3rd), save (1st), store (K)

hoarse (5th): cracked (1st), dry (1st), gruff (1st), loud (1st), rough (4th)

hoary (6th): aged (2nd), ancient (3rd), bearded (4th), crusty (4th), elderly (5th), grizzly (4th), old (K)

hoax (5th): A. deception (6th), fake (1st), fraud (6th), imitation (5th) **B.** cheat (3rd), deceive (5th), fool (2nd), joke (1st), trick (1st)

hobby (3rd): amusement (4th), collection (3rd), entertainment (4th), pastime (3rd), recreation (5th), sport (1st)

hockey (3rd)

hoe (2nd): cultivate (6th), dig (1st), farm (K), garden (K), rake (1st), till (1st)

hog (K): A. pig (K) **B.** amass (3rd), be selfish (5th), keep (K)

hogan (2nd): house (K)

hoist (6th): elevate (2nd), erect (4th), heave (5th), lift (1st), raise (1st)

hold (1st): bear (K), carry (K), clasp (4th), clutch (4th), contain (5th), embrace (4th), grip (4th), hug (1st), keep (K), maintain (4th), reserve (3rd), restrict (6th), seize (3rd), support (4th)

hole (K): cavity (5th), dent (1st), dip (1st), gap (K), hollow (3rd), opening (1st), rut (1st), space (1st), vent (4th), void (6th)

holiday (K): celebration (5th), ceremony (5th), festival (5th), observance (5th), vacation (2nd)

hollow (3rd): A. senseless (2nd), useless (2nd), worthless (3rd) **B.** depression (5th), pocket (1st), sunk (3rd) **C.** empty (3rd), vacant (6th)

Holocene (5th): of or belonging to the geologic time, rock series, or sedimentary deposits of the more recent of the two epochs of the Quaternary Period

holy (5th): blessed (3rd), celestial (5th), divine (5th), heavenly (2nd), moral (3rd), pious (6th), pure (3rd), religious (4th), saintly (4th)

homage (6th): admiration (5th), awe (6th), esteem (5th), honor (1st), respect (2nd), reverence (4th), tribute (5th), worship (4th)

home (K): abode (5th), address (K), domicile (5th), dwelling (4th), habitat (6th), habitation (6th), hearth (5th), house (K), location (3rd), quarters (2nd), residence (5th), shelter (4th)

homespun (5th): homemade (1st), homey (1st), modest (4th), plain (2nd), simple (2nd)

homework (1st): lessons (3rd), studies (2nd)

honest (3rd): fair (1st), frank (4th), honorable (3rd), just (1st), moral (3rd), sincere (4th), trustworthy (3rd), truthful (2nd), worthy (3rd)

honey (1st)

honeysuckle (5th)

honk (1st)

honor (1st): admire (5th), celebrate (4th), esteem (5th), fame (3rd), glorify (4th), glory (3rd), hail (4th), respect (2nd), salute (4th), tribute (5th), worship (4th)

hood (4th): bonnet (6th), cap (K), hat (K), scarf (6th), veil (3rd)

hoof (1st): foot (K), paw (1st)

hook (4th): angle (3rd), bend (K), bow (1st), catch (1st), curve (3rd), sickle (6th), snare (6th), trap (1st), turn (1st)

hoop (5th): band (1st), circle (K), ring (1st), wheel (1st)

hoot (1st): bawl (5th), cry (K), howl (4th), roar (1st), shout (1st)

hop (K): bound (2nd), jump (K), leap (3rd), skip (2nd), spring (K), vault (5th)

hope (K): await (5th), believe (1st), desire (5th), dream (K), expect (3rd), foresee (6th), long (1st), longing (2nd), suppose (2nd), trust (1st), want (K), wish (K), yearn (6th)

hopped (1st)

horde (6th): band (1st), herd (2nd), host (4th), lot (K), mass (3rd), mob (4th), pack (1st), throng (5th), tribe (3rd)

horizon (4th): distance (4th), prospect (4th), range (3rd), scope (6th), skyline (5th), view (1st)

horizontal (6th): flat (2nd), level (3rd), plane (1st), sideways (1st)

horrible (1st): See horrid.

horn (3rd)

hornet (5th)

horrible (1st): awful (3rd), dreadful (6th), horrible (1st), terrible (1st)

horrid (4th): See horrible.

horrify (4th): alarm (3rd), frighten (2nd), scare (1st), startle (4th), terrify (3rd)

horror (4th): dread (6th), fear (1st), terror (3rd)

hose (6th): A. sock (1st), stocking (4th), tights (1st) **B.** channel (4th), pipe (1st), spray (2nd), tube (3rd), water (1st)

hospital (3rd): clinic (1st), medical center (5th)

host (4th): army (1st), band (1st), herd (2nd), horde (6th), legion (6th), mob (4th), pack (1st), throng (5th)

hostile (4th): angry (1st), contrary (4th), fighting (1st), mad (K), malicious (6th), mean (1st), unfriendly (3rd), unkind (1st)

hot (K): angry (1st), baking (2nd), blazing (2nd), burning (3rd), eager (5th), earnest (4th), fiery (5th), furious (5th), keen (4th), scorching (6th), spicy (4th), strong (K), tart (5th), warm (1st)

hotel (3rd): inn (4th), lodging (4th), motel (3rd), tavern (5th)

hothouse (5th): greenhouse (1st), pavilion (5th)

hotspot (5th): geographical region covered by one or several access points where computers, cell phones, or other devices can connect to the Internet or other Wi-Fi–enabled equipment

hound (2nd): A. dog (K), pup (K) **B.** badger (2nd), bait (3rd), force (1st),

heel (3rd), hunt (2nd), pursue (5th), stalk (4th), tail (1st)

hour (1st): time (1st)

house (K): abode (5th), address (K), domicile (5th), dwelling (4th), habitat (6th), habitation (6th), home (K), lodge (4th), quarters (2nd), residence (5th), shelter (4th)

housekeeper (3rd): cleaner (1st), help (K), maid (3rd), servant (3rd)

housework (3rd): clean (1st),

hover (3rd): float (1st), fly (K), hang (2nd), linger (4th), suspend (4th), wait near (2nd)

hovercraft (3rd): a craft capable of moving over water or land on a cushion of air

how (K): how come (1st), whereby (4th), wherefore (4th), why (K)

however (1st): although (2nd), anyway (1st), but (K), even though (2nd), in any case (2nd), nevertheless (4th), regardless (4th)

howl (4th): bark (3rd), growl (4th), roar (1st), shout (1st), wail (5th), yell (K), yelp (6th)

hue (6th): color (K), shade (2nd), tint (5th), tone (3rd)

hug (1st): clasp (4th), clutch (4th), cuddle (5th), embrace (4th), grip (4th), hold (1st), snuggle (5th), squeeze (5th)

huge (1st): big (K), enormous (4th), grant (2nd), infinite (5th), large (K), massive (5th), tremendous (4th), unlimited (4th)

hull (4th): body (1st), case (2nd), frame (3rd), outside (1st), shell (1st), skeleton (4th), structure (4th)

hum (1st): buzz (5th), murmur (4th), sing (1st), vibrate (5th), vibration (5th)

human (3rd): being (1st), individual (3rd), mortal (4th), person (1st), soul (3rd)

humble (4th): A. put down (2nd), shame (3rd) **B.** base (1st), belittle (4th), common (2nd), dishonor (3rd), lower (1st), lowly (1st), mean (1st), meek (2nd), mild (4th), modest (4th), plain (2nd), simple (1st)

humor (4th): comedy (5th), heart (K), jest (4th), joke (1st), mood (3rd), nature (1st), soul (3rd), spirit (2nd), wit (1st)

hump (3rd): bulge (4th), bump (2nd), hunch (6th), lump (4th), mass (3rd), swelling (3rd)

hunch (6th): A. bet (1st), feeling (1st) **B.** bend (K), squat (5th), stoop (5th)

hundred (1st)

hunger (2nd): appetite (4th), craving (6th), desire (5th), longing (1st), urge (4th), want (K)

hungry (2nd): craving (6th), longing (1st), starving (5th), yearning (6th)

hunker (6th): crouch (5th), stoop (5th)

hunt (2nd): chase (1st), comb (2nd), follow (1st), look for (1st), pursue (5th), search (1st), seek (1st), stalk (4th), track (1st)

hurl (5th): cast (2nd), fling (6th), heave (5th), launch (5th), pitch (2nd), send (K), shoot (3rd), throw (1st), toss (2nd)

hurried (1st): careless (5th), feverish (4th), hasty (2nd), rushed (3rd), urgent (6th)

hurry (1st): drive on (1st), fly (K), hasten (2nd), provoke (6th), rush (2nd), speed (3rd), sprint (5th), stimulate (6th)

hurt (K): A. ache (5th), ill (1st), pain (2nd), woe (4th) **B.** abuse (6th), damage (5th), harm (3rd), injure (5th), injury (5th), ruin (5th), wound (3rd)

husband (1st): groom (5th), mate (4th), partner (5th)

hush (3rd): lull (5th), quiet (K), rest (1st), silence (4th), solitude (5th), still (1st)

hut (4th): cabin (1st), cottage (4th), house (K)

hydrogen (6th)

hyena (4th)

hymn (5th): carol (3rd), chant (5th), melody (4th), psalm (6th), song (K), tune (1st)

hysteria (6th): craze (4th), eruption (4th), explosion (4th), fit (K), madness (3rd)

hysterical (6th): crazed (4th), emotional (4th), funny (1st), mad (2nd), raving (6th)

I (K): me (K)

ice (K): frost (4th), frozen (4th)

iceberg (3rd)

icebox (1st): refrigerator (2nd)

icon (1st): picture (K), image (4th), symbol (5th)

I'd (1st)

idea (1st): belief (1st), concept (4th), feeling (K), notion (5th), opinion (3rd), thought (1st), viewpoint (5th)

ideal (3rd): A. example (2nd), model (3rd), original (3rd), pattern (3rd) **B.** aim (3rd), goal (4th), objective (2nd) **C.** abstract (6th), perfect (3rd), truth (1st)

identical (6th): alike (1st), duplicate (6th), equal (2nd), equivalent (6th), same (1st)

identify (4th): call (K), know (1st), label (3rd), point out (1st), prove (1st), recognize (3rd), select (4th), term (3rd)

identity (5th): itself (2nd), myself (1st), name (K), oneself (3rd), person (1st), self (3rd), uniqueness (6th)

idiot (6th): fool (2nd), silly (1st), simple (2nd), stupid (4th)

idle (4th): A. do nothing (1st), laze (4th), loaf (4th) **B.** inactive (3rd), lazy (4th), not working (1st), unoccupied (3rd)

idol (6th): dream (K), god (1st), hero (1st), vision (4th)

idolize (6th): adore (4th), magnify (3rd), worship (4th)

if (K): although (2nd), provided (3rd), though (1st), whether (1st)

igneous (5th): relating to or characteristic of rocks formed by solidification from a molten state such as lava

ignite (6th): burn (3rd), fire (K), light (K), set on fire (K)

ignorant (4th): blind (3rd), in the dark (2nd), unaware (3rd), uneducated (3rd), unknowing (2nd), unschooled (1st)

ignore (5th): disregard (4th), neglect (4th), overlook (4th), push aside (3rd)

ill (1st): A. bad (K), evil (3rd), sinful (2nd), wicked (4th) **B.** poorly (1st), sick (1st), sickly (1st), unwell (1st)

I'll (1st)

illegal (1st): forbidden (4th), lawless (2nd), unlawful (3rd)

illuminate (6th): A. educate (3rd), explain (2nd), guide (1st), inform (5th), tell (K) **B.** light (K), light up (1st), shine (1st)

illusion (6th): false idea (3rd), fancy (3rd), fantasy (6th), imagination (2nd), vision (4th)

illustration (4th): A. example (2nd), explanation (2nd), sample (5th) **B.** drawing (1st), photograph (5th), sketch (5th)

illustrious (6th): celebrated (5th), famous (2nd), popular (3rd), renowned (5th)

I'm (1st)

image (4th): likeness (2nd), photograph (5th), picture (K), portrait (5th), statue (4th)

imagine (2nd): conceive (4th), dream up (1st), envision (4th), fancy (3rd), picture (K), think (1st)

imitate (5th): ape (5th), copy (3rd), mimic (6th), mock (4th), simulate (6th)

immaculate (6th): clean (1st), fresh (2nd), perfect (3rd), pure (3rd), spotless (1st)

immature (5th): childish (1st), new (K), not ripe (1st)

immediate (3rd): abrupt (5th), direct (1st), nearest (2nd), now (K), prompt (4th), sudden (1st)

immense (4th): big (K), broad (3rd), enormous (4th), giant (2nd), great (K), huge (1st), large (K), vast (4th), wide (1st)

immigrant (6th): alien (5th), foreigner (5th), stranger (1st)

immobile (6th): constant (4th), firm (2nd), fixed (1st), stationary (3rd), steady (3rd), unmoving (3rd)

immortal (4th): constant (4th), everlasting (5th), never-ending (1st), undying (4th), without end (1st)

immunity (4th): resistance (4th)

imp (5th): demon (4th), devil (1st), dwarf (4th), elf (1st), gnome (6th), spirit (2nd)

impart (6th): communicate (4th), give (K), pass on (K), reveal (4th), tell (1st)

impatient (5th): jumpy (1st), nervous (1st), restless (4th), rude (2nd), short (1st), uneasy (2nd), unquiet (1st)

imperial (5th): kingly (1st), queenly (1st), regal (6th), royal (3rd), ruling (1st)

impetus (6th): drive (K), energy (4th), force (1st), momentum (6th), push (1st), speed (3rd)

implement (6th): A. instrument (3rd), tool (1st), utensil (6th) **B.** enforce (5th), execute (5th), follow (1st)

imply (5th): assume (5th), hint (1st), include (3rd), involve (6th), mean (1st), suggest (2nd), suppose (2nd)

import (5th): A. bring in (K), carry (K), introduce (5th) **B.** concern (3rd), meaning (1st), sense (1st), value (2nd), worth (3rd)

important (1st): large (K), main (3rd), major (3rd), matters (1st), needed (1st), significant (6th)

impose (4th): ask (K), demand (5th), direct (1st), order (1st), put on (K), require (1st)

impossible (3rd): absurd (6th), can't (1st), out of the question (2nd), unable (3rd)

impoverished (6th): backwards (4th), deprived (6th), disadvantaged (3rd), poor (K), underprivileged (5th), reduced to poverty (5th), poverty-stricken (5th)

impress (5th): A. affect (4th), influence (5th), move (K), reach (1st), touch (1st) **B.** imprint (4th), print (1st), push (1st), stamp (2nd), strike (2nd)

impression (5th): A. imprint (4th), mark (1st), print (1st) **B.** concept (4th), idea (1st), image (4th), opinion (3rd), sense (1st), thought (1st), view (2nd)

imprint (4th): impression (5th), print (1st), stamp (2nd)

imprison (6th): cage (1st), capture (3rd), catch (1st), close in (1st), jail (4th), put in prison (3rd)

improve (3rd): better (1st), clean (K), develop (5th), fix (1st), help (K), put right (K), repair (4th)

impulse (5th): desire (5th), liking (1st), motive (5th), passion (6th), spur (4th), stimulus (6th)

in (K): at (K), inside (1st), on (K)

incapable (6th): helpless (1st), incompetent (6th), powerless (2nd), unable (3rd), weak (3rd)

incense (5th): anger (1st), enrage (6th), fire up (2nd), irritate (6th), provoke (6th)

inch (1st): creep (1st), move slowly (1st)

incident (5th): episode (6th), event (3rd), happening (1st), matter (1st), occurrence (3rd)

incline (5th): A. grade (2nd), slant (6th) **B.** prefer (3rd), tend (K) **C.** cant (6th), hill (K), incline (5th), lean (3rd), list (2nd), tilt (5th), slant (6th), rake (1st), slope (3rd), tip (1st)

inclined (5th): apt (5th), eager (5th), likely (1st)

include (3rd): cover (1st), embrace (4th), involve (6th), take in (1st)

income (4th): fee (4th), pay (K), salary (3rd), wages (3rd)

inconvenient (6th): awkward (6th), ill timed (2nd), out of the way (K)

increase (3rd): enlarge (5th), expand (5th), gain (2nd), multiply (4th), raise (1st)

incredible (6th): absurd (6th), crazy (4th), doubtful (5th), strange (1st), unbelievable (3rd), unreal (2nd)

incredulous (6th): doubtful (5th), unbelieving (2nd), uncertain (1st)

indeed (1st): certainly (1st), in fact (1st), surely (K), truly (K), yes (K)

independent (3rd): A. alone (1st), lone (2nd), separate (3rd), unconnected (3rd) **B.** confident (6th), direct (1st), free (K), self-reliant (5th), self-sufficient (3rd)

index (6th): A. label (3rd), mark (1st), sort (2nd) **B.** guide (1st), key (K)

Indian (1st)

indicate (4th): A. point (1st), point out (1st), show (1st), signal (4th) **B.** express (5th), hint (1st), imply (5th), mean (1st), state (1st), suggest (2nd), tell (K)

indifferent (5th): detached (5th), disinterested (3rd), distant (4th), uncaring (1st), unconcerned (3rd), unemotional (4th)

indignant (5th): angry (1st), annoyed (5th), irritated (6th), mad (K)

indispensable (6th): basic (5th), important (1st), necessary (1st), significant (6th)

individual (3rd): A. being (1st), creature (3rd), person (1st) **B.** characteristic (6th), distinct (5th), one (K), separate (3rd), single (3rd), sole (4th), special (2nd), specific (5th), unique (6th)

indoor (6th): enclosed (4th), in (K), inside (1st), sheltered (4th)

induce (5th): convince (4th), motivate (6th), persuade (5th), prompt (4th), provoke (6th), spur (4th)

indulge (5th): baby (K), fulfill (4th), humor (4th), oblige (6th), satisfy (3rd), spoil (4th)

industry (5th): business (2nd), commerce (5th), employment (5th), labor (1st), trade (2nd), work (K)

infant (5th): babe (5th), baby (K), newborn (2nd)

infect (6th): A. affect (4th), influence (5th), inspire (4th) **B.** contaminate (6th), poison (3rd), spoil (4th), taint (6th)

inferior (5th): below (1st), dependent (3rd), lesser (2nd), lower (1st), poorer (1st), secondary (2nd), second class (2nd), under (K)

infinite (5th): boundless (4th), constant (4th), continuous (2nd), eternal (4th), innumerable (5th), limitless (3rd), never ending (1st), nonstop (1st), ongoing (1st), unlimited (3rd), vast (4th)

inflect (6th): arch (4th), bend (K), curve (3rd), loop (5th), turn (1st)

influence (5th): A. affect (4th), change (2nd), direct (1st), impress (5th), manage (4th), sway (3rd) **B.** authority (3rd), effect (3rd), force (1st), power (1st), strength (1st)

inform (5th): acquaint (4th), animate (6th), announce (3rd), communicate (4th), educate (3rd), inspire (4th), teach (1st), tell (K)

informal (5th): casual (5th), common (2nd), easygoing (1st), every day (K), off hand (K), plain (2nd)

information (5th): advice (3rd), facts (1st), knowledge (2nd), report (1st)

ingenious (6th): clever (3rd), creative (3rd), cunning (6th), inventive (3rd), skillful (2nd), smart (1st)

ingredient (4th): component (4th), element (3rd), factor (5th), item (5th), member (1st), unit (5th)

inhabit (6th): abide (5th), dwell (4th), live (1st), live in (1st), occupy (3rd), reside (5th)

inherit (5th): get (K), receive (2nd)

initial (6th): beginning (2nd), first (1st), primary (5th)

initiate (5th): A. educate (3rd), instruct (4th), teach (1st) **B.** begin (1st), establish (3rd), found (2nd), install (6th), open (K), start (1st)

initiative (6th): A. beginning (2nd), first step (1st), lead (1st) **B.** ambition (4th), desire (5th), drive (K)

injure (5th): abuse (6th), bruise (5th), damage (5th), harm (3rd), hurt (1st), wound (3rd), wrong (1st)

injury (5th): bruise (5th), hurt (1st), ill (1st), pain (2nd), wound (3rd)

ink (2nd)

inland (5th): interior (5th), internal (6th), offshore (1st)

inlet (4th): bay (K), nook (6th)

inn (4th): hotel (3rd), tavern (5th)

inner (5th): inside (1st), interior (5th), internal (6th), inward (6th), within (3rd)

innocent (5th): A. blameless (2nd), guiltless (4th), pure (3rd) **B.** harmless (3rd)

innumerable (5th): countless (5th), infinite (5th), many (K), unlimited (3rd)

inquire (3rd): ask (K), examine (5th), question (1st), search (1st)

insane (6th): crazy (4th), lunatic (6th), mad (K), unbalanced (3rd)

inscribe (5th): address (K), autograph (6th), mark (1st), print (1st), sign (1st), write (K)

inscription (6th): address (K), caption (6th), legend (5th), message (1st), name (K), note (1st)

insect (4th): bug (1st), fly (K)

insert (6th): add in (K), introduce (5th), place (1st), put in (K)

inside (1st): inner (5th), interior (5th), internal (6th)

insist (5th): assure (3rd), compel (3rd), demand (5th), press (1st), stress (6th), urge (4th)

inspect (5th): examine (5th), observe (3rd), scan (6th), study (1st)

inspire (4th): cheer (3rd), encourage (4th), enliven (6th), fire (K), impress (5th)

install (6th): establish (3rd), initiate (5th), put in (K), set up (1st)

instance (5ᵗʰ): case (2ⁿᵈ), example (2ⁿᵈ), illustration (4ᵗʰ), sample (5ᵗʰ)

instant (3ʳᵈ): A. immediate (3ʳᵈ), prompt (4ᵗʰ), quick (1ˢᵗ), urgent (6ᵗʰ) **B.** flash (2ⁿᵈ), minute (1ˢᵗ), moment (1ˢᵗ), second (1ˢᵗ)

instead (1ˢᵗ): in place of (1ˢᵗ), rather (1ˢᵗ)

instinct (5ᵗʰ): impulse (5ᵗʰ), leaning (3ʳᵈ), reaction (5ᵗʰ), tendency (5ᵗʰ)

institute (5ᵗʰ): A. establish (3ʳᵈ), found (2ⁿᵈ), organize (4ᵗʰ) **B.** association (5ᵗʰ), clinic (1ˢᵗ), school (K)

instruct (4ᵗʰ): A. command (2ⁿᵈ), direct (1ˢᵗ), order (1ˢᵗ) **B.** acquaint (4ᵗʰ), educate (3ʳᵈ), school (K), teach (1ˢᵗ), train (K)

instrument (3ʳᵈ): agent (5ᵗʰ), channel (4ᵗʰ), device (4ᵗʰ), machine (1ˢᵗ), method (2ⁿᵈ), tool (1ˢᵗ)

insult (5ᵗʰ): abuse (6ᵗʰ), offend (4ᵗʰ), put down (2ⁿᵈ), shame (3ʳᵈ)

insure (5ᵗʰ): assure (3ʳᵈ), guarantee (6ᵗʰ), make sure (1ˢᵗ), protect (4ᵗʰ), secure (3ʳᵈ)

intelligence (4ᵗʰ): brain (3ʳᵈ), cleverness (3ʳᵈ), mind (1ˢᵗ), mentality (5ᵗʰ), reason (1ˢᵗ), sense (1ˢᵗ)

intelligent (4ᵗʰ): alert (5ᵗʰ), aware (3ʳᵈ), bright (1ˢᵗ), brilliant (4ᵗʰ), clever (3ʳᵈ), mental (5ᵗʰ), quick (1ˢᵗ), sharp (1ˢᵗ), smart (1ˢᵗ)

intend (6ᵗʰ): A. aim (3ʳᵈ), mean (1ˢᵗ), purpose (1ˢᵗ), scheme (5ᵗʰ) **B.** design (5ᵗʰ), plan (1ˢᵗ)

intense (6ᵗʰ): fierce (4ᵗʰ), harsh (5ᵗʰ), passionate (6ᵗʰ), stressed (6ᵗʰ), strong (K), violent (5ᵗʰ)

intensive (6ᵗʰ): See intense.

intent (5ᵗʰ): A. aim (3ʳᵈ), design (5ᵗʰ), end (K), intention (6ᵗʰ), objective (2ⁿᵈ), purpose (2ⁿᵈ) **B.** absorbed (5ᵗʰ), firm (2ⁿᵈ), fixed (1ˢᵗ), rapt (6ᵗʰ)

intention (6ᵗʰ): aim (3ʳᵈ), goal (4ᵗʰ), objective (2ⁿᵈ), purpose (2ⁿᵈ)

interactive (4ᵗʰ): the ability for a person to interact with a computer, or deal with another person when both are using computers

interest (1ˢᵗ): A. absorb (5ᵗʰ), amuse (4ᵗʰ), engage (5ᵗʰ), excite (4ᵗʰ), stimulate (6ᵗʰ) **B.** business (2ⁿᵈ), care (K), concern (3ʳᵈ)

interface (4ᵗʰ): program that controls how users interact with a device

interfere (4ᵗʰ): block (1ˢᵗ), butt in (1ˢᵗ), hinder (6ᵗʰ), intrude (6ᵗʰ), meddle (6ᵗʰ), obstruct (5ᵗʰ)

interior (5ᵗʰ): hidden (1ˢᵗ), inner (5ᵗʰ), inside (1ˢᵗ), internal (6ᵗʰ), inward (6ᵗʰ), personal (3ʳᵈ), secret (1ˢᵗ), within (3ʳᵈ)

internal (6ᵗʰ): inborn (2ⁿᵈ), native (1ˢᵗ), natural (2ⁿᵈ), true (K). See interior.

international (5ᵗʰ): general (2ⁿᵈ), global (4ᵗʰ), universal (4ᵗʰ), worldly (2ⁿᵈ)

Internet (2ⁿᵈ)

interpret (5ᵗʰ): comment (5ᵗʰ), demonstrate (6ᵗʰ), explain (2ⁿᵈ), illustrate (5ᵗʰ), show (1ˢᵗ), spell out (1ˢᵗ), translate (5ᵗʰ)

interrupt (3ʳᵈ): arrest (3ʳᵈ), cease (3ʳᵈ), check (1ˢᵗ), end (K), halt (4ᵗʰ), interfere (4ᵗʰ), postpone (6ᵗʰ), stop (K), suspend (4ᵗʰ)

interval (6th): break (1st), era (6th), gap (K), interruption (3rd), lull (5th), pause (3rd), period (2nd)

interview (5th): A. consult (4th), examine (5th), question (1st) **B.** conference (4th), discussion (5th), meeting (1st)

intestine (4th): guts (1st), organs (4th), stomach (2nd)

intimate (5th): A. buddy (4th), companion (3rd), comrade (4th), friend (1st) **B.** comfortable (3rd), small (K), warm (1st) **C.** buddy-buddy (4th), close (K), dear (1st), friendly (2nd)

into (1st)

intricate (6th): complex (6th), complicated (6th), involved (6th), obscure (6th), puzzling (4th), tangled (3rd)

introduce (5th): A. begin (K), found (2nd), invent (2nd), originate (3rd) **B.** acquaint (4th), make known (2nd), meet (K), present (K)

intrude (6th): bother (2nd), impose (4th), interfere (4th), invade (5th), push in (1st)

invade (5th): aggress (6th), attack (3rd), enter (2nd), intrude (6th), trespass (6th)

invent (2nd): begin (K), coin (3rd), conceive (4th), create (3rd), design (5th), devise (4th), make (K), originate (3rd)

invest (5th): fund (4th), give (1st), grant (2nd), install (6th), support (4th)

investigate (5th): examine (5th), inquire (3rd), question (1st), research (5th), search (1st)

invisible (6th): ghostly (1st), imaginary (2nd), unseen (2nd)

invite (3rd): appeal (3rd), ask (K), bid (1st), call (1st), plead (3rd), request (4th)

involve (6th): affect (4th), commit to (4th), confuse (4th), connect (3rd), contain (5th), embrace (4th), engage (5th), entail (6th), envelop (6th), include (3rd), occupy (3rd)

inward (6th): inborn (3rd), inner (5th), inside (1st), interior (5th), internal (6th), within (3rd)

ion (5th): an atom that has acquired a net electric charge by gaining or losing one or more electrons

iris (5th)

irk (6th): agitate (5th), anger (1st), annoy (5th), bother (2nd), irritate (6th), provoke (6th), vex (5th)

iron (2nd): press (1st), smooth (2nd), straighten (3rd)

irregular (6th): different (1st), not normal (5th), odd (4th), peculiar (4th), strange (1st), unusual (3rd)

irrigate (5th): flush (4th), water (K), wet (K)

irritate (6th): See irk.

Islam (5th)

island (2nd)

isn't (1st)

issue (4th): A. child (K), heir (4th) **B.** declare (5th), originate (4th), proclaim (4th), put out (1st), send (K) **C.** conclusion (3rd), controversy (6th), effect (3rd), outcome (4th), point (1st), proceed (4th), result (2nd), subject (3rd)

it (K)

itch (5th): A. crave (6th), desire (5th), want (K), wish (K), yearn (6th) **B.** annoy (5th), irritate (6th), sting (2nd)

item (5th): article (2nd), aspect (5th), detail (5th), feature (3rd), ingredient (4th), point (1st)

its (K)

it's (1st)

itself (2nd)

I've (1st)

ivory (3rd): beige (3rd), bone (1st), cream (1st), tan (K), tooth (1st), tusk (5th)

ivy (2nd)

jab (1st): hit (K), poke (1st), punch (4th), push (1st), slap (2nd), smack (6th), stick (K), strike (2nd)

jack (1st): A. banner (3rd), flag (3rd), streamer (3rd) **B.** hoist (6th), lift (1st), raise (1st)

jackal (5th)

jackdaw (5th)

jacket (3rd): cloak (4th), clothing (1st), coat (1st), cover (1st), sweater (3rd)

jagged (5th): irregular (6th), sharp (1st), zigzag (3rd)

jail (4th): A. imprison (6th), intern (6th) **B.** cell (1st), dungeon (5th), fortress (5th), prison (3rd)

jam (K): A. gelatin (5th), jelly (1st), preserves (4th) **B.** block (1st), cram (5th), crowd (2nd), fix (1st), pack (1st), press (1st), problem (1st), push (1st), squeeze (5th)

January (1st)

jar (K): A. clash (5th), shock (1st), strike (2nd) **B.** container (5th), glass (1st), pot (K)

jasper (5th)

jaunty (6th): alive (3rd), bouncy (6th), gay (1st), happy (K), showy (1st), stylish (3rd)

jaw (4th): A. criticize (5th), scold (5th), talk (K) **B.** chin (1st), chops (2nd), mouth (1st)

jay (1st)

jealous (5th): covetous (6th), distrustful (2nd), doubtful (1st), envious (4th), suspicious (4th)

jeans (1st): pants (1st)

jeep (1st): military car (3rd), vehicle (6th)

jeer (5th): ridicule (6th), scoff (6th), sneer (6th), tease (3rd)

jell (1st): set (K), stick (K)

jelly (1st): gelatin (5th), jam (K), preserves (4th)

jellybean (4th)

jellyfish (2nd)

jersey (5th): shirt (1st)

jest (4th): A. fool (2nd), mock (4th), tease (3rd) **B.** gag (1st), joke (1st), prank (5th)

jet (K): A. airplane (1st), plane (1st) **B.** fly (1st), hurry (1st), speed (3rd)

Jew (K)

jewel (5th): ornament (4th), precious (4th), stone (2nd), treasure (4th)

jewelry (5th): jewels (5th), ornament (4th), treasures (4th)

jibe (6th): agree (2nd), conform (6th), fit (K), harmonize (4th), match (3rd)

jingle (2nd): A. chime (6th), ring (1st), sing (1st) **B.** advertisement (4th), poem (3rd), rhyme (6th), song (K), verse (4th)

job (K): activity (3rd), duty (1st), employment (5th), function (4th), labor (1st), occupation (6th), project (4th), role (6th), task (3rd), trade (1st), work (K)

jog (2nd): A. brisk walk (6th), run (K), trot (5th) **B.** bump (2nd), poke (1st), prod (6th), push (1st), shake (1st)

join (3rd): add (K), adhere (6th), adjoin (6th), associate (5th), attach (5th), combine (3rd), connect (3rd), embrace (4th), link (5th), tie (1st), unite (5th)

joined (3rd): allied (6th), combined (3rd), together (1st)

joint (4th): A. hinge (5th), seam (5th) **B.** combination (3rd), connection (3rd), link (5th)

joke (1st): gag (1st), humor (5th), jest (4th), prank (5th)

jolly (4th): bright (1st), cheery (3rd), gay (1st), glad (K), happy (K)

jostle (6th): A. hurry (1st), rush (2nd) **B.** bump (2nd), knock (3rd), push (1st), shake (1st)

jot (1st): A. note (1st), write (K) **B.** atom (5th), bit (1st), scant (6th), smallness (1st), tiny (2nd)

journal (2nd): book (K), diary (3rd), log (K), magazine (3rd), newspaper (1st), record (2nd), review (4th)

journey (3rd): adventure (3rd), expedition (4th), tour (3rd), travel (1st), trip (1st), voyage (4th)

joust (6th): fence (1st), fight (K), strive (5th), wrestle (6th)

jovial (5th): cheerful (3rd), gay (1st), happy (K), high spirits (2nd), jolly (4th), merry (3rd), witty (2nd)

joy (1st): cheer (3rd), delight (3rd), ecstasy (6th), gladness (1st), happiness (2nd), merriment (3rd), pleasure (2nd)

judge (1st): A. critic (5th), officer (1st), protector (4th) **B.** choose (3rd), condemn (4th), decide (1st), decision maker (3rd), expert (5th), merit (4th), try (4th), weigh (1st)

jug (1st): container (5th), jar (K), pot (K)

juice (K): extract (4th), fluid (6th), liquid (3rd), sap (1st), syrup (4th)

jump (K): bounce (6th), bound (2nd), hop (K), leap (3rd), pounce (5th), skip (2nd), spring (K), vault (5th)

jumped (1st)

jungle (4th): A. confusion (4th), disarray (5th), mess (1st) **B.** rain forest (2nd), thicket (4th), woods (1st)

junior (4th): child (K), heir (4th), juvenile (5th), lesser (2nd), minor (5th), newer (1st), undergraduate (4th), younger (2nd)

junk (3rd): A. garbage (5th), trash (2nd) **B.** discard (6th), scrap (3rd), throw away (1st)

Jurassic (5th): of or belonging to the geologic time, rock series, or sedimentary deposits of the second period of the Mesozoic Era

jury (4th): A. court (3rd), panel (6th) **B.** choose (3rd), decide (1st), judge (1st)

just (1st): correct (3rd), earned (2nd), fair (1st), honest (3rd), honorable (3rd), legal (5th), legitimate (6th), right (K), true (K), virtuous (4th)

justice (3rd): fairness (2nd), ideal (3rd), lawfulness (2nd), legality (5th), right (K)

justification (5th): alibi (6th), excuse (3rd), reason (2nd)

juvenile (5th): minor (5th), junior (4th), teen (2nd), under age (1st), youngster (2nd), youth (2nd)

(K)aiser (5th): emperor (4th), king (1st), ruler (3rd)

kangaroo (1st): A. unjust (2nd) **B.** jump (K)

kangaroo (1st)

keen (4th): A. sorrow (4th), wail (5th), weep (4th) **B.** acute (6th), eager (5th), intense (6th), larger (5th), sharp (1st), smart (1st)

keep (K): A. castle (3rd), fort (5th) **B.** accumulate (6th), celebrate (4th), conserve (5th), hold (1st), obey (3rd), observe (3rd), possess (3rd), preserve (4th), save (1st), support (4th)

keeper (1st): guard (1st), guardian (3rd), manager (4th), owner (1st)

keg (1st): barrel (4th)

kettle (4th): pot (K)

key (K): A. important (1st), main (3rd), principal (3rd) **B.** access (6th), opener (1st) **C.** input (1st), type (1st)

keyboard (1st): piano (4th), typewriter (1st)

khaki (6th): brown (K), tan (K)

kick (1st): A. object (1st), oppose (3rd), protest (4th) **B.** blow (1st), boot (1st), hit (K), move (K), tap (K)

kid (K): A. goat (K) **B.** joke (1st), mock (4th), rib (1st), tease (3rd) **C.** boy (K), child (K), girl (K), youth (2nd)

kill (1st): execute (5th), murder (3rd), slay (4th)

kilo (6th)

kilogram (2nd)

kin (1st): ally (6th), family (K), relative (4th)

kind (K): A. mode (5th), sort (1st), type (1st) **B.** charitable (4th), gentle (3rd), tolerant (5th), warm (1st)

kindle (5th): burn (3rd), fire (K), ignite (6th), light (K)

king (K): crown (1st), emperor (4th), (K)aiser (5th), noble (3rd), ruler (3rd)

kingbird (3rd)

kingdom (3rd): country (1st), estate (4th), land (K)

kingfisher (5th)

kiss (K): embrace (4th), greet (3rd)

kit (1st): gear (1st), set (K), supplies (1st), tools (1st)

kitchen (1st)

kite (K): fly (1st), glide (4th), sail (1st), soar (6th)

kitten (K): cat (K), kitty (1st)

knapsack (4th): backpack (4th), bag (1st), tote bag (5th)

knave (5th): chessman (4th), noble (3rd), rascal (5th), villain (5th)

knead (4th): fold (1st), pound (2nd), push (1st), shape (1st), work (K)

kneel (1st)

kneel (4th): bow (1st)

knew (1st)

knife (1st): blade (2nd), cut (K), pierce (4th), stab (5th), stick (K), sword (4th)

knight (2nd): noble (3rd), prince (1st), soldier (3rd)

knit (4th): plait (5th), weave (4th)

knock (3rd): bang (3rd), pound (2nd), rap (1st), strike (2nd), tap (K)

knot (4th): loop (5th), problem (1st), tie (1st)

know (1st): comprehend (5th), realize (2nd), recognize (3rd), understand (1st)

know-how (2nd): ability (3rd), competence (6th), intelligence (4th), knowledge (2nd), skill (2nd)

knowledge (2nd): information (5th), learning (1st), scholarship (5th), understanding (3rd)

known (1st): learned (2nd), recognized (3rd), understood (2nd)

knuckle (4th): hit (K), punch (4th)

koala (K)

Koran (5th)

lab (1st): laboratory (4th), study (1st), workshop (2nd)

label (3rd): brand (2nd), mark (1st), stamp (2nd),

labor (1st): effort (2nd), job (K), toil (4th), work (K)

laboratory (4th): lab (1st), study (1st), workshop (2nd)

lace (4th): A. secure (3rd), string (2nd), thread (2nd), tie (1st) B. braid (2nd), crochet (4th), tatting (4th) C. pull through (1st), pass through (1st) D. add (K) E. attack (3rd), assail (6th)

lack (1st): absence (5th), need (1st), want (K)

lad (K): boy (K), youth (2nd)

ladder (2nd): stairs (2nd), stairway (3rd)

laden (6th): filled (1st), full (K), loaded (2nd), packed (2nd), weighted (2nd)

ladle (4th): dish (1st), scoop (4th), spoon (1st)

lady (1st): female (4th), woman (K)

lag (1st): delay (5th), linger (4th), slow (1st), wait (1st)

lagoon (5th): bay (K), inlet (4th), lake (1st), pond (1st), swamp (4th)

lair (5th): cave (1st), den (1st)

lake (1st): lagoon (5th), pond (1st), pool (1st)

lamb (K): gentle (3rd), meek (2nd), mild (4th)

lame (4th): disabled (3rd), hurt (K), injured (5th), sore (4th)

lament (6th): cry (1st), grieve (5th), mourn (4th), sorrow (4th), weep (4th)

lamp (1st): bulb (2nd), illumination (6th), light (K)

lance (4th): spear (4th), open (K), pierce (4th)

land (K): A. dirt (1st), earth (1st), ground (1st), perch (5th), plot (4th), roost (5th), sod (6th), yard (1st) **B.** achieve (5th), alight (5th), gain (2nd), reach (1st)

landing (1st): arrival (3rd)

landslide (5th): mudslide (2nd)

lane (4th): alley (6th), drive (1st), path (1st), road (K), street (1st), way (K)

language (2nd): dialect (5th), speech (2nd), vocabulary (6th), words (K)

lanky (5th): lean (3rd), long (1st), tall (K), thin (1st)

lantern (5th): lamp (1st), light (K)

lap (K): seat (1st)

lapse (6th): break (1st), error (4th), fall (K), mistake (1st), pause (3rd), slip (3rd)

lard (6th): butter (2nd), fat (1st)

large (K): big (K), giant (2nd), great (K), huge (1st), mammoth (5th), vast (4th)

lark (5th): adventure (3rd), fun (K), game (K)

larvae (2nd)

lash (4th): beat (1st), bind (2nd), tie (1st), whip (4th)

lass (1st): girl (K), young woman (1st)

lasso (4th): A. rope (1st) **B.** catch (1st), grab (4th)

last (K): A. endure (4th), persist (5th), remain (2nd), stay (1st), survive (3rd) **B.** end (K), final (3rd), latest (1st)

latch (4th): buckle (6th), clasp (4th), close (K), lock (1st)

latchkey (4th)

late (K): behind (1st), contemporary (5th), dead (1st), delayed (5th), modern (2nd), old (K), overdue (3rd), recent (3rd)

later (1st): after (1st), afterward (4th), behind (1st), next (K)

latitude (4th)

latter (3rd): end (K), last (K), later (1st), second (1st)

laugh (1st): joke (1st)

launch (5th): begin (K), float (1st), push (1st), send off (1st), start (1st)

laundry (6th): clothes (1st), dirty clothes (1st), wash (1st)

laurel (5th): award (5th), honor (1st), prize (3rd), reward (4th)

lavish (6th): abundant (5th), bountiful (5th), extravagant (6th), generous (4th), lush (6th), luxuriant (4th)

law (1st): regulation (5th), rule (2nd)

lawn (2nd): grass (1st), landscape (5th), sod (6th), yard (1st)

lawyer (5th): advocate (5th), counsel (5th)

lay (1st): A. aim (3rd), direct (1st), point (1st) **B.** leave (1st), place (1st), put (K), rest (1st), set (K)

layer (4th): coat (1st), level (3rd), wrapping (3rd)

lazy (4th): idle (4th), inactive (3rd), listless (6th)

lead (1st): guide (1st), pilot (5th), steer (5th)

leaf (1st)

league (3rd): association (5th), federation (5th), partnership (5th)

leak (6th): drain (5th), drip (2nd), hold (K)

lean (3rd): A. skinny (1st), thin (2nd) **B.** angle (4th), cant (6th), incline (5th), list (2nd), rake (1st), recline (6th), slant (6th), slope (3rd), tilt (5th)

leaning (3rd): bias (6th), tendency (5th)

leap (3rd): hop (K), jump (K), spring (1st)

learn (1st): comprehend (5th), master (1st), realize (2nd)

lease (6th): hire (3rd), rent (K)

least (1st): last (K), littlest (1st), smallest (1st)

leather (1st): hide (1st)

leave (1st): abandon (4th), allow (2nd), assign (5th), depart (5th), desert (1st), go (K), let (K), permit (3rd), quit (1st), will (K), yield (4th)

lecture (5th): address (K), speech (1st), talk (K)

led (K)

ledge (5th): bluff (6th), edge (3rd), shelf (6th)

lee (5th): calm (3rd), protection (4th), safety (2nd), shelter (4th)

leech (4th): sponge (5th), suck (1st), take (1st)

leek (5th): onion (2nd)

left (1st)

leg (K): lap (K), limb (4th)

legal (5th): allowable (5th), lawful (2nd), right (K)

legend (5th): adventure (3rd), caption (6th), myth (4th), saga (6th), story (K), tale (3rd)

legion (6th): army (1st), military (3rd)

legislation (5th): laws (1st)

legitimate (6th): honest (3rd), lawful (2nd), legal (5th), proper (3rd), right (K)

leisure (5th): comfort (3rd), ease (3rd), freedom (3rd), holiday (K), liberty (3rd), rest (1st), vacation (2nd)

lemon (2nd)

lend (K): give (K), loan (4th), provide (3rd)

length (2nd): distance (4th), extent (4th), measure (2nd), size (1st)

lens (1st): glass (1st)

Lent (4th)

leopard (1st)

less (1st): fewer (1st), smaller (1st)

lessen (3rd): A. ease (3rd), lighten (1st), soften (1st) **B.** abbreviate (6th), abstract (6th), condense (6th), contract (3rd), cut (K), cut down (K), reduce (3rd), shorten (2nd), shrink (5th) **C.** relieve (4th), smooth (3rd)

lesson (3rd): assignment (5th), homework (1st), knowledge (2nd), learning (1st), lecture (5th), studies (2nd), teaching (1st)

lest (4th): unless (2nd)

let (K): A. charter (2nd), hire (3rd), lease (6th), rent (K) **B.** allow (2nd), permit (3rd), sanction (6th)

letter (1st): message (1st), note (1st), report (2nd)

letters (1st): alphabet (2nd)

levee (6th): bank (1st), dam (K), dock (1st), pier (4th), wharf (5th)

level (3rd): A. aim (3rd), direct (1st), point (1st) **B.** even (1st), flat (2nd), plane (1st), smooth (2nd)

liable (6th): answerable (4th), exposed (4th), open (K), responsible (4th)

liberal (4th): abundant (5th), ample (5th), generous (4th), tolerant (5th)

liberty (3rd): freedom (3rd), independence (3rd), license (5th)

library (3rd)

lice (2nd)

license (5th): A. allow (2nd), permit (3rd) **B.** allowance (5th), commission (2nd), freedom (3rd), liberty (3rd)

lichen (5th): A. any of several skin diseases characterized by a papular eruption **B.** any of numerous complex thallophytic plants made up of an alga and a fungus growing in symbiotic association on a solid surface

lick (1st): A. taste (1st) **B.** beat (1st), conquer (4th), defeat (5th)

lid (1st): cover (1st), seal (K), top (K)

lie (1st): falsehood (4th), fib (1st), untruth (3rd)

lieutenant (4th)

life (1st): animation (6th), biography (6th), nature (1st), soul (3rd), spirit (2nd)

lift (1st): arise (4th), elevate (2nd), raise (1st)

light (K): A. ignite (6th), illuminate (6th) **B.** easy (1st), simple (2nd) **C.** fair (2nd), lightweight (4th), pale (3rd), small (K), tiny (2nd), weightless (2nd) **D.** fire (K), glow (1st), lamp (1st), lantern (5th)

lighthouse (2nd): guide (1st), signal (4th), warning (3rd)

lightweight (4th)

like (K): A. equal (2nd), same (1st), similar (4th) **B.** enjoy (2nd), fancy (3rd), love (K), prefer (3rd)

likely (1st): apt (5th), inclined (5th), liable (6th)

likes (1st)

lilac (5th)

lily (1st)

limb (4th): arm (K), branch (2nd), leg (K), part (1st)

limber (4th): agile (6th), flexible (6th), supple (6th)

lime (4th)

limestone (4th)

limit (3rd): A. bound (2nd), check (1st), restrict (6th) **B.** border (1st), curb (3rd), edge (1st), end (K), margin (5th)

limp (5th): floppy (1st), loose (3rd), soft (K), weak (3rd)

limpet (3rd)

limpid (6th): clear (2nd), pure (3rd), transparent (5th)

line (K): A. chain (3rd), file (1st), row (K), series (4th), strip (3rd), stripe (1st) **B.** arrange (3rd), draw (K)

linen (4th): cloth (1st), fabric (5th), sheets (1st), towels (6th)

linger (4th): remain (1st), stay (1st), wait (K)

link (5th): adhere (6th), associate (5th), connect (3rd), join (3rd), tie (1st)

lion (K)

lip (1st): mouth (1st)

liquid (3rd): drink (1st), fluid (6th)

liquor (5th): alcohol (4th), spirits (2nd)

list (2nd): A. schedule (6th), table (1st) **B.** catalog (5th), record (2nd), roll (1st) **C.** angle (4th), cant (6th),incline (5th), lean (3rd), list (2nd), slant (6th), tilt (5th),rake (1st), slope (3rd), tip (1st)

listen (1st): attend (3rd), hear (1st), pay attention (3rd)

listless (6th): idle (4th), inactive (4th), lazy (4th)

lit (K)

liter (6th)

literal (6th): exact (2nd)

literature (5th): book (K), writing (1st)

lithosphere (5th): the outer part of the earth, consisting of the crust and upper mantle, approximately 100 km (62 mi.) thick

litter (2nd): A. clutter (4th), junk (3rd), mess (1st), trash (2nd) **B.** dump (2nd), pollute (3rd), scatter (3rd)

little (K): miniature (6th), small (K), tiny (2nd)

live (1st): alive (3rd), be (K), breathe (1st), endure (4th), exist (3rd)

lived (1st)

lives (1st)

livestock (3rd): cattle (3rd), cows (K), herds (2nd)

living (1st): active (3rd), alive (3rd), energetic (4th), strong (K)

lizard (1st)

llama (1st)

load (2nd): burden (5th), cargo (5th), charge (2nd), contents (3rd), duty (1st), freight (4th), responsibility (4th), weight (1st)

loaf (4th): idle (4th), linger (4th), lounge (6th), relax (4th), rest (1st)

loan (4th): A. advance (2nd), credit (5th) **B.** lease (6th), lend (K)

lobster (3rd)

local (3rd): close by (1st), domestic (5th), folk (3rd), native (1st), near (1st), nearby (2nd), regional (4th)

locality (4th): area (3rd), district (4th), neighborhood (2nd), place (1st), region (4th)

locate (3rd): catch (1st), detect (4th), discover (1st), establish (3rd), find (K), lay (1st), place (1st), position (2nd), put (K), set (K), situate (4th), spot (1st), uncover (2nd)

location (3rd): address (K), area (3rd), district (4th), place (1st), position (2nd), region (4th)

lock (1st): bolt (4th), clamp (5th), clasp (4th), corner (2nd), hook (4th), latch (4th), restrain (5th), trap (1st)

locomotive (5th): engine (3rd), mobile (6th), moving (1st)

locust (5th)

lodge (4th): association (5th), brotherhood (4th), cabin (1st), club (1st), community (2nd), hotel (3rd), hut (4th), inn (4th), resort (5th), shelter (4th)

loft (5th): attic (2nd), balcony (6th)

lofty (5th): ambitious (4th), elevated (2nd), excellent (1st), grand (2nd), heavenly (1st), high (K), prominent (5th), soaring (6th), splendid (4th), tall (K)

log (K): A. chart (1st), journal (2nd), record (2nd), report (2nd) **B.** beam (3rd), board (1st), branch (2nd), plank (5th), pole (K), trunk (4th)

logger (4th): lumberman (2nd), woodsman (3rd)

logic (6th): judgment (4th), reason (2nd), sense (1st), thought (1st), wisdom (2nd)

logo (4th): seal (K), stamp (2nd), symbol (5th)

loincloth (6th)

lone (2nd): alone (1st), apart (3rd), exclusive (6th), free (K), independent (3rd), individual (3rd), one (K), separate (3rd), single (3rd), solitary (5th), unique (6th)

lonely (2nd): lonesome (2nd), separate (3rd), solitary (5th)

long (1st): A. covet (6th), crave (6th), desire (5th), lust (6th), want (K), yearn (6th) **B.** extended (4th), lengthy (3rd), tedious (6th)

longing (1st): desire (5th), hope (K), lust (6th), want (K), wish (K)

longitude (4th): lengthwise (2nd), length (2nd)

look (K): A. appear (2nd), gaze (5th), glance (3rd), inspect (5th), observe (3rd), peek (2nd), see (K), seem (1st), watch (1st) **B.** appearance (3rd), aspect (5th), front (1st), sight (1st), view (2nd)

looked (1st)

looking (1st)

loom (5th): A. weave (4th) **B.** appear (2nd), arise (4th), emerge (5th), hover (3rd), spin (1st), threaten (5th)

loop (5th): band (1st), bow (1st), circle (K), coil (5th), curl (2nd), hoop (5th), ring (1st)

loose (3rd): casual (5th), easy (1st), feeble (4th), floppy (1st), limp (5th), reckless (5th), relaxed (4th), vague (5th), wild (2nd), untied (5th)

lope (5th): bound (2nd), hop (K), hurry (1st), jaunt (6th), jump (K), sprint (5th)

lord (2nd): chief (1st), king (K), leader (2nd), master (1st), noble (3rd), president (1st), ruler (2nd)

lose (K): drop (1st), fail (2nd), forget (1st), give up (1st), misplace (3rd), sacrifice (4th), surrender (5th)

loss (K): casualty (5th), cost (1st), damage (5th), hurt (K), injury (5th), penalty (5th), ruin (2nd)

lost (K): absent (5th), confused (4th), dead (1st), extinct (5th), forgotten (2nd), gone (1st), missing (1st)

lot (K): A. land (K), mass (3rd), plot (4th), property (3rd) **B.** batch (2nd), bunch (3rd), chance (2nd), destiny (5th), division (4th), fate (3rd), fortune (3rd), luck (1st), much (1st), part (K), piece (1st)

lots (5th): enough (1st), full (K), plenty (1st)

lotus (5th)

loud (1st): conspicuous (5th), flashy (2nd), glaring (4th), noisy (5th), shrill (5th), vocal (2nd)

lounge (6th): A. loaf (4th), recline (6th), relax (4th), repose (6th), rest (1st) **B.** bar (3rd), couch (4th), den (1st), idle (4th), inn (4th), pub (1st), saloon (6th), tavern (5th)

love (K): A. adore (4th), cherish (5th), desire (5th), honor (1st), idolize (6th), like (K), prize (3rd), treasure (4th), value (2nd), worship (4th) **B.** affection (4th), care (K), devotion (5th), emotion (4th), friendship (2nd), passion (6th), romance (5th), sympathy (4th)

loved (1st)

lovely (1st): attractive (5th), beautiful (1st), delicate (5th), elegant (5th), pretty (1st)

low (K): A. sad (K) **B.** base (1st), beneath (1st), cheap (3rd), down (K), economical (4th), humble (4th), inferior (5th), inexpensive (4th), short (1st), under (K)

lowland (6th): flat (2nd), meadow (3rd), plain (2nd), prairie (4th)

loyal (5th): constant (4th), dedicated (6th), devoted (5th), faithful (3rd), honest (3rd), sincere (4th), steady (3rd), true (1st), trusted (2nd)

luck (1st): chance (2nd), destiny (5th), fate (3rd), fortune (3rd)

lucky (K): fortunate (4th), happy (K)

lug (1st): carry (1st), drag (5th), haul (4th), pack (1st), pull (K), transport (5th)

luggage (4th): bag (1st), case (2nd), packs (1st), suitcases (1st)

lull (5th): break (1st), delay (5th), gap (K), idle (4th), pause (3rd), rest (1st), wait (1st)

lumber (1st): A. boards (1st), logs (K), wood (1st) **B.** drag (3rd), persist (5th), plod (5th)

lumbering (2nd): awkward (6th), clumsy (6th)

lumberman (2nd): logger (4th), woodsman (3rd)

lump (4th): A. blend (5th), combine (3rd), group (1st), mix (1st), unite (5th) **B.** ball (K), batch (2nd), bulge (4th), mass (3rd), stack (6th), swelling (3rd)

lunatic (6th): absurd (6th), crazy (4th), foolish (2nd), insane (6th), mad (K)

lunch (1st): buffet (6th), fare (3rd), food (K), meal (3rd)

lung (4th)

lunge (6th): dive (1st), drive (1st), leap (3rd), lurch (5th), plunge (4th), poke (1st)

lurch (5th): drive (1st), fall (K), lunge (6th), reel (5th), stagger (4th), stumble (4th)

lure (5th): attract (5th), bait (3rd), charm (3rd), flirt (6th), invite (3rd), tempt (4th), trap (1st)

lurk (5th): hide (1st), prowl (2nd), sneak (4th), tiptoe (4th)

lush (6th): generous (4th), lavish (6th), rich (1st), sensual (5th)

lust (6th): A. craving (6th), hunger (2nd), longing (1st), need (1st) **B.** covet (6th), crave (6th), desire (5th), long (1st), need (1st), passion (6th)

luster (4th): brilliance (4th), glitter (4th), glory (3rd), glow (1st), polish (4th), shimmer (5th), shine (1st)

luxury (4th): comfort (3rd), ease (3rd), elegance (5th), pleasure (2nd), treat (2nd), wealth (3rd)

lye (2nd)

lynx (4th)

lyre (6th)

Lystrosaurus (5th)

ma'am (6th): lady (1st), madam (4th), Mrs. (K)

machine (1st): device (4th), engine (3rd), instrument (3rd), mechanism (6th), motor (4th), tool (1st)

machinery (1st): equipment (5th), gear (1st)

mackerel (5th)

mad (K): A. absurd (6th), crazy (4th), foolish (2nd), insane (6th) **B.** angry (1st), annoyed (5th), enraged (6th), fierce (4th), stormy (2nd), upset (3rd), violent (5th), wild (2nd)

madam (4th): lady (1st), ma'am (6th), Mrs. (K)

made (K)

madness (3rd)

magazine (3rd): journal (2nd), publication (4th)

magic (1st): spell (1st), witchcraft (3rd)

magician (5th): witch (K), wizard (6th)

magistrate (6th): judge (1st)

magnet (3rd)

magnetize (3rd): attract (5th), drag (3rd), lure (5th), pull (K)

magnetron (5th): a microwave tube in which electrons generated from a heated cathode are affected by magnetic and electric fields in such a way as to produce microwave radiation used in radar and in microwave ovens

magnificent (4th): awesome (6th), beautiful (1st), brilliant (4th), glorious (3rd), grand (2nd), great (1st), splendid (4th), terrific (5th), wonderful (1st)

magnify (3rd): enhance (5th), enlarge (5th), expand (5th), increase (3rd), maximize (6th)

magnitude (5th)

magnolia (5th)

magpie (5th)

maid (3rd): girl (K), housekeeper (3rd), servant (3rd)

maiden (4th): A. girl (K), maid (3rd) **B.** earliest (2nd), first (1st), initial (6th), original (3rd)

mail (1st): A. letter (1st), package (4th) **B.** deliver (5th), post (1st), send (1st), ship (1st)

mailbox (1st)

mailman (1st): postal carrier (5th), postman (1st)

maim (4th): cripple (5th), disable (3rd), harm (3rd), hurt (K), injure (5th)

main (3rd): central (3rd), chief (1st), dominant (5th), first (1st), foremost (6th), leading (1st), major (3rd), most (1st), primary (5th), prime (5th), principal (3rd), supreme (5th), top (K)

mainland (5th): continent (4th), shore (2nd)

maintain (4th): argue (3rd), assert (6th), believe (1st), claim (2nd), contend (5th), continue (2nd), encourage (4th), fix (1st), keep (K), preserve (4th), provide (3rd), repair (4th), save (1st), say (K), service (5th), support (4th)

maize (2nd): corn (2nd), yellow (K)

majesty (4th): magnificence (4th), royalty (3rd)

major (3rd): big (K), critical (5th), dominant (5th), grand (2nd), huge (1st), important (1st), key (K), large (K), leading (1st), main (3rd), primary (5th), principal (3rd), serious (4th), sizeable (2nd), vital (5th)

majority (3rd): bulk (4th), mass (3rd), most (1st)

make (K): assemble (4th), build (1st), cause (2nd), compel (3rd), construct (3rd), craft (2nd), create (3rd), develop (5th), earn (2nd), erect (4th), force (K), form (1st), manufacture (3rd), prepare (1st), produce (2nd)

maker (1st): builder (1st), creator (4th), manufacturer (3rd), producer (3rd)

making (K)

male (4th): boy (K), chap (4th), gentleman (3rd), fellow (1st), guy (1st), lad (K), man (K)

malice (6th): anger (1st), dislike (3rd), grudge (5th), hate (2nd), spite (3rd)

malignant (6th): bad (K), harmful (3rd), ominous (6th)

malinger (6th): delay (5th), idle (4th), lag (1st), linger (4th), loaf (4th), lounge (6th)

mall (K): business (2nd), market (1st), shop (1st), store (K)

mallard (4th)

malt (2nd): dessert (1st), ice cream (1st), milkshake (2nd)

mama (1st): mom (K), mother (K)

mammal (5th)

mammoth (5th): giant (2nd), great (K), huge (1st), immense (4th), massive (5th), vast (4th)

man (K): chap (4th), citizen (3rd), fellow (1st), gentleman (3rd), guy (1st), human (3rd), individual (3rd), male (4th), person (1st)

manage (4th): contend (5th), control (2nd), cope (6th), direct (1st), govern (1st), handle (2nd), lead (1st), operate (3rd), oversee (3rd), run (K), supervise (6th)

manager (4th)

mandarin (5th): A. bureaucrat (6th), official (3rd) **B.** elite (6th), intellectual (4th) **C.** elaborate (5th)

mane (1st): fur (K), hair (K)

mango (5th)

manifest (5th): A. appear (2nd), develop (5th), display (3rd), exhibit (4th), express (5th), happen (1st), occur (3rd), reveal (4th), show (1st) **B.** apparent (3rd), clear (2nd), distinct (5th), plain (2nd), obvious (5th), true (1st)

mankind (4th): humanity (3rd), people (K), world (1st)

manly (K): bold (2nd), brave (1st), male (4th), mighty (1st), powerful (2nd), strong (K), tough (5th)

manner (1st): code (3rd), custom (6th), fashion (3rd), habit (3rd), method (2nd), mode (5th), practice (1st), routine (6th), style (3rd), tone (3rd), use (K), way (K)

mansion (5th): castle (3rd), estate (4th), palace (1st)

mantel (4th): A. cloak (4th), cover (1st), drape (5th) **B.** ledge (5th), shelf (6th) **C.** the layer of the earth between the crust and the core

mantle (4th): cape (4th), cloak (4th), coat (1st), jacket (3rd), shawl (6th), wrap (4th)

manufacture (3rd): assemble (4th), build (1st), construct (3rd), develop (5th), fabricate (5th), form (1st), make (K), produce (2nd)

manure (5th): fertilizer (5th), feces (6th)

manuscript (6th): book (K)

many (K): enough (1st), host (4th), legion (6th), lots (1st), numerous (4th), plenty (1st)

map (1st): chart (1st), design (5th), outline (4th), plan (1st), plot (4th)

maple (2nd)

mar (6th): damage (5th), harm (3rd), hurt (1st), injure (5th), spoil (4th)

marble (4th): A. agate (4th), alabaster (4th) **B.** ball (K), orb (4th), sphere (6th)

March (1st)

march (1st): advance (2nd), continue (2nd), depart (5th), go (K), hike (3rd), leave (1st), parade (2nd), progress (4th), stride (5th), tramp (4th), walk (K)

mare (4th): horse (K), mount (2nd)

margin (5th): border (1st), boundary (4th), edge (1st), limit (3rd), rim (1st)

marine (5th): sea (K), water (1st)

marigold (5th)

marine (5th): maritime (6th), oceanic (4th)

Marines (1st)

mark (1st): A. brand (2nd), imprint (4th), note (1st), print (1st), sign (1st), stamp (2nd) **B.** accent (6th), approval (4th), clue (2nd), dent (1st), emblem (5th), feature (3rd), flag (3rd), grade (2nd), level (3rd), name (K), notice (1st), quality (4th), signature (6th), spot (1st)

market (1st): bazaar (5th), fair (1st), shop (1st), store (K)

marquis (6th): nobleman (3rd)

marrow (5th): center (2nd), core (6th), essence (6th), heart (K), spirit (2nd)

marry (1st): attach (5th), blend (5th), bond (3rd), combine (3rd), couple (3rd), cross (1st), join (3rd), mate (4th), pair (1st), unite (5th), wed (K)

marsh (5th): bog (5th), mud (1st), swamp (4th)

marshal (5th): A. officer (1st), police (1st) **B.** assemble (4th), call (1st), gather (1st), group (1st), order (1st), organize (4th), rally (5th)

marsupial (1st)

martyr (6th): A. sacrifice (4th) **B.** victim (4th)

marvel (4th): miracle (5th), wonder (1st)

marvelous (4th): excellent (1st), good (K), great (1st), mysterious (3rd), super (1st), unique (6th), wonderful (1st)

mash (4th): beat (1st), crush (4th), pound (2nd), squash (2nd), squeeze (5th)

mask (2nd): A. costume (4th), cover (1st), disguise (5th) **B.** camouflage (5th), conceal (4th), cover (1st), disguise (5th), hide (1st), obscure (6th), pretend (2nd), shield (4th)

mason (5th): bricklayer (4th)

mass (3rd): abundance (5th), bulk (4th), collection (4th), lot (K), lump (4th), majority (3rd), much (1st), plenty (1st), size (1st), stack (3rd), stock (1st), total (2nd), whole (1st)

massacre (6th): butcher (4th), destroy (2nd), kill (1st), murder (3rd), slaughter (5th), slay (4th)

massive (5th): big (K), giant (2nd), huge (1st), immense (4th), large (K), mammoth (5th), powerful (2nd)

mast (4th)

master (1st): A. conquer (4th), defeat (5th), dominate (5th), learn (1st) **B.** ace (2nd), artist (1st), champion (4th), expert (5th), guide (1st), leader (2nd), lord (2nd), ruler (2nd), teacher (1st)

mastiff (5th)

mastodon (1st)

mat (K): carpet (4th), mattress (6th), pad (K), rug (1st)

match (3rd): A. compare (3rd), copy (3rd), equal (2nd), meet (K), sort (2nd) **B.** bout (6th), competition (5th), contest (4th), copy (3rd), equal (2nd), for (4th), game (1st), like (K), mate (4th), opponent (5th), tie (1st)

matching (3rd): alike (1st), comparable (3rd), equal (2nd), same (1st), similar (4th)

mate (4th): A. join (3rd), marry (1st), unite (5th), wed (K) **B.** associate (5th), blend (5th), buddy (4th), equal (2nd), friend (1st), match (3rd), pal (1st)

material (5th): A. important (1st), physical (5th), real (1st), vital (5th) **B.** cloth (1st), fabric (5th), matter (1st), substance (5th)

mathematical (5th): exact (2nd), numerical (5th), precise (5th)

mathematics (5th): addition (3rd), arithmetic (3rd), math (3rd)

matter (1st): affair (2nd), business (2nd), concern (3rd), elements (3rd), issue (4th), material (5th), stuff (1st), substance (5th)

mattress (6th): bed (K), mat (K), pad (K)

mature (5th): A. age (1st), develop (5th), evolve (5th), grow (1st), unfold (2nd) **B.** adult (1st), aged (1st), experienced (3rd), grown (1st), mellow (6th), ripe (1st)

maturity (6th): adulthood (2nd), age (1st)

maxim (6th): moral (3rd), proverb (3rd), rule (2nd), saying (1st), teaching (1st), truth (1st)

maximum (6th): A. ceiling (4th), extreme (5th), most (1st) **B.** best (K), biggest (1st), greatest (1st), largest (1st), most (1st), top (K)

May (1st)

may (K): allowed (2nd), can (K)

maybe (1st): perhaps (1st), possibly (2nd)

mayonnaise (4th)

mayor (1st): leader (2nd), manager (4th)

me (K): I (K), myself (1st), self (3rd)

meadow (3rd): field (2nd), grassland (1st), mead (6th)

meal (3rd): banquet (4th), breakfast (1st), dinner (2nd), feast (1st), food (K), lunch (1st), supper (2nd)

mean (1st): A. imply (5th), intend (6th), plan (1st) **B.** awful (3rd), bad (K), base (1st), cheap (3rd), common (2nd), cruel (5th), little (K), small (1st), tough (5th), unkind (2nd)

mean (average) (5th): average (3rd), halfway (3rd), middle (2nd), standard (3rd)

meaning (3rd): content (3rd), explanation (2nd), goal (4th), importance (1st), intent (5th), message (1st), purpose (1st), sense (1st), significance (6th)

measure (2nd): A. divide (4th) **B.** degree (5th), extent (4th), fit (K), guide (1st), law (1st), length (2nd), portion

(4th), rule (2nd), scope (6th), share (2nd), size (1st), standard (3rd), test (3rd)

meat (1st): beef (2nd), food (K)

meatloaf (5th)

mechanic (5th): engineer (4th), operator (5th)

mechanical (5th): automatic (6th), robotic (2nd)

mechanism (6th): apparatus (6th), engine (3rd), machine (1st), motor (4th)

medal (4th): award (5th), honor (1st), prize (3rd), recognition (4th), reward (4th), ribbon (4th), trophy (6th)

meddle (6th): fiddle (4th), interfere (4th), intrude (6th), poke (1st), pry (6th)

mediate (5th): arrange (3rd), bargain (4th), settle (2nd), umpire (1st)

medicine (4th): cure (4th), drug (1st), prescription (6th), remedy (4th), treatment (5th)

meditate (6th): consider (2nd), contemplate (6th), ponder (6th), reflect (4th), think (1st)

medium (5th): A. average (3rd), common (2nd), mean (1st), middle (2nd), ordinary (3rd) **B.** agency (5th), agent (5th), channel (4th), instrument (3rd), psychic (6th)

meek (2nd): humble (4th), mild (4th), modest (4th), tame (4th)

meet (K): A. adjoin (6th), confer (4th), connect (3rd), date (1st), encounter (4th), fill (1st), fit (K), fulfill (4th), greet (3rd), join (3rd), link (5th), match (3rd), satisfy (3rd), see (K), unite (5th), visit (1st), welcome (1st) **B.** competition (4th), contest (4th), encounter (4th), game (1st) **C.** desirable (5th), equal

(2nd), just (1st), proper (3rd), right (K), useful (2nd)

melancholy (6th): depressed (5th), gloomy (3rd), meditative (6th), sad (K), sorrow (4th), woeful (4th)

mellow (6th): A. soften (2nd), tame (4th), temper (4th) **B.** aged (1st), gentle (3rd), mature (5th), mild (4th), musical (5th), ripe (1st), soft (K), tame (4th)

melody (4th): harmony (4th), music (K), song (K), tune (1st)

melon (3rd): fruit (2nd)

melt (2nd): defrost (4th), warm (1st)

member (1st): associate (5th), individual (3rd), limb (4th), part (1st)

membrane (4th): skin (1st), surface (3rd)

memory (3rd): recall (3rd), reminder (3rd)

men (1st)

menace (5th): A. attack (3rd), frighten (2nd), threaten (5th) **B.** danger (1st), hazard (6th), threat (5th)

mend (1st): correct (3rd), cure (4th), fix (1st), heal (3rd), patch (4th), remedy (4th), repair (4th)

mental (5th): logical (6th), psychological (6th), thinking (2nd)

mention (5th): indicate (4th), quote (5th), refer to (5th)

menu (6th): fare (3rd), list (2nd)

meow (K)

merchandise (6th): goods (K), products (4th), stock (1st), wares (5th)

merchant (3rd): dealer (2nd), seller (1st), trader (2nd)

mercy (4ᵗʰ): care (K), charity (4ᵗʰ), forgiveness (3ʳᵈ), grace (3ʳᵈ), kindness (2ⁿᵈ), tenderness (3ʳᵈ)

mere (3ʳᵈ): only (K), simply (2ⁿᵈ)

merit (4ᵗʰ): A. deserve (4ᵗʰ) **B.** excellence (2ⁿᵈ), quality (4ᵗʰ), value (2ⁿᵈ), worth (3ʳᵈ)

mermaid (4ᵗʰ)

merry (3ʳᵈ): bright (1ˢᵗ), cheerful (3ʳᵈ), festive (5ᵗʰ), gay (1ˢᵗ), happy (K), joyful (2ⁿᵈ), sunny (1ˢᵗ)

mesa (6ᵗʰ)

Mesosaurus (5ᵗʰ)

Mesozoic (5ᵗʰ): of, belonging to, or designating the era of geologic time that includes the Triassic, Jurassic, and Cretaceous periods

mess (1ˢᵗ): confusion (4ᵗʰ), clutter (4ᵗʰ), difficulty (5ᵗʰ), disorder (2ⁿᵈ), jam (K), tangle (3ʳᵈ)

message (1ˢᵗ): intent (5ᵗʰ), letter (1ˢᵗ), meaning (1ˢᵗ), understanding (1ˢᵗ)

met (1ˢᵗ)

metal (3ʳᵈ)

meteor (5ᵗʰ)

meter (2ⁿᵈ): A. dial (5ᵗʰ) **B.** indicate (4ᵗʰ), measure (2ⁿᵈ)

metal (3ʳᵈ): ore (4ᵗʰ)

method (2ⁿᵈ): action (1ˢᵗ), fashion (3ʳᵈ), form (1ˢᵗ), mode (5ᵗʰ), order (1ˢᵗ), plan (1ˢᵗ), procedure (4ᵗʰ), process (4ᵗʰ), routine (6ᵗʰ), system (2ⁿᵈ), way (K)

metropolitan (6ᵗʰ): central (2ⁿᵈ), downtown (2ⁿᵈ)

micro (4ᵗʰ): little (K), mini (6ᵗʰ), miniature (6ᵗʰ), minute (1ˢᵗ), tiny (2ⁿᵈ)

microchip (4ᵗʰ)

microscope (4ᵗʰ): lens (1ˢᵗ), magnifier (4ᵗʰ)

microwave (4ᵗʰ)

middle (2ⁿᵈ): A. center (2ⁿᵈ), core (6ᵗʰ), halfway (3ʳᵈ) **B.** central (3ʳᵈ), halfway (3ʳᵈ), medium (5ᵗʰ)

midge (5ᵗʰ)

midnight (3ʳᵈ)

might (1ˢᵗ): authority (3ʳᵈ), force (1ˢᵗ), muscle (4ᵗʰ), power (1ˢᵗ), strength (2ⁿᵈ)

migrant (4ᵗʰ): drifter (2ⁿᵈ), traveler (2ⁿᵈ), wanderer (4ᵗʰ)

mike (1ˢᵗ)

mild (4ᵗʰ): gentle (3ʳᵈ), kind (K), mellow (6ᵗʰ), soft (K), tender (3ʳᵈ)

mile (1ˢᵗ)

milestone (5ᵗʰ): event (3ʳᵈ), marker (1ˢᵗ), occasion (3ʳᵈ)

military (3ʳᵈ): army (1ˢᵗ), soldiers (3ʳᵈ)

milk (1ˢᵗ)

mill (1ˢᵗ): A. crush (4ᵗʰ), grind (4ᵗʰ) **B.** factory (1ˢᵗ), plant (K)

millimeter (2ⁿᵈ)

million (3ʳᵈ)

mimic (6ᵗʰ): ape (K), copy (3ʳᵈ), imitate (5ᵗʰ), mime (6ᵗʰ)

mimosa (5ᵗʰ)

mince (6ᵗʰ): chop (2ⁿᵈ), slice (5ᵗʰ)

mind (1st): A. attend (3rd), care (1st), comply (6th), consider (2nd), heed (4th), listen (1st), look (K), obey (3rd), object (1st), observe (3rd), watch (1st) **B.** attitude (5th), bent (K), brain (3rd), brilliance (4th), head (1st), intellect (4th), learning (1st), mood (3rd), self (3rd), sense (1st), slant (6th), spirit (2nd), wit (1st)

mine (1st)

mineral (5th)

mingle (4th): blend (5th), combine (3rd), connect (3rd), join (3rd), mix (1st), stir (3rd), unite (5th)

miniature (6th): little (K), small (1st), tiny (2nd)

minimalist (6th): expressing only the fundamental features or bare minimum to communicate an idea such as in painting or writing

minimum (6th): base (1st), bottom (1st), least (2nd), lowest (2nd), smallest (2nd)

minister (4th): aid (2nd), clergy (6th), cleric (6th), pastor (4th), priest (4th)

mink (3rd)

minnow (4th): fish (K)

minor (5th): A. assistant (4th), child (K), teenager (3rd), youth (2nd) **B.** casual (5th), lesser (1st), little (K), low (K), petty (6th), picky (1st), secondary (3rd), slight (4th), small (1st)

minority (6th)

minstrel (5th): musician (4th), singer (1st)

mint (5th): A. fortune (3rd) **B.** fresh (2nd), new (K), perfect (3rd), unused (2nd)

minus (1st): deduct (2nd), from (K), less (1st), subtract (1st), take (1st)

minute (1st): invisible (6th), little (K), small (1st), tiny (2nd)

miracle (5th): blessing (3rd), marvel (4th), wonder (1st)

Miocene (5th): from 25 million to 13 million years ago; at this time grazing mammals appeared.

miraculous (6th)

mirror (4th): glass (1st), lens (1st), reflection (4th)

mirth (5th): amusement (4th), cheer (3rd), delight (3rd), glee (5th), happiness (2nd), joy (1st), laughter (2nd), merriment (3rd)

mischief (4th): adventure (3rd), harm (3rd), joke (1st), prank (5th), trouble (1st)

miser (5th)

miserable (4th): burden (5th), misfortune (5th), pitiful (3rd), poor (K), sad (K), sadness (1st), shabby (4th), sorrow (4th)

misery (4th): agony (5th), distress (5th), pain (2nd), suffering (2nd)

misfortune (5th): accident (4th), burden (5th), curse (3rd), disaster (6th), evil (3rd), hardship (5th), tragedy (5th), trouble (1st)

mislead (5th): cheat (3rd), deceive (5th), misdirect (2nd), trick (1st)

miss (K): A. girl (K), lass (1st) **B.** long for (1st), regret (5th) **C.** disregard (4th), fail (K), fall short (1st), overlook (4th)

mission (5th): assignment (5th), commission (2nd), concern (3rd), effort

(2nd), goal (4th), job (K), purpose (2nd), task (3rd)

Mississippian (5th): of or belonging to the geologic time, system of rocks, or sedimentary deposits of the fifth period of the Paleozoic Era

mist (1st): cloud (1st), fog (1st), light rain (1st), steam (2nd), vapor (3rd)

mistake (1st): error (4th), misunderstanding (2nd), slip (3rd)

mistreat (3rd): abuse (6th), hurt (K), wrong (1st)

mistress (4th): female (4th), lady (1st), lover (1st), woman (K)

misunderstanding (2nd): disagreement (2nd), dispute (6th), falling out (2nd), mistake (1st)

misuse (3rd): abuse (6th), mistreat (3rd)

mitten (1st): glove (4th)

mix (1st): A. combination (3rd), compound (4th), mess (1st) **B.** blend (5th), combine (3rd), merge (4th), mingle (4th), scramble (4th), stir (3rd), unite (5th)

mixed (1st): amid (4th), between (1st)

mixture (4th): blend (5th), combination (3rd), compound (4th)

mix-up (2nd): complicate (6th), confuse (4th), rearrange (3rd), scramble (4th)

moan (5th): cry (1st), groan (3rd), sigh (3rd), wail (5th), weep (4th), whine (5th)

mob (4th): crowd (2nd), gang (1st), group (1st), herd (2nd), horde (6th), pack (1st)

mobile (6th): loose (3rd), moveable (2nd), moving (1st), restless (4th)

mobilize (6th): drive (1st), motivate (6th), move (K), propel (6th), push (1st), rally (5th), start (1st)

moccasin (2nd): boot (1st), shoe (1st), slipper (5th)

mock (4th): A. fake (1st), false (3rd), imitation (5th), pretend (2nd), sham (5th) **B.** ape (5th), copy (3rd), imitate (5th), jeer (5th), mimic (6th), sneer (6th), tease (3rd)

mode (5th): A. fad (K), fashion (3rd), style (3rd) **B.** agency (5th), channel (4th), condition (3rd), instrument (3rd), manner (2nd), means (1st), mechanism (6th), method (2nd), process (4th), state (1st), tone (3rd), vein (4th), way (K)

model (3rd): A. demonstrate (6th), pose (2nd) **B.** classic (5th), hero (1st), ideal (3rd), idol (6th) **C.** copy (3rd), example (2nd), image (4th), miniature (6th), mock-up (6th), pattern (3rd), reproduction (5th), sample (5th), symbol (5th), test (3rd), typical (6th)

moderate (4th): A. cheap (3rd), inexpensive (3rd), reasonable (3rd) **B.** chair (K), lead (1st), preside (6th), regulate (5th) **C.** gradual (3rd), mild (4th), reasonable (1st), temperate (4th) **D.** ease (3rd), lessen (3rd), lighten (1st), soften (1st)

modern (2nd): contemporary (5th), late (K), new (K), recent (3rd)

modest (4th): humble (4th), meek (2nd), moderate (4th), plain (2nd), proper (3rd), pure (3rd), reasonable (1st), shy (1st), simple (2nd), temperate (5th), timid (5th)

modify (5th): adapt (4th), adjust (5th), alter (4th), change (2nd), edit (3rd), fix (1st), move (K), reform (5th), vary (4th)

226

moist (4th): damp (5th), juicy (1st), misty (1st), watery (1st), wet (K)

moisture (3rd): dampness (5th), mist (1st), water (K), wetness (2nd)

mold (5th): A. decay (5th), fungus (5th) **B.** cast (2nd), fashion (3rd), form (1st), shape (1st)

mole (2nd)

molecule (5th): particle (5th), piece (1st)

molten (5th): A. liquefied (3rd), melted (2nd), fluid (6th) **B.** hot (K)

mom (K)

mommy (K)

moment (1st): A. importance (1st) **B.** instant (3rd), minute (1st), occasion (3rd), second (1st)

momentum (6th): energy (4th), impulse (5th), movement (2nd)

monarch (5th): king (1st), lord (3rd), queen (1st), ruler (2nd)

monastery (5th): abbey (6th), convent (6th)

Monday (1st)

money (K): cash (2nd), coins (3rd), currency (3rd), funds (4th)

mongoose (5th)

monk (4th): abbot (6th), brother (1st), friar (5th), hermit (5th)

monkey (K)

monopoly (6th): controlling (2nd), exclusive (6th)

Monsieur (4th)

monster (1st): beast (3rd), creature (3rd), giant (2nd)

monstrous (5th): A. giant (2nd), gigantic (5th), huge (1st), immense (4th), massive (5th), vast (4th) **B.** awful (3rd), offensive (4th), enormous (5th), outrageous (6th), uncivilized (4th), wicked (4th)

month (1st)

monument (2nd): legacy (5th), memorial (5th), shrine (5th), statue (4th)

moo (K)

mood (3rd): attitude (5th), climate (4th), feeling (1st), humor (4th), outlook (2nd), spirit (2nd), temper (4th)

moon (1st): satellite (6th)

moonbeam (4th)

moonlight (4th)

moor (5th): anchor (4th), secure (3rd)

moose (K)

mop (1st): bathe (3rd), clean (1st), launder (6th), scour (6th), scrub (6th), wash (1st), wipe (1st)

mope (5th): brood (4th), sulk (5th)

moral (3rd): A. belief (1st), ethic (5th), truth (1st), virtue (4th) **B.** decent (6th), ethical (5th), honest (3rd), honorable (3rd), pure (3rd), responsible (4th), right (K), stable (4th), upright (4th), virtuous (4th)

more (K): above (1st), added (1st), additional (3rd), besides (1st), extra (1st), further (2nd), greater (1st), other (1st), over (1st), superior (4th), surplus (6th)

moreover (3rd): additionally (3rd), also (K), besides (1st), furthermore (3rd)

Mormon (4th)

morning (1st): a.m. (6th), daylight (1st), morn (1st), sunrise (2nd)

morsel (5th): bit (1st), bite (1st), dab (1st), dot (K), particle (5th), piece (1st), sample (5th), snack (2nd), speck (4th), taste (1st)

mortal (4th): A. deadly (1st), fatal (4th) **B.** alive (3rd), human (3rd), living (1st)

mortgage (6th): borrow (2nd), debt (3rd), loan (4th), obligation (6th), payment (1st)

Moslem (5th)

mosque (5th): church (1st), house of God (1st), sanctuary (6th), temple (3rd)

moss (1st): algae (5th), fungus (5th)

most (1st): almost all (K), best (K), greatest (1st), larger (1st), majority (3rd), prime (5th), superior (4th), usually (3rd)

moth (1st)

mother (K): A. care (1st), protect (4th), raise (1st), root (3rd), source (4th), start (1st) **B.** mama (1st), mom (K), parent (3rd)

motion (3rd): A. bid (1st), offer (2nd), proposal (4th), request (4th) **B.** change (2nd), flow (1st), gesture (4th), move (K), movement (2nd), progress (4th), signal (4th)

motivate (6th): animate (6th), compel (3rd), drive (1st), encourage (4th), excite (4th), force (1st), inspire (4th), move (K), persuade (5th), prompt (4th), propel (6th), provoke (6th), rouse (4th), spark (5th), spur (4th), start (1st), stimulate (6th), urge (4th)

motive (5th): aim (3rd), cause (2nd), goal (4th), intention (6th), motivation (6th), principle (4th), reason (2nd)

motor (4th): engine (3rd), machine (1st)

motto (6th): saying (1st)

mound (2nd): heap (3rd), hill (1st), hump (3rd), mount (2nd), pile (1st), stack (6th)

mount (2nd): A. horse (K), steed (4th) **B.** ascend (4th), climb (1st), crest (4th), hill (1st), increase (3rd), rise (1st), scale (3rd)

mountain (2nd): hill (1st), mount (2nd), peak (4th)

mourn (4th): cry (1st), grieve (5th), lament (6th), sorrow (4th), weep (4th)

mouse (K)

mouth (1st): access (6th), entrance (3rd), inlet (4th), opening (1st)

move (K): A. strategy (6th), tactic (6th) **B.** impress (5th), motivate (6th), persuade (5th), sadden (3rd) **C.** adjust (5th), advance (2nd), change (2nd), continue (2nd), leave (1st), plan (1st), push (1st), shift (4th)

movement (2nd): action (1st), animation (6th), change (2nd), drift (2nd), gesture (4th), motion (3rd), progress (4th), traffic (5th)

movie (1st): film (4th), moving picture (1st)

moving (1st): active (3rd), animated (6th), mobile (6th)

Mr. (K)

Mrs. (K)

Ms. (K)

much (1st): full (K), lot (K), many (K), myriad (6th), plenty (1st)

mud (1st): dirt (1st)

muffin (4th)

mug (1st)

mulberry (4th)

mule (2nd)

multiply (2nd): breed (4th), double (3rd), enlarge (5th), expand (5th), grow (K), increase (3rd)

mumble (4th): babble (6th), murmur (4th), mutter (4th), whisper (1st)

mums (4th)

mummy (2nd)

municipal (6th): city (K), civic (3rd), civil (3rd), public (1st)

murder (3rd): butcher (4th), execute (5th), finish (1st), kill (1st), shooting (3rd), slaughter (5th), slay (4th), strangle (6th)

murmur (4th): babble (6th), gossip (5th), mumble (4th), mutter (4th), rumor (5th), whisper (1st)

muscle (4th): energy (4th), force (1st), might (1st), power (1st), strength (2nd)

muse (4th)

museum (4th): exhibit hall (4th), gallery (5th)

mush (5th)

mushroom (4th)

music (K): harmony (4th), melody (4th), rhythm (6th), song (K), tune (1st)

musical (5th): harmonious (4th), melodious (4th), tuneful (1st)

musician (4th): performer (4th), player (1st), singer (1st)

musk (5th)

musket (5th): gun (K), rifle (4th)

muskrat (5th)

muss (1st): crease (5th), disorder (3rd), displace (2nd), disturb (6th), fold (1st), mess (1st), wrinkle (3rd)

mussel (3rd)

must (1st): essential (6th), have to (K), requirement (3rd)

mustang (4th)

mustard (4th)

muster (6th): assemble (4th), call (1st), cause (2nd), collect (3rd), crowd (2nd), enlist (6th), gather (1st), generate (4th), group (1st), mass (3rd), rally (5th), recruit (6th)

mutate (4th): alter (4th), change (2nd), convert (4th), modify (5th), transform (5th), translate (5th), turn (1st), vary (4th)

mute (6th): dumb (1st), gag (1st), quiet (K), silence (3rd), silent (3rd), speechless (2nd)

mutiny (6th): challenge (4th), dare (2nd), defy (6th), revolt (5th), treason (4th)

mutt (4th): canine (5th), dog (K), hound (2nd)

mutter (4th): babble (6th), grumble (5th)

mutton (5th): lamb (1st), sheep (1st)

mutual (5th): common (2nd), joint (4th), shared (2nd)

muzzle (6ᵗʰ): A. mouth (1ˢᵗ), nose (1ˢᵗ), snout (5ᵗʰ) **B.** gag (1ˢᵗ), restraint (5ᵗʰ), silence (3ʳᵈ)

my (K)

myriad (6ᵗʰ): bunch (3ʳᵈ), extensive (4ᵗʰ), legion (6ᵗʰ), many (K), numerous (4ᵗʰ), plenty (1ˢᵗ), thousands (1ˢᵗ), tons (1ˢᵗ)

myself (1ˢᵗ): me (K), I (K)

mystery (1ˢᵗ): A. miracle (5ᵗʰ), secret (1ˢᵗ), wonder (1ˢᵗ) **B.** problem (1ˢᵗ), puzzle (4ᵗʰ), question (1ˢᵗ), riddle (1ˢᵗ)

mystic (4ᵗʰ): concealed (4ᵗʰ), hidden (1ˢᵗ), mysterious (4ᵗʰ), private (3ʳᵈ), secret (1ˢᵗ), spiritual (5ᵗʰ)

myth (4ᵗʰ): fable (5ᵗʰ), fantasy (5ᵗʰ), fiction (5ᵗʰ), legend (5ᵗʰ), tale (3ʳᵈ)

nab (1ˢᵗ): arrest (3ʳᵈ), capture (3ʳᵈ), catch (1ˢᵗ), clutch (4ᵗʰ), get (K), grab (4ᵗʰ), seize (3ʳᵈ), steal (3ʳᵈ), take (1ˢᵗ)

nag (1ˢᵗ): annoy (5ᵗʰ), badger (2ⁿᵈ), bother (2ⁿᵈ), complain (4ᵗʰ), fault (3ʳᵈ), fuss (1ˢᵗ), gripe (5ᵗʰ), grumble (5ᵗʰ), mutter (4ᵗʰ), object (1ˢᵗ), pester (2ⁿᵈ), scold (5ᵗʰ)

nail (2ⁿᵈ): A. attach (5ᵗʰ), connect (3ʳᵈ), fasten (4ᵗʰ), join (3ʳᵈ), staple (6ᵗʰ), tack (1ˢᵗ) **B.** capture (3ʳᵈ), catch (1ˢᵗ), get (K), seize (3ʳᵈ) **C.** grab (4ᵗʰ), hit (K), nab (1ˢᵗ), peg (1ˢᵗ), pin (K), strike (2ⁿᵈ)

naked (4ᵗʰ): bare (3ʳᵈ), exposed (4ᵗʰ), plain (2ⁿᵈ), stark (1ˢᵗ), stripped (3ʳᵈ), uncovered (2ⁿᵈ)

name (K): A. alias (6ᵗʰ), reputation (5ᵗʰ), signature (6ᵗʰ), term (3ʳᵈ), title (3ʳᵈ) **B.** celebrity (5ᵗʰ), star (K) **C.** appoint (3ʳᵈ), call (1ˢᵗ), identify (4ᵗʰ), label (3ʳᵈ), select (4ᵗʰ), specify (5ᵗʰ)

nanites (4ᵗʰ): very small machines measured in nanometers

nano (4ᵗʰ): miniature (4ᵗʰ), minute (1ˢᵗ), tiny (2ⁿᵈ), small (K), wee (1ˢᵗ)

nanometer (4ᵗʰ): one billionth of a meter

nanoparticle (4ᵗʰ): a microscopic particle whose size is measured in nanometers

nanowires (4ᵗʰ): wires that are 100 times thinner than a human hair

nap (K): recline (6ᵗʰ), rest (1ˢᵗ), sleep (1ˢᵗ)

napkin (5ᵗʰ): cloth (1ˢᵗ), towel (6ᵗʰ)

napping (1ˢᵗ): asleep (3ʳᵈ), resting (1ˢᵗ), sleeping (1ˢᵗ)

narcissus (4ᵗʰ)

narrate (6ᵗʰ): explain (2ⁿᵈ), express (5ᵗʰ), inform (5ᵗʰ), read (K), recite (5ᵗʰ), relate (4ᵗʰ), report (1ˢᵗ), reveal (4ᵗʰ), review (4ᵗʰ), state (1ˢᵗ), tell (K)

narrow (2ⁿᵈ): A. limit (3ʳᵈ), reduce (3ʳᵈ), select (4ᵗʰ), taper (5ᵗʰ) **B.** ignorant (4ᵗʰ), limited (3ʳᵈ), strict (6ᵗʰ) **C.** focused (5ᵗʰ), slender (4ᵗʰ), small (1ˢᵗ), thin (2ⁿᵈ), tight (1ˢᵗ)

NASA (1ˢᵗ): National Aeronautics and Space Administration

nasturtium (4ᵗʰ)

nation (1ˢᵗ): clan (5ᵗʰ), country (K), empire (4ᵗʰ), government (1ˢᵗ), land (K), race (1ˢᵗ), realm (4ᵗʰ), society (3ʳᵈ), state (1ˢᵗ), tribe (3ʳᵈ)

native (1ˢᵗ): citizen (3ʳᵈ), domestic (5ᵗʰ), local (3ʳᵈ), national (2ⁿᵈ), natural (2ⁿᵈ), original (3ʳᵈ)

natural (2ⁿᵈ): A. basic (5ᵗʰ), common (2ⁿᵈ), genuine (5ᵗʰ), honest (3ʳᵈ), native (1st), normal (5th), plain (2nd), real (1st), simple (2nd), wild (2nd) **B.** automatic (6th), expected (3rd), instinct (5th), unforced (3rd), usual (3rd)

naturalist (6th): nature lover (1st), ranger (1st)

nature (1st): A. outside (1st), universe (4th), world (1st) **B.** character (2nd), core (6th), disposition (5th), division (4th), essence (6th), fiber (3rd), heart (K), make up (K), personality (5th), quality (4th), spirit (2nd), substance (5th), temperament (4th), tendency (5th), tone (3rd), type (1st)

naught (5th): defeat (5th), empty (3rd), failure (2nd), none (1st), nothing (1st), ruin (2nd), void (6th), zero (K)

naughty (5th): bad (1st), bratty (3rd), playful (1st), wicked (4th)

navigate (5th): command (2nd), direct (1st), guide (1st), journey (3rd), pilot (5th), sail (1st), steer (5th)

Navy (1st)

nay (4th): against (1st), no (K)

Nazareth (4th)

Neanderthal (5th)

near (1st): about (K), approach (3rd), around (1st), beside (1st), close (K), nearby (1st)

nearing (1st): approaching (3rd), coming (K)

nearly (1st): almost (1st), barely (3rd), hardly (1st)

neat (K): clean (K), ordered (1st), plain (2nd), straight (3rd), tidy (2nd)

nebula (4th)

necessary (1st): basic (5th), essential (6th), important (1st), must (1st), needed (1st), required (2nd), vital (5th)

neck (1st)

nectar (2nd)

need (1st): A. charge (2nd), duty (1st) **B.** demand (5th), desire (5th), emergency (5th), lack (1st), miss (K), necessity (3rd), poverty (5th), require (1st), want (K) **C.** defect (5th), fault (3rd), flaw (2nd)

needle (3rd): A. annoy (5th), bug (K), pester (2nd), pick on (1st), tease (3rd) **B.** pin (K), point (1st), sew (2nd)

negative (6th): against (1st), complaining (4th), critical (5th), denying (5th), harmful (3rd), opposing (3rd), opposite (3rd), unfavorable (3rd)

neglect (4th): abandon (4th), absence (5th), carelessness (5th), disregard (4th), exclude (6th), forget (1st), ignore (5th), laziness (4th), miss (K), negligence (4th), omission (6th), omit (6th), overlook (4th), pass (2nd), shirk (6th), slight (4th)

neighbor (2nd): A. acquaintance (4th), person next door (1st) **B.** border (1st), connect (3rd), meet (K), touch (1st)

neighborhood (2nd): area (3rd), closeness (1st), district (4th), locale (3rd), nearness (2nd), region (4th), section (4th), suburbs (6th)

neither (1st)

nephew (4th)

nerve (6th)

nervous (1st): afraid (1st), alarmed (3rd), anxious (4th), concerned (3rd), edgy (2nd), excitable (4th), excited (4th), hysterical (6th), restless (4th), scared (1st), tense (5th), timid (5th), troubled (1st), uncertain (3rd), uneasy (3rd), upset (3rd), worried (1st)

nest (1st): brood (4th), den (1st), dwelling (4th), home (K), refuge (5th), retreat (4th), roost (2nd), shelter (4th)

nestle (3rd): bundle (5th), cradle (4th), cuddle (5th), embrace (4th), snuggle (5th)

net (3rd): A. bag (1st), catch (1st), trap (1st) **B.** attain (6th), earn (2nd), gain (2nd), get (K), obtain (5th), profit (4th), return (2nd), take (1st), win (1st), worth (3rd), yield (4th)

nettle (4th): anger (3rd), annoy (5th), bother (2nd), disturb (6th), irk (6th), irritate (6th), pester (2nd), pick on (1st), upset (3rd), vex (5th)

neuron (6th): nerve cell (6th)

neutral (6th): A. pale (3rd), uncolored (3rd) **B.** detached (5th), fair (1st), free (K), impartial (6th), impersonal (3rd), independent (3rd), indifferent (3rd), objective (2nd), peaceful (2nd)

never (K): at no time (1st), not ever (K)

nevertheless (4th): anyway (1st), but (K), however (3rd), nonetheless (5th), notwithstanding (4th), so (K), still (1st)

new (K): contemporary (5th), first (1st), fresh (2nd), green (K), latest (1st), modern (2nd), novel (5th), original (3rd), pioneer (4th), raw (1st), recent (3rd), unique (6th), unknown (3rd), unused (3rd), unusual (3rd), young (1st)

newspaper (1st): bulletin (3rd), journal (2nd), publication (4th)

Newtonian (5th)

next (K): A. following (1st), future (5th), latter (3rd) **B.** adjoining (6th), beside (1st), closest (1st), later (1st), nearest (2nd)

nibble (4th): bite (1st), chew (1st), eat (K), gnaw (1st), snack (2nd)

nice (1st): agreeable (2nd), charming (3rd), cordial (6th), correct (3rd), good (K), likable (1st), pleasant (3rd), polite (4th), refined (6th), sweet (K)

nickel (1st)

niece (3rd)

night (1st): dark (1st), evening (1st), sunset (1st), twilight (1st)

nightingale (4th)

nine (K)

nineteen (1st)

ninety (1st)

nip (1st): A. cut (K), snip (2nd), stop (K), stunt (6th), wither (5th) **B.** piece (1st), pinch (4th), sample (5th) **C.** bite (1st), consume (4th), drink (1st), gulp (1st), sip (1st), snack (2nd)

nitrogen (6th)

no (K): denial (5th), deny (5th), nay (4th), never (K), refusal (2nd), rejection (5th)

noble (3rd): A. aristocrat (6th), gallant (4th), gentleman (3rd), gentlewoman (3rd), grand (2nd), imperial (5th), lady (1st), lofty (5th), lordly (3rd), majestic (4th), regal (6th), royal (3rd) **B.** ethical (5th), heroic (5th), honest (3rd), honorable (3rd), pure (3rd), true (1st), worthy (3rd)

nobody (1st): no one (K), not anyone (1st)

nod (1ˢᵗ): assent (6ᵗʰ), consent (3ʳᵈ), cue (2ⁿᵈ), gesture (4ᵗʰ), greet (3ʳᵈ), motion (3ʳᵈ), salute (4ᵗʰ), signal (4ᵗʰ)

noise (1ˢᵗ): blast (2ⁿᵈ), clamor (6ᵗʰ), commotion (5ᵗʰ), din (6ᵗʰ), racket (2ⁿᵈ), shout (1ˢᵗ), sound (1ˢᵗ), yell (K)

noisy (5ᵗʰ): babbling (6ᵗʰ), blasting (2ⁿᵈ), harsh (5ᵗʰ), loud (1ˢᵗ), loud-mouthed (1ˢᵗ), riotous (6ᵗʰ), shouting (1ˢᵗ)

nominate (5ᵗʰ): appoint (3ʳᵈ), choose (3ʳᵈ), designate (5ᵗʰ), elect (3ʳᵈ), induct (5ᵗʰ), name (K), ordain (6ᵗʰ), present (K), select (4ᵗʰ), submit (4ᵗʰ)

none (1ˢᵗ): no one (K), not a one (K), nothing (1ˢᵗ), zero (K)

nonetheless (5ᵗʰ): anyway (1ˢᵗ), but (K), however (3ʳᵈ), notwithstanding (4ᵗʰ), still (1ˢᵗ), yet (1ˢᵗ)

nonfiction (5ᵗʰ): actual (3ʳᵈ), fact (1ˢᵗ), history (2ⁿᵈ)

nonsense (5ᵗʰ): absurdity (6ᵗʰ), babble (6ᵗʰ), folly (4ᵗʰ), foolishness (4ᵗʰ), garbage (6ᵗʰ), junk (3ʳᵈ), ridiculousness (6ᵗʰ), senselessness (3ʳᵈ), silliness (1ˢᵗ), stupidity (4ᵗʰ)

nook (6ᵗʰ): cabinet (4ᵗʰ), cave (1ˢᵗ), chest (2ⁿᵈ), closet (2ⁿᵈ), crack (4ᵗʰ), cubby (4ᵗʰ), gap (K), hole (1ˢᵗ)

nook (6ᵗʰ)

nor (3ʳᵈ)

normal (5ᵗʰ): average (3ʳᵈ), common (2ⁿᵈ), customary (6ᵗʰ), everyday (1ˢᵗ), familiar (3ʳᵈ), healthy (1ˢᵗ), medium (5ᵗʰ), natural (2ⁿᵈ), ordinary (3ʳᵈ), regular (3ʳᵈ), routine (6ᵗʰ), standard (3ʳᵈ), typical (6ᵗʰ), usual (3ʳᵈ)

north (1ˢᵗ)

nose (1ˢᵗ): A. beak (4ᵗʰ), muzzle (6ᵗʰ), snout (5ᵗʰ) **B.** feel (K), flair (6ᵗʰ), gift (K), insight (2ⁿᵈ), knack (4ᵗʰ), talent (2ⁿᵈ)

nostril (5ᵗʰ)

not (K)

notable (5ᵗʰ): A. big shot (1ˢᵗ), celebrity (5ᵗʰ), name (K), star (K) **B.** celebrated (4ᵗʰ), famous (2ⁿᵈ), outstanding (2ⁿᵈ), rare (4ᵗʰ), remarkable (4ᵗʰ), significant (6ᵗʰ), special (2ⁿᵈ), strange (1ˢᵗ), unusual (3ʳᵈ), well-known (1ˢᵗ)

notch (5ᵗʰ): A. degree (5ᵗʰ), grade (2ⁿᵈ) **B.** carve (4ᵗʰ), chip (5ᵗʰ), cut (K), dent (1ˢᵗ), groove (5ᵗʰ), mark (1ˢᵗ), tab (K)

note (1ˢᵗ): A. bill (1ˢᵗ), check (1ˢᵗ), currency (3ʳᵈ), money (K) **B.** card (1ˢᵗ), letter (1ˢᵗ), memo (3ʳᵈ), reminder (3ʳᵈ) **C.** comment (5ᵗʰ), notice (1ˢᵗ), observe (3ʳᵈ), record (2ⁿᵈ), remark (4ᵗʰ), see (K), state (1ˢᵗ), watch (1ˢᵗ) **D.** honor (1ˢᵗ), recognize (3ʳᵈ)

nothing (1ˢᵗ): empty (3ʳᵈ), naught (6ᵗʰ), none (1ˢᵗ), void (6ᵗʰ), zero (K)

notice (1ˢᵗ): A. announcement (4ᵗʰ), poster (3ʳᵈ) **B.** be aware (3ʳᵈ), concern (3ʳᵈ), consider (2ⁿᵈ), feel (K), mark (1ˢᵗ), observe (3ʳᵈ), recognize (3ʳᵈ), regard (4ᵗʰ), remark (4ᵗʰ), see (K), sense (1ˢᵗ), watch (1ˢᵗ), witness (3ʳᵈ)

noticeable (3ʳᵈ): apparent (3ʳᵈ), clear (2ⁿᵈ), evident (5ᵗʰ), observable (3ʳᵈ), recognizable (3ʳᵈ)

notify (3ʳᵈ): alert (5ᵗʰ), caution (5ᵗʰ), let know (1ˢᵗ), remind (3ʳᵈ), report (1ˢᵗ), tell (K), warn (3ʳᵈ)

notion (5ᵗʰ): belief (2ⁿᵈ), clue (2ⁿᵈ), concept (4ᵗʰ), fancy (3ʳᵈ), idea (1ˢᵗ), guess (1ˢᵗ), guide (1ˢᵗ), hint (1ˢᵗ), idea (1ˢᵗ), impulse (5ᵗʰ), judgment (3ʳᵈ), mind (1st), opinion (3rd), thought (1st), view (2nd), whim (6th)

nourish (6th): feed (1st), help (K), maintain (4th), mother (K), parent (3rd), promote (5th), protect (4th), support (4th), sustain (5th)

novel (5th): A. different (4th), fresh (2nd), latest (1st), modern (2nd), new (K), original (3rd), strange (1st) **B.** book (K), history (2nd), fiction (5th), story (1st), tale (3rd)

November (1st)

novice (5th): amateur (5th), beginner (2nd), student (3rd)

now (K): at once (1st), current (3rd), immediately (3rd), instantly (3rd), promptly (4th), quickly (1st), right away (K), soon (K)

nuclear (4th): A. atomic (5th) **B.** central (3rd), core (6th), focal (5th)

nucleus (4th): center (2nd), core (6th), essence (6th), focus (5th), heart (K), marrow (2nd), mass (3rd)

nuisance (6th): annoyance (5th), bother (2nd), pain (2nd), pest (1st), problem (1st), worry (1st)

number (K): A. itemize (5th), list (2nd) **B.** amount (2nd), calculation (5th), count (1st), figure (2nd), numeral (5th), quantity (4th), sum (1st), total (2nd)

numeral (5th): figure (2nd), number (K)

numerous (4th): abundant (5th), assorted (5th), countless (5th), extensive (4th), great (K), infinite (5th), many (K), numberless (1st), several (1st), various (4th)

nun (1st): sister (1st)

nurse (K): A. attendant (4th), governess (2nd) **B.** aid (2nd), attend (3rd), care for (1st), feed (1st), help (K), nourish (6th), suckle (6th)

nut (K): A. bolt (4th), peg (1st), pin (K), stud (6th) **B.** acorn (4th), grain (3rd), seed (1st) **C.** zealot (6th)

nutmeg (4th)

nutrino (5th)

nuzzle (1st): caress (1st), cuddle (5th), hold (1st), hug (1st), nestle (2nd), pet (1st), snuggle (5th)

nymph (6th): elf (1st), fairy (2nd), mermaid (4th), sea-maiden (4th)

oak (1st)

oar (1st)

oarlock (2nd)

oat (1st)

oath (5th): declaration (5th), pledge (5th), promise (1st), vow (4th), word (K)

oatmeal (5th)

obey (3rd): comply (6th), conform (6th), execute (5th), follow (1st), mind (1st), observe (3rd), serve (1st)

object (1st): A. argue (3rd), complain (4th), disagree (3rd), grumble (5th), mind (1st), protest (4th) **B.** aim (3rd), goal (4th), intention (5th), target (5th) **C.** article (2nd), body (1st), element (3rd), item (5th), piece (1st), thing (K)

objective (2nd): A. fair (1st), impartial (6th) **B.** aim (3rd), end (K), goal (4th), intent (5th)

obligation (6th): burden (5th), commitment (4th), duty (1st), guarantee (6th), pledge (5th), promise (1st), responsibility (4th), tie (1st)

oblige (6th): accommodate (6th), aid (2nd), assist (4th), help (K), please (K)

obscure (6th): A. clouded (1st), dark (1st), dim (1st), gloomy (3rd) **B.** doubtful (5th), mysterious (3rd), mystic (4th), puzzling (4th), unclear (2nd), unknown (K), vague (5th), veiled (3rd) **C.** concealed (4th), invisible (6th), nameless (3rd), remote (5th), secret (1st)

observe (3rd): A. eye (1st), examine (5th), inspect (5th), notice (1st), see (K), spy (4th), study (2nd), view (2nd), watch (1st) **B.** comply (6th), mind (1st), obey (3rd), understand (1st) **C.** celebrate (4th), honor (1st), keep (K), remember (1st)

obstacle (5th): bar (3rd), barrier (6th), challenge (4th), fence (1st), hurdle (5th), interference (4th), plight (6th), problem (1st), restriction (6th)

obstinate (5th): determined (5th), firm (2nd), inflexible (6th), persistent (5th), rigid (5th), stubborn (5th), unbending (3rd)

obtain (5th): accomplish (2nd), achieve (5th), acquire (4th), attain (6th), buy (K), earn (2nd), gain (2nd), get (K), procure (5th), secure (3rd), win (1st)

obvious (5th): apparent (3rd), clear (2nd), distinct (5th), evident (5th), marked (1st), noticeable (3rd), plain (2nd), prominent (5th), visible (4th)

occasion (3rd): A. celebration (4th), festivity (5th), holiday (K) **B.** cause (2nd), chance (2nd), event (3rd), incident (5th), moment (1st), occurrence (4th)

occupation (6th): business (2nd), career (4th), employment (5th), job (K), profession (5th), task (3rd), trade (2nd), work (K)

occupy (3rd): A. capture (3rd), conquer (4th), seize (3rd) **B.** absorb (5th), dwell (4th), fill (1st), live (1st), reside (5th)

occur (3rd): appear (2nd), come about (2nd), develop (5th), exist (3rd), happen (1st), pass (2nd)

ocean (1st): A. immense (4th), infinity (5th), lots (K) **B.** deep (1st), sea (1st), tide (1st)

o'clock (4th)

October (1st)

octopus (1st)

odd (4th): funny (1st), lone (2nd), one (K), only (K), peculiar (4th), single (3rd), sole (4th), strange (1st), uncommon (3rd), unique (6th), unusual (3rd), weird (1st)

odor (3rd): fragrance (5th), scent (3rd), smell (3rd)

odor (3rd): aroma (4th), scent (3rd), smell (3rd)

of (K)

off (K): A. inaccurate (6th), incorrect (4th), wrong (1st) **B.** disconnected (4th), not on (1st) **C.** odd (4th), strange (1st), unusual (3rd) **D.** distant (4th), far (1st), far away (3rd)

offend (4th): anger (1st), annoy (5th), insult (5th), irritate (6th), outrage (6th), provoke (6th), shock (1st), sin (1st), slight (4th), upset (3rd)

offensive (4th): A. aggressive (6th), attacking (4th), hostile (4th) **B.** abusive (6th), disagreeable (3rd), disgusting (5th), displeasing (3rd), irritating (6th)

offer (2nd): A. extend (4th), give (1st), present (K), volunteer (5th) **B.** attempt (2nd), try (K), venture (4th) **C.** approach (3rd), bid (1st), proposal (4th), suggest (2nd)

office (1st): A. department (2nd), division (4th), job (K), position (2nd), post (1st) **B.** appointment (3rd), branch (2nd), capacity (6th), duty (1st), rank (3rd), task (3rd), unit (5th)

officer (1st): director (2nd), executive (5th), official (3rd)

official (3rd): A. real (1st), standard (3rd) **B.** authority (3rd), clerk (2nd) **C.** established (3rd)

often (1st): common (2nd), frequently (4th), much (1st), regular (3rd), repeated (4th), routine (6th),

usual (3rd)

oh (K): goodness (1st), my (K)

oil (K): A. canvas (6th), painting (2nd), picture (K) **B.** anoint (6th) **C.** fat (1st), grease (5th)

O.K. (K): acceptable (4th), accurate (6th), all right (K), correct (3rd), good (K), satisfactory (4th), well (K)

okay (1st): see O.K.

old (K): aged (1st), ancient (3rd), antique (6th), dead (1st), elderly (5th), former (6th), late (1st), long-lived (1st), ongoing (2nd), past (1st), primitive (5th), stale (2nd), worn (3rd)

older (1st): advanced (2nd), elder (5th), first (1st), mature (5th), senior (6th)

Oligocene (5th): of or belonging to the geologic time, rock series, or sedimentary deposits of the third epoch of the Tertiary Period

olive (4th)

omen (6th): indication (4th), sage (5th), sign (1st), warning (3rd)

ominous (6th): bad (K), fearful (2nd), ghostly (1st), malignant (6th), menacing (5th), odd (4th), scary (1st), strange (1st), threatening (5th)

omit (6th): bar (3rd), cancel (6th), exclude (6th), forget (1st), leave out (1st), miss (K), neglect (4th), remove (2nd), skip (2nd)

omnivore (5th)

on (K): at (K), atop (3rd)

once (1st): before (1st), earlier (2nd), former (6th), late (1st), one time (2nd), past (1st)

one (K): A. entire (3rd), undivided (4th), united (5th), whole (1st) **B.** individual (3rd), single (3rd)

oneself (3rd): myself (2nd), yourself (2nd)

onion (2nd)

only (K): a (K), alone (1st), but (K), except (2nd), exclusive (6th), however (3rd), individual (3rd), just (1st), lone (2nd), merely (3rd), odd (4th), one (K), simply (2nd), single (3rd), sole (4th), unique (6th), yet (1st)

onto (1st)

onward (3rd): ahead (1st), along (1st), before (1st), beyond (1st), forth (2nd), forward (3rd), in front (1st)

onyx (5th)

opal (5th)

open (K): A. earnest (4th), frank (4th), honest (3rd), sincere (4th) **B.** accessible (6th), bare (3rd), begin (1st), big (K), due (2nd), expand (5th), exposed (4th), launch (5th), naked (4th), natural (2nd), owed (3rd), plain (2nd), roomy (2nd), simple (2nd), spacious (3rd), start (1st), unblock (2nd), uncover (2nd), unlock

(2nd), vast (4th), visible (4th), wide (1st), widen (1st), windy (1st)

opera (4th): music drama (5th)

operate (3rd): act (K), behave (4th), conduct (3rd), function (4th), manage (4th), work (K)

operation (3rd): action (1st), battle (2nd), engagement (5th), function (4th), method (2nd), performing (4th), process (4th), use (K)

operator (5th): conductor (3rd), flier (2nd), manager (4th), mechanic (5th), pilot (5th), user (1st), worker (1st)

opinion (3rd): advice (3rd), angle (3rd), belief (1st), bias (6th), conviction (5th), counsel (5th), feeling (1st), judgment (2nd), ruling (2nd), slant (6th), suggestion (2nd), view (2nd), voice (1st)

opossum (3rd)

opponent (5th): challenger (4th), competitor (4th), contestant (4th), enemy (2nd), foe (4th), rival (4th)

opportunity (3rd): break (1st), chance (2nd), freedom (3rd), means (4th), moment (1st), occasion (3rd), opening (1st), possibility (2nd), room (1st)

oppose (3rd): argue (3rd), attack (3rd), challenge (4th), contest (4th), contrast (4th), counter (5th), defy (6th), dispute (6th), resist (4th)

opposite (3rd): conflicting (4th), contrary (4th), counter (5th), different (1st), opposed (3rd), reverse (5th), unlike (2nd)

oppress (6th): abuse (6th), beat down (1st), burden (5th), crush (4th), exploit (6th), persecute (6th)

optical (5th)

or (K): else (1st), if not (1st), otherwise (3rd),

oracle (6th): authority (3rd), mastermind (2nd), prophecy (4th), prophet (4th), psychic (6th), revelation (4th), seer (1st), vision (4th), visionary (5th), wizard (6th)

orange (K)

orbit (4th): circle (K), course (3rd), curve (3rd), distance (4th), extent (4th), flight path (2nd), length (2nd), reach (1st), route (4th), scope (6th)

orchard (5th)

orchestra (6th)

orchid (4th)

ordain (6th): approve (4th), authorize (3rd), establish (3rd), legislate (5th), order (1st), rule (K)

order (1st): A. arrange (3rd), direction (1st), group (1st), method (2nd), organize (4th), pattern (3rd), plan (1st), rank (3rd), series (4th) **B.** ask for (K), boss (K), command (2nd), demand (5th), summon (4th) **C.** contract (3rd)

ordinary (3rd): average (3rd), common (2nd), familiar (3rd), normal (5th), regular (3rd), standard (3rd), typical (6th), usual (3rd)

Ordovician (5th): of or belonging to the geologic time, system of rocks, or sedimentary deposits of the second period of the Paleozoic Era

ore (4th): metal (3rd), rock (1st)

organ (4th): journal (2nd), newspaper (1st), publication (4th), voice (1st)

organic (4th): live (1st), living (1st), natural (2nd)

organism (4ᵗʰ): animal (K), being (1ˢᵗ), body (1ˢᵗ), cell (1ˢᵗ), creature (3ʳᵈ), thing (K)

organize (4ᵗʰ): arrange (3ʳᵈ), catalog (5ᵗʰ), classify (5ᵗʰ), group (1ˢᵗ), order (1ˢᵗ), plan (1ˢᵗ), sort (1ˢᵗ), structure (4ᵗʰ)

orient (5ᵗʰ): locate (3ʳᵈ), place (1ˢᵗ)

original (3ʳᵈ): A. basic (5ᵗʰ), earliest (2ⁿᵈ), first (1ˢᵗ), fundamental (4ᵗʰ), introductory (5ᵗʰ), primary (5ᵗʰ)
B. clever (3ʳᵈ), creative (4ᵗʰ), different (1ˢᵗ), new (K), novel (5ᵗʰ), unique (6ᵗʰ)

oriole (3ʳᵈ)

ornament (4ᵗʰ): accessory (6ᵗʰ), adorn (6ᵗʰ), decoration (3ʳᵈ), garnish (6ᵗʰ), trim (4ᵗʰ), trimming (5ᵗʰ)

ornithischians (5ᵗʰ): bird-hipped dinosaurs

orphan (5ᵗʰ): lone (2ⁿᵈ)

osprey (5ᵗʰ)

ostrich (1ˢᵗ)

other (1ˢᵗ): added (1ˢᵗ), additional (2ⁿᵈ), another (1ˢᵗ), different (1ˢᵗ), distinct (5ᵗʰ), extra (1ˢᵗ), further (2ⁿᵈ), more (K), separate (3ʳᵈ), spare (3ʳᵈ), surplus (6ᵗʰ)

otherwise (3ʳᵈ): else (1ˢᵗ), if not (1ˢᵗ), or (1ˢᵗ)

otter (1ˢᵗ)

ought (1ˢᵗ): should (1ˢᵗ)

ounce (2ⁿᵈ)

our (K)

ourselves (3ʳᵈ): us (K), we (K)

out (K): dead (1ˢᵗ), done (1ˢᵗ), expired (6ᵗʰ), free (K), not in (K), outside (1ˢᵗ), over (K), unconscious (6ᵗʰ)

outcome (4ᵗʰ): consequence (4ᵗʰ), effect (3ʳᵈ), end (K), payoff (2ⁿᵈ), result (2ⁿᵈ)

outcry (4ᵗʰ): demonstration (6ᵗʰ), noise (1ˢᵗ), protest (4ᵗʰ), scream (1ˢᵗ), yell (K)

outer (5ᵗʰ): exterior (5ᵗʰ), outside (1ˢᵗ), outward (6ᵗʰ)

outer space (3ʳᵈ)

outlandish (6ᵗʰ): excessive (5ᵗʰ), extravagant (6ᵗʰ), extreme (5ᵗʰ), outrageous (6ᵗʰ), peculiar (4ᵗʰ), strange (1ˢᵗ), unbelievable (2ⁿᵈ), weird (1ˢᵗ)

outline (4ᵗʰ): chart (1ˢᵗ), essence (6ᵗʰ), form (1ˢᵗ), format (4ᵗʰ), framework (4ᵗʰ), pattern (3ʳᵈ), plan (1ˢᵗ), profile (5ᵗʰ), shape (1ˢᵗ), skeleton (4ᵗʰ), sketch (5ᵗʰ)

outrage (6ᵗʰ): anger (1ˢᵗ), corruption (6ᵗʰ), cruelty (5ᵗʰ), dishonor (3ʳᵈ), fury (4ᵗʰ), offense (4ᵗʰ), range (4ᵗʰ), scandal (6ᵗʰ), uproar (5ᵗʰ), wrath (4ᵗʰ)

outright (6ᵗʰ): absolute (3ʳᵈ), complete (3ʳᵈ), crashing (2ⁿᵈ), out-and-out (1ˢᵗ), perfect (3ʳᵈ), plain (2ⁿᵈ), pure (3ʳᵈ), sheer (5ᵗʰ), thorough (4ᵗʰ), thoroughgoing (4ᵗʰ), total (2ⁿᵈ), unbounded (6ᵗʰ), unlimited (3ʳᵈ), unqualified (4ᵗʰ), utter (4ᵗʰ)

outside (1ˢᵗ): beyond (1ˢᵗ), exterior (5ᵗʰ), farther (3ʳᵈ), front (1ˢᵗ), outdoor (2ⁿᵈ), past (1ˢᵗ), surface (3ʳᵈ)

outstanding (2ⁿᵈ): A. celebrated (4ᵗʰ), dominant (5ᵗʰ), excellent (1ˢᵗ), famous (2ⁿᵈ), great (1ˢᵗ), important (1ˢᵗ), super (1ˢᵗ), wonderful (1ˢᵗ)
B. due (2ⁿᵈ), owed (3ʳᵈ), unpaid (2ⁿᵈ)

outward (6th): evident (5th), exterior (5th), outer (5th), outside (1st), visible (4th)

outwit (6th): best (K), defeat (5th), fool (2nd), outsmart (K), trick (1st), win (1st)

oval (1st)

oven (1st)

ovenbird (2nd)

over (K): above (1st), across (1st), complete (3rd), done (1st), ended (1st), finished (1st), gone (1st), greater (1st), more (K), past (1st), through (1st)

overflow (5th): excess (5th), flood (2nd), run over (1st), spill (1st), submerge (5th), surplus (6th), swamp (4th)

overlook (4th): A. direct (1st), manage (4th), oversee (1st), supervise (6th) **B.** forget (1st), ignore (5th), miss (K), neglect (4th), omit (6th), pass (2nd), skip (2nd)

overseas (2nd)

oversee (1st): direct (1st), manage (4th), overlook (4th), regulate (5th), run (K), supervise (6th), watch over (1st)

overtake (5th): advance (2nd), approach (3rd), come up (1st), equal (2nd), match (3rd), near (1st), outdo (2nd), pass (K), reach (1st)

overthrow (2nd): conquer (4th), crush (4th), defeat (5th), destroy (2nd), down (K), lick (1st), overcome (3rd), ruin (2nd), topple (6th), upset (3rd), vanquish (6th)

overwhelm (5th): amaze (5th), awe (6th), conquer (4th), crush (4th), daze (5th), defeat (5th), destroy (2nd), drown (1st), flood (2nd), overpower (2nd), shock (1st), stun (4th), swamp (4th)

owe (3rd): payable (2nd)

owl (K)

own (K): admit (4th), allow (2nd), confess (4th), concede (6th), have (K), individual (3rd), keep (K), personal (3rd), possess (3rd), retain (5th)

ox (K)

oxygen (4th): air (1st)

oyster (4th)

ozone (5th): air (1st), atmosphere (4th)

ozone hole (5th): a loss in ozone; ozone blocks some of the suns UV-B rays from reaching the earth's surface

pace (3rd): A. rate (1st), speed (3rd), stride (5th) **B.** step (1st), walk (K)

pack (1st): A. bag (1st), batch (2nd), bundle (5th), gear (1st), kit (1st), pouch (1st), sack (1st), team (1st) **B.** bag (1st), box (K), bunch (3rd), carry (1st), crowd (2nd), fill (K), haul (4th), insert (6th), load (2nd), stow (6th), stuff (1st), tote (5th)

package (4th): A. bundle (5th), parcel (4th) **B.** box (K), close (K), enclose (4th), pack (1st), seal (K), wrap (3rd)

pad (K): A. pack (1st) **B.** carpet (4th), mat (5th), pallet (5th), pillow (4th)

paddle (1st): A. spank (2nd) **B.** oar (1st)

page (1st): A. paper (K), sheet (1st) **B.** announce (3rd), call (1st), summon (4th)

pageant (6th): celebration (4th), ceremony (5th), festival (5th), parade (2nd), show (1st)

pagoda (5th): temple (3rd)

paid (2ⁿᵈ): compensated (6ᵗʰ), settled (2ⁿᵈ)

pail (2ⁿᵈ): bucket (3ʳᵈ), pan (K), pot (K), tin (1ˢᵗ), tub (1ˢᵗ)

pain (2ⁿᵈ): A. annoy (5ᵗʰ), bother (2ⁿᵈ), distress (5ᵗʰ), hurt (1ˢᵗ) **B.** ache (5ᵗʰ), agony (5ᵗʰ), anguish (6ᵗʰ), bother (2ⁿᵈ), distress (5ᵗʰ), grief (5ᵗʰ), hurt (1ˢᵗ), injury (5ᵗʰ), sorrow (4ᵗʰ), suffering (2ⁿᵈ), trouble (1ˢᵗ), woe (4ᵗʰ)

paint (2ⁿᵈ): A. color (K), cover (1ˢᵗ), dye (2ⁿᵈ) **B.** color (K), dye (2ⁿᵈ)

pair (1ˢᵗ): A. couple (3ʳᵈ), two (K) **B.** combine (3ʳᵈ), join (3ʳᵈ), set (K), unite (5ᵗʰ), wed (K)

pal (K): buddy (4ᵗʰ), friend (1ˢᵗ)

palace (1ˢᵗ): castle (3ʳᵈ), estate (4ᵗʰ), mansion (5ᵗʰ)

pale (3ʳᵈ): dim (1ˢᵗ), light (K), weak (3ʳᵈ), white (K)

paleontologist (5ᵗʰ)

Paleocene (5ᵗʰ): of or belonging to the geologic time, rock series, or sedimentary deposits of the first epoch of the Tertiary Period

Paleozoic (5ᵗʰ): designating the era of geologic time that includes the Cambrian, Ordovician, Silurian, Devonian, Mississippian, Pennsylvanian, and Permian periods

pallet (5ᵗʰ): bed (K), cot (1ˢᵗ), pad (K)

palm (4ᵗʰ): hand (1ˢᵗ)

pamphlet (6ᵗʰ): booklet (1ˢᵗ), circular (4ᵗʰ), program (4ᵗʰ)

pan (K): container (5ᵗʰ), pot (K)

panda (K)

pane (5ᵗʰ): glass (1ˢᵗ), part (1ˢᵗ), sheet (1ˢᵗ), window (1ˢᵗ)

panel (6ᵗʰ): A. curtain (5ᵗʰ), divider (4ᵗʰ), part (1ˢᵗ) **B.** committee (5ᵗʰ), jury (4ᵗʰ)

pang (6ᵗʰ): ache (5ᵗʰ), pain (2ⁿᵈ), regret (5ᵗʰ)

Pangea (5ᵗʰ): a hypothetical supercontinent that included all the landmasses of the earth before the Triassic Period

panic (1ˢᵗ): alarm (3ʳᵈ), fear (1ˢᵗ), fright (2ⁿᵈ), horror (4ᵗʰ), scare (1ˢᵗ), terror (3ʳᵈ)

panther (3ʳᵈ)

pantry (5ᵗʰ): closet (2ⁿᵈ), food room (1ˢᵗ)

pants (1ˢᵗ): jeans (1ˢᵗ), trousers (5ᵗʰ)

papa (1ˢᵗ): dad (K), daddy (K), father (K), pop (K)

paper (K): A. page (1ˢᵗ), stationery (5ᵗʰ) **B.** composition (4ᵗʰ), essay (5ᵗʰ), papyrus (4ᵗʰ), report (1ˢᵗ), theme (4ᵗʰ)

papier-mâché (6ᵗʰ)

paprika (4ᵗʰ)

papyrus (4ᵗʰ)

parasite (4ᵗʰ)

parade (2ⁿᵈ): display (3ʳᵈ), exhibit (4ᵗʰ), march (1ˢᵗ), procession (4ᵗʰ), show (1ˢᵗ), walk (K)

paradise (4ᵗʰ): delight (3ʳᵈ), glory (3ʳᵈ), heaven (1ˢᵗ), joy (1ˢᵗ)

paragraph (6ᵗʰ): part (1ˢᵗ), passage (4ᵗʰ), verse (4ᵗʰ)

parakeet (5ᵗʰ)

parallel (5th): associated (5th), equal (2nd), even (1st), like (K), related (4th), same (K), similar (4th), uniform (1st)

paralysis (6th): disability (3rd), immovable (3rd), inaction (2nd), rigid (5th)

paralyze (6th): daze (5th), disable (3rd), freeze (4th), shock (1st), stun (4th)

paranormal (5th): psychic (6th)

parcel (4th): A. assign (5th), divide (4th) **B.** box (K), bunch (3rd), bundle (5th), carton (4th), lot (K), package (4th), plot (4th), portion (4th)

pardon (4th): clear (2nd), excuse (3rd), forgive (2nd), free (K), release (5th), relief (4th)

parent (3rd): A. nourish (6th), raise (1st) **B.** creator (3rd), elder (5th), founder (2nd), guardian (2nd), inventor (2nd)

parish (6th): district (4th), region (4th), ward (5th)

park (1st): field (2nd), forest (1st), garden (K), green (K), square (2nd), woods (1st)

parlor (4th): living room (1st), salon (6th)

parrot (1st): copy (3rd), echo (4th), imitate (5th), mimic (6th), repeat (4th)

parsley (4th)

parsnip (4th)

parson (6th): clergy (6th), minister (4th), pastor (4th), priest (4th), reverend (4th)

part (1st): A. divide (4th), divorce (4th), go (K), leave (1st), separate (3rd), share (2nd) **B.** break (1st), detail (5th), measure (2nd), percentage (4th), piece (1st), portion (4th), role (6th), section (4th), unit (5th)

partial (6th): A. biased (6th), favored (2nd), inclined (5th), prejudiced (6th), unfair (3rd) **B.** incomplete (3rd), unfinished (3rd)

particle (5th): atom (5th), bit (1st), dot (K), fragment (6th), grain (2nd), morsel (5th), scrap (3rd), shred (5th), speck (4th), spot (1st)

particular (4th): careful (1st), cautious (5th), choosy (3rd), exact (2nd), individual (3rd), part (1st), personal (3rd), select (4th), selective (4th), single (3rd), special (2nd), specific (5th), unique (6th)

partition (6th): A. assign (5th), divide (4th), separate (3rd) **B.** curtain (5th), division (4th), fence (1st), exclude (6th), panel (6th), portion (4th), wall (1st)

partner (5th): associate (5th), friend (1st), mate (4th)

partridge (1st)

part-time (3rd)

party (K): A. bunch (3rd), group (1st), member (1st), partner (5th), team (1st) **B.** affair (2nd), ball (K), celebration (4th), ceremony (5th), festival (5th)

pass (K): A. overtake (5th), better (K), exceed (4th), excel (6th), outdo (1st), outrun (1st), surpass (6th), top (K), transcend (6th) **B.** carry (K), communicate (4th), convey (4th), impart (6th), report (1st), tell (K), transmit (4th) **C.** bequeath (6th), hand down (1st), hand on (1st), transmit (4th) **D.** happen (1st), occur (3rd), transpire (6th) **E.** impersonate (6th), masquerade (6th), pose (4th) **F.** affirm (6th), approve (4th), confirm (4th), ratify, sanction (6th) **G.** ticket (1st)

passion (6th): desire (5th), emotion (4th), excitement (4th), intensity (6th), love (K), rage (4th), temper (4th)

passport (6th): identification (4th), pass (2nd), permit (3rd)

past (1st): A. beyond (1st), farther (3rd) **B.** ancient (3rd), before (1st), behind (1st), earlier (2nd), extinct (5th), former (6th), gone (1st), late (1st), left (1st), old (K), once (1st), previous (5th), prior (5th)

paste (1st): A. adhere (6th), bond (3rd), fasten (4th), join (3rd), seal (K), stick (K) **B.** adhesive (6th), cement (4th), glue (1st)

pastel (4th): delicate (5th), pale (3rd), soft (K)

pastime (6th): amusement (4th), entertainment (4th), game (K), hobby (3rd), play (K), sport (1st)

pastor (4th): clergy (6th), minister (4th), parson (6th), priest (4th), reverend (4th)

pasty (5th): doughy (5th), gluey (2nd), sticky (K)

pat (K): dab (1st), tap (K), touch (1st)

patch (4th): A. cover (1st), fix (1st), mend (1st), repair (4th) **B.** land (K), piece (1st), rag (1st), scrap (3rd)

patent (4th): A. claim (2nd), grant (2nd), invention (3rd), license (5th), permission (3rd), register (4th), right (K) **B.** apparent (3rd), evident (5th), obvious (5th), open (K), plain (2nd), true (1st)

path (1st): direction (1st), journey (3rd), passage (4th), road (K), route (4th), street (1st), trail (2nd)

pathetic (6th): emotional (4th), moving (1st), sad (K), touching (1st)

patient (4th): calm (3rd), cooperative (5th), easy (1st), quiet (K), sympathetic (4th), tolerant (5th)

patriot (4th): loyalist (5th), nationalist (2nd)

patrol (1st): A. guard (1st), policeman (1st) **B.** defend (5th), explore (4th), guard (1st), invade (5th), police (1st), protect (4th), watch (1st)

patron (5th): backer (1st), buyer (1st), client (6th), customer (5th)

patter (6th): routine (6th), speech (2nd), talk (K)

pattern (3rd): A. copy (3rd), follow (1st), imitate (5th), match (3rd), mimic (6th) **B.** copy (3rd), design (5th), example (2nd), form (1st), guide (1st), model (3rd), order (1st), outline (4th), plan (1st), series (4th), standard (3rd), system (2nd), trend (2nd)

pause (3rd): A. break (1st), delay (5th), rest (1st), stay (1st), stop (K), wait (1st) **B.** break (1st), delay (5th), gap (K), halt (4th), lag (1st), period (2nd), rest (1st), stop (K), wait (1st)

pave (5th): cement (4th), cover (1st)

pavilion (5th): canopy (6th), shelter (4th)

paw (1st): foot (1st), hit (K), strike (2nd)

pay (K): A. spend (2nd), yield (4th) **B.** payment (1st), salary (3rd), wage (3rd)

paying (1st)

payment (1ˢᵗ)

pea (1ˢᵗ): dab (1ˢᵗ), dot (K), pellet (6ᵗʰ), speck (K)

peace (1ˢᵗ): calm (3ʳᵈ), harmony (4ᵗʰ), quiet (K), rest (1ˢᵗ)

peach (1ˢᵗ)

peacock (1ˢᵗ)

peak (4ᵗʰ): crest (4ᵗʰ), crown (1ˢᵗ), height (4ᵗʰ), hill (1ˢᵗ), summit (5ᵗʰ), top (K)

peal (6ᵗʰ): chime (6ᵗʰ), clang (4ᵗʰ), ring (1ˢᵗ)

peanut (3ʳᵈ)

pear (4ᵗʰ)

pearl (4ᵗʰ): drop (K), jewel (5ᵗʰ), seed (1ˢᵗ)

peasant (4ᵗʰ): commoner (3ʳᵈ), farmer (K), worker (1ˢᵗ)

pebble (4ᵗʰ): gravel (4ᵗʰ), pellet (6ᵗʰ), rock (K), stone (2ⁿᵈ)

peck (1ˢᵗ): fault (3ʳᵈ), pick (1ˢᵗ), poke (1ˢᵗ), scold (5ᵗʰ)

peculiar (4ᵗʰ): curious (3ʳᵈ), funny (1ˢᵗ), odd (4ᵗʰ), outstanding (2ⁿᵈ), puzzle (4ᵗʰ), special (2ⁿᵈ), strange (1ˢᵗ), unique (6ᵗʰ), unusual (3ʳᵈ), weird (1ˢᵗ)

peddler (5ᵗʰ): merchant (3ʳᵈ), salesman (6ᵗʰ), seller (1ˢᵗ)

peek (2ⁿᵈ): eye (1ˢᵗ), glance (3ʳᵈ), look (K)

peel (2ⁿᵈ): A. open (K), strip (3ʳᵈ) **B.** bark (3ʳᵈ), case (2ⁿᵈ), crust (4ᵗʰ), shell (1ˢᵗ), skin (1ˢᵗ) peep **(4ᵗʰ):** crack (4ᵗʰ), glance (3ʳᵈ), peek (2ⁿᵈ)

peep (4ᵗʰ): A. cheep (1ˢᵗ) **B.** emerge (5ᵗʰ), hatch (4ᵗʰ), protrude (6ᵗʰ) **C.**

sandpiper (4ᵗʰ) **D.** glance (3ʳᵈ), peek (2ⁿᵈ), peer (1ˢᵗ)

peer (1ˢᵗ): A. equal (2ⁿᵈ), friend (1ˢᵗ), like (K), match (3ʳᵈ), partner (5ᵗʰ) **B.** classmate (4ᵗʰ), examine (5ᵗʰ), explore (4ᵗʰ), gape (5ᵗʰ), gaze (5ᵗʰ), hunt (2ⁿᵈ), inquire (3ʳᵈ), look (K), observe (3ʳᵈ), stare (3ʳᵈ)

peg (1ˢᵗ): A. connect (3ʳᵈ), join (3ʳᵈ), nail (2ⁿᵈ), pin (K), spike (4ᵗʰ), tack (1ˢᵗ) **B.** bolt (4ᵗʰ), nail (2ⁿᵈ), pin (K), spike (4ᵗʰ), tack (1ˢᵗ)

pelican (1ˢᵗ)

pellet (6ᵗʰ): bead (K), dot (K), pea (1ˢᵗ), pebble (4ᵗʰ)

pen (1ˢᵗ): A. marker (2ⁿᵈ), quill (6ᵗʰ) **B.** barn (K), cage (1ˢᵗ), jail (4ᵗʰ), stable (4ᵗʰ) **C.** author (3ʳᵈ), compose (4ᵗʰ), write (K)

penalty (5ᵗʰ): loss (K), pain (2ⁿᵈ), punishment (4ᵗʰ)

pencil (1ˢᵗ)

penetrate (5ᵗʰ): enter (2ⁿᵈ), move (K), pierce (4ᵗʰ), poke (1ˢᵗ), stab (5ᵗʰ), stir (3ʳᵈ)

peninsula (6ᵗʰ): cape (4ᵗʰ), point (1ˢᵗ)

penguin (1ˢᵗ)

penny (1ˢᵗ): cent (1ˢᵗ)

pension (6ᵗʰ): allowance (5ᵗʰ), retirement (4ᵗʰ)

people (K): community (2ⁿᵈ), humans (3ʳᵈ), public (1ˢᵗ), society (3ʳᵈ)

pepper (4ᵗʰ)

peppermint (4ᵗʰ)

perceive (6ᵗʰ): comprehend (5ᵗʰ), detect (4ᵗʰ), feel (K), know (1ˢᵗ), notice

(1st), observe (3rd), realize (2nd), recognize (3rd), see (K), sense (1st), understand (1st), view (2nd)

percent (4th): part (1st), portion (4th), section (4th)

perch (4th): A. sit (K) **B.** bar (3rd), seat (1st)

perfect (3rd): accurate (6th), best (K), complete (3rd), exact (2nd), excellent (1st), faultless (3rd), ideal (3rd), model (3rd), proper (3rd), pure (3rd), whole (1st)

perform (4th): accomplish (2nd), achieve (5th), act (K), complete (4th), do (K), execute (5th), fulfill (2nd), gain (2nd), run (K), work (K)

perfume (3rd): cologne (5th), fragrance (5th), scent (3rd), smell (3rd)

perhaps (1st): maybe (1st), possibly (2nd)

peril (5th): danger (1st), hazard (6th), menace (5th), risk (4th), threat (5th)

period (2nd): age (1st), cycle (6th), era (6th), pause (3rd), term (3rd), time (1st)

periodic (4th): alternate (5th), occasional (4th), rare (4th), regular (3rd)

perish (4th): cease (3rd), decay (5th), die (2nd), pass (2nd)

permanent (5th): constant (4th), continuous (2nd), durable (6th), enduring (4th), eternal (4th), fastened (4th), fixed (1st), lasting (1st), set (K), stable (4th)

Permian (5th): of or belonging to the geologic time, system of rocks, or sedimentary deposits of the seventh and last period of the Paleozoic Era

permit (3rd): allow (2nd), let (K), license (5th), pass (2nd), support (4th), tolerate (5th)

perpetual (6th): constant (4th), continuous (4th), endless (2nd), eternal (4th), permanent (5th), undying (4th)

perplex (6th): bewilder (3rd), confuse (4th), puzzle (4th), stump (3rd)

persecute (6th): harass (2nd), oppress (6th), pick on (1st), provoke (6th), tease (3rd), torture (5th)

persimmon (4th)

persist (5th): assert (6th), continue (2nd), endure (4th), insist (5th), last (K), remain (1st), stay (1st), survive (3rd)

person (1st): human (3rd), individual (3rd)

personal (3rd): close (K), individual (3rd), intimate (5th), near (1st), own (K), private (3rd), secret (1st)

personality (5th): celebrity (5th), identity (5th), influence (5th), name (K), spirit (2nd)

perspire (6th): glow (1st), sweat (3rd)

persuade (5th): affect (4th), bend (K), cause (2nd), convert (4th), convince (4th), influence (5th), inspire (4th), lead (1st), motivate (6th), move (1st)

pest (1st)

pester (2nd): annoy (5th), badger (2nd), bother (2nd), irk (6th), irritate (6th), nettle (5th), vex (5th)

pestilence (6th): curse (3rd), disease (5th), plague (5th)

pet (1st): A. favorite (3rd), special (2nd) **B.** cuddle (5th), pat (K), stroke (1st)

petal (5th)

petrify (4th): frighten (2nd), horrify (1st), scare (1st), shock (1st), surprise (1st), terrify (3rd)

petroleum (6th): fuel (4th), gas (1st), oil (K)

petticoat (6th): slip (3rd), underwear (2nd)

petty (6th): light (K), little (K), meaningless (3rd), minor (5th), poor (K), scant (6th), slight (4th), small (1st), sparse (3rd), worthless (3rd)

pewter (5th): lead and tin (1st), metal (3rd), tin (1st)

Pharaoh (6th)

phase (6th): aspect (5th), condition (3rd), level (3rd), side (K), stage (3rd), state (1st), step (1st)

pheasant (4th)

phenomenon (6th): event (3rd), experience (4th), marvel (4th), miracle (5th), wonder (1st)

philosophy (5th): belief (1st), knowledge (2nd), logic (6th), principles (4th), thinking (1st)

phone (2nd)

phonograph (5th): record player (2nd)

photograph (5th): photo (5th), picture (K), slide (2nd), snapshot (2nd)

photon (4th)

photosynthesis (5th)

phrase (5th): A. put into words (1st), say (K), speak (1st), state (1st) **B.** expression (5th), sentence (1st), words (K)

physical (5th): body (1st), concrete (4th), material (5th), real (1st), substantial (5th)

physics (6th)

piano (4th)

pick (1st): A. choose (3rd), elect (3rd), remove (2nd), select (4th), separate (3rd), sort (2nd) **B.** jab (1st), peck (1st) **C.** best (K), decide (1st), favorite (3rd), finest (1st), preference (3rd)

picket (3rd): A. protest (4th), strike (2nd) **B.** fence (1st), guard (1st)

pickle (1st)

picnic (5th): cookout (2nd), outing (1st)

picture (K): A. imagine (2nd), see (K), view (2nd) **B.** art (K), drawing (1st), illustration (4th), image (4th), painting (2nd), photograph (5th), print (1st), sketch (5th)

pie (K)

piece (1st): bit (1st), bite (1st), fragment (6th), ingredient (4th), measure (2nd), morsel (5th), object (1st), part (1st), patch (4th), portion (4th), rag (1st), scrap (3rd), section (4th), strip (3rd)

piecemeal (6th): gradually (3rd)

pier (4th): dock (1st), landing (1st), wharf (5th)

pierce (4th): cut (K), drill (2nd), penetrate (5th), poke (1st), punch (4th), stab (5th), wound (3rd)

pig (K)

pigeon (1st)

pike (4th)

pile (1st): A. collect (3rd), gather (1st), group (1st), heap (4th), stack (6th) **B.** hill (1st), mound (2nd), reserve (3rd), store (K), supply (2nd)

pilgrim (5th): pioneer (4th), settler (2nd), traveler (1st)

pill (1ˢᵗ): bead (K), dot (K), pea (1ˢᵗ)

pillar (5ᵗʰ): column (4ᵗʰ), pole (1ˢᵗ), post (1ˢᵗ), support (4ᵗʰ)

pillow (4ᵗʰ): A. soften (2ⁿᵈ), support (5ᵗʰ) **B.** pad (K)

pilot (5ᵗʰ): A. flyer (1ˢᵗ), guide (1ˢᵗ) **B.** experiment (3ʳᵈ), test (3ʳᵈ), untested (3ʳᵈ)

pimento (4ᵗʰ)

pimple (5ᵗʰ): blemish (5ᵗʰ), boil (3ʳᵈ), bump (2ⁿᵈ), spot (1ˢᵗ)

pin (K): A. attach (5ᵗʰ), buckle (6ᵗʰ), clasp (4ᵗʰ), clip (2ⁿᵈ), connect (3ʳᵈ), fasten (4ᵗʰ), join (3ʳᵈ), staple (6ᵗʰ) **B.** bolt (4ᵗʰ), brooch (4ᵗʰ), buckle (6ᵗʰ), fastener (4ᵗʰ), peg (1ˢᵗ), shaft (4ᵗʰ)

pinch (4ᵗʰ): A. difficulty (5ᵗʰ), hardship (5ᵗʰ), trouble (1ˢᵗ) **B.** bit (1ˢᵗ), dab (1ˢᵗ), piece (1ˢᵗ), spot (1ˢᵗ) **C.** bind (2ⁿᵈ), catch (1ˢᵗ), pull (K), squeeze (5ᵗʰ)

pine (1ˢᵗ): crave (6ᵗʰ), desire (5ᵗʰ), long (1ˢᵗ), want (K), yearn (6ᵗʰ)

pineapple (4ᵗʰ)

pinecone (2ⁿᵈ)

pink (1ˢᵗ)

pint (2ⁿᵈ)

pioneer (4ᵗʰ): A. create (3ʳᵈ), invent (2ⁿᵈ), lead (1ˢᵗ), start (1ˢᵗ) **B.** first (1ˢᵗ), introductory (5ᵗʰ), original (3ʳᵈ) **C.** guide (1ˢᵗ), scout (1ˢᵗ)

pious (6ᵗʰ): devoted (5ᵗʰ), holy (5ᵗʰ), religious (4ᵗʰ), spiritual (5ᵗʰ)

pipe (1ˢᵗ): channel (4ᵗʰ), cylinder (6ᵗʰ), hose (6ᵗʰ), tube (3ʳᵈ)

pipeline (1ˢᵗ): channel (4ᵗʰ), conduit (6ᵗʰ)

pirate (5ᵗʰ): robber (1ˢᵗ), rogue (5ᵗʰ)

pistol (5ᵗʰ): gun (1ˢᵗ), revolver (5ᵗʰ)

pit (1ˢᵗ): A. compete (4ᵗʰ), match (3ʳᵈ), oppose (3ʳᵈ) **B.** hole (1ˢᵗ), mine (1ˢᵗ), tomb (5ᵗʰ), trap (1ˢᵗ)

pitch (2ⁿᵈ): A. fling (6ᵗʰ), send (K), throw (1ˢᵗ), toss (2ⁿᵈ) **B.** angle (3ʳᵈ), incline (5ᵗʰ), slant (6ᵗʰ), slope (3ʳᵈ) **C.** frequency (4ᵗʰ), tone (3ʳᵈ)

piteous (6ᵗʰ): emotional (4ᵗʰ), sad (K), tender (3ʳᵈ), to be pitied (3ʳᵈ), touching (1ˢᵗ)

pity (3ʳᵈ): A. dishonor (2ⁿᵈ), regret (5ᵗʰ), shame (3ʳᵈ) **B.** compassion (6ᵗʰ), kindness (3ʳᵈ), mercy (4ᵗʰ), sympathy (4ᵗʰ), understanding (1ˢᵗ)

pivot (5ᵗʰ): turn (1ˢᵗ), turning point (1ˢᵗ), wheel (1ˢᵗ)

pizza (K)

place (1ˢᵗ): A. class (1ˢᵗ), position (2ⁿᵈ), rank (3ʳᵈ), standing (1ˢᵗ) **B.** put (K), set (K), sit (K) **C.** identify (4ᵗʰ), recall (3ʳᵈ), recognize (3ʳᵈ) **D.** area (3ʳᵈ), facility (5ᵗʰ), location (3ʳᵈ), office (1ˢᵗ), point (1ˢᵗ), scene (1ˢᵗ), site (5ᵗʰ), spot (1ˢᵗ)

plague (5ᵗʰ): A. annoy (5ᵗʰ), bother (2ⁿᵈ), pester (2ⁿᵈ), tease (3ʳᵈ), torment (5ᵗʰ) **B.** curse (3ʳᵈ), disease (5ᵗʰ), evil (3ʳᵈ), trouble (1ˢᵗ)

plain (2ⁿᵈ): A. bare (3ʳᵈ), naked (4ᵗʰ), natural (2ⁿᵈ), pure (3ʳᵈ), simple (2ⁿᵈ) **B.** average (3ʳᵈ), basic (5ᵗʰ), modest (4ᵗʰ), ordinary (3ʳᵈ), regular (3ʳᵈ), usual (3ʳᵈ) **C.** candid (4ᵗʰ), frank (4ᵗʰ) **D.** ugly (4ᵗʰ), unattractive (5ᵗʰ) **E.** clear (2ⁿᵈ), evident (5ᵗʰ)

plait (5ᵗʰ): braid (2ⁿᵈ), weave (4ᵗʰ)

plan (1st): A. design (5th), map (1st), procedure (4th) **B.** arrange (3rd), intend (6th), organize (4th), scheme (5th), shape (1st)

plane (1st): A. aircraft (1st), airplane (1st), jet (K), **B.** even (1st), flat (2nd), flat surface (3rd), level (3rd)

planet (4th): satellite (6th), world (1st)

plank (5th): beam (3rd), block (1st), board (1st)

plant (K): A. flora (6th), flower (K), greenery (3rd), root (3rd), seed (1st) **B.** bury (3rd), cultivate (6th), farm (K), grow (1st), raise (1st) **C.** anchor (4th), moor (5th) **D.** establish (3rd), insert (6th), place (1st), promote (5th)

plantation (5th): farm (K), ranch (5th)

plaque (5th): award (5th), badge (5th), sign (1st)

plaster (4th): cement (4th), coat (1st), cover (1st)

plastic (3rd): A. artificial (4th), manmade (1st) **B.** adjustable (5th), elastic (6th), flexible (6th), soft (K), yielding (4th)

plate (K): A. dish (1st), platter (6th) **B.** armor (4th), coat (1st), cover (1st), shell (1st), shield (4th)

plateau (6th): level (3rd), mesa (6th), plane (1st)

platform (4th): deck (1st), landing (1st), stage (3rd)

platter (6th): dish (1st), plate (K)

play (K): A. act (K), entertainment (4th), show (1st) **B.** amusement (4th), pastime (6th), recreation (5th) **C.** excess (5th), give (1st), leeway (5th), stretch (4th) **D.** amuse oneself (3rd), compete (4th), have fun (K)

player (1st): athlete (5th), sportsman (2nd), sportswoman (2nd)

playground (1st): park (1st), recreation area (5th)

plea (5th): A. argument (3rd), defense (5th) **B.** excuse (3rd), reason (1st) **C.** appeal (3rd), beg (1st), prayer (3rd), request (4th)

plead (3rd): appeal (3rd), argue (3rd), ask (K), beg (1st), beseech (5th), request (4th)

pleasant (3rd): agreeable (2nd), fair (1st), friendly (1st), mild (4th), nice (1st), pleasing (2nd)

please (K): amuse (4th), content (3rd), delight (3rd), entertain (4th), gratify (4th), satisfy (3rd), soothe (5th)

pleasure (2nd): amusement (4th), contentment (3rd), delight (3rd), enjoy (2nd), joy (1st)

pleat (5th): crease (5th), fold (1st)

pledge (5th): A. declare (5th), guarantee (6th), promise (1st), swear (4th), vow (4th) **B.** agreement (3rd), commitment (4th), compact (5th), contract (3rd), oath (5th), obligation (6th), promise (1st)

plentiful (2nd): more than enough (1st). See plenty.

plenty (1st): abundant (5th), ample (5th), armload (2nd), enough (1st), excess (5th) full (K), heaps (4th), loads (2nd), lots (K), luxury (4th), many (K), much (1st), numerous (4th), quantity (4th), resources (5th), wealth (3rd)

pliers (3rd)

plight (6th): circumstances (6th), condition (3rd), difficulty (5th), problem (1st), situation (4th), state (1st)

Pliocene (5th): of or belonging to the geologic time, rock series, or sedimentary deposits of the last epoch of the Tertiary Period

plod (5th): continue (2nd), grind (4th), lumber (1st), persist (5th), walk (K)

plop (1st): collapse (5th), drop (K), fall (1st)

plot (4th): A. land (K), lot (K), parcel (4th), property (3rd) **B.** bring about (1st), devise (4th), figure (4th), plan (1st), scheme (5th) **C.** chart (1st), design (5th), frame (3rd), plan (1st), scheme (5th), strategy (6th)

plow (4th): A. plunge (4th), push (1st), shove (5th) **B.** cultivate (6th), farm (K), prepare (1st), till (1st)

pluck (1st): A. backbone (4th), nerve (1st), spirit (2nd), vigor (5th) **B.** persist (5th), pick (1st), pull (K), remove (2nd), tug (1st)

plug (5th): A. ad (4th), commercial (5th), promotion (5th) **B.** block (1st), close (K), cork (6th), cover (1st), stop (K), stuff (1st) **C.** grind (4th), persist (5th), plod (5th), publicize (4th)

plum (4th)

plumber (5th)

plume (6th): A. boast (4th), brag (3rd), glory (3rd), preen (2nd) **B.** feather (2nd), quill (6th)

plump (6th): chubby (2nd), fat (1st), heavy (1st), stout (4th)

plunder (5th): A. fortune (3rd), reward (4th), spoils (4th), take (1st), treasure (4th) **B.** devastate (6th), ravage (6th), rob (K), seize (3rd)

plunge (4th): dip (1st), dive (1st), drive (1st), fall (K), hurry (1st), leap (3rd), rush (2nd), sink (3rd), stab (5th), submerge (5th)

plural (4th): many (K), more than one (K)

plus (1st): add (K), addition (3rd), also (K), and (K), besides (1st), extra (1st), further (2nd), increase (3rd), too (1st)

ply (6th): A. handle (2nd), practice (1st), use (K) **B.** layer (4th), thickness (2nd) **C.** furnish (4th), give (K), provide (3rd), supply (1st) **D.** follow (1st), inclination (5th), prejudice (6th), turn (1st)

p.m. (6th): afternoon (1st), evening (1st)

pneumatic (4th)

poach (6th): A. hunt (2nd), raid (6th), steal (3rd) **B.** boil (3rd), cook (1st)

pocket (1st): A. bag (1st), pouch (1st), purse (4th) **B.** rob (K), steal (3rd), take (1st)

pod (1st)

poem (3rd): rhyme (6th), sonnet (6th), verse (4th)

point (1st): A. focus (5th), issue (4th), question (1st) **B.** address (K), location (3rd), place (1st), position (2nd), spot (1st) **C.** dot (K), end (K), peak (4th), tip (1st) **D.** aim (3rd), intent (5th), meaning (3rd), purpose (1st), reason (1st) **E.** aim (3rd), direct (1st), show (1st)

poise (6th): A. attitude (5th), bearing (1st), presence (2nd) **B.** balance (3rd), calm (3rd), confidence (6th), coolness (2nd), ease (3rd), self-control (3rd), tact (6th)

poison (3rd): A. harmful substance (5th), impurity (4th) **B.** contaminate (6th), foul (4th), pollute (3rd)

poke (1ˢᵗ): force (1ˢᵗ), jog (2ⁿᵈ), push (1ˢᵗ), shove (5ᵗʰ)

polar (3ʳᵈ): conflicting (4ᵗʰ), contrary (4ᵗʰ), different (1ˢᵗ), opposed (3ʳᵈ), opposite (3ʳᵈ)

pole (K): bar (3ʳᵈ), column (4ᵗʰ), post (1ˢᵗ), rod (1ˢᵗ), shaft (4ᵗʰ)

polar (3ʳᵈ): A. opposite (3ʳᵈ) **B.** cold (K)

police (1ˢᵗ): A. guard (1ˢᵗ), patrol (1ˢᵗ), protect (4ᵗʰ), regulate (5ᵗʰ), watch (1ˢᵗ) **B.** authority (3ʳᵈ), cop (K), guard (1ˢᵗ), officer (1ˢᵗ), the law (1ˢᵗ)

policeman (1ˢᵗ): authority (3ʳᵈ), cop (K), guard (1ˢᵗ), law enforcer (5ᵗʰ), officer (1ˢᵗ), lawman (1ˢᵗ), law enforcement officer (5ᵗʰ)

policewoman (1ˢᵗ)

policy (5ᵗʰ): course (3ʳᵈ), direction (1ˢᵗ), guarantee (6ᵗʰ), guide (1ˢᵗ), instruction (4ᵗʰ), manner (1ˢᵗ), rule (2ⁿᵈ), strategy (6ᵗʰ), system (2ⁿᵈ), way (K)

polish (4ᵗʰ): A. clean (K), refine (6ᵗʰ), rub (1ˢᵗ), smooth (2ⁿᵈ), wax (K) **B.** elegance (5ᵗʰ), poise (6ᵗʰ), refinement (6ᵗʰ), style (3ʳᵈ) **C.** glaze (6ᵗʰ), gleam (1ˢᵗ), luster (4ᵗʰ), radiance (6ᵗʰ), shine (1ˢᵗ), sparkle (5ᵗʰ)

polite (4ᵗʰ): kind (K), mannerly (2ⁿᵈ), pleasant (3ʳᵈ), refined (6ᵗʰ), respectful (2ⁿᵈ)

political (4ᵗʰ): civil (3ʳᵈ), official (3ʳᵈ), public (1ˢᵗ)

politics (4ᵗʰ)

poll (5ᵗʰ): A. ask (K), examine (5ᵗʰ), gather (1ˢᵗ), inquire (3ʳᵈ), question (1ˢᵗ), survey (5ᵗʰ), test (3ʳᵈ) **B.** cast a ballot (6ᵗʰ), elect (3ʳᵈ), vote (2ⁿᵈ)

pollen (2ⁿᵈ)

pollute (3ʳᵈ): contaminate (6ᵗʰ), destroy (2ⁿᵈ), dirty (1ˢᵗ), harm (3ʳᵈ), poison (3ʳᵈ), taint (6ᵗʰ)

pomegranate (4ᵗʰ)

pomp (6ᵗʰ): display (3ʳᵈ), glory (3ʳᵈ), parade (2ⁿᵈ), ritual (6ᵗʰ), splendor (4ᵗʰ)

pond (1ˢᵗ): basin (4ᵗʰ), lagoon (5ᵗʰ), lake (1ˢᵗ), pool (1ˢᵗ)

ponder (6ᵗʰ): consider (2ⁿᵈ), contemplate (6ᵗʰ), examine (5ᵗʰ), meditate (5ᵗʰ), think (1ˢᵗ), weigh (1ˢᵗ)

pony (K)

poodle (4ᵗʰ)

pool (1ˢᵗ): A. lagoon (5ᵗʰ), lake (1ˢᵗ), pond (1ˢᵗ) **B.** combine (3ʳᵈ), gather (3ʳᵈ), mound (2ⁿᵈ), share (2ⁿᵈ)

poor (K): A. ill (1ˢᵗ), lean (3ʳᵈ), sick (1ˢᵗ) **B.** bad (K), scarce (4ᵗʰ), slight (4ᵗʰ) **C.** needy (1ˢᵗ), not rich (1ˢᵗ), pitiful (3ʳᵈ), unfortunate (4ᵗʰ)

pop (K): A. dad (K), father (K) **B.** break (1ˢᵗ), burst (3ʳᵈ), explode (3ʳᵈ)

popcorn (1ˢᵗ)

Pope (5ᵗʰ)

poplar (4ᵗʰ)

poppy (2ⁿᵈ)

popular (3ʳᵈ): A. common (2ⁿᵈ), current (3ʳᵈ), familiar (3ʳᵈ), normal (5ᵗʰ), ordinary (3ʳᵈ), standard (3ʳᵈ), usual (3ʳᵈ) **B.** admired (5ᵗʰ), approved (4ᵗʰ), desired (5ᵗʰ), liked (K), wanted (1ˢᵗ)

population (3ʳᵈ): census (6ᵗʰ), inhabitants (6ᵗʰ), natives (1ˢᵗ), people (K), residents (5ᵗʰ)

porch (3ʳᵈ): balcony (6ᵗʰ), walk (K)

porcupine (2ⁿᵈ)

pore (6th): consider (2nd), dwell (4th), examine (5th), read (K), search (1st)

pork (6th)

porpoise (1st)

porridge (5th): cereal (1st), gruel (6th), mush (5th)

port (3rd): dock (1st), harbor (2nd), landing (1st), pier (4th), shelter (4th), wharf (5th)

porter (5th): bearer (1st), carrier (5th), doorman (2nd), loader (2nd), servant (3rd)

portion (4th): A. destiny (5th), fate (3rd), fortune (3rd), future (5th), luck (1st) **B.** cut (K), fraction (4th), parcel (4th), part (K), piece (1st), section (4th), serving (1st), share (2nd)

portrait (5th): drawing (1st), figure (4th), image (4th), likeness (1st), mask (2nd), model (3rd), painting (2nd), photograph (5th), picture (K), profile (5th), sketch (5th)

position (2nd): A. level (3rd), rank (3rd) **B.** duty (1st), job (K), occupation (6th) **C.** manner (1st), pose (2nd), stance (2nd) **D.** belief (1st), opinion (3rd), policy (5th), stand (1st) **E.** angle (3rd), location (3rd), place (1st), post (1st), site (5th), slant (6th), spot (1st)

positive (2nd): A. beneficial (3rd), helpful (2nd), production (4th) **B.** absolute (3rd), agreement (2nd), certain (1st), conclusion (3rd), confident (6th), decided (1st), for (K), good (K), sound (1st), sure (1st)

possess (3rd): cling (4th), control (2nd), have (K), hold (1st), keep (K), maintain (4th), occupy (3rd), own (K), retain (5th)

possible (1st): able (3rd), chance (2nd), imaginable (2nd), likely (1st), may (K), thinkable (2nd)

post (1st): A. after (1st), later (1st) **B.** base (1st), camp (1st), headquarters (3rd), position (2nd), station (1st) **C.** advise (3rd), inform (5th), mail (1st), notify (3rd), send (K) **D.** column (4th), leg (1st), pillar (5th), pole (1st), stake (1st), stud (6th)

postcard (1st): note (1st), scene (1st), view (2nd)

postpone (6th): delay (5th), put off (1st)

pot (K): cauldron (6th), container (5th), kettle (4th), pan (K), saucepan (3rd)

potato (4th)

pouch (1st): bag (1st), cheek (2nd), pocket (1st), purse (4th), sack (1st)

poultry (6th): chickens (1st), fowl (4th), hens (1st)

pounce (5th): attack (3rd), dine (1st), fall (K), jump (K), leap (3rd), spring (1st), surprise (1st)

pound (2nd): batter (1st), beat (1st), bruise (5th), buffet (6th), hit (K), smash (3rd)

pour (3rd): A. crowd (2nd), stampede (5th), swarm (4th) **B.** empty (3rd), flow (1st), serve (1st), spill (1st), tip (1st)

poverty (5th): distress (5th), need (1st), poor (K), scarce (4th), shortage (2nd), want (K)

powder (3rd): A. beat (1st), pound (2nd), refine (6th) **B.** dust (2nd), flour (3rd), grain (3rd), sand (1st)

power (1st): ability (3rd), authority (3rd), capacity (6th), command (2nd), control (2nd), energy (4th), force (1st), might (1st), muscle (4th), strength (1st), talent (2nd)

powerful (2nd): authoritative (3rd), forceful (2nd), intense (6th), mighty (1st), strong (K), supreme (5th)

practical (4th): functional (4th), performable (4th), plain (2nd), possible (2nd), realistic (5th), reasonable (2nd), useful (2nd), workable (3rd)

practice (1st): A. business (2nd), profession (5th), trade (1st) **B.** exercise (1st), habit (3rd), method (2nd), perform (4th), polish (4th), repeat (4th), sharpen (1st), study (1st), train (K), work (K)

prairie (4th): flat land (1st), meadow (3rd)

praise (4th): adore (4th), commend (6th), compliment (5th), flatter (4th), glorify (3rd), honor (1st)

prank (5th): caper (4th), joke (1st), mischief (4th), sport (1st), trick (1st)

pray (3rd): appeal (3rd), ask (K), beg (1st), beseech (5th), plead (3rd), request (4th)

prayer (3rd): appeal (3rd), devotion (5th), plea (5th), request (4th), worship (4th)

preach (4th): advice (3rd), caution (5th), lecture (5th), moralize (3rd), sermon (5th)

Precambrian (5th): of or belonging to the geologic time period between Hadean Time and the Cambrian Period

precaution (5th): anticipation (6th), care (1st), caution (5th), preparation (2nd)

precede (6th): anticipate (6th), begin (1st), go before (1st), head (1st), introduce (5th), lead (1st), preface (6th), start (1st), usher (6th)

precious (4th): beloved (4th), cherished (5th), costly (1st), dear (1st), expensive (3rd), exquisite (6th), loved (1st), priceless (2nd), rare (4th), sweet (1st), valuable (3rd)

precipice (6th): brink (6th), cliff (2nd), drop (1st), edge (1st), ledge (5th), rim (1st)

precise (5th): accurate (6th), correct (3rd), exact (2nd), literal (6th), neat (K), specific (5th), strict (6th)

predator (2nd)

predict (6th): anticipate (6th), estimate (5th), expect (2nd), figure (2nd), forecast (4th), foresee (6th), foretell (6th), guess (1st), judge (1st), prophesy (4th), see (K)

preen (2nd): adorn (6th), dress (1st), groom (5th), plume (6th), take pride (3rd)

preface (6th): begin (1st), beginning (2nd), foreword (1st), introduce (5th), lead (1st), precede (6th), start (1st)

prefer (3rd): A. advance (2nd), offer (2nd), promote (5th), raise (1st) **B.** choose (3rd), elect (3rd), fancy (3rd), favor (2nd), like (K), pick (1st), select (4th)

prehistoric (5th): ancestral (5th), ancient (3rd), early (1st), original (3rd), primitive (5th)

prejudice (6th): assumption (5th), belief (1st), bias (6th), partial (6th), sexism (3rd), slant (6th), subjective (2nd)

prehistory (5th)

prejudice (6th): bias (6th), discrimination (6th), predisposition (6th)

preliminary (6th): basic (5th), beginning (1st), elementary (3rd), introductory (5th), opening (1st), presume (6th), prior (6th), surmise (6th), theory (5th)

premise (6th): argument (3rd), assumption (5th), basis (5th), given (1st), idea (1st), presume (6th), surmise (6th), theory (5th)

preoccupy (5th): absorb (5th), abstract (6th), bother (1st), engage (5th), forget (1st), involved (6th), lost (K), occupied (3rd)

prepare (1st): arrange (3rd), create (3rd), equip (5th), form (1st), furnish (3rd), make (K), provide (3rd), qualify (4th), ready (1st), study (2nd), supply (2nd)

prescribe (6th): assign (5th), command (2nd), direct (1st), impose (4th), offer (2nd), order (1st), require (2nd), suggest (2nd)

present (K): A. favor (2nd), gift (1st), grant (2nd), offering (2nd) **B.** award (5th), bestow (5th), confer (4th), contribute (4th), display (3rd), exhibit (4th), give (K), offer (2nd), show (1st) **C.** alive (3rd), attending (3rd), existing (3rd) **D.** now (K), this moment (1st), today (K)

preserve (4th): A. can (K), jam (K), jelly (1st) **B.** care for (1st), conserve (5th), guard (1st), protect (4th), rescue (4th), save (1st), secure (3rd), shelter (4th), treat (2nd)

preside (6th): captain (2nd), chair (K), control (2nd), direct (1st), head (K), judge (1st), lead (1st), manage (4th), organize (4th), run (K)

president (1st): boss (K), chief (1st), head (1st)

press (1st): A. journalist (3rd), reporter (2nd) **B.** clasp (4th), condense (6th), cram (5th), crowd (2nd), depress (5th), flatten (2nd), grip (4th), iron (2nd), jam (K), level (3rd), pack (1st), pat (K), poke (1st), push (1st), shove (5th), squeeze (5th)

pressure (4th): demand (5th), press (1st), push (1st), strain (4th), stress (6th), tension (5th), weight (1st)

presume (6th): assume (5th), conclude (3rd), gather (1st), guess (1st), judge (1st), suppose (2nd), surmise (6th), think (1st)

pretend (2nd): act (K), deceive (5th), fake (1st), imagine (2nd), imitate (5th), lie (1st), make believe (1st), mask (2nd), play (K)

pretext (5th): alibi (6th), cover up (1st), deception (5th), defense (5th), device (4th), excuse (3rd), reason (1st), trick (1st)

pretty (1st): A. fairly (1st), reasonably (2nd), somewhat (1st) **B.** attractive (5th), beautiful (1st), delicate (5th), fair (1st), good-looking (1st), handsome (3rd)

prevail (5th): affect (4th), conquer (4th), dominate (5th), endure (4th), get (K), induce (5th), overcome (2nd), reign (4th), succeed (2nd), win (1st)

prevent (3rd): avert (6th), avoid (3rd), ban (K), bar (3rd), block (1st), dam (K), deter (6th), forbid (4th), head off (1st), hinder (6th), prohibit (6th), stop (K)

prevention (3rd)

previous (5th): earlier (1st), first (1st), former (6th), preceding (6th)

prey (4th): catch (1st), chase (1st), game (K), kill (1st), stalk (4th), target (5th), use (K), victim (4th)

price (K): amount (2nd), charge (2nd), cost (1st), expense (3rd), fee (4th), payment (1st), penalty (5th), tab (K), toll (6th), value (2nd), wages (3rd), worth (3rd)

prick (5th): bore (2nd), compel (3rd), cut (K), drill (2nd), excite (4th), move (K), pierce (4th), provoke (6th), punch (4th), slit (5th), stab (5th), stick (K), stimulate (6th)

pride (2nd): arrogance (6th), conceit (5th), self-importance (3rd), vanity (5th)

priest (4th): clergy (6th), cleric (6th), father (K), minister (4th), pastor (4th), rabbi (4th)

prim (5th): clean (1st), formal (4th), grim (4th), modest (4th), neat (K), proper (3rd), pure (3rd), rigid (5th), sour (2nd), straight (3rd)

primary (5th): base (1st), beginning (1st), earliest (1st), first (1st), fundamental (4th), head (K), initial (6th), key (K), leading (1st), oldest (1st), original (3rd), primitive (5th), start (1st)

prime (5th): basic (5th), beginning (1st), best (K), bloom (4th), excellent (1st), first (1st), good (K), health (K), primary (5th), principal (3rd), splendid (4th), superb (6th), superior (4th), top (K), youth (2nd)

primitive (5th): basic (5th), early (1st), original (3rd), plain (2nd), primary (5th), savage (5th), simple (2nd), uncivilized (4th)

prince (1st): monarch (5th), nobleman (3rd), royalty (3rd)

princess (1st): monarch (5th), noblewoman (3rd), royalty (3rd)

principal (3rd): capital (2nd), central (3rd), director (1st), ethic (5th), head (1st), idea (1st), main (3rd), major (3rd), master (1st), money (K), most important (1st), prime (5th), star (K), superior (4th)

principle (4th): basis (5th), ethics (5th), fundamentals (4th), guide (1st), law (1st), regulation (5th), rule (K), source (4th), standard (3rd), truth (1st)

print (1st): impress (5th), imprint (4th), mark (1st), stamp (2nd), type (1st)

prior (5th): before (1st), earlier (2nd), former (6th), preceding (6th), previous (5th)

prison (3rd): cage (4th), cell (1st), dungeon (5th), jail (4th), vault (5th)

private (3rd): A. exclusive (6th), individual (3rd), nonpublic (2nd), restricted (6th) **B.** alone (1st), confidential (6th), quiet (K), remote (5th), secret (1st), solitary (5th), withdrawn (2nd) **C.** confidential (6th), hidden (1st), intimate (5th), personal (3rd), secret (1st)

privateer (6th): pirate (5th)

privilege (5th): advantage (3rd), allowance (5th), authority (3rd), benefit (3rd), due (2nd), entitle (5th), entitlement (5th), freedom (3rd), liberty (3rd), license (5th), permission (3rd), power (1st), right (K)

prize (3rd): A. appreciate (5th), cherish (5th), desire (5th), hope (K), treasure (4th), value (2nd) **B.** aim (3rd), award (5th), gift (1st), honor (1st), payment (1st), present (K), recognition (3rd), reward (4th), trophy (6th), winnings (1st)

pro (4th): A. affirmative (6th), for (K) **B.** professional (5th)

probably (4th): chance (2nd), expectation (2nd), likely (1st), possible (1st), risky (4th), surely (1st)

problem (1st): challenge (4th), complexity (6th), mystery (1st), puzzle (4th), question (1st), riddle (1st), unknown (1st)

proceed (4th): advance (2nd), continue (2nd), extend (4th), go (K), move along (1st), pass (2nd), progress (4th), pursue (5th)

process (4th): A. develop (5th), grow (K), handle (2nd), make (K), prepare (1st), refine (6th) **B.** action (1st), development (5th), formula (6th), growth (1st), mechanism (6th), method (2nd), movement (2nd), procedure (4th), routine (6th), style (3rd), system (2nd), way (1st)

procession (4th): line (K), march (1st), parade (2nd), stream (1st), train (1st)

proclaim (4th): advertise (4th), announce (3rd), broadcast (5th), declare (5th), inform (5th), report (1st), state (1st)

procure (5th): acquire (4th), attain (6th), buy (K), earn (2nd), gain (2nd), gather (1st), get (K), obtain (5th), pick up (1st), receive (1st), secure (3rd)

prod (6th): bug (1st), drive (1st), poke (1st), prick (5th), prompt (4th), push (1st), remind (3rd), stick (K), stimulate (6th)

produce (2nd): A. construct (3rd), create (3rd), generate (4th), make (K), manufacture (3rd), turn out (1st) **B.** crops (2nd), food (K), product (4th), yield (4th)

product (4th): crop (2nd), goods (K), item (5th), result (2nd)

production (4th): creation (3rd), formation (4th), goods (K), making (1st)

profess (5th): allege (6th), assert (6th), aver (6th), claim (2nd), declare (5th), state (1st)

profession (5th): business (2nd), career (4th), employment (5th), job (K), occupation (6th), pursuit (5th), specialty (3rd), work (K)

professor (4th): doctor (1st), educator (3rd), instructor (4th), teacher (1st)

profile (5th): biography (6th), portrait (5th), shape (1st), sketch (5th), side view (1st)

profit (4th): benefit (3rd), gain (2nd), income (4th), yield (4th)

profound (6th): deep (1st), important (1st), intense (6th), moving (1st), thoughtful (2nd), wise (1st)

program (4th): A. aim (3rd), approach (3rd), design (5th), intent (5th), plan (1st) **B.** calendar (1st), entertainment (4th), event (3rd), presentation (4th), schedule (6th)

progress (4th): A. breakthrough (2nd), growth (1st), movement (2nd) **B.** advance (2nd), change (2nd), develop (5th), go on (K), grow (1st), improve (3rd), proceed (4th)

prohibit (6th): ban (K), bar (3rd), block (1st), deny (5th), forbid (4th), prevent (3rd), stop (K)

project (4th): A. aim (3rd), intend (6th) **B.** cast (2nd), shoot (3rd), stick out (1st), throw (1st) **C.** design (5th), program (4th), scheme (5th), undertaking (3rd), work (K)

prolong (5th): carry on (1st), continue (2nd), draw out (1st), lengthen (2nd), pull (K), stretch (4th)

promenade (5th): A. path (1st), sidewalk 1, walkway (2nd) **B.** march (1st),

254

parade (2nd), saunter (6th), stroll (5th), walk (K)

prominent (5th): A. projecting (4th), raised (1st) **B.** famous (2nd), important (1st), outstanding (2nd), well-known (K)

promise (1st): A. assurance (3rd), commitment (4th), contract (3rd), guarantee (6th), oath (5th), pledge (5th), vow (4th), word (K) **B.** assure (3rd), commit (4th), profess (5th), swear (4th), vow (4th)

promote (5th): A. advance (2nd), further (2nd), graduate (4th) **B.** advertise (4th), encourage (4th), support (4th), uphold (6th)

promotion (5th): A. advance (2nd), move up (K), raise (1st) **B.** help (K), encouragement (4th), support (4th) **C.** ad (4th), advertisement (4th)

prompt (4th): A. animate (6th), force (1st), push (1st), stimulate (6th), urge (4th) **B.** alert (5th), fast (1st), instant (3rd), on time (1st), rapid (4th), ready (1st), timely (1st)

pronghorn (5th)

pronounce (4th): announce (3rd), declare (5th), proclaim (4th), report (1st), say (K), speak (1st), talk (K), voice (1st)

proof (4th): demonstration (6th), evidence (5th), show (1st), support (4th)

prop (5th): A. lean against (3rd), rest (1st) **B.** assurance (3rd), hold up (1st), support (4th), sustain (5th), uphold (6th)

propel (6th): compel (3rd), move (K), prod (6th), project (4th), push (1st), send (K), start (1st)

proper (3rd): correct (3rd), fitting (2nd), formal (4th), mannerly (2nd), right (K), strict (6th), suitable (2nd)

property (3rd): A. character (2nd), feature (3rd), mark (1st), quality (4th), trait (6th) **B.** belongings (2nd), capital (2nd), holdings (1st), land (K)

prophet (4th): forecaster (2nd), preacher (4th), predictor (6th), seer (1st)

proportion (4th): balance (3rd), part (1st), percent (4th), portion (4th), ratio (6th), relationship (4th), share (2nd), uniform (1st)

propose (4th): advance (2nd), aim (3rd), ask (K), design (5th), intend (5th), plan (1st), present (K), submit (4th), suggest (2nd)

proprietor (6th): manager (4th), owner (2nd), possessor (3rd)

prospect (4th): chance (2nd), expectation (3rd), forecast (4th), intention (5th), outlook (2nd), possibility (2nd), probability (4th), view (2nd)

prosper (5th): benefit (3rd), bloom (4th), do well (1st), flourish (4th), gain (2nd), money (K), profit (4th), succeed (2nd), thrive (6th)

protect (4th): conserve (5th), defend (5th), guard (1st), keep (K), preserve (4th), save (1st), secure (3rd), shelter (4th), shield (4th)

protection (4th): armor (4th), defense (5th), guard (1st), security (3rd)

protein (5th)

protest (4th): A. demonstration (6th), strike (2nd), walk out (1st) **B.** complain (4th), demonstrate (6th), gripe (5th), object (1st), oppose (3rd)

protostar (5th): a star that is in the process of forming

proud (2nd): A. pleased (1st), satisfied (3rd) B. arrogant (6th), lofty (5th), vain (4th)

prove (1st): demonstrate (6th), show (1st)

provide (3rd): distribute (6th), furnish (3rd), give (1st), maintain (4th), stock (1st), supply (2nd), yield (4th)

province (6th): area (3rd), domain (5th), orbit (4th), realm (4th), region (4th), sphere (6th), territory (3rd)

provision (4th): equipment (5th), means (1st), stock (1st), supplies (1st)

provoke (6th): anger (1st), disturb (6th), move (K), press (1st), prompt (4th), push (1st), start (1st), torment (5th)

prow (5th): bow (1st), front (1st), nose (1st)

prowess (6th): bravery (1st), courage (4th), force (1st), power (1st), strength (1st), talent (2nd)

prowl (2nd): roam (4th), rove (6th), search (1st), sneak (6th), stroll (5th), wander (3rd)

prudent (6th): careful (1st), cautious (5th), economical (4th), moderate (4th), modest (4th), polite (4th), proper (3rd), reasonable (1st), sensible (6th)

prune (3rd): cut (K), shape (1st), shorten (1st), thin (2nd), trim (4th)

pry (6th): A. examine (5th), impose (4th), inquire (3rd), investigate (5th), question (1st), spy (4th) B. force (1st), lift (1st), open (K), tear (4th)

psalm (6th): chant (5th), hymn (5th), poem (3rd), song (K), verse (4th)

psychedelic (5th): a substance generating hallucinations, distortions of perception, altered states of awareness, and occasionally states resembling psychosis

psychic (6th): mental (5th), spiritual (5th), supernatural (3rd)

psychology (6th)

Pteranodon (2nd): a type of flying dinosaur

pub (1st): bar (3rd), inn (4th), tavern (5th)

public (1st): common (2nd), general (2nd), national (2nd), not secret (1st), open (K), outside (1st), society (3rd), universal (4th)

publication (4th): ad (4th), announcement (3rd), issue (4th), printed material (5th)

publicity (4th): ad (4th), advertisement (4th), notice (1st), promotion (5th)

publicize (4th): advertise (4th), announce (3rd), broadcast (5th), publish (4th)

publish (4th): advertise (4th), air (1st), broadcast (5th), declare (5th), issue (4th), make public (1st), print (1st), produce (2nd), report (1st) reveal (4th)

puff (2nd): A. boast (4th), magnify (3rd), praise (4th), publicize (4th), show off (1st) B. air (1st), blow up (1st), breath (1st), gasp (4th)

pull (K): draw (K), haul (4th), lower (2nd), lug (1st), tow (1st), transport (5th)

pulp (6th): batter (1st), flesh (3rd), fruit (2nd), jam (K), mash (4th), paste (1st), squash (2nd), wood (1st)

pulse (5ᵗʰ): beat (1ˢᵗ), heart rate (1ˢᵗ), pace (3ʳᵈ), throb (5ᵗʰ)

pulsars (5ᵗʰ)

puma (4ᵗʰ)

pump (4ᵗʰ): A. cross-examine (5ᵗʰ), question (1ˢᵗ) **B.** blow up (1ˢᵗ), enlarge (5ᵗʰ), expand (5ᵗʰ), swell (3ʳᵈ)

pumpkin (K)

punch (4ᵗʰ): beat (1ˢᵗ), box (K), cuff (1ˢᵗ), drill (2ⁿᵈ), hit (K), pound (2ⁿᵈ), smash (3ʳᵈ), strike (2ⁿᵈ)

punish (4ᵗʰ): correct (3ʳᵈ), discipline (6ᵗʰ), fine (1ˢᵗ), imprison (6ᵗʰ), penalize (5ᵗʰ)

pup (K): dog (K), puppy (K)

pupa (2ⁿᵈ)

pupil (4ᵗʰ): beginner (2ⁿᵈ), devotee (5ᵗʰ), follower (1ˢᵗ), scholar (5ᵗʰ), student (3ʳᵈ), trainee (2ⁿᵈ)

puppy (K)

purchase (3ʳᵈ): A. grasp (4ᵗʰ), hold (1ˢᵗ), perch (4ᵗʰ), stand (1ˢᵗ) **B.** acquire (4ᵗʰ), attain (6ᵗʰ), buy (K), gain (2ⁿᵈ), invest (5ᵗʰ), trade (2ⁿᵈ)

pure (3ʳᵈ): A. innocent (5ᵗʰ), moral (3ʳᵈ), proper (3ʳᵈ), sincere (4ᵗʰ), virtuous (4ᵗʰ) **B.** clean (1ˢᵗ), clear (2ⁿᵈ), complete (3ʳᵈ), genuine (5ᵗʰ), perfect (3ʳᵈ), spotless (2ⁿᵈ)

Puritan (1ˢᵗ): moralist (3ʳᵈ), prim (5ᵗʰ), proper (3ʳᵈ), prude (6ᵗʰ), strict (6ᵗʰ)

purple (K)

purpose (1ˢᵗ): aim (3ʳᵈ), design (5ᵗʰ), goal (4ᵗʰ), idea (1ˢᵗ), intent (6ᵗʰ), meaning (1ˢᵗ), mission (5ᵗʰ), object (1ˢᵗ), objective (2ⁿᵈ), plan (1ˢᵗ), reason (2ⁿᵈ), resolve (5ᵗʰ), target (5ᵗʰ), will (K)

purse (4ᵗʰ): A. award (5ᵗʰ), gift (K), means (5ᵗʰ), prize (3ʳᵈ) **B.** bag (1ˢᵗ), pouch (1ˢᵗ), wallet (6ᵗʰ)

pursuit (5ᵗʰ): chase (1ˢᵗ), hunt (2ⁿᵈ), quest (3ʳᵈ), run (K)

push (1ˢᵗ): get going (1ˢᵗ), move (K), press (1ˢᵗ), propel (6ᵗʰ), shove (5ᵗʰ)

push-up (1ˢᵗ)

pushy (1ˢᵗ): aggressive (6ᵗʰ), bossy (1ˢᵗ), forceful (2ⁿᵈ)

put (K): drop (K), lay (1ˢᵗ), locate (3ʳᵈ), place (1ˢᵗ), position (2ⁿᵈ), set (K), stand (K)

puzzle (4ᵗʰ): A. game (1ˢᵗ), mystery (1ˢᵗ), riddle (1ˢᵗ) **B.** bewilder (3ʳᵈ), challenge (4ᵗʰ), confuse (4ᵗʰ), consider (2ⁿᵈ), ponder (6ᵗʰ), question (1ˢᵗ), study (1ˢᵗ), think (1ˢᵗ)

pyramid (5ᵗʰ): A. cone (1ˢᵗ), triangle (1ˢᵗ) **B.** build (1ˢᵗ), compound (4ᵗʰ), increase (3ʳᵈ), rise (1ˢᵗ), soar (6ᵗʰ)

quack (K): A. cheat (3ʳᵈ), hoaxer (5ᵗʰ), pretender (2ⁿᵈ) **B.** affected (4ᵗʰ), fake (1ˢᵗ), false (3ʳᵈ), put-on (K) **C.** gobble (1ˢᵗ), honk (1ˢᵗ)

quail (1ˢᵗ)

quaint (5ᵗʰ): A. charming (3ʳᵈ), homey (1ˢᵗ), picturesque (2ⁿᵈ), small-town (K) **B.** curious (3ʳᵈ), odd (4ᵗʰ), peculiar (4ᵗʰ), queer (4ᵗʰ), ridiculous (6ᵗʰ), strange (1ˢᵗ), unusual (3ʳᵈ), weird (1ˢᵗ)

quake (4ᵗʰ): A. shock (1ˢᵗ), tremor (6ᵗʰ) **B.** jar (K), jostle (6ᵗʰ), reel (5ᵗʰ), rock (K), shake (1ˢᵗ), shudder (4ᵗʰ), stir (3ʳᵈ), tremble (3ʳᵈ), wobble (4ᵗʰ)

Quaker (1ˢᵗ): puritan

qualify (4ᵗʰ): A. adapt (4ᵗʰ), coach (4ᵗʰ), enable (4ᵗʰ), instruct (4ᵗʰ), prepare (1ˢᵗ), ready (1ˢᵗ), supply (1ˢᵗ), teach (1st), test (3rd), train (K) **B.** distinguish (6th), name (K), regard (4th) **C.** able (3rd), capable (4th), pass (2nd)

quality (4th): A. excellence (2nd), greatness (1st), superior (4th) **B.** characteristic (6th), class (1st), condition (3rd), grade (2nd), feature (3rd), property (3rd), rank (3rd), tone (3rd), worth (3rd)

quantity (4th): A. amount (2nd), capacity (6th), content (3rd), extent (4th), large amount (2nd), mass (4th), measure (2nd), number (K), sum (1st), volume (3rd), weight (1st) **B.** allowance (5th), dose (1st), handful (1st), portion (4th)

quasars (5th)

quarrel (4th): A. argue (3rd), blow up (1st), contest (4th), disagree (3rd), dispute (6th), have words (K) **B.** broil (4th), conflict (4th), difference of opinion (4th), feud (6th), variance (4th)

quarry (6th): A. dig (1st), mine (1st), pit (1st), seek (1st) **B.** game (K), hunted animal (2nd), prey (4th), victim (4th)

quart (2nd)

quarter (1st): A. area (3rd), neighborhood (2nd), part (1st), region (4th), territory (3rd) **B.** fourth (1st), one-fourth (1st), twenty-five percent (4th) **C.** ease (3rd), help (K), locate (3rd), mercy (4th), pity (3rd)

quasars (5th)

Quaternary (5th): of or belonging to the geologic time, system of rocks, or sedimentary deposits of the second period of the Cenozoic Era

quay (5th): dock (1st), landing (1st), pier (4th), wharf (5th)

queen (K): A. empress (4th), majesty (4th), noble (3rd), princess (1st), ruler (2nd) **B.** ideal (3rd), perfection (3rd), pink (1st), star (K)

queer (4th): abnormal (5th), astonishing (4th), comical (5th), curious (3rd), faint (3rd), gamble (5th), insane (6th), odd (4th), original (3rd), peculiar (4th), quaint (5th), ruin (2nd), spoil (4th), strange (1st), suspicious (4th), uncommon (2nd), unusual (3rd)

quench (6th): choke (1st), crush (4th), defeat (5th), drown (1st), ease (3rd), extinguish (5th), fill (1st), flood (2nd), hit the spot (1st), nip (1st), put out (K), quiet (K), satisfy (3rd), smother (6th), subdue (6th), topple (6th)

query (6th): A. ask (K), challenge (4th), examine (5th), inquire (3rd), investigate (5th), raise (1st), suspect (5th) **B.** confusion (4th), doubt (1st), question (1st), reservation (3rd), survey (5th)

quest (3rd): A. aim (3rd), campaign (3rd), goal (4th), hunt (2nd), journey (3rd), objective (2nd), point (1st), pursuit (5th) **B.** chase (1st), hunt (2nd), pursue (5th), search (1st), seek (1st)

question (1st): A. ask (K), challenge (4th), doubt (1st), examine (5th), inquire (3rd), raise (1st), suspect (5th) **B.** issue (4th), mystery (1st), problem (1st), puzzle (4th), query (6th), uncertainty (2nd)

quick (1st): A. active (3rd), alert (5th), alive (3rd), energetic (4th), keen (4th), lively (1st), skillful (2nd), spirited (2nd), vigorous (5th) **B.** apt (5th), brief (3rd), fast (1st), immediate (3rd), prompt (4th), rapid (4th), speedy (3rd), sudden (1st)

quicksand (1st)

quiet (K): A. calm (3rd), grave (3rd), hushed (3rd), immobile (6th), inactive (3rd), meek (2nd), modest (4th), motionless (3rd), mute (3rd), noiseless (2nd), peaceful (2nd), reserved (3rd), secretive (2nd), silent (3rd), simple (2nd), sleeping (K), sleepy (1st), slumbering (4th), soundless (2nd), still (1st), unexcited (4th) **B.** break (1st), delay (5th), interval (6th), pause (3rd), rest (1st), silence (3rd) **C.** choke (1st), prevent (3rd), quench (6th), smother (6th)

quill (6th): feather (2nd), needle (3rd), nib (4th), pen (1st), plume (6th), point (1st), spine (4th)

quirt (6th): blacksnake (1st), cat-o'-nine-tails (1st), crop (2nd), stick (K), whip (4th)

quilt (6th): A. piece (1st), sew (2nd) **B.** bedspread (2nd), blanket (3rd), comforter (3rd), cover (1st)

quit (1st): abandon (4th), cease (3rd), depart (5th), discard (6th), discontinue (4th), down (K), emigrate (6th), end (K), flee (5th), give up (1st), leave (1st), lessen (3rd), move (K), pause (3rd), quiet down (K), reject (5th), resign (5th), stop (K), surrender (5th), vacate (2nd), yield (4th)

quite (1st): actually (3rd), certainly (1st), completely (3rd), considerably (2nd), excessively (5th), highly (1st), in fact (K), indeed (1st), really (1st), totally (2nd), truly (1st), very (K)

quiver (4th): A. container (5th), holder (1st) **B.** beating (1st), flapping (4th), jump (K), move (K), pounding (2nd), shake (1st), shiver (1st), start (1st), tremble (3rd), tremor (6th), vibrate (5th), waving (1st)

quote (5th): A. chorus (5th), passage (4th), selection (4th), words (K) **B.**

charge (2nd), evaluate (2nd), price (K), value (2nd) **C.** call to mind (1st), cite (6th), copy (3rd), mimic (6th), note (1st), parrot (1st), proclaim (4th), recite (5th), refer to (5th), remember (1st), repeat (4th), reproduce (4th), retell (3rd), state (1st)

RNA (4th)

rabbi (4th)

rabbit (K)

raccoon (1st)

race (1st): A. competition (3rd), contest (4th) **B.** clan (5th), family (K), nation (1st), people (K), stock (1st), tribe (3rd) **C.** bolt (4th), dart (1st), hurry (1st), run (K), speed (3rd)

rack (1st): A. agonize (5th), extend (4th), hang (2nd), hurt (K), pain (2nd), torment (5th), torture (5th), wound (3rd) **B.** display (3rd), form (1st), frame (3rd), holder (1st), stand (K), structure (4th)

radar (5th): A. a method of detecting distant objects and determining their position, velocity, or other characteristics by analysis of very high frequency radio waves reflected from their surfaces **B.** the radio waves in the radar spectrum

radiant (6th): bright (1st), brilliant (4th), dazzling (5th), gleaming (1st), glowing (1st), lighted (1st), magnificent (4th), shining (3rd), sparkling (5th), splendid (4th), sunny (1st)

radiate (6th): A. beam (3rd), glitter (4th), glow (1st), sparkle (5th) **B.** circulate (4th), scatter (3rd), send out (1st), spread (2nd)

radical (6th): complete (3rd), extreme (5th), far (1st), severe (4th), total (2nd)

259

radio (1st): beam (3rd), broadcast (5th), transmit (4th)

radioactive (6th)

radish (1st)

radius (6th): arc (4th), arch (4th), circle (K), section (4th)

raft (6th): A. float (1st) **B.** many (K)

rafter (6th): beam (3rd), support (4th)

rag (1st): fragment (6th), part (1st), patch (4th), piece (1st), scrap (3rd), shred (5th), towel (6th)

rage (4th): A. rave (5th), roar (1st), storm (2nd), yell (K) **B.** anger (1st), craze (4th), fad (4th), fit (K), fury (4th), madness (3rd), passion (6th), violence (5th), wrath (4th)

ragged (5th): jagged (5th), ripped (1st), shabby (4th), torn (2nd), worn (3rd)

raid (6th): A. attack (3rd), invade (5th), storm (2nd) **B.** assault (4th), invasion (5th), seizure (3rd)

rail (2nd): fence (1st), picket (3rd), post (1st), track (1st)

railroad (2nd): rails (2nd), tracks (1st), train (K)

rain (1st): flood (2nd), mist (1st), pour (3rd), raindrops (2nd), rainfall (2nd), shower (4th), sprinkle (3rd), storm (2nd)

raindrops (2nd)

rainfall (2nd)

raise (1st): A. cultivate (6th), develop (5th), farm (K), grow (K), hoe (2nd), nurse (K), plant (K), rear (3rd), spade (6th) **B.** build (1st), construct (3rd), erect (4th), fabricate (5th) **C.** elevate (2nd), heave (5th), hoist up (6th), lift (1st)

rake (1st): comb (2nd), dig (1st)

rally (5th): A. collect (3rd), gather (1st), muster 6, unite (5th) **B.** assembly (4th), conference (4th), convention (6th), group (1st), meeting (1st)

ram (K): beat (1st), cram (5th), crowd (2nd), drive (K), force (1st), hammer (2nd), hit (K), pack (1st), pound (2nd), push (1st), strike (2nd)

ramble (6th): babble (6th), chatter (1st), rave (5th), rove (6th), stroll (5th), talk (K), walk (K), wander (3rd)

ramp (6th): access (6th), elevate (2nd), grade (2nd), hill (K), incline (5th), slant (6th), slope (3rd)

rampart (6th): barrier (6th), block (1st), wall (1st)

ranch (5th): farm (K)

ran (K)

ranch (5th)

random (6th): accidental (4th), aimless (3rd), careless (5th), casual (5th), chance (2nd), stray (3rd)

range (3rd): A. grass (K), meadow (3rd) **B.** roam (4th), rove (6th), sweep (4th), wander (3rd) **C.** arrange (3rd), classify (2nd), file (1st), grade (2nd), group (1st), order (1st), rank (3rd), rate (1st) **D.** circuit (4th), distance (4th), extent (4th), reach (1st)

ranger (1st): forester (2nd)

rank (3rd): class (1st), grade (2nd), level (3rd), place (1st), position (2nd), range (3rd), station (1st)

ransom (6th): A. bribe (5th), cost (K), penalty (5th), price (K), purchase

(3rd) **B.** buy back (1st), free (K), pay off (1st), redeem (6th) **C.** freedom (3rd), redemption (6th), release (5th), rescue (4th)

rap (1st): belt (2nd), crack (4th), hit (K), knock (3rd), pat (K), slap (2nd), strike (2nd), tap (K)

rapid (4th): brisk (6th), fast (1st), hasty (2nd), prompt (4th), quick (1st), speedy (3rd), swift (4th), urgent (6th)

raptor (5th): bird (K)

rapture (6th): happiness (2nd), joy (1st), paradise (4th), pleasure (2nd), thrill (4th)

rare (4th): A. bloody (1st), uncooked (2nd), underdone (2nd) **B.** excellent (1st), exceptional (2nd), extraordinary (5th), few (1st), fine (1st), infrequent (4th), marvelous (4th), remarkable (4th), scarce (4th), uncommon (2nd), unique (6th), unusual (3rd)

rascal (5th): bad boy (1st), brat (3rd), creep (1st), imp (5th), rat (K), rogue (5th), scamp (4th), villain (5th)

rash (6th): A. break out (2nd), hives (2nd), irritation (6th) **B.** bold (2nd), careless (5th), hasty (2nd), thoughtless (2nd)

raspberry (2nd)

rat (K)

rate (1st): A. grade (2nd), judge (1st), place (1st), rank (3rd), sort (1st) **B.** pace (3rd) **C.** charge (2nd), cost (K), estimate (5th), fare (3rd), price (K), toll (6th), value (2nd)

rather (1st): A. better (1st), preferably (3rd), sooner (1st) **B.** quite (1st), somewhat (1st), very (K)

ratify (6th): approve (4th), certify (6th), support (4th)

ratio (6th): fraction (4th), part (1st), percentage (4th), proportion (4th), quota (5th), share (2nd)

rattle (2nd): bewilder (3rd), clatter (5th), confuse (4th), disturb (6th), racket (2nd), upset (3rd)

rattlesnake (1st)

ravage (6th): damage (5th), desolate (6th), destroy (2nd), devastate (6th), lay waste (2nd), ruin (2nd), wreck (4th)

rave (5th): go mad (K), howl (4th), rage (4th), roar (1st), storm (2nd), wander (3rd), yell (K)

ravenous (6th): devouring (5th), fierce (4th), greedy (5th), hungry (2nd), piggish (1st), starving (5th)

ravine (5th): gorge (5th), gulf (4th), valley (2nd)

ravish (6th): A. charm (3rd), delight (3rd), enchant (6th) **B.** abduct (6th), abuse (6th), assault (4th), attack (3rd), kidnap (2nd), seize (3rd), steal (3rd)

raw (1st): A. bloody (1st), fresh (2nd), rare (4th), uncooked (2nd) **B.** green (K), not ripe (1st) **C.** exposed (4th), natural (2nd), rough (4th), untrained (2nd)

ray (1st): beam (3rd), flame (3rd), gleam (1st), radiation (6th), stream (3rd)

razor (6th): blade (2nd), edge (1st), knife (1st), shaver (1st)

reach (1st): A. distance (4th), expanse (5th), extension (4th), space (1st), stretch (4th), sweep (4th) **B.** approach (3rd), extend (4th), gain (2nd), get (K), grasp (4th), seize (3rd), span (6th), stretch out (4th), touch (1st)

react (5ᵗʰ): answer (K), reply (1ˢᵗ), respond (5ᵗʰ), return (1ˢᵗ)

read (K): go over (1ˢᵗ), review (4ᵗʰ), skim (6ᵗʰ), study (2ⁿᵈ)

ready (1ˢᵗ): A. equipped (5ᵗʰ), fit (K), prepared (1ˢᵗ), willing (1ˢᵗ) **B.** arrange (3ʳᵈ), done (1ˢᵗ), order (1ˢᵗ), prepare (1ˢᵗ), provide (3ʳᵈ)

real (1ˢᵗ): A. concrete (4ᵗʰ), material (5ᵗʰ), natural (2ⁿᵈ), physical (5ᵗʰ) **B.** actual (3ʳᵈ), genuine (5ᵗʰ), just (1ˢᵗ), pure (3ʳᵈ), simple (1ˢᵗ), sincere (4ᵗʰ), true (K)

reality (5ᵗʰ): actual (3ʳᵈ), concrete (4ᵗʰ), fact (1ˢᵗ), life (1ˢᵗ), realness (2ⁿᵈ), truth (1ˢᵗ)

realize (2ⁿᵈ): comprehend (5ᵗʰ), discover (1ˢᵗ), figure out (2ⁿᵈ), know (1ˢᵗ), perceive (6ᵗʰ), recognize (3ʳᵈ), take in (1ˢᵗ)

realm (4ᵗʰ): area (3ʳᵈ), empire (4ᵗʰ), kingdom (3ʳᵈ), orbit (4ᵗʰ), place (1ˢᵗ), province (6ᵗʰ), region (4ᵗʰ), section (4ᵗʰ), territory (3ʳᵈ), zone (4ᵗʰ)

reap (4ᵗʰ): crop (2ⁿᵈ), cut (K), gather (1ˢᵗ), harvest (4ᵗʰ), prune (3ʳᵈ), trim (4ᵗʰ)

rear (3ʳᵈ): A. back (1ˢᵗ), behind (1ˢᵗ), heel (3ʳᵈ), tail (1ˢᵗ) **B.** bring up (1ˢᵗ), erect (4ᵗʰ), raise (1ˢᵗ)

reason (1ˢᵗ): A. alibi (6ᵗʰ), basis (5ᵗʰ), cause (2ⁿᵈ), excuse (3ʳᵈ) **B.** deduce (6ᵗʰ), explain (2ⁿᵈ), figure (4ᵗʰ), review (4ᵗʰ), think (1ˢᵗ), understand (1ˢᵗ) **C.** intelligence (4ᵗʰ), sanity (6ᵗʰ), sense (1ˢᵗ)

reassure (6ᵗʰ): assure (3ʳᵈ), back up (1ˢᵗ), encourage (4ᵗʰ), hearten (1ˢᵗ), inspire (4ᵗʰ), support (4ᵗʰ), uplift (2ⁿᵈ)

rebuke (4ᵗʰ): A. refutation (5ᵗʰ), reproach (6ᵗʰ), scolding (5ᵗʰ) **B.** lecture (5ᵗʰ), refute (3ʳᵈ), reproach (6ᵗʰ), scold (5ᵗʰ)

recall (3ʳᵈ): recognize (3ʳᵈ), recollect (6ᵗʰ), remember (1ˢᵗ), review (4ᵗʰ)

receipt (5ᵗʰ): bill (1ˢᵗ), ticket (1ˢᵗ)

receive (1ˢᵗ): accept (3ʳᵈ), acquire (4ᵗʰ), catch (1ˢᵗ), gain (2ⁿᵈ), get (K), inherit (5ᵗʰ), obtain (5ᵗʰ), take in (1ˢᵗ)

recent (3ʳᵈ): current (3ʳᵈ), fresh (2ⁿᵈ), late (K), latest (1ˢᵗ), modern (2ⁿᵈ), new (K)

reception (5ᵗʰ): A. greeting (3ʳᵈ), welcome (1ˢᵗ) **B.** acceptance (3ʳᵈ), admission (4ᵗʰ), gathering (1ˢᵗ), party (K)

recess (2ⁿᵈ): break (1ˢᵗ), holiday (K), interval (6ᵗʰ), lull (5ᵗʰ), pause (3ʳᵈ), rest (1ˢᵗ), vacation (2ⁿᵈ)

recipe (4ᵗʰ): directions (1ˢᵗ), formula (6ᵗʰ), plan (1ˢᵗ), process (4ᵗʰ), system (2ⁿᵈ)

recite (5ᵗʰ): A. narrate (6ᵗʰ), recount (6ᵗʰ), relate (4ᵗʰ), speak (1ˢᵗ), state (1ˢᵗ) **B.** chant (5ᵗʰ), mimic (6ᵗʰ), perform (4ᵗʰ), quote (5ᵗʰ), rehearse (6ᵗʰ), repeat (4ᵗʰ), say by heart (1ˢᵗ)

reckless (5ᵗʰ): careless (5ᵗʰ), dangerous (6ᵗʰ), daring (2ⁿᵈ), foolish (2ⁿᵈ), impulsive (5ᵗʰ), rash (6ᵗʰ), thoughtless (2ⁿᵈ), wild (2ⁿᵈ)

reckon (5ᵗʰ): A. add (K), calculate (5ᵗʰ), compute (1ˢᵗ), count (1ˢᵗ), figure (4ᵗʰ), number (K) **B.** conclude (3ʳᵈ), consider (2ⁿᵈ), judge (1ˢᵗ), rate (1ˢᵗ), think (1ˢᵗ), value (2ⁿᵈ)

reclaim (6ᵗʰ): clean (1ˢᵗ), recover (4ᵗʰ), reform (5ᵗʰ), rescue (4ᵗʰ), restore (5ᵗʰ), save (1ˢᵗ)

recline (6th): lay (1st), lie (1st), lounge (6th), repose (6th)

recognize (3rd): comprehend (5th), identify (4th), know (1st), perceive (6th), realize (2nd), recall (3rd), remember (1st), see (K), understand (1st)

recollect (6th): recall (3rd), recognize (3rd), remember (1st), review (4th)

recommend (5th): advise (3rd), approve (4th), back (1st), favor (1st), offer (2nd), promote (5th), propose (4th), suggest (2nd), support (4th)

recompense (6th): A. compensation (6th), fee (4th), payment (1st), reward (4th), salary (3rd), satisfaction (3rd), wages (3rd) **B.** compensate (6th), pay (K), recover (4th), repay (3rd), reward (4th)

reconcile (6th): A. harmonize (4th), heal (3rd), make up (1st), mend (1st), reunite (5th) **B.** accept (3rd), adjust (5th), resign (5th), resolve (5th), settle (2nd), submit (4th)

record (2nd): A. chronicle (6th), log (K), note (1st), register (4th), report (1st), set down (K), write (K) **B.** account (3rd), achievement (5th), chronicle (6th), diary (3rd), history (2nd), journal (2nd), register (4th), report (1st)

recount (6th): narrate (6th), recite (5th), relate (4th), report (1st), review (4th), tell (K)

recourse (6th): A. backup (1st), retreat (4th) **B.** action (1st), course (3rd), plan (1st), resource (5th), way (K)

recover (4th): A. find (K), get back (1st), regain (6th), rescue (4th), restore (5th), retrieve (6th), save (1st) **B.** get better (1st), get well (1st), heal (3rd), mend (1st), revive (6th)

recreation (5th): entertainment (4th), exercise (1st), fun (K), game (K), hobby (3rd), pastime (2nd), play (K), relaxation (4th), rest (1st)

recruit (6th): call (1st), enlist (6th), gather (1st), impress (5th), summon (4th)

rectangle (1st)

recur (6th): continue (2nd), persist (5th), reappear (2nd), repeat (4th), return (2nd)

recycle (1st): reuse (1st)

red (K)

redeem (6th): exchange (4th), free (K), offset (2nd), pay off (1st), purchase (3rd), ransom (6th), recover (4th), regain (6th), restore (5th), retrieve (6th), save (1st)

redouble (6th): concentrate (5th), heighten (4th), intensify (6th), try harder (1st)

reduce (3rd): A. abbreviate (6th), cut (K), diminish (6th), lessen (3rd), limit (3rd), shorten (1st), trim (4th) **B.** ease (3rd), relax (4th), restrain (5th)

redwood (4th)

reed (4th)

reef (5th): bank (1st), bar (3rd), flat (2nd), ledge (5th), ridge (5th)

reel (5th): A. bobbin (4th), spool (2nd), wheel (1st) **B.** lurch (5th), pitch (2nd), rock (K), roll (1st), rotate (4th), spin (1st), sway (3rd), waver (5th), whirl (4th)

refer (5th): ask (K), call on (1st), direct (1st), indicate (4th), mean (1st), mention (5th), quote (5th), signify (6th), site (5th), specify (5th)

refine (6th): civilize (4th), clean (1st), clear (2nd), cultivate (6th), elevate (2nd), finish (1st), improve (3rd), polish (4th), purify (3rd), sensitize (5th), sharpen (1st)

reflect (4th): contemplate (6th), copy (3rd), deliberate (6th), display (3rd), exhibit (4th), illustrate (4th), intimate (5th), mirror (4th), remember (1st), reproduce (4th), reverse (5th), show (1st), think (1st), turn (1st)

reflex (6th): habit (3rd), reaction (5th), response (6th)

reform (5th): better (1st), change (2nd), correct (3rd), improve (3rd), make over (1st), redo (1st), repair (4th), reshape (3rd), restore (5th), revolutionize (5th)

refrain (6th): A. avoid (3rd), cease (3rd), discontinue (4th), halt (4th), hold (1st), quit (1st), renounce (6th), resist (4th), restrain (5th), stop (K) **B.** chorus (5th), repetition (4th)

refresh (6th): awaken (3rd), energize (4th), motivate (6th), pick up (1st), prompt (4th), renew (2nd), rest (1st), restore (5th), revive (6th)

refrigerator (2nd): cooler (1st), freezer (4th), icebox (1st)

refuge (5th): hiding (1st), protection (4th), retreat (4th), sanctuary (6th), security (3rd), shelter (4th)

refuse (2nd): decline (6th), forbid (4th), reject (5th)

refute (5th): deny (5th), expose (4th)

regain (6th): get back (1st), recover (4th), repossess (3rd), retrieve (6th)

regal (6th): imperial (5th), majestic (4th), noble (3rd), royal (3rd), stately (2nd)

regard (4th): A. behold (3rd), detect (4th), look (K), notice (1st), perceive (6th), see (K), view (1st), witness (3rd) **B.** contemplate (6th), think (1st) **C.** admire (5th), cherish (5th), esteem (5th), honor (1st), praise (4th), respect (2nd), treasure (4th), value (2nd), worship (4th)

regiment (5th): company (2nd)

region (4th): area (3rd), arena (5th), district (4th), location (3rd), place (1st), quarter (1st), realm (4th), section (4th), site (5th), sphere (6th), territory (3rd), zone (4th)

register (4th): A. catalog (5th), enlist (6th), enter (2nd), list (2nd), record (2nd), sign (1st) **B.** journal (2nd), record (2nd), roll (1st)

registration (5th): certificate (6th), list (2nd), permit (3rd), record (2nd), ticket (1st)

regret (5th): A. apologies (6th), grief (5th), remorse (6th), shame (3rd), sorrow (4th), woe (4th), worry (1st) **B.** grieve (5th), lament (6th), miss (K), mourn (4th), repent (6th)

regular (3rd): common (2nd), customary (6th), even (1st), habitual (3rd), normal (5th), orderly (2nd), ordinary (3rd), routine (6th), typical (6th), uniform (1st), usual (3rd)

regulate (5th): accustom (4th), adapt (4th), adjust (5th), alter (4th), control (2nd), correct (3rd), direct (1st), govern (1st), manage (4th), modify (5th), operate (3rd), rule (K), run (K)

rehearse (6th): drill (2nd), practice (1st), prepare (1st), recite (5th), repeat (4th), review (4th), train (6th)

reheat (6th): cook (1st), warm (1st)

reign (4ᵗʰ): A. administer (6ᵗʰ), control (2ⁿᵈ), dominate (5ᵗʰ), govern (1ˢᵗ), lead (1ˢᵗ), prevail (5ᵗʰ), rule (2ⁿᵈ) **B.** era (6ᵗʰ), period (2ⁿᵈ)

reindeer (K)

reins (1ˢᵗ): bridle (4ᵗʰ), control (2ⁿᵈ), hold (1ˢᵗ), restrain (5ᵗʰ)

reject (5ᵗʰ): A. decline (6ᵗʰ), forbid (4ᵗʰ), refuse (2ⁿᵈ), say no to (K), turn down (1ˢᵗ) **B.** discard (6ᵗʰ), eliminate (5ᵗʰ), rid (1ˢᵗ), toss (2ⁿᵈ)

rejoice (4ᵗʰ): celebrate (4ᵗʰ), delight (3ʳᵈ), glory (3ʳᵈ), party (K), triumph (5ᵗʰ)

relate (4ᵗʰ): A. communicate (4ᵗʰ), narrate (6ᵗʰ), recite (5ᵗʰ), repeat (4ᵗʰ), say (K), tell (K) **B.** associate (5ᵗʰ), connect (3ʳᵈ), link (5ᵗʰ)

relation (4ᵗʰ): A. association (5ᵗʰ), connection (3ʳᵈ), similarity (4ᵗʰ), tie-in (1ˢᵗ) **B.** family (K), relative (K)

relative (4ᵗʰ): A. fitting (2ⁿᵈ), regarding (4ᵗʰ), related (4ᵗʰ), relating to (4ᵗʰ) **B.** blood (1ˢᵗ), family (K), kin (1ˢᵗ), relation (4ᵗʰ)

relax (4ᵗʰ): bend (K), ease (3ʳᵈ), free (K), lessen (3ʳᵈ), loosen (5ᵗʰ), release (5ᵗʰ), soften (1ˢᵗ), weaken (3ʳᵈ), yield (4ᵗʰ)

relay (6ᵗʰ): A. communicate (4ᵗʰ), report (1ˢᵗ), say (K), tell (K) **B.** give (1ˢᵗ), hand off (1ˢᵗ)

release (5ᵗʰ): A. announcement (3ʳᵈ) **B.** freedom (3ʳᵈ), loosening (5ᵗʰ) **C.** excuse (3ʳᵈ), free (K), let out (K), liberate (3ʳᵈ), lose (K), unfasten (4ᵗʰ), untie (3ʳᵈ)

relic (5ᵗʰ): antique (6ᵗʰ), fossil (4ᵗʰ), heirloom (5ᵗʰ), remains (1ˢᵗ), trace (3ʳᵈ)

relief (4ᵗʰ): A. break (1ˢᵗ), recess (2ⁿᵈ), rest (1ˢᵗ) **B.** aid (2ⁿᵈ), assistance (4ᵗʰ), comfort (3ʳᵈ), help (K), rescue (4ᵗʰ), support (4ᵗʰ)

relieve (4ᵗʰ): aid (2ⁿᵈ), assist (4ᵗʰ), calm (3ʳᵈ), ease (3ʳᵈ), help (K), lessen (3ʳᵈ), lose (K), relax (4ᵗʰ), rest (1ˢᵗ), soothe (5ᵗʰ)

religion (4ᵗʰ): belief (1ˢᵗ), church (1ˢᵗ), creed (6ᵗʰ), cult (5ᵗʰ), faith (3ʳᵈ), sect (5ᵗʰ)

relish (6ᵗʰ): A. appetite (4ᵗʰ), delight (3ʳᵈ), enjoyment (2ⁿᵈ), liking (1ˢᵗ), pleasure (2ⁿᵈ), taste (1ˢᵗ), zest (6ᵗʰ) **B.** approve (4ᵗʰ), delight in (3ʳᵈ), enjoy (2ⁿᵈ) **C.** appetizer (4ᵗʰ), pickle (1ˢᵗ)

reluctant (6ᵗʰ): afraid (1ˢᵗ), cautious (5ᵗʰ), hesitant (4ᵗʰ), resistant (4ᵗʰ), shy (1ˢᵗ), unwilling (3ʳᵈ)

rely (5ᵗʰ): believe in (1ˢᵗ), count on (1ˢᵗ), depend (3ʳᵈ), lean on (3ʳᵈ), trust (1ˢᵗ)

remain (1ˢᵗ): abide (5ᵗʰ), continue (2ⁿᵈ), dwell (4ᵗʰ), endure (4ᵗʰ), exist (3ʳᵈ), inhabit (6ᵗʰ), last (K), linger (4ᵗʰ), reside (5ᵗʰ), rest (1ˢᵗ), stay (1ˢᵗ), survive (3ʳᵈ), tarry (5ᵗʰ), wait (1ˢᵗ)

remark (4ᵗʰ): A. comment (5ᵗʰ), declare (5ᵗʰ), mention (5ᵗʰ), note (1ˢᵗ), notice (1ˢᵗ), observe (3ʳᵈ), perceive (6ᵗʰ), say (K), speak (1ˢᵗ), state (1ˢᵗ), voice (1ˢᵗ) **B.** comment (5ᵗʰ), saying (1ˢᵗ), statement (2ⁿᵈ)

remedy (4ᵗʰ): A. correct (3ʳᵈ), cure (4ᵗʰ), heal (3ʳᵈ) **B.** cure (4ᵗʰ), medicine (4ᵗʰ), tonic (2ⁿᵈ), treatment (5ᵗʰ)

remember (1ˢᵗ): recall (3ʳᵈ), recognize (3ʳᵈ), recollect (6ᵗʰ), recover (4ᵗʰ), reflect (4ᵗʰ), retrieve (6ᵗʰ)

remind (3rd): cue (2nd), hint (1st), prompt (4th), review (4th), suggest (2nd)

remnant (6th): carry-over (1st), piece (1st), remains (2nd), rest (1st), scrap (3rd), trace (3rd), waste (1st)

remonstrate (6th): A. scold (5th) **B.** argue (3rd), challenge (4th), complain (4th), oppose (3rd), protest (4th)

remorse (6th): grief (5th), guilt (4th), regret (5th), repentance (6th), sadness (1st), shame (1st), sorrow (4th), woe (4th), worry (1st)

remote (5th): A. obscure (6th), pointless (2nd), strange (1st), vague (5th) **B.** distant (4th), far (1st), foreign (5th), removed (2nd) **C.** slight (4th), slim (5th), small (K), tiny (2nd)

remove (2nd): A. dethrone (6th), kill (1st), cut (K), subtract (1st), take away (1st) **B.** bare (3rd), clean (1st)

renaissance (5th): awakening (3rd), rebirth (3rd), renewal (4th), revival (6th)

rend (4th): divide (4th), rip (K), shred (5th), slice (5th), split (4th), tear (2nd)

renew (4th): A. begin again (1st), repeat (4th), resume (5th) **B.** make anew (3rd), modernize (3rd), refresh (6th), repair (4th)

renounce (6th): abandon (4th), avoid (3rd), deny (5th), disown (3rd), forego (5th), forsake (6th), give up (1st), shun (6th), stop (K)

renown (5th): eminence (6th), fame (3rd), importance (1st), noted (2nd), popularity (3rd), respect (2nd)

rent (K): A. hire (3rd), lease (6th), let (K) **B.** fee (4th), payment (1st) **C.** crack

(4th), damage (5th), hole (K), rip (1st), tear (2nd)

repair (4th): A. correction (3rd), improvement (3rd), renewal (4th), restoration (5th) **B.** correct (3rd), cure (4th), fix (1st), mend (1st), renew (4th), restore (5th), right (K)

repeat (4th): A. duplicate (6th), playback (1st) **B.** copy (3rd), duplicate (6th), echo (4th), recur (6th), redo (1st), reproduce (4th)

repel (6th): A. disgust (5th), revolt (5th), sicken (2nd) **B.** oppose (3rd), push (1st), put off (1st), reject (5th), repulse (6th), resist (4th)

repent (6th): A. make amends (4th), make up for (1st) **B.** grieve (5th), lament (6th), mourn (4th), regret (5th)

replace (5th): A. follow (1st), substitute (5th), succeed (2nd) **B.** displace (3rd), replenish (6th), restore (5th)

replenish (6th): provide (3rd), refill (1st), reload (2nd), renew (1st), replace (5th), supply (1st)

reply (1st): A. acknowledgment (5th), answer (1st), comment (5th), reaction (5th), response (5th) **B.** answer (1st), comment (5th), respond (5th)

report (1st): A. announce (3rd), communicate (4th), relay (6th), repeat (4th), tell (K) **B.** account (3rd), article (2nd), log (K), news (1st), paper (K), relation (4th), review (4th), rumor (5th), telling (1st)

repose (6th): A. lounge (6th), relax (4th) **B.** ease (3rd), nap (K), peace (1st), recess (2nd), rest (1st), sleep (K), vacation (2nd)

represent (4th): illustrate (4th), image (4th), picture (K), portray (5th), present (K), symbolize (5th), typify (6th)

reproach (6th): A. blame (2nd), disapproval (4th), scolding (5th) **B.** blame (2nd), criticize (5th), disapprove (4th), scold (5th), shame (3rd)

reproduce (4th): breed (4th), copy (3rd), duplicate (6th), match (3rd), multiply (2nd), redo (1st), renew (4th), repeat (4th), restore (5th)

reptile (4th): lizard (1st), serpent (5th), snake (5th)

repulse (6th): A. deny (5th), put off (1st) **B.** denial (5th), rejection (5th), repelling (6th) **C.** defeat (5th), drive away (1st), repel (6th)

reputation (5th): fame (3rd), honor (1st), name (K), rank (3rd), repute (5th), standing (1st)

request (4th): A. appeal (3rd), ask (K), beg (1st), demand (5th), plead (5th) **B.** appeal (3rd), demand (5th), plea (5th)

require (1st): demand (5th), force (1st), lack (1st), need (1st), order (1st), want (K)

requisition (6th): A. call (K), command (2nd), demand (5th), order (1st), request (4th) **B.** ask (K), order (1st), request (4th), seize (3rd), take over (1st)

rescue (4th): A. delivery (5th), freedom (3rd), liberty (3rd), salvation (6th) **B.** deliver (5th), free (K), liberate (3rd), release (5th), save (1st)

research (5th): A. exploration (4th), investigation (5th), search (1st), study (1st) **B.** explore (4th), inquire (3rd), investigate (5th)

resemble (4th): be like (1st), be similar to (4th), favor (2nd), look like (1st), match (3rd), mimic (6th), seem like (1st)

resent (5th): be irritated (6th), dislike (3rd), envy (4th)

reserve (3rd): A. conserve (5th), put aside (3rd), retain (5th), save (1st), withhold (2nd) **B.** backup (2nd), extra (1st), spare (3rd) **C.** composure (4th), formality (4th) **D.** stock (1st), store (K), supply (2nd)

reside (5th): dwell (4th), inhabit (6th), live (1st), occupy (3rd)

residence (5th): address (K), domicile (5th), dwelling (4th), habitation (6th), home (K), house (K), location (3rd), lodging (4th)

resident (5th): A. dwelling (4th), inhabiting (6th), living (1st) **B.** dweller (4th), inhabitant (6th), lodger (5th), occupant (3rd), tenant (5th)

resign (5th): A. depart (5th), leave (1st), quit (1st), retire (4th) **B.** accept (3rd), give up (1st), submit (4th), surrender (5th), yield (4th)

resin (5th): amber (5th), copal (5th), gum (1st), pitch (2nd), tar (1st)

resist (4th): defy (6th), fight (K), interfere (4th), oppose (3rd), repel (6th), stop (K), withstand (2nd)

resolution (5th): A. bill (1st), declaration (5th), outcome (4th), proposal (2nd), ruling (1st), verdict (6th) **B.** desire (5th), determination (5th), proposal (2nd), purpose (2nd), resolve (5th), will (K)

resolve (5th): A. decide (1st), determine (5th), propose (4th), solve (4th), will (K) **B.** break up (1st), separate (3rd) **C.** determination (5th), effort (2nd), purpose (2nd), resolution (5th), stubbornness (5th)

resort (5th): A. aid (2nd), choice (3rd), recourse (6th) **B.** hotel (3rd), refuge (5th), retreat (4th) **C.** come to (1st), lower (1st), try (K), use (K)

resource (5th): aid (2nd), backup (2nd), help (K), reserve (3rd), support (4th)

resourceful (5th): clever (3rd), creative (3rd), enterprising (5th), inventive (2nd), original (3rd)

respect (2nd): A. admiration (5th), consideration (2nd), courtesy (4th), politeness (4th), reverence (4th) **B.** compliment (5th), esteem (5th), honor (1st), regard (4th), venerate (6th)

respecting (4th): A. concerning (3rd), considering (2nd) **B.** admiring (5th), honoring (2nd), venerating (6th)

respiration (6th): breath (1st), breathing (1st), gasping (4th), wheezing (5th)

respite (6th): A. internal (6th), pause (3rd), rest (1st) **B.** ease (3rd), relax (4th), relieve (4th)

respond (5th): acknowledge (5th), answer (1st), react (5th), reply (2nd), retort (5th)

responsible (4th): accountable (3rd), answerable (2nd), dependable (3rd), liable (6th), reasonable (2nd), reliable (5th), sensible (6th), stable (4th)

rest (1st): A. ease (3rd), pause (3rd), peace (1st), quiet (K), sleep (K) **B.** place (1st), put (K), relax (4th), remain (2nd), settle (2nd)

restaurant (5th): cafe (4th), cafeteria (5th), coffeehouse (2nd), delicatessen (5th)

restless (4th): A. sleepless (1st) **B.** agitated (5th), excitable (4th), nervous (1st), restive (5th), uneasy (3rd) **C.** changing (2nd), moving (1st), wandering (3rd)

restore (5th): cure (4th), fix (1st), mend (1st), patch (4th), re-establish (3rd), remodel (3rd), renew (3rd), repair (4th), replace (5th)

restrain (5th): contain (5th), control (2nd), delay (5th), deter (5th), hinder (6th), hold back (1st), prevent (3rd), stop (K)

restrict (6th): bound (2nd), cage (1st), limit (3rd), localize (3rd)

result (2nd): A. conclude (3rd), finish (1st) **B.** arise (4th), emerge (5th), follow (1st) **C.** answer (K), conclusion (3rd), consequence (4th), effect (3rd), end (K), out come (4th), product (4th)

resume (5th): advance (2nd), continue (2nd), proceed (4th), restart (1st), return (2nd)

retain (5th): A. employ (5th), hire (3rd) **B.** memorize (3rd), remember (1st) **C.** hold (1st), keep (K), reserve (3rd), save (1st)

retire (4th): A. go to bed (K), rest (1st) **B.** give up work (1st), resign (5th) **C.** depart (5th), leave (1st), retreat (4th), withdraw (2nd)

retort (5th): A. answer (K), reply (2nd), response (5th) **B.** answer (K), reply (2nd), respond (5th)

retreat (4th): A. flee (5th), leave (1st), retire (4th), withdraw (2nd) **B.** departure (5th), escape (1st), privacy (3rd), protection (4th), rest (1st), sanctuary (6th), shelter (4th)

retrieve (6th): acquire (4th), recover (4th), redeem (6th), remedy (4th), rescue (4th), restore (5th)

return (1st): A. give back (1st), replace (5th), restore (5th) **B.** gain (2nd), profits (4th), yield (4th) **C.** reverse (5th) **D.** reappear (2nd), reoccur (3rd) **E.** duplication (6th), recurrence (6th) **F.** answer (K), response (5th) **G.** reply (2nd), respond (5th)

reveal (4th): A. acknowledge (5th), tell (K) **B.** bare (3rd), exhibit (4th), expose (4th), show (1st)

revenge (5th): bitterness (3rd), get back at (1st), get even with (1st), repayment (1st), satisfaction (3rd), spite (3rd)

revenue (6th): cash (2nd), earnings (2nd), gain (2nd), income (4th), payment (1st), profits (4th), wealth (3rd)

reverence (4th): awe (6th), honor (1st), regard (4th), respect (2nd), worship (4th)

reverend (4th): A. holy (5th), honorable (3rd), worthy (3rd) **B.** clergy (6th), minister (4th), pastor (4th), priest (4th)

reverse (5th): A. backward (4th), contrasting (4th), opposite (3rd) **B.** contrary (4th), opposite (3rd) **C.** cancel (6th), change (2nd), conflict (4th), counter (5th), turn (1st)

review (4th): A. examine (5th), reconsider (2nd), skim (6th) **B.** study (1st), survey (5th)

revive (6th): A. recall (3rd) **B.** freshen (2nd), heal (3rd), mend (1st), rally (5th), rebuild (3rd), recover (4th), remodel (3rd), renew (4th), restore (5th), start (1st)

revolt (5th): A. go against (1st), oppose (3rd) **B.** disgust (5th), dislike (1st), sicken (2nd) **C.** mutiny (6th), riot (6th), uprising (5th)

revolution (5th): A. mutiny (6th), revolt (5th), riot (6th), uprising (5th) **B.** circulation (4th), curl (2nd), loop (5th), rotation (6th), turn (1st)

revolve (5th): A. recur (6th), return (1st) **B.** circle (1st), circulate (4th), rotate (4th), spin (1st), turn (1st)

revolver (5th): gun (K), pistol (5th)

reward (4th): A. compensate (6th), pay (K), tip (1st) **B.** award (5th), bonus (6th), gain (2nd), gift (1st), outcome (4th), payment (1st), present (2nd), result (2nd)

rhinoceros (3rd)

rhubarb (4th)

rhyme (6th): lyric (6th), poem (3rd), song (K), verse (4th)

rhythm (5th): A. flow (1st), harmony (4th) **B.** beat (1st), pulse (5th), rate (1st), time (1st), throb (5th)

rib (1st): joke (1st), needle (3rd), tease (3rd)

ribbon (4th): band (1st), headband (2nd), sash (6th), strip (3rd)

ribbon (4th): line (K), strip (3rd)

rice (1st)

rich (K): A. bright (1st), vivid (6th), **B.** wealthy (3rd) **C.** fattening (2nd), heavy (1st), sweet (1st) **D.** elegant (5th), extravagant (6th), lavish (6th), ornate (4th), precious (4th), valuable (4th)

rid (1st): eliminate (5th), free (K), relieve (4th), remove (2nd)

riddle (1st): mystery (1st), problem (1st), puzzle (4th), question (1st), secret (1st)

ride (K): A. drive (K), journey (3rd), spin (1st), trip (1st) **B.** mount (2nd), sit on (K) **C.** annoy (5th), bother (2nd), tease (3rd) **D.** drive (K), journey (3rd), tour (3rd), travel (3rd)

ridge (5th): crest (4th), hill (1st), ledge (5th), mound (5th)

ridicule (6th): A. contempt (5th), mockery (4th), teasing (3rd) **B.** mock (4th), scorn (4th), tease (3rd)

ridiculous (6th): absurd (6th), comical (5th), foolish (2nd), impossible (3rd), senseless (2nd), stupid (4th), unreasonable (2nd), untrue (1st)

rifle (4th): A. look (K), sort (2nd) **B.** shotgun (2nd)

rig (1st): A. clothe (1st), dress (K), equip (5th), furnish (4th), supply (2nd) **B.** equipment (5th), outfit (2nd) **C.** carriage (5th), vehicle (6th) **D.** adapt (4th), convert (4th), fit (K), modify (5th), tailor (4th)

right (K): A. accurate (6th), correct (3rd), exact (2nd), precise (5th), true (1st) **B.** ethical (5th), good (K), honest (3rd), moral (3rd), polite (4th), proper (3rd) **C.** license (5th), permission (3rd), privilege (5th), title (3rd) **D.** adjust (5th), fix (1st), mend (1st), remedy (4th)

rigid (5th): A. harsh (5th), severe (4th), stern (4th), strict (6th), stubborn (5th), unbending (2nd) **B.** controlled (2nd), exact (2nd), firm (2nd), hard (1st), set (K), solid (3rd), stiff (3rd), tight (1st)

rim (1st): border (1st), boundary (4th), brink (6th), curb (3rd), edge (1st), limit (3rd), lip (1st)

ring (1st): A. gang (1st), group (1st) **B.** band (1st), circle (K), loop (5th), **C.** clang (4th), chime (6th), toll (6th) **D.** revolve (5th), spin (1st) **E.** sound (1st), tone (3rd) **F.** encircle (5th), surround (3rd)

rinse (3rd): A. bath (1st), cleaning (K), shower (4th), wash (1st) **B.** clean (K), launder (6th), wash (1st), wet (K), wipe (1st)

riot (6th): A. celebration (4th), merrymaking (3rd), party (K) **B.** fight (K), revolt (5th) **C.** crazy (4th), disorder (3rd), fun (3rd), panic (1st), wild (2nd)

rip (K): A. crack (4th), cut (K), slit (5th), tear (2nd) **B.** cut (K), rend (4th), shred (5th), slash (6th), tear (2nd)

ripe (1st): aged (1st), mature (5th), mellow (6th), ready (1st)

ripen (1st): age (1st), develop (5th), mature (5th), mellow (6th), season (2nd)

ripple (4th): A. ruffle (6th), wrinkle (3rd) **B.** splash (1st), swell (3rd), wave (K)

rise (1st): A. arise (4th), ascend (4th), climb (1st), go up (K), stand (1st) **B.** happen (1st), occur (3rd), pass (2nd) **C.** hill (1st), incline (5th), lift (1st), mound (2nd), slope (3rd) **D.** appearance (2nd), coming (K) **E.** awaken (3rd), get up (K) **F.** expansion (5th), gain (2nd) **G.** come up (1st), develop (5th), expand (5th), grow (K), increase (3rd), raise (1st), swell (3rd)

risk (4th): A. endanger (6th), threaten (5th) **B.** adventure (3rd), chance (2nd), danger (1st), gamble (5th), hazard (6th), menace (5th), peril (5th) **C.** attempt (2nd), bet (1st), dare (2nd), gamble (5th), try (K), wager (3rd)

rite (6th): A. command (2nd), law (1st), order (1st), rule (2nd) **B.** celebration (4th), ceremony (5th), custom (6th), ritual (6th), tradition (5th)

ritual (6ᵗʰ): ceremony (5ᵗʰ), custom (6ᵗʰ), rite (6ᵗʰ), service (5ᵗʰ), tradition (5ᵗʰ)

rival (4ᵗʰ): A. competing (5ᵗʰ), competitive (5ᵗʰ), opposing (5ᵗʰ) **B.** equal (2ⁿᵈ), match (3ʳᵈ) **C.** challenger (4ᵗʰ), enemy (2ⁿᵈ), opponent (5ᵗʰ) **D.** challenge (4ᵗʰ), contend (5ᵗʰ), fight (K)

river (K): branch (2ⁿᵈ), creek (4ᵗʰ), waterway (2ⁿᵈ), stream (1ˢᵗ)

road (K): A. freeway (2ⁿᵈ), highway (4ᵗʰ), lane (4ᵗʰ), street (1ˢᵗ) **B.** means (1ˢᵗ), method (2ⁿᵈ), path (1ˢᵗ), route (4ᵗʰ), way (K)

roadbed (1ˢᵗ): A. path (1ˢᵗ), route (4ᵗʰ) **B.** base (1ˢᵗ), foundation (5ᵗʰ)

roam (4ᵗʰ): drift (2ⁿᵈ), ramble (6ᵗʰ), rove (6ᵗʰ), stroll (5ᵗʰ), travel (1ˢᵗ), walk (K), wander (3ʳᵈ)

roar (1ˢᵗ): A. boom (1ˢᵗ), crash (2ⁿᵈ), rumble (3ʳᵈ), thunder (3ʳᵈ) **B.** bellow (4ᵗʰ), cry (K), growl (4ᵗʰ), howl (4ᵗʰ), laugh loudly (1ˢᵗ), scream (1ˢᵗ), shriek (4ᵗʰ), wail (5ᵗʰ), yell (K)

roast (4ᵗʰ): A. joke (1ˢᵗ), mock (4ᵗʰ), tease (3ʳᵈ) **B.** bake (1ˢᵗ), broil (4ᵗʰ), cook (1ˢᵗ), heat (1ˢᵗ)

rob (K): cheat (3ʳᵈ), plunder (5ᵗʰ), steal (3ʳᵈ), take (1ˢᵗ), thieve (3ʳᵈ)

robe (4ᵗʰ): A. adorn (6ᵗʰ), attire (6ᵗʰ), clothe (1ˢᵗ), drape (5ᵗʰ), garb (5ᵗʰ) **B.** cape (4ᵗʰ), cloak (4ᵗʰ), coat (1ˢᵗ), dress (K), frock (4ᵗʰ), gown (4ᵗʰ), tunic (6ᵗʰ)

robin (K)

robot (K)

robust (5ᵗʰ): athletic (5ᵗʰ), dynamic (5ᵗʰ), energetic (4ᵗʰ), hardy (5ᵗʰ), healthy (1ˢᵗ), hearty (5ᵗʰ), powerful

(2ⁿᵈ), sound (1ˢᵗ), stout (4ᵗʰ), sturdy (2ⁿᵈ), well (1ˢᵗ)

rock (K): A. disturb (6ᵗʰ), stun (4ᵗʰ), upset (3ʳᵈ) **B.** roll (1ˢᵗ), shake (1ˢᵗ), sway (3ʳᵈ), swing (1ˢᵗ), wobble (4ᵗʰ) **C.** boulder (5ᵗʰ), pebble (4ᵗʰ), stone (2ⁿᵈ)

rocket (K): A. fire (K), launch (5ᵗʰ), shoot (3ʳᵈ) **B.** spacecraft (2ⁿᵈ) **C.** hurry (1ˢᵗ), rush (2ⁿᵈ), speed (3ʳᵈ)

rod (1ˢᵗ): A. gun (K), pistol (5ᵗʰ), revolver (5ᵗʰ) **B.** bar (3ʳᵈ), cane (3ʳᵈ), pole (1ˢᵗ), staff (4ᵗʰ), stick (K), wand (3ʳᵈ), whip (4ᵗʰ)

roe (5ᵗʰ)

rogue (5ᵗʰ): knave (5ᵗʰ), rascal (5ᵗʰ), troublemaker (2ⁿᵈ), villain (5ᵗʰ), wretch (6ᵗʰ)

role (6ᵗʰ): character (2ⁿᵈ), part (1ˢᵗ), position (2ⁿᵈ), use (K)

roll (1ˢᵗ): A. coil (5ᵗʰ), scroll (5ᵗʰ) **B.** ripple (4ᵗʰ), rock (K), rotate (4ᵗʰ), spill (1ˢᵗ), spin (1ˢᵗ), toss (2ⁿᵈ), turn (1ˢᵗ), upset (3ʳᵈ), wave (K) **C.** list (2ⁿᵈ) **D.** roar (1ˢᵗ), rumble (3ʳᵈ), thunder (3ʳᵈ), thundering (3ʳᵈ) **E.** reel (5ᵗʰ), spool (2ⁿᵈ) **F.** biscuit (6ᵗʰ), bun (2ⁿᵈ) **G.** circle (K), loop (5ᵗʰ), revolve (5ᵗʰ)

romance (5ᵗʰ): A. affair (2ⁿᵈ), wooing (6ᵗʰ) **B.** fiction (5ᵗʰ), novel (5ᵗʰ), story (K), tale (3ʳᵈ) **C.** court (3ʳᵈ), flirt (6ᵗʰ), love (K)

roof (1ˢᵗ): A. dwelling (4ᵗʰ), home (K), house (K) **B.** canopy (6ᵗʰ), ceiling (4ᵗʰ), cover (1ˢᵗ), shade (2ⁿᵈ), top (K)

room (K): A. capacity (6ᵗʰ) **B.** expanse (5ᵗʰ), freedom (3ʳᵈ), space (1ˢᵗ) **C.** dwell (4ᵗʰ), live (1ˢᵗ), lodge (4ᵗʰ), rent (K), reside (5ᵗʰ) **D.** apartment (1ˢᵗ), chamber (5ᵗʰ), compartment (6ᵗʰ)

roost (2ⁿᵈ): A. perch (4ᵗʰ), sit on (1ˢᵗ)
B. home (1ˢᵗ), perch (4ᵗʰ), rest (1ˢᵗ),
seat (1ˢᵗ)

rooster (1ˢᵗ)

root (3ʳᵈ): A. fasten (4ᵗʰ), plant (K),
set (K), settle (2ⁿᵈ) **B.** dig (K), pry (6ᵗʰ),
search (1ˢᵗ) **C.** cheer (3ʳᵈ), support
(4ᵗʰ) **D.** beginning (2ⁿᵈ), fundamental
(4ᵗʰ), heart (K), origin (3ʳᵈ), principle
(3ʳᵈ), source (4ᵗʰ) **E.** anchor (4ᵗʰ), base
(1ˢᵗ), footing (1ˢᵗ), foundation (5ᵗʰ),
ground (1ˢᵗ)

rope (1ˢᵗ): A. bind (2ⁿᵈ), catch (1ˢᵗ),
fasten (4ᵗʰ), join (3ʳᵈ), lash (4ᵗʰ), tie
(1ˢᵗ) **B.** cable (1ˢᵗ), cord (4ᵗʰ), line (K)

rose (1ˢᵗ)

rot (1ˢᵗ): A. decay (5ᵗʰ), spoil (4ᵗʰ) **B.**
corrupt (6ᵗʰ), poison (3ʳᵈ), ruin (2ⁿᵈ) **C.**
nonsense (5ᵗʰ) **D.** contamination (6ᵗʰ),
infection (6ᵗʰ), pollution (3ʳᵈ)

rotate (4ᵗʰ): A. change (2ⁿᵈ), shift
(4ᵗʰ), switch (4ᵗʰ) **B.** circle (K), cycle
(6ᵗʰ), revolve (5ᵗʰ), spin (1ˢᵗ), turn (1ˢᵗ)

rote (2ⁿᵈ): by memory (3ʳᵈ), groove
(5ᵗʰ), habit (3ʳᵈ), ritual (6ᵗʰ), routine
(6ᵗʰ)

rotorcraft (1ˢᵗ): a flying machine
that gets its lift and thrust from rotor
blades

rough (4ᵗʰ): A. basic (5ᵗʰ), brief
(3ʳᵈ), plain (1ˢᵗ), simple (2ⁿᵈ), sketchy
(5ᵗʰ), unfinished (3ʳᵈ) **B.** difficult (5ᵗʰ),
tough (5ᵗʰ) **C.** bumpy (2ⁿᵈ), coarse
(4ᵗʰ), harsh (5ᵗʰ), irregular (6ᵗʰ), rugged (5ᵗʰ), uneven (3ʳᵈ) **D.** primitive
(5ᵗʰ) **E.** impolite (4ᵗʰ), rude (2ⁿᵈ), un-
mannered (2ⁿᵈ)

round (K): A. circuit (4ᵗʰ), revolution
(5ᵗʰ), turn (1ˢᵗ) **B.** arch (4ᵗʰ), bend (K),
curve (3ʳᵈ) **C.** circular (4ᵗʰ), oval (1ˢᵗ)

D. complete (3ʳᵈ), entire (3ʳᵈ) **E.** circle
(K), disk (2ⁿᵈ), sphere (6ᵗʰ)

roundhouse (1ˢᵗ)

rouse (4ᵗʰ): call (K), challenge (4ᵗʰ),
excite (4ᵗʰ), inspire (4ᵗʰ), provoke (6ᵗʰ),
rally (5ᵗʰ), stimulate (6ᵗʰ), stir (3ʳᵈ),
thrill (4ᵗʰ), wake up (1ˢᵗ)

roust (5ᵗʰ): awaken rudely (3ʳᵈ),
prod (6ᵗʰ)

route (4ᵗʰ): A. direct (1ˢᵗ), guide (1ˢᵗ),
send (1ˢᵗ), steer (5ᵗʰ) **B.** course (3ʳᵈ),
highway (4ᵗʰ), passage (4ᵗʰ), path (1ˢᵗ),
road (K), trail (2ⁿᵈ), way (K)

routine (6ᵗʰ): A. habit (3ʳᵈ), method
(2ⁿᵈ), procedure (4ᵗʰ), process (4ᵗʰ),
practice (1ˢᵗ), rote (2ⁿᵈ), system (2ⁿᵈ)
B. accustomed (4ᵗʰ), automatic (6ᵗʰ),
average (3ʳᵈ), common (2ⁿᵈ), established (3ʳᵈ), familiar (3ʳᵈ), normal (5ᵗʰ),
regular (3ʳᵈ), typical (6ᵗʰ), usual (3ʳᵈ)

rove (6ᵗʰ): ramble (6ᵗʰ), roam (4ᵗʰ),
stroll (5ᵗʰ), travel (1ˢᵗ), walk (K), wander (3ʳᵈ)

row (K): A. chain (3ʳᵈ), column (4ᵗʰ),
layer (4ᵗʰ), line (K), order (1ˢᵗ), rank
(3ʳᵈ), series (4ᵗʰ) **B.** oar (1ˢᵗ), paddle
(1ˢᵗ) **C.** argue (3ʳᵈ), fight (K), quarrel
(4ᵗʰ) **D.** argument (3ʳᵈ), battle (2ⁿᵈ),
dispute (6ᵗʰ), fight (1ˢᵗ)

royal (3ʳᵈ): imperial (5ᵗʰ), majestic
(4ᵗʰ), noble (3ʳᵈ), regal (6ᵗʰ)

rub (1ˢᵗ): brush (2ⁿᵈ), clean (1ˢᵗ),
knead (4ᵗʰ), pet (1ˢᵗ), polish (4ᵗʰ),
scour (6ᵗʰ), scrub (6ᵗʰ), stroke, (1ˢᵗ),
wipe (1ˢᵗ)

rubber (1ˢᵗ)

rubbish (5ᵗʰ): A. debris (5ᵗʰ), garbage (5ᵗʰ), junk (3ʳᵈ), litter (2ⁿᵈ), remains (2ⁿᵈ), rot (1ˢᵗ), trash (2ⁿᵈ), waste

(1st) **B.** foolishness (2nd), garbage (5th), nonsense (5th), trash (2nd)

ruby (6th)

rude (2nd): abrupt (5th), fresh (2nd), impolite (4th), rough (4th), thoughtless (2nd), uncivil (3rd), unmannerly (2nd)

ruffle (6th): A. disorder (3rd) **B.** agitate (5th), bewilder (3rd), confuse (4th), disturb (6th), upset (3rd) **C.** crease (5th), ripple (4th) **D.** edging (1st), trim (4th) **rug (1st):** carpet (4th), mat (K), pad (K)

rug (1st)

rugged (5th): A. durable (6th), powerful (2nd), strong (K), sturdy (3rd), tough (5th) **B.** rocky (1st), rough (4th), uneven (2nd) **C.** demanding (5th), difficult (5th), forceful (3rd), harsh (5th)

ruin (2nd): A. destruction (6th), downfall (3rd), failure (3rd), fall (K), finish (1st) **B.** collapse (5th), corrupt (6th), decay (5th), destroy (2nd), spoil (4th), upset (3rd)

ruinous (5th): A. destructive (5th), disastrous (6th) **B.** destructive (5th) **C.** rundown (2nd), tumbledown (4th)

rule (K): A. code (3rd), guide (1st), rite (6th), saying (1st), standard (3rd), truth (1st) **B.** law (1st), policy (5th), principle (4th) **C.** administer (6th), command (2nd), control (2nd), decide (1st), dominate (5th), find (K), govern (1st), judge (1st), manage (4th)

rum (1st)

rumble (3rd): A. boom (1st), crash (2nd), thunder (3rd) **B.** growl (4th), roar (1st)

rumor (5th): A. gossip (5th), tell (K) **B.** gossip (5th), news (1st), report (1st), tale (3rd), talk (K)

run (K): A. escape (2nd), flee (5th) **B.** course (3rd), trip (1st), way (K) **C.** chain (3rd), pattern (3rd), series (4th) **D.** competition (4th), event (3rd), game (1st), meet (K) **E.** conduct (3rd), direct (1st), manage (4th), operate (3rd) **F.** flow (1st), leak (6th), melt (2nd) **G.** gallop (4th), jog (2nd), race (1st), rush (2nd), speed (3rd), sprint (5th)

running (1st)

rural (5th): country (1st), farm (K), outback (1st), outland (2nd), rustic (3rd)

rush (2nd): A. flow (1st), motion (3rd), surge (5th) **B.** assault (4th), attack (3rd) **C.** fast (1st), hasty (2nd), quick (1st) **D.** hurry (1st), race (1st), run (K), scramble (4th), speed (3rd)

rust (2nd): A. age (1st), decay (5th), wear (1st) **B.** stain (4th)

rustle (3rd): disturb (6th), move (K), ripple (4th), whisper (1st)

rut (1st): A. habit (3rd), routine (6th), system (2nd) **B.** crack (4th), groove (5th), path (1st)

Sabbath (5th)

saber (5th): blade (2nd), knife (1st), sword (4th)

saber-toothed (5th)

sable (5th): black (K), dark (K), jet (K)

sack (1st): A. bag (1st), case (2nd), pack (1st), pouch (1st) **B.** discharge (3rd), fire (K), terminate (6th) **C.** abuse (6th), attack (3rd), plunder (5th), ravage (6th), rob (K)

sacred (4th): blessed (3rd), godly (1st), holy (5th), pure (3rd), religious (4th), spiritual (5th)

sacrifice (4th): A. forfeit (6th), give up (1st), offer (2nd), reject (5th), surrender (5th), yield (4th) **B.** gift (K), loss (K), offering (2nd)

sad (K): depressed (5th), down (K), grim (4th), pitiful (3rd), serious (4th), unhappy (1st), woeful (4th)

saddle (4th): A. perch (4th), seat (1st) **B.** burden (5th), impose (4th), load (2nd), strain (4th)

sadness (1st): depression (6th), gloom (3rd), grief (5th), sorrow (4th)

safe (K): A. guarded (1st), protected (4th), secure (3rd), sound (1st), unharmed (3rd), unhurt (2nd) **B.** cautious (5th), harmless (3rd), wary (5th) **C.** strong box (2nd), vault (5th) **D.** accurate (6th), believable (3rd), certain (1st), dependable (3rd), reliable (5th), true (1st)

saffron (4th)

sag (1st): dip (1st), drip (2nd), droop (5th), fall (K), lower (1st), sink (3rd), slide (2nd), slip (3rd), slump (5th), wilt (4th)

saga (6th): adventure (3rd), fantasy (6th), legend (5th), story (K), tale (3rd)

sage (4th): clever (3rd), enlightened (4th), just (1st), knowing (1st), prudent (6th), wise (1st)

sagebrush (4th)

said (K)

sail (1st): A. outing (1st), trip (1st), voyage (4th) **B.** coast (2nd), drift (2nd), float (1st)

sailor (3rd): mariner (5th), seaman (2nd)

saint (3rd): angel (4th), holy person (5th), model (3rd)

sake (3rd): account (3rd), behalf (6th), benefit (3rd), cause (2nd), gain (2nd), goal (4th), good (K), interest (1st), motive (5th), objective (2nd), purpose (2nd), reason (2nd), welfare (5th)

salamander (3rd)

salary (3rd): commission (2nd), earnings (1st), income (4th), pay (K), wage (3rd)

sale (1st): A. bargain (4th), discount (3rd), special (2nd) **B.** deal (2nd), exchange (4th), trade (2nd)

salesperson (6th): clerk (2nd), representative (4th), seller (1st)

sally (5th): A. depart (5th), go (K), leave (1st), set out (1st) **B.** expedition (4th), journey (3rd), trip (1st), venture (4th)

saloon (6th): bar (3rd), lounge (6th), pub (1st), tavern (5th)

salmon (3rd)

saloon (6th): bar (3rd), pub (1st), tavern (5th)

salt (1st): flavor (4th), season (2nd)

salute (4th): address (K), bow (1st), cheer (3rd), greet (3rd), hail (4th), honor (1st), nod (1st), recognize (3rd), welcome (1st)

salvation (6th): deliverance (5th), freedom (3rd), liberation (3rd), release (5th), rescue (4th)

same (K): alike (1st), constant (4th), duplicate (6th), equal (2nd), equivalent

(6th), even (1st), identical (6th), like (K), matching (3rd)

sample (5th): A. taste (1st), test (3rd), try (K) **B.** case (2nd), example (2nd), illustration (4th), member (2nd), model (3rd), part (1st), piece (1st), portion (4th), section (4th)

sanction (6th): approve (4th), authorize (3rd), back (1st), conform (6th), consent (3rd), license (5th), permit (3rd), support (4th), warrant (5th)

sand (1st): A. gravel (4th) **B.** finish (1st), grate (4th), grind (4th), polish (4th)

sandstone (2nd): sedimentary rock formed by the consolidation and compaction of sand

sane (6th): logical (6th), normal (5th), reasonable (2nd), sensible (6th), sound (1st), stable (4th)

sap (1st): drain (5th), exhaust (4th), wear (1st)

sapling (5th): bush (2nd), tree (K), young tree (1st)

sapphire (6th)

sardine (4th)

sash (6th): band (1st), belt (2nd), ribbon (4th)

sassafras (4th)

satellite (6th): A. moon (1st), orbiter (4th) **B.** adherent (6th), attendant (3rd), disciple (6th), follower (2nd), supporter (4th) **C.** dependent (3rd), subordinate (6th)

satin (3rd)

satisfy (3rd): A. baby (K), comfort (3rd), content (3rd), delight (3rd), please (K), spoil (4th) **B.** achieve (5th),

answer (1st), complete (3rd), do (K), fill (1st), finish (1st), fulfill (2nd), meet (K), pay (K), settle (2nd)

Saturday (1st)

satyr (6th)

sauce (3rd): flavoring (4th), relish (6th), seasoning (2nd), topping (1st)

saunter (6th): ramble (6th), roam (4th), rove (6th), stroll (5th), walk (K), wander (3rd)

Saurischians (5th): lizard-hipped dinosaurs

sausage (4th): breakfast meat (1st), frank (4th), meat (1st)

sauté (4th): cook (1st), fry (1st)

savage (5th): angry (1st), fierce (4th), primitive (5th), uncivilized (4th), not tame (4th), violent (5th), wild (2nd)

save (1st): A. rescue (4th), salvage (6th) **B.** economize (4th), maintain (4th), preserve (4th) **C.** but (K), except (2nd) **D.** accumulate (6th), collect (3rd), protect (4th), store (K)

savior (6th): deliverer (5th), liberator (3rd), rescuer (4th)

savor (6th): A. flavor (4th), salt (1st), season (2nd) **B.** enjoy (2nd), sample (5th), taste (1st)

savory (6th): flavorful (4th), juicy (1st), moist (4th), tasty (1st), tender (3rd)

saw (K): cut (K), divide (4th), split (4th)

sawmill (1st)

say (K): A. choice (3rd), opinion (3rd), turn (1st) **B.** announce (3rd), assert (6th), claim (2nd), express (5th), speak (1st), state (1st), swear (4th), talk (K)

scabbard (6th)

scale (3rd): A. coat (1st), cover (1st), peel (2nd), skin (1st) **B.** climb (1st)

scamper (4th): dart (1st), move quickly (2nd), run (K), rush (2nd), sprint (5th)

scan (5th): browse (6th), dip into (1st), glance (3rd), view (1st)

scandal (6th): crime (2nd), dishonor (2nd), disturbance (6th), misconduct (3rd), outrage (6th), shame (3rd)

scant (6th): bare (3rd), few (1st), inferior (5th), lacking (1st), limited (3rd), scarce (1st), short (1st)

scar (5th): fault (3rd), flaw (2nd)

scarce (4th): barely (3rd), few (1st), hardly (1st), rare (4th), scant (6th), seldom (4th), uncommon (3rd), unusual (3rd), wanting (1st)

scare (1st): alarm (3rd), fright (2nd), frighten (2nd), horrify (4th), shock (1st), startle (4th), terrify (3rd)

scarecrow (1st)

scared (1st): frightened (2nd), nervous (1st), on edge (1st)

scarf (6th): sash (6th), shawl (6th), tie (1st)

scatter (3rd): drop (1st), litter (2nd), spread (2nd)

scene (1st): A. area (3rd), arena (5th), locale (4th), place (1st), setting (1st), site (5th), theater (3rd) **B.** event (3rd), incident (5th), occurrence (3rd), spectacle (5th), background (2nd), setting (1st), situation (4th), tableau (6th)

scent (3rd): bouquet (6th), fragrance (5th), odor (3rd), perfume (3rd), smell (3rd)

schedule (6th): A. arrange (3rd), organize (4th), plan (1st) **B.** book (K), calendar (1st), dates (1st), list (2nd), listing (2nd), program (4th)

scheme (5th): A. organize (4th), plan (1st), prepare (1st), think out (1st) **B.** design (5th), intent (5th), plan (1st), project (4th), purpose (1st), strategy (6th)

scholar (5th): intellectual (4th), learner (1st), pupil (4th), student (3rd)

school (K): A. educate (3rd), teach (1st), train (K), tutor (6th) **B.** group (1st), institute (5th)

schoolwork (1st): homework (1st)

science (3rd): information (5th), knowledge (2nd), methods (2nd), principles (4th)

scientist (3rd)

scissors (5th)

scoff (6th): jeer (5th), laugh at (1st), ridicule (6th), sneer (6th)

scold (5th): accuse (4th), blame (2nd), charge (2nd), complain (4th), criticize (5th), fault (3rd)

scoop (4th): A. facts (1st), information (5th), report (2nd) **B.** ladle (4th), spoon (1st) **C.** bucket (3rd), dig (1st), shovel (1st)

scope (6th): A. glass (1st), lens (1st), microscope (4th), telescope (4th) **B.** amount (2nd), degree (5th), extent (4th), measure (2nd), range (3rd), size (1st), span (6th)

scorch (6th): bake (1st), burn (3rd), roast (4th), toast (5th)

score (1st): amount (2nd), count (1st), grade (2nd), mark (1st), rate (1st), record (2nd), sum (1st), total (2nd)

scorn (4th): attack (3rd), contempt (5th), insult (5th), mock (4th), reject (5th), slight (4th), tease (3rd)

scorpion (5th)

scour (6th): A. look (K), search (1st), separate (3rd), sift (4th), sort (1st) **B.** clean (1st), scrape (4th), scrub (6th), wash (1st)

scourge (6th): bad luck (1st), curse (3rd), evil (3rd), misfortune (3rd), plague (5th)

scout (1st): A. escort (5th), guide (1st), leader (1st) **B.** examine (5th), explore (4th), investigate (5th), observe (3rd), spy (4th), survey (5th)

scow (6th)

scramble (4th): A. hurry (1st), race (1st), rush (2nd) **B.** clash (5th), fight (K), struggle (1st) **C.** blend (5th), confuse (4th), disorder (3rd), mix (1st)

scrap (3rd): A. abandon (4th), discard (6th), junk (3rd) **B.** argument (3rd), battle (2nd), disagreement (3rd), quarrel (4th) **C.** fragment (6th), part (1st), patch (4th), piece (1st), rag (1st), remainder (2nd), shred (5th)

scrapbook (3rd): album (1st), chronicle (6th), record (2nd)

scrape (4th): A. bind (2nd), difficulty (5th), fix (1st), trouble (1st) **B.** brush (2nd), clean (1st), cut (K), graze (5th), hurt (1st), irritate (6th), rub (1st), scour (6th), scratch (4th), scrub (6th), shave (1st)

scratch (4th): A. cut (K), scrape (4th), shave (1st) **B.** cut (K), scar (5th), wound (3rd)

scream (1st): cry (1st), roar (1st), screech (5th), shout (1st), yell (K)

screech (1st): See scream.

screen (5th): A. barrier (6th), blind (3rd), cover (1st), shade (2nd) **B.** guard (1st), hide (1st), protect (4th), shield (4th) **C.** filter (5th), sieve (5th)

screw (3rd): A. fasten (4th), turn (1st), twist (1st) **B.** bolt (4th), clamp (5th), fastener (4th)

screwdriver (3rd)

scroll (5th): A. list (2nd), manuscript (6th), paper (K) **B.** move (K), unroll (1st)

scrub (6th): brush (2nd), clean (1st), rub (1st), scour (6th), scrape (4th), wash (1st), wipe (1st)

scuff (5th): brush (2nd), rub (1st), scrape (4th)

scull (6th): A. racer (1st), shell (1st) **B.** propel (6th), row (K)

sculptor (4th): artist (2nd), carver (4th)

sculpture (4th): figure (2nd), statue (4th)

scuttle (4th): damage (5th), destroy (2nd), ruin (5th), wreck (4th)

scurvy (6th)

sea (K): abundance (5th), a lot (K), host (4th), ocean (1st)

seal (K): A. brand (2nd), label (3rd), mark (1st), stamp (2nd) **B.** cement (4th), close (K), glue (1st), secure (3rd), shut (1st), stick (K), tape (1st)

seam (5th): connection (3rd), joint (4th)

search (1st): A. quest (3rd), scouting (1st) **B.** examine (5th), explore (4th), hunt (2nd), inspect (5th), investigate (5th)

277

season (2ⁿᵈ): A. flavor (4ᵗʰ), salt (1ˢᵗ), spice (3ʳᵈ) **B.** age (1ˢᵗ), cycle (5ᵗʰ), period (2ⁿᵈ), span (6ᵗʰ), term (3ʳᵈ), time (1ˢᵗ) **C.** accustom (4ᵗʰ), harden (2ⁿᵈ), ripen (2ⁿᵈ), toughen (5ᵗʰ)

seat (1ˢᵗ): A. lead (1ˢᵗ), place (1ˢᵗ), put (K) **B.** assign (5ᵗʰ), elect (3ʳᵈ) **C.** bench (4ᵗʰ), chair (K), couch (4ᵗʰ)

second (1ˢᵗ): A. instant (3ʳᵈ), moment (1ˢᵗ) **B.** following (1ˢᵗ), next (K), other (1ˢᵗ), runner-up (2ⁿᵈ)

secret (1ˢᵗ): A. code (3ʳᵈ), mystery (1ˢᵗ), puzzle (4ᵗʰ) **B.** concealed (4ᵗʰ), covered (1ˢᵗ), hidden (1ˢᵗ), private (3ʳᵈ), unknown (2ⁿᵈ)

secretary (4ᵗʰ): assistant (4ᵗʰ), clerk (2ⁿᵈ), helper (1ˢᵗ)

secretary (4ᵗʰ)

section (4ᵗʰ): area (3ʳᵈ), division (4ᵗʰ), part (1ˢᵗ), piece (1ˢᵗ), portion (4ᵗʰ)

secure (3ʳᵈ): A. acquire (4ᵗʰ), get (K) **B.** attach (5ᵗʰ), close (K), fix (1ˢᵗ), lock (1ˢᵗ), tape (1ˢᵗ) **C.** defend (5ᵗʰ), guard (1ˢᵗ), protect (4ᵗʰ) **D.** comfortable (3ʳᵈ), guarded (1ˢᵗ), protected (4ᵗʰ), safe (1ˢᵗ)

see (K): look (K), notice (1ˢᵗ), observe (3ʳᵈ), view (2ⁿᵈ), watch (1ˢᵗ)

sedimentary (5ᵗʰ): of or relating to rocks formed by the deposition of sediment

see (K): notice (1ˢᵗ), observe (3ʳᵈ)

seed (1ˢᵗ): A. child (K), heir (4ᵗʰ), offspring (2ⁿᵈ) **B.** beginning (1ˢᵗ), start (1ˢᵗ) **C.** center (2ⁿᵈ), core (6ᵗʰ), pit (1ˢᵗ)

seek (1ˢᵗ): explore (4ᵗʰ), hunt (2ⁿᵈ), investigate (5ᵗʰ), look (K), pursue (5ᵗʰ), search (1ˢᵗ)

seem (1ˢᵗ): appear (2ⁿᵈ), look like (K)

seep (4ᵗʰ): drain (5ᵗʰ), drip (2ⁿᵈ), leak (6ᵗʰ), soak (5ᵗʰ)

seesaw (1ˢᵗ): bounce (6ᵗʰ), change (2ⁿᵈ), shift (4ᵗʰ), rotate (4ᵗʰ), up and down (K)

Seismosaurus (5ᵗʰ): literally "earth-shaking lizard;" a type of large plant-eating dinosaur

seize (3ʳᵈ): catch (1ˢᵗ), clasp (4ᵗʰ), get (K), grab (4ᵗʰ), grasp (4ᵗʰ), handle (2ⁿᵈ), hold (1ˢᵗ), pull (K), steal (3ʳᵈ), take (1ˢᵗ)

seizures (6ᵗʰ)

seldom (4ᵗʰ): few (1ˢᵗ), not often (1ˢᵗ), not usual (3ʳᵈ), occasional (3ʳᵈ), rarely (4ᵗʰ), scarce (4ᵗʰ), uncommon (3ʳᵈ), unusual (3ʳᵈ)

select (4ᵗʰ): choose (1ˢᵗ), put aside (3ʳᵈ)

self (3ʳᵈ): being (1ˢᵗ), I (K), individual (3ʳᵈ), me (K), person (1ˢᵗ)

selfish (5ᵗʰ): childish (4ᵗʰ), grabby (4ᵗʰ), greedy (5ᵗʰ), mean (1ˢᵗ), miserly (5ᵗʰ), taking (1ˢᵗ),

sell (K): bargain (4ᵗʰ), market (1ˢᵗ), merchandise (6ᵗʰ), offer (2ⁿᵈ), trade (2ⁿᵈ)

Senate (1ˢᵗ): legislature (5ᵗʰ), ruling body (2ⁿᵈ)

senate (1ˢᵗ): A. assembly (6ᵗʰ), council (5ᵗʰ) **B.** chamber (5ᵗʰ), hall (1ˢᵗ)

semitropical (5ᵗʰ): subtropical (5ᵗʰ)

send (K): convey (4ᵗʰ), deliver (5ᵗʰ), direct (1ˢᵗ), mail (1ˢᵗ), ship (1ˢᵗ), transmit (4ᵗʰ)

senior (6ᵗʰ): aged (1ˢᵗ), chief (1ˢᵗ), elder (5ᵗʰ), first (1ˢᵗ), higher (1ˢᵗ), older (1ˢᵗ), over (K), superior (4ᵗʰ)

sensation (5ᵗʰ): A. marvel (4ᵗʰ), spectacle (5ᵗʰ), wonder (1ˢᵗ) **B.** awareness (3ʳᵈ), emotion (4ᵗʰ), feeling (1ˢᵗ), impression (5ᵗʰ), passion (6ᵗʰ), sense (1ˢᵗ)

sense (1ˢᵗ): A. feeling (1ˢᵗ), instinct (5ᵗʰ), judgment (3ʳᵈ), opinion (3ʳᵈ) **B.** intent (5ᵗʰ), meaning (1ˢᵗ), message (1ˢᵗ) **C.** intelligence (4ᵗʰ), mind (1ˢᵗ), understanding (1ˢᵗ)

sensible (6ᵗʰ): intelligent (4ᵗʰ), objective (2ⁿᵈ), practical (4ᵗʰ), realistic (5ᵗʰ), reasonable (3ʳᵈ), sane (6ᵗʰ), thoughtful (2ⁿᵈ), wise (1ˢᵗ)

sensitive (5ᵗʰ): A. irritated (6ᵗʰ), painful (3ʳᵈ), sore (4ᵗʰ), touchy (1ˢᵗ) **B.** clever (3ʳᵈ), delicate (5ᵗʰ), emotional (4ᵗʰ), feeling (1ˢᵗ), knowing (1ˢᵗ), psychic (6ᵗʰ), secret (1ˢᵗ)

sensitivity (5ᵗʰ): A. allergy (5ᵗʰ), reaction (5ᵗʰ) **B.** compassion (6ᵗʰ), concern (3ʳᵈ), emotion (4ᵗʰ), sympathy (4ᵗʰ), understanding (1ˢᵗ)

sent (K)

sentence (1ˢᵗ): A. condemn (4ᵗʰ), fine (1ˢᵗ), judge (1ˢᵗ) **B.** finding (1ˢᵗ), judgment (3ʳᵈ), ruling (2ⁿᵈ), tax (K), verdict (6ᵗʰ)

sentiment (5ᵗʰ): A. attitude (5ᵗʰ), belief (1ˢᵗ), feeling (1ˢᵗ), opinion (3ʳᵈ) **B.** affection (4ᵗʰ), caring (1ˢᵗ), emotion (4ᵗʰ), passion (6ᵗʰ), warmth (1ˢᵗ)

sentinel (5ᵗʰ): guard (1ˢᵗ), lookout (2ⁿᵈ), patrol (1ˢᵗ), sentry (5ᵗʰ), watch (1ˢᵗ)

sentry (5ᵗʰ): guard (1ˢᵗ), lookout (2ⁿᵈ), watch (1ˢᵗ)

separate (3ʳᵈ): A. divide (4ᵗʰ), part (1ˢᵗ), pull apart (3ʳᵈ), sort (1ˢᵗ) **B.** different (1ˢᵗ), distinct (5ᵗʰ), exclusive (6ᵗʰ), free (K), independent (3ʳᵈ), individual (3ʳᵈ), lone (2ⁿᵈ), sole (4ᵗʰ)

September (1ˢᵗ)

sequoia (2ⁿᵈ)

serene (6ᵗʰ): calm (3ʳᵈ), composed (4ᵗʰ), even (1ˢᵗ), gentle (3ʳᵈ), peaceful (2ⁿᵈ), quiet (K), still (1ˢᵗ), tranquil (6ᵗʰ), unchanging (3ʳᵈ)

serf (6ᵗʰ): peasant (4ᵗʰ), servant (3ʳᵈ), slave (3ʳᵈ), worker (1ˢᵗ)

serge (6ᵗʰ)

sergeant (5ᵗʰ)

series (4ᵗʰ): chain (3ʳᵈ), line (K), order (1ˢᵗ), pattern (3ʳᵈ), routine (6ᵗʰ), row (K), run (K), trend (2ⁿᵈ)

serious (4ᵗʰ): A. earnest (4ᵗʰ), grim (4ᵗʰ), sad (K), sober (4ᵗʰ), solemn (5ᵗʰ), stern (4ᵗʰ), thoughtful (2ⁿᵈ) **B.** acute (6ᵗʰ), alarming (3ʳᵈ), critical (5ᵗʰ), dangerous (6ᵗʰ), scary (1ˢᵗ) **C.** important (1ˢᵗ), significant (6ᵗʰ)

sermon (5ᵗʰ): instruction (4ᵗʰ), lecture (5ᵗʰ), lesson (3ʳᵈ), preaching (4ᵗʰ), talk (K)

serpent (5ᵗʰ): asp (4ᵗʰ), snake (5ᵗʰ)

servant (3ʳᵈ): aide (5ᵗʰ), assistant (4ᵗʰ), attendant (3ʳᵈ), employee (5ᵗʰ), helper (K)

serve (1ˢᵗ): assist (4ᵗʰ), attend (3ʳᵈ), help (K), lend a hand (1ˢᵗ), obey (3ʳᵈ), provide (3ʳᵈ), supply (1ˢᵗ), wait on (1ˢᵗ)

service (1ˢᵗ): A. install (6ᵗʰ), maintain (4ᵗʰ), repair (4ᵗʰ), upkeep (2ⁿᵈ) **B.** ceremony (5ᵗʰ), observance (3ʳᵈ), rite (6ᵗʰ), ritual (6ᵗʰ) **C.** assistance (4ᵗʰ), attention (2ⁿᵈ), courtesy (4ᵗʰ), favor (2ⁿᵈ), kindness (2ⁿᵈ)

session (6th): assembly (4th), conference (4th), meeting (1st), period (2nd)

set (K): A. agreed (2nd), established (3rd), regular (3rd), routine (6th), usual (3rd) **B.** group (1st), series (4th) **C.** prepared (1st), primed (5th), ready (1st)

settle (2nd): A. decide (1st), determine (5th), find (K), judge (1st) **B.** drop (1st), lower (1st), sink (3rd) **C.** arrange (3rd), calm (3rd), establish (3rd), order (1st), quiet (K), set (K), straighten (3rd)

seven (K)

seventeen (1st)

seventy (1st)

several (1st): few (1st), numerous (4th), some (K), three (K), various (4th)

severe (4th): A. plain (2nd), prim (5th), prudish (6th), unadorned (6th) **B.** hard (K), harsh (5th), rigid (5th), stern (4th), strict (6th) **C.** dangerous (6th), extreme (5th), violent (5th) **D.** demanding (5th), difficult (5th), hard (K), intense (6th)

sew (2nd): fix (1st), mend (1st), stitch (6th)

sex (3rd)

shabby (4th): dirty (1st), faded (1st), inferior (5th), poor (K), run down (K), worn (3rd)

shade (2nd): A. blend (5th), color (K), hue (6th), tone (3rd) **B.** blind (3rd), protect (4th), screen (1st), shield (4th) **C.** degree (5th), slight (4th), touch (1st) **D.** blot out (4th), cloud (1st), obscure (6th), shadow (3rd)

shadow (3rd): A. chase (1st), follow (1st), tail (1st), trace (3rd), track (1st), trail (2nd) **B.** dim (1st), shade (2nd) **C.** cloud (1st), confuse (4th), obscure

(6th) **D.** darkness (1st), gloom (3rd), sadness (1st)

shaft (4th): A. beam (3rd), glimmer (6th), ray (1st) **B.** passage (4th), path (1st), tunnel (2nd) **C.** pole (1st), rod (1st), tube (3rd) **D.** cheat (3rd), deceive (5th), offend (4th)

shaggy (5th): hairy (1st), raggedy (5th)

shake (1st): agitate (5th), jar (K), jog (2nd), loosen (5th), move (K), quake (4th), rattle (2nd), rock (K), stir (3rd), upset (3rd), vibrate (5th)

shale (5th): an easily broken rock composed of layers of claylike sediments

shall (1st): should (1st), will (K), would (1st)

shallow (4th): A. not deep (1st) **B.** meaningless (3rd), silly (1st), surface (3rd), vain (4th)

shaman (5th): A. healer (3rd), magician (5th), sorcerer (4th), witch (1st), wizard (6th)

shame (3rd): A. burden (5th), guilt (4th), remorse (6th), sorrow (4th) **B.** blame (2nd), disgrace (4th), dishonor (3rd), fault (3rd), humiliate (4th)

shape (1st): A. figure (4th), form (1st), outline (4th) **B.** carve (1st), conceive (4th), craft (2nd), design (5th), devise (4th), fashion (3rd), make (K), mold (5th), sculpt (5th) **C.** condition (3rd), fitness (3rd), state (1st)

share (2nd): A. due (2nd), portion (4th) **B.** cooperate (5th), lend (K), use (K)

shark (1st)

sharp (1st): A. alert (5th), bright (1st), clever (3rd), crafty (2nd), keen (4th),

280

knowing (1st), quick (1st), sly (4th), smart (1st) **B.** acid (4th), sour (2nd), tart (5th) **C.** accurate (6th), acute (6th), clear (2nd), exact (2nd), precise (5th) **D.** high (K), piercing (4th), pointed (1st) **E.** cutting (1st), harsh (5th), hurtful (1st)

shatter (5th): break (1st), burst (3rd), destroy (2nd), fracture (4th), fragment (6th), smash (3rd)

shave (1st): A. brush (2nd), graze (5th), scrape (4th), skim (6th), touch (1st) **B.** crop (2nd), cut (K), reduce (3rd), trim (4th)

shawl (6th): cape (4th), cloak (4th), scarf (6th), wrap (3rd)

she (K): female (4th), girl (K), her (K)

sheaf (6th): batch (2nd), bundle (5th), pile (1st)

shear (5th): clip (2nd), crop (2nd), cut (K), lop (1st), shave (1st), trim (4th)

sheep (K)

sheer (5th): A. absolute (3rd), full (K), perfect (3rd), pure (3rd), total (2nd), very (K) **B.** sharp (1st), steep (2nd), vertical (1st) **C.** delicate (5th), filmy (4th), transparent (5th)

sheet (1st): A. coating (1st), cover (1st), film (4th), layer (4th), top (K) **B.** page (1st), paper (K), tissue (5th)

shelf (6th): ledge (5th), reef (5th), sill (1st)

shell (1st): A. bullet (4th), shot (1st) **B.** armor (4th), covering (1st), plate (K), protection (4th), shield (4th) **C.** bark (3rd), body (1st), case (2nd), coat (1st), frame (3rd), skin (1st)

shellfish (5th)

shelter (4th): A. conceal (4th), cover (1st), harbor (2nd), hide (1st), protect

(4th), shield (4th) **B.** enclosure (4th), housing (1st), lodging (4th), port (3rd), refuge (5th), retreat (4th), room (K)

shepherd (4th): conduct (3rd), direct (1st), guide (1st), lead (1st), pilot (5th), steer (4th)

sherbet (5th)

sheriff (4th)

shield (4th): A. armor (4th), barrier (6th), defense (5th), protection (4th), shell (1st) **B.** mask (2nd), plate (K) **C.** conceal (4th), cover (1st), defend (5th), disguise (5th), protect (4th), screen (1st), shelter (4th)

shift (4th): adjust (5th), alter (4th), change (2nd), move (K), rearrange (3rd), reverse (5th), transfer (5th), turn (1st), vary (4th)

shimmer (5th): gleam (1st), glitter (4th), luster (4th), radiance (6th), reflect (4th), shine (1st), sparkle (5th)

shine (1st): glaze (6th), gleam (1st), glitter (4th), polish (4th), reflect (4th), shimmer (5th), sparkle (5th)

shiny (3rd)

ship (1st): A. export (5th), mail (1st), move (K), send (1st), shift (4th), transfer (5th) **B.** ark (2nd), boat (1st), craft (2nd), freighter (4th), liner (K), vessel (4th)

shipment (5th): cargo (5th), freight (4th), load (2nd), package (4th)

shipwreck (5th)

shirk (6th): avoid (3rd), duck (K), put off (1st)

shirt (1st): blouse (1st), tee (1st), top (K)

shiver (1ˢᵗ): quake (4ᵗʰ), shake (1ˢᵗ), shudder (4ᵗʰ), tremble (3ʳᵈ), vibrate (5ᵗʰ)

shock (1ˢᵗ): A. horror (4ᵗʰ), surprise (1ˢᵗ), thrill (4ᵗʰ) **B.** amaze (5ᵗʰ), astonish (4ᵗʰ), jar (K), offend (4ᵗʰ), scare (1ˢᵗ), startle (4ᵗʰ), stun (4ᵗʰ)

shoe (K): boot (1ˢᵗ), footwear (1ˢᵗ), slipper (5ᵗʰ)

shoemaker (2ⁿᵈ)

shoot (3ʳᵈ): A. branch (2ⁿᵈ), growth (2ⁿᵈ), spurt (5ᵗʰ) **B.** fling (6ᵗʰ), launch (5ᵗʰ), throw (2ⁿᵈ), toss (2ⁿᵈ) **C.** fire (K), hit (K), kill (1ˢᵗ), wound (3ʳᵈ)

shop (1ˢᵗ): A. buy (K), purchase (3ʳᵈ), seek (1ˢᵗ) **B.** booth (5ᵗʰ), business (2ⁿᵈ), market (1ˢᵗ), store (K)

shoplift (3ʳᵈ): pocket (1ˢᵗ), rob (K), steal (3ʳᵈ), take (1ˢᵗ)

shoplift (3ʳᵈ)

shore (1ˢᵗ): A. beach (1ˢᵗ), coast (2ⁿᵈ) **B.** base (1ˢᵗ), brace (5ᵗʰ), foundation (5ᵗʰ), prop (5ᵗʰ), strengthen (2ⁿᵈ), support (4ᵗʰ)

short (1ˢᵗ): A. brief (3ʳᵈ), low (K), small (K) **B.** incomplete (3ʳᵈ), lacking (1ˢᵗ) **C.** abrupt (5ᵗʰ), rude (2ⁿᵈ), sharp (1ˢᵗ), tactless (6ᵗʰ) **D.** fast (1ˢᵗ), hasty (2ⁿᵈ), sudden (1ˢᵗ)

shortly (1ˢᵗ): directly (1ˢᵗ), immediately (3ʳᵈ), presently (2ⁿᵈ), promptly (4ᵗʰ), quickly (1ˢᵗ), soon (K)

shot (1ˢᵗ): A. attempt (2ⁿᵈ), chance (2ⁿᵈ), effort (2ⁿᵈ), opportunity (3ʳᵈ), try (1ˢᵗ) **B.** tired (2ⁿᵈ), useless (2ⁿᵈ) **C.** bullet (4ᵗʰ), lead (1ˢᵗ), round (1ˢᵗ), shell (1ˢᵗ)

should (1ˢᵗ)

shoulder (1ˢᵗ): bear (K), burden (5ᵗʰ), carry (1ˢᵗ), lift (1ˢᵗ), push (1ˢᵗ), shove (5ᵗʰ), trans port (5ᵗʰ)

shouldn't (1ˢᵗ)

shout (1ˢᵗ): A. cheer (3ʳᵈ), cry (K), howl (4ᵗʰ), yelp (6ᵗʰ) **B.** bellow (4ᵗʰ), call (1ˢᵗ), hail (4ᵗʰ), scream (1ˢᵗ), yell (K)

shove (5ᵗʰ): A. push (1ˢᵗ), thrust (4ᵗʰ) **B.** drive (1ˢᵗ), force (1ˢᵗ), move (K), press (1ˢᵗ), push (1ˢᵗ)

shovel (1ˢᵗ): A. dig (1ˢᵗ), groove (5ᵗʰ), mine (1ˢᵗ), trench (5ᵗʰ) **B.** backhoe (2ⁿᵈ), bulldozer (1ˢᵗ), plow (4ᵗʰ), scoop (4ᵗʰ), spade (6ᵗʰ)

show (1ˢᵗ): A. act (K), drama (5ᵗʰ), performance (4ᵗʰ), theater (3ʳᵈ) **B.** demonstration (6ᵗʰ), display (3ʳᵈ), exhibition (4ᵗʰ), pretense (2ⁿᵈ) **C.** demonstrate (6ᵗʰ), display (3ʳᵈ), exhibit (4ᵗʰ), present (K), prove (1ˢᵗ), reveal (4ᵗʰ)

showroom (4ᵗʰ): display room (3ʳᵈ), merchandise display (6ᵗʰ), sales floor (1ˢᵗ)

shred (5ᵗʰ): A. rip (1ˢᵗ), slice (5ᵗʰ), splinter (6ᵗʰ), tear (2ⁿᵈ) **B.** bit (1ˢᵗ), dab (1ˢᵗ), end (K), fragment (6ᵗʰ), particle (5ᵗʰ), piece (1ˢᵗ), rag (1ˢᵗ), scrap (3ʳᵈ)

shrewd (6ᵗʰ): careful (1ˢᵗ), clever (1ˢᵗ), crafty (2ⁿᵈ), intelligent (4ᵗʰ), prudent (6ᵗʰ), sharp (1ˢᵗ), sly (4ᵗʰ), smart (1ˢᵗ), wary (5ᵗʰ)

shriek (4ᵗʰ): cry (1ˢᵗ), scream (1ˢᵗ), shout (1ˢᵗ), yell (K)

shrill (5ᵗʰ): acute (6ᵗʰ), high (K), piercing (4ᵗʰ), sharp (1ˢᵗ)

shrine (5ᵗʰ): memorial (4ᵗʰ), monument (2ⁿᵈ), statue (4ᵗʰ), temple (3ʳᵈ), tomb (5ᵗʰ)

shrink (5th): A. hesitate (4th), recoil (5th), retire (4th), retreat (4th) **B.** collapse (5th), compress (4th), contract (3rd), dry (1st), reduce (3rd), waste (1st), wilt (4th), wither (5th)

shroud (6th): A. camouflage (5th), cloak (4th), conceal (4th), cover (1st), darken (2nd), disguise (5th), envelope (5th), hide (1st) **B.** mask (2nd), pretense (2nd), sheet (1st), shield (4th), veil (3rd), wrap (3rd) **shrub (4th):** bush (2nd), hedge (4th), thicket (4th)

shrug (4th): show indifference (5th), toss one's head (3rd), turn aside (3rd)

shudder (4th): A. pulse (5th), shake (1st), shiver (1st), vibrate (5th) **B.** quake (4th), quiver (4th), tremble (3rd)

shun (6th): avoid (3rd), disregard (4th), exclude (6th), ignore (5th), neglect (4th), omit (6th), pass (2nd), skip (2nd)

shut (1st): A. block (1st), stop (K) **B.** closed (1st), fastened (4th), latched (4th) **C.** close (1st), lock (1st), secure (3rd), slam (5th)

shutter (4th): blind (3rd), shade (2nd), window cover (2nd)

shuttle (5th): carry (1st), haul (4th), transport (5th)

shutter (4th)

shuttle (5th)

shy (K): A. avoid (3rd), retreat (3rd), shrink (5th) **B.** insufficient (3rd), scant (6th), scarce (4th), short (1st) **C.** afraid (1st), bashful (4th), doubtful (5th), hesitant (4th), modest (4th), reluctant (6th), timid (5th), uncertain (2nd), unsure (2nd)

sick (K): A. offended (4th), revolted (5th), shocked (1st), upset (3rd) **B.** hurt (K), ill (1st), injured (5th), not healthy (1st), unwell (2nd)

sickle (6th): blade (2nd), knife (1st), reaper blade (4th)

side (K): A. angle (3rd), aspect (5th), view (2nd) **B.** squad (6th), support (4th), team (1st) **C.** back (1st), border (1st), curb (3rd), edge (1st), face (1st), margin (5th), surface (3rd), wall (K)

sidekick (2nd): companion (3rd), friend (1st), pal (K), partner (5th)

sidewalk (1st): path (1st), pavement (5th), walk (K)

siege (5th): A. contain (5th), surround (3rd) **B.** attack (3rd), campaign (3rd), encirclement (5th)

sieve (5th): filter (5th), screen (1st), sifter (4th), strainer (4th)

sift (4th): comb (2nd), filter (5th), pick (1st), screen (1st), select (4th), separate (3rd), search (1st), sieve (5th), sort (2nd)

sigh (3rd): A. deep breath (1st), sob (1st), wail (5th) **B.** groan (3rd), moan (5th), sob (1st)

sight (1st): A. perception (6th), picture (K), scene (1st), spot (1st), view (2nd), vision (4th) **B.** rarity (4th), spectacle (5th), wonder (1st) **C.** focus (5th), look (K), notice (1st), see (K)

sign (1st): A. clue (2nd), hint (1st), indicator (4th), key (K), lead (1st), mark (1st), pointer (1st), signal (4th), symbol (5th), tip (1st), token (5th), trace (3rd) **B.** autograph (6th), character (2nd) **C.** flag (3rd), indicate (4th), show (1st), signal (4th) **D.** announcement (4th), banner (3rd)

signal (4th): A. alarm (3rd), bell (K), clue (2nd), cue (2nd), hint (1st), pointer (1st), sign (1st), symptom (6th) **B.** indicate (4th), warn (3rd) **C.** caution (5th), directional (1st), guiding (1st), warning (3rd)

signature (6th): A. acceptance (3rd), approval (4th) **B.** autograph (6th), label (3rd), logo (4th), mark (1st), name (K), symbol (5th)

significant (6th): essential (6th), formidable (6th), huge (1st), important (1st), impressive (5th), meaningful (3rd), momentous (6th), substantial (5th), vital (5th)

signify (6th): identify (4th), indicate (4th), mean (1st), represent (4th), show (1st), signal (4th), symbolize (5th)

silent (3rd): A. dumb (1st), mute (6th), speechless (2nd) **B.** calm (3rd), peaceful (1st), quiet (K), still (1st)

silk (3rd): fiber (3rd), soft fabric (5th)

silkworm (3rd)

silly (1st): absurd (6th), comic (5th), crazy (4th), foolish (3rd), funny (1st), humorous (4th), mindless (2nd)

Silurian (5th): of or belonging to the geologic time, system of rocks, or sedimentary deposits of the third period of the Paleozoic Era

silver (1st)

similar (4th): alike (1st), comparable (3rd), equal (2nd), like (K), matching (3rd), parallel (5th), related (4th), same (1st), uniform (1st)

simmer (4th): boil (3rd), bubble (2nd), cook (1st), stew (2nd)

simple (1st): A. natural (2nd), primitive (5th), undeveloped (5th) **B.** foolish (2nd), innocent (5th), modest (4th), slow (1st), stupid (4th) **C.** basic (6th), childish (3rd), clear (2nd), direct (1st),

easy (1st), elementary (3rd), frank (4th), logical (6th), plain (2nd), understandable (3rd)

simulate (6th): affect (4th), copy (3rd), imitate (5th), pretend (2nd)

sin (1st): A. err (6th), misbehave (4th), offend (4th), wrong (1st) **B.** crime (2nd), dishonor (3rd), evil (3rd), fault (3rd), offense (4th), vice (4th)

since (1st): A. because (K), due to (2nd) **B.** after (K). subsequent (6th)

sincere (4th): direct (1st), earnest (4th), frank (4th), genuine (5th), honest (3rd), open (K), real (1st), true (1st), truthful (2nd)

sinew (6th): muscle (4th), power (1st), strength (1st)

sing (1st): A. glorify (3rd), honor (1st), praise (4th) **B.** carol (3rd), chant (5th), chirp (2nd), harmony (4th)

single (3rd): A. divorced (4th), unmarried (2nd), widowed (4th) **B.** alone (1st), distinct (5th), exclusive (6th), lone (2nd), odd (4th), one (K), only (K), separate (3rd), sole (4th), solitary (5th), solo (5th), unique (6th)

sink (3rd): A. collapse (5th), drop (K), fall (K), settle (2nd), tilt (5th) **B.** basin (4th), tub (1st), washbowl (2nd)

sip (1st): A. drink (1st), lick (1st), nip (1st), sample (5th) **B.** drink (1st), sample (5th), suck (1st), taste (1st)

sir (1st): knight (2nd), man (K)

sire (4th): A. father (K), mate (4th), parent (3rd) **B.** breed (4th), create (3rd), originate (3rd)

sister (1st): female (4th), girl (K)

sit (K): model (3rd), perch (4th), pose (2nd), relax (4th), rest (1st), roost (2nd)

site (5th): area (3rd), arena (5th), location (3rd), place (1st), scene (1st), spot (1st)

sitting (1st): A. period (2nd), session (6th) **B.** lounging (6th), relaxing (4th), resting (1st)

situation (4th): A. environment (6th), place (1st), setting (1st) **B.** circumstance (6th), condition (3rd), difficulty (5th), position (2nd), problem (1st), rank (3rd), state (1st)

sit-up (1st)

six (K)

sixteen (1st)

sixth (1st)

sixty (1st)

size (1st): amount (2nd), extent (4th), magnitude (4th), measure (2nd), quantity (4th), scope (6th)

skate (1st): coast (2nd), glide (4th), skim (6th), slide (2nd)

skateboard (2nd)

skeleton (4th): bones (1st), frame (3rd), outline (4th), shape (1st), structure (4th)

sketch (5th): A. draw (K), outline (4th) **B.** drawing (1st), illustration (4th), study (1st) **C.** performance (4th), scene (1st), story (K)

skill (2nd): ability (3rd), aptitude (5th), art (K), craft (2nd), education (3rd), grace (5th), knowledge (2nd), mastery (2nd), practice (1st), talent (2nd)

skim (6th): A. brush (2nd), scrape (4th), touch (1st) **B.** cream (1st), remove (2nd), take (1st) **C.** coast (2nd), fly (1st), glide (4th), skate (1st), slide (2nd) **D.** glance at (3rd), scan (6th)

skin (1st): A. cut (K), hurt (K), scrape (4th) **B.** peel (2nd), shave (1st), strip (3rd) **C.** bark (3rd), case (2nd), coating (1st), covering (1st), fur (K), hide (1st), outside (1st), peel (2nd), shell (1st), surface (3rd), wrapper (3rd)

skinny (1st): bony (1st), gaunt (6th), lean (3rd), narrow (2nd), slender (4th), slim (5th), thin (2nd)

skip (2nd): A. disregard (4th), exclusion (6th), oversight (2nd) **B.** bounce (6th), caper (1st), jump (K), hop (K), leap (3rd), spring (1st) **C.** exclude (6th), ignore (5th), miss (K), omit (6th), pass (2nd)

skirt (3rd): A. avoid (3rd), hedge (4th) **B.** clothing (1st), garment (4th) **C.** approach (3rd), border (1st), edge (1st)

skull (5th): face (1st), head (1st), skeleton (4th)

skunk (K): A. beat (1st), best (K), outdo (K), win (1st) **B.** cheat (3rd), fool (2nd), trick (1st)

sky (K): atmosphere (4th), heavens (1st), space (1st)

Skylab (4th): the United States' first space station

skyline (5th): horizon (4th), outline of buildings (4th)

skyrocket (3rd): bomb (5th), explosive (3rd), fireworks (1st), rocket (K)

slab (5th): block (1st), board (1st), piece (1st), plank (5th), slice (5th)

slam (5th): A. close (K), fling (6th), shut (1st) **B.** hit (K), knock (3rd) **C.** bang (3rd), crash (2nd) **D.** smash (3rd), strike (2nd)

slant (6th): A. incline (5th), misrepresent (4th), pitch (2nd) **B.** angle (3rd), attitude (5th), belief (1st), bias (6th), hill (1st), leaning (3rd), opinion (3rd), ramp (6th), view (2nd) **C.** angle (4th), cant (6th),incline (5th), lean (3rd), list (2nd), rake (1st), slope (3rd), tilt (5th), tip (1st)

slap (2nd): A. box (K), cuff (1st), strike (2nd) **B.** clap (2nd), hit (K), knock (3rd), rap (1st), smack (6th), spank (2nd) **C.** insult (5th), jeer (5th)

slash (6th): A. break (1st), crack (4th), wound (3rd) **B.** condense (6th), edit (3rd), reduce (3rd), shorten (1st) **C.** beat (1st), lash (4th), whip (4th) **D.** drop (K), reduction (3rd) **E.** line (K), streak (5th), stroke (1st) **F.** cut (K), pierce (4th), punch (4th), rip (1st), slice (5th), slit (5th), tear (2nd)

slate (1st): A. book (K), plan (1st), program (4th), schedule (6th) **B.** arrange (3rd), list (2nd), organize (4th), register (4th) **C.** blackboard (2nd), chalkboard (5th)

slaughter (5th): A. butchering (4th), killing (1st), massacre (6th), murder (3rd) **B.** butcher (4th), execute (5th), kill (1st), slay (4th)

slave (3rd): A. labor (2nd), toil (4th), work (K) **B.** bondsman (3rd), serf (6th), servant (3rd)

slay (4th): execute (5th), kill (1st), murder (3rd), slaughter (5th)

sled (5th): A. glide (4th), ride (K), slide (2nd) **B.** sledge (6th)

sledge (6th): hammer (2nd), sled (5th)

sleek (3rd): A. polish (4th), shine (1st) **B.** elegant (5th), neat (K), oily (1st), polished (4th), shiny (1st), smooth (2nd)

sleep (K): A. nap (K), repose (6th), rest (1st), slumber (4th) **B.** nap (K), nod (1st), retire (4th), snooze (4th)

sleeve (5th): envelope (5th), file (1st), folder (1st)

slender (4th): A. bony (1st), gaunt (6th), lank (5th), light (K), narrow (2nd), skinny (1st), slight (4th), slim (5th), small (1st), thin (2nd)

slice (5th): A. bit (1st), lot (K), part (1st), piece (1st), portion (4th), section (4th), share (2nd) **B.** carve (4th), cut (K), measure (2nd), rip (1st), shred (5th), slash (6th), tear (2nd)

slide (2nd): A. chute (5th), shaft (4th), trough (6th), tube (3rd) **B.** picture (K), transparency (5th) **C.** coast (2nd), descend (6th), dip (1st), dive (1st), drop (1st), fall (K), float (1st), glide (4th), plunge (4th), skim (6th), slip (3rd), sneak (4th), tumble (4th)

slight (4th): A. attack (3rd), insult (5th), offend (4th) **B.** casual (5th), minor (5th), petty (6th), unimportant (2nd) **C.** ignore (5th), omit (6th) **D.** delicate (5th), faint (3rd), feeble (4th), frail (6th), light (K), little (K), narrow (2nd), slender (4th), slim (5th), thin (2nd), weak (3rd)

slim (5th): A. diet (4th), reduce (3rd) **B.** casual (5th), marginal (5th), petty (6th) **C.** lank (5th), narrow (2nd), skinny (1st), slender (4th), slight (4th), thin (2nd)

slip (3rd): A. accident (4th), error (4th), mistake (1st) **B.** stumble (4th), trip (1st), tumble (4th) **C.** drift (2nd), glide (4th), skim (6th), slide (2nd) **D.** drop (1st), fall (K), settle (2nd) **E.** fall (K), spill (1st) **F.** err (6th), fumble (5th) **G.** decline (6th), dip (1st) **H.** card (1st), note (1st), paper (K) **I.** petticoat (6th), under-dress (2nd), underwear (1st) **J.** lapse (6th), miss (K), pass (K)

slipper (5th): house shoe (1st), moccasin (2nd), shoe (4th)

slit (5th): A. crack (4th), opening (1st), tear (2nd), trench (5th) **B.** cut (K), rip (1st), slash (6th), slice (5th)

slither (4th): crawl (1st), creep (1st), glide (4th), skim (6th), slide (2nd), snake (5th), sneak (4th)

slob (5th): messy person (1st), tramp (4th)

slope (3rd): A. bluff (6th), hill (1st), ramp (6th), rise (1st), slant (6th), tilt (5th) **B.** angle (3rd), bank (1st), grade (2nd), incline (5th), pitch (2nd)

sloth (5th)

slouch (6th): A. lazybones (4th), loafer (4th), lounger (6th) **B.** bend (K), droop (5th), hunch over (6th), slump (5th), stoop (5th)

slow (1st): A. backward (4th), dull (1st), stupid (4th) **B.** inactive (3rd), unhurried (2nd) **C.** endless (2nd), long (1st) **D.** crawling (1st), gradual (3rd), hesitant (4th), methodical (4th), not hasty (2nd)

slug (5th)

slugger (5th): batter (1st), fighter (1st), hitter (1st)

slumber (4th): A. repose (6th), snooze (4th) **B.** nap (K), nod (1st), rest (1st), sleep (K)

slump (5th): A. decline (6th), fall (K), plunge (4th) **B.** bend (K), bow (1st), collapse (5th), dip (1st), drop (1st), lower (1st), sag (1st), slide (2nd), slip (3rd)

sly (4th): A. secret (1st), sneaky (4th), subtle (6th), tricky (1st) **B.** artful (3rd), clever (3rd), crafty (2nd), foxy (1st), sharp (1st), shifty (4th), shrewd (6th)

smack (6th): A. accurate (6th), exact (2nd), right (K) **B.** blow (K), hit (K), punch (4th), slap (2nd) **C.** bang (3rd), box (K), clap (2nd), knock (3rd), jar (K), rap (1st), spank (2nd), strike (2nd)

small (K): A. minor (5th), unimportant (2nd) **B.** brief (3rd), compact (5th), limited (3rd), nominal (5th), token (5th) **C.** grudging (5th), mean (1st), petty (6th) **D.** little (K), mini (6th), miniature (6th), narrow (2nd), slight (4th), thin (1st), tiny (2nd)

smart (1st): A. hurt (K), pinch (4th), sting (2nd) **B.** painful (2nd), sore (4th) **C.** fashionable (3rd), stylish (3rd), trendy (2nd) **D.** alert (5th), brilliant (4th), clever (3rd), intelligent (4th), knowing (1st), quick (1st), sharp (1st), sly (4th), wise (1st), witty (2nd)

smart house (1st): A. homes equipped with networks that allow users to regulate and control devices in their home with ease **B.** houses or buildings where many systems such as temperature, lighting, alarms, and some chores are automated

smash (3rd): A. accident (4th), blow (1st), crash (2nd), hit (K), impact (6th), wreck (4th) **B.** defeat (5th), overthrow (2nd) **C.** break (1st), destroy (2nd), destruct (6th), knock (3rd), shatter (5th), slam (5th), splinter (6th), strike (2nd)

smear (3rd): A. blacken (1st), defame (4th), libel (6th) **B.** defamation (4th), false accusation (4th) **C.** blot (4th), soil (2nd), spot (1st) **D.** blur (4th), dirty (1st), spread (2nd), stain (4th)

smell (3rd): A. scent (3rd), sniff (4th) **B.** detect (4th), perceive (6th), sense (1st) **C.** fragrance (5th), odor (3rd), savor (6th)

smile (1st): A. beam (3rd), grin (1st), laugh (1st) **B.** grin (1st), laugh (1st)

smite (5th): attack (3rd), beat (1st), hit (K), strike (2nd)

smog (5th): fog (1st), fumes (3rd), gases (1st), pollution (3rd)

smoke (1st): A. breath in (1st), puff (2nd) **B.** burn (3rd), rage (4th), steam (2nd) **C.** cloud (1st), exhaust (4th), fog (1st), smog (5th)

smooth (2nd): A. polished (4th), silky (3rd), shiny (1st), sleek (3rd), soft (K) **B.** mellow (6th), mild (4th), poised (6th) **C.** even (1st), flat (2nd), level (3rd) **D.** flatten (4th), plane (1st) **E.** easy (K), simple (1st) **F.** improve (3rd), polish (4th), soften (1st) **G.** calm (3rd), hush (3rd), soothe (5th) **H.** charming (3rd), cultured (6th), elegant (5th), flowing (1st), refined (6th)

smother (6th): A. dampen (5th), put out (1st) **B.** cover (1st), wrap (3rd) **C.** conceal (4th), mask (2nd), suppress (5th) **D.** dull (1st), mute (6th), soften (K) **E.** choke (1st), gag (1st), strangle (6th), suffocate (6th)

smuggle (6th): sneak in (4th), transport illegally (5th)

snack (2nd): A. nip (1st), taste (1st) **B.** bite (1st), food (K), meal (3rd)

snail (1st): crawl (1st), creep (1st), inch (1st)

snake (1st)

snap (2nd): A. catch (1st), clip (2nd), fastener (4th), pin (K) **B.** clasp (4th), hook (4th), link (5th) **C.** crack (4th), pop (K) **D.** break (1st), click (2nd)

snare (6th): A. bag (1st), hook (4th), pit (1st), trap (1st) **B.** attract (5th), bait (3rd), capture (3rd), catch (1st), entrap (3rd), lure (5th), tangle (3rd), tempt (4th)

snarl (5th): A. confusion (4th), disarray (5th), disorder (3rd), mess (1st), tangle (3rd) **B.** bark (3rd) **C.** menace (5th), snap at (2nd), threaten (5th) **D.** complicate (6th), entangle (4th), knot (4th), twist (1st)

snatch (4th): catch (1st), grab (4th), nab (1st), seize (3rd), steal (3rd), take (1st)

sneak (4th): A. prowler (2nd), snake (5th) **B.** creep (1st), glide (4th), hide (1st), shrink (5th), slip (3rd), slither (4th), steal (3rd)

sneer (6th): A. insult (5th), jeer (5th), put-down (1st) **B.** mock (4th), taunt (5th), torment (5th)

sneeze (5th)

sniff (4th): perceive (6th), scent (3rd), smell (3rd), track (1st), whiff (5th)

snooze (4th): A. sleep (K), slumber (4th) **B.** nap (K), rest (1st)

snore (6th): breathe loudly (1st), saw logs (1st)

snorkel (5th): A. dive (1st), swim (K) **B.** breathing tube (3rd), swimmer's air supplier (1st)

snort (5th): A. grunt (3rd), honk (1st) **B.** grunt (3rd), honk (1st), sniff (4th)

snout (5th): beak (4th), bill (1st), muzzle (6th), nose (1st)

snow (K): A. blizzard (4th), white ice (K) **B.** coax (6th), deceive (5th), trick (1st)

snowball (K): A. enlarge (5th), grow (1st), increase (3rd) **B.** pressed snow (1st), rolled snow (1st)

snowman (K)

288

snowstorm (2nd): blizzard (4th), heavy downpour (3rd)

snuff (6th): A. scent (3rd), smell (3rd), sniff (4th) **B.** dampen (5th), put out (1st)

snug (6th): comfortable (3rd), content (3rd), secure (3rd), soft (K)

snuggle (5th): cradle (4th), cuddle (5th), hold (1st), hug (1st), love (K), nuzzle (1st)

so (K): A. extremely (5th), very (K) **B.** positive (2nd), real (1st), true (K) **C.** also (K), consequently (4th), hence (3rd), therefore (2nd), thus (1st), too (1st)

soak (5th): spray (2nd), water down (K), wet (K)

soap (4th): A. cleaner (1st), scrub (6th) **B.** clean (K), wash (1st)

soar (6th): arise (4th), ascend (4th), fly (K), lift (1st), rise (1st)

sob (1st): cry (1st), moan (5th), wail (5th), weep (4th)

sober (4th): A. calm (3rd), quiet (K), subdue (6th) **B.** earnest (4th), grave (3rd), logical (6th), moderate (4th), reasonable (3rd), sensible (6th), serious (4th), solemn (5th)

soccer (1st): ball game (1st), field game (2nd), football (1st)

social (1st): collective (4th), friendly (1st), neighborly (2nd), public (1st)

society (3rd): association (5th), club (1st), colony (3rd), community (2nd), company (2nd), institution (5th), organization (4th), people (K), public (1st), tribe (3rd), union (3rd), culture (6th)

sock (1st): A. foot covering (1st), slipper (5th) **B.** hit (K), punch (4th), strike (2nd)

socket (6th): holder (1st), hollow (3rd), opening (1st)

socks (1st)

sod (6th): grass (1st), land (K), mud (1st), turf (5th)

sodden (6th): A. dull (1st), lifeless (2nd), sober (4th), solemn (5th) **B.** dripping (1st), soaked (5th), spongy (3rd), wet (K)

soft (K): calm (3rd), comfortable (3rd), cottony (2nd), flexible (6th), gentle (3rd), luxurious (4th), mild (4th), movable (2nd), mushy (5th), silky (3rd), smooth (2nd), tender (3rd), velvety (4th)

soil (2nd): A. blot (4th), darken (2nd), dirty (1st), smear (3rd), stain (4th), taint (6th) **B.** dirt (1st), earth (1st), ground (1st), land (K), mud (1st)

solar (4th)

solar system (4th)

soldier (3rd): brave (1st), fighter (K), hero (1st), knight (2nd), trooper (3rd), warrior (4th)

sole (4th): exclusive (6th), individual (3rd), lone (2nd), odd (4th), one (K), particular (4th), separate (3rd), single (3rd), solitary (5th), unique (6th)

solemn (5th): dire (6th), earnest (4th), grave (3rd), important (1st), profound (6th), serious (4th), sober (4th)

solid (3rd): close (K), compact (5th), firm (2nd), hard (1st), reliable (5th), rigid (5th), secure (3rd), set (K), sound (1st), strong (K), thick (2nd), tight (1st), trusted (1st)

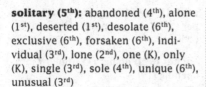

solitary (5ᵗʰ): abandoned (4ᵗʰ), alone (1ˢᵗ), deserted (1ˢᵗ), desolate (6ᵗʰ), exclusive (6ᵗʰ), forsaken (6ᵗʰ), individual (3ʳᵈ), lone (2ⁿᵈ), one (K), only (K), single (3ʳᵈ), sole (4ᵗʰ), unique (6ᵗʰ), unusual (3ʳᵈ)

solution (5ᵗʰ): A. fluid (6ᵗʰ), liquid (3ʳᵈ), mixture (4ᵗʰ) **B.** answer (1ˢᵗ), conclusion (3ʳᵈ), cure (4ᵗʰ), explanation (4ᵗʰ), key (K), relief (4ᵗʰ), remedy (4ᵗʰ), resolution (5ᵗʰ), result (2ⁿᵈ)

solve (4ᵗʰ): determine (5ᵗʰ), examine (5ᵗʰ), explain (2ⁿᵈ), penetrate (5ᵗʰ), resolve (5ᵗʰ)

sombrero (6ᵗʰ)

some (K): a few (1ˢᵗ), any (1ˢᵗ), several (1ˢᵗ), various (4ᵗʰ)

somebody (1ˢᵗ): being (1ˢᵗ), human (3ʳᵈ), individual (3ʳᵈ), person (1ˢᵗ), someone (1ˢᵗ)

someday (1ˢᵗ): at last (1ˢᵗ), eventually (5ᵗʰ), finally (3ʳᵈ), ultimately (6ᵗʰ)

someone (1ˢᵗ): being (1ˢᵗ), human (3ʳᵈ), individual (3ʳᵈ), person (1ˢᵗ), somebody (1ˢᵗ)

something (1ˢᵗ): article (2ⁿᵈ), element (3ʳᵈ), item (5ᵗʰ), object (1ˢᵗ), part (1ˢᵗ), thing (K)

sometimes (1ˢᵗ): now and then (1ˢᵗ), occasionally (6ᵗʰ), once in a while (1ˢᵗ)

somewhere (1ˢᵗ): place (1ˢᵗ), unspecified location (5ᵗʰ)

son (K): boy (K), junior (4ᵗʰ), heir (4ᵗʰ), lad (K)

song (K): air (1ˢᵗ), melody (4ᵗʰ), poem (3ʳᵈ), rhyme (6ᵗʰ), tune (1ˢᵗ), verse (4ᵗʰ)

sonic (2ⁿᵈ): audible (6ᵗʰ), noisy (1ˢᵗ), of the speed of sound (3ʳᵈ)

sonnet (6ᵗʰ): poem (3ʳᵈ), rhyme (6ᵗʰ), verse (4ᵗʰ)

soon (K): directly (1ˢᵗ), presently (2ⁿᵈ), promptly (4ᵗʰ), quickly (1ˢᵗ), rapidly (4ᵗʰ), shortly (1ˢᵗ), swiftly (4ᵗʰ)

soothe (5ᵗʰ): calm (3ʳᵈ), comfort (3ʳᵈ), compose (4ᵗʰ), lull (1ˢᵗ), quiet (K), relieve (4ᵗʰ), soften (1ˢᵗ)

sorcerer (4ᵗʰ): healer (3ʳᵈ), magician (5ᵗʰ), shaman (5ᵗʰ), witch (1ˢᵗ), wizard (6ᵗʰ)

sore (4ᵗʰ): A. annoyed (5ᵗʰ), irritated (6ᵗʰ), mad (K) **B.** aching (5ᵗʰ), painful (2ⁿᵈ), sensitive (5ᵗʰ), tender (3ʳᵈ)

sorrow (4ᵗʰ): ache (5ᵗʰ), agony (5ᵗʰ), care (1ˢᵗ), distress (5ᵗʰ), grief (5ᵗʰ), heartache (6ᵗʰ), pain (2ⁿᵈ), regret (5ᵗʰ), remorse (6ᵗʰ), sadness (2ⁿᵈ), suffering (2ⁿᵈ), torment (5ᵗʰ), trouble (1ˢᵗ), woe (4ᵗʰ), worry (1ˢᵗ)

sorry (2ⁿᵈ): A. hopeless (2ⁿᵈ), inferior (5ᵗʰ), poor (K), shabby (4ᵗʰ) **B.** contrite (5ᵗʰ), depressed (5ᵗʰ), gloomy (3ʳᵈ), remorseful (6ᵗʰ), repentant (6ᵗʰ), sad (K)

sort (1ˢᵗ): A. group (1ˢᵗ), organize (4ᵗʰ), systemize (2ⁿᵈ) **B.** class (1ˢᵗ), division (4ᵗʰ), kind (K), order (1ˢᵗ), section (4ᵗʰ), type (1ˢᵗ)

soul (3ʳᵈ): center (2ⁿᵈ), heart (K), individual (3ʳᵈ), mind (1ˢᵗ), personality (5ᵗʰ), self (3ʳᵈ), spirit (2ⁿᵈ)

sound (1ˢᵗ): A. express (5ᵗʰ), pronounce (4ᵗʰ), say (K) **B.** chime (6ᵗʰ), ring (1ˢᵗ), toll (6ᵗʰ) **C.** chord (5ᵗʰ), music (K), noise (1ˢᵗ), note (1ˢᵗ), tone (3ʳᵈ) **D.** complete (3ʳᵈ), correct (3ʳᵈ), logical (6ᵗʰ), reasonable (3ʳᵈ), whole (1ˢᵗ), wise (1ˢᵗ) **E.** firm (2ⁿᵈ), fit (K), healthy (1ˢᵗ), intact (6ᵗʰ), safe (1ˢᵗ), secure (3ʳᵈ), solid (3ʳᵈ), strong (K), well (1ˢᵗ)

soup (1st): broth (4th), chowder (5th)

sour (2nd): A. disenchant (6th), disillusion (6th) **B.** acidify (4th), spoil (4th) **C.** acid (4th), sharp (1st), spoiled (4th), tart (5th) **D.** gloomy (3rd), glum (4th), sulky (5th), unhappy (2nd)

source (4th): author (3rd), authority (3rd), basis (5th), beginning (2nd), cause (2nd), creation (3rd), foundation (5th), fund (4th), maker (1st), origin (3rd), parent (3rd), reason (2nd), reference (5th), root (3rd), seed (1st), start (1st), store (K), supply (2nd)

south (1st)

sovereign (4th): A. emperor (4th), king (1st), master (1st), ruler (2nd) **B.** dominant (5th), free (K), independent (3rd), lone (2nd), separate (3rd)

space (1st): A. break (1st), crack (4th), gap (K), opening (1st), split (4th) **B.** arrange (3rd), rank (3rd) **C.** area (3rd), atmosphere (4th), capacity (6th), region (4th), room (1st)

spade (6th): A. dig (1st), trench (5th) **B.** scoop (4th), shovel (1st)

span (6th): A. continuation (2nd), depth (5th), distance (4th), interval (6th), length (2nd) **B.** cross (1st), range (3rd), reach (1st), stretch (4th) **C.** age (1st), cycle (5th), era (6th), life (1st), period (2nd), season (2nd), stage (3rd), survival (5th), term (3rd)

spank (2nd): hit (K), paddle (1st), slap (2nd), smack (6th)

spar (5th): A. battle (2nd), fight (K), quarrel (4th) **B.** beam (3rd), plank (5th) **C.** argue (3rd), box (K), combat (5th), struggle (1st)

spare (3rd): A. free (K), rescue (4th), save (1st) **B.** extra (1st), more (K), other (1st), surplus (6th) **C.** conserve (5th), hold onto (1st) **D.** bare (3rd), few (1st), poor (K), scant (6th) **E.** lank (5th), skinny (1st), thin (2nd)

spark (3rd): A. life (1st), spirit (2nd) **B.** beam (3rd), flicker (5th), glimmer (6th), hint (1st), light (K), trace (3rd) **C.** activate (3rd), awaken (3rd), cause (2nd), excite (4th), generate (4th), ignite (6th), motivate (6th), prompt (4th), stimulate (6th)

sparkle (5th): A. flash (2nd), gleam (1st), glimmer (6th) **B.** glisten (6th), glitter (4th), shimmer (5th), shine (1st), twinkle (4th) **C.** animation (6th), energy (4th), spirit (2nd), vigor (5th)

sparrow (5th)

spasm (6th): attack (3rd), contraction (3rd), cramp (6th), fit (K), seizure (3rd)

speak (1st): address (K), chat (1st), express (5th), lecture (5th), preach (4th), say (K), talk (K)

spear (4th): A. pierce (4th), stab (5th) **B.** lance (4th), sword (4th)

spearhead (5th): A. lead (1st), pioneer (4th) **B.** forefront (4th), front (1st), head (1st)

special (2nd): A. bargain (4th), deal (2nd), sale (1st) **B.** different (1st), favorite (3rd), individual (3rd), odd (4th), personal (3rd), pet (1st), remarkable (4th), select (4th), specific (5th), unique (6th), unusual (3rd)

species (5th): class (1st), division (4th), family (K), group (1st), kind (K), order (1st), set (K), type (1st), variety (4th)

specific (5th): certain (1st), clear (2nd), detailed (5th), distinct (5th), exact (2nd), individual (3rd), particular (4th), precise (5th), special (2nd)

specimen (5th): case (2nd), example (2nd), illustration (4th), representative (4th), sample (5th)

speck (4th): bit (1st), dab (1st), dot (K), drop (1st), fragment (6th), particle (5th), pinch (4th), scrap (3rd), tad (1st)

spectacle (5th): demonstration (6th), event (3rd), marvel (4th), scene (1st), sensation (5th), vision (4th), wonder (1st)

spectacles (5th): eyeglasses (4th), glasses (1st)

spectator (5th): attendee (3rd), onlooker (2nd), patron (5th), tourist (5th), viewer (2nd), watcher (1st)

spectrum (6th): assortment (5th), extent (4th), range (3rd), reach (1st), scope (6th), variety (4th)

speculate (6th): assume (5th), bet (1st), chance (2nd), consider (2nd), contemplate (6th), gamble (5th), imagine (2nd), ponder (6th), presume (6th), propose (4th), suggest (2nd), suppose (2nd), surmise (6th), theorize (5th), think (1st), wager (3rd)

speech (2nd): address (K), conversation (5th), language (2nd), lecture (5th), speaking (1st), statement (3rd), talk (K)

speed (3rd): A. haste (3rd), hurry (1st), rate (1st), swiftness (4th) **B.** race (1st), run (K), rush (2nd), sprint (5th), zoom (4th)

spell (1st): A. mean (1st), signify (6th), write out (1st) **B.** cycle (5th), period (2nd), span (6th), term (3rd) **C.** charm (3rd), enchantment (6th), magic (1st) **D.** relieve (4th), replace (5th), substitute (5th)

spend (2nd): consume (4th), dispose of (5th), employ (5th), exhaust (4th), expend (3rd), finish (1st), use (K), waste (1st)

sphere (6th): A. ball (K), globe (4th), orb (4th) **B.** area (3rd), domain (5th), kingdom (3rd), realm (4th), territory (3rd)

spice (3rd): A. flavor (4th), improve (3rd), season (2nd) **B.** herb (5th), incense (5th), perfume (3rd), scent (3rd)

spider (K)

spike (4th): A. pierce (4th), prick (5th), stick (K) **B.** bolt (4th), nail (2nd), peg (1st), pin (K), stud (6th)

spill (1st): A. fall (K), tumble (4th) **B.** confess (4th), exclaim (3rd), report (1st) **C.** flood (2nd), overflow (5th), pour (3rd), surge (5th)

spin (1st): A. circle (K), curl (2nd), loop (5th), revolve (5th), rotate (4th), turn (1st), twirl (3rd) **B.** drive (1st), ride (K)

spinach (2nd)

spine (4th): A. backbone (4th), ridge (5th) **B.** courage (4th), determination (5th), resolution (5th)

spire (6th): crown (1st), peak (4th), point (1st), summit (5th), tip (1st)

spirit (2nd): A. bravery (2nd), courage (4th), daring (2nd), initiative (6th), strength (1st) **B.** heart (K), mind (1st), nature (1st), soul (3rd), wit (1st) **C.** atmosphere (4th), attitude (5th), character (2nd), mood (3rd)

spirits (2nd): alcohol (4th), liquor (5th)

spiritual (5th): goodly (1st), heavenly (1st), pure (3rd), sacred (4th), unearthly (3rd)

spit (3rd): A. sprinkle (3rd), sputter (3rd) **B.** point (1st), spear (4th) **C.** hiss (3rd), jeer (5th), sneer (6th) **D.** pierce (4th), spear (4th)

spite (3rd): A. grudge (5th), hate (2nd), hostility (4th), malice (6th), resentment (5th) **B.** annoy (5th), hurt (K), injure (5th), needle (3rd), pester (2nd), plague (5th), tease (3rd)

splash (1st): A. shower (4th), squirt (4th), stain (4th) **B.** smear (3rd), spot (1st), spray (2nd), sprinkle (3rd)

splendid (4th): beautiful (1st), brilliant (4th), elegant (5th), glorious (3rd), great (1st), magnificent (4th), outstanding (2nd), superb (6th), terrific (5th), wonderful (1st)

splendor (4th): brilliance (4th), distinction (5th), glory (3rd), luster (4th)

splinter (6th): A. bit (1st), fragment (6th), piece (1st), shred (5th) **B.** break (1st), shatter (5th), smash (3rd)

split (4th): A. apart (3rd), parted (1st) **B.** break (1st), crack (4th), gap (K), space (1st) **C.** chop (2nd), cut (K), divide (4th), divorce (4th), escape (2nd), flee (5th), leave (1st), open (K), run (K), separate (3rd), slice (5th)

splotch (5th): A. smear (3rd), soil (2nd), splash (1st) **B.** blot (4th), patch (4th), spot (1st), stain (4th)

spoil (4th): A. baby (K), humor (4th), indulge (5th) **B.** corrupt (6th), decay (5th), destroy (2nd), devastate (6th), disintegrate (5th), harm (3rd), ravage (6th), rot (1st), ruin (5th)

spoke (1st): A. addressed (1st), chatted (1st), conversed (5th), said (K), talked (1st) **B.** handle (2nd), ladder bar (3rd), rod (1st)

sponge (3rd)

spool (2nd): cylinder (6th), wheel (1st)

spoon (1st): dipper (1st), ladle (4th), scoop (4th)

sport (1st): A. frolic (6th), play (K) **B.** cheer (3rd), contest (4th), exercise (1st), fun (K), game (1st)

sportsman (2nd): athlete (5th), fair player (1st), fisherman (1st), good loser (1st), graceful winner (3rd), hunter (2nd)

sportswoman (2nd): athlete (5th), fair player (1st), good loser (1st), graceful winner (3rd)

spot (1st): A. area (3rd), location (3rd), place (1st), point (1st), position (2nd), scene (1st), site (5th) **B.** blemish (5th), blot (4th), dab (1st), mess (1st) **C.** detect (4th), glimpse (4th), locate (3rd), see (K), sight (1st) **D.** mark (1st), smear (3rd), stain (4th) **E.** ad (4th), commercial (5th), promotion (5th)

spout (5th): A. chute (5th), drain (5th), lip (1st), nose (1st), tube (3rd) **B.** erupt (4th), explode (3rd), jet (K), shoot (3rd), spurt (5th), squirt (4th), tap (K)

sprawl (6th): expand (5th), extend (4th), fan out (K), flare (6th), spread (2nd), stretch (4th), unfold (2nd)

spray (2nd): A. explode (3rd), hose (6th), spout (5th), sprinkle (3rd), spurt (5th), squirt (4th) **B.** jet (K), mist (1st), shower (4th), splash (1st)

spread (2nd): A. apply (2nd), rub (1st) **B.** depth (5th), distance (4th), expansion (5th), range (3rd), sprawl (6th) **C.** array (5th), organize (4th), set (K) **D.** farm (K), ranch (5th) **E.** blanket (3rd), cover (1st) **F.** arrangement (3rd), layout (2nd) **G.** broaden (3rd), enlarge (5th), expand (5th), extend (4th), fan

(K), flare (6th), open (K), scatter (3rd), stretch (4th)

spring (K): A. coil (5th), flexibility (6th), hop (4th), skip (2nd), stretchiness (4th) **B.** appear (2nd), jump (K), leap (3rd), pop up (1st)

sprinkle (3rd): A. misting (1st), scattering (3rd), spitting (3rd) **B.** dust (2nd), powder (3rd), rain (1st), shower (4th), spray (2nd), spread (2nd)

sprint (5th): A. race (1st), run (K) **B.** hurry (1st), speed (3rd)

spruce (3rd): A. evergreen tree (4th), pine (1st) **B.** neat (K), sleek (3rd), trim (3rd)

spur (4th): A. arouse (4th), dig (1st), encourage (4th), prod (6th), prompt (4th), urge (4th) **B.** claw (1st), hook (4th), spike (4th), stimulus (6th)

spurt (5th): A. flow (1st), jet (K), squirt (4th) **B.** ejaculate (6th), shoot (3rd), spout (5th), surge (5th)

sputter (3rd): bubble (2nd), foam (4th), shower (4th), spit (3rd), spray (2nd)

spy (4th): A. agent (5th), detective (4th), informer (5th) **B.** bug (1st), examine (5th), investigate (5th), observe (3rd), scout (1st)

squadron (6th): division (4th), fleet (6th), formation (4th), troop (3rd)

square (2nd): A. block (1st), cube (4th) **B.** fair (1st), honest (3rd), just (1st) **C.** park (1st), place (1st) **D.** accurate (6th), equal (2nd), even (1st), exact (2nd), right (K) **E.** agree (2nd), conform (6th), correspond (5th), fit (K), harmonize (4th)

squash (2nd): bruise (5th), compact (5th), compress (4th), crush (4th), jam (K), mash (4th), pack (1st), press (1st),

push (1st), squeeze (5th), stomp (4th), trample (5th)

squat (5th): A. fat (1st), short (1st), stout (4th) **B.** bend (K), crouch (5th), hunch (6th), shrink (5th), sit (K)

squawk (2nd): complain (4th), cry (1st), howl (4th), scream (1st), shriek (4th), wail (5th), whine (5th), yell (K)

squeak (2nd): A. creak (4th), peep (4th) **B.** cry (K), whimper (5th), yelp (6th)

squeeze (5th): A. clasp (4th), compression (4th), crowding (2nd), hug (1st) **B.** compact (5th), compress (4th), crush (4th), drain (5th), embrace (4th), hold (1st), mash (4th), milk (1st), press (1st), squash (2nd), wring (5th)

squid (3rd)

squire (4th): A. gentleman (3rd), landlord (4th), owner (2nd) **B.** attendant (3rd), escort (5th), partner (5th), servant (3rd) **C.** boss (K), conduct (3rd), usher (6th)

squirm (2nd): move (K), slither (4th), snake (5th), writhe (6th)

squirrel (1st): accumulate (6th), collect (3rd), gather (1st), save (1st)

squirt (4th): A. flow (1st), fountain (3rd), spray (2nd) **B.** jet (K), shoot (3rd), splash (1st), spout (5th), spurt (5th), surge (5th), wet (K)

stab (5th): A. cut (K), lunge (6th), pain (2nd), punch (4th), slash (6th) spasm (6th), throb (5th) **B.** hurt (K), lance (4th), penetrate (5th), pierce (4th), spear (4th), thrust (4th), wound (3rd) **C.** attempt (2nd), chance (2nd), guess (1st), try (1st)

stable (4th): A. barn (K), stall (5th) **B.** consistent (3rd), constant (4th), durable (6th), enduring (4th), even (1st), firm (4th), lasting (1st), permanent (5th), reliable (5th), resolute (5th), sane (6th), secure (3rd), solid (3rd), sound (1st), steady (3rd)

stack (6th): A. pile (1st), rank (3rd), rate (1st), sort (2nd) **B.** bank (1st), cluster (4th), group (1st), heap (4th), mass (3rd), mound (2nd)

staff (4th): A. equip (5th), furnish (4th), supply (1st) **B.** crew (2nd), employees (5th), faculty (6th) **C.** baton (5th), cane (3rd), pole (1st), rod (1st), stick (K), wand (3rd)

stag (1st)

stage (3rd): A. level (3rd), place (1st), platform (4th), site (5th) **B.** perform (4th), present (K), produce (2nd) **C.** condition (3rd), cycle (5th), period (2nd), phase (6th), span (6th), step (1st), time (1st)

stagger (4th): A. falter (1st), halt (4th), hesitate (4th), lurch (5th), reel (5th), stumble (4th), sway (3rd), totter (6th), waver (5th) **B.** amaze (5th), astonish (4th), awe (6th), confound (6th)

stain (4th): A. dirty (1st), spot (1st), taint (6th), tint (5th) **B.** blemish (5th), blot (4th), color (K), dye (2nd), paint (2nd), smear (3rd), soil (2nd)

stair (2nd): steps (1st), riser (2nd)

stake (1st): A. bet (1st), claim (2nd), finance (4th), risk (4th) **B.** cane (3rd), pole (1st), post (1st), rod (1st), stick (K) **C.** bankroll (2nd), fortune (3rd), fund (4th), interest (3rd), money (K), prize (3rd), reward (4th), share (2nd)

stalagmite (5th): calcium deposit (6th), cave floor formation (4th)

stale (2nd): foul (4th), musty (2nd), old (K), rusty (2nd), spoiled (4th), sour (2nd), tired (2nd)

stalk (4th): A. bunch (3rd), stem (2nd), trunk (4th) **B.** chase (1st), follow (1st), hunt (2nd), pursue (5th), seek (1st), shadow (3rd), track (1st), trail (2nd)

stall (5th): A. barn (K), bed (K), crib (2nd), pen (1st) **B.** delay (5th), pause (3rd) **C.** cage (1st), park (1st), room (K) **D.** arrest (3rd), block (1st), falter (1st), halt (4th), hesitate (4th), put off (1st), stop (K), waver (5th)

stallion (4th)

stalwart (6th): A. hero (1st), loyalist (5th), soldier (3rd) **B.** bold (2nd), brave (1st), courageous (4th), daring (2nd), fearless (3rd), firm (2nd), forceful (3rd), gallant (4th), hearty (5th), heroic (5th), mighty (1st), powerful (2nd), robust (5th), rugged (5th), stout (4th), strong (K), sturdy (3rd), tough (5th), valiant (6th)

stamen (6th)

stammer (6th): echo (4th), hesitate (4th), pause (3rd), repeat (4th)

stamp (2nd): A. pound (2nd), strike (2nd) **B.** imprint (4th), mint (5th), press (1st), print (1st) **C.** brand (2nd), impression (5th), mark (1st), seal (5th)

stampede (5th): A. flee (5th), run (K), scatter (3rd) **B.** race (1st), riot (6th), rush (2nd)

stand (K): A. abide (5th), accept (3rd), allow (3rd), endure (4th), permit (3rd), remain (1st), tolerate (5th) **B.** belief (1st), policy (5th), post (1st), station (1st) **C.** position (2nd), put (K), rise (1st), set (K)

standard (3rd): A. flag (3rd) **B.** example (2nd), guideline (3rd), ideal (3rd), mean (1st), model (3rd), normal (5th), pattern (3rd), plan (1st), principle (4th), rule (K) **C.** accepted (3rd), average (3rd), basic (5th), common (2nd), conventional (6th), established (3rd), official (3rd), regular (3rd), traditional (5th), uniform (1st)

stanza (5th): chapter (3rd), paragraph (6th), passage (4th), verse (4th)

staple (6th): A. essence (6th), product (4th), resource (5th) **B.** peg (1st), pin (K), spike (4th), tack (1st) **C.** attach (5th), bolt (4th), clip (2nd), fasten (4th), nail (2nd) **D.** basic (5th), core (6th), essential (6th)

star (K): A. heavenly body (2nd), planet (4th) **B.** celebrity (5th), lead (1st), principal (3rd) **C.** feature (3rd), present (K), promote (5th) **D.** chief (1st), famed (3rd), superior (4th)

starch (6th): A. make rigid (5th), stiffen (3rd) **B.** formality (4th), manners (1st), precision (5th), stiffness (3rd)

stare (3rd): A. blank look (4th), gaze (5th) **B.** eye (1st), gape (5th), observe (3rd), peer (1st), study (1st)

starfish (1st)

start (1st): A. scare (1st), shock (1st), surprise (1st) **B.** activate (4th), begin (1st), bolt (4th), create (3rd), ignite (6th), invent (2nd), jump (K), launch (5th), originate (3rd) **C.** introduction (5th), outset (1st)

startle (4th): alarm (3rd), bolt (4th), bump (2nd), jar (K), jump (K), panic (1st), scare (1st), shock (1st), surprise (1st)

starve (5th): die (2nd), fast (1st), hunger (2nd), perish (4th)

state (1st): A. allege (6th), argue (3rd), assert (6th), claim (2nd), comment (5th), declare (5th), explain (2nd), express (5th), narrate (6th), remark (4th), tell (K) **B.** condition (3rd), disposition

(5th), feeling (K), level (3rd), mode (5th), phase (6th), plight (6th), quality (4th), situation (4th), standing (1st), temper (4th) **C.** federal (4th), formal (4th), national (1st), solemn (5th) **D.** country (1st), land (K), nation (2nd), province (6th)

station (1st): A. establish (3rd), install (6th) **B.** location (3rd), office (1st), position (2nd), rank (3rd), standing (1st), stop (K)

statue (4th): bust (6th), figure (4th), image (4th), monument (2nd)

stature (6th): fame (3rd), height (4th), merit (4th), rank (3rd), reputation (5th), size (1st), standing (1st)

stay (1st): A. delay (5th), interval (6th), lull (5th), standstill (1st) **B.** suspension (5th) **C.** brace (5th), column (4th), support (4th) **D.** halt (4th), pause (3rd), postpone (6th), stop (K), wait (1st) **E.** dwell (4th), live (1st), persist (5th), remain (2nd), reside (5th), visit (1st)

steady (3rd): A. fix (1st), settle (2nd), stabilize (4th) **B.** balanced (3rd), calm (3rd), composed (4th), consistent (3rd), constant (4th), cool (1st), dependable (3rd), endless (2nd), even (1st), faithful (4th), loyal (5th), orderly (1st), ready (1st), regular (3rd), reliable (5th), routine (6th), stable (4th), trusty (1st), uniform (1st)

steak (2nd): beef (2nd), fish (K), meat (1st), slice (5th)

steal (3rd): A. bargain (4th), sale (1st) **B.** creep (1st), defraud (6th), grab (4th), plunder (5th), rob (K), seize (3rd), sneak (4th), take (1st), thieve (3rd)

steam (2nd): A. boil (3rd), drive (1st) **B.** energy (4th), might (1st), power (1st) **C.** fog (1st), fume (3rd), mist (1st), vapor (3rd)

steed (4th): horse (K), mount (2nd), stallion (5th)

steel (2nd): A. brace (5th), toughen (5th) **B.** blade (2nd), knife (1st), sword (4th)

steep (2nd): A. brew (6th), soak (5th), wet (K) **B.** cliff (2nd), height (4th), hill (K) **C.** sheer (5th), sudden (1st) **D.** costly (1st), expensive (3rd)

steer (4th)

Stegosaurus (2nd)

stem (2nd): A. base (1st), origin (3rd), source (4th), stalk (4th) **B.** check (1st), oppose (3rd), resist (4th), stop (K)

step (1st): A. go (K), move (K), stride (5th), walk (K) **B.** action (1st), degree (5th), grade (2nd), interval (6th), level (3rd), phase (6th), rank (3rd), stage (3rd) **C.** riser (2nd), stair (2nd)

stereoscope (5th): depth simulator (6th), eye test instrument (3rd)

stern (4th): brutal (6th), fierce (4th), firm (2nd), grim (4th), hard (1st), harsh (5th), resolute (5th), rigid (5th), serious (4th), severe (4th), steadfast (4th), stiff (3rd), strict (6th), tough (5th)

stew (2nd): A. chowder (5th), soup (1st) **B.** boil (3rd), brood (4th), fret (5th), fuss (1st), simmer (4th), worry (1st)

stick (K): A. bar (3rd), bat (K), cane (3rd), pole (1st), rod (1st), staff (4th), stake (1st) **B.** adhere (6th), bond (3rd), cement (4th), fasten (4th), glue (1st), join (3rd), paste (1st), seal (5th) **C.** pierce (4th), stab (5th)

sticker (K): adhesive paper (6th), label (3rd)

sticky (K): A. awkward (6th), delicate (5th), tricky (1st) **B.** adhesive (6th), gummy (1st), tacky (1st)

stiff (3rd): A. body (1st), dead person (1st) **B.** awkward (6th), firm (2nd), formal (4th), hard (1st), obstinate (5th), rigid (5th), solid (3rd), stern (4th), tense (5th), tight (1st), tough (5th)

still (1st): A. subsequently (6th), until now (1st) **B.** gag (1st), hush (3rd), quiet (K), silence (3rd), suppress (5th) **C.** calm (3rd), dead (1st), fixed (1st), idle (4th), inactive (3rd), silent (3rd), stationary (3rd), steady (3rd) **D.** but (K), however (3rd), though (1st), yet (1st)

stimulate (6th): amuse (4th), arouse (4th), cue (2nd), entertain (4th), excite (4th), inspire (4th), interest (3rd), prompt (4th), provoke (6th), rouse (4th), spark (3rd), start (K), stir (3rd), thrill (4th)

sting (2nd): A. cheat (3rd), scheme (5th) **B.** bite (1st), injury (5th) **C.** hurt (1st), pain (2nd)

stink (2nd)

stir (3rd): A. agitate (5th), animate (6th), arouse (4th), awaken (3rd), bother (2nd), convince (4th), cue (2nd), excite (4th), prompt (4th), remind (3rd), suggest (2nd), upset (3rd) **B.** beat (1st), blend (5th), mix (1st), shake (1st) **C.** action (1st), activity (3rd), bustle (6th), commotion (5th), excitement (4th), fuss (1st), interest (3rd), movement (2nd), turmoil (5th)

stitch (6th): A. pain (2nd), pang (6th) **B.** embroider (5th), fix (1st), repair (4th), sew (2nd)

stock (1st): A. ancestry (5th), breed (4th), ownership (3rd), relation (4th) **B.** basic (5th), essential (6th), staple (6th) **C.** animals (K), cattle (3rd) **D.** goods

(1st), store (K), supply (1st), wares (5th) **E.** fill (1st), furnish (3rd), pile (1st), replace (5th)

stockade (6th): A. block (1st), surround (3rd) **B.** brig (6th), defense (5th), enclosure (4th), fort (5th), jail (4th), pen (1st), prison (3rd)

stocking (4th): footwear (2nd), hose (6th), sock (1st)

stomach (2nd): A. accept (3rd), allow (2nd), bear (K), endure (4th), permit (3rd), tolerate (5th) **B.** appetite (4th), desire (5th), liking (1st) **C.** abdomen (6th), belly (5th)

stomp (4th): crush (4th), stamp (2nd), trample (5th)

stone (2nd): boulder (5th), jewel (5th), pebble (4th), rock (K)

stood (K)

stool (2nd): bench (4th), chair (K), seat (1st), toilet (2nd)

stoop (5th): A. bow (1st), droop (5th), humility (4th), slouch (6th), yielding (4th) **B.** deck (1st), porch (3rd) **C.** bend (K), descend (6th), duck (1st), hunch (6th), lower (1st), patronize (5th), sink (3rd), submit (4th)

stoop (5th)

stop (K): A. stay (1st), visit (1st) **B.** location (3rd), station (1st) **C.** block (1st), cancel (6th), conclude (3rd), finish (1st), quit (1st), suspend (4th), terminate (6th) **D.** end (K), halt (4th), pause (3rd), rest (1st)

stoplight (1st): brake light (1st), traffic signal (5th)

store (K): A. business (2nd), market (1st), shop (1st) **B.** put away (1st), reserve (3rd), save (1st) **C.** bank (1st),

deposit (5th), fund (4th), goods (1st), source (4th), stock (1st), supply (1st)

stork (2nd)

storm (2nd): A. anger (1st), charge (2nd), rage (4th) **B.** attack (3rd), commotion (5th), disorder (3rd) **C.** rain (1st), thundershower (3rd), torrent (5th)

story (K): A. deck (1st), floor (2nd), level (3rd) **B.** adventure (3rd), fable (5th), fantasy (6th), fib (1st), gossip (5th), legend (5th), lie (2nd), narration (6th), novel (5th), saga (6th), tale (3rd), yarn (2nd)

stout (4th): A. ale (2nd), beer (5th) **B.** athletic (5th), chubby (2nd), fat (1st), firm (2nd), heavy (1st), large (K), muscular (4th), powerful (2nd), strong (K), sturdy (3rd)

stove (1st): burner (3rd), furnace (4th), oven (1st), range (3rd)

stovepipe (4th): chimney (2nd), smoke chute (5th)

stow (6th): A. carry (K), contain (5th), hold (1st) **B.** box (K), crate (5th), pack (1st), store (K)

straight (3rd): A. fair (1st), honest (3rd), just (1st), proper (3rd), traditional (5th) **B.** frankly (4th), honestly (3rd) **C.** direct (1st), even (1st), neat (K), ordered (1st), plain (2nd), pure (3rd)

strain (4th): A. injure (5th), labor (2nd), pull (K), stretch (4th), struggle (1st), tense (5th), tighten (1st), try (K), work (K) **B.** melody (4th), subject (1st), theme (4th) **C.** burden (5th), effort (2nd), pressure (4th), stress (6th), tension (5th) **D.** family (K), stock (1st), tribe (3rd)

strait (5th): A. difficult (5th), tight (1st) **B.** difficulty (5th), problem (1st) **C.** arm (K), bay (K), channel (4th), inlet

(4th), narrows (2nd), road (K), street (1st)

strand (5th): A. abandon (4th), desert (1st) **B.** braid (2nd), twine (3rd), weave (4th) **C.** beach (1st), coast (2nd) **D.** cable (1st), cord (4th), fiber (3rd), line (K), rope (1st), string (1st)

strand (5th)

strange (1st): foreign (5th), not known (1st), novel (5th), odd (4th), peculiar (4th), queer (4th), unusual (3rd), weird (1st)

stranger (1st): foreigner (5th), outsider (1st)

strangle (6th): choke (1st), smother (6th), suffocate (6th)

strap (5th): A. beat (1st), whip (4th) **B.** band (1st), belt (2nd), tie (1st) **C.** bind (2nd), fasten (4th), lash (4th)

strategy (6th): course (3rd), design (5th), direction (1st), logic (6th), plan (1st), plot (4th), proposal (4th), scheme (5th), tactics (6th)

straw (2nd): hay (K), reed (4th), stalk (4th), stem (2nd)

strawberry (2nd)

stray (3rd): A. deserter (1st), homeless (2nd), orphan (5th) **B.** lost (K), roaming (4th) **C.** drift (2nd), roam (4th), wander (3rd)

streak (5th): A. layer (4th), line (K), mark (1st), strip (3rd) **B.** hurry (1st), run (K) **C.** bleach (4th), stain (4th)

stream (1st): A. flow (1st), glide (4th), march (1st), pour (3rd) **B.** brook (2nd), creek (4th), current (3rd), movement (2nd)

street (1st): access (6th), avenue (3rd), lane (4th), path (1st), road (K), route (4th)

strength (1st): A. ability (3rd), gift (1st), skill (2nd), talent (2nd) **B.** concentration (5th), endurance (4th), force (1st), magnitude (4th), might (1st), muscle (4th), power (1st), spirit (2nd)

strenuous (6th): demanding (5th), difficult (5th), hard (1st), heavy (1st), labored (2nd), rough (4th), severe (4th), tough (5th), trying (1st)

stress (6th): A. annoy (5th), bother (2nd) **B.** anxiety (4th), burden (5th), distress (5th), pressure (4th), strain (4th), weight (1st), worry (1st) **C.** accent (6th), emphasis (5th), importance (1st) **D.** feature (3rd), highlight (2nd)

stretch (4th): A. period (2nd), term (3rd) **B.** enlarge (5th), expand (5th), extend (4th), flex (6th), prolong (5th), span (6th), tense (5th), tighten (2nd) **C.** excess (5th), give (1st), reach (1st)

stricken (6th): hit (K), overwhelmed (5th), tortured (5th), wounded (3rd)

strict (6th): careful (1st), exact (2nd), firm (2nd), harsh (5th), narrow (2nd), precise (5th), prim (5th), rigid (5th), severe (4th), stern (4th), tough (5th), zealous (6th)

stride (5th): A. gait (6th), step (1st) **B.** march (1st), pace (3rd), walk (K)

strife (5th): battle (2nd), clash (5th), conflict (4th), dispute (6th), fight (1st)

strike (2nd): A. assault (4th), attack (3rd), club (1st), dispute (6th), hammer (2nd), invade (5th), raid (6th), storm (2nd), surprise (1st) **B.** coin (3rd), imprint (4th), mint (5th), print (1st), stamp (2nd) **C.** blow (1st), hit (K), knock (3rd), slap (2nd) **D.** boycott (6th), picket (3rd), walkout (K) **E.** ignite (6th), light (K), spark (3rd)

string (1st): A. row (K), run (K), series (4th), train (K) **B.** arrange (3rd), order (1st), rank (3rd) **C.** cable (1st), chain (3rd), cord (4th), line (K), rope (1st), row (K), run (K), series (4th), thread (2nd) **D.** bind (2nd), fasten (4th), tie (1st) **E.** a group of printable characters used in computer programming

strip (3rd): A. band (1st), bar (3rd), ribbon (4th), tape (1st) **B.** bare (3rd), expose (4th), peel (2nd), remove (2nd), reveal (4th), skin (1st), uncover (2nd), undress (2nd)

stripe (1st): A. blaze (1st), line (K), streak (5th) **B.** band (1st), layer (4th), ribbon (4th), stream (1st)

strive (5th): advance (2nd), aim (3rd), argue (3rd), attempt (2nd), compete (4th), contend (5th), contest (4th), dispute (6th), fight (K), labor (2nd), oppose (3rd), progress (4th), resist (4th), struggle (1st), toil (4th), try (K), work (K)

stroke (1st): A. attack (3rd), seizure (3rd), spasm (6th) **B.** blow (1st), hit (K), kick (1st) **C.** feel (K), pet (1st), rub (1st) **D.** cheer (3rd), commend (6th), flatter (4th), preen (2nd), recognize (3rd)

stroll (5th): A. hike (3rd), saunter (6th), walk (K) **B.** ramble (6th), roam (4th), wander (3rd)

strong (K): athletic (5th), durable (6th), effective (4th), forceful (3rd), heavy (1st), intense (6th), massive (5th), mighty (1st), muscular (4th), powerful (2nd), severe (4th), sturdy (3rd), vital (5th)

structure (4th): A. arrange (3rd), build (1st), form (1st), organize (4th)

B. building (1st), frame (3rd), pattern (3rd), shape (1st)

struggle (1st): A. battle (2nd), clash (5th), combat (5th), effort (2nd), fight (K), quarrel (4th), trial (4th) **B.** compete (4th), conflict (4th), contest (4th), dispute (6th), oppose (3rd), scramble (4th), spar (5th), strive (5th), toil (4th), try (K), war (1st), work (K), wrestle (6th)

strut (5th): boast (4th), brag (3rd), crow (2nd), march (1st), parade (2nd), step (1st), stride (5th), swagger (5th), walk (K)

stubble (6th): beard (4th), grass (K), growth (1st)

stubborn (5th): arrogant (6th), defiant (6th), determined (5th), firm (2nd), hard (1st), obstinate (5th), persistent (5th), pushy (1st), resolute (5th), rigid (5th), tough (5th), unbending (3rd)

stuck (4th)

stud (6th): A. buck (1st), horse (K) **B.** bolt (4th), button (1st), cleat (5th), peg (1st), pin (K), spike (4th)

student (3rd): beginner (2nd), learner (1st), pupil (4th), scholar (5th)

studio (5th): broadcast station (5th), school (K), work space (1st)

study (1st): A. consider (2nd), explore (4th), inquire (3rd), investigate (5th), search (1st) **B.** class (1st), course (3rd), research (5th), subject (3rd) **C.** den (1st), sanctuary (6th), school (K)

stuff (1st): A. cram (5th), fill (1st), jam (K), load (2nd), pack (1st) **B.** content (3rd), matter (1st), property (3rd), substance (5th), things (K)

stumble (4th): bewilder (3rd), err (6th), fall (K), hesitate (4th), stagger

(4th), stump (3rd), trip (1st), tumble (4th)

stump (3rd): A. clip (2nd), shorten (1st), trim (4th) **B.** amaze (5th), bewilder (3rd), puzzle (4th) **C.** base (1st), behind (1st), bottom (1st), end (K), stem (2nd), trunk (4th)

stun (4th): amaze (5th), astonish (4th), awe (6th), confound (6th), dazzle (5th), disable (3rd), freeze (4th), horrify (4th), outrage (6th), shock (1st), stagger (4th), stop (K), surprise (1st)

stunt (6th): A. check (1st), shorten (1st) **B.** act (K), deed (1st), event (3rd), exploit (6th), feat (1st), trick (1st)

stupid (4th): dull (1st), dumb (1st), foolish (3rd), pointless (2nd), silly (1st), simple (2nd), slow (1st)

sturdy (3rd): durable (6th), fit (K), forceful (3rd), hardy (5th), healthy (1st), powerful (2nd), robust (5th), sound (1st), stout (4th), strong (K), tough (5th), well (1st)

stutter (1st)

style (3rd): A. design (5th), make (K), plan (1st) **B.** elegance (5th), fad (K), flair (6th), polish (4th) **C.** approach (3rd), class (1st), fashion (3rd), manner (2nd), tone (3rd), type (1st)

subdue (6th): calm (3rd), conquer (4th), crush (4th), defeat (5th), dominate (5th), exploit (6th), hush (3rd), quiet (K), reduce (3rd), silence (3rd), suppress (5th), soften (1st), vanquish (6th)

subject (1st): A. course (3rd), issue (4th), object (1st), study (2nd), target (5th), text (6th), theme (4th), topic (5th) **B.** citizen (3rd), dependent (3rd), national (2nd) **C.** expose (4th), humble (4th), treat (2nd)

sublime (6th): A. ideal (3rd), model (3rd), perfection (3rd) **B.** elevated (2nd), great (1st), heavenly (1st), lofty (5th), magnificent (4th), superb (6th)

submarine (5th): ship (1st), underwater vessel (4th)

submerge (5th): cover (1st), drown (1st), lower (1st), sink (3rd), subside (6th)

submit (4th): A. present (K), propose (4th), refer (5th) **B.** comply (6th), conform (6th), fall (K), follow (1st), obey (3rd), surrender (5th), yield (4th)

subsequent (6th): after (1st), behind (1st), beyond (1st), following (1st), future (5th)

subside (6th): cease (3rd), decline (6th), ease (3rd), fall (K), reduce (3rd), relax (4th), settle (2nd), shrink (5th), sink (3rd), slide (2nd), submerge (5th)

substance (5th): basis (2nd), content (3rd), depth (5th), elements (3rd), essence (6th), fiber (3rd), heart (K), ingredients (4th), intent (5th), mass (3rd), material (5th), matter (1st), nature (1st), significance (6th), weight (1st)

substantial (5th): ample (5th), generous (4th), important (1st), impressive (5th), objective (3rd), real (1st)

substitute (5th): A. agent (5th), alternate (5th), equivalent (6th), fake (1st), false (3rd), mock (4th), recourse (6th), stand-in (1st) **B.** exchange (4th), replace (5th), switch (4th)

subtle (6th): careful (1st), crafty (2nd), delicate (5th), gentle (3rd), logical (6th), mysterious (2nd), refined (6th), sensitive (5th), skillful (3rd), slight (4th), sly (4th), tactful (6th), vague (5th)

subtract (1st): minus (1st), reduce (3rd), take away (1st)

suburb (6th): border (1st), edge (1st), fringe (5th)

success (2nd): achievement (5th), fame (3rd), triumph (5th), victory (4th), win (1st)

succession (6th): A. descent (6th), family (K) **B.** chain (3rd), following (1st), line (K), order (1st), pattern (3rd), procession (4th), row (K), run (K), series (4th), string (1st)

such (1st): akin (1st), alike (1st), comparable (3rd), equivalent (6th), like (K), related (4th), same (1st), similar (4th)

suck (1st): drain (5th), draw (K), drink (1st), pull (K), sip (1st)

suckling (6th): baby (K), newborn (2nd)

sudden (1st): abrupt (5th), fast (1st), impulsive (5th), immediate (3rd), instant (3rd), quick (1st), rapid (4th), startling (4th), surprising (1st), swift (4th), unexpected (3rd)

suffer (2nd): accept (3rd), allow (2nd), bear (K), concede (6th), endure (4th), experience (4th), grieve (5th), hurt (1st), let (K), permit (3rd), tolerate (5th), undergo (2nd)

suffering (2nd): agony (5th), distress (5th), endurance (4th), misery (4th), pain (2nd), patience (4th), trial (4th), grief (5th)

suffice (6th): answer (1st), do (K), meet (K), qualify (4th), satisfy (3rd)

sufficient (3rd): ample (5th), competent (6th), effective (4th), enough (1st), plenty (1st)

suffocate (6th): choke (1st), smother (6th), strangle (6th), suppress (5th)

sugar (1st): flavor (4th), sweeten (K)

suggest (2nd): convey (4th), hint (1st), imply (5th), indicate (4th), mention (5th), offer (2nd),

resemble (4th)

suggestion (2nd): A. advice (3rd), idea (1st), opinion (3rd), thought (1st) **B.** hint (1st), sprinkling (3rd), tinge (5th), trace (3rd)

suit (1st): A. adapt (4th), adjust (5th), content (3rd), fit (K), modify (5th), please (K), satisfy (3rd) **B.** clothes (1st), costume (4th), fashion (3rd), outfit (2nd) **C.** case (2nd), legal action (5th), trial (4th) **D.** attire (6th), dress (K), equip (5th)

suitcase (1st): bag (1st), baggage (3rd), case (2nd), grip (4th), luggage (4th)

suitor (5th): admirer (5th), boyfriend (1st), lover (1st)

sulky (5th): angry (1st), brooding (4th), cross (1st), gloomy (3rd), glum (4th), moody (3rd), sour (2nd), sullen (5th), surly (6th)

sullen (5th): angry (1st), brooding (4th), crabby (2nd), cross (1st), glum (4th), moody (3rd), sulky (5th), surly (6th), touchy (1st)

sulfur (4th): brimstone (5th)

sultan (5th): king (K), sovereign (4th)

sum (1st): A. add (K), count (1st) **B.** addition (3rd), all (K), amount (2nd), balance (3rd), result (2nd), total (2nd), whole (1st)

sumac (4th)

summer (K)

summit (5th): crest (4th), crown (1st), height (4th), hill (1st), peak (4th), top (K)

summon (4th): A. recall (3rd), remember (1st), revive (6th) **B.** announce (3rd), assemble (4th), call (1st), cluster (4th), collect (3rd), gather (1st), greet (3rd), group (1st), marshal (5th), mass (3rd), muster (6th), order (1st), page (1st), rally (5th)

sun (K): daylight (1st), fireball (2nd), light (K), star (K)

Sunday (1st)

sundown (2nd): dusk (5th), nightfall (2nd), sunset (1st)

sundry (6th): assorted (5th), many (K), various (4th)

sunlit (2nd): bright (1st), clear (2nd), fair (1st), glowing (1st), light (K)

sunny (1st): A. bright (1st), glowing (1st), radiant (6th), shining (1st) **B.** cheerful (3rd), cheery (3rd), fair (1st), favorable (3rd), merry (3rd), promising (1st), warm (1st)

sunrise (2nd)

sunset (1st): dusk (5th), nightfall (2nd), sundown (2nd)

suntan (2nd): browning (1st), tan (K)

super (1st): excellent (1st), exceptional (3rd), fantastic (6th), great (1st), marvelous (4th), remarkable (4th), stunning (4th), terrific (5th), tremendous (4th), wonderful (1st)

superb (6th): excellent (1st), fine (1st), outstanding (2nd), superior (4th)

superintendent (5th): boss (K), chief (1st), director (1st), foreman (6th), manager (4th)

superior (4th): A. boss (K), chief (1st), foreman (6th), senior (6th), supervisor (6th) **B.** champion (4th), standout (2nd) **C.** above (1st), best (K), better (1st), excellent (1st), finest (1st), greater (1st), leading (1st), outstanding (2nd), over (1st), prime (5th), principal (3rd), select (4th), superb (6th), top (K)

supernatural (5th): ghostly (1st), magical (1st), marvelous (4th), mystical (4th)

superstition (5th): belief (1st), fable (5th), illusion (6th), myth (4th), tradition (5th), witchcraft (2nd)

supervise (6th): administer (6th), boss (K), direct (1st), govern (1st), guide (1st), lead (1st), manage (4th), oversee (2nd), regulate (5th)

supper (2nd): dinner (2nd), meal (3rd)

supple (6th): agile (6th), elastic (6th), flexible (6th), movable (3rd), plastic (3rd), pliable (6th), soft (K)

supply (1st): A. arm (K), deliver (5th), equip (5th), fill (1st), furnish (3rd), give (1st), nourish (6th), outfit (2nd), provide (3rd) **B.** fund (4th), reserve (3rd), stock (1st), store (K), source (4th)

support (4th): A. approval (4th), base (1st), beam (3rd), comfort (3rd), foundation (5th), helper (1st) **B.** aid (2nd), assist (4th), back (1st), brace (5th), keep (K), lift (1st), maintain (4th), nourish (6th), persuade (5th), promote (5th), sustain (5th)

suppose (2nd): assume (5th), believe (1st), dream (1st), guess (1st), imagine (2nd), infer (5th), presume (6th), suggest (2nd), suspect (5th), think (1st), trust (1st)

suppress (5th): ban (K), bar (3rd), choke (1st), crush (4th), dominate (5th), forbid (4th), outlaw (2nd), prevent (3rd), prohibit (6th), put down (2nd), smother (6th), stop (K), subdue (6th)

supreme (5th): best (K), chief (1st), dominant (5th), first (1st), foremost (4th), greatest (1st), head (1st), highest (2nd), primary (5th), principal (3rd), top (K)

sure (K): accurate (6th), certain (1st), confident (6th), convinced (4th), dependable (3rd), effective (3rd), positive (2nd), reliable (5th), secure (3rd), stable (4th)

surf (4th): current (3rd), surge (5th), tide (1st), waves (2nd)

surface (3rd): appearance (2nd), cover (1st), face (1st), front (1st), outside (1st), rise (1st), side (K), skin (1st), tip (K)

surge (5th): A. flow (1st), rise (1st), stream (1st), swell (3rd) **B.** crest (4th), flood (2nd), pulse (5th), rush (2nd), wave (1st)

surgeon (5th): doctor (1st), operator (5th)

surly (6th): angry (1st), brooding (4th), gloomy (3rd), impolite (4th), mean (1st), rude (2nd), sullen (5th)

surmise (6th): A. guess (1st), opinion (3rd), view (2nd) **B.** assume (5th), believe (1st), conclude (3rd), consider (2nd), gather (1st), imagine (2nd), judge (1st), presume (6th), suggest (2nd), suppose (2nd), think (1st)

surmount (6th): ascend (4th), clear (2nd), climb (1st), conquer (4th), defeat (5th), leap (3rd), mount (2nd), overcome (2nd), scale (3rd), vault (5th)

surpass (6th): beat (1st), better (1st), eclipse (4th), exceed (4th), excel (6th), pass (2nd), top (K)

surplus (6th): A. excess (5th), extra (1st), unused (1st) **B.** overflow (5th), spare (3rd)

surprise (1st): A. blow (1st), marvel (4th), sensation (5th), wonder (1st) **B.** alarm (3rd), amaze (5th), ambush (6th), astonish (4th), shock (1st), stagger (4th), stun (4th)

surrender (5th): A. compliance (6th), concession (6th), fall (K), submission (4th) **B.** bow (1st), comply (6th), concede (6th), forfeit (6th), give up (1st), resign (5th), submit (4th), yield (4th)

surround (3rd): circle (K), compass (4th), enclose (4th), frame (3rd)

surrounding (3rd): A. around (1st), circling (1st), near (1st) **B.** belt (2nd), border (1st), enclosure (4th)

survey (5th): A. report (1st), research (5th) **B.** examine (5th), explore (4th), inquire (3rd), inspect (5th), investigate (5th), question (1st), review (4th), study (1st)

survive (3rd): continue (2nd), endure (4th), last (K), live (1st), outlast (2nd), outlive (2nd), persist (5th), stay (1st)

suspect (5th): A. distrust (3rd), fear (1st), mistrust (3rd), question (1st), suspect (5th) **B.** doubtful (5th), uncertain (1st) **C.** guess (1st), imagine (2nd), suppose (2nd), think (1st) **D.** accused (4th), prisoner (3rd)

suspend (4th): A. dangle (5th), hang (2nd) **B.** bar (3rd), delay (5th), halt (4th), interrupt (3rd), postpone (6th), stop (K)

suspicion (4th): clue (2nd), concern (3rd), distrust (3rd), doubt (5th), fear (1st), feeling (1st), guess (1st), hint (1st), hunch (6th), instinct (5th), mistrust (3rd), sense (1st)

sustain (5th): defend (5th), feed (1st), maintain (4th), nourish (6th), provide (3rd), support (4th), uphold (6th)

swagger (5th): boast (4th), brag (3rd), march (1st), parade (2nd), strut (5th)

swallow (1st): A. consume (4th), drink (1st), eat (K) **B.** bite (1st), consumption (4th), drinking (1st), eating (1st) **C.** accept (3rd), allow (2nd), believe (1st), endure (4th), permit (3rd), tolerate (5th)

swamp (4th): A. drown (1st), flood (2nd), overflow (5th) **B.** bog (5th), marsh (5th)

swarm (4th): A. crowd (2nd), overrun (2nd), throng (5th) **B.** cluster (4th), horde (6th), host (4th), many (K), mass (3rd), mob (4th), numerous (4th)

swarthy (6th): black (K), brown (K), chocolate (4th), dark (1st)

sway (3rd): A. authority (3rd), bend (K), influence (5th), tilt (5th), vibration (5th) **B.** affect (4th), charm (3rd), convert (4th), convince (4th), persuade (5th), pitch (2nd), reel (5th), rock (K), roll (1st), swing (1st), toss (2nd), wave (1st), wheel (1st), win (1st)

swear (4th): A. condemn (4th), curse (3rd) **B.** aver (6th), promise (1st) **C.** guarantee (6th), pledge (5th), promise (1st), vow (4th)

sweat (3rd): A. fret (5th), slavery (3rd), toil (4th), work (K) **B.** labor (2nd), perspire (6th), strain (4th), strive (5th), worry (1st)

sweater (3rd): jacket (3rd), pullover (1st)

sweep (4th): A. drive (K), movement (2nd), stroke (1st) **B.** blow (1st), carry (K), force (1st), move (K) **C.** brush (2nd), clean (K), mop (1st), wipe (1st) **D.** range (3rd), reach (1st), realm (4th), scope (6th), width (4th)

sweet (K): appealing (3rd), dear (1st), fresh (2nd), honey (1st), pleasant (3rd), precious (4th), pure (3rd), sugary (1st)

sweetmeat (5th): candy (K), cream (1st), kiss (K), pie (K), sweet (K)

sweetness (2nd): gentleness (3rd), perfume (3rd), sugariness (2nd), tastiness (2nd)

sweets (1st): candy (K), treats (2nd)

swell (3rd): A. elegant (5th), fine (1st), stylish (3rd), superior (4th) **B.** hill (K), increase (3rd), lump (4th), spread (2nd) **C.** enlarge (5th), expand (5th), fatten (2nd), grow (1st), peak (4th), rise (1st), roll (1st), surge (5th)

swift (4th): A. alert (5th), bright (1st), intelligent (4th), smart (1st) **B.** brief (3rd), fast (1st), hasty (2nd), immediate (3rd), instant (3rd), quick (1st), rapid (4th), speedy (3rd), sudden (1st)

swim (K): crawl (1st), float (1st), glide (4th), skim (6th)

swine (5th): animal (K), boar (5th), hog (K), monster (1st), pig (K), slob (5th)

swing (1st): A. jab (1st), punch (4th) **B.** lurch (5th), reel (5th), wave (K) **C.** direct (1st), guide (1st), manage (4th) **D.** range (3rd), scope (6th), sweep (4th) **E.** beat (1st), pulse (5th), rhythm (5th) **F.** dangle (5th), hang (2nd), move (K), pitch (2nd), rock (K), suspend (4th), sway (3rd), turn (1st)

swish (2nd): A. swing (1st), wave (K), whip (4th), whisk (4th) **B.** hiss (3rd), hum (1st), murmur (4th), rustle (3rd), sigh (3rd), whir (6th), whisper (1st), whistle (4th)

switch (4th): A. exchange (4th), replace (5th), turn (1st) **B.** rod (1st), stick (K), whip (4th) **C.** hit (K), strike (2nd)

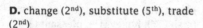

D. change (2nd), substitute (5th), trade (2nd)

swoop (4th): A. descent (6th), dive (1st), plunge (4th) **B.** clutch (4th), grab (4th), lift (1st), seize (3rd) **C.** descend (6th), dip (1st), pounce (5th)

sword (4th): blade (2nd), cutlass (6th), knife (1st), saber (5th)

sycamore (4th)

syllable (6th): letters (1st), word part (1st)

symbol (5th): character (2nd), emblem (5th), image (4th), model (3rd), sign (1st), signal (4th), token (5th)

sympathy (4th): accord (4th), approval (4th), compassion (6th), harmony (4th), kindness (2nd), mercy (4th), pity (3rd), sensitivity (5th), understanding (1st), unity (5th)

symphony (6th): music (K), orchestra (6th), performance (6th), piece (1st), recital (5th)

symptom (6th): evidence (5th), feature (3rd), sign (1st), signal (4th), symbol (5th), trait (6th)

syrup (4th): A. sap (1st), sugary water (1st) **B.** sentimentality (5th), sweetness (2nd)

system (2nd): arrangement (3rd), method (2nd), order (1st), pattern (3rd), plan (1st), procedure (4th), routine (6th), scheme (5th)

tab (K): A. account (3rd), bill (1st), credit (5th), statement (3rd) **B.** flap (4th), label (3rd), loop (5th), mark (1st), notch (5th)

table (K): A. chart (1st), column (4th), list (2nd) **B.** board (1st), desk (2nd), shelf (6th), stand (K)

tablecloth (4th): covering (1st), linen (4th), spread (2nd)

tablespoon (4th): ladle (4th), measurer (2nd), scoop (4th), server (1st)

tack (1st): A. bolt (4th), nail (2nd), pin (K), staple (6th) **B.** angle (3rd), course (3rd), direction (1st), path (1st) **C.** shift (4th), turn (1st) **D.** attach (5th), connect (3rd), fasten (4th)

tackle (4th): A. equipment (5th), gear (1st), outfit (2nd) **B.** attack (3rd), attempt (2nd), seize (3rd), take on (1st), try (1st)

tact (6th): diplomacy (5th), grace (3rd), poise (6th), polish (4th), regard (4th), skill (2nd), subtlety (6th)

tactics (6th): execution (5th), handling (2nd), plans (1st), strategies (6th)

tag (K): A. follow (1st), pursue (5th), trail (2nd) **B.** flap (4th), name (K), sticker (K), tab (K), term (3rd) **C.** call (1st), label (3rd), ticket (1st), title (3rd), touch (1st)

tail (1st): A. back (1st), end (K), last 1 **B.** chase (1st), follow (1st), hunt (2nd), pursue (5th), near (3rd), shadow (3rd), track (1st), trail (2nd)

tailor (4th): A. costumer (4th), dressmaker (2nd), seamstress (5th) **B.** adapt (4th), create (3rd), conform (6th), fashion (3rd), fit (K), modify (5th), sew (2nd), shape (1st)

taint (6th): A. flaw (2nd), infection (6th), pollution (3rd), stain (4th), trace (3rd) **B.** contaminate (6th), corrupt (6th), defile (6th), dirty (1st), discolor (3rd), poison (3rd), ruin (5th), soil (4th), spoil (4th)

take (K): A. bear (K), bring (1st), carry (1st) **B.** endure (4th), put up with (K), stand (K), tolerate (5th) **C.** earnings

(2nd), obtainment (2nd), profits (4th), seizure (3rd) **D.** consume (4th), eat (K) **E.** accept (3rd), acquire (4th), collect (3rd), rob (K), seize (3rd), steal (3rd)

taken (1st)

tale (3rd): fable (5th), fantasy (6th), fib (1st), fiction (5th), invention (2nd), legend (5th), lie (2nd), myth (4th), story (K)

talent (2nd): ability (3rd), aptitude (5th), art (K), craft (2nd), flair (6th), genius (4th), gift (1st), skill (2nd)

talk (K): A. chat (1st), conference (4th), lecture (5th), presentation (4th), speech (2nd) **B.** address (K), discuss (5th), gossip (5th), rumor (5th), speak (1st)

tall (K): big (K), elevated (2nd), giant (2nd), high (K), long (1st), soaring (6th)

tame (4th): A. meek (2nd), mild (4th), yielding (4th) **B.** govern (1st), restrict (6th), temper (4th), train (K)

tan (K): A. darken (1st), sun (K), toast (5th) **B.** beige (3rd), bronze (4th), brown (K), copper (4th)

tangle (3rd): A. involve (6th), snare (6th), twist (1st) **B.** confusion (4th), disorder (3rd), mess (1st), snarl (5th)

tank (5th): A. armored car (4th), combat vehicle (6th) **B.** bowl (1st), container (5th), holder (1st), jug (1st), pool (1st), vessel (4th)

tankard (6th): cup (1st), glass (1st), mug (1st), vessel (1st)

Taoist (5th)

tap (K): A. drain (5th), explore (4th), open (K) **B.** knock (3rd), rap (1st) **C.** plug (5th), valve (6th) **D.** bump (2nd), knock (3rd), rap (1st) **E.** hit (K), pat (K), strike (2nd)

tape (1st): A. photograph (5th), record (2nd) **B.** adhesive (6th), band (1st), roll (1st), seal (K), strip (3rd) **C.** adhere (6th), bind (2nd), close (K), wrap (3rd)

taper (5th): A. compress (4th), ease (3rd), narrow (2nd), slow down (1st), thin (1st) **B.** candle (2nd), light (K), wick (1st)

tapestry (6th): curtain (5th), hanging (2nd), weaving (4th)

tar (1st): asphalt (5th), gum (K), resin (5th)

target (5th): aim (3rd), center (2nd), goal (4th), focus (5th), mission (5th), prey (4th), quarry (6th), subject (1st), task (3rd), victim (4th)

tariff (5th): fee (4th), tax (K), toll (6th)

taro (4th)

tarpaulin (6th): canvas (6th), covering (1st)

tarry (5th): await (5th), delay (5th), linger (4th), remain (2nd), stay (1st), wait (1st)

tart (5th): A. pie (K), puff (2nd) **B.** acid (4th), biting (1st), sharp (1st), sour (2nd)

task (3rd): assignment (5th), goal (4th), job (K), labor (1st), mission (5th), objective (2nd), work (K)

taste (1st): A. appetite (4th), flavor (4th), fondness (4th), liking (1st) **B.** fashion (3rd), style (3rd) **C.** experience (4th), sample (5th), savor (6th), sip (1st)

taught (2nd): coached (4th), explained (2nd), instructed (4th), trained (1st), tutored (6th)

taunt (5th): A. insult (5th), jeer (5th), scorn (4th), sneer (6th) **B.** annoy (5th), badger (2nd), bother (2nd), mock (4th), needle (3rd), tease (3rd), torment (5th)

tavern (5th): bar (3rd), pub (1st), saloon (6th)

tawny (6th): dark (1st), golden (1st), light brown (1st), tan (K)

tax (K): A. burden (5th), charge (2nd), duty (1st), fee (4th), tariff (5th) **B.** demand (5th), load (2nd), strain (4th), toll (6th)

taxi (1st): A. glide (4th), ride (K) **B.** cab (K), fare (3rd)

tea (1st)

teach (1st): acquaint (4th), coach (4th), educate (3rd), explain (2nd), inform (5th), instruct (4th), school (K), train (K), tutor (6th)

teacher (1st): educator (3rd), example (2nd), guide (1st), instructor (4th), model (3rd), professor (4th), tutor (6th)

team (1st): band (1st), crew (2nd), group (1st), pack (1st), unit (5th)

tear (2nd): A. break (1st), cut (K) **B.** cry (K), weep (4th) **C.** bead (K), drop (K) **D.** divide (4th), pull (K), remove (2nd), rip (1st), shred (5th), split (4th), tug (1st)

tease (3rd): annoy (5th), badger (2nd), bait (3rd), bother (2nd), jeer (5th), kid (1st), mock (4th), needle (3rd), pester (2nd), taunt (5th)

teaspoon (2nd): ladle (4th), measurer (2nd), scoop (4th), stirrer (3rd)

tectonic (5th): relating to the structural deformation of the earth's crust

tedious (6th): boring (2nd), dull (1st), long (1st), slow (1st), tiresome (3rd)

tee (1st): A. begin (1st), set up (K), start (1st) **B.** holder (1st), mound (2nd), peg (1st), support (4th)

teen (2nd): adolescent (5th), juvenile (5th), minor (5th), teenager (3rd), youth (2nd)

teenager (3rd): adolescent (5th), juvenile (5th), minor (5th), teen (2nd), youth (2nd)

teeth (1st): fangs (5th), points (1st), spikes (4th), tips (1st), tusks (5th)

telecommunications (4th)

telegram (4th): bulletin (3rd), cable (1st), message (1st), wire (3rd)

telephone (2nd): A. line (K), phone (2nd) **B.** call (1st), dial (5th), ring (1st)

telescope (4th): A. condense (6th), cut (K), reduce (3rd), shorten (1st) **B.** binoculars (6th), glass (1st), lens (1st), scope (6th)

television (4th): A. broadcast (5th), transmission (6th) **B.** cabinet (4th), set (K), TV (K)

tell (K): announce (3rd), brief (3rd), confide (6th), expose (4th), express (5th), gossip (5th), inform (5th), mention (5th), recount (6th), reveal (4th), share (2nd), state (1st)

telling (1st): convincing (4th), forceful (3rd), influential (5th), persuasive (5th), revealing (4th)

temper (4th): A. mellow (6th), moderate (4th), regulate (5th), restrain (5th), soften (2nd), tame (4th) **B.** anger (1st), emotions (4th), feeling (1st), mood (3rd), passion (6th), rage (4th)

temperature (4th): climate (4th), condition (3rd), heat (1st), warmth (3rd)

temple (3rd): chapel (4th), church (1st), sanctuary (6th), shrine (5th)

temporary (5ᵗʰ): brief (3ʳᵈ), fleeting (6ᵗʰ), passing (2ⁿᵈ), reserve (3ʳᵈ), short (1ˢᵗ)

tempt (4ᵗʰ): appeal (3ʳᵈ), attract (5ᵗʰ), charm (3ʳᵈ), coax (6ᵗʰ), court (3ʳᵈ), draw (K), encourage (4ᵗʰ), excite (4ᵗʰ), influence (5ᵗʰ), invite (3ʳᵈ), lure (5ᵗʰ), magnetize (3ʳᵈ), prompt (4ᵗʰ), summon (4ᵗʰ), tease (3ʳᵈ), woo (6ᵗʰ)

temptation (5ᵗʰ): attraction (5ᵗʰ), bait (3ʳᵈ), coaxing (6ᵗʰ), dare (2ⁿᵈ), fascination (5ᵗʰ), invitation (3ʳᵈ), lure (5ᵗʰ), magnet (3ʳᵈ), persuasion (5ᵗʰ), trap (1ˢᵗ)

ten (K)

tenant (5ᵗʰ): A. lease (6ᵗʰ), pay (K), rent (1ˢᵗ) **B.** guest (3ʳᵈ), holder (2ⁿᵈ), inhabitant (6ᵗʰ), lodger (4ᵗʰ), occupant (6ᵗʰ), occupier (6ᵗʰ), owner (2ⁿᵈ), renter (1ˢᵗ), resident (5ᵗʰ)

tend (K): A. incline (5ᵗʰ), influence (5ᵗʰ), look to (K), point to (1ˢᵗ) **B.** care for (1ˢᵗ), comfort (3ʳᵈ), guard (1ˢᵗ), help (K), nurse (K), protect (4ᵗʰ), relieve (4ᵗʰ), serve (1ˢᵗ)

tendency (5ᵗʰ): appetite (4ᵗʰ), attraction (5ᵗʰ), bearing (K), bent (K), course (3ʳᵈ), direction (1ˢᵗ), drift (2ⁿᵈ), impression (5ᵗʰ), leaning (3ʳᵈ), likeliness (2ⁿᵈ), path (1ˢᵗ), pattern (3ʳᵈ), tone (3ʳᵈ), trend (2ⁿᵈ)

tender (3ʳᵈ): A. affectionate (4ᵗʰ), agreeable (2ⁿᵈ), caring (1ˢᵗ), gentle (3ʳᵈ), kind (K), loving (1ˢᵗ), mild (4ᵗʰ), romantic (5ᵗʰ), soft (K) **B.** caretaker (4ᵗʰ), observer (3ʳᵈ), sitter (2ⁿᵈ) **C.** delicate (5ᵗʰ), painful (3ʳᵈ), sensitive (5ᵗʰ), shaky (2ⁿᵈ), sore (4ᵗʰ), touchy (1ˢᵗ) **D.** extend (4ᵗʰ), offer (2ⁿᵈ), present (K), yield (4ᵗʰ)

tenement (6ᵗʰ): apartment (1ˢᵗ), dwelling (4ᵗʰ), house (K), lodge (4ᵗʰ), residence (5ᵗʰ), room (1ˢᵗ)

tense (5ᵗʰ): A. frightened (2ⁿᵈ), nervous (1ˢᵗ), restless (4ᵗʰ), shy (K), timid (5ᵗʰ), trembling (3ʳᵈ), uneasy (2ⁿᵈ), worried (1ˢᵗ) **B.** draw (K), firm (2ⁿᵈ), flex (6ᵗʰ), pull (K), rigid (5ᵗʰ), stiff (3ʳᵈ), stretch (4ᵗʰ), tight (1ˢᵗ), unyielding (4ᵗʰ)

tent (1ˢᵗ): booth (5ᵗʰ), canopy (6ᵗʰ), canvas (6ᵗʰ)

term (3ʳᵈ): A. call (1ˢᵗ), expression (5ᵗʰ), label (3ʳᵈ), name (K), phrase (5ᵗʰ), word (K) **B.** administration (6ᵗʰ), cycle (5ᵗʰ), interval (6ᵗʰ), length (2ⁿᵈ), period (2ⁿᵈ), rule (K), season (2ⁿᵈ), span (6ᵗʰ), stage (2ⁿᵈ), time (1ˢᵗ)

terminate (6ᵗʰ): close (K), complete (3ʳᵈ), conclude (3ʳᵈ), end (K), finish (1ˢᵗ), fire (K), halt (4ᵗʰ), kill (1ˢᵗ), lapse (6ᵗʰ), limit (3ʳᵈ), stop (K)

termites (2ⁿᵈ)

terrace (5ᵗʰ): plain (2ⁿᵈ), platform (4ᵗʰ), porch (3ʳᵈ)

terraform (4ᵗʰ): A. to transform a nonterrestrial planet to one having the characteristics of landscapes on earth **B.** to transform areas with harsh climates on earth to an area capable of farming or sustaining life

terrible (1ˢᵗ): awful (3ʳᵈ), dreadful (6ᵗʰ), fearful (2ⁿᵈ), foul (4ᵗʰ), frightful (3ʳᵈ), grim (4ᵗʰ), gross (3ʳᵈ), hateful (3ʳᵈ), horrible (4ᵗʰ), offensive (4ᵗʰ), shocking (1ˢᵗ), violent (5ᵗʰ), ugly (4ᵗʰ)

terrier (5ᵗʰ)

terrific (5ᵗʰ): delightful (3ʳᵈ), excellent (1ˢᵗ), fantastic (6ᵗʰ), glorious (4ᵗʰ), great (1ˢᵗ), magnificent (4ᵗʰ), marvelous (4ᵗʰ), outstanding (2ⁿᵈ), splendid

(4th), super (1st), superb (6th), superior (4th), wonderful (1st)

terrified (3rd): frightened (2nd), horrified (4th), scared (1st), stunned (4th)

terrify (3rd): alarm (3rd), frighten (2nd), horrify (4th), panic (1st), scare (1st), shock (1st), stun (4th)

territory (3rd): area (4th), neighborhood (2nd), quarter (1st), region (4th), zone (4th)

terror (3rd): A. beast (3rd), monster (1st) **B.** alarm (3rd), fear (1st), fright (2nd), horror (4th), panic (1st), shock (1st)

test (3rd): A. criteria (5th), examination (5th), guideline (2nd) **B.** attempt (2nd), examine (5th), experiment (3rd), explore (4th), judge (1st), measure (2nd), question (1st), search (1st), trial (4th), try (K)

tether (6th): A. cable (1st), chain (3rd), connection (3rd), rope (1st), tie (1st) **B.** attach (5th), bind (2nd), bridle (6th), check (1st), fasten (4th), line (K), restrain (5th), secure (3rd)

text (6th): book (K), contents (3rd), grammar (6th), idea (1st), matter (1st), subject (1st), words (K), writing (1st)

texture (6th): build (1st), composition (4th), feel (K), formation (4th), frame (3rd), grain (3rd), make (K), net (3rd), pile (1st), touch (1st), weave (4th)

thank (K): acknowledge (5th), appreciate (5th), credit (5th), recognize (3rd), reward (4th), tip (1st)

Thanksgiving (K)

that (K): it (K), thing (K)

that's (1st): that is (1st), that was (1st)

thatch (4th): cover (1st), plants (1st), roof (1st), shelter (4th)

the (K): a (K), it (K), one (K)

theater (3rd): A. company (2nd), drama (5th) **B.** arena (5th), hall (1st), movie palace (1st)

theater (3rd)

thee (2nd): you (K)

their (K)

them (K)

theme (4th): A. issue (4th), main idea (1st), opinion (3rd), point (1st), strain (4th), subject (1st), substance (5th), thread (2nd), topic (5th) **B.** composition (4th), essay (5th), paper (K), report (1st), story (K)

then (K): after (1st), behind (1st), beyond (1st), following (1st), later (1st)

thence (4th): from here (K), since (1st), therefore (1st)

theory (5th): assumption (5th), belief (1st), code (3rd), idea (1st), opinion (3rd), philosophy (5th), principle (4th), school (K), science (3rd)

there (1st): away (K), not here (K)

therefore (1st): so (K), thence (4th), thus (1st)

thermodynamics (4th): a division of physics that deals with the relationships and conversions between heat and other forms of energy

thermometer (6th): instrument (3rd), temperature (4th)

theropod (5th): beast-footed dinosaurs

these (K)

they (K): the boys (K), the girls (K), the group (1st), the individuals (3rd), them (1st), the people over there (1st)

they'll (1st)

they're (1st)

thick (2nd): A. abundant (5th), crowded (2nd), full (K), plentiful (2nd) **B.** slow (1st), stupid (4th) **C.** broad (3rd), compact (5th), jelled (5th), solid (3rd), tight (1st), wide (1st) **D.** chummy (6th), intimate (5th) **E.** deep (1st), extreme (5th), mysterious (2nd)

thicket (4th): bush (2nd), jungle (4th), shrubbery (4th), woods (1st)

thief (3rd): bandit (3rd), burglar (1st), pirate (5th), robber (1st), smuggler (6th), sneak (4th), trickster (5th)

thigh (3rd)

thin (1st): A. light (K), watery (2nd) **B.** delicate (5th), sheer (5th), transparent (5th) **C.** gentle (3rd), little (K), quiet (K), scarce (4th), weak (3rd) **D.** bony (1st), fragile (6th), lean (3rd), narrow (2nd), skinny (1st), slender (4th), slim (5th), withered (5th)

thing (K): action (1st), anything (1st), article (2nd), calling (1st), design (5th), element (3rd), fashion (3rd), goal (4th), ingredient (4th), item (5th), object (1st), situation (4th), task (3rd), trend (2nd)

things (K): doings (1st), equipment (5th), goods (K), matters (1st), possessions (3rd), stuff (1st), tools (1st), utensils (6th), works (K)

think (1st): acknowledge (5th), assert (6th), assume (5th), believe (1st), conceive (4th), consider (2nd), contend (5th), feel (K), imagine (2nd), intend (6th), maintain (4th), ponder (6th), propose (4th), reason (2nd), speculate (6th), suppose (2nd), view (1st)

third (1st)

thirsty (2nd): arid (6th), craving (6th), dry (1st), eager (5th), longing (2nd), needing moisture (3rd), yearning (6th)

thirteen (1st)

thirty (1st)

this (K): it (K), that (K)

thistle (4th)

thorn (3rd)

thorough (4th): careful (1st), complete (3rd), deliberate (6th), entire (3rd), exact (2nd), fine (1st), global (4th), nice (1st), patient (4th), perfect (3rd), total (2nd)

those (1st): them (1st)

though (1st): although (2nd), but (K), however (3rd)

thought (1st): concept (4th), guess (1st), hope (K), idea (1st), imagination (3rd), judgment (2nd), memory (3rd), mind (1st), notion (5th), purpose (1st), suspicion (4th)

thoughtful (2nd): A. deep (1st), focusing (5th), pondering (6th), serious (4th), substantial (5th), thinking (1st) **B.** careful (1st), considerate (3rd), generous (4th), kind (K), sympathetic (4th), tender (3rd)

thousand (1st)

thrash (4th): batter (1st), beat (1st), blow (1st), crush (4th), defeat (5th), overwhelm (5th), spank (2nd), trample (5th), whip (4th)

thread (2nd): A. braid (2nd), fuse (4th) **B.** plot (4th), subject (1st), theme (4th), thought (1st) **C.** cord (4th), fiber (3rd), line (K), strain (4th), strand (1st), string (1st), twine (3rd), yarn (2nd)

threat (5th): alarm (3rd), danger (1st), hazard (6th), menace (5th), notice (1st), peril (5th), quicksand (1st), risk (4th), warning (3rd)

three (K)

three-fourths (5th)

thresh (6th): A. clean (1st), seed (1st), separate (3rd) **B.** beat (1st), paddle (1st), spanking (2nd), thrash (4th), whipping (4th)

threshold (5th): A. approach (3rd), door (1st), entrance (3rd), frontier (5th), opening (1st) **B.** beginning (1st), edge (1st), start (1st), verge (6th)

threw (1st)

thrift (6th): cheapness (3rd), conservative (5th), economy (4th), moderation (4th), tightness (2nd)

thrill (4th): arouse (4th), charm (3rd), delight (3rd), excitement (4th), impress (5th), inspire (4th), move (K), please (K), stimulate (6th), stir (3rd), throb (5th), tickle pink (2nd), tingle (4th), touch (1st)

thrive (6th): develop (5th), flourish (4th), flower (K), grow (K), progress (4th), prosper (5th), ripen (2nd), succeed (2nd)

throat (1st): neck (1st)

throb (5th): beat (1st), pound (2nd), pulse (5th), surge (5th), tremble (3rd)

throne (4th): emperor (4th), king (K), queen (K), royal seat (3rd), ruler (1st)

throng (5th): crowd (2nd), flock (2nd), gang (1st), group (1st), herd (2nd), jam (K), mass (3rd), mob (4th), pack (1st), press (1st), shove (5th), swarm (4th)

through (1st): A. complete (3rd), conclude (3rd), done (1st), ended (K), finished (1st), over (1st) **B.** direct (1st), straight (3rd) **C.** among (1st), between (1st), beyond (1st), inside (K), under (K)

throughout (2nd)

throw (1st): A. blanket (3rd), comforter (3rd), cover (1st), quilt (6th) **B.** bounce (6th), bump (2nd), cast (2nd), deliver (5th), fling (6th), hurl (5th), launch (5th), pitch (2nd), rid (1st), toss (2nd), unseat (3rd)

thrush (5th)

thrust (4th): A. assault (4th), attack (3rd), offensive (4th) **B.** ambition (4th), drive (K), force (1st), jab (1st), plunge (4th), propel (6th), punch (4th), push (1st), ram (K), shove (5th), stab (5th)

thud (3rd)

thunder (3rd): bellow (4th), boom (1st), clap (2nd), crash (2nd), roar (1st), rumble (3rd), shout (1st), yell (K)

Thursday (1st)

thus (1st): for example (2nd), so (K), thence (4th), therefore (2nd), wherefore (4th), whereupon (4th)

thy (3rd): your (1st)

thyme (4th)

thyself (5th): yourself (2nd)

tick (1st): beat (1st), check (1st), click (2nd), go (K), snap (2nd), sound (1st), strike (2nd), stroke (1st), succeed (2nd), tap (K), throb (5th), work (K)

ticket (1st): admission (4th), ballot (6th), citation (6th), fare (3rd), label (3rd), notice (1st), tag (K), token (5th)

tickets (1st): attaches (5th), designates (5th), labels (3rd)

tide (1st): breakers (4th), current (3rd), direction (1st), drift (2nd), flow (1st), stream (1st), swell (3rd), tendency (5th)

tie (1st): A. association (5th), bond (3rd), connection (3rd), membership (5th), obligation (6th) **B.** draw (K), equal (2nd), even (1st) **C.** attach (5th), band (1st), bind (2nd), chain (3rd), fasten (4th), join (3rd), lash (4th), link (5th), marry (1st), restrain (5th), restrict (6th), secure (3rd), wrap (3rd) **D.** cord (4th), deadlock (3rd), strap (5th)

tiger (K)

tight (1st): A. cheap (3rd) **B.** close (K), confining (6th), fixed (1st), limited (3rd), restricted (6th), sealed (1st), secure (3rd) **C.** compact (5th), crowded (2nd), difficult (5th), fast (1st), firm (2nd), hard (1st), mean (1st), rigid (5th), solid (3rd), stiff (3rd), tense (5th), thick (2nd)

tile (1st): A. clay (1st), stone (2nd) **B.** cover (1st)

till (1st): A. box (K), drawer (2nd), safe (K) **B.** before (K), until (1st) **C.** cultivate (6th), dig up (1st), farm (K), plant (K), plow (4th), weed (1st)

tilt (5th): A. bank (1st), grade (2nd), hill (K), incline (5th), slope (3rd) **B.** angle (3rd), bend (K), flex (6th), lean (3rd), list (2nd), rise (1st), roll (1st), slant (6th), tip (1st), twist (1st)

timber (5th): A. duck (2nd), look out (K) **B.** beam (3rd), board (1st), log (1st), lumber (1st), plank (5th), pole (K), rafter (6th), wood (1st)

time (1st): A. count (K), measure (2nd), set (K) **B.** beat (1st), pulse (5th), rhythm (5th) **C.** age (1st), break (1st), era (6th), instant (3rd), interval (6th), leisure (5th), length (2nd), moment (1st), occasion (3rd), opportunity (3rd), pause (3rd), period (2nd), point (1st),

season (2nd), span (6th), stage (3rd), term (3rd)

timid (5th): A. afraid (1st), cowardly (4th), fearful (1st), frightened (2nd), scared (1st) **B.** bashful (4th), demure (5th), hesitant (4th), quiet (K), reluctant (6th), sheepish (1st), shy (1st)

tin (1st): can (K), package (4th), metal (3rd)

tinge (5th): A. glimmer (6th), little bit (1st), nip (1st), pinch (4th), touch (1st), trace (3rd) **B.** flavor (4th), season (2nd), smell (3rd), spice (3rd), sprinkle (3rd), suggest (2nd), whisper (1st) **C.** color (K), dye (2nd), hint (1st), shade (2nd), stain (4th)

tingle (4th): A. crawl (1st), quake (4th), quiver (4th), shake (1st), tickle (2nd) **B.** excitement (4th), thrill (4th), tremor (6th)

tinker (5th): A. mend (2nd), patch (4th), repair (4th) **B.** dabble (2nd), fiddle (4th), toy (1st), trifle (5th) **C.** fixer (2nd), mender (2nd) **D.** bungle (6th), damage (5th)

tinkle (5th): chime (6th), jingle (2nd), murmur (4th), ring (1st), sound (1st), whisper (1st)

tint (5th): bleach (4th), cast (2nd), color (K), darken (1st), dye (2nd), hue (6th), paint (2nd), pastel (3rd), shade (2nd), stain (4th), tinge (5th), tone (3rd)

tiny (2nd): delicate (5th), little (K), miniature (6th), minor (5th), minute (1st), petty (6th), slight (4th), small (1st)

tip (1st): A. clue (2nd), cue (2nd), guide (1st), hint (1st), key (K), lead (1st), warn (3rd) **B.** bend (K), tilt (5th), turn (1st) **C.** bonus (6th), commission (2nd), reward (4th) **D.** crest (4th), edge (1st), end (K), peak (4th), point (1st), summit (5th), top (K)

tiptoe (4th): creep (1st), sneak (4th)

tire (2nd): annoy (5th), bore (2nd), bother (2nd), disable (3rd), drain (5th), exhaust (4th), fatigue (5th), irritate (6th), weary (4th)

tired (2nd): drained (5th), drooping (5th), exhausted (4th), sleepy (1st), spent (2nd), weary (4th), worn out (3rd)

tissue (5th): cloth (1st), coat (1st), cover (1st), fabric (5th), film (4th), lace (1st), layer (4th), net (3rd), sheet (1st)

title (3rd): A. claim (2nd), deed (1st), right (K), share (2nd) **B.** call (1st), label (3rd), name (K), term (3rd) **C.** banner (3rd), heading (1st)

to (K): into (1st), opposite (3rd)

toast (5th): A. celebrate (4th), drink (1st), honor (1st), pledge (5th), praise (4th), roast (4th), salute (4th) **B.** bake (1st), bread (2nd), brown (K), warm (1st)

tobacco (4th): cigar (4th), cigarette (4th), smoke (1st)

today (K): current (3rd), now (1st), present (2nd)

toe (K)

toenail (4th)

together (1st): as one (K), collective (4th), jointly (4th), mutual (5th), side by side (1st), successive (2nd), united (5th)

toil (4th): A. net (3rd), snare (6th), trap (1st) **B.** effort (2nd), exertion (6th), grind (4th), labor (2nd), persist (5th), strain (4th), struggle (1st), work (K)

toilet (2nd): bathroom (1st), outhouse (K), potty (1st), throne (4th)

token (5th): A. indifferent (5th), little (K), slight (4th), small (1st), unenthusiastic (4th) **B.** badge (5th), emblem (5th), example (2nd), gift (1st), guarantee (6th), keepsake (3rd), mark (1st), omen (6th), pledge (5th), relic (5th), reminder (3rd), sign (1st), symbol (5th)

told (K): informed (5th), remarked (4th), reported (2nd), said (K)

tolerate (5th): accept (3rd), admit (4th), allow (2nd), endure (4th), favor (1st), ignore (5th), let (K), permit (3rd), stand (K), suffer (2nd)

toll (6th): A. chime (6th), peal (6th), ring (1st), sound (1st), strike (2nd) **B.** cost (1st), duty (1st), expense (3rd), fee (4th), pay (1st), penalty (5th), tax (K)

tomato (4th)

tomb (5th): grave (3rd), memorial (3rd), resting place (1st), shrine (5th)

tomfoolery (5th): folly (4th), joking (2nd), mischief (4th), monkey business (2nd), nonsense (5th), oddity (4th), rot (1st), silliness (3rd), strangeness (2nd)

tomorrow (1st): future (5th), the next day (K)

ton (1st): abundance (5th), huge (1st), mass (3rd), weighty (2nd)

tone (3rd): A. attitude (5th), feeling (1st), humor (4th), impression (5th), manner (2nd), mood (3rd), quality (4th), spirit (2nd), temper (4th) **B.** cast (2nd), chime (6th), color (K), flavor (4th), hue (6th), peal (6th), shade (2nd), tinge (5th), tint (5th) **C.** jingle (2nd), noise (1st), note (1st), pitch (2nd), ring (1st), sound (1st), swing (1st)

tongue (3rd): accent (6th), dialect (5th), language (2nd), lick (1st), speech (2nd), taste (1st), vocabulary (6th), voice (1st)

tonic (2ⁿᵈ): healthful (1ˢᵗ), medicine (4ᵗʰ), refresher (6ᵗʰ), stimulating (6ᵗʰ), strengthening (2ⁿᵈ)

tonight (1ˢᵗ): now (K), this evening (1ˢᵗ), today (K)

too (1ˢᵗ): also (K), and (K), as well (1ˢᵗ), besides (1ˢᵗ), furthermore (3ʳᵈ), likewise (2ⁿᵈ), moreover (2ⁿᵈ), plus (1ˢᵗ), with (K)

took (1ˢᵗ): achieved (5ᵗʰ), captured (3ʳᵈ), gained (2ⁿᵈ), swallowed (1ˢᵗ), used (1ˢᵗ)

tool (1ˢᵗ): agent (5ᵗʰ), alter (4ᵗʰ), device (4ᵗʰ), drill (2ⁿᵈ), fit (K), implement (6ᵗʰ), instrument (3ʳᵈ), machine (1ˢᵗ), medium (5ᵗʰ), utensil (6ᵗʰ), vehicle (6ᵗʰ)

toolbox (5ᵗʰ): compartment (6ᵗʰ), holder (1ˢᵗ), storage box (2ⁿᵈ)

toot (1ˢᵗ): blow (1ˢᵗ), honk (1ˢᵗ), sound (1ˢᵗ)

toot (1ˢᵗ)

tooth (1ˢᵗ): dent (1ˢᵗ), fang (5ᵗʰ), point (1ˢᵗ), spine (4ᵗʰ), tusk (5ᵗʰ)

toothpaste (2ⁿᵈ): brush (2ⁿᵈ), cleaner (1ˢᵗ), soap (4ᵗʰ)

top (K): A. cover (1ˢᵗ), lid (1ˢᵗ) **B.** ace (2ⁿᵈ), best (K), better (1ˢᵗ), champion (4ᵗʰ), chief (1ˢᵗ), dominant (5ᵗʰ), finest (1ˢᵗ), first (1ˢᵗ), greatest (2ⁿᵈ), key (K), leading (1ˢᵗ), main (3ʳᵈ), major (3ʳᵈ), maximum (6ᵗʰ), primary (5ᵗʰ), principal (3ʳᵈ), supreme (5ᵗʰ) **C.** beat (1ˢᵗ), pass (2ⁿᵈ), surpass (6ᵗʰ) **D.** cap (K), crest (4ᵗʰ), crown (1ˢᵗ), head (1ˢᵗ), peak (4ᵗʰ), point (1ˢᵗ), summit (5ᵗʰ), tip (1ˢᵗ)

topic (5ᵗʰ): argument (3ʳᵈ), idea (1ˢᵗ), issue (4ᵗʰ), question (1ˢᵗ), statement (2ⁿᵈ), subject (1ˢᵗ), theme (4ᵗʰ), theory (5ᵗʰ)

topple (6ᵗʰ): collapse (5ᵗʰ), cut (K), defeat (5ᵗʰ), fall (K), knock down (3ʳᵈ), spill (1ˢᵗ), tip (1ˢᵗ), tumble (4ᵗʰ), upset (3ʳᵈ)

torch (5ᵗʰ): burn (3ʳᵈ), flame (3ʳᵈ), flashlight (3ʳᵈ)

torment (5ᵗʰ): A. agony (5ᵗʰ), anguish (6ᵗʰ), distress (5ᵗʰ), misery (4ᵗʰ), pain (2ⁿᵈ), sorrow (4ᵗʰ), suffering (2ⁿᵈ), torture (5ᵗʰ), woe (4ᵗʰ) **B.** annoy (5ᵗʰ), badger (2ⁿᵈ), bend (K), corrupt (6ᵗʰ), persecute (6ᵗʰ), punish (4ᵗʰ), twist (1ˢᵗ)

tornado (6ᵗʰ): funnel cloud (3ʳᵈ), gale (2ⁿᵈ), storm (2ⁿᵈ), twister (1ˢᵗ), winds (1ˢᵗ)

torrent (5ᵗʰ): abundance (5ᵗʰ), flood (2ⁿᵈ), flow (1ˢᵗ), rush (2ⁿᵈ), stream (1ˢᵗ)

tortoise (3ʳᵈ)

torture (5ᵗʰ): A. abuse (6ᵗʰ), agony (5ᵗʰ), misery (4ᵗʰ), suffering (2ⁿᵈ), torment (5ᵗʰ) **B.** hurt (1ˢᵗ), injure (5ᵗʰ), persecute (6ᵗʰ), punish (4ᵗʰ)

toss (2ⁿᵈ): A. fling (6ᵗʰ), pitch (2ⁿᵈ), throw (1ˢᵗ) **B.** cast (2ⁿᵈ), lurch (5ᵗʰ), mingle (4ᵗʰ), mix (1ˢᵗ), rock (K), roll (1ˢᵗ), stir (3ʳᵈ), sway (3ʳᵈ)

total (2ⁿᵈ): A. complete (3ʳᵈ), entire (3ʳᵈ), whole (1ˢᵗ) **B.** addition (3ʳᵈ), all (K), amount (2ⁿᵈ), balance (3ʳᵈ), mass (3ʳᵈ), quantity (4ᵗʰ), result (2ⁿᵈ), score (1ˢᵗ) **C.** add (K), count (1ˢᵗ), number (K), plus (1ˢᵗ), sum (1ˢᵗ)

tote (5ᵗʰ): A. bag (1ˢᵗ), load (2ⁿᵈ), suitcase (1ˢᵗ) **B.** bear (K), carry (1ˢᵗ), haul (4ᵗʰ), transport (5ᵗʰ)

totter (6ᵗʰ): limp (5ᵗʰ), lurch (5ᵗʰ), pitch (2ⁿᵈ), reel (5ᵗʰ), rock (K), stagger (4ᵗʰ), sway (3ʳᵈ), toss (2ⁿᵈ)

touch (1ˢᵗ): A. hint (1ˢᵗ), shade (2ⁿᵈ), sprinkle (3ʳᵈ), suggestion (2ⁿᵈ), tinge

(5th), trace (3rd), whisper (1st) **B.** brush (2nd), dab (1st), explore (4th), feel (K), handle (2nd) **C.** contact (4th), pat (K), sensation (5th), stroke (1st)

touching (1st): A. against (1st), meeting (1st) **B.** affecting (4th), exciting (4th), thrilling (4th)

tough (5th): bad (K), cruel (5th), demanding (5th), difficult (5th), durable (6th), firm (2nd), hard (1st), harsh (5th), mean (1st), rigid (5th), rough (4th), rugged (5th), severe (4th), stern (4th), stiff (3rd), strict (6th), strong (K), taxing (1st), trying (1st)

tour (3rd): A. explore (4th), survey (5th), travel (1st), visit (1st) **B.** circuit (4th), journey (3rd), trip (1st)

tourist (5th): foreigner (5th), traveler (1st), visitor (2nd)

tournament (5th): competition (4th), contest (4th), game (1st), match (3rd), meet (K), race (1st)

tow (1st): drag (5th), draw (K), haul (4th), pull (K), tug (1st)

toward (1st): A. almost (K), near (1st) **B.** onward (3rd), to (K)

towel (6th): A. dry (1st), rub (1st) **B.** cloth (1st), linen (4th), paper (K)

tower (3rd): A. ascend (4th), go up (K), soar (6th) **B.** castle (3rd), column (4th), high-rise (1st), pillar (5th), pyramid (5th) **C.** overlook (4th), overshadow (3rd),

towhead (4th): blond (5th), flaxenhaired (6th)

town (K): city (K), downtown (2nd), metropolis (6th), village (2nd)

toxic (2nd): dangerous (6th), deadly (1st), harmful (3rd), poisonous (3rd)

toy (K): A. game (1st), plaything (1st) **B.** imaginary (2nd), miniature (6th) **C.** fiddle (4th), flirt (6th), fool (2nd), jest (4th), kid (1st), play (K), sport (1st), tease (3rd), tinker (5th)

trace (3rd): A. copy (3rd), draw (K) **B.** chase (1st), hunt (2nd), pursue (5th), seek (1st), tail (1st), track (1st), trail (2nd) **C.** image (4th), sketch (5th) **D.** breath (1st), clue (2nd), glimmer (6th), hint (1st), lead (1st), mark (1st), relic (5th), remnant (6th), shade (2nd), shadow (3rd), sign (1st), spark (3rd), sprinkle (3rd), suggestion (2nd), touch (1st), whisper (1st)

track (1st): A. line (K), path (1st), railway (2nd), road (K), route (4th) **B.** chase (1st), follow (1st), hunt (2nd), pursue (5th), seek (1st), shadow (3rd), trace (3rd), trail (2nd)

tractor (K)

trade (1st): A. deal (2nd), exchange (4th), sell (K), switch (4th), transfer (5th) **B.** business (2nd), commerce (6th), enterprise (5th), industry (5th), job (K), profession (5th), work (K)

tradition (5th): belief (1st), custom (6th), habit (3rd), practice (1st), rite (6th), ritual (6th), routine (6th), superstition (5th), way (K)

traffic (5th): A. conveyance (4th), movement (2nd), transport (5th) **B.** bargain (4th), deal (2nd), trade (2nd) **C.** business (2nd), commerce (6th)

tragedy (5th): calamity (6th), disaster (6th), drama (5th), misfortune (5th)

trail (2nd): A. path (1st), road (K), route (4th), track (1st) **B.** chase (1st), drag (5th), follow (1st), hunt (2nd), pursue (5th), seek (1st), shadow (3rd), tail (1st), trace (3rd)

train (K): A. locomotive (5th), rail (2nd) **B.** chain (3rd), line (K), order (1st), row (K), run (K), series (4th), string (1st) **C.** aim (3rd), condition (3rd), drill (2nd), educate (3rd), focus (5th), instruct (4th), point (1st), teach (1st)

trained (1st)

trait (6th): characteristic (6th), feature (3rd), manner (2nd), mark (1st), quality (4th), sign (1st), symptom (6th)

traitor (4th): betrayer (5th), informer (5th)

tramp (4th): A. beggar (2nd), derelict (6th), drifter (2nd) **B.** firm walk (2nd), plodding (5th), stroll (5th) **C.** hike (3rd), march (1st), stomp (4th), tread (4th), walk (K)

trample (5th): crush (4th), defy (6th), squash (2nd), stomp (4th), tramp (4th)

trample (5th): crush (4th), stamp (2nd), stomp (4th), tromp (4th)

tranquil (6th): calm (3rd), collected (3rd), cool (1st), peaceful (2nd), quiet (K), relaxed (4th), serene (6th), still (1st)

transfer (5th): A. relocation (3rd), removal (2nd), sale (1st) **B.** deed (1st), lease (6th) **C.** assign (5th), convey (4th), exchange (4th), move (K), sell (K), shift (4th), ship (1st), trade (2nd)

transform (5th): alter (4th), change (2nd), evolve (6th), modify (5th)

transit (6th): change (2nd), going (1st), journey (3rd), movement (2nd), shift (4th), transport (5th)

translate (5th): explain (2nd), interpret (5th), render (4th)

transmit (4th): air (1st), beam (3rd), broadcast (5th), carry (1st), conduct (3rd), convey (4th), forward (3rd), fun-nel (3rd), pass (2nd), radiate (6th), relay (6th), send (1st), ship (1st), spread (2nd)

transmission (4th)

transom (6th): crosspiece (2nd), window (1st)

transparent (5th): A. direct (1st), honest (3rd), obvious (5th), plain (2nd) **B.** clear (2nd), crystal (3rd), filmy (4th), sheer (5th)

transport (5th): A. charm (3rd), delight (3rd), fascinate (5th) **B.** ecstasy (6th), thrill (4th) **C.** bus (K), ship (1st), transit (6th), truck (1st) **D.** carry (1st), convey (4th), haul (4th), move (K), send (1st)

trap (1st): A. lure (5th), snare (6th), trick (1st) **B.** bag (1st), cage (1st), capture (3rd), catch (1st), imprison (5th), tempt (4th)

trash (2nd): A. destroy (2nd), wreck (4th) **B.** garbage (5th), junk (3rd), litter (2nd), refuse (2nd), rubbish (5th), waste (1st)

travel (1st): A. movement (2nd), transit (6th) **B.** go (K), journey (3rd), move (K), roam (4th), tour (3rd), venture (4th), wander (3rd)

traverse (5th): cross (1st), pass (2nd), roam (4th), rove (6th), stray (3rd), tour (3rd), travel (1st), wander (3rd), voyage (4th)

tray (1st): base (1st), dish (1st), plate (K), platter (6th), server (1st)

treacherous (6th): dangerous (6th), dishonest (3rd), evil (3rd), false (3rd), hostile (4th), shaky (1st), sneaky (4th), traitorous (4th)

tread (4th): A. step (1st), stomp (4th), walk (K) **B.** march (1st), oppress (6th), pace (3rd), plod (5th), trample (5th)

treason (4th): betrayal (5th), mutiny (6th), revolt (5th), riot (6th)

treasure (4th): A. bank (1st), collect (3rd), save (1st) **B.** fortune (3rd), prize (3rd), riches (1st), wealth (3rd) **C.** adore (4th), cherish (5th), honor (1st), idolize (6th), love (K), value (2nd)

treat (2nd): A. cure (4th), heal (3rd) **B.** cope (6th), handle (2nd), manage (4th), use (K) **C.** prepare (1st), process (4th), ready (1st) **D.** extra (1st), gift (1st) **E.** amuse (4th), cheer (3rd), entertain (4th) **F.** candy (K), morsel (5th), snack (2nd) **G.** buy (K), finance (1st), fund (4th)

treatment (5th): A. behavior (4th), handling (2nd), use (K) **B.** cure (4th), remedy (4th) **C.** preparation (2nd), processing (4th)

treaty (4th): agreement (3rd), bargain (4th), compact (5th), contract (4th), deal (2nd), pledge (5th), promise (1st), understanding (1st)

treble (6th): high (K), shrill (5th)

tree (K): A. evergreen (4th), sapling (5th), shrub (4th) **B.** corner (2nd), trap (1st)

tremble (3rd): pulse (5th), quake (4th), quiver (4th), shake (1st), vibrato (5th)

tremendous (4th): A. excellent (1st), extraordinary (5th), fantastic (6th), great (1st), marvelous (4th), super (1st), superb (6th), terrific (5th), wonderful (1st) **B.** big (K), enormous (4th), giant (2nd), huge (1st), immense (4th), massive (5th), vast (4th)

tremor (6th): quake (4th), quiver (4th), shake (1st), shudder (4th), tremble (3rd), vibrate (5th)

trench (5th): A. gorge (5th), groove (5th), furrow (5th) **B.** canal (4th), chan-

nel (4th), cut (K), furrow (6th), rut (1st), slit (5th)

trend (2nd): A. drift (2nd), incline (5th), lean (3rd), tend (K) **B.** course (3rd), direction (1st), drift (2nd), fad (K), fashion (3rd), mood (3rd), pattern (3rd), run (K), tendency (5th)

trespass (6th): A. intrude (6th), invade (5th), sin (1st) **B.** crime (2nd), intrusion (6th), invasion (5th), offense (4th), wrong (1st)

trial (4th): A. developmental (6th), experimental (4th) **B.** examination (5th), inquiry (3rd), study (1st) **C.** attempt (2nd), care (1st), struggle (1st), test (3rd), try (K), worry (1st)

triangle (1st)

Triassic (5th)

tribe (3rd): clan (5th), class (1st), company (2nd), family (K), group (1st), race (1st), species (5th), stock (1st)

tribunal (6th): court (3rd), panel (6th), session (6th), trial (4th)

tribute (5th): award (5th), compliment (5th), credit (5th), honor (1st), medal (4th), praise (4th), recognition (3rd), reward (4th)

Triceratops (2nd)

trick (1st): A. cheat (3rd), confuse (4th), fool (2nd), trap (1st) **B.** act (K), deception (5th), feat (1st), hoax (5th), joke (1st), lie (2nd), plot (4th), prank (5th)

trickery (5th): betrayal (5th), deceit (5th), fraud (6th), shrewdness (6th)

tried (K): dependable (3rd), proved (1st), reliable (5th), sure (1st), tested (3rd)

trifle (5th): A. fragment (6th), hint (1st), suggestion (2nd), tease (3rd), tinge (5th), trace (3rd) **B.** chatter (1st), talk (K) **C.** junk (3rd), plaything (1st), toy (K) **D.** flirt (6th), play (K), tinker (5th)

trigger (6th): A. starter (1st), stimulus (6th) **B.** activate (4th), generate (4th), prompt (4th), provoke (6th), spark (3rd), start (1st)

trim (4th): A. adorn (6th), decorate (3rd), garnish (6th) **B.** border (1st), edge (1st), fringe (5th), lace (4th), ornament (4th), ribbon (4th), ruffle (6th) **C.** clip (2nd), crop (2nd), cut (K), fit (K), shave (1st) **D.** neatness (1st), organization (4th) **E.** clip (2nd), scrap (3rd) **F.** conditioned (3rd), neat (K), orderly (1st), sleek (3rd)

trinket (6th): amusement (4th), decoration (3rd), ornament (4th), plaything (1st), toy (K)

trio (3rd)

trip (1st): A. drop (K), error (4th), fall (K), mistake (1st), slip (3rd), stumble (4th) **B.** adventure (3rd), expedition (4th), journey (3rd), tour (3rd), voyage (4th) **C.** err (6th), lurch (5th), spill (1st), tumble (4th)

tripod (6th)

triumph (5th): A. master (1st), prevail (5th), rejoice (4th), win (1st) **B.** achievement (5th), celebration (4th), conquest (4th), defeat (5th), success (2nd), victory (4th)

troll (1st): beast (3rd), creature (3rd), dwarf (4th), fairy (4th), monster (1st)

troop (3rd): A. assemble (4th), gather (1st), swarm (4th), unite (5th) **B.** band (1st), company (2nd), crowd (2nd), group (1st), herd (2nd), mass (3rd), mob (4th)

trophy (6th): award (5th), keepsake (4th), prize (3rd), relic (5th), token (5th)

tropic (6th)

tropical (5th): boiling (3rd), burning (3rd), hot (1st), oppressive (6th), warm (1st)

trot (5th): A. gallop (4th), jog (2nd), pace (3rd) **B.** hurry (1st), ride (K), run (K), step (1st)

troth (6th): engagement (5th), fidelity (6th), pledge (5th), promise (1st)

trouble (1st): A. annoy (5th), bother (2nd), concern (3rd), distress (5th), worry (1st) **B.** bind (2nd), care (1st), conflict (4th), difficulty (5th), dispute (6th), effort (2nd), misfortune (5th), pain (2nd), problem (1st), sorrow (4th), struggle (1st), trial (4th), upset (3rd), vex (5th)

troublemaker (1st): agitator (5th), gossip (5th), meddler (6th), provoker (6th), rioter (6th)

trough (6th): A. canal (4th), channel (4th), cut (K), furrow (6th), gorge (5th), groove (5th), gully (6th), ravine (5th), trench (5th) **B.** feedbox (2nd), manger (4th)

trousers (5th): breeches (5th), jeans (1st), pants (1st)

trout (4th)

truant (6th): A. avoider (3rd), deserter (1st), neglecter (4th) **B.** absent (5th), gone (1st), missing (1st)

truce (6th): agreement (2nd), peace (1st), rest (1st), treaty (4th)

truck (1st): A. van (K), vehicle (6th) **B.** carry (1st), cart (1st), convey (4th), freight (4th), haul (4th), move (K), ship (1st), transport (5th)

trudge (5th): A. march (1st), tramp (4th), walk (K) **B.** creep (1st), lag (1st), plod (5th), walk (K)

true (K): A. accurate (6th), actual (3rd), constant (4th), devoted (5th), direct (1st), exact (2nd), factual (2nd), faithful (3rd), genuine (5th), honest (3rd), legitimate (6th), loyal (5th), precise (5th), real (1st), right (K), rightful (2nd) **B.** honestly (3rd), sincerely (4th)

trunk (4th): A. box (K), chest (2nd), luggage (4th), suitcase (1st) **B.** nose (1st), snout (5th) **C.** body (1st), framework (4th), stalk (4th), stem (2nd)

trust (1st): A. belief (1st), confidence (6th), faith (3rd) **B.** expect (3rd), rely (5th), understand (1st)

truth (1st): actuality (4th), fact (1st), honesty (3rd), reality (5th)

try (K): A. annoy (5th), bother (2nd), distress (5th), disturb (6th), irritate (6th), strain (4th), worry (1st) **B.** attempt (2nd), judge (1st), tackle (4th), test (3rd) **C.** chance (2nd), effort (2nd), struggle (1st)

tryout (2nd): attempt (2nd), demonstration (6th), performance (4th), test (3rd)

tsunami (5th): a very large ocean wave caused by an underwater earthquake or volcanic eruption

tub (1st): barrel (4th), basin (4th), bath (1st), bowl (1st), bucket (3rd), pail (2nd), vessel (4th)

tube (3rd): channel (4th), cylinder (6th), pipe (1st), shaft (4th), straw (4th), tunnel (2nd)

tuck (1st): A. crease (5th), dart (1st), fold (1st), pleat (5th) **B.** cover (1st), hide (1st), insert (6th), pin (K), stuff (1st)

Tuesday (1st)

tuft (3rd): bunch (3rd), bush (2nd), cluster (4th), puff (2nd), stand (K)

tug (1st): A. effort (2nd), labor (1st), pull (K) **B.** drag (5th), draw (K), haul (4th), tow (1st)

tulip (2nd)

tumble (4th): A. collapse (5th), slip (3rd), stumble (4th), trip (1st) **B.** dive (1st), drop (1st), fall (K), flow (1st), plunge (4th), topple (6th), upset (3rd)

tummy (K): abdomen (6th), belly (5th), stomach (2nd)

tumor (6th): cancer (6th), growth (1st), swelling (3rd)

tumult (6th): agitation (5th), commotion (5th), confusion (4th), disorder (3rd), excitement (4th), fury (4th), fuss (1st), noise (1st), passion (6th), turmoil (5th), uproar (5th), violence (5th)

tune (1st): harmony (4th), melody (4th), song (K), strain (4th)

tunic (6th): garment (4th), jacket (3rd), robe (4th)

tunnel (2nd): A. build (1st), make (K), mine (1st) **B.** burrow (5th), chute (5th), tube (3rd)

turban (5th): headdress (2nd), scarf (6th)

turbulent (5th): agitated (5th), excited (4th), fierce (4th), frantic (5th), furious (4th), stormy (2nd), violent (5th), wild (2nd)

turf (5th): area (3rd), grass (1st), land (K), region (4th), sod (6th), space (1st), territory (3rd), zone (4th)

turkey (K)

turmoil (5th): bother (2nd), confusion (4th), disorder (3rd), excitement (4th), fight (K), noise (1st), stir (3rd), tangle (3rd), whirl (4th)

turn (1st): A. revolve (5th), rotate (4th), spin (1st), swing (1st), twirl (3rd), twist (1st), veer (6th) **B.** attempt (2nd), chance (2nd), opportunity (3rd), try (K) **C.** circle (K), movement (2nd) **D.** difference (1st), shift (4th) **E.** alter (4th), change (2nd), deviate (4th), reverse (5th)

turnip (3rd)

turquoise (5th)

turret (5th): spire (6th), tower (3rd)

turtle (K)

tusk (5th): fang (5th), tooth (1st)

tussle (6th): A. combat (5th), conflict (4th), contest (4th) **B.** fight (K), struggle (1st), wrestle (6th)

tutor (6th): A. coach (4th), drill (2nd), guide (1st), prepare (1st), school (K) **B.** educator (3rd), instructor (4th), leader (1st), teacher (1st), trainer (K)

TV (K): screen (1st), television (5th)

twain (6th): couple (3rd), pair (1st), two (K)

twang (6th): A. ringing (1st), shrillness (5th) **B.** chime (6th), pang (6th), pluck (1st), ring (1st) **C.** suggestion (2nd), trace (3rd)

twang (6th): vibrate (5th)

twelve (1st)

twenty (1st)

twice (3rd): double (3rd), two times (1st)

twig (4th): branch (2nd), limb (4th), sprout (5th), stem (2nd), stick (4th)

twine (3rd): A. braid (2nd), knit (4th), weave (4th) **B.** cord (4th), line (K), rope (1st), string (1st)

twinkle (4th): A. flash (2nd), flicker (5th), glimmer (6th), sparkle (5th), wink (2nd) **B.** blink (6th), gleam (1st), glisten (6th), glitter (4th), pulse (5th), shimmer (5th), shine (1st)

twirl (3rd): A. coil (5th), spin (1st), turn (1st), whirl (4th) **B.** curl (2nd), loop (5th), reel (5th), revolve (5th), ring (1st), rotate (4th)

twist (1st): A. bend (K), cord (4th), twine (3rd) **B.** coil (5th), connect (3rd), curl (2nd), join (3rd), loop (5th), revolve (5th), rotate (4th), snarl (5th), spin (1st), tangle (3rd), tighten (2nd), turn (1st), twirl (3rd), wind (1st)

two (K)

type (1st): A. class (1st), copy (3rd), grade (2nd), order (1st), sort (1st) **B.** breed (4th), division (4th), family (K), flavor (4th), group (1st), kind (K), set (K), species (5th), style (3rd), variety (4th)

typewriter (1st): keyboard (1st), writing machine (1st)

typical (6th): average (3rd), characteristic (6th), common (2nd), general (2nd), model (3rd), normal (5th), ordinary (3rd), regular (3rd), routine (6th), usual (3rd)

Tyrannosaurus Rex (2nd)

tyranny (5th): cruelty (5th), domination (5th), harshness (5th), oppression (6th), sovereignty (4th)

tyrant (5th): emperor (4th), king (K), master (1st), monarch (5th), sovereign (4th)

udder (5th)

ugh (4th)

ugly (4th): awful (3rd), bad (K), evil (3rd), frightening (2nd), grim (4th), hideous (6th), horrible (1st), plain (2nd), repulsive (6th), revolting (5th), shocking (1st), terrible (1st), unattractive (6th), vile (6th)

ultimate (6th): A. best (K) **B.** crest (4th), height (4th), summit (5th), terminal (6th) **C.** extreme (5th), farthest (3rd), final (3rd), furthest (3rd), last (K), peak (4th), remotest (5th), top (K)

umbrella (2nd)

umpire (1st): A. judge (1st), mediator (5th), moderator (4th) **B.** decide (1st), judge (1st), mediate (5th), settle (2nd)

unanimous (6th): agreed (2nd), complete (3rd), solid (3rd), uniform (1st), united (5th)

unbidden (6th): A. free (K), voluntary (5th), willing (5th) **B.** unasked (2nd), uninvited (3rd), unwelcome (2nd)

uncanny (6th): A. amazing (5th), astonishing (4th), extraordinary (5th), fantastic (6th), incredible (6th), marvelous (4th), remarkable (4th), unbelievable (2nd), wonderful (1st) **B.** odd (4th), ominous (6th), peculiar (4th), queer (4th), strange (1st), unreal (2nd), unusual (3rd), weird (1st)

unceremonious (4th): A. casual (5th), easy (K), familiar (3rd), free (K), informal (5th), natural (2nd), relaxed (4th) **B.** abrupt (5th), brief (3rd), careless (5th), hasty (2nd), inconsiderate (3rd), quick (1st), rude (2nd), sharp (1st),

short (1st), tactless (6th), unrefined (6th)

uncertain (1st): A. borderline (2nd), chancy (2nd), clouded (2nd), doubtful (1st), dubious (6th), nebulous (4th), obscure (6th), questionable (2nd), vague (5th) **B.** arguable (3rd), contested (4th), debatable (4th), disputable (6th), open (K), problematic (6th), shady (2nd), suspect (5th), suspicious (5th) **C.** changeable (2nd), fantastic (6th), fickle (6th), temperamental (5th), ticklish (2nd), variable (4th)

uncle (1st)

under (K): below (1st), beneath (1st), lower (1st), sunken (3rd)

underground (4th): A. buried (3rd), sunken (3rd) **B.** concealed (4th), hidden (1st), secret (1st), undercover (1st)

understand (1st): believe (1st), comprehend (5th), conceive (4th), conclude (3rd), decode (5th), determine (5th), estimate (5th), fathom (6th), figure (2nd), grasp (4th), interpret (5th), know (1st), learn (1st), master (1st), perceive (6th), presume (6th), realize (3rd), think (1st)

undertaking (3rd): adventure (3rd), enterprise (5th), feat (1st), job (K), project (4th), task (3rd), venture (4th)

undoubtedly (5th): absolutely (3rd), certainly (1st), positively (2nd), really (1st), surely (1st), truly (1st)

unfit (1st): forlorn (6th), ill (1st), improper (3rd), melancholy (6th), out of shape (2nd), sickly (1st), unable (3rd), unsuitable (3rd), weak (3rd)

unhappy (1st): blue (K), cursed (3rd), dejected (5th), depressed (5th), difficult (5th), down (K), foolish (2nd), gloomy (3rd), mournful (4th), ominous (6th), sad (K), threatening (5th), unfor-

322

tunate (4th), unlucky (1st), unpleasant (3rd)

unidentified (5th): A. mysterious (2nd), strange (1st), supernatural (5th), unexplained (3rd), unfamiliar (3rd) **B.** disguised (5th), hidden (1st), masked (2nd), nameless (2nd), secret (1st), unknown (2nd), veiled (3rd)

uniform (1st): A. suit (1st), costume (4th), habit (3rd) **B.** alike (1st), certain (1st), consistent (3rd), constant (4th), equivalent (6th), even (1st), identical (6th), like (K), matching (3rd), regular (3rd), same (1st), similar (4th), stable (4th), standard (3rd), steady (3rd)

union (3rd): A. marriage (1st), wedding (3rd) **B.** association (5th), blend (5th), bond (3rd), connection (3rd), league (3rd), society (3rd)

unique (6th): alone (1st), different (1st), distinctive (5th), exceptional (2nd), extraordinary (5th), individual (3rd), lone (2nd), matchless (3rd), odd (4th), only (K), particular (4th), peculiar (4th), rare (4th), select (4th), singular (4th), solitary (5th), special (2nd), strange (1st), uncommon (3rd), unusual (3rd)

unison (6th): accord (4th), agreement (3rd), harmony (4th), union (3rd), unity (5th)

unit (5th): item (5th), measure (2nd), member (1st), one (K), part (1st), piece (1st), portion (4th), quantity (4th)

unite (5th): adhere (6th), attach (3rd), band (1st), blend (5th), bond (3rd), cement (4th), clump (3rd), combine (3rd), connect (3rd), couple (3rd), fasten (4th), fuse (4th), join (3rd), knot (4th), link (5th), lock (1st), marry (1st), mate (4th), mix (1st), pool (1st), tie (1st), wed (K)

unity (5th): accord (4th), agreement (2nd), cooperation (5th), entirety (3rd), harmony (4th), individuality (4th), oneness (2nd), teamwork (2nd), union (3rd), unison (6th), wholeness (2nd)

universal (4th): common (2nd), entire (3rd), general (2nd), total (2nd), unlimited (3rd), worldwide (2nd), catholic (5th)

universe (4th): creation (3rd), heavens (1st), infinity (5th), nature (1st), vast (4th)

university (4th): college (4th), institute (5th), school (K)

unless (2nd): aside (3rd), bar (3rd), but (K), except (2nd), excluding (6th), leaving out (2nd), save (1st), without (1st)

unlimited (3rd): boundless (3rd), countless (1st), endless (1st), eternal (4th), infinite (5th)

unpaid (2nd): amateur (5th), free (K)

unreal (1st): artificial (4th), false (3rd), imaginary (3rd), imitation (5th), pretend (2nd)

unruly (6th): aggressive (6th), disorderly (2nd), lawless (2nd), restless (4th), stubborn (5th), uncontrollable (3rd), wild (2nd)

until (1st)

unto (3rd): until (1st), to (K)

unusual (3rd): abnormal (5th), alien (5th), curious (3rd), distinct (5th), extraordinary (5th), irregular (3rd), lone (2nd), new (K), novel (5th), occasional (3rd), odd (4th), quaint (5th), queer (4th), rare (4th), scarce (1st), singular (4th), special (2nd), strange (1st), uncommon (2nd), unique (6th), weird (1st)

unzip (1st): air (1st), expose (4th), loosen (5th), open (K), peel (2nd), reveal (4th), speak (1st), unbind (2nd), undo (2nd), unfasten (4th)

up (K): alert (5th), aware (3rd), excited (4th), familiar (3rd), high (K), increase (3rd), informed (5th), intensify (6th), lift (1st), prepared (2nd), raise (1st), ready (1st)

uphill (1st): angled (3rd), banked (1st), difficult (5th), hard (1st), inclined (5th), pitched (2nd), slanted (6th), sloped (3rd), steep (2nd), strenuous (6th), tilted (5th), trying (1st)

uphold (6th): aid (2nd), back (1st), bolster (4th), brace (5th), carry (1st), champion (4th), defend (5th), maintain (4th), promote (5th), prop (5th), side (K), support (4th), sustain (5th)

upholster (6th): cover (1st), pad (K)

upholstery (6th): covering (1st), fabric (5th), padding (1st)

upon (1st): at (K), atop (3rd), on (K), when (K)

upper (3rd): above (1st), excitement (4th), greatest (1st), higher (1st), leading (2nd), principal (3rd), supreme (5th)

upright (4th): A. erect (4th), stand up (1st), straight (3rd), upstanding (2nd), vertical (1st) **B.** ethical (5th), fair (1st), honest (3rd), just (1st), moral (3rd), noble (3rd), proper (3rd), true (K)

uproar (5th): agitation (5th), clamor (6th), commotion (5th), conflict (4th), confusion (4th), craze (4th), din (6th), disturbance (6th), excitement (4th), fury (4th), fuss (1st), noise (1st), riot (6th), tumult (6th)

upset (3rd): agitate (5th), alarm (3rd), angry (1st), annoyed (5th), anxious (4th), blow (1st), bother (2nd), collapse (5th), confuse (4th), cross (1st), defeat (5th), disorder (2nd), distressed (5th), disturb (6th), excited (4th), failure (3rd), fall (K), fluster (6th), fuming (3rd), mad (K), overthrow (6th), shake (1st), shock (1st), startle (4th), tip (1st), topple (6th), troubled (1st), turnover (1st)

upstairs (3rd)

uptown (1st)

upward (4th): alone (K), high (K), overhead (1st), rising (1st), striving (5th)

uranium (6th)

urchin (3rd): brat (3rd), child (K), kid (K), stray (3rd)

urge (4th): A. desire (5th), hunger (2nd), impulse (5th), longing (1st), yearning (6th) **B.** agitate (5th), arouse (4th), assert (6th), coax (6th), demand (5th), drive (K), encourage (4th), excite (4th), force (1st), insist (5th), itch (5th), motivate (6th), move (K), persuade (5th), prod (6th), prompt (4th), provoke (6th), push (1st), recommend (5th), spur (4th), stimulate (6th), urgency (6th)

urgent (6th): acute (6th), burning (3rd), critical (5th), demanding (5th), desperate (5th), dire (6th), grave (3rd), immediate (3rd), important (1st), pressing (1st), serious (4th), severe (4th), vital (5th)

us (K)

use (K): apply (2nd), assistance (4th), benefit (3rd), control (2nd), custom (6th), employ (5th), exercise (1st), exploit (6th), function (4th), handle (2nd), help (K), manage (4th), operate (3rd), profit (4th), purpose (2nd), routine (6th), service (6th), tradition (5th), utility (6th), utilize (6th)

used (K): hand-me-down (2nd), old (K), ragged (2nd), second hand (1st), worn (3rd), worn out (3rd)

useful (2nd): beneficial (3rd), convenient (4th), effective (4th), fitting (1st), good (K), handy (1st), helpful (1st), practical (4th), productive (4th), suitable (2nd), usable (1st), valuable (4th), working (1st), worthwhile (3rd)

useless (2nd): fruitless (3rd), hopeless (1st), impractical (4th), ineffective (4th), unhelpful (2nd), vain (4th), worthless (3rd)

usher (6th): A. accompany (3rd), attend (3rd), conduct (3rd), direct (1st), escort (5th), guide (1st), lead (1st), pilot (5th) **B.** escort (5th), guide (2nd)

usual (3rd): accepted (3rd), average (3rd), casual (5th), common (2nd), established (3rd), everyday (1st), expected (2nd), familiar (3rd), frequent (4th), general (2nd), habitual (4th), normal (5th), ordinary (3rd), predictable (6th), regular (3rd), routine (6th), traditional (5th), typical (6th)

utensil (6th): appliance (2nd), container (5th), device (4th), fork (1st), holder (2nd), instrument (3rd), knife (1st), spoon (1st), tool (1st)

utilize (6th): adopt (3rd), apply (2nd), control (2nd), employ (5th), exercise (1st), exploit (6th), handle (2nd), manage (4th), occupy (3rd), operate (3rd), service (1st), use (K)

utter (4th): A. air (K), express (5th), pronounce (4th), say (K), tell (K), vent (4th), voice (1st) **B.** absolute (3rd), complete (3rd), downright (1st), pure (3rd), total (2nd)

vacant (6th): bare (3rd), barren (3rd), blank (4th), clear (2nd), deserted (1st), empty (3rd), free (K), hollow (3rd), idle

(4th), uninhabited (6th), unused (2nd), void (6th)

vacation (2nd): A. break (1st), holiday (K), jaunt (6th), recess (2nd), repose (6th), rest (1st), trip (1st) **B.** explore (4th), travel (1st)

vaccine (4th)

vaccination (4th)

vacuum (5th): A. clean (1st), suck (1st), sweep (4th) **B.** emptiness (3rd), void (6th)

vague (5th): blurry (4th), clouded (1st), doubtful (5th), dubious (6th), faint (3rd), foggy (1st), lost (K), mysterious (2nd), obscure (6th), pale (3rd), puzzling (4th), questionable (2nd), remote (5th), suspect (5th), uncertain (1st), unclear (2nd), weak (3rd)

vain (4th): A. arrogant (6th), conceited (5th), haughty (6th), proud (2nd) **B.** empty (3rd), foolish (2nd), hollow (3rd), idle (4th), meaningless (3rd), pointless (3rd), shallow (4th), unsuccessful (3rd), useless (3rd), valueless (2nd), worthless (3rd)

vale (4th): glen (6th), valley (2nd)

valentine (K)

valiant (6th): bold (2nd), brave (1st), courageous (4th), daring (2nd), fearless (3rd), gallant (4th), heroic (5th), resolute (5th), spirited (2nd), stalwart (6th), sturdy (3rd)

valley (2nd): basin (4th), hollow (3rd), ravine (5th), vale (4th)

valuable (4th): costly (1st), dear (1st), expensive (3rd), important (1st), lavish (6th), precious (4th), priceless (2nd), prized (3rd), rare (4th), rich (K), treasured (4th), useful (2nd), valued (2nd), worthwhile (3rd)

value (2ⁿᵈ): A. admire (5ᵗʰ), cherish (5ᵗʰ), esteem (5ᵗʰ), honor (1ˢᵗ), prize (3ʳᵈ), regard (4ᵗʰ), respect (2ⁿᵈ), treasure (4ᵗʰ), worship (4ᵗʰ) **B.** estimate (5ᵗʰ), price (K) **C.** meaning (3ʳᵈ), purpose (1ˢᵗ), significance (6ᵗʰ) **D.** cost (1ˢᵗ), gain (2ⁿᵈ), importance (2ⁿᵈ), merit (4ᵗʰ), price (K), profit (4ᵗʰ), use (K), worth (3ʳᵈ)

valve (6ᵗʰ)

vamoose (6ᵗʰ): bolt (4ᵗʰ), depart (5ᵗʰ), exit (3ʳᵈ), flee (5ᵗʰ), go (K), leave (1ˢᵗ)

van (K): bus (K), car (K), truck (1ˢᵗ), vehicle (6ᵗʰ), wagon (2ⁿᵈ)

vanish (3ʳᵈ): die out (2ⁿᵈ), disappear (2ⁿᵈ), dissolve (4ᵗʰ), expire (6ᵗʰ), fade (1ˢᵗ), perish (4ᵗʰ), retire (4ᵗʰ)

vanity (5ᵗʰ): A. arrogance (6ᵗʰ), conceit (5ᵗʰ), haughtiness (6ᵗʰ), pride (2ⁿᵈ) **B.** emptiness (3ʳᵈ), hollowness (3ʳᵈ), worthlessness (3ʳᵈ)

vanquish (6ᵗʰ): beat (1ˢᵗ), conquer (4ᵗʰ), crush (4ᵗʰ), defeat (5ᵗʰ), destroy (2ⁿᵈ), dominate (5ᵗʰ), eliminate (5ᵗʰ), enslave (3ʳᵈ), master (1ˢᵗ), overpower (2ⁿᵈ), over throw (2ⁿᵈ), ruin (5ᵗʰ), subdue (6ᵗʰ), surpass (6ᵗʰ)

vapor (3ʳᵈ): breath (1ˢᵗ), cloud (1ˢᵗ), fog (1ˢᵗ), fume (3ʳᵈ), gas (1ˢᵗ), mist (1ˢᵗ), smoke (1ˢᵗ), steam (2ⁿᵈ)

various (4ᵗʰ): A. abundant (5ᵗʰ), many (K), multiple (2ⁿᵈ), numerous (4ᵗʰ), several (1ˢᵗ), some (K) **B.** alternate (5ᵗʰ), assorted (5ᵗʰ), different (1ˢᵗ)

vary (4ᵗʰ): adjust (5ᵗʰ), alter (4ᵗʰ), assort (5ᵗʰ), change (2ⁿᵈ), contrast (4ᵗʰ), depart (5ᵗʰ), disagree (3ʳᵈ), dispute (6ᵗʰ), evolve (6ᵗʰ), mix (1ˢᵗ), modify (5ᵗʰ), transform (5ᵗʰ), tune (1ˢᵗ)

vase (2ⁿᵈ): jar (K), pitcher (2ⁿᵈ), pot (K)

vast (4ᵗʰ): big (K), endless (2ⁿᵈ), enormous (4ᵗʰ), extensive (4ᵗʰ), giant (2ⁿᵈ), gigantic (5ᵗʰ), grand (2ⁿᵈ), great (1ˢᵗ), huge (1ˢᵗ), immense (4ᵗʰ), infinite (5ᵗʰ), large (K), mammoth (5ᵗʰ), massive (5ᵗʰ), monstrous (2ⁿᵈ), monumental (2ⁿᵈ), roomy (1ˢᵗ), tremendous (4ᵗʰ), wide (1ˢᵗ)

vault (5ᵗʰ): A. bound (2ⁿᵈ), hop (K), jump (K), leap (3ʳᵈ) **B.** arch (4ᵗʰ), bend (K), curve (3ʳᵈ) **C.** basement (3ʳᵈ), cellar (1ˢᵗ), chest (2ⁿᵈ), safe (1ˢᵗ), strongbox (2ⁿᵈ), tomb (5ᵗʰ), treasury (4ᵗʰ)

veal (4ᵗʰ)

veer (6ᵗʰ): bend (K), curve (3ʳᵈ), shift (4ᵗʰ), swing (1ˢᵗ), turn (1ˢᵗ), twist (1ˢᵗ), wheel (1ˢᵗ)

vegetable (2ⁿᵈ): green (K), plant (K), produce (2ⁿᵈ)

vehicle (6ᵗʰ): A. automobile (3ʳᵈ), car (K), carriage (5ᵗʰ), cart (1ˢᵗ) **B.** agency (5ᵗʰ), agent (5ᵗʰ), channel (1ˢᵗ), instrument (3ʳᵈ), mechanism (6ᵗʰ), medium (5ᵗʰ), method (2ⁿᵈ), way (K)

veil (3ʳᵈ): A. camouflage (5ᵗʰ), cloak (4ᵗʰ), curtain (5ᵗʰ), mantle (4ᵗʰ), mask (2ⁿᵈ), scarf (6ᵗʰ), shield (4ᵗʰ), shroud (6ᵗʰ) **B.** camouflage (5ᵗʰ), cloud (1ˢᵗ), conceal (4ᵗʰ), cover (1ˢᵗ), cover up (1ˢᵗ), curtain (5ᵗʰ), envelope (5ᵗʰ), hide (1ˢᵗ), mask (2ⁿᵈ), obscure (6ᵗʰ), shade (2ⁿᵈ), shroud (6ᵗʰ)

vein (4ᵗʰ): A. blood vessel (4ᵗʰ) **B.** bed (K), mine (1ˢᵗ), seam (5ᵗʰ) **C.** channel (4ᵗʰ), vessel (4ᵗʰ) **D.** attitude (5ᵗʰ), fashion (3ʳᵈ), feeling (1ˢᵗ), flavor (4ᵗʰ), manner (2ⁿᵈ), mind (1ˢᵗ), mode (5ᵗʰ), mood (3ʳᵈ), spirit (2ⁿᵈ), style (3ʳᵈ), temper (4ᵗʰ), tone (3ʳᵈ)

vengeance (6ᵗʰ): punishment (4ᵗʰ), revenge (5ᵗʰ)

venison (5th)

vent (4th): A. express (5th), proclaim (4th), reveal (4th), tell (K), utter (4th), voice (1st) **B.** air (1st)

venture (4th): A. attempt (2nd), bet (1st), chance (2nd), dare (2nd), endanger (6th), endeavor (4th), gamble (5th), hazard (6th), imperil (5th), risk (4th), speculate (6th), try (K), wager (3rd) **B.** advance (2nd), presume (6th) **C.** adventure (3rd), chance (2nd), enterprise (3rd), experiment (5th), exploration (4th), journey (3rd), project (4th), quest (3rd), stake (1st), trial (4th), undertaking (3rd)

venue (6th): address (K), area (3rd), place (1st), spot (K)

verdict (6th): conclusion (3rd), decision (1st), finding (1st), judgment (3rd), opinion (3rd), ruling (2nd), sentence (1st)

verge (6th): approach (3rd), border (1st), boundary (4th), brim (5th), brink (6th), edge (1st), end (K), fringe (5th), hem (1st), limit (3rd), margin (5th), outline (4th), rim (1st), side (K), skirt (3rd), thicket (4th), threshold (5th)

verse (4th): line (K), poem (3rd), rhyme (6th), song (K), stanza (5th)

version (6th): account (3rd), edition (3rd), interpretation (5th), rendition (4th), story (K), variation (4th)

vertebrate (5th): having a backbone or spinal column

vertical (1st): erect (4th), high (K), sheer (5th), steep (2nd), straight (3rd), upright (4th)

vertiport (1st): a landing area for rotocars; essentially a heliport

very (K): actually (3rd), exactly (2nd), extremely (5th), genuinely (5th), greatly (1st), highly (1st), quite (1st), rather (2nd), really (1st), sincerely (4th), terribly (1st), thoroughly (1st), truly (1st), unusually (3rd), well (1st)

vessel (4th): A. boat (1st), ship (1st), **B.** container (5th), cup (1st), drum (1st), keg (1st), pan (K), pot (K), tub (1st), vase (2nd) **C.** vein (4th)

vest (3rd): waistcoat (4th)

vet (1st): A. veteran (6th) **B.** veterinarian (4th) **C.** check (1st), evaluate (6th), examine (5th)

veteran (6th): chief (1st), experienced (4th), expert (5th), master (1st), practiced (1st), professional (5th), ranking (3rd), seasoned (2nd), senior (6th), soldier (3rd), superior (4th)

veterinarian (4th)

vex (5th): anger (1st), annoy (5th), bother (2nd), bug (K), condemn (4th), curse (3rd), enrage (6th), irk (6th), irritate (6th), pester (2nd), provoke (6th), upset (3rd), worry (1st)

vexation (5th): anger (1st), annoyance (5th), bother (2nd), care (1st), concern (3rd), discontent (3rd), displeasure (2nd), dissatisfaction (3rd), irritation (6th), nuisance (6th), pest (1st), problem (1st), regret (5th), worry (1st)

vibrant (5th): active (3rd), alive (3rd), bright (1st), dynamic (5th), energetic (4th), lively (2nd), spirited (2nd), strong (K), vigorous (5th), vital (5th)

vibrate (5th): beat (1st), echo (4th), jar (K), pulsate (5th), quake (4th), quiver (4th), shake (1st), shiver (1st), shudder (4th), surge (5th), sway (3rd), throb (5th), tremble (3rd), wave (K), waver (5th), wobble (4th)

vice (4th): corruption (6th), crime (2nd), dishonor (3rd), evil (3rd), fault (3rd), immorality (4th), impurity (4th), offense (4th), sin (1st), weakness (3rd), wickedness (4th), wrong (1st)

vicinity (6th): area (3rd), closeness (2nd), district (4th), field (2nd), locality (3rd), nearness (2nd), neighborhood (2nd), range (3rd), reach (1st), section (4th), sphere (6th), surroundings (3rd), zone (4th)

vicious (6th): angry (1st), bad (K), brutal (6th), cruel (5th), deadly (1st), evil (3rd), fierce (4th), foul (4th), hateful (3rd), horrible (4th), hostile (4th), intense (6th), mean (1st), savage (5th), violent (5th), wicked (4th), wild (2nd)

victim (4th): casualty (5th), injured (5th), prey (4th), sufferer (2nd), target (5th)

victory (4th): success (2nd), triumph (5th), win (1st)

video (4th): movie (1st)

videoconference (4th)

view (1st): A. look (K), notice (1st), observe (3rd), see (K), watch (1st), witness (3rd) **B.** picture (K), prospect (4th), scene (2nd) **C.** comprehend (5th), sight (1st), understand (1st), vision (4th) **D.** attitude (5th), belief (1st), bias (6th), opinion (3rd), perception (6th) **E.** angle (3rd), aspect (5th), observance (3rd), side (1st)

viewpoint (5th): angle (3rd), aspect (5th)

vigor (5th): animation (6th), drive (1st), energy (4th), enthusiasm (4th), flair (6th), force (1st), health (K), intensity (6th), might (1st), power (1st), punch (4th), spark (3rd), spirit (2nd),

strength (1st), tolerance (5th), vitality (5th)

vigorous (5th) active (3rd), brisk (6th), energetic (4th), forceful (2nd), lively (1st)

Viking (5th): Scandinavian (5th)

vile (6th): awful (3rd), bad (K), base (1st), corrupt (6th), dreadful (6th), evil (3rd), hateful (3rd), horrible (1st), immoral (4th), low (K), sinful (2nd), terrible (1st), wicked (4th), wretched (6th)

village (2nd): community (2nd), settlement (2nd), town (1st)

villain (5th): brute (6th), creep (1st), rat (K), rogue (5th), snake (1st)

violent (5th): brutal (6th), cruel (5th), destructive (5th), fierce (4th), frantic (5th), furious (4th), intense (6th), out of control (2nd), powerful (2nd), savage (5th), severe (4th), stormy (2nd), strong (K), terrible (1st), turbulent (5th), wild (2nd)

violet (2nd)

violin (4th)

virgin (6th): clean (1st), first (1st), inexperienced (4th), new (K), original (3rd), pure (3rd), unused (1st)

virtual environment (also VE) (4th): simulated 3-D environment; a seemingly real artificial environment

virtual reality (4th): a computer simulation that lets users interact with a simulated environment in real time

virtually (4th): almost (K), essentially (6th), nearly (1st), practically (4th), substantially (5th)

virtue (4th): character (2nd), charity (4th), goodness (1st), honor (1st), innocence (5th), morality (3rd), purity (3rd)

virus (2nd)

visible (4th): apparent (3rd), evident (5th), exposed (4th), noticeable (3rd), observable (3rd), obvious (5th), open (K), public (1st), uncovered (2nd), visual (4th)

vision (4th): A. daydream (2nd), dream (1st), fantasy (6th), illusion (6th) **B.** eyesight (1st), sight (1st) **C.** ghost (1st), soul (3rd), spirit (2nd) **D.** image (4th), perception (6th), prophecy (4th), revelation (4th), visualization (4th)

visit (1st): A. chat (1st), stop (K), talk (K) **B.** call (K), stay (1st), tour (3rd) **C.** appear (2nd), attend (3rd), chat (1st), meet (K), talk (K)

vital (5th): A. active (3rd), alive (3rd), dynamic (5th), intense (6th), lively (2nd), living (1st), powerful (2nd), spirited (2nd), strong (K), vibrant (5th), vigorous (5th) **B.** central (3rd), critical (5th), essential (6th), important (1st), key (K), necessary (1st), needed (1st), required (2nd), significant (6th), urgent (6th)

vivid (6th): A. bright (1st), brilliant (4th), colorful (1st), expressive (5th), radiant (6th), splendid (4th), vibrant (5th) **B.** detailed (5th), dramatic (5th), impressive (5th), intense (6th), powerful (2nd), striking (2nd), strong (1st)

vocabulary (6th): dialect (5th), language (2nd), terms (3rd)

voice (1st): A. call (K), language (2nd), sound (1st) **B.** air (K), announce (3rd), express (5th), mouth (1st), proclaim (4th), pronounce (4th), reveal (4th), say (K), speak (1st), state (1st), utter (4th),

vent (4th) **C.** expression (5th), utterance (4th)

void (6th): A. nothing (1st), opening (1st), space (1st), vacancy (6th), vacuum (5th), zero (K) **B.** useless (2nd), vain (4th) **C.** bare (3rd), blank (4th), empty (3rd), hollow (3rd), vacant (6th)

volcano (5th)

volume (3rd): A. amount (2nd), bulk (4th), capacity (6th), content (3rd), mass (3rd), quantity (4th), scope (6th), size (1st) **B.** amount (2nd), number (K), sum (1st), total (2nd) **C.** book (K), edition (3rd), publication (4th), text (6th) **D.** loudness (2nd), sound (1st)

volunteer (5th): A. bestow (5th), give (1st), grant (2nd), offer (2nd), present (K), propose (4th) **B.** communicate (4th), tell (K)

vomit (6th): throw up (1st)

vote (2nd): A. appoint (3rd), choose (3rd), elect (3rd), pick (1st), select (4th) **B.** ballot (6th), count (K), election (3rd), poll (5th)

vow (4th): A. assure (3rd), commit (4th), guarantee (6th), pledge (5th), promise (1st), swear (4th) **B.** guarantee (6th), oath (5th), pledge (5th), promise (1st)

voyage (4th): A. adventure (3rd), journey (3rd), passage (4th), sail (1st), trip (1st), travel (3rd) **B.** adventure (3rd), journey (3rd), roam (4th), tour (3rd), travel (3rd)

vulture (3rd)

waddle (5th): rock (K), roll (1st), stagger (4th), step (1st), sway (3rd), swing (1st), walk (K)

wade (4th)

waft (5th): blow (1st), breath (1st), carry (K), convey (4th), current (3rd), float (1st), fly (K), glide (4th), sail (1st)

wag (1st): shake (1st), sway (3rd), swing (1st), wave (K)

wage (3rd): compensation (6th), conduct (3rd), earnings (2nd), fee (4th), hire (3rd), income (4th), pay (K), salary (3rd)

wagon (2nd): buggy (6th), carriage (5th), cart (1st), coach (4th), stagecoach (4th), van (K)

wail (5th): bawl (5th), cry (1st), grieve (5th), howl (4th), lament (6th), moan (5th), mourn (4th), scream (1st), shriek (4th), sob (1st), sorrow (4th), weep (4th), whine (5th)

wait (K): abide (5th), anticipate (6th), attend (3rd), await (5th), delay (5th), expect (2nd), help (K), linger (4th), look for (1st), lull (5th), pause (3rd), postpone (6th), remain (2nd), rest (1st), serve (1st), stay (1st), suspend (4th), table (1st)

wake (1st): A. funeral (4th), session (6th) **B.** arouse (4th), awaken (3rd), excite (4th), kindle (5th), rise (1st), rouse (4th), stir (3rd)

walk (K): A. lane (4th), pathway (2nd), sidewalk (1st), trail (2nd) **B.** hike (3rd), march (1st), pace (3rd), step (1st), stride (5th), stroll (5th), strut (5th)

walked (1st)

walking (1st)

wall (K): barrier (6th), curtain (5th), divider (4th), face (1st), fence (1st), panel (6th), partition (6th), railing (2nd), screen (1st), side (K), surface (3rd)

wallet (6th): case (2nd), purse (4th)

wallow (6th): A. delight (3rd), enjoy (2nd), indulge (5th), relish (6th) **B.** flop (1st), pitch (2nd), roll (1st), toss (2nd), tumble (4th)

walnut (1st)

walrus (1st)

waltz (6th): dance (2nd), glide (4th)

wan (6th): ashen (3rd), colorless (1st), dim (1st), faint (3rd), gentle (3rd), ghostly (1st), pale (3rd), peaked (5th), thin (1st), weak (3rd)

wand (3rd): baton (5th), rod (1st), staff (4th), stick (K)

wander (3rd): drift (2nd), ramble (6th), range (3rd), roam (4th), rove (6th), shift (4th), stray (3rd), stroll (5th), travel (3rd), veer (6th)

want (K): absence (5th), crave (6th), demand (5th), desire (5th), fancy (3rd), fault (3rd), flaw (2nd), hunger (2nd), lack (1st), longing (2nd), miss (K), need (1st), passion (6th), poverty (5th), require (2nd), shortage (2nd), thirst (2nd), wish (1st), yearn (6th)

wanted (1st): desired (5th), marketable (4th), needed (1st), salable (4th)

war (1st): arms (2nd), battle (2nd), clash (5th), combat (5th), contest (4th), conflict (4th), fight (1st)

warble (6th): chirp (2nd), sing (1st)

ward (5th): area (3rd), chamber (5th), district (4th), dormitory (5th), guard (1st), hall (1st), region (4th), room (K), section (4th), sentinel (5th), watch (1st), zone (4th)

wardrobe (6th): A. attire (6th), clothes (1st), costume (4th), dress (K), outfit (1st) **B.** bureau (4th), cabinet

(4th), chest (2nd), closet (2nd), dresser (2nd)

ware (5th): goods (1st), line (K), merchandise (6th), products (4th), stock (2nd)

warehouse (5th): stock (1st), stockroom (2nd), store (K), vault (5th)

warm (1st): A. heat (1st), hot (K), stuffy (2nd) **B.** eager (5th), emotional (4th), enthusiastic (4th), lively (1st), violent (5th) **C.** affectionate (4th), comfortable (3rd), friendly (1st), kind (K), loving (1st)

warn (3rd): advise (3rd), alarm (3rd), alert (5th), caution (5th), flag (3rd), inform (5th), notify (3rd), recommend (5th), signal (4th), threaten (5th), tip (1st), urge (4th)

warning (3rd): advice (3rd), caution (5th), notification (3rd), sign (1st), signal (4th), threat (5th)

warp (4th): bend (K), bias (6th), corrupt (6th), infect (6th), misrepresent (4th), prejudice (6th), poison (3rd), slant (6th), twist (1st)

warrant (5th): assure (3rd), authorize (3rd), believe (1st), certificate (6th), establish (3rd), guarantee (6th), license (5th), permit (3rd), right (K), support (4th)

warrior (4th): brave (1st), fighter (1st), soldier (3rd), veteran (6th)

wary (5th): alert (5th), artful (1st), awake (3rd), careful (1st), cautious (5th), clever (3rd), guarded (1st), prudent (6th), suspect (5th), watchful (2nd), wise (1st)

was (K)

wash (1st): bathe (1st), clean (1st), drift (2nd), float (1st), launder (6th),

rinse (3rd), scour (6th), scrub (6th), shower (4th), wet (K)

wasn't (1st)

wasp (2nd)

waste (1st): debris (5th), garbage (5th), junk (3rd), litter (2nd), misuse (3rd), rubbish (5th), scraps (3rd), throw away (2nd), trash (2nd), wasteland (6th), wilderness (4th), wilt (4th)

wasteland (6th): barren (4th), desert (1st), waste (1st), wild (2nd), wilderness (4th)

watch (1st): A. clock (1st) **B.** anticipate (6th), beware (6th), examine (5th), eye (K), guard (1st), inspect (5th), lookout (2nd), mind (1st), observe (3rd), patrol (1st), police (1st), protect (4th), regard (4th), see (K), study (2nd), view (1st), witness (3rd)

watchful (2nd): alert (5th), attentive (2nd), cautious (5th), on guard (1st)

water (K)

watercress (4th)

watermelon (3rd)

wave (K): alert (5th), breaker (4th), curl (2nd), curve (3rd), flag (3rd), flap (4th), indicate (4th), motion (3rd), move (K), rise (1st), rush (2nd), shake (1st), signal (4th), surge (5th), sway (3rd), swell (3rd), swing (1st), tide (1st), twist (1st), wag (1st), warn (3rd)

waver (5th): delay (5th), falter (1st), hesitate (4th), pause (3rd), shift (4th), stagger (4th), stall (5th), stumble (4th), sway (3rd), waffle (4th), weave (4th)

wax (K): build (1st), develop (5th), enlarge (5th), expand (5th), glaze (6th), grow (1st), increase (3rd), polish (4th), shine (1st), spread (2nd), stretch (4th), swell (3rd)

way (K): A. approach (3rd), custom (6th), fashion (3rd), manner (2nd), method (2nd), practice (1st), process (4th), style (3rd), tradition (5th) **B.** access (6th), avenue (3rd), code (3rd), course (3rd), direction (1st), distance (4th), lane (4th), length (2nd), path (1st), road (K), route (4th), street (1st), system (2nd), trail (2nd), use (K)

we (K)

wee (1st): tiny (2nd), small (K)

weak (3rd): defenseless (5th), delicate (5th), dependent (3rd), exposed (4th), feeble (4th), fragile (6th), frail (6th), helpless (2nd), hesitant (4th), ineffective (4th), lacking (2nd), powerless (2nd), reduced (3rd), slight (4th), spineless (4th)

wealth (3rd): abundance (5th), capital (2nd), fortune (3rd), money (K), plenty (1st), prosperity (5th), resources (5th), riches (1st), treasure (4th)

weapon (4th): ammunition (6th), arm (K), defense (5th), shot (1st)

wear (1st): A. decay (5th), destruction (5th), erosion (5th), wear-and-tear (3rd) **B.** attire (6th), clothes (1st), display (3rd), dress (K), exhibit (4th), have on (1st), outfit (1st), show (1st), use (K), weary (4th)

weary (4th): beat (1st), bored (2nd), drain (5th), exhausted (4th), fatigued (5th), impatient (5th), sick (K), spent (2nd), tired (2nd), wear (1st), worn (1st)

weasel (3rd)

weather (1st): A. climate (4th), temperature (4th) **B.** bear (K), overcome (1st), resist (4th), stand (K), suffer (2nd), survive (3rd)

weave (4th): build (1st), compose (4th), create (3rd), design (5th), invent (2nd), knot (4th), lace (4th), loom (5th), loop (5th), make up (2nd), produce (2nd), thread (2nd), twist (1st)

wed (K): associate (5th), attach (5th), blend (5th), bond (3rd), combine (3rd), connect (3rd), couple (3rd), fasten (4th), fuse (4th), join (3rd), link (5th), marry (1st), mate (4th), pair (1st), tie (1st), unite (5th)

wedding (1st): ceremony (5th), marriage (2nd), vows (4th)

wedge (4th): A. crowd (2nd), force (1st), jam (K), lodge (4th), press (1st), squeeze (5th), stuff (1st) **B.** access (6th), cut (K), crack (4th), device (4th), gap (K), groove (5th), notch (5th), opening (1st), opportunity (3rd), prop (5th), slot (5th), split (4th), step (1st), void (6th)

Wednesday (1st)

weed (1st): clear (2nd), dig (1st), hoe (2nd), pick (1st), pluck (1st), pull (K)

week (K)

weep (4th): bawl (5th), cry (1st), grieve (5th), lament (6th), mourn (4th), sob (1st), wail (5th), whimper (5th), whine (5th)

weevil (5th)

weigh (1st): A. consider (2nd), contemplate (6th), ponder (6th), reason (2nd), reflect (4th), study (2nd), think (1st) **B.** balance (3rd), measure (2nd) **C.** mark (1st), note (1st), observe (3rd)

weight (1st): A. gravity (4th), mass (3rd), pounds (2nd), volume (3rd) **B.** concern (3rd), emphasis (5th), importance (2nd), significance (6th), value (2nd) **C.** burden (5th), load (2nd), responsibility (4th), stress (6th) **D.** anchor (4th)

weird (1ˢᵗ): crazy (4ᵗʰ), creepy (2ⁿᵈ), curious (3ʳᵈ), fantastic (6ᵗʰ), ghostly (1ˢᵗ), odd (4ᵗʰ), peculiar (4ᵗʰ), queer (4ᵗʰ), strange (1ˢᵗ), unaccountable (3ʳᵈ), unusual (3ʳᵈ), wild (2ⁿᵈ)

welcome (1ˢᵗ): A. agreeable (2ⁿᵈ), comfortable (3ʳᵈ), pleasing (1ˢᵗ) **B.** address (K), embrace (4ᵗʰ), greet (3ʳᵈ), hail (4ᵗʰ), hello (K), meet (K), receive (1ˢᵗ), toast (5ᵗʰ)

weld (6ᵗʰ): attach (5ᵗʰ), bolt (4ᵗʰ), bond (3ʳᵈ), connect (3ʳᵈ), fasten (4ᵗʰ), link (5ᵗʰ), pin (K), fuse (4ᵗʰ), unite (5ᵗʰ)

welfare (5ᵗʰ): A. financial aid (2ⁿᵈ), public assistance (4ᵗʰ) **B.** advantage (3ʳᵈ), benefit (3ʳᵈ), good (K), interest (3ʳᵈ), sake (3ʳᵈ) **C.** fortune (3ʳᵈ), happiness (1ˢᵗ), health (K), prosperity (5ᵗʰ), success (2ⁿᵈ)

well (K): A. acceptable (3ʳᵈ), favorable (3ʳᵈ), satisfactory (3ʳᵈ), suitable (3ʳᵈ) **B.** fit (K), hardy (5ᵗʰ), healthy (1ˢᵗ), sound (1ˢᵗ), sturdy (3ʳᵈ) **C.** fortunate (4ᵗʰ), good (K), happy (K), nice (1ˢᵗ), very (K) **D.** flow (1ˢᵗ), run (K), spring (K)

we'll (1ˢᵗ)

well built (2ⁿᵈ): durable (6ᵗʰ), solid (3ʳᵈ), strong (K), sturdy (3ʳᵈ)

went (K)

were (K)

we're (1ˢᵗ)

west (1ˢᵗ)

westward (3ʳᵈ)

wet (K): A. damp (5ᵗʰ), dripping (2ⁿᵈ), fluid (6ᵗʰ), liquid (3ʳᵈ), misty (2ⁿᵈ), moist (4ᵗʰ), rainy (1ˢᵗ), soaked (5ᵗʰ), watery (1ˢᵗ) **B.** flood (2ⁿᵈ), rain (1ˢᵗ), shower (4ᵗʰ), vapor (3ʳᵈ)

whale (1ˢᵗ)

wharf (5ᵗʰ): breakwater (4ᵗʰ), dock (1ˢᵗ), landing (1ˢᵗ), pier (4ᵗʰ)

what (K)

whatever (1ˢᵗ)

wheat (1ˢᵗ)

wheel (1ˢᵗ): A. drive (1ˢᵗ), move (K), push (1ˢᵗ), reel (5ᵗʰ), roll (1ˢᵗ), spin (1ˢᵗ), stagger (4ᵗʰ), sway (3ʳᵈ), turn (1ˢᵗ), veer (6ᵗʰ), whirl (4ᵗʰ) **B.** band (1ˢᵗ), circle (K), disk (2ⁿᵈ), round (K)

wheeze (5ᵗʰ): cough (5ᵗʰ), gasp (4ᵗʰ), sneeze (5ᵗʰ)

when (K): at the time (1ˢᵗ), then (1ˢᵗ)

whence (4ᵗʰ): from (K), where (1ˢᵗ)

whenever (3ʳᵈ): anytime (1ˢᵗ), every time (1ˢᵗ)

where (1ˢᵗ): direction (1ˢᵗ), position (2ⁿᵈ), what place (1ˢᵗ)

whereas (4ᵗʰ): although (2ⁿᵈ), because (K), since (1ˢᵗ), while (1ˢᵗ)

wherefore (4ᵗʰ): therefore (1ˢᵗ)

whereupon (4ᵗʰ): in consequence of (4ᵗʰ), on which (1ˢᵗ)

whether (1ˢᵗ): or (1ˢᵗ)

which (1ˢᵗ): that (K)

whiff (5ᵗʰ): A. clue (2ⁿᵈ), hint (1ˢᵗ), suspicion (4ᵗʰ), trace (3ʳᵈ) **B.** blow (1ˢᵗ), breath (1ˢᵗ), breeze (4ᵗʰ), puff (2ⁿᵈ), smell (3ʳᵈ), sniff (4ᵗʰ)

while (1ˢᵗ): A. period (2ⁿᵈ), spell (1ˢᵗ), time (1ˢᵗ) **B.** although (2ⁿᵈ), as (K), at the same time (1ˢᵗ), during (4ᵗʰ), whereas (2ⁿᵈ)

whim (6ᵗʰ): craze (4ᵗʰ), dream (K), fancy (3ʳᵈ), impulse (5ᵗʰ), notion (5ᵗʰ)

whimper (5th): cry (1st), groan (3rd), moan (5th), sigh (3rd), sob (1st), wail (5th), weep (4th), whine (5th)

whine (5th): A. beg (1st), bemoan (5th), cry (1st), groan (3rd), lament (6th), moan (5th), plead (3rd), wail (5th), whimper (5th) **B.** complain (4th), gripe (5th), grumble (5th), nag (1st)

whip (4th): A. batter (1st), beat (1st), blend (5th), mix (1st), stir (3rd) **B.** conquer (4th), defeat (5th), lash (4th), pound (2nd), thrash (4th) **C.** route (4th), swing (1st), turn (1st), veer (6th)

whippoorwill (4th)

whir (6th): A. buzz (5th) **B.** fly (K), revolve (5th)

whirl (4th): circle (K), fling (6th), rotate (4th), round (K), spin (1st), turn (1st)

whisk (4th): A. hurry (1st), quickly (1st), rush (2nd), speed (3rd) **B.** brush (2nd), clean (1st), dust (2nd), sweep (4th) **C.** beat (1st), mix (1st)

whiskey (6th): alcohol (4th), liquor (5th), sauce (3rd)

whisper (1st): A. breathe (1st), hum (1st), mumble (4th), murmur (4th), mutter (4th), sigh (3rd), tell (K) **B.** shade (2nd), sprinkle (3rd), tinge (5th), touch (1st) **C.** clue (2nd), hint (1st), suggestion (2nd), suspicion (4th)

whistle (4th): chirp (2nd), hum (1st), sound (1st)

white (K)

White House (K)

who (K)

whoever (1st): anybody (1st), anyone (1st), everybody (3rd), everyone (1st)

whole (1st): A. all (K), complete (3rd), entire (3rd), full (K), sum (1st), total (2nd), undivided (4th) **B.** hearty (5th), perfect (3rd), solid (3rd), strong (K)

wholesome (5th): clean (1st), fit (K), hardy (5th), healthy (1st), helpful (1st), pure (3rd), robust (5th), sound (1st), spotless (2nd), sturdy (3rd), well (1st)

wholly (5th): completely (3rd), entirely (3rd), fully (1st), thoroughly (1st), totally (2nd)

whom (2nd): who (K)

whoop (6th): call (1st), cheer (3rd), cry (1st), roar (1st), scream (1st), shout (1st), yell (K)

why (K): because (K), cause (2nd), reason (2nd)

wick (1st): cord (4th), fibers (3rd), fuse (4th)

wicked (4th): A. awful (3rd), bad (K), corrupt (6th), criminal (4th), dishonest (3rd), evil (3rd), immoral (3rd), monstrous (5th), sinful (2nd), unethical (5th), vile (6th), villainous (5th), wrong (1st) **B.** dangerous (6th), harsh (5th), severe (4th)

wide (1st): ample (5th), broad (3rd), catholic (4th), full (K), large (4th), thick (2nd), vast (4th)

widespread (5th): broad (3rd), common (2nd), current (3rd), general (2nd), global (4th), fashionable (4th), popular (3rd), rampant (6th), universal (4th)

widow (4th)

width (4th): capacity (6th), degree (5th), extent (4th), measure (2nd), range (3rd), reach (1st), scope (6th), size (1st), space (1st), span (6th)

Wi-Fi (4ᵗʰ): (sometimes written Wi-fi, WiFi, Wifi, wifi): short for "Wireless Fidelity;" technically Wi-Fi is a trademark for sets of product compatibility standards for wireless local area networks that connect electronic machines to each other or to the Internet; used for computers, cameras, telephones, PDAs and other devices

wield (6ᵗʰ): control (2ⁿᵈ), exercise (1ˢᵗ), handle (2ⁿᵈ), ply (6ᵗʰ), raise (1ˢᵗ), shake (1ˢᵗ), swing (1ˢᵗ), use (K)

wife (1ˢᵗ): bride (4ᵗʰ), lady (1ˢᵗ), mate (4ᵗʰ)

wig (1ˢᵗ): carpet (4ᵗʰ), fall (K), hairpiece (2ⁿᵈ), rug (1ˢᵗ)

wigwam (5ᵗʰ): home (K), house (K), hut (4ᵗʰ)

wild (2ⁿᵈ): A. barren (4ᵗʰ), desert (1ˢᵗ), waste (1ˢᵗ), wasteland (4ᵗʰ), wilderness (4ᵗʰ) **B.** agitated (5ᵗʰ), confused (4ᵗʰ), disorderly (3ʳᵈ), excited (4ᵗʰ), extravagant (6ᵗʰ), fantastic (6ᵗʰ), fierce (4ᵗʰ), frantic (5ᵗʰ), free (K), mad (K), rambling (6ᵗʰ), reckless (5ᵗʰ), savage (5ᵗʰ), stubborn (5ᵗʰ), uncivilized (4ᵗʰ)

wildcat (2ⁿᵈ)

wilderness (4ᵗʰ): barren (4ᵗʰ), desert (1ˢᵗ), wasteland (4ᵗʰ)

wile (6ᵗʰ): attraction (5ᵗʰ), charm (3ʳᵈ), design (5ᵗʰ), device (4ᵗʰ), lure (5ᵗʰ), snare (6ᵗʰ), temptation (5ᵗʰ), trap (1ˢᵗ)

will (K): A. ambition (4ᵗʰ), choice (3ʳᵈ), discipline (6ᵗʰ), goal (4ᵗʰ), persistence (5ᵗʰ), purpose (1ˢᵗ) **B.** command (2ⁿᵈ), decide (1ˢᵗ), desire (5ᵗʰ), determine (5ᵗʰ), effect (3ʳᵈ), order (1ˢᵗ), wish (K) **C.** free (K), impart (6ᵗʰ), leave (1ˢᵗ), resolve (5ᵗʰ)

willing (5ᵗʰ): agreeable (2ⁿᵈ), compliant (6ᵗʰ), content (3ʳᵈ), cooperative (5ᵗʰ), eager (5ᵗʰ), glad (1ˢᵗ), happy (K), inclined (5ᵗʰ), obedient (4ᵗʰ), pleased (K), unforced (3ʳᵈ), voluntary (5ᵗʰ)

wilt (4ᵗʰ): decay (5ᵗʰ), die (2ⁿᵈ), droop (5ᵗʰ), dry (1ˢᵗ), fade (1ˢᵗ), faint (3ʳᵈ), sag (1ˢᵗ), shrink (5ᵗʰ), waste (1ˢᵗ), wither (5ᵗʰ)

win (K): A. success (2ⁿᵈ), triumph (5ᵗʰ), victory (4ᵗʰ) **B.** ace (2ⁿᵈ), acquaint (4ᵗʰ), best (K), capture (3ʳᵈ), conquer (4ᵗʰ), conquest (4ᵗʰ), defeat (5ᵗʰ), earn (2ⁿᵈ), gain (2ⁿᵈ), get (K), master (1ˢᵗ), score (1ˢᵗ), secure (3ʳᵈ)

wince (5ᵗʰ): quiver (4ᵗʰ), shudder (4ᵗʰ), shy (K), start (1ˢᵗ), startle (4ᵗʰ), tremble (K)

wind (1ˢᵗ): A. blow (1ˢᵗ), breeze (4ᵗʰ), current (3ʳᵈ), gale (2ⁿᵈ), gust (5ᵗʰ), puff (2ⁿᵈ), storm (2ⁿᵈ) **B.** circle (K), coil (5ᵗʰ), curl (2ⁿᵈ), curve (3ʳᵈ), screw (3ʳᵈ), turn (1ˢᵗ), twist (1ˢᵗ)

window (1ˢᵗ): bull's-eye (1ˢᵗ), opening (1ˢᵗ), port (3ʳᵈ)

wine (1ˢᵗ): alcohol (4ᵗʰ), liquor (5ᵗʰ), spirits (2ⁿᵈ)

wing (1ˢᵗ): A. branch (2ⁿᵈ), division (4ᵗʰ), extension (4ᵗʰ), section (4ᵗʰ) **B.** fly (1ˢᵗ), glide (4ᵗʰ), soar (6ᵗʰ) **C.** harm (3ʳᵈ), hit (K), hurt (K), injure (5ᵗʰ)

wink (2ⁿᵈ): A. instant (3ʳᵈ), moment (1ˢᵗ) **B.** hint (1ˢᵗ), sign (1ˢᵗ), signal (4ᵗʰ) **C.** blink (6ᵗʰ), flash (2ⁿᵈ), flicker (5ᵗʰ), shine (1ˢᵗ), sparkle (5ᵗʰ), twinkle (4ᵗʰ)

winter (K)

wipe (1ˢᵗ): brush (2ⁿᵈ), clean (1ˢᵗ), dry (1ˢᵗ), polish (4ᵗʰ), rub (1ˢᵗ), scour (6ᵗʰ), stroke (1ˢᵗ)

wire (3rd): cable (1st), rigging (1st), telegraph (4th)

wise (1st): A. competent (6th), educated (3rd), intelligent (4th), just (1st), knowledgeable (3rd), politic (4th), prudent (6th), reasonable (3rd), sage (5th), sensible (6th) **B.** fashion (3rd), manner (1st), method (2nd), way (K)

wish (K): aim (3rd), desire (5th), fancy (3rd), goal (4th), hope (1st), hunger (2nd), longing (1st), request (4th), want (K), whim (6th), will (K), yearn (6th)

wit (1st): A. comedy (5th), humor (4th), jest (4th), joke (1st) **B.** awareness (3rd), intelligence (4th), keenness (4th), perception (6th), reason (2nd), sense (1st)

witch (K): enchantress (6th), medium (5th), nag (1st), old bat (1st)

with (K): along (1st), also (K), amid (4th), among (1st), and (K), besides (1st), furthermore (3rd), inside (1st), moreover (2nd), plus (1st), too (1st), within (3rd)

withal (6th): also (K), besides (2nd), everything (1st), nevertheless (4th), too (1st)

withdraw (2nd): depart (5th), exit (3rd), go (K), leave (1st), pull out (K), recall (3rd), remove (2nd), resign (5th), retreat (4th), subtract (K), surrender (5th), yield (4th)

wither (5th): decay (5th), decline (6th), droop (5th), dry (1st), fade (1st), sag (1st), shrink (5th), starve (5th), weaken (3rd), wilt (4th)

within (1st): inside (1st), into (1st), inwardly (6th)

without (1st): lacking (1st), not (K)

witness (3rd): A. behold (3rd), note (1st), observe (3rd), see (K), sight (1st), view (1st), watch (1st) **B.** approve (4th), certify (6th), proof (4th), speak (1st), swear (4th), warrant (5th)

wizard (6th): authority (3rd), expert (5th), genius (4th), magician (5th), master (5th), witch (K)

wobble (4th): flex (6th), lean (3rd), quiver (4th), shake (1st), stagger (4th), tilt (5th), tip (1st), twist (1st)

woe (4th): A. agony (5th), anguish (6th), care (1st), depression (6th), distress (5th), grief (5th), misery (4th), pain (2nd), regret (5th), remorse (6th), sadness (1st), sorrow (4th), suffering (2nd), torment (5th) **B.** burden (5th), disaster (6th), trial (4th), trouble (1st)

woman (K): bride (4th), female (4th), individual (3rd), lady (1st), mistress (4th), person (1st), wife (1st)

women (K)

wonder (1st): A. marvel (4th), miracle (5th), novelty (5th), phenomenon (6th), sight (1st), spectacle (5th) **B.** awe (6th), curiosity (3rd), doubt (5th), question (1st), suspicion (4th) **C.** amazement (5th), astonishment (4th), sensation (5th), stare (3rd)

wonderful (1st): delightful (3rd), excellent (1st), fantastic (6th), good (K), glorious (3rd), great (1st), magnificent (4th), marvelous (4th), outstanding (2nd), phenomenal (6th), splendid (4th), superb (6th), super (1st), terrific (5th), tremendous (4th)

won't (1st)

wont (5th): custom (6th), fashion (3rd), habit (3rd), manner (2nd), observance (3rd), practice (1st), routine (6th), tradition (5th), use (K)

woo (6th): attract (5th), beg (1st), court (3rd), encourage (4th), flirt (6th), lure (5th), pursue (5th), romance (5th), tempt (4th), urge (4th)

wood (1st): forest (2nd), lumber (1st), trees (K), timber (5th), wilderness (4th)

woodbine (3rd)

woodchuck (2nd)

woodpecker (2nd)

wool (3rd)

word (K): A. oath (5th), pledge (5th), promise (1st), vow (4th) **B.** account (3rd), expression (5th), gossip (5th), name (K), report (1st), story (K), talk (K), term (3rd) **C.** demand (5th), law (1st), order (1st), rule (K)

work (K): A. business (2nd), employment (5th), job (K), occupation (6th), profession (5th), role (6th), task (3rd), trade (2nd) **B.** act (1st), answer (1st), do (K), effort (2nd), grind (K), labor (2nd), operation (3rd), perform (4th), qualify (4th), run (K), satisfy (3rd), toil (4th) **C.** action (1st), book (K), composition (4th), essay (5th), manuscript (6th), text (6th)

worked (1st)

worker (1st): employee (5th), laborer (2nd), master (1st), operator (5th)

workman (1st): employee (5th), laborer (2nd), operator (5th)

workstation (4th): A. an area, as in an office, outfitted with equipment and furnishings for one worker and usually including a computer **B.** a sophisticated standalone computer used for a specific purpose, such as imaging

world (1st): globe (4th), nations (1st), sphere (6th)

worm (K)

worn (3rd): aged (1st), exhausted (4th), faded (1st), old (K), shabby (4th), spent (2nd), tired (2nd), used (1st), weary (4th)

worrisome (5th): annoying (5th), provoking (6th), tormenting (5th), troublesome (2nd)

worry (1st): A. alarm (3rd), bother (2nd), concern (3rd), confuse (4th), distress (5th), fret (5th), fuss (1st), sweat (3rd), torment (5th), unease (3rd), woe (4th) **B.** anxiety (4th), care (1st), doubt (5th), fear (1st), pain (2nd), stress (6th), trial (4th), trouble (1st)

worse (1st): inferior (5th), meaner (1st), poorer (1st), weaker (3rd)

worship (4th): A. church (K), temple (3rd) **B.** adore (4th), beseech (5th), cherish (5th), devotion (5th), glory (3rd), hail (4th), honor (1st), love (K), praise (4th), pray (3rd), respect (2nd), reverence (4th)

worst (3rd): A. last (K), least (2nd), lowest (K), poorest (1st) **B.** beat (1st), best (K), break (1st), defeat (5th), quench (6th)

worth (3rd): A. cost (1st), merit (4th), price (K), rate (1st), significance (6th), value (2nd) **B.** character (2nd), excellence (1st), honor (1st), quality (4th), stature (6th)

worthless (3rd): fruitless (3rd), immaterial (5th), ineffective (3rd), insignificant (6th), unimportant (2nd), useless (2nd), vain (4th)

would (1st)

wouldn't (1st)

wouldst (5th): will (K)

wound (3rd): A. cut (K), damage (5th), hurt (1st), injure (5th), pierce (4th), shoot (3rd): **B.** ache (5th), blow (1st), bump (2nd), injury (5th), pain (2nd)

wow (K): amaze (5th), astonish (4th), awe (6th), delight (3rd), floor (2nd), impress (5th)

wrap (3rd): A. cape (4th), cloak (4th), coat (1st), shawl (6th) **B.** close (1st), cover (1st), enclose (4th), envelop (5th), package (4th), tape (1st)

wrath (4th): anger (1st), fury (4th), indignation (5th), madness (3rd), outrage (6th), rage (4th), revenge (5th)

wreath (4th): circle (K), crown (1st), garland (6th), ring (1st)

wreck (4th): A. crash (2nd), crush (4th), destroy (2nd), devastate (6th), ruin (5th), shatter (5th), sink (3rd), smash (3rd), trash (2nd) **B.** accident (4th), collision (6th) **C.** remains (2nd), ruins (5th), shell (1st)

wren (5th)

wrench (6th): A. pull (K), tear (2nd), tug (1st), turn (1st), twist (1st), yank (2nd) **B.** hurt (K), pain (2nd), sadness (1st), trouble (1st), worry (1st)

wrest (6th): abduct (6th), clutch (4th), grab (4th), grapple (6th), grasp (4th), grip (4th), hold (1st), nab (1st), seize (3rd), snatch (4th), steal (3rd), take (1st), wrench (6th)

wrestle (6th): battle (2nd), contend (5th), fight (K), grab (4th), grapple (6th), squeeze (5th), struggle (1st), tackle (4th)

wretched (6th): broken (1st), crushed (4th), depressed (5th), difficult (5th), fatal (4th), poor (K), rotten (1st), sorry (2nd), tragic (5th)

wriggle (5th): crawl (1st), slither (4th), snake (5th), squirm (2nd), turn (1st), twist (1st), writhe (6th)

wring (5th): exact (2nd), pierce (4th), pull (K), rend (4th), squeeze (5th), tug (1st), twist (1st), wound (3rd), wrench (6th), wrest (6th), yank (2nd)

wrinkle (3rd): crease (5th), fold (1st), gather (1st), knit (4th), muss (1st), pleat (5th), ridge (5th)

writ (6th): citation (6th), summons (4th), ticket (1st)

write (K): author (3rd), communicate (4th), compose (4th), inscribe (5th), note (1st), rhyme (6th), scratch (4th)

writer (1st): author (3rd), composer (4th), correspondent (5th)

writhe (6th): bend (K), crawl (1st), glide (4th), misshape (1st), slither (4th), snake (5th), squirm (2nd), twist (1st), wriggle (5th)

written (3rd)

wrong (1st): A. corrupt (6th), crime (2nd), error (4th), evil (3rd), fraud (6th), illegal (1st), immoral (3rd), improper (3rd), injustice (3rd), mistake (1st), offense (4th), sin (1st), unethical (2nd), unfair (2nd), unjust (2nd) **B.** abuse (6th), exploit (6th), fault (3rd), harm (3rd), injure (5th), persecute (6th), victimize (4th) **C.** amiss (3rd), bad (K), false (3rd), incorrect (3rd), untrue (2nd), wicked (4th)

wrought (5th): A. excited (4th) **B.** fashioned (3rd), formed (1st), hammered (2nd), manufactured (3rd), turned (1st)

yam (1st)

yank (2nd): drag (5th), draw (K), pull (K), tug (1st), wrench (6th)

yard (K): garden (K), grounds (1st), park (1st), pen (1st), plot (4th)

yarn (2nd): A. cord (4th), fiber (3rd), strand (5th), thread (2nd) **B.** fable (5th), fantasy (6th), fiction (5th), myth (4th), story (K), tale (3rd)

yawn (5th): gape (5th), open wide (1st), stretch (4th), tired (2nd)

ye (4th): you (K)

yea (K): yes (K)

yeah (1st): yes (K)

year (1st): period (2nd), session (6th), span (6th), term (3rd), time (1st), twelve months (1st)

yearly (2nd)

yearn (6th): ache (5th), covet (6th), crave (6th), desire (5th), hunger (2nd), long (1st), need (1st), thrust (4th), want (K), wish for (K)

yeast (2nd): A. bubble (2nd), foam (K), rise (1st) **B.** agitation (5th), confusion (4th), fuss (1st)

yell (K): alarm (3rd), bellow (4th), call (1st), cry (1st), exclaim (3rd), howl (4th), roar (1st), scream (1st), shout (1st), shrick (4th), signal (4th), wail (5th)

yellow (K)

yelp (6th): bark (3rd), bay (K), cry (1st), howl (4th), shout (1st). See yell.

yes (K): yea (K), yeah (1st)

yesterday (3rd): day before (K), last night (1st)

yet (1st): but (K), except (2nd), further (2nd), however (3rd), just (1st), merely (3rd), only (K), simply (2nd), still (1st), through (5th)

yew (2nd)

yield (4th): A. earnings (2nd), gain (2nd), pay (K), profit (4th), result (2nd), return (2nd) **B.** crop (2nd), harvest (4th), produce (2nd), product (4th) **C.** abandon (4th), bend (K), buckle (6th), cave (1st), comply (6th), concede (6th), generate (4th), give (1st), resign (5th), submit (4th), surrender (5th)

yip (1st): bark (3rd), cry (1st), yelp (6th)

yoke (6th): A. band (1st), collar (4th), frame (3rd) **B.** chain (3rd), connect (3rd), group (1st), join (3rd), link (5th), team (1st), tie (1st)

yon (4th): that (K), there (1st), yonder (4th)

yonder (4th): beyond (1st), distant (4th), far (1st), far away (3rd), further (2nd), overseas (2nd), over there (1st), past (1st), yon (4th)

yore (6th): ancient (3rd), earlier (2nd), forgotten (2nd), former (6th), gone (1st), late (1st), long ago (1st), lost (1st), old (K), once (1st), past (1st), preceding (6th), prior (5th), time past (1st), vague (5th)

you (K): thee (2nd), ye (4th)

you'll (1st)

young (1st): A. active (3rd), cheerful (3rd), confident (6th), keen (4th), laughing (1st) **B.** early (1st), fresh (2nd), green (K), immature (5th), innocent (5th), new (K), youthful (2nd)

your (K)

yourself (2nd): oneself (3rd), you (K)

youth (2nd): A. child (K), juvenile (5th), kid (1st), lad (K), minor (5th), teen (2nd) **B.** freshness (2nd), vigor (5th) **C.** early life (1st)

yucca (1st)

Yule (2nd): Christmas (K), New Year (1st)

zeal (6th): delight (3rd), devotion (5th), ecstasy (6th), enjoyment (3rd), enthusiasm (4th), excitement (4th), fire (K), glow (1st), passion (6th), relish (6th), spirited (2nd), warmth (1st), zest (6th)

zealous (6th): ambitious (4th), ardent (6th), devoted (5th), eager (5th), emotional (4th), energetic (4th), extreme (5th), fervent (6th), fiery (5th), intense (6th), loyal (5th), passionate (6th), radical (6th), revolutionary (5th)

zebra (K)

zephyr (6th)

zero (K): bottom (1st), none (1st), nothing (1st)

zest (6th): A. bite (1st), edge (1st), flavor (4th), seasoning (2nd), spice (3rd) **B.** delight (3rd), enjoyment (3rd), fer-vor (6th), fire (K), passion (6th), relish (6th), thrill (4th), zeal (6th), zip (K)

zigzag (3rd): abrupt (5th), angled (3rd), cross (1st), curve (3rd), forked (2nd)

zinc (5th)

zip (K): A. close (1st) **B.** barrel (4th), drive (1st), hurry (1st), rush (2nd), speed (3rd), streak (5th) **C.** easy (1st), energy (4th), spirit (2nd), vigor (5th), vitality (5th), zest (6th)

zipper (K): close (K), fastener (4th), seal (2nd), slide (2nd)

zone (4th): area (3rd), arena (5th), belt (2nd), district (4th), field (2nd), part (1st), quarter (1st), range (3rd), realm (4th), region (4th), section (4th), space (1st), sphere (6th), territory (3rd), ward (5th)

zoo (K): A. confusion (4th), disorder (1st) **B.** garden (K), park (1st)

RESOURCES

RECOMMENDED READINGS

- Dils, Tracey E. *You Can Write Children's Books*. Writer's Digest Books.

- Pope, Alice, ed. *Children's Writer's and Illustrator's Market*. Writer's Digest Books, 2003.

- Wyndham, Lee. *Writing for Children & Teenagers*. Writer's Digest Books.

SOURCES USED FOR WORD LISTS

- Ainsworth, Norma Ruedi. *The Ghost at Peaceful End*. Scholastic, 1977.

- Batchelor de Garcia, Karen and Randi Slaughter. *An Integrated Skills Approach in Plain English*. Addison-Wesley, 1986.

- Beech, Linda Ward and Tara McCarthy. *Communication for Today*. Steck-Vaughn, 1987.

- Bolognese, Don. *Squeak Parker*. Scholastic, 1977.

- Borisoff, Norman. *Dangerous Fortune*. Scholastic, 1976.

- Bunting, Eve. *Going Against Cool Calvin*. Scholastic, 1978.

- Granbeck, Marilyn. *Summer at Ravenswood*. Scholastic, 1977.

- Henney, R. Lee. *Basic Education: Reading Book 1*. Cambridge, 1977.

- Katz, Bobbi. *Action on Ice*. Scholastic, 1976.

- Kimberly, Gail. *Star Jewel*. Scholastic, 1979.

- Martel, Cruz. *Pirate Kite*. Scholastic, 1978.

- Purification, Les. *Karate Ace*. Scholastic, 1976.

- *Reading for Today, a Sequential Program for Adults*. Steck-Vaughn, 1987.

- *Reading 720* (a sequential reading program for children: levels 5–12). Ginn and Company (Xerox Corp.), 1976.

- Roth, Arthur. *Black and White Jones*. Scholastic, 1978.

- Stamper, Judith Bauer. *Ghost Town*. Scholastic, 1979.

- Stevens, Claire. *Mr. Marvel*. Scholastic, 1978.

- Stine, H. William and Megan. *Frozen Danger*. Scholastic, 1978.

- Stine, Megan and H. William. *The Mad Doctor*. Scholastic, 1978.

- Sunshine, Madeline. *Adventure at the Wax Museum*. Scholastic, 1980.

- Sunshine, Madeline. *Midnight Lantern*. Scholastic, 1979.

- Thorndike, Edward L., Irving Lorge. *The Teacher's Word Book of 30,000 Words*. Columbia University, 1944.

- Tivenan, Bonnie. *Contemporary's New Beginnings in Reading*. Contemporary Books, 1985.

- *Word List B*. Minneapolis Public Schools, 1962.

ADDRESSES FOR THE DEPARTMENTS OF EDUCATION FOR U.S. STATES AND TERRITORIES

Alabama

Alabama Department of Education
Gordon Persons Office Building
50 North Ripley Street
P.O. Box 302102
Montgomery, AL 36130-2101
(334) 242-9700
Fax: (334) 242-9708
http://www.alsde.edu/html/
|home.asp

Alaska

Alaska Department of Education
and Early Development
Suite 200
801 West 10th Street
Juneau, AK 99801-1894
(907) 465-2800
TTY: (907) 465-2800
Fax: (907) 465-3452
http://www.eed.state.ak.us/

Arizona

Arizona Department of Education
1535 West Jefferson Street
Phoenix, AZ 85007
(602) 542-4361
(800) 352-4558
Fax: (602) 542-5440
http://www.ade.state.az.us/

Arkansas

Arkansas Department of Education
General Education Division
Room 304A
Four State Capitol Mall
Little Rock, AR 72201-1071
(501) 682-4475
Fax: (501) 682-1079
http://arkedu.state.ar.us/

California

California Department of Education
1430 N Street
Sacramento, CA 95814
(916) 657-2451
Fax: (916) 657-2682
http://www.cde.ca.gov/

Colorado

Colorado Department of Education
201 East Colfax Avenue
Denver, CO 80203-1799
(303) 866-6600
Fax: (303) 830-0793
http://www.cde.state.co.us/

Connecticut

Connecticut Department of
    Education
P.O. Box 2219
Hartford, CT 06145-2219
(860) 566-5061
Fax: (860) 566-8964
http://www.state.ct.us/sde/

Delaware

Delaware Department of Education
John G. Townsend Building
P.O. Box 1402
Federal and Lockerman Streets
Dover, DE 19903-1402
(302) 739-4601
Fax: (302) 739-4654
E-Mail: vwoodruff@state.de.us
http://www.doe.state.de.us/

District of Columbia

District of Columbia Public Schools
Union Square
825 North Capitol Street, NE,
    9th floor
Washington, DC 20002
(202) 442-4289
Fax: (202) 442-5026
http://www.k12.dc.us/dcps/
    home.html

Florida

Florida Department of Education
Turlington Building
325 West Gaines Street
Tallahassee, FL 32399-0400
(850) 487-1785
Fax: (850) 413-0378
http://www.fldoe.org/

Georgia

Georgia Department of Education
2054 Twin Towers East
205 Butler Street
Atlanta, GA 30334-5001
(404) 656-2800
(800) 311-3627

Toll Free Restrictions:
  GA residents only
Fax: (404) 651-6867
http://www.doe.k12.ga.us/
  index.asp

Hawaii
Hawaii Department of Education
P.O. Box 2360
Honolulu, HI 96804
(808) 586-3230
Fax: (808) 586-3234
http://doe.k12.hi.us/

Idaho
Idaho Department of Education
Len B. Jordan Office Building
650 West State Street
P.O. Box 83720
Boise, ID 83720-0027
(208) 332-6800
(800) 432-4601
Toll Free Restrictions:
  ID residents only
TTY: (800) 377-3529
Fax: (208) 334-2228
http://www.sde.state.id.us/Dept/

Illinois
Illinois State Board of Education
100 North First Street
Springfield, IL 62777
(217) 782-4321
Toll Free: (866) 262-6663
TTY: (217) 782-1900
Fax: (217) 524-4928
http://www.isbe.net/

Indiana
Indiana Department of Education
State House, Room 229
Indianapolis, IN 46204-2798
(317) 232-0808
Fax: (317) 233-6326
http://ideanet.doe.state.in.us/

Iowa
Iowa Department of Education
Grimes State Office Building
East 14th and Grand Streets
Des Moines, IA 50319-0146
(515) 281-5294
Fax: (515) 242-5988
http://www.state.ia.us/educate/

Kansas
Kansas Department of Education
120 Southeast 10th Avenue
Topeka, KS 66612-1182
(785) 296-3201
Fax: (785) 296-7933
http://www.ksde.org/

Kentucky
Kentucky Department of Education
19th Floor
500 Mero Street
Frankfort, KY 40601
(502) 564-4770
(800) 533-5372
Toll Free Restrictions:
  KY residents only
Fax: (502) 564-6470
http://www.kde.state.ky.us/

Louisiana

Louisiana Department of Education
626 North Fourth Street
P.O. Box 94064
Baton Rouge, LA 70704-9064
(225) 342-4411
(877) 453-2721
Fax: (225) 342-7316
http://www.doe.state.la.us/lde/
index.html

Maine

Maine Department of Education
23 State House Station
Augusta, ME 04333-0023
(207) 624-6600
TTY: (207) 287-2550
Fax: (207) 287-5802
http://www.state.me.us/
education/homepage.htm

Maryland

Maryland Department of Education
200 West Baltimore Street
Baltimore, MD 21201
(410) 767-0100
Fax: (410) 333-6033
http://www.maryland
publicschools.org/MSDE

Massachusetts

Massachusetts Department of
Education
Educational Improvement Group
350 Main Street
Malden, MA 02148-5023
(781) 338-3000

TTY: (800) 439-2370
Fax: (781) 338-3395
http://www.doe.mass.edu/

Michigan

Michigan Department of Education
Hannah Building
Fourth Floor
608 West Allegan Street
Lansing, MI 48933
(517) 373-3324
Fax: (517) 335-4565
http://www.mde.state.mi.us/

Minnesota

Minnesota Department of Children,
Families, and Learning
1500 Highway 36 West
Roseville, MN 55113-4266
(651) 582-8200
TTY: (651) 582-8201
Fax: (651) 582-8727
http://cfl.state.mn.us/

Mississippi

Mississippi State Department of
Education
P.O. Box 7711
359 North West Street
Jackson, MS 39205
(601) 359-3513
Fax: (601) 359-3242
http://www.mde.k12.ms.us/

Missouri

Missouri Department of Elementary
and Secondary Education

P.O. Box 480
Jefferson City, MO 65102-0480
(573) 751-4212
TTY: (800) 735-2966
Fax: (573) 751-8613
http://www.dese.state.mo.us

Montana

Montana Office of Public
  Instruction
P.O. Box 202501
Helena, MT 59620-2501
(406) 444-3680
(888) 231-9393
Toll Free Restrictions:
  MT residents only
Fax: (406) 444-3924
http://www.opi.state.mt.us/

Nebraska

Nebraska Department of Education
301 Centennial Mall South
P.O. Box 94987
Lincoln, NE 68509-4987
(402) 471-2295
TTY: (402) 471-7295
Fax: (402) 471-0117
http://www.nde.state.ne.us/

Nevada

Nevada State Department of
  Education
700 East Fifth Street
Carson City, NV 89701
(775) 687-9200
Fax: (775) 687-9101
http://www.doe.nv.gov/

New Hampshire

New Hampshire Department of
  Education
101 Pleasant Street
State Office Park South
Concord, NH 03301
(603) 271-3494
(800) 339-9900
TTY: (800) 735-2964
Fax: (603) 271-1953
http://www.ed.state.nh.us/

New Jersey

New Jersey Department of
  Education
P.O. Box 500
100 River View Plaza
Trenton, NJ 08625-0500
(609) 292-4041
Fax: (609) 777-4099
http://www.state.nj.us/education/

New Mexico

New Mexico State Department of
  Education
Education Building
300 Don Gaspar
Santa Fe, NM 87501-2786
(505) 827-6516
TTY: (505) 827-6541
Fax: (505) 827-6696
http://www.sde.state.nm.us/

New York

New York Education Department
Education Building
Room 111

89 Washington Avenue

Albany, NY 12234

(518) 474-3852

Fax: (518) 473-4909

http://www.nysed.gov/

North Carolina

North Carolina Department of
Public Instruction

Education Building

301 North Wilmington Street

Raleigh, NC 27601-2825

(919) 807-3300

Fax: (919) 715-1278

http://www.ncpublicschools.org/

North Dakota

North Dakota Department of Public
Instruction

11th Floor

Department 201

600 East Boulevard Avenue

Bismarck, ND 58505-0440

(701) 328-2260

Fax: (701) 328-2461

http://www.dpi.state.nd.us/

Ohio

Ohio Department of Education

25 South Front Street

Columbus, OH 43215-4183

(877) 644-6338

Fax: (614) 752-3956

http://www.ode.state.oh.us/

Oklahoma

Oklahoma State Department of
Education

2500 North Lincoln Boulevard

Oklahoma City, OK 73105-4599

(405) 521-3301

Fax: (405) 521-6205

http://sde.state.ok.us/home/
defaultie.html

Oregon

Oregon Department of Education

255 Capitol Street, NE

Salem, OR 97310-0203

(503) 378-3569

TTY: (503) 378-2892

Fax: (503) 378-5156

http://www.ode.state.or.us/

Pennsylvania

Pennsylvania Department of
Education

10th Floor

333 Market Street

Harrisburg, PA 17126-0333

(717) 783-6788

Fax: (717) 787-7222

http://www.pde.state.pa.us/

Rhode Island

Rhode Island Department of
Elementary and Secondary
Education

255 Westminster Street

Providence, RI 02903-3400

(401) 222-4600

TTY: (800) 745-5555

Fax: (401) 222-4044

http://www.ridoe.net/

South Carolina

South Carolina Department of
    Education
1006 Rutledge Building
1429 Senate Street
Columbia, SC 29201
(803) 734-8500
Fax: (803) 734-3389
http://www.myscschools.com/

South Dakota

South Dakota Department of
    Education and Cultural Affairs
700 Governors Drive
Pierre, SD 57501-2291
(605) 773-3134
TTY: (605) 773-6302
Fax: (605) 773-6139
http://www.state.sd.us/deca/

Tennessee

Tennessee State Department of
    Education
Andrew Johnson Tower, Sixth Floor
710 James Robertson Parkway
Nashville, TN 37243-0375
(615) 741-2731
Fax: (615) 532-4791
http://www.state.tn.us/education/

Texas

Texas Education Agency
William B. Travis Building
1701 North Congress Avenue
Austin, TX 78701-1494
(512) 463-9734

Fax: (512) 463-9008
http://www.tea.state.tx.us/

Utah

Utah State Office of Education
250 East 500 South
Salt Lake City, UT 84111
(801) 538-7500
Fax: (801) 538-7521
http://www.usoe.k12.ut.us/

Vermont

Vermont Department of Education
120 State Street
Montpelier, VT 05620-2501
(802) 828-3135
TTY: (802) 828-2755
Fax: (802) 828-3140
http://www.state.vt.us/educ/

Virginia

Virginia Department of Education
P.O. Box 2120
101 North 14th Street
Richmond, VA 23218-2120
(804) 225-2020
(800) 292-3820
Toll Free Restrictions:
    VA residents only
Fax: (804) 371-2455
http://www.pen.k12.va.us/go/
    VDOE/

Washington

Office of Superintendent of Public
    Instruction

Old Capitol Building
600 South Washington
P.O. Box 47200
Olympia, WA 98504-7200
(360) 725-6000
TTY: (360) 664-3631
Fax: (360) 753-6712
http://www.k12.wa.us/

West Virginia

West Virginia Department of
  Education
Building 6
1900 Kanawha Boulevard East
Charleston, WV 25305-0330
(304) 558-0304
Fax: (304) 558-2584
http://wvde.state.wv.us/

Wisconsin

Wisconsin Department of Public
  Instruction
125 South Webster Street
P.O. Box 7841
Madison, WI 53707-7841
(608) 266-3390
(800) 441-4563
TTY: (608) 267-2427
Fax: (608) 267-1052
http://www.dpi.state.wi.us/

Wyoming

Wyoming Department of Education
Second Floor
2300 Capitol Avenue
Cheyenne, WY 82002
(307) 777-7675

TTY: (307) 777-6221
Fax: (307) 777-6234
http://www.k12.wy.us/

TERRITORIES

American Samoa

American Samoa Department of
  Education
Pago Pago, AS 96799
(684) 633-5237
Fax: (684) 633-4240
http://www.asg-gov.com/depart-
  ments/doe.home/doe.htm

Commonwealth of the Northern
Mariana Islands

Commonwealth of the Northern
  Mariana Islands Public School
  System
P.O. Box 501370
Saipan, MP 96950
(670) 664-3721
Fax: (670) 664-3796
http://www.pss.cnmi.mp/
  PSSCentralOffice/index2.cfm

Federated States of Micronesia

Department of Health, Education,
  and Social Services
PS70, Palikir, Pohnpei State, FM
  96941
(691) 320-2872
Fax: (691) 320-5263
http://www.literacynet.org/
  |micronesia/doe1.html

Guam
Guam Department of Education
P.O. Box DE
Agana, GU 96932
(671) 475-0457
http://www.doe.edu.gu

Puerto Rico
Puerto Rico Department of
  Education
P.O. Box 190759
San Juan, PR 00919-0759
(787) 759-2000

Republic of Palau
Palau Ministry of Education
P.O. Box 189

Korror, PW 96940
http://www.pacificls.com/MOE/

**Republic of the Marshall
  Islands**
http://www.rmiembassyus.org/
  education/overview.html

Virgin Islands
Virgin Islands Department of
  Education
44-46 Kongens Gade
Charlotte Amalie, VI 00802
(340) 774-0100
Fax: (340) 779-7153
http://www.usvi.org/education/
  index.html

a

abacus (5th)
abandon (4th)
abbey (6th)
abbot (6th)
abbreviate (6th)
abdomen (6th)
abduct (6th)
abhor (6th)
abide (5th)
ablaze (6th)
able (3rd)
aboard (2nd)
abode (5th)
abolish (5th)
abolition (5th)
abominable (6th)
about (K)
above (K)
abroad (5th)
abrupt (5th)
absence (5th)
absent (5th)
absolute (3rd)
absorb (5th)
abstain (6th)
abstract (6th)
absurd (6th)
abundant (5th)
abuse (6th)
accent (6th)
accept (3rd)
access (6th)
accessory (6th)
accident (4th)
accommodate (6th)
accompany (3rd)
accomplish (2nd)

accord (4th)
according to (4th)
account (3rd)
accumulate (6th)
accurate (6th)
accuse (4th)
accustom (4th)
ace (2nd)
ache (5th)
achieve (5th)
acid (4th)
acknowledge (5th)
acorn (4th)
acquaint (4th)
acquire (4th)
acquit (6th)
acrobat (5th)
across (1st)
act (K)
acts (K)
action (1st)
active (3rd)
actor (2nd)
actual (3rd)
acute (6th)
A.D. (5th)
ad (4th)
adapt (4th)
add (K)
adder (5th)
addict (5th)
addition (3rd)
additionally (3rd)
address (K)
adept (4th)
adhere (6th)
adhesive (6th)
adjective (6th)

adjoin (6th)
adjourn (6th)
adjust (5th)
adjustment (5th)
administer (6th)
admiral (5th)
admire (5th)
admit (4th)
adobe (4th)
adolescent (5th)
adopt (3rd)
adore (4th)
adorn (6th)
adrift (6th)
adult (1st)
advance (2nd)
advantage (3rd)
adventure (3rd)
advertise (4th)
advertisement (4th)
advice (3rd)
advise (3rd)
aerial (4th)
aerosol (4th)
affair (2nd)
affect (4th)
affection (4th)
afford (3rd)
afire (2nd)
aflame (2nd)
afloat (2nd)
afraid (1st)
after (K)
afternoon (1st)
afterward (4th)
again (K)
against (1st)
agate (4th)

age (1st)
aged (1st)
agent (5th)
aggress (6th)
aggressive (6th)
agile (6th)
agitate (5th)
ago (1st)
agony (5th)
agree (2nd)
agriculture (4th)
ahead (1st)
aid (2nd)
aide (5th)
AIDS (4th)
aim (3rd)
air (K)
Air Force (1st)
aircraft (1st)
airfield (1st)
airfoil (4th)
airplane (1st)
airport (1st)
airship (1st)
airtight (5th)
alarm (3rd)
alas (4th)
albatross (5th)
album (1st)
alcohol (4th)
alder (tree) (3rd)
ale (2nd)
alert (5th)
alfalfa (3rd)
algae (5th)
alias (6th)
alibi (6th)
alien (5th)

alight (5th)
alike (1st)
alive (3rd)
alkaline (6th)
all (K)
Allah (5th)
allege (6th)
allergic (5th)
allergy (5th)
alley (6th)
allied (6th)
alligator (1st)
allow (2nd)
allowance (5th)
alloy (6th)
ally (6th)
almond (1st)
almost (K)
aloe (4th)
alone (K)
along (1st)
aloud (4th)
alphabet (2nd)
alphanumeric (4th)
already (1st)
also (K)
altar (4th)
alter (4th)
alternate (5th)
although (2nd)
altitude (5th)
alto (6th)
alum (6th)
aluminum (6th)
always (K)
a.m. (6th)
am (K)
amateur (5th)

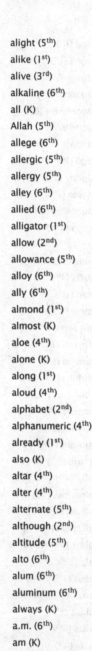

amaze (5th)
Amazon (river)
   (5th)
Amazon (5th)
ambassador (5th)
amber (4th)
ambergris (5th)
ambition (4th)
ambulance (6th)
ambush (6th)
amen (4th)
amend (4th)
amid (4th)
amethyst (4th)
amiss (3rd)
ammonia (6th)
ammunition (6th)
among (1st)
amount (2nd)
amphibian (3rd)
ample (5th)
amplify (6th)
amuse (4th)
an (K) one (K)
analog (4th)
anarchy (5th)
ancestor (5th)
anchor (4th)
anchovy (4th)
ancient (3rd)
and (K)
anemone (3rd)
anew (3rd)
angel (4th)
anger (1st)
angle (3rd)
angry (1st)
anguish (6th)

animal (K)
animate (6th)
animated (6th)
ankle (4th)
announce (3rd)
announcement
   (3rd)
annoy (5th)
annual (4th)
anoint (6th)
another (1st)
answer (K)
ant (K)
antennae (2nd)
antibiotic (4th)
antibodies (4th)
anticipate (6th)
antique (6th)
antler (4th)
anvil (6th)
anxiety (4th)
anxious (4th)
any (K)
anybody (1st)
anyone (1st)
anything (1st)
anyway (1st)
apart (3rd)
apartment (1st)
Apatosaurus (2nd)
ape (5th)
apologize (6th)
apology (6th)
apparatus (6th)
apparent (3rd)
appeal (3rd)
appear (2nd)
appearance (2nd)

appetite (4th)
apple (K)
applesauce (3rd)
apply (2nd)
appoint (3rd)
appreciate (5th)
approach (3rd)
approve (4th)
April (1st)
apron (3rd)
apt (5th)
aquarium (1st)
Arab (5th)
arc (4th)
arch (4th)
archaeology (5th)
Archaeozic Era
   (5th)
archer (5th)
arctic (3rd)
ardent (6th)
are (K)
area (3rd)
arena (5th)
aren't (1st)
argue (3rd)
arid (6th)
arise (4th)
aristocrat (6th)
arithmetic (3rd)
ark (2nd)
arm (K)
armadillo (1st)
armload (2nd)
armor (4th)
arms (1st)
Army (1st)
army (1st)

around (1st)
arouse (4th)
arrange (3rd)
array (5th)
arrest (3rd)
arrive (2nd)
arrogant (6th)
arrow (2nd)
arrowhead (2nd)
art (K)
artichoke (4th)
article (2nd)
artificial (4th)
artificial
   intelligence
   (4th)
artist (2nd)
as (K)
ascend (4th)
ash (3rd)
ashamed (4th)
ashore (2nd)
aside (3rd)
ask (K)
asleep (3rd)
aspect (5th)
aspen (tree) (4th)
asphalt (5th)
assault (4th)
assemble (4th)
assert (6th)
assertive (6th)
assign (5th)
assist (4th)
assistance (4th)
assistant (4th)
associate (5th)
association (5th)

assort (5th)
assume (5th)
assure (3rd)
asteroid (2nd)
asthenosphere
   (5th)
asthma (6th)
astonish (4th)
astound (4th)
astray (3rd)
astride (6th)
astrology (4th)
astronaut (4th)
astronomy (4th)
at (K)
ate (K)
athlete (5th)
atmosphere (4th)
atom (2nd)
atop (3rd)
attach (5th)
attack (3rd)
attain (6th)
attempt (2nd)
attend (3rd)
attention (2nd)
attire (6th)
attitude (5th)
attract (5th)
au Pair (4th)
audible (6th)
August (1st)
aunt (1st)
aurora (5th)
austere (5th)
author (3rd)
authority (3rd)
authorize (3rd)

autobiography
   (6th)
autograph (6th)
automatic (6th)
automobile (3rd)
autumn (3rd)
avenge (5th)
avenue (3rd)
average (3rd)
aviation (6th)
avocado (3rd)
avoid (3rd)
await (5th)
awake (3rd)
awaken (3rd)
award (5th)
aware (3rd)
away (K)
awe (6th)
awful (3rd)
awhile (5th)
awkward (6th)
ax (K)
axis (4th)

b

B.C. (5th)
B.C.E. (5th)
babble (6th)
babe (5th)
baboon (1st)
baby (K)
bachelor (6th)
back (K)
backbone (4th)
background (4th)
backing (1st)
backpack (4th)
backward (4th)

backwoods (4th)
bacon (4th)
bacteria (2nd)
bad (K)
badge (5th)
badger (2nd)
badger (2nd)
bag (1st)
bagpipe (3rd)
bait (3rd)
bake (1st)
balance (3rd)
balcony (6th)
bald (6th)
ball (K)
ballad (5th)
ballast (4th)
ballet (4th)
balloon (1st)
ballot (6th)
bamboo (3rd)
ban (K)
banana (2nd)
band (1st)
bandit (3rd)
bane (5th)
baneberry (4th)
bang (3rd)
banister (5th)
bank (1st)
banner (3rd)
banquet (4th)
banyan (4th)
bar (3rd)
bar code (3rd)
barbecue (5th)
barber (2nd)
bare (3rd)

bareback (4th)

bargain (4th)

barge (5th)

bark (3rd)

barley (4th)

barn (K)

barnacle (3rd)

baron (4th)

barrel (4th)

barren (4th)

barrier (6th)

basalt (5th)

base (1st)

baseball (1st)

basement (3rd)

bashful (4th)

basic (2nd)

basin (4th)

basis (2nd)

basket (1st)

basketball (1st)

bass (1st)

bass (1st)

bat (K)

batch (2nd)

bath (1st)

bathe (1st)

bathroom (1st)

bathtub (1st)

baton (5th)

batter (1st)

battery (5th)

battle (2nd)

bawl (5th)

bay (K)

bayonet (5th)

bayou (5th)

bazaar (5th)

be (K)

beach (K)

beached (1st)

bead (K)

beak (3rd)

beam (3rd)

bear (K)

beard (4th)

beast (3rd)

beat (1st)

beautiful (1st)

beautify (2nd)

beaver (1st)

because (K)

become (1st)

bed (K)

bedraggled (5th)

bedroom (3rd)

bee (K)

beech (4th)

beef (5th)

been (K)

beep (K)

beer (5th)

beet (4th) red (K)

beetle (1st)

before (K)

befriend (6th)

beg (1st)

begin (K)

beginner (2nd)

behalf (6th)

behave (4th)

behavior (4th)

behind (1st)

behold (3rd)

being (1st)

belief (1st)

believe (1st)

bell (K)

belle (6th)

bellow (4th)

belly (5th)

belong (1st)

beloved (4th)

below (1st)

belt (2nd)

bench (4th)

bend (1st)

beneath (1st)

beneficial (3rd)

benefit (3rd)

bent (K)

berate (5th)

berry (1st)

beseech (5th)

beside (1st)

besides (1st)

best (K)

bestow (5th)

bet (1st)

betray (5th)

better (K)

between (1st)

beverage (6th)

beware (6th)

bewilder (3rd)

beyond (1st)

bias (6th)

bib (1st)

Bible (K)

bicycle (2nd)

bid (1st)

big (K)

bike (1st)

bill (1st)

billboard (3rd)

billiards (6th)

billion (5th)

bin (1st)

bind (2nd)

binoculars (6th)

biography (6th)

biology (4th)

biosphere (6th)

birch (4th)

bird (K)

birthday (K)

biscuit (4th)

bishop (5th)

bison (4th)

bit (1st)

bite (1st)

bitter (3rd)

black (K)

blackberry (2nd)

blackbird (1st)

blackboard (3rd)

blackmail (4th)

blacksmith (4th)

blacktop (1st)

blade (2nd)

blame (2nd)

blank (4th)

blanket (3rd)

blast (2nd)

blaze (1st)

bleach (4th)

bleat (4th)

blemish (5th)

blend (5th)

bless (3rd)

blimp (5th)

blind (3rd)

blink (6th)
blister (5th)
blizzard (4th)
block (1st)
blond (5th)
blood (1st)
bloodhound (3rd)
bloodshed (4th)
bloodthirsty (4th)
bloom (4th)
blossom (4th)
blot (4th)
blotch (6th)
blouse (1st)
blow (1st)
blue (K)
blue jay (1st)
bluebell (2nd)
blueberry (2nd)
bluebird (1st)
bluebottle (3rd)
bluff (6th)
blunt (6th)
blur (4th)
blush (4th)
boar (5th)
board (1st)
boast (4th)
boat (1st)
bobbin (4th)
bobcat (1st)
bobolink (5th)
bodily (5th)
body (1st)
bodyguard (4th)
bog (5th)
boil (3rd)
bold (2nd)

bolt (4th)
bomb (5th)
bonbon (4th)
bond (3rd)
bondage (6th)
bone (1st)
bonfire (3rd)
bonnet (6th)
bonus (6th)
boo (K)
boob (2nd)
book (K)
bookcase (3rd)
bookkeeper (3rd)
boom (1st)
boomerang (5th)
boon (5th)
boot (1st)
booth (5th)
borax (5th)
border (1st)
bore (2nd)
born (1st)
borrow (2nd)
boss (K)
both (K)
bother (2nd)
bottle (3rd)
bottom (1st)
bought (2nd)
boulder (5th)
boulevard (4th)
bounce (6th)
bound (2nd)
boundary (4th)
boundless (4th)
bouquet (6th)
bout (6th)

bow (1st)
bowl (1st)
box (K)
boxer (1st)
boy (K)
boycott (6th)
boyfriend (4th)
boyhood (4th)
brace (5th)
bracelet (5th)
brag (3rd)
Brahman (5th)
braid (2nd)
brain (3rd)
brake (1st)
branch (2nd)
brand (2nd)
brandish (6th)
brass (2nd)
brat (3rd)
bravado (6th)
brave (1st)
bravo (6th)
bread (2nd)
breadfruit (2nd)
break (1st)
breakers (4th)
breakfast (1st)
breakwater (4th)
breast (3rd)
breath (1st)
breathe (1st)
breeches (5th)
breed (4th)
breeze (4th)
brew (6th)
bribe (5th)
brick (4th)

bride (4th)
bridesmaid (4th)
bridge (1st)
brief (3rd)
brier (6th)
brig (6th)
brigantine (6th)
bright (1st)
brilliant (4th)
brim (5th)
bring (K)
brink (6th)
brisk (6th)
bristle (6th)
broad (3rd)
broadcast (5th)
broadcloth (5th)
broadsword (4th)
brocade (5th)
broccoli (4th)
broil (4th)
bronco (6th)
bronze (4th)
brooch (4th)
brood (4th)
brook (2nd)
hroom (2nd)
broth (4th)
brother (1st)
brow (4th)
brown (K)
brownie (2nd)
bruise (5th)
brush (2nd)
brutal (6th)
brute (6th)
bubble (2nd)
buck (1st)

bucket (3rd)
buckeye (4th)
buckle (6th)
buckskin (6th)
bud (1st)
buddy (4th)
budge (4th)
budget (5th)
buffet (6th)
bug (K)
buggy (6th)
bugle (6th)
build (1st)
building (1st)
bulb (2nd)
bulge (4th)
bulk (4th)
bull (K)
bulldog (1st)
bulldozer (1st)
bullet(s) (4th)
bulletin (3rd)
bullfrog (1st)
bull's-eye (1st)
bully (1st)
bumble (4th)
bumblebee (4th)
bump (2nd)
bun (2nd)
bunch (3rd)
bundle (5th)
bung (6th)
bunk (4th)
bunny (K)
bunt (2nd)
burden (5th)
bureau (4th)
burglar (1st)

burlap (6th)
burn (3rd)
burning (3rd)
burnoose (5th)
burrow (5th)
burst (3rd)
bury (3rd)
bus (K)
bush (2nd)
business (2nd)
bust (6th)
bustle (6th)
busy (1st)
busybody (3rd)
but (K)
butcher (4th)
butter (2nd)
button (1st)
buttonhole (4th)
buy (K)
buyer (1st)
buzz (5th)
buzzard (4th)
by (K)

C

Common Era (C.E.)
    (5th)
cab (K)
cabbage (4th)
cabin (1st)
cabinet (4th)
cable (1st)
cafe (4th)
cafeteria (5th)
cage (1st)
cake (K)
calamity (6th)
calcium (6th)

calculate (5th)
calendar (1st)
calf (K)
calico (6th)
call (K)
calm (3rd)
calories (3rd)
Cambrian (5th)
came (K)
camel (K)
camera (1st)
cameo (4th)
camouflage (5th)
camp (1st)
campaign (3rd)
campfire (1st)
campus (6th)
can (K)
canal (4th)
canary (1st)
cancel (6th)
cancer (6th)
candidate (4th)
candle (2nd)
candy (K)
cane (3rd)
canine (5th)
cannibal (4th)
cannon (4th)
cannot (1st)
canoe (4th)
canopy (6th)
can't (1st)
canter (5th)
canvas (6th)
canyon (4th)
cap (K)
capable (4th)

capacity (6th)
cape (4th)
caper (4th)
capital (2nd)
capitalize (3rd)
captain (2nd)
caption (6th)
capture (3rd)
car (K)
caramel (5th)
caravan (6th)
carbon (4th)
Carboniferous (5th)
carcass (5th)
card (1st)
cardboard (2nd)
cardinal (3rd)
care (K)
career (4th)
carefree (3rd)
careful (1st)
careless (5th)
caretaker (4th)
cargo (5th)
carload (4th)
carnation (4th)
carnival (2nd)
carnivore (5th)
carol (3rd)
carp (5th)
carpenter (4th)
carpet (4th)
carriage (5th)
carrot (2nd)
carry (K)
cart (1st)
carton (4th)
cartoon (2nd)

cartridge (6th)	cell (1st)	charge (2nd)	Christmas (K)
carve (4th)	cell phone (2nd)	chariot (6th)	circle (1st)
case (2nd)	cellar (1st)	charity (4th)	chirp (2nd)
cash (2nd)	cellophane (5th)	charm (3rd)	chivalry (6th)
cask (4th)	cement (4th)	chart (1st)	chocolate (4th)
casserole (4th)	cemetery (6th)	chase (1st)	choice (3rd)
cast (2nd)	census (6th)	chat (1st)	choir (5th)
castle (3rd)	cent (1st)	chatter (1st)	choke (1st)
casual (5th)	center (2nd)	chauffeur (6th)	choose (3rd)
cat (K)	centigrade (2nd)	cheap (3rd)	chop (2nd)
cat scan (5th)	centimeter (2nd)	cheat (3rd)	chord (5th)
catalog (5th)	central (3rd)	check (1st)	chorus (5th)
catalogue (5th)	century (2nd)	checkers (2nd)	chow (5th)
catbird (1st)	cereal (6th)	cheek (2nd)	chowder (5th)
catch (1st)	ceremony (5th)	cheer (3rd)	Christ (4th)
caterpillar (1st)	certain (1st)	cheese (3rd)	Christian (4th)
cathedral (5th)	certainly (1st)	chef (4th)	Christmas (K)
catholic (4th)	certificate (6th)	chemical (4th)	chrome (2nd)
catnip (3rd)	certify (6th)	Cenozoic (5th)	chronicle (6th)
cattle (3rd)	chagrin (5th)	cherish (5th)	chubby (2nd)
cauldron (6th)	chain (3rd)	cherry (2nd)	chum (6th)
cauliflower (4th)	chair (K)	chess (4th)	church (K)
cause (2nd)	chalk (5th)	chest (2nd)	churn (3rd)
caution (5th)	challenge (4th)	chestnut (4th)	chute (5th)
cautious (5th)	chamber (5th)	chew (1st)	cider (2nd)
cavalry (6th)	champion (4th)	chick (K)	cigar (4th)
cave (1st)	chance (2nd)	chickadee (5th)	cigarette (4th)
cavity (5th)	chancellor (6th)	chicken (K)	cinch (6th)
Cayuse (6th)	chandelier (5th)	chief (1st)	cinnamon (2nd)
cayuse (6th)	change (2nd)	child (K)	circle (K)
cease (3rd)	channel (4th)	childhood (4th)	circuit (4th)
cedar (2nd)	chant (5th)	children (K)	circular (4th)
ceiling (4th)	chap (4th)	chili (4th)	circumstance (6th)
celebrate (4th)	chapel (4th)	chill (3rd)	circus (1st)
celebration (5th)	chapter (3rd)	chime (6th)	cite (6th)
celebrity (5th)	character (2nd)	chin (1st)	citizen (3rd)
celery (4th)	characteristic (6th)	chip (5th)	city (K)
celestial (5th)	charcoal (6th)	chipmunk (2nd)	civil (3rd)

civilization (4th)
claim (2nd)
clam (1st)
clambake (5th)
clamor (6th)
clamp (5th)
clan (5th)
clang (4th)
clank (4th)
clap (2nd)
clash (5th)
clasp (4th)
class (1st)
classic (5th)
classroom (1st)
clatter (5th)
clause (6th)
claw (1st)
clay (1st)
clean (K)
clear (2nd)
cleat (5th)
clergyman (6th)
clerk (2nd)
clever (3rd)
click (2nd)
client (6th)
cliff (2nd)
climate (4th)
climate-controlled
   (4th)
climb (1st)
cling (4th)
clinic (1st)
clip (2nd)
cloak (4th)
clock (1st)
clog (5th)

clone (4th)
close (K)
closet (2nd)
clot (5th)
clothes (1st)
cloud (1st)
clown (1st)
club (1st)
clue (2nd)
clump (3rd)
clumsy (6th)
cluster (4th)
clutch (4th)
clutter (4th)
coach (4th)
coal (2nd)
coarse (4th)
coast (2nd)
coat (1st)
coax (6th)
cob (1st)
cobra (1st)
cobweb (3rd)
cocaine (6th)
cock (4th)
cockpit (2nd)
cocoa (1st)
cocoon (2nd)
code (3rd)
coffee (2nd)
coffin (6th)
cog (6th)
coil (5th)
coin (3rd)
coke (1st)
cold (K)
coliseum (5th)
collapse (5th)

collar (4th)
collect (3rd)
college (4th)
collie (2nd)
collision (6th)
cologne (5th)
colonel (3rd)
colonial (4th)
colony (3rd)
color (K)
colorful (2nd)
colt (K)
column (4th)
comb (2nd)
coma (6th)
combat (5th)
combine (3rd)
combustion (6th)
come (K)
comedian (5th)
comedy (5th)
comet (5th)
comfort (3rd)
comfortable (3rd)
comic (5th)
coming (K)
comma (2nd)
command (2nd)
commence (6th)
commend (6th)
comment (5th)
commentator (5th)
commercial (5th)
commissar (5th)
commission (2nd)
commit (4th)
committee (5th)
commodity (5th)

common (2nd)
commonwealth
   (5th)
commotion (5th)
communicate (4th)
communism (5th)
community (2nd)
commute (4th)
compact (5th)
companion (3rd)
company (2nd)
comparable (3rd)
compare (3rd)
compartment (6th)
compass (4th)
compassion (5th)
compassionate
   (5th)
compel (3rd)
compensation (6th)
compete (4th)
competent (6th)
competition (5th)
complain (4th)
complete (3rd)
complex (6th)
complicate (6th)
compliment (5th)
comply (6th)
composition (4th)
compound (4th)
comprehend (5th)
compress (4th)
comprise (6th)
compromise (5th)
computer (1st)
comrade (4th)
con (3rd)

conceal (4th)
concede (6th)
conceited (5th)
conceive (4th)
concentrate (5th)
concern (3rd)
concerning (3rd)
concession (6th)
conclude (3rd)
concord (6th)
concrete (4th)
condemn (4th)
condo (4th)
condominium (4th)
condense (6th)
condition (3rd)
condor (3rd)
conduct (3rd)
cone(1st)
confederate (6th)
conference (4th)
confess (4th)
confide (6th)
confident (6th)
confidential (6th)
conflict (4th)
conform (6th)
confound (6th)
confront (5th)
confuse (4th)
congratulate (6th)
congregation (6th)
Congress (1st)
congress (4th)
connect (3rd)
conquer (4th)
conscience (4th)
conscious (6th)

conscript (6th)
conscription (6th)
consent (3rd)
consequence (4th)
conserve (5th)
consider (2nd)
consist (3rd)
console (5th)
conspicuous (5th)
constable (6th)
constant (4th)
constantly (4th)
constellation (5th)
consternation (6th)
constitute (4th)
contraceptive (5th)
construct (3rd)
consul (5th)
consult (4th)
consume (4th)
consumerism (5th)
contact (4th)
contaminated (6th)
contagious (6th)
contain(ed) (5th)
contaminate (6th)
contemplate (6th)
contemporary (5th)
contempt (5th)
contend (5th)
content (3rd)
contest (4th)
continent (4th)
continue (2nd)
contract (3rd)
contrary (4th)
contrast (4th)
contribute (4th)

contrite (5th)
contrive (6th)
control (2nd)
controversy (6th)
convenient (4th)
convent (6th)
convention (6th)
conventional (6th)
conversation (5th)
convert (4th)
convey (4th)
convict (5th)
convince (4th)
cook (1st)
cookie (K)
cool (1st)
cooperate (5th)
copal (5th)
cope (6th)
copper (4th)
copy (3rd)
coral (3rd)
cord (4th)
cordial (6th)
core (6th)
cork (6th)
corn (2nd)
corner (2nd)
corny (2nd)
corporal (4th)
corporation (4th)
corps (6th)
correct (3rd)
correspond (5th)
corridor (5th)
corrupt (6th)
cosmetics (6th)

cost (K)
costume (4th)
cot (1st)
cottage (4th)
cotton (2nd)
couch (4th)
cough (5th)
could (K)
couldn't (1st)
council (5th)
counsel (5th)
count (K)
counter (5th)
countless (5th)
country (1st)
couple (3rd)
courage (4th)
course (3rd)
court (3rd)
courtesy (4th)
courtier (6th)
courtroom (3rd)
cover (1st)
covert (6th)
covet (6th)
cow (K)
cowardly (4th)
cowboy (4th)
cowpuncher (6th)
coyote (1st)
crab (K)
crack (4th)
cracker (4th)
crackle (3rd)
cradle (4th)
craft (2nd)
craftsmanship (6th)
crag (6th)

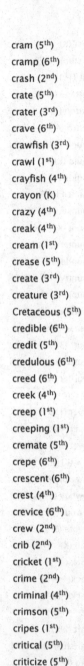

cram (5th)
cramp (6th)
crash (2nd)
crate (5th)
crater (3rd)
crave (6th)
crawfish (3rd)
crawl (1st)
crayfish (4th)
crayon (K)
crazy (4th)
creak (4th)
cream (1st)
crease (5th)
create (3rd)
creature (3rd)
Cretaceous (5th)
credible (6th)
credit (5th)
credulous (6th)
creed (6th)
creek (4th)
creep (1st)
creeping (1st)
cremate (5th)
crepe (6th)
crescent (6th)
crest (4th)
crevice (6th)
crew (2nd)
crib (2nd)
cricket (1st)
crime (2nd)
criminal (4th)
crimson (5th)
cripes (1st)
critical (5th)
criticize (5th)

crocodile (1st)
Cro-Magnon (5th)
crop (2nd)
cross (1st)
crosswise (2nd)
crotch (6th)
crouch (5th)
crow (2nd)
crowd (2nd)
crown (1st)
cruel (5th)
crunch (4th)
crush (4th)
crust (4th)
cry (K)
crystal (3rd)
cub (K)
cube (4th)
cuddle (5th)
cue (2nd)
cuff (1st)
cultivate (6th)
cultivation (6th)
culture (6th)
cunning (6th)
cup (K)
curb (3rd)
cure (4th)
curfew (6th)
curious (3rd)
curl (2nd)
current (3rd)
curse (3rd)
curtain (5th)
curve (3rd)
custom (6th)
customer (5th)
cut (K)

cute (1st)
cutlass (6th)
cutting (1st)
cyber (4th)
cybernetics (4th)
Cyberpunk (4th)
Cyberspace (4th)
cylinder (6th)
Cynognathus (5th)

d

DNA (4th)
dab (1st)
dad (K)
daft (6th)
daily (4th)
dairy (1st)
dam (K)
damage (5th)
damp (5th)
damsel (6th)
dance (1st)
dandy (1st)
danger (1st)
dangerous (6th)
dangle (5th)
dare (2nd)
dark (K)
dart (1st)
data (4th)
database (4th)
datamining (4th)
date (1st)
daughter (1st)
day (K)
daydream (2nd)
daylight (1st)
dazzle (5th)
dead (1st)

deal (2nd)
dear (1st)
debris (5th)
decapitate (6th)
decay (5th)
deceive (5th)
December (1st)
descendant (5th)
decide (1st)
decision (3rd)
deck (1st)
declare (5th)
decline (6th)
decode (5th)
decorate (3rd)
decoration (3rd)
dedicate (6th)
deduce (6th)
deed (1st)
deep (1st)
deer (K)
defeat (5th)
defend (5th)
deform (4th)
defy (6th)
degree (5th)
dehydrate (6th)
deity (5th)
dejected (5th)
delay (5th)
delegate (5th)
delegation (5th)
deliberate (6th)
delicate (5th)
delicatessen (5th)
delight (3rd)
deliver (5th)
demand (5th)

demigod (6th)

demonstrate (6th)

demure (5th)

den (1st)

dent (1st)

deny (5th)

depart (5th)

department (2nd)

depend (3rd)

depose (6th)

deposit (5th)

depress (5th)

depression (6th)

depth (5th)

derelict (6th)

descend (5th)

descendant (5th)

desert (1st)

deserve (4th)

design (5th)

desire (5th)

desk (2nd)

desolate (6th)

desperate (5th)

despise (5th)

destiny (5th)

destroy (2nd)

destruction (5th)

destructive (5th)

detail (5th)

detect (4th)

detective (4th)

determine (5th)

detest (6th)

dethrone (6th)

devastate (6th)

develop (5th)

device (4th)

Devonian (5th)

devote (5th)

devotee (5th)

devour (5th)

dew (1st)

dial (5th)

dialect (5th)

diamond (4th)

diarrhea (6th)

diary (3rd)

did (K)

didn't (1st)

die (2nd)

diet (4th)

differ (4th)

different (1st)

difficult (5th)

dig (1st)

digits (4th)

digital (4th)

dill (1st)

dim (1st)

dime (1st)

diminutive (6th)

din (6th)

dine (1st)

dinosaur (K)

dinner (1st)

dip (1st)

diplomat (5th)

dire (6th)

direct (1st)

direction (1st)

dirt (1st)

disabled (3rd)

disagree (2nd)

disappoint (5th)

disaster (6th)

disbelief (5th)

discard (6th)

discipline (6th)

discontinue (4th)

discourage (5th)

discover (1st)

discuss (5th)

disease (5th)

disguise (5th)

disgust (5th)

dish (1st)

dishearten (5th)

disintegrate (5th)

disk (2nd)

dispense (5th)

display (3rd)

dispose (5th)

disposition (5th)

dispute (6th)

distance (4th)

distant (4th)

distaste (6th)

distinctive (5th)

distinguish (6th)

distress (5th)

distribute (6th)

district (4th)

disturb (6th)

dive (1st)

divide (4th)

divorce (4th)

do (K)

dock (1st)

doctor (1st)

does (1st)

doesn't (1st)

dog (K)

doing (1st)

doll (K)

dolphin (1st)

domicile (5th)

dominant (5th)

dominate (5th)

done (1st)

donkey (K)

don't (1st)

door (K)

doorway (2nd)

dope (1st)

dormitory (5th)

dose (1st)

dot (K)

double (3rd)

doubt (1st)

doubtful (1st)

dough (5th)

down (K)

doughnut (2nd)

dove (K)

down (K)

downhearted (5th)

downstairs (2nd)

downtown (2nd)

Dr. (K)

drag (3rd)

dragon (1st)

drain (5th)

drake (5th)

drama (5th)

dramatize (5th)

drape (5th)

draught (6th)

draw (K)

dread (6th)

dream (K)

dress (K)

dresser (2nd)
drift (2nd)
drill (2nd)
drink (1st)
drip (2nd)
drive (K)
droop (5th)
drop (K)
dropped (1st)
drove (1st)
drown (1st)
drug (1st)
drum (1st)
dry (1st)
dubious (6th)
duck (K)
due (2nd)
dull (1st)
dumb (1st)
dummy (1st)
dump (2nd)
dumpling (4th)
dune (5th)
dungeon (5th)
duplicate (6th)
durable (6th)
during (1st)
dusk (5th)
dust (2nd)
duty (1st)
dwarf (4th)
dwell (4th)
dwelling (4th)
dye (2nd)
dynamic (5th)
dynamite (6th)

e

each (K)

eager (5th)
eagle (1st)
ear (1st)
earl (4th)
early (1st)
earn (2nd)
earnest (4th)
earth (1st)
earthenware (5th)
earthquake (5th)
ease (3rd)
east (1st)
Easter (K)
easy (K)
eat (K)
eating (1st)
eaves (6th)
echo (4th)
eclipse (5th)
ecotourism (5th)
ecology (5th)
ecosystem (5th)
economy (4th)
ecstasy (6th)
eddy (6th)
edge (1st)
edit (3rd)
educate (3rd)
education (3rd)
eel (K)
effect (3rd)
effective (4th)
effort (2nd)
egg (K)
egret (3rd)
eight (K)
eighteen (1st)
eighty (1st)

either (2nd)
ejaculate (6th)
elaborate (5th)
elastic (6th)
elbow (4th)
elder (5th)
elderly (5th)
elect (3rd)
electric (3rd)
electricity (3rd)
electron (4th)
electronic (4th)
elegant (5th)
element (3rd)
elephant (K)
elevate (2nd)
elevation (4th)
elevator (2nd)
elf (1st)
eliminate (5th)
e-mail (4th)
elk (K)
elm (2nd)
else (1st)
elsewhere (4th)
embrace (4th)
embarrass (5th)
embarrassed (5th)
emblem (5th)
embryo (4th)
embroider (5th)
emerge (5th)
emergency (5th)
emigrant (6th)
eminent (6th)
emission (5th)
emotion (4th)
emperor (4th)

emphasize (5th)
emphatic (6th)
empire (4th)
employ (5th)
empress (4th)
empty (3rd)
enable (4th)
enamel (6th)
enchant (6th)
encircle (5th)
enclose (4th)
encode (5th)
encounter (4th)
encourage (4th)
encrust (6th)
encyclopedia (5th)
end (K)
endanger (6th)
endeavor (4th)
endow (6th)
endure (4th)
enemy (2nd)
energy (4th)
enforce (5th)
engage (5th)
engine (3rd)
engineer (4th)
English (1st)
engrave (5th)
enjoy (2nd)
enlarge (5th)
enlist (6th)
enliven (6th)
enormous (4th)
enough (1st)
enrage (6th)
enraged (6th)
enrich (6th)

enter (1st)
enterprise (5th)
entertain (4th)
enthusiasm (4th)
entire (3rd)
entitle (5th)
entrance (3rd)
entrap (3rd)
envelope (5th)
environment (6th)
envy (4th)
Eocene (5th)
epidemic (4th)
episode (6th)
Epoch (5th)
equal (2nd)
equator (4th)
equip (5th)
equipment (5th)
equinox (5th)
equivalent (6th)
era (6th)
erase (2nd)
ere (4th)
erect (4th)
erode (5th)
err (6th)
errand (4th)
error (4th)
erupt (4th)
escape (1st)
escort (5th)
Eskimo (3rd)
especially (4th)
essay (5th)
essential (6th)
establish (3rd)
estate (4th)

esteem (5th)
estimate (5th)
et cetera (6th)
etc. (6th)
eternal (4th)
E.U. (5th)
European
    Community
    (5th)
evacuate (5th)
eve (5th)
even (1st)
evening (1st)
event (3rd)
eventually (5th)
ever (K)
evergreen (4th)
every (K)
everybody (3rd)
everyone (1st)
everything (1st)
everywhere (2nd)
evidence (5th)
evident (5th)
evil (3rd)
evolution (6th)
exact (2nd)
exaggerate (6th)
examine (5th)
example (2nd)
excavate (5th)
exceed (4th)
excel (6th)
excellent (1st)
except (1st)
excess (5th)
exchange (4th)
excite (4th)

exclaim (3rd)
exclude (6th)
exclusive (6th)
excuse (3rd)
execute (5th)
executive (5th)
exercise (1st)
exert (6th)
exhaust (4th)
exhibit (4th)
exhilarate (6th)
exile (5th)
exist (3rd)
exit (3rd)
expand (5th)
expect (2nd)
expedition (4th)
expel (6th)
expense (3rd)
experience (4th)
experiment (3rd)
expert (5th)
expire (6th)
explain (2nd)
explode (3rd)
exploit (6th)
explore (4th)
export (5th)
expose (4th)
express (5th)
exquisite (6th)
extend (4th)
exterminate (6th)
extinct (5th)
extra (1st)
extraordinary (5th)
extraterrestrial
    (5th)

extravagant (6th)
extreme (5th)
extremist (5th)
eye (K)
eyeglasses (4th)

f

fable (5th)
fabric (5th)
face (K)
facility (5th)
fact (1st)
factor (5th)
factory (1st)
faculty (6th)
fad (K)
fade (1st)
Fahrenheit (4th)
fail (2nd)
faint (3rd)
fair (1st)
fairy (4th)
faith (3rd)
fake (1st)
falcon (3rd)
fall (K)
false (3rd)
falter (3rd)
fame (3rd)
familiar (3rd)
families (1st)
family (K)
famine (6th)
famous (2nd)
fan (K)
fancy (3rd)
fang (5th)
fantastic (6th)
far (1st)

faraway (3rd)	fell (1st)	filter (5th)	flat (2nd)
fare (3rd)	fellow (1st)	fin (1st)	flatter (4th)
farm (K)	female (4th)	final (3rd)	flavor (4th)
farmer (K)	fence (1st)	finance (1st)	flaw (2nd)
farming (1st)	fend (6th)	find (K)	flea (5th)
farther (3rd)	ferret (5th)	finding (1st)	flee (5th)
fascinate (5th)	ferry (6th)	fine (1st)	fleece (6th)
fashion (3rd)	fertile (5th)	finger (1st)	fleet (6th)
fast (1st)	fertilizer (5th)	fingernail (4th)	flesh (3rd)
fasten (4th)	fervor (6th)	fingerprint (5th)	flew (1st)
fat (1st)	festive (5th)	finish (1st)	flexible (6th)
fatal (4th)	festivity (5th)	fire (K)	flicker (5th)
fate (3rd)	fetch (4th)	firecracker (5th)	flight (2nd)
father (K)	fetish (5th)	fireman (K)	fling (6th)
fathom (6th)	feud (6th)	fireworks (2nd)	flint (5th)
fatigue (5th)	fever (4th)	firm (2nd)	flip (2nd)
fault (3rd)	few (K)	first (1st)	flipper (4th)
faultless (3rd)	fez (5th)	fish (K)	flirt (6th)
fauna (6th)	fib (1st)	fishing (1st)	float (1st)
favor (1st)	fiber (3rd)	fission (4th)	flock (2nd)
favorite (3rd)	fiber-optics (4th)	fist (2nd)	flood (2nd)
fax (4th)	fiction (5th)	fit (K)	floor (K)
fear (1st)	fiddle (4th)	fitness (3rd)	flop (1st)
fearful (1st)	fidelity (6th)	fitting (2nd)	floppy disk (1st)
feast (1st)	field (2nd)	five (K)	flora (6th)
feat (1st)	fierce (4th)	fix (1st)	floss (2nd)
feather (2nd)	fiery (5th)	fixture (6th)	floatation (6th)
feature (3rd)	fife (5th)	fizz (5th)	flotsam (6th)
feces (6th)	fifteen (1st)	flag (3rd)	flounder (5th)
February (1st)	fifth (1st)	flail (6th)	flour (3rd)
fed (K)	fifty (1st)	flair (6th)	flourish (4th)
federal (4th)	fig (1st)	flake (1st)	flow (1st)
fee (4th)	fight (K)	flame (3rd)	flower (K)
feeble (4th)	figure (2nd)	flamingo (5th)	fluid (6th)
feed (1st)	filch (5th)	flank (5th)	fluorescent (6th)
feel (K)	file (1st)	flap (4th)	flush (4th)
feeling (K)	fill (K)	flare (6th)	fluster (6th)
feet (1st)	film (4th)	flash (2nd)	flute (5th)

fly (K)

foam (4th)

foal (2nd)

foam (4th)

focal (5th)

focus (5th)

foe (4th)

fog (1st)

fold (1st)

foliage (6th)

folk (3rd)

folklore (5th)

follow (1st)

following (1st)

folly (4th)

fond (4th)

food (K)

fool (2nd)

foolish (2nd)

foot (K)

football (1st)

footstep (3rd)

for (K)

forbid (4th)

force (1st)

forceful (2nd)

ford (5th)

fore (6th)

forecast (4th)

forefather (6th)

forego (5th)

forehead (4th)

foreign (5th)

foreigner (5th)

foreman (6th)

foresight (6th)

forest (1st)

foretell (6th)

forever (3rd)

forfeit (6th)

forge (5th)

forget (1st)

forgive (2nd)

fork (1st)

forlorn (6th)

form (1st)

formal (4th)

formation (4th)

former (6th)

formidable (6th)

formula (6th)

forsake (6th)

fort (5th)

forth (2nd)

forthright (5th)

fortnight (6th)

fortress (5th)

fortunate (4th)

fortune (3rd)

forty (1st)

forward (3rd)

fossil (4th)

foul (4th)

found (K)

foundation (5th)

fountain (3rd)

four (K)

fourteen (1st)

fourth (1st)

fowl (4th)

fox (K)

foxglove (5th)

fraction (4th)

fragile (6th)

fragment (6th)

fragrance (5th)

fragrant (5th)

frail (6th)

frame (3rd)

framework (4th)

France (1st)

frank (4th)

frantic (5th)

fraud (6th)

freckles (1st)

free (K)

freedom (3rd)

freely (K)

freeze (4th)

freezing (4th)

freight (4th)

French (1st)

frequent (4th)

fresco (5th)

fresh (2nd)

freshwater (4th)

fret (5th)

friar (5th)

friction (6th)

Friday (1st)

fried (5th)

friend (1st)

friendship (2nd)

fright (2nd)

frighten (ed) (2nd)

frigid (6th)

fringe (5th)

frizz (5th)

fro (5th)

frock (4th)

frog (K)

frolic (6th)

from (K)

front (1st)

frontier (5th)

frost (4th)

frown (2nd)

fruit (2nd)

fry (1st)

fuel (4th)

fugitive (4th)

fulfill (4th)

fulfillment (4th)

full (K)

fumble (5th)

fume (3rd)

fun (K)

function (4th)

fund (4th)

fundamental (4th)

funeral (4th)

fungus (5th)

funnel (3rd)

funny (1st)

fur (K)

furious (4th)

furnace (4th)

furnish (4th)

furniture (3rd)

furrow (6th)

further (2nd)

fury (4th)

fuse (4th)

fusion (4th)

fuss (1st)

future (5th)

g

gab (1st)

gag (1st)

gaia (5th)

gaia theory (5th)

gain (2nd)

gait (6th)
gale (2nd)
gallant (4th)
gallery (5th)
gallop (4th)
gallows (6th)
gamble (5th)
game (K)
gang (1st)
gap (K)
gape (5th)
garage (6th)
garb (5th)
garbage (6th)
garden (K)
gargle (6th)
garland (6th)
garment (4th)
garnish (6th)
garrison (5th)
gas (1st)
gasp (4th)
gate (1st)
gather (1st)
gave (K)
gaunt (6th)
gay (1st)
gaze (5th)
gazelle (5th)
gear (1st)
gee (K)
gelatin (5th)
gene (4th)
general (2nd)
generation (4th)
generous (4th)
genial (5th)
genius (4th)

genome (5th)
gentle (3rd)
gentleman (3rd)
genuine (5th)
geographic (5th)
geography (5th)
geology (5th)
germ (6th)
German (2nd)
Germany (2nd)
gesture (4th)
get (K)
ghastly (6th)
ghost (K)
giant (2nd)
gift (K)
gigantic (5th)
gild (6th)
gill (4th)
gin (6th)
ginger (1st)
gingerbread (1st)
gingerly (6th)
giraffe (K)
girdle (6th)
girl (K)
girlfriend (4th)
give (K)
glacier (3rd)
glad (K)
glance (3rd)
gland (5th)
glare (4th)
glass (1st)
glasses (1st)
glaze (6th)
gloss (5th)
gleam (1st)

glee (5th)
gleeful (5th)
glen (6th)
glide (4th)
glimmer (6th)
glimpse (4th)
glisten (6th)
glitter (4th)
globe (4th)
gloom (3rd)
glory (3rd)
gloss (5th)
Glossopteris (5th)
glove (4th)
glow (1st)
glue (1st)
glum (4th)
gnarled (5th)
gnash (4th)
gnat (5th)
gnaw (1st)
gnome (6th)
go (K)
goal (4th)
goat (K)
gobble (1st)
goblin (4th)
god (1st)
goddess (1st)
godfather (3rd)
godmother (3rd)
goes (1st)
goggle (4th)
goggles (4th)
gold (K)
golden (K)
goldenrod (5th)
goldfinch (5th)

goldfish (K) carp
   (5th)
golf (4th)
gone (1st)
good (K)
good-bye (1st)
good-natured (5th)
good-night (2nd)
goose (K)
gooseberry (5th)
gopher (1st)
gorge (5th)
gorgeous (5th)
gorilla (1st)
gospel (6th)
gossip (5th)
got (K)
gourd (5th)
govern (2nd)
government (1st)
gown (4th)
grab (4th)
grace (3rd)
grade (2nd)
gradual (3rd)
graduate (4th)
graham (6th)
grain (3rd)
grammar (6th)
grand (2nd)
grandfather (1st)
grandmother (1st)
grant (2nd)
grape (2nd)
grapefruit (5th)
grapeshot (6th)
grapple (6th)
grasp (4th)

grass (K)
grasshopper (1st)
grateful (4th)
grave (3rd)
gravel (4th)
gravity (4th)
gray (1st)
graze (5th)
grease (5th)
great (K)
greed (4th)
green (K)
greenery (3rd)
greenhouse (3rd)
greenhouse effect
    (3rd)
greet (3rd)
grey (3rd)
greyhound (3rd)
grief (5th)
grim (4th)
grin (1st)
grind (4th)
grip (4th)
gripe (5th)
grizzly (4th)
groan (3rd)
groom (5th)
groove (5th)
grope (6th)
gross (3rd)
ground (1st)
group (1st)
grove (4th)
grow (K)
growl (4th)
grown-up (1st)
grub (5th)

grudge (5th)
grudgingly (5th)
gruel (6th)
gruff (1st)
grumble (5th)
guarantee (6th)
guard (1st)
guess (1st)
guest (3rd)
guide (1st)
guidepost (6th)
guilt (4th)
guilty (4th)
guitar (4th)
gulf (4th)
gully (6th)
gulp (1st)
gum (K)
gun (K)
gust (5th)
gut (1st)
guts (1st)
gutter (6th)
guttural (6th)
guy (1st)
gym (1st)
gymnasium (5th)
gymnast (5th)
gypsy (6th)

h

habit (3rd)
habitable (6th)
habitat (6th)
hackle (6th)
had (K)
hadn't (1st)
hail (4th)
hair (K)

hale (2nd)
half (1st)
half-mast (5th)
hall (1st)
Halloween (K)
halt (4th)
ham (K)
hamburger (4th)
hammer (2nd)
hamster (1st)
hand (K)
handcuffs (2nd)
handkerchief (4th)
handle (2nd)
handsome (3rd)
hang (2nd)
happen (1st)
happy (K)
harbor (2nd)
hard (K)
hard drive (1st)
harden (2nd)
hardship (5th)
hardy (5th)
hare (3rd)
hark (6th)
harm (3rd)
harmonize (4th)
harmony (4th)
harness (4th)
harp (4th)
harsh (5th)
harvest (4th)
harvesting (4th)
has (K)
hasn't (1st)
haste (2nd)
hasty (2nd)

hat (K)
hatch (4th)
hate (2nd)
hateful (3rd)
haughty (6th)
haul (4th)
haunch (5th)
haunt (2nd)
have (K)
hay (K)
hazard (6th)
he (K)
he'd (1st)
head (K)
headache (6th)
headquarters (3rd)
heal (3rd)
health (K)
heap (4th)
hear (K)
heard (K)
heart (K)
heartache (6th)
hearth (5th)
hearty (5th)
heat (1st)
heathen (6th)
heave (5th)
heaven (1st)
heavenly (2nd)
heavy (1st)
hectic (3rd)
hedge (4th)
heed (4th)
heel (3rd)
height (4th)
heir (4th)
hello (K)

helm (6th)
helmet (1st)
help (K)
helper (1st)
hem (1st)
hemisphere (6th)
hemlock (6th)
hemp (5th)
hen (K)
hence (3rd)
her (K)
herald (3rd)
herb (5th)
herbivore (5th)
herd (2nd)
here (K)
hereafter (6th)
here's (1st)
hermit (5th)
hero (1st)
heroic (5th)
herring (5th)
hers (K)
herself (2nd)
hesitate (4th)
hew (6th)
hey (K)
hi (K)
hidden (1st)
hide (1st)
hideous (6th)
high (K)
highway (4th)
hike (3rd)
hill (K)
hillside (4th)
him (K)
himself (2nd)

hind (4th)
hinder (6th)
hindquarter (5th)
Hindu (5th)
hinge (5th)
hint (1st)
hip (1st)
hippo (K)
hippopotamus
   (3rd)
hire (3rd)
his (K)
hiss (3rd)
history (2nd)
hit (K)
hither (6th)
HIV (4th)
hive (2nd)
hoarfrost (6th)
hoard (6th)
hoarse (5th)
hoary (6th)
hoax (5th)
hobby (3rd)
hockey (3rd)
hoe (2nd)
hog (K)
hogan (2nd)
hoist (6th)
hold (1st)
hole (K)
holiday (K)
hollow (3rd)
Holocene (5th)
holy (5th)
homage (6th)
home (K)
homespun (5th)

homework (1st)
honest (3rd)
honey (1st)
honeysuckle (5th)
honk (1st)
honor (1st)
hood (4th)
hoof (1st)
hook (4th)
hoop (5th)
hoot (1st)
hop (K)
hope (K)
hopped (1st)
horde (6th)
horizon (4th)
horizontal (6th)
horrible (1st)
horn (3rd)
hornet (5th)
horrible (1st)
horrid (4th)
horrify (4th)
horror (4th)
hose (6th)
hospital (3rd)
host (4th)
hostile (4th)
hot (K)
hotel (3rd)
hothouse (5th)
hotspot (5th)
hound (2nd)
hour (1st)
house (K)
housekeeper (3rd)
housework (3rd)
hover (3rd)

hovercraft (3rd)
how (K)
however (1st)
howl (4th)
hue (6th)
hug (1st)
huge (1st)
hull (4th)
hum (1st)
human (3rd)
humble (4th)
humor (4th)
hump (3rd)
hunch (6th)
hundred (1st)
hunger (2nd)
hungry (2nd)
hunker (6th)
hunt (2nd)
hurl (5th)
hurried (1st)
hurry (1st)
hurt (K)
husband (1st)
hush (3rd)
hut (4th)
hydrogen (6th)
hyena (4th)
hymn (5th)
hysteria (6th)
hysterical (6th)

i

I (K)
ice (K)
iceberg (3rd)
icebox (1st)
icon (1st)
I'd (1st)

idea (1st)
ideal (3rd)
identical (6th)
identify (4th)
identity (5th)
idiot (6th)
idle (4th)
idol (6th)
idolize (6th)
if (K)
igneous (5th)
ignite (6th)
ignorant (4th)
ignore (5th)
ill (1st)
I'll (1st)
illegal (1st)
illuminate (6th)
illusion (6th)
illustration (4th)
illustrious (6th)
I'm (1st)
image (4th)
imagine (2nd)
imitate (5th)
immaculate (6th)
immature (5th)
immediate (3rd)
immense (4th)
immigrant (6th)
immobile (6th)
immortal (4th)
immunity (4th)
imp (5th)
impart (6th)
impatient (5th)
imperial (5th)
impetus (6th)

implement (6th)
imply (5th)
import (5th)
important (1st)
impose (4th)
impossible (3rd)
impoverished (6th)
impress (5th)
impression (5th)
imprint (4th)
imprison (6th)
improve (3rd)
impulse (5th)
in (K)
incapable (6th)
incense (5th)
inch (1st)
incident (5th)
incline (5th)
inclined (5th)
include (3rd)
income (4th)
inconvenient (6th)
increase (3rd)
incredible (6th)
incredulous (6th)
indeed (1st)
independent (3rd)
index (6th)
Indian (1st)
indicate (4th)
indifferent (5th)
indignant (5th)
indispensable (6th)
individual (3rd)
indoor (6th)
induce (5th)
indulge (5th)

industry (5th)
infant (5th)
infect (6th)
inferior (5th)
infinite (5th)
inflect (6th)
influence (5th)
inform (5th)
informal (5th)
information (5th)
ingenious (6th)
ingredient (4th)
inhabit (6th)
inherit (5th)
initial (6th)
initiate (5th)
initiative (6th)
injure (5th)
injury (5th)
ink (2nd)
inland (5th)
inlet (4th)
inn (4th)
inner (5th)
innocent (5th)
innumerable (5th)
inquire (3rd)
insane (6th)
inscribe (5th)
inscription (6th)
insect (4th)
insert (6th)
inside (1st)
insist (5th)
inspect (5th)
inspire (4th)
install (6th)
instance (5th)

instant (3rd)
instead (1st)
instinct (5th)
institute (5th)
instruct (4th)
instrument (3rd)
insult (5th)
insure (5th)
intelligence (4th)
intelligent (4th)
intend (6th)
intense (6th)
intensive (6th)
intent (5th)
intention (6th)
interactive (4th)
interest (1st)
interface (4th)
interfere (4th)
interior (5th)
internal (6th)
international (5th)
internet (2nd)
interpret (5th)
interrupt (3rd)
interval (6th)
interview (5th)
intestine (4th)
intimate (5th)
into (1st)
intricate (6th)
introduce (5th)
intrude (6th)
invade (5th)
invent (2nd)
invest (5th)
investigate (5th)
invisible (6th)

invite (3rd)
involve (6th)
inward (6th)
ion (5th)
iris (5th)
irk (6th)
iron (2nd)
irregular (6th)
irrigate (5th)
irritate (6th)
Islam (5th)
island (2nd)
isn't (1st)
issue (4th)
it (K)
itch (5th)
item (5th)
its (K)
it's (1st)
itself (2nd)
I've (1st)
ivory (3rd)
ivy (2nd)

j

jab (1st)
jack (1st)
jackal (5th)
jackdaw (5th)
jacket (3rd)
jagged (5th)
jail (4th)
jam (K)
January (1st)
jar (K)
jasper (5th)
jaunty (6th)
jaw (4th)
jay (1st)

jealous (5th)
jeans (1st)
jeep (1st)
jeer (5th)
jell (1st)
jelly (1st)
jellybean (4th)
jellyfish (2nd)
jersey (5th)
jest (4th)
jet (K)
Jew (K)
jewel (5th)
jewelry (5th)
jibe (6th)
jingle (2nd)
job (K)
jog (2nd)
join (3rd)
joined (3rd)
joint (4th)
joke (1st)
jolly (4th)
jostle (6th)
jot (1st)
journal (2nd)
journey (3rd)
joust (6th)
jovial (5th)
joy (1st)
judge (1st)
jug (1st)
juice (K)
jump (K)
jumped (1st)
jungle (4th)
junior (4th)
junk (3rd)

Jurassic (5th)
jury (4th)
just (1st)
justice (3rd)
justification (5th)
juvenile (5th)

k

(K)aiser (5th)
kangaroo (1st)
kangaroo (1st)
keen (4th)
keep (K)
keeper (1st)
keg (1st)
kettle (4th)
key (K)
keyboard (1st)
khaki (6th)
kick (1st)
kid (K)
kill (1st)
kilo (6th)
kilogram (2nd)
kin (1st)
kind (K)
kindle (5th)
king (K)
kingbird (3rd)
kingdom (3rd)
kingfisher (5th)
kiss (K)
kit (1st)
kitchen (1st)
kite (K)
kitten (K)
knapsack (4th)
knave (5th)
knead (4th)

kneel (1st)
kneel (4th)
knew (1st)
knife (1st)
knight (2nd)
knit (4th)
knock (3rd)
knot (4th)
know (1st)
know-how (2nd)
knowledge (2nd)
known (1st)
knuckle (4th)
koala (K)
(K)oran (5th)

l

lab (1st)
label (3rd)
labor (1st)
laboratory (4th)
lace (4th)
lack (1st)
lad (K)
ladder (2nd)
laden (6th)
ladle (4th)
lady (1st)
lag (1st)
lagoon (5th)
lair (5th)
lake (1st)
lamb (K)
lame (4th)
lament (6th)
lamp (1st)
lance (4th)
land (K)
landslide (5th)

lane (4th)	led (K)	lie (1st)	live (1st)
language (2nd)	ledge (5th)	lieutenant (4th)	lived (1st)
lantern (5th)	lee (5th)	life (1st)	lives (1st)
lap (K)	leech (4th)	lift (1st)	livestock (3rd)
lapse (6th)	leek (5th)	light (K)	living (1st)
lard (6th)	left (1st)	lighthouse (2nd)	lizard (1st)
large (K)	leg (K)	lightweight (4th)	llama (1st)
larvae (2nd)	legal (5th)	like (K)	load (2nd)
lash (4th)	legend (5th)	likely (1st)	loaf (4th)
lass (1st)	legion (6th)	likes (1st)	loan (4th)
lasso (4th)	legislation (5th)	lilac (5th)	lobster (3rd)
last (K)	legitimate (6th)	lily (1st)	local (3rd)
latch (4th)	leisure (5th)	limb (4th)	locality (4th)
latchkey (4th)	lemon (2nd)	limber (4th)	locate (3rd)
late (K)	lend (K)	lime (4th)	location (3rd)
later (1st)	length (2nd)	limestone (4th)	lock (1st)
latitude (4th)	lens (1st)	limit (3rd)	locomotive (5th)
launch (5th)	Lent (4th)	limp (5th)	locust (5th)
lavish (6th)	leopard (1st)	limpet (3rd)	lodge (4th)
law (1st)	less (1st)	limpid (6th)	loft (5th)
lawn (2nd)	lessen (3rd)	line (K)	lofty (5th)
lawyer (5th)	fade (1st)	linen (4th)	log (K)
lay (1st)	lesson (3rd)	linger (4th)	logger (4th)
layer (4th)	lest (4th)	link (5th)	logic (6th)
lazy (4th)	let (K)	lion (K)	logo (4th)
lead (1st)	letter (1st)	lip (1st)	loincloth (6th)
leaf (1st)	letters (1st)	liquid (3rd)	lone (2nd)
league (3rd)	levee (6th)	liquor (5th)	lonely (2nd)
leak (6th)	level (3rd)	list (2nd)	long (1st)
lean (3rd)	liable (6th)	listen (1st)	longing (1st)
leaning (3rd)	liberal (4th)	listless (6th)	longitude (4th)
leap (3rd)	liberty (3rd)	lit (K)	look (K)
learn (1st)	library (3rd)	liter (6th)	looked (1st)
lease (6th)	lice (2nd)	literal (6th)	looking (1st)
least (1st)	license (5th)	literature (5th)	loom (5th)
leather (1st)	lichen (5th)	lithosphere (5th)	loop (5th)
leave (1st)	lick (1st)	litter (2nd)	loose (3rd)
lecture (5th)	lid (1st)	little (K)	lope (5th)

lord (2nd)
lose (K)
loss (K)
lost (K)
lot (K)
lots (5th)
lotus (5th)
loud (1st)
lounge (6th)
love (K)
loved (1st)
lovely (1st)
low (K)
lowland (6th)
loyal (5th)
luck (1st)
lucky (K)
lug (1st)
luggage (4th)
lull (5th)
lumber (1st)
lumbering (2nd)
lumberman (2nd)
lump (4th)
lunatic (6th)
lunch (1st)
lung (4th)
lunge (6th)
lurch (5th)
lure (5th)
lurk (5th)
lush (6th)
lust (6th)
luster (4th)
luxury (4th)
lye (2nd)
lynx (4th)
lyre (6th)

Lystrosaurus (5th)

m

ma'am (6th)
machine (1st)
machinery (1st)
mackerel (5th)
mad (K)
madam (4th)
made (K)
madness (3rd)
magazine (3rd)
magic (1st)
magician (5th)
magistrate (6th)
magnet (3rd)
magnetize (3rd)
magnetron (5th)
magnificent (4th)
magnify (3rd)
magnitude (5th)
magnolia (5th)
magpie (5th)
maid (3rd)
maiden (4th)
mail (1st)
mailbox (1st)
mailman (1st)
maim (4th)
main (3rd)
mainland (5th)
maintain (4th)
maize (2nd)
majesty (4th)
major (3rd)
majority (3rd)
make (K)
maker (1st)
making (K)

male (4th)
malice (6th)
malignant (6th)
malinger (6th)
mall (K)
mallard (4th)
malt (2nd)
mama (1st)
mammal (5th)
mammoth (5th)
man (K)
manage (4th)
manager (4th)
mandarin (5th)
mane (1st)
mango (5th)
manifest (5th)
mankind (4th)
manly (K)
manner (1st)
mansion (5th)
mantel (4th)
mantle (4th)
manufacture (3rd)
manure (5th)
manuscript (6th)
many (K)
map (1st)
maple (2nd)
mar (6th)
marble (4th)
March (1st)
march (1st)
mare (4th)
margin (5th)
marine (5th)
marigold (5th)
marine (5th)

Marines (1st)
mark (1st)
market (1st)
marquis (6th)
marrow (5th)
marry (1st)
marsh (5th)
marshal (5th)
marsupial (1st)
martyr (6th)
marvel (4th)
marvelous (4th)
mash (4th)
mask (2nd)
mason (5th)
mass (3rd)
massacre (6th)
massive (5th)
mast (4th)
master (1st)
mastiff (5th)
mastodon (1st)
mat (K)
match (3rd)
matching (3rd)
mate (4th)
material (5th)
mathematical (5th)
mathematics (5th)
matter (1st)
mattress (6th)
mature (5th)
maturity (6th)
maxim (6th)
maximum (6th)
May (1st)
may (K)
maybe (1st)

mayonnaise (4th)

mayor (1st)

me (K)

meadow (3rd)

meal (3rd)

mean (1st)

mean (average)
   (5th)

meaning (3rd)

measure (2nd)

meat (1st)

meatloaf (5th)

mechanic (5th)

mechanical (5th)

mechanism (6th)

medal (4th)

meddle (6th)

mediate (5th)

medicine (4th)

meditate (6th)

medium (5th)

meek (2nd)

meet (K)

melancholy (6th)

mellow (6th)

melody (4th)

melon (3rd)

melt (2nd)

member (1st)

membrane (4th)

memory (3rd)

men (1st)

menace (5th)

mend (1st)

mental (5th)

mention (5th)

menu (6th)

meow (K)

merchandise (6th)

merchant (3rd)

mercy (4th)

mere (3rd)

merit (4th)

mermaid (4th)

merry (3rd)

mesa (6th)

Mesosaurus (5th)

Mesozoic (5th)

mess (1st)

message (1st)

met (1st)

metal (3rd)

meteor (5th)

meter (2nd)

metal (3rd)

method (2nd)

metropolitan (6th)

micro (4th)

microchip (4th)

microscope (4th)

microwave (4th)

middle (2nd)

midge (5th)

midnight (3rd)

might (1st)

migrant (4th)

mike (1st)

mild (4th)

mile (1st)

milestone (5th)

military (3rd)

milk (1st)

mill (1st)

millimeter (2nd)

million (3rd)

mimic (6th)

mimosa (5th)

mince (6th)

mind (1st)

mine (1st)

mineral (5th)

mingle (4th)

miniature (6th)

minimalist (6th)

minimum (6th)

minister (4th)

mink (3rd)

minnow (4th)

minor (5th)

minority (6th)

minstrel (5th)

mint (5th)

minus (1st)

minute (1st)

miracle (5th)

Miocene (5th)

miraculous (6th)

mirror (4th)

mirth (5th)

mischief (4th)

miser (5th)

miserable (4th)

misery (4th)

misfortune (5th)

mislead (5th)

miss (K)

mission (5th)

Mississippian (5th)

mist (1st)

mistake (1st)

mistreat (3rd)

mistress (4th)

misunder-standing
   (2nd)

misuse (3rd)

mitten (1st)

mix (1st)

mixed (1st)

mixture (4th)

mix-up (2nd)

moan (5th)

mob (4th)

mobile (6th)

mobilize (6th)

moccasin (2nd)

mock (4th)

mode (5th)

model (3rd)

moderate (4th)

modern (2nd)

modest (4th)

modify (5th)

moist (4th)

moisture (3rd)

mold (5th)

mole (2nd)

molecule (5th)

molten (5th)

mom (K)

mommy (K)

moment (1st)

momentum (6th)

monarch (5th)

monastery (5th)

Monday (1st)

money (K)

mongoose (5th)

monk (4th)

monkey (K)

monopoly (6th)

Monsieur (4th)

monster (1st)

monstrous (5th)

month (1st)

monument (2nd)

moo (K)

mood (3rd)

moon (1st)

moonbeam (4th)

moonlight (4th)

moor (5th)

moose (K)

mop (1st)

mope (5th)

moral (3rd)

more (K)

moreover (3rd)

Mormon (4th)

morning (1st)

morsel (5th)

mortal (4th)

mortgage (6th)

Moslem (5th)

mosque (5th)

moss (1st)

most (1st)

moth (1st)

mother (K)

motion (3rd)

motivate (6th)

motive (5th)

motor (4th)

motto (6th)

mound (2nd)

mount (2nd)

mountain (2nd)

mourn (4th)

mouse (K)

mouth (1st)

move (K)

movement (2nd)

movie (1st)

moving (1st)

Mr. (K)

Mrs. (K)

Ms. (K)

much (1st)

mud (1st)

muffin (4th)

mug (1st)

mulberry (4th)

mule (2nd)

multiply (2nd)

mumble (4th)

mums (4th)

mummy (2nd)

municipal (6th)

murder (3rd)

murmur (4th)

muscle (4th)

muse (4th)

museum (4th)

mush (5th)

mushroom (4th)

music (K)

musical (5th)

musician (4th)

musk (5th)

musket (5th)

muskrat (5th)

muss (1st)

mussel (3rd)

must (1st)

mustang (4th)

mustard (4th)

muster (6th)

mutate (4th)

mute (6th)

mutiny (6th)

mutt (4th)

mutter (4th)

mutton (5th)

mutual (5th)

muzzle (6th)

my (K)

myriad (6th)

myself (1st)

mystery (1st)

mystic (4th)

myth (4th)

n

nab (1st)

nag (1st)

nail (2nd)

naked (4th)

name (K)

nanites (4th)

nano (4th)

nanometer (4th)

nanoparticle (4th)

nanowires (4th)

nap (K)

napkin (5th)

napping (1st)

narcissus (4th)

narrate (6th)

narrow (2nd)

NASA (1st)

nasturtium (4th)

nation (1st)

native (1st)

natural (2nd)

naturalist (6th)

nature (1st)

naught (5th)

naughty (5th)

navigate (5th)

Navy (1st)

nay (4th)

Nazareth (4th)

Neanderthal (5th)

near (1st)

nearing (1st)

nearly (1st)

neat (K)

nebula (4th)

necessary (1st)

neck (1st)

nectar (2nd)

need (1st)

needle (3rd)

negative (6th)

neglect (4th)

neighbor (2nd)

neighborhood
(2nd)

neither (1st)

nephew (4th)

nerve (6th)

nervous (1st)

nest (1st)

nestle (3rd)

net (3rd)

nettle (4th)

neuron (6th)

neutral (6th)

never (K)

nevertheless (4th)

new (K)

newspaper (1st)

Newtonian (5th)

next (K)

nibble (4th)

nice (1st)

nickel (1st)
niece (3rd)
night (1st)
nightingale (4th)
nine (K)
nineteen (1st)
ninety (1st)
nip (1st)
nitrogen (6th)
no (K)
noble (3rd)
nobody (1st)
nod (1st)
noise (1st)
noisy (5th)
nominate (5th)
none (1st)
nonetheless (5th)
nonfiction (5th)
nonsense (5th)
nook (6th)
nor (3rd)
normal (5th)
north (1st)
nose (1st)
nostril (5th)
not (K)
notable (5th)
notch (5th)
note (1st)
nothing (1st)
notice (1st)
noticeable (3rd)
notify (3rd)
notion (5th)
nourish (6th)
novel (5th)
November (1st)

novice (5th)
now (K)
nuclear (4th)
nucleus (4th)
nuisance (6th)
number (K)
numeral (5th)
numerous (4th)
nun (1st)
nurse (K)
nut (K)
nutmeg (4th)
nutrino (5th)
nuzzle (1st)
nymph (6th)

O

oak (1st)
oar (1st)
oarlock (2nd)
oat (1st)
oath (5th)
oatmeal (5th)
obey (3rd)
object (1st)
objective (2nd)
obligation (6th)
oblige (6th)
obscure (6th)
observe (3rd)
obstacle (5th)
obstinate (5th)
obtain (5th)
obvious (5th)
occasion (3rd)
occupation (6th)
occupy (3rd)
occur (3rd)
ocean (1st)

o'clock (4th)
October (1st)
octopus (1st)
odd (4th)
odor (3rd)
of (K)
off (K)
offend (4th)
offensive (4th)
offer (2nd)
office (1st)
officer (1st)
official (3rd)
often (1st)
oh (K)
oil (K)
O.(K). (K)
okay (1st)
old (K)
older (1st)
Oligocene (5th)
olive (4th)
omen (6th)
ominous (6th)
omit (6th)
omnivore (5th)
on (K)
once (1st)
one (K)
oneself (3rd)
onion (2nd)
only (K)
onto (1st)
onward (3rd)
onyx (5th)
opal (5th)
open (K)
opera (4th)

operate (3rd)
operation (3rd)
operator (5th)
opinion (3rd)
opossum (3rd)
opponent (5th)
opportunity (3rd)
oppose (3rd)
opposite (3rd)
oppress (6th)
optical (5th)
or (K)
oracle (6th)
orange (K)
orbit (4th)
orchard (5th)
orchestra (6th)
orchid (4th)
ordain (6th)
order (1st)
ordinary (3rd)
Ordovician (5th)
ore (4th)
organ (4th)
organic (4th)
organism (4th)
organize (4th)
orient (5th)
original (3rd)
oriole (3rd)
ornament (4th)
ornithischians (5th)
orphan (5th)
osprey (5th)
ostrich (1st)
other (1st)
otherwise (3rd)
otter (1st)

ought (1st)
ounce (2nd)
our (K)
ourselves (3rd)
out (K)
outcome (4th)
outcry (4th)
outer (5th)
outer space (3rd)
outlandish (6th)
outline (4th)
outrage (6th)
outright (6th)
outside (1st)
outstanding (2nd)
outward (6th)
outwit (6th)
oval (1st)
oven (1st)
ovenbird (2nd)
over (K)
overflow (5th)
overlook (4th)
overseas (2nd)
oversee (1st)
overtake (5th)
overthrow (2nd)
overwhelm (5th)
owe (3rd)
owl (K)
own (K)
ox (K)
oxygen (4th)
oyster (4th)
ozone (5th)
ozone hole (5th)

p

pace (3rd)

pack (1st)
package (4th)
pad (K)
paddle (1st)
page (1st)
pageant (6th)
pagoda (5th)
paid (2nd)
pail (2nd)
pain (2nd)
paint (2nd)
pair (1st)
pal (K)
palace (1st)
pale (3rd)
paleontologist (5th)
Paleocene (5th)
Paleozoic (5th)
pallet (5th)
pamphlet (6th)
pan (K)
panda (K)
pane (5th)
panel (6th)
pang (6th)
Pangea (5th)
panic (1st)
panther (3rd)
pantry (5th)
pants (1st)
papa (1st)
paper (K)
papier-mâché (6th)
paprika (4th)
papyrus (4th)
parasite (4th)
parade (2nd)
paradise (4th)

paragraph (6th)
parakeet (5th)
parallel (5th)
paralysis (6th)
paralyze (6th)
paranormal (5th)
parcel (4th)
pardon (4th)
parent (3rd)
parish (6th)
park (1st)
parlor (4th)
parrot (1st)
parsley (4th)
parsnip (4th)
parson (6th)
part (1st)
partial (6th)
particle (5th)
particular (4th)
partition (6th)
partner (5th)
partridge (1st)
part-time (3rd)
party (K)
pass (K)
passion (6th)
passport (6th)
past (1st)
paste (1st)
pastel (4th)
pastime (6th)
pastor (4th)
pasty (5th)
pat (K)
patch (4th)
patent (4th)
path (1st)

pathetic (6th)
patient (4th)
patriot (4th)
patrol (1st)
patron (5th)
patter (6th)
pattern (3rd)
pause (3rd)
pave (5th)
pavilion (5th)
paw (1st)
pay (K)
paying (1st)
payment (1st)
pea (1st)
peace (1st)
peach (1st)
peacock (1st)
peak (4th)
peal (6th)
peanut (3rd)
pear (4th)
pearl (4th)
peasant (4th)
pebble (4th)
peck (1st)
peculiar (4th)
peddler (5th)
peek (2nd)
peel (2nd)
peep (4th)
peer (1st)
peg (1st)
pelican (1st)
pellet (6th)
pen (1st)
penalty (5th)
pencil (1st)

penetrate (5th)
peninsula (6th)
penguin (1st)
penny (1st)
pension (6th)
people (K)
pepper (4th)
peppermint (4th)
perceive (6th)
percent (4th)
perch (4th)
perfect (3rd)
perform (4th)
perfume (3rd)
perhaps (1st)
peril (5th)
period (2nd)
periodic (4th)
perish (4th)
permanent (5th)
Permian (5th)
permit (3rd)
perpetual (6th)
perplex (6th)
persecute (6th)
persimmon (4th)
persist (5th)
person (1st)
personal (3rd)
personality (5th)
perspire (6th)
persuade (5th)
pest (1st)
pester (2nd)
pestilence (6th)
pet (1st)
petal (5th)
petrify (4th)

petroleum (6th)
petticoat (6th)
petty (6th)
pewter (5th)
Pharaoh (6th)
phase (6th)
pheasant (4th)
phenomenon (6th)
philosophy (5th)
phone (2nd)
phonograph (5th)
photograph (5th)
photon (4th)
photosynthesis
    (5th)
phrase (5th)
physical (5th)
physics (6th)
piano (4th)
pick (1st)
picket (3rd)
pickle (1st)
picnic (5th)
picture (K)
pie (K)
piece (1st)
piecemeal (6th)
pier (4th)
pierce (4th)
pig (K)
pigeon (1st)
pike (4th)
pile (1st)
pilgrim (5th)
pill (1st)
pillar (5th)
pillow (4th)
pilot (5th)

pimento (4th)
pimple (5th)
pin (K)
pinch (4th)
pine (1st)
pineapple (4th)
pinecone (2nd)
pink (1st)
pint (2nd)
pioneer (4th)
pious (6th)
pipe (1st)
pipeline (1st)
pirate (5th)
pistol (5th)
pit (1st)
pitch (2nd)
piteous (6th)
pity (3rd)
pivot (5th)
pizza (K)
place (1st)
plague (5th)
plain (2nd)
plait (5th)
plan (1st)
plane (1st)
planet (4th)
plank (5th)
plant (K)
plantation (5th)
plaque (5th)
plaster (4th)
plastic (3rd)
plate (K)
plateau (6th)
platform (4th)
platter (6th)

play (K)
player (1st)
playground (1st)
plea (5th)
plead (3rd)
pleasant (3rd)
please (K)
pleasure (2nd)
pleat (5th)
pledge (5th)
plentiful (2nd)
plenty (1st)
pliers (3rd)
plight (6th)
Pliocene (5th)
plod (5th)
plop (1st)
plot (4th)
plow (4th)
pluck (1st)
plug (5th)
plum (4th)
plumber (5th)
plume (6th)
plump (6th)
plunder (5th)
plunge (4th)
plural (4th)
plus (1st)
ply (6th)
p.m. (6th)
pneumatic (4th)
poach (6th)
pocket (1st)
pod (1st)
poem (3rd)
point (1st)
poise (6th)

poison (3rd)
poke (1st)
polar (3rd)
pole (K)
polar (3rd)
police (1st)
policeman (1st)
policewoman (1st)
policy (5th)
polish (4th)
polite (4th)
political (4th)
politics (4th)
poll (5th)
pollen (2nd)
pollute (3rd)
pomegranate (4th)
pomp (6th)
pond (1st)
ponder (6th)
pony (K)
poodle (4th)
pool (1st)
poor (K)
pop (K)
popcorn (1st)
Pope (5th)
poplar (4th)
poppy (2nd)
popular (3rd)
population (3rd)
porch (3rd)
porcupine (2nd)
pore (6th)
pork (6th)
porpoise (1st)
porridge (5th)
port (3rd)

porter (5th)
portion (4th)
portrait (5th)
position (2nd)
positive (2nd)
possess (3rd)
possible (1st)
post (1st)
postcard (1st)
postpone (6th)
pot (K)
potato (4th)
pouch (1st)
poultry (6th)
pounce (5th)
pound (2nd)
pour (3rd)
poverty (5th)
powder (3rd)
power (1st)
powerful (2nd)
practical (4th)
practice (1st)
prairie (4th)
praise (4th)
prank (5th)
pray (3rd)
prayer (3rd)
preach (4th)
Precambrian (5th)
precaution (5th)
precede (6th)
precious (4th)
precipice (6th)
precise (5th)
predator (2nd)
predict (6th)
preen (2nd)

preface (6th)
prefer (3rd)
prehistoric (5th)
prejudice (6th)
prehistory (5th)
prejudice (6th)
preliminary (6th)
premise (6th)
preoccupy (5th)
prepare (1st)
prescribe (6th)
present (K)
preserve (4th)
preside (6th)
president (1st)
press (1st)
pressure (4th)
presume (6th)
pretend (2nd)
pretext (5th)
pretty (1st)
prevail (5th)
prevent (3rd)
prevention (3rd)
previous (5th)
prey (4th)
price (K)
prick (5th)
pride (2nd)
priest (4th)
prim (5th)
primary (5th)
prime (5th)
primitive (5th)
prince (1st)
princess (1st)
principal (3rd)
principle (4th)

print (1st)
prior (5th)
prison (3rd)
private (3rd)
privateer (6th)
privilege (5th)
prize (3rd)
pro (4th)
probably (4th)
problem (1st)
proceed (4th)
process (4th)
procession (4th)
proclaim (4th)
procure (5th)
prod (6th)
produce (2nd)
product (4th)
production (4th)
profess (5th)
profession (5th)
professor (4th)
profile (5th)
profit (4th)
profound (6th)
program (4th)
progress (4th)
prohibit (6th)
project (4th)
prolong (5th)
promenade (5th)
prominent (5th)
promise (1st)
promote (5th)
promotion (5th)
prompt (4th)
pronghorn (5th)
pronounce (4th)

proof (4th)
prop (5th)
propel (6th)
proper (3rd)
property (3rd)
prophet (4th)
proportion (4th)
propose (4th)
proprietor (6th)
prospect (4th)
prosper (5th)
protect (4th)
protection (4th)
protein (5th)
protest (4th)
protostar (5th)
proud (2nd)
prove (1st)
provide (3rd)
province (6th)
provision (4th)
provoke (6th)
prow (5th)
prowess (6th)
prowl (2nd)
prudent (6th)
prune (3rd)
pry (6th)
psalm (6th)
psychedelic (5th)
psychic (6th)
psychology (6th)
Pteranodon (2nd)
pub (1st)
public (1st)
publication (4th)
publicity (4th)
publicize (4th)

publish (4th)
puff (2nd)
pull (K)
pulp (6th)
pulse (5th)
pulsars (5th)
puma (4th)
pump (4th)
pumpkin (K)
punch (4th)
punish (4th)
pup (K)
pupa (2nd)
pupil (4th)
puppy (K)
purchase (3rd)
pure (3rd)
Puritan (1st)
purple (K)
purpose (1st)
purse (4th)
pursuit (5th)
push (1st)
push-up (1st)
pushy (1st)
put (K)
puzzle (4th)
pyramid (5th)

q

quack (K)
quail (1st)
quaint (5th)
quake (4th)
Quaker (1st)
qualify (4th)
quality (4th)
quantity (4th)
quasars (5th)

quarrel (4th)
quarry (6th)
quart (2nd)
quarter (1st)
quasars (5th)
Quaternary (5th)
quay (5th)
queen (K)
queer (4th)
quench (6th)
query (6th)
quest (3rd)
question (1st)
quick (1st)
quicksand (1st)
quiet (K)
quill (6th)
quirt (6th)
quilt (6th)
quit (1st)
quite (1st)
quiver (4th)
quote (5th)

r

RNA (4th)
rabbi (4th)
rabbit (K)
raccoon (1st)
race (1st)
rack (1st)
radar (5th)
radiant (6th)
radiate (6th)
radical (6th)
radio (1st)
radioactive (6th)
radish (1st)
radius (6th)

raft (6th)
rafter (6th)
rag (1st)
rage (4th)
ragged (5th)
raid (6th)
rail (2nd)
railroad (2nd)
rain (1st)
raindrops (2nd)
rainfall (2nd)
raise (1st)
rake (1st)
rally (5th)
ram (K)
ramble (6th)
ramp (6th)
rampart (6th)
ran (K)
ranch (5th)
random (6th)
range (3rd)
ranger (1st)
rank (3rd)
ransom (6th)
rap (1st)
rapid (4th)
raptor (5th)
rapture (6th)
rare (4th)
rascal (5th)
rash (6th)
raspberry (2nd)
rat (K)
rate (1st)
rather (1st)
ratify (6th)
ratio (6th)

rattle (2nd)

rattlesnake (1st)

ravage (6th)

rave (5th)

ravenous (6th)

ravine (5th)

ravish (6th)

raw (1st)

ray (1st)

razor (6th)

reach (1st)

react (5th)

read (K)

ready (1st)

real (1st)

reality (5th)

realize (2nd)

realm (4th)

reap (4th)

rear (3rd)

reason (1st)

reassure (6th)

rebuke (4th)

recall (3rd)

receipt (5th)

receive (1st)

recent (3rd)

reception (5th)

recess (2nd)

recipe (4th)

recite (5th)

reckless (5th)

reckon (5th)

reclaim (6th)

recline (6th)

recognize (3rd)

recollect (6th)

recommend (5th)

recompense (6th)

reconcile (6th)

record (2nd)

recount (6th)

recourse (6th)

recover (4th)

recreation (5th)

recruit (6th)

rectangle (1st)

recur (6th)

recycle (1st)

redeem (6th)

redouble (6th)

reduce (3rd)

redwood (4th)

reed (4th)

reef (5th)

reel (5th)

refer (5th)

refine (6th)

reflect (4th)

reflex (6th)

reform (5th)

refrain (6th)

refresh (6th)

refrigerator (2nd)

refuge (5th)

refuse (2nd)

refute (5th)

regain (6th)

regal (6th)

regard (4th)

regiment (5th)

region (4th)

register (4th)

registration (5th)

regret (5th)

regular (3rd)

regulate (5th)

rehearse (6th)

reheat (6th)

reign (4th)

reindeer (K)

reins (1st)

reject (5th)

rejoice (4th)

relate (4th)

relation (4th)

relative (4th)

relax (4th)

relay (6th)

release (5th)

relic (5th)

relief (4th)

relieve (4th)

religion (4th)

relish (6th)

reluctant (6th)

rely (5th)

remain (1st)

remark (4th)

remedy (4th)

remember (1st)

remind (3rd)

remnant (6th)

remonstrate (6th)

remorse (6th)

remote (5th)

remove (2nd)

renaissance (5th)

rend (4th)

renew (4th)

renounce (6th)

renown (5th)

rent (K)

repair (4th)

repeat (4th)

repel (6th)

repent (6th)

replace (5th)

replenish (6th)

reply (1st)

report (1st)

repose (6th)

represent (4th)

reproach (6th)

reproduce (4th)

reptile (4th)

repulse (6th)

reputation (5th)

request (4th)

require (1st)

requisition (6th)

rescue (4th)

research (5th)

resemble (4th)

resent (5th)

reserve (3rd)

reside (5th)

residence (5th)

resident (5th)

resign (5th)

resin (5th)

resist (4th)

resolution (5th)

resolve (5th)

resort (5th)

resource (5th)

resourceful (5th)

respect (2nd)

respecting (4th)

respiration (6th)

respite (6th)

respond (5th)

responsible (4th)
rest (1st)
restaurant (5th)
restless (4th)
restore (5th)
restrain (5th)
restrict (6th)
result (2nd)
resume (5th)
retain (5th)
retire (4th)
retort (5th)
retreat (4th)
retrieve (6th)
return (1st)
reveal (4th)
revenge (5th)
revenue (6th)
reverence (4th)
reverend (4th)
reverse (5th)
review (4th)
revive (6th)
revolt (5th)
revolution (5th)
revolve (5th)
revolver (5th)
reward (4th)
rhinoceros (3rd)
rhubarb (4th)
rhyme (6th)
rhythm (5th)
rib (1st)
ribbon (4th)
rice (1st)
rich (K)
rid (1st)
riddle (1st)

ride (K)
ridge (5th)
ridicule (6th)
ridiculous (6th)
rifle (4th)
rig (1st)
right (K)
rigid (5th)
rim (1st)
ring (1st)
rinse (3rd)
riot (6th)
rip (K)
ripe (1st)
ripen (1st)
ripple (4th)
rise (1st)
risk (4th)
rite (6th)
ritual (6th)
rival (4th)
river (K)
road (K)
roadbed (1st)
roam (4th)
roar (1st)
roast (4th)
rob (K)
robe (4th)
robin (K)
robot (K)
robust (5th)
rock (K)
rocket (K)
rod (1st)
roe (5th)
rogue (5th)
role (6th)

roll (1st)
romance (5th)
roof (1st)
room (K)
roost (2nd)
rooster (1st)
root (3rd)
rope (1st)
rose (1st)
rot (1st)
rotate (4th)
rote (2nd)
rotorcraft (1st)
rough (4th)
round (K)
roundhouse (1st)
rouse (4th)
roust (5th)
route (4th)
routine (6th)
rove (6th)
row (K)
royal (3rd)
rub (1st)
rubber (1st)
rubbish (5th)
ruby (6th)
rude (2nd)
ruffle (6th)
rug (1st)
rugged (5th)
ruin (2nd)
ruinous (5th)
rule (K)
rum (1st)
rumble (3rd)
rumor (5th)
run (K)

running (1st)
rural (5th)
rush (2nd)
rust (2nd)
rustle (3rd)
rut (1st)

S

Sabbath (5th)
saber (5th)
saber-toothed (5th)
sable (5th)
sack (1st)
sacred (4th)
sacrifice (4th)
sad (K)
saddle (4th)
sadness (1st)
safe (K)
saffron (4th)
sag (1st)
saga (6th)
sage (4th)
sagebrush (4th)
said (K)
sail (1st)
sailor (3rd)
saint (3rd)
sake (3rd)
salamander (3rd)
salary (3rd)
sale (1st)
salesperson (6th)
sally (5th)
salmon (3rd)
saloon (6th)
salt (1st)
salute (4th)
salvation (6th)

same (K)	scare (1st)	scrub (6th)	sensation (5th)
sample (5th)	scarecrow (1st)	scuff (5th)	sense (1st)
sanction (6th)	scared (1st)	scull (6th)	sensible (6th)
sand (1st)	scarf (6th)	sculptor (4th)	sensitive (5th)
sandstone (2nd)	scatter (3rd)	sculpture (4th)	sensitivity (5th)
sane (6th)	scene (1st)	scurvy (6th)	sent (K)
sap (1st)	scent (3rd)	scuttle (4th)	sentence (1st)
sapling (5th)	schedule (6th)	sea (K)	sentiment (5th)
sapphire (6th)	scheme (5th)	seal (K)	sentinel (5th)
sardine (4th)	scholar (5th)	seam (5th)	sentry (5th)
sash (6th)	school (K)	search (1st)	separate (3rd)
sassafras (4th)	schoolwork (1st)	season (2nd)	September (1st)
satellite (6th)	science (3rd)	seat (1st)	sequoia (2nd)
satin (3rd)	scientist (3rd)	second (1st)	serene (6th)
satisfy (3rd)	scissors (5th)	secret (1st)	serf (6th)
Saturday (1st)	scoff (6th)	secretary (4th)	serge (6th)
satyr (6th)	scold (5th)	section (4th)	sergeant (5th)
sauce (3rd)	scoop (4th)	secure (3rd)	series (4th)
saunter (6th)	scope (6th)	sedimentary (5th)	serious (4th)
Saurischians (5th)	scorch (6th)	see (K)	sermon (5th)
sausage (4th)	score (1st)	seed (1st)	serpent (5th)
sauté (4th)	scorn (4th)	seek (1st)	servant (3rd)
savage (5th)	scorpion (5th)	seem (1st)	serve (1st)
save (1st)	scour (6th)	seep (4th)	service (1st)
savior (6th)	scourge (6th)	seesaw (1st)	session (6th)
savor (6th)	scout (1st)	Seismosaurus (5th)	set (K)
savory (6th)	scow (6th)	seize (3rd)	settle (2nd)
saw (K)	scramble (4th)	seizures (6th)	seven (K)
sawmill (1st)	scrap (3rd)	seldom (4th)	seventeen (1st)
say (K)	scrapbook (3rd)	select (4th)	seventy (1st)
scabbard (6th)	scrape (4th)	self (3rd)	several (1st)
scale (3rd)	scratch (4th)	selfish (5th)	severe (4th)
scamper (4th)	scream (1st)	sell (K)	sew (2nd)
scan (5th)	screech (1st)	Senate (1st)	sex (3rd)
scandal (6th)	screen (5th)	senate (1st)	shabby (4th)
scant (6th)	screw (3rd)	semitropical (5th)	shade (2nd)
scar (5th)	screwdriver (3rd)	send (K)	shadow (3rd)
scarce (4th)	scroll (5th)	senior (6th)	shaft (4th)

shaggy (5th)
shake (1st)
shale (5th)
shall (1st)
shallow (4th)
shaman (5th)
shame (3rd)
shape (1st)
share (2nd)
shark (1st)
sharp (1st)
shatter (5th)
shave (1st)
shawl (6th)
she (K)
sheaf (6th)
shear (5th)
sheep (K)
sheer (5th)
sheet (1st)
shelf (6th)
shell (1st)
shellfish (5th)
shelter (4th)
shepherd (4th)
sherbet (5th)
sheriff (4th)
shield (4th)
shift (4th)
shimmer (5th)
shine (1st)
shiny (3rd)
ship (1st)
shipment (5th)
shipwreck (5th)
shirk (6th)
shirt (1st)
shiver (1st)

shock (1st)
shoe (K)
shoemaker (2nd)
shoot (3rd)
shop (1st)
shoplift (3rd)
shore (1st)
short (1st)
shortly (1st)
shot (1st)
should (1st)
shoulder (1st)
shouldn't (1st)
shout (1st)
shove (5th)
shovel (1st)
show (1st)
showroom (4th)
shred (5th)
shrewd (6th)
shriek (4th)
shrill (5th)
shrine (5th)
shrink (5th)
shroud (6th)
shrug (4th)
shudder (4th)
shun (6th)
shut (1st)
shutter (4th)
shuttle (5th)
shy (K)
sick (K)
sickle (6th)
side (K)
sidekick (2nd)
sidewalk (1st)
siege (5th)

sieve (5th)
sift (4th)
sigh (3rd)
sight (1st)
sign (1st)
signal (4th)
signature (6th)
significant (6th)
signify (6th)
silent (3rd)
silk (3rd)
silkworm (3rd)
silly (1st)
Silurian (5th)
silver (1st)
similar (4th)
simmer (4th)
simple (1st)
simulate (6th)
sin (1st)
since (1st)
sincere (4th)
sinew (6th)
sing (1st)
single (3rd)
sink (3rd)
sip (1st)
sir (1st)
sire (4th)
sister (1st)
sit (K)
site (5th)
sitting (1st)
situation (4th)
sit-up (1st)
six (K)
sixteen (1st)
sixth (1st)

sixty (1st)
size (1st)
skate (1st)
skateboard (2nd)
skeleton (4th)
sketch (5th)
skill (2nd)
skim (6th)
skin (1st)
skinny (1st)
skip (2nd)
skirt (3rd)
skull (5th)
skunk (K)
sky (K)
Skylab (4th)
skyline (5th)
skyrocket (3rd)
slab (5th)
slam (5th)
slant (6th)
slap (2nd)
slash (6th)
slate (1st)
slaughter (5th)
slave (3rd)
slay (4th)
sled (5th)
sledge (6th)
sleek (3rd)
sleep (K)
sleeve (5th)
slender (4th)
slice (5th)
slide (2nd)
slight (4th)
slim (5th)
slip (3rd)

slipper (5th)
slit (5th)
slither (4th)
slob (5th)
slope (3rd)
sloth (5th)
slouch (6th)
slow (1st)
slug (5th)
slugger (5th)
slumber (4th)
slump (5th)
sly (4th)
smack (6th)
small (K)
smart (1st)
smart house (1st)
smash (3rd)
smear (3rd)
smell (3rd)
smile (1st)
smite (5th)
smog (5th)
smoke (1st)
smooth (2nd)
smother (6th)
smuggle (6th)
snack (2nd)
snail (1st)
snake (1st)
snap (2nd)
snare (6th)
snarl (5th)
snatch (4th)
sneak (4th)
sneer (6th)
sneeze (5th)
sniff (4th)

snooze (4th)
snore (6th)
snorkel (5th)
snort (5th)
snout (5th)
snow (K)
snowball (K)
snowman (K)
snowstorm (2nd)
snuff (6th)
snug (6th)
snuggle (5th)
so (K)
soak (5th)
soap (4th)
soar (6th)
sob (1st)
sober (4th)
soccer (1st)
social (1st)
society (3rd)
sock (1st)
socket (6th)
socks (1st)
sod (6th)
sodden (6th)
soft (K)
soil (2nd)
solar (4th)
solar system (4th)
soldier (3rd)
sole (4th)
solemn (5th)
solid (3rd)
solitary (5th)
solution (5th)
solve (4th)
sombrero (6th)

some (K)
somebody (1st)
someday (1st)
someone (1st)
something (1st)
sometimes (1st)
somewhere (1st)
son (K)
song (K)
sonic (2nd)
sonnet (6th)
soon (K)
soothe (5th)
sorcerer (4th)
sore (4th)
sorrow (4th)
sorry (2nd)
sort (1st)
soul (3rd)
sound (1st)
soup (1st)
sour (2nd)
source (4th)
south (1st)
sovereign (4th)
space (1st)
spade (6th)
span (6th)
spank (2nd)
spar (5th)
spare (3rd)
spark (3rd)
sparkle (5th)
sparrow (5th)
spasm (6th)
speak (1st)
spear (4th)
spearhead (5th)

special (2nd)
species (5th)
specific (5th)
specimen (5th)
speck (4th)
spectacle (5th)
spectacles (5th)
spectator (5th)
spectrum (6th)
speculate (6th)
speech (2nd)
speed (3rd)
spell (1st)
spend (2nd)
sphere (6th)
spice (3rd)
spider (K)
spike (4th)
spill (1st)
spin (1st)
spinach (2nd)
spine (4th)
spire (6th)
spirit (2nd)
spiritual (5th)
spit (3rd)
spite (3rd)
splash (1st)
splendid (4th)
splendor (4th)
splinter (6th)
split (4th)
splotch (5th)
spoil (4th)
spoke (1st)
sponge (3rd)
spool (2nd)
spoon (1st)

sport (1st)

sportsman (2nd)

sportswoman (2nd)

spot (1st)

spout (5th)

sprawl (6th)

spray (2nd)

spread (2nd)

spring (K)

sprinkle (3rd)

sprint (5th)

spruce (3rd)

spur (4th)

spurt (5th)

sputter (3rd)

spy (4th)

squadron (6th)

square (2nd)

squash (2nd)

squat (5th)

squawk (2nd)

squeak (2nd)

squeeze (5th)

squid (3rd)

squire (4th)

squirm (2nd)

squirrel (1st)

squirt (4th)

stab (5th)

stable (4th)

stack (6th)

staff (4th)

stag (1st)

stage (3rd)

stagger (4th)

stain (4th)

stair (2nd)

stake (1st)

stalagmite (5th)

stale (2nd)

stalk (4th)

stall (5th)

stallion (4th)

stalwart (6th)

stamen (6th)

stammer (6th)

stamp (2nd)

stampede (5th)

stand (K)

standard (3rd)

stanza (5th)

staple (6th)

star (K)

starch (6th)

stare (3rd)

starfish (1st)

start (1st)

startle (4th)

starve (5th)

state (1st)

station (1st)

statue (4th)

stature (6th)

stay (1st)

steady (3rd)

steak (2nd)

steal (3rd)

steam (2nd)

steed (4th)

steel (2nd)

steep (2nd)

steer (4th)

Stegosaurus (2nd)

stem (2nd)

step (1st)

stereoscope (5th)

stern (4th)

stew (2nd)

stick (K)

sticker (K)

sticky (K)

stiff (3rd)

still (1st)

stimulate (6th)

sting (2nd)

stink (2nd)

stir (3rd)

stitch (6th)

stock (1st)

stockade (6th)

stocking (4th)

stomach (2nd)

stomp (4th)

stone (2nd)

stood (K)

stool (2nd)

stoop (5th)

stop (K)

stoplight (1st)

store (K)

stork (2nd)

storm (2nd)

story (K)

stout (4th)

stove (1st)

stovepipe (4th)

stow (6th)

straight (3rd)

strain (4th)

strait (5th)

strand (5th)

strange (1st)

strangle (6th)

strap (5th)

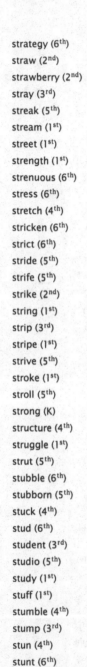

strategy (6th)
straw (2nd)
strawberry (2nd)
stray (3rd)
streak (5th)
stream (1st)
street (1st)
strength (1st)
strenuous (6th)
stress (6th)
stretch (4th)
stricken (6th)
strict (6th)
stride (5th)
strife (5th)
strike (2nd)
string (1st)
strip (3rd)
stripe (1st)
strive (5th)
stroke (1st)
stroll (5th)
strong (K)
structure (4th)
struggle (1st)
strut (5th)
stubble (6th)
stubborn (5th)
stuck (4th)
stud (6th)
student (3rd)
studio (5th)
study (1st)
stuff (1st)
stumble (4th)
stump (3rd)
stun (4th)
stunt (6th)

stupid (4th)
sturdy (3rd)
stutter (1st)
style (3rd)
subdue (6th)
subject (1st)
sublime (6th)
submarine (5th)
submerge (5th)
submit (4th)
subsequent (6th)
subside (6th)
substance (5th)
substantial (5th)
substitute (5th)
subtle (6th)
subtract (1st)
success (2nd)
succession (6th)
such (1st)
suck (1st)
suckling (6th)
sudden (1st)
suffer (2nd)
suffering (2nd)
suffice (6th)
sufficient (3rd)
suffocate (6th)
sugar (1st)
suggest (2nd)
suggestion (2nd)
suit (1st)
suitcase (1st)
sulky (5th)
sullen (5th)
sulfur (4th)
sultan (5th)
sum (1st)

sumac (4th)
summer (K)
summit (5th)
summon (4th)
sun (K)
Sunday (1st)
sundown (2nd)
sundry (6th)
sunlit (2nd)
sunny (1st)
sunrise (2nd)
sunset (1st)
suntan (2nd)
super (1st)
superb (6th)
superintendent
 (5th)
superior (4th)
supernatural (5th)
superstition (5th)
supervise (6th)
supper (2nd)
supple (6th)
supply (1st)
support (4th)
suppose (2nd)
suppress (5th)
supreme (5th)
sure (K)
surf (4th)
surface (3rd)
surge (5th)
surgeon (5th)
surly (6th)
surmise (6th)
surmount (6th)
surpass (6th)
surplus (6th)

surprise (1st)
surrender (5th)
surround (3rd)
surrounding (3rd)
survey (5th)
survive (3rd)
suspect (5th)
suspend (4th)
suspicion (4th)
sustain (5th)
swagger (5th)
swallow (1st)
swamp (4th)
swarm (4th)
swarthy (6th)
sway (3rd)
swear (4th)
sweat (3rd)
sweater (3rd)
sweep (4th)
sweet (K)
sweetmeat (5th)
sweetness (2nd)
sweets (1st)
swell (3rd)
swift (4th)
swim (K)
swine (5th)
swing (1st)
swish (2nd)
switch (4th)
swoop (4th)
sword (4th)
sycamore (4th)
syllable (6th)
symbol (5th)
sympathy (4th)
symphony (6th)

symptom (6th)

syrup (4th)

system (2nd)

t

tab (K)

table (K)

tablecloth (4th)

tablespoon (4th)

tack (1st)

tackle (4th)

tact (6th)

tactics (6th)

tag (K)

tail (1st)

tailor (4th)

taint (6th)

take (K)

taken (1st)

tale (3rd)

talent (2nd)

talk (K)

tall (K)

tame (4th)

tan (K)

tangle (3rd)

tank (5th)

tankard (6th)

Taoist (5th)

tap (K)

tape (1st)

taper (5th)

tapestry (6th)

tar (1st)

target (5th)

tariff (5th)

taro (4th)

tarpaulin (6th)

tarry (5th)

tart (5th)

task (3rd)

taste (1st)

taught (2nd)

taunt (5th)

tavern (5th)

tawny (6th)

tax (K)

taxi (1st)

tea (1st)

teach (1st)

teacher (1st)

team (1st)

tear (2nd)

tease (3rd)

teaspoon (2nd)

tectonic (5th)

tedious (6th)

tee (1st)

teen (2nd)

teenager (3rd)

teeth (1st)

telecommunica-

    tions (4th)

telegram (4th)

telephone (2nd)

telescope (4th)

television (4th)

tell (K)

telling (1st)

temper (4th)

temperature (4th)

temple (3rd)

temporary (5th)

tempt (4th)

temptation (5th)

ten (K)

tenant (5th)

tend (K)

tendency (5th)

tender (3rd)

tenement (6th)

tense (5th)

tent (1st)

term (3rd)

terminate (6th)

termites (2nd)

terrace (5th)

terraform (4th)

terrible (1st)

terrier (5th)

terrific (5th)

terrified (3rd)

terrify (3rd)

territory (3rd)

terror (3rd)

test (3rd)

tether (6th)

text (6th)

texture (6th)

thank (K)

Thanksgiving (K)

that (K)

that's (1st)

thatch (4th)

the (K)

theater (3rd)

thee (2nd)

their (K)

them (K)

theme (4th)

themselves (1st)

then (K)

thence (4th)

theory (5th)

there (1st)

therefore (1st)

thermodynamics

    (4th)

thermometer (6th)

theropod (5th)

these (K)

they (K)

they'll (1st)

they're (1st)

thick (2nd)

thicket (4th)

thief (3rd)

thigh (3rd)

thin (1st)

thing (K)

things (K)

think (1st)

third (1st)

thirsty (2nd)

thirteen (1st)

thirty (1st)

this (K)

thistle (4th)

thorn (3rd)

thorough (4th)

those (1st)

though (1st)

thought (1st)

thoughtful (2nd)

thousand (1st)

thrash (4th)

thread (2nd)

threat (5th)

three (K)

three-fourths (5th)

thresh (6th)

threshold (5th)

threw (1st)

thrift (6th)	tiny (2nd)	topple (6th)	trample (5th)
thrill (4th)	tip (1st)	torch (5th)	tranquil (6th)
thrive (6th)	tiptoe (4th)	torment (5th)	transfer (5th)
throat (1st)	tire (2nd)	tornado (6th)	transform (5th)
throb (5th)	tired (2nd)	torrent (5th)	transit (6th)
throne (4th)	tissue (5th)	tortoise (3rd)	translate (5th)
throng (5th)	title (3rd)	torture (5th)	transmit (4th)
through (1st)	to (K)	toss (2nd)	transmission (4th)
throughout (2nd)	toast (5th)	total (2nd)	transom (6th)
throw (1st)	tobacco (4th)	tote (5th)	transparent (5th)
thrush (5th)	today (K)	totter (6th)	transport (5th)
thrust (4th)	toe (K)	touch (1st)	trap (1st)
thud (3rd)	toenail (4th)	touching (1st)	trash (2nd)
thunder (3rd)	together (1st)	tough (5th)	travel (1st)
Thursday (1st)	toil (4th)	tour (3rd)	traverse (5th)
thus (1st)	toilet (2nd)	tourist (5th)	tray (1st)
thy (3rd)	token (5th)	tournament (5th)	treacherous (6th)
thyme (4th)	told (K)	tow (1st)	tread (4th)
thyself (5th)	tolerate (5th)	toward (1st)	treason (4th)
tick (1st)	toll (6th)	towel (6th)	treasure (4th)
ticket (1st)	tomato (4th)	tower (3rd)	treat (2nd)
tickets (1st)	tomb (5th)	towhead (4th)	treatment (5th)
tide (1st)	tomfoolery (5th)	town (K)	treaty (4th)
tie (1st)	tomorrow (1st)	toxic (2nd)	treble (6th)
tiger (K)	ton (1st)	toy (K)	tree (K)
tight (1st)	tone (3rd)	trace (3rd)	tremble (3rd)
tile (1st)	tongue (3rd)	track (1st)	tremendous (4th)
till (1st)	tonic (2nd)	tractor (K)	tremor (6th)
tilt (5th)	tonight (1st)	trade (1st)	trench (5th)
timber (5th)	too (1st)	tradition (5th)	trend (2nd)
time (1st)	took (1st)	traffic (5th)	trespass (6th)
timid (5th)	tool (1st)	tragedy (5th)	trial (4th)
tin (1st)	toolbox (5th)	trail (2nd)	triangle (1st)
tinge (5th)	toot (1st)	train (K)	Triassic (5th)
tingle (4th)	tooth (1st)	trained (1st)	tribe (3rd)
tinker (5th)	toothpaste (2nd)	trait (6th)	tribunal (6th)
tinkle (5th)	top (K)	traitor (4th)	tribute (5th)
tint (5th)	topic (5th)	tramp (4th)	Triceratops (2nd)

trick (1st)
trickery (5th)
tried (K)
trifle (5th)
trigger (6th)
trim (4th)
trinket (6th)
trio (3rd)
trip (1st)
tripod (6th)
triumph (5th)
troll (1st)
troop (3rd)
trophy (6th)
tropic (6th)
tropical (5th)
trot (5th)
troth (6th)
trouble (1st)
troublemaker (1st)
trough (6th)
trousers (5th)
trout (4th)
truant (6th)
truck (1st)
trudge (5th)
true (K)
trunk (4th)
trust (1st)
truth (1st)
try (K)
tryout (2nd)
tsunami (5th)
tub (1st)
tube (3rd)
tuck (1st)
Tuesday (1st)
tuft (3rd)

tug (1st)
tulip (2nd)
tumble (4th)
tummy (K)
tumor (6th)
tumult (6th)
tune (1st)
tunic (6th)
tunnel (2nd)
turban (5th)
turbulent (5th)
turf (5th)
turkey (K)
turmoil (5th)
turn (1st)
turnip (3rd)
turquoise (5th)
turret (5th)
turtle (K)
tusk (5th)
tussle (6th)
tutor (6th)
TV (K)
twain (6th)
twang (6th)
twelve (1st)
twenty (1st)
twice (3rd)
twig (4th)
twine (3rd)
twinkle (4th)
twirl (3rd)
twist (1st)
two (K)
type (1st)
typewriter (1st)
typical (6th)
Tyrannosaurus Rex

(2nd)
tyranny (5th)
tyrant (5th)

u

udder (5th)
ugh (4th)
ugly (4th)
ultimate (6th)
umbrella (2nd)
umpire (1st)
unanimous (6th)
unbidden (6th)
uncanny (6th)
uncertain (1st)
unceremonious
   (4th)
uncertain (1st)
uncle (1st)
under (K)
underground (4th)
understand (1st)
undertaking (3rd)
undoubtedly (5th)
unfit (1st)
unhappy (1st)
unidentified (5th)
uniform (1st)
union (3rd)
unique (6th)
unison (6th)
unit (5th)
unite (5th)
unity (5th)
universal (4th)
universe (4th)
university (4th)
unless (2nd)
unlimited (3rd)

unpaid (2nd)
unreal (1st)
unruly (6th)
until (1st)
unto (3rd)
unusual (3rd)
unzip (1st)
up (K)
uphill (1st)
uphold (6th)
upholster (6th)
upholstery (6th)
upon (1st)
upper (3rd)
upright (4th)
uproar (5th)
upset (3rd)
upstairs (3rd)
uptown (1st)
upward (4th)
uranium (6th)
urchin (3rd)
urge (4th)
urgent (6th)
us (K)
use (K)
used (K)
useful (2nd)
useless (2nd)
usher (6th)
usual (3rd)
utensil (6th)
utilize (6th)
utter (4th)

v

vacant (6th)
vacation (2nd)
vaccine (4th)

vaccination (4th)
vacuum (5th)
vague (5th)
vain (4th)
vale (4th)
valentine (K)
valiant (6th)
valley (2nd)
valuable (4th)
value (2nd)
valve (6th)
vamoose (6th)
van (K)
vanish (3rd)
vanity (5th)
vanquish (6th)
vapor (3rd)
various (4th)
vary (4th)
vase (2nd)
vast (4th)
vault (5th)
veal (4th)
veer (6th)
vegetable (2nd)
vehicle (6th)
veil (3rd)
vein (4th)
vengeance (6th)
venison (5th)
vent (4th)
venture (4th)
venue (6th)
verdict (6th)
verge (6th)
verse (4th)
version (6th)
vertebrate (5th)

vertical (1st)
vertiport (1st)
very (K)
vessel (4th)
vest (3rd)
vet (1st)
veteran (6th)
veterinarian (4th)
vex (5th)
vexation (5th)
vibrant (5th)
vibrate (5th)
vice (4th)
vicinity (6th)
vicious (6th)
victim (4th)
victory (4th)
video (4th)
video-conference
    (4th)
view (1st)
viewpoint (5th)
vigor (5th)
vigorous (5th)
Viking (5th)
vile (6th)
village (2nd)
villain (5th)
violent (5th)
violet (2nd)
violin (4th)
virgin (6th)
Virtual
    Environment
    (also V.E.) (4th)
virtual reality (4th)
virtually (4th)
virtue (4th)

virus (2nd)
visible (4th)
vision (4th)
visit (1st)
vital (5th)
vivid (6th)
vocabulary (6th)
voice (1st)
void (6th)
volcano (5th)
volume (3rd)
volunteer (5th)
vomit (6th)
vote (2nd)
vow (4th)
voyage (4th)
vulture (3rd)

W

waddle (5th)
wade (4th)
waft (5th)
wag (1st)
wage (3rd)
wagon (2nd)
wail (5th)
wait (K)
wake (1st)
walk (K)
walked (1st)
walking (1st)
wall (K)
wallet (6th)
wallow (6th)
walnut (1st)
walrus (1st)
waltz (6th)
wan (6th)
wand (3rd)

wander (3rd)
want (K)
wanted (1st)
war (1st)
warble (6th)
ward (5th)
wardrobe (6th)
ware (5th)
warehouse (5th)
warm (1st)
warn (3rd)
warning (3rd)
warp (4th)
warrant (5th)
warrior (4th)
wary (5th)
was (K)
wash (1st)
wasn't (1st)
wasp (2nd)
waste (1st)
wasteland (6th)
watch (1st)
watchful (2nd)
water (K)
watercress (4th)
watermelon (3rd)
wave (K)
waver (5th)
wax (K)
way (K)
we (K)
wee (1st)
weak (3rd)
wealth (3rd)
weapon (4th)
wear (1st)
weary (4th)

weasel (3rd)
weather (1st)
weave (4th)
wed (K)
wedding (1st)
wedge (4th)
Wednesday (1st)
weed (1st)
week (K)
weep (4th)
weevil (5th)
weigh (1st)
weight (1st)
weird (1st)
welcome (1st)
weld (6th)
welfare (5th)
well (K)
we'll (1st)
well built (2nd)
went (K)
were (K)
we're (1st)
west (1st)
westward (3rd)
wet (K)
whale (1st)
wharf (5th)
what (K)
whatever (1st)
wheat (1st)
wheel (1st)
wheeze (5th)
when (K)
whence (4th)
whenever (3rd)
where (1st)
whereas (4th)

wherefore (4th)
whereupon (4th)
whether (1st)
which (1st)
whiff (5th)
while (1st)
whim (6th)
whimper (5th)
whine (5th)
whip (4th)
whippoorwill (4th)
whir (6th)
whirl (4th)
whisk (4th)
whiskey (6th)
whisper (1st)
whistle (4th)
white (K)
White House (K)
who (K)
whoever (1st)
whole (1st)
wholesome (5th)
wholly (5th)
whom (2nd)
whoop (6th)
why (K)
wick (1st)
wicked (4th)
wide (1st)
widespread (5th)
widow (4th)
width (4th)
Wi-Fi (4th)
wield (6th)
wife (1st)
wig (1st)
wigwam (5th)

wild (2nd)
wildcat (2nd)
wilderness (4th)
wile (6th)
will (K)
willing (5th)
wilt (4th)
win (K)
wince (5th)
wind (1st)
window (1st)
wine (1st)
wing (1st)
wink (2nd)
winter (K)
wipe (1st)
wire (3rd)
wise (1st)
wish (K)
wit (1st)
witch (K)
with (K)
withal (6th)
withdraw (2nd)
wither (5th)
within (1st)
without (1st)
witness (3rd)
wizard (6th)
wobble (4th)
woe (4th)
woman (K)
women (K)
wonder (1st)
wonderful (1st)
won't (1st)
wont (5th)
woo (6th)

wood (1st)
woodbine (3rd)
woodchuck (2nd)
woodpecker (2nd)
wool (3rd)
word (K)
work (K)
worked (1st)
worker (1st)
workman (1st)
workstation (4th)
world (1st)
worm (K)
worn (3rd)
worrisome (5th)
worry (1st)
worse (1st)
worship (4th)
worst (3rd)
worth (3rd)
worthless (3rd)
would (1st)
wouldn't (1st)
wouldst (5th)
wound (3rd)
wow (K)
wrap (3rd)
wrath (4th)
wreath (4th)
wreck (4th)
wren (5th)
wrench (6th)
wrest (6th)
wrestle (6th)
wretched (6th)
wriggle (5th)
wring (5th)
wrinkle (3rd)

writ (6th)
write (K)
writer (1st)
writhe (6th)
written (3rd)
wrong (1st)
wrought (5th)

y

yam (1st)
yank (2nd)
yard (K)
yarn (2nd)
yawn (5th)
ye (4th)
yea (K)
yeah (1st)
year (1st)
yearly (2nd)
yearn (6th)
yeast (2nd)
yell (K)
yellow (K)
yelp (6th)
yes (K)
yesterday (3rd)
yet (1st)
yew (2nd)
yield (4th)
yip (1st)
yoke (6th)
yon (4th)
yonder (4th)
yore (6th)
you (K)
you'll (1st)
young (1st)
your (K)
yourself (2nd)

youth (2nd)
yucca (1st)
Yule (2nd)

z

zeal (6th)
zealous (6th)
zebra (K)
zephyr (6th)
zero (K)
zest (6th)
zigzag (3rd)
zinc (5th)
zip (K)
zipper (K)
zone (4th)
zoo (K)